AF361514

The History of Courts and Procedure in Medieval Canon Law

HISTORY OF MEDIEVAL CANON LAW

Edited by Wilfried Hartmann and Kenneth Pennington

Canonical Collections of the Early Middle Ages (ca. 400–1140):
A Bibliographical Guide to the Manuscripts and Literature

Papal Letters in the Early Middle Ages

The History of Western Canon Law to 1140

The History of Byzantine and Eastern Canon Law to 1500

The History of Medieval Canon Law in the Classical Period,
1140–1234

The History of Medieval Canon Law in the Late Middle Ages,
1234–1500

The History of Courts and Procedure in Medieval Canon Law

A Guide to Medieval Canon Law Jurists and Collections, 1140–1500

The History of Courts and Procedure in Medieval Canon Law

Edited by Wilfried Hartmann and
Kenneth Pennington

The Catholic University of America Press
Washington, D.C.

LIBRARY OF CONGRESS CATALOGING-IN-PUBLICATION DATA
Names: Hartmann, Wilfried, 1942– editor. | Pennington, Kenneth,
editor. | Title: The history of courts and procedure in medieval Canon
law / edited by Wilfried Hartmann and Kenneth Pennington.
Description: Washington, DC : The Catholic University of America
Press, 2016. | Series: History of medieval canon law | Includes biblio-
graphical references and index.
Identifiers: LCCN 2016036446 | ISBN 9780813229041 (cloth : alk. paper)
Subjects: LCSH: Ecclesiastical courts—History. | Justice, Administra-
tion of (Canon law)—History. | Procedure (Canon law)—History. |
Catholic Church. | Rota Romana—History. | Canon law—History.
Classification: LCC KBU3782 .H57 2016 | DDC 262.909/02—dc23
LC record available at https://lccn.loc.gov/2016036446

Contents

Preface

Understanding the rules of procedure and the practices of medieval and early modern courts is a subject that is of great importance for historians of every stripe. The authors and editors of this volume wish to present readers with a description of court procedure, the sources for investigating the work of the courts, the jurisprudence and the norms that regulated the courts, and a survey of the variety of courts that populated the European landscape. Not least, they wish to show the relationship between the jurisprudence that governed judicial procedure and what happened in the court room.

Like the other volumes in this series, this book is the collaborative effort of scholars from different countries. In spite of its international profile, it does not cover every court system in all parts of Europe. This absence of complete coverage is not as serious as it may first appear. By the end of the thirteenth century, court procedure on the continent in both secular and ecclesiastical courts shared many characteristics. As the jurists of the Ius commune began to excavate the norms of procedure from Justinian's great codification and then expound them in the classroom and in their writings, they shaped the structure of the courts not only in ecclesiastical courts but in secular courts as well.

The editors are thankful to Caroline Levine, University of Wisconsin, Madison, for her translation of Antonio García y García's chapter and to Steven Rowan, University of Missouri, Kansas City, for his translations of His Eminence, Péter Cardinal Erdö's and Brigide Schwarz' chapters. Schwarz' chapter was then thoroughly revised by Dr. Brigitte Flug. The chapters then were revised by the editors who are responsible for their final form. The editors are also grateful to the support that this volume has received from the National Endowment for the Humanities, the Werner

Reimers Stiftung in Bad Homberg where many of these essays were first presented for discussion, the Alexander von Humboldt Stiftung, and the Gerda Henkel Stiftung. The universities of Tübingen and Syracuse and the Catholic University of America have also provided substantial support for the project and to the editors. The Catholic University of America Press has supported the publication of all the volumes in this series. We are particularly grateful to Charles Donahue who helped us immensely and well beyond the call of duty with the editorial work of putting this volume together.

In the time during which this volume was being assembled, Antonio García y García has died. Antonio was one of the most prominent and productive Spanish legal historians of his generation. In addition, Charles Duggan, who had written an essay for a previous volume that has also been published posthumously, publishes his final essay in this volume. We are in debt to Anne Duggan who prepared the final version of his essay for publication. Antonio García y García and Charles Duggan: Resquiescant in pace.

September 2014
Wilfried Hartmann and Kenneth Pennington
Tübingen and Washington D.C.

Abbreviations

The following sigla are used without further explanation:

ACA	*Archivo de la Corona d'Aragon / Arxiu de la Corona d'Arago*
AHC	*Annuarium historiae conciliorum*
AHDE	*Anuario de Historia del Derecho Español*
AHP	*Archivum historiae pontificiae*
AJLH	*American Journal of Legal History*
AKKR	*Archiv für katholisches Kirchenrecht*
BAV	Biblioteca Apostolica Vaticana
BDHI	*Bibliothek des Deutschen Historischen Instituts in Rom*
BC	Bibliotheca / Archivio capitolare, capitular, chapter, kapitoly etc.
BEC	*Bibliothèque de l'Ecole des Chartes*
BIDR	*Bullettino dell'Istituto di Diritto Romano*
BISM	*Bullettino dell'Istituto Storico Italiano per il Medio Evo e Archivio Muratoriano*
BL	British Library
BM	Bibliothèque municipale, Stadtsbibliothek, Biblioteca comume, Landesbibliothek, civica, etc.
BMCL	*Bulletin of Medieval Canon Law,* New series
BNF / BN	Bibliothèque nationale de France / Biblioteca nazionale
BSB	Bayerische Staatsbibliothek
BU	Bibliothèque universitaire, Universitätsbibliothek, Biblioteca di Università, etc.
C.	Causa in Gratian's *Decretum*
c.	capitulum
CCL	*Corpus Christianorum, Series latina*

CCCM	*Corpus Christianorum, Continuatio mediaevalis*
CHR	*Catholic Historical Review*
CID	*Cuadernos informativos de derecho histórico publico, procesal y de la navigación*
Clm	Codices latini monacenses-Bayerische Staatsbibliothek Munich
COD	Conciliorum oecumenicorum generaliumque decreta, 2.1: *The General Councils of Latin Christendom: From Constantinople IV to Pavia-Siena (869–1424),* ed. Giuseppe Alberigo, Alberto Melloni (Corpus Christianorum; Turnhout: Brepols Publishers, 2013)
Cod.	Justinian's *Codex*
Comp.	*Compilatio antiqua*
CSEL	*Corpus scriptorum ecclesiasticorum latinorum*
D.	Distinction in Gratian's *Decretum*
DA	*Deutsches Archiv für Erforschung des Mittelalters*
DBI	*Dizionario biografico degli Italiani*
DDC	*Dictionnaire de droit canonique*
DGI	*Dizionario biografico dei giuristi italiani (XII–XX secolo),* ed. Italo Birocchi, Ennio Cortese, Antonello Mattone, Marco Nicola Miletti (2 vols. Bologna: Mulino, 2013)
DHEE	*Diccionario de historia eclesiástica de España*
DHGE	*Dictionnaire d'histoire et de géographie ecclésiastiques*
Dig.	Justinian's *Digest*
DMA	*Dictionary of the Middle Ages*
DThC	*Dictionnaire de théologie catholique*
EHR	*English Historical Review*
EncD	*Enciclopedia del diritto*
HDIE	*Histoire du droit et des institutions de l'Eglise en Occident*
HJb	*Historische Jahrbuch*
HLF	*Histoire littéraire de la France*
HRG	*Handwörterbuch zur deutschen Rechtsgeschichte*
HZ	*Historische Zeitschrift*
IRMAe	*Ius romanum medii aevi*
JEH	*Journal of Ecclesiastical History*
JK, JE, JL	Jaffé, *Regesta pontificum romanorum* ... ed. secundam curaverunt F. Kaltenbrunner (JK: an. ?–590), P. Ewald (JE: an. 590–882), S. Loewenfeld (JL: an. 882–1198)
JMH	*Journal of Medieval History*
JTS	*Journal of Theological Studies*
l.	lex, leges
LHR	*Law and History Review*

LMA	*Lexikon des Mittelalters*
LThK	*Lexikon für Theologie unk Kirche* (LThK²: ed. 2)
Mansi	Mansi, *Sacrorum conciliorum nova et amplissima collectio*
Mazzatinti	G. Mazzatinti (continued by A. Sorbelli et al.), *Inventari dei manoscritti delle biblioteche d'Italia*
MEFR	*Mélanges de l'École française de Rome: Moyen âge – Temps modernes*
MGH	Monumenta Germaniae historica

- Capit.   Capitularia
- Conc.   Concilia
- Const.   Constitutiones
  - Ldl   Libelli de lite imperatorum et pontificum
  - LL   Leges (in Folio)
- LL nat. Germ.   Leges nationum Germanicarum

MIC	Monumenta iuris canonici

- Ser. A   Series A: Corpus Glossatorum
- Ser. B   Series B: Corpus Collectionum
- Ser. C   Series C: Subsidia

MIÖG	*Mitteilungen des Instituts für österreichische Geschichts-forschung*
ML	Monastic Library, Stiftsbibliothek, etc.
NA	*Neues Archiv der Gesellschaft für ältere deutsche Geschichtskunde*
NCE	*The New Catholic Encyclopedia*
NDI	*Novissimo Digesto Italiano*
ÖAKR	*Österreichisches Archiv für Kirchenrecht*
ÖNB	*Österreichische Nationalbibliothek*
PG	Migne, *Patrologia graeca*
PL	Migne, *Patrologia latina*
Potth.	Potthast, *Regesta pontificum romanorum*
QF	*Quellen und Forschungen aus italienischen Archiven und Bibliotheken*
QL	Schulte, *Quellen und Literatur*
RDC	*Revue de droit canonique*
REDC	*Revista español de derecho canónico*
RHD	*Revue historique de droit français et étranger* (4ᵉ série unless otherwise indicated)
RHE	*Revue d'histoire ecclésiastique*
RHM	*Römische historische Mitteilungen*
RIDC	*Rivista internazionale di diritto comune*
RIS²	Muratori, *Rerum italicarum scriptores: Raccolta degli storici italiani*, nuova edizione…
RQ	*Römische Quartalschrift für christliche Altertumskunde und Kirchengeschichte*

RS	Rolls Series (Rerum Britannicarum medii aevi scriptores)
RSCI	*Rivista di storia della Chiesa in Italia*
RSDI	*Rivista di storia del diritto italiano*
RTAM	*Recherches de théologie ancienne et médiévale*
SB	Staatsbibliothek
SCH	*Studies in Church History*
SDHI	*Studia et documenta historiae et iuris*
SG	*Studia Gratiana*
SH	*Synodicon Hispanum*, ed. Antonio García y García et alii (5 vols. Madrid 1981–1991).
TRE	*Theologische Realenzyklopädie*
TRG	*Tijdschrift voor Rechtsgeschiedenis*
TUI	*Tractatus universi iuris* (18 vols. Venice 1584–1586)
Vat.	Biblioteca Apostolica Vaticana
VI	*Liber Sextus of Boniface VIII*
X	*Decretals of Gregory IX*
ZKG	*Zeitschrift für Kirchengeschichte*
ZRG Kan. Abt.	*Zeitschrift der Savigny-Stiftung für Rechtsgeschichte*, Kanonistische Abteilung
ZRG Rom. Abt.	*Zeitschrift der Savigny-Stiftung für Rechtsgeschichte*, Romanistische) Abteilung

The Proceedings of the International Congresses of Medieval Canon Law will be referred to as (e.g.): *Proceedings Boston 1965, 1968, 1972* etc.

For the serial publications of the great academies:

Abh. Akad. … followed by name of city, e.g. *Berlin, München, etc. = Abhandlungen der … preussischen, bayerischen, etc. Akademie der Wissenschaften, philosophisch-historische Klasse.*

Similarly for *Mémoires, Memorie, Proceedings, Rendiconti, Sitzungsberichte,* etc. the abridged form is always understood as referring to the series covering philosophy and the humanities where several classes or sections exist in a single academy; e.g.:

Mém. Acad. Inscr.	*Rendic. Istit. Lombardo*
Proceed. Brit. Acad.	*Sb. Akad. Wien*

Short Titles

Adams/Donahue, *Canterbury Cases*   *Select Cases from the Ecclesiastical Courts
of the Province of Canterbury c. 1200–1301,* ed. Norma Adams and Charles
Donahue Jr. (Selden Society 95; London, 1981).

Beaulande/Charageat, *Officialités*   Beaulande-Barraud, Véronique and Martine
Charageat, *Les officialités dans l'Europe médiévale et moderne: Des tribunaux pour
une société chrétienne* (Actes du colloque international de Troyes, 27–29 mai
2010; Turnhout 2014).

Bethmann-Hollweg, *Civilprozeß*   Moritz August von Bethmann-Hollweg, *Der
Civilprozeß des gemeinen Rechts in geschichtlicher Entwicklung,: Der germanisch-
romanische Civilprozeß im Mittelalter vom 12. bis 15. Jahrhundert* (6 vols. Bonn
1864–1874).

Brundage, *Medieval Origins*   James A. Brundage, *The Medieval Origins of the Legal Profession* (Chicago 2008).

Coing, *Handbuch* 1   *Handbuch der Quellen und Literatur der neueren europäischen
Privatrechtsgeschichte, 1: Mittelalter (1100–1500): Die Gelehrten Rechte und die Gesetzgebung,* ed. Helmut Coing (Munich 1973).

Cortese, 'Scienza di guidici'   Ennio Cortese, 'Scienza di giudici e scienza di
professori tra xii e xiii secolo', *Legge, Giudici, Giuristi: Atti del Convegno tenuto
a Cagliari nei giorni 18–21 maggio 1981* (Pubblicazioni della Facoltà di Giurisprudenza, Università di Cagliari: Serie 1, Giuridica 26; Milan 1982) 93–148.

Donahue, Records 1, 2   *The Records of the Medieval Ecclesiastical Courts: Reports
of the Working Group on Church Court Records. 1: The Continent; 2: England,* ed.
Charles Donahue Jr. (Comparative Studies in Continental and Anglo-American
Legal History, 6–7; Berlin 1989–1994).

Einfluss der Kanonistik 1, 3, 4   *Der Einfluss der Kanonistik auf die europäische
Rechtskultur,. 1: Zivil- und Zivilprozessrecht,* ed. Orazio Condorelli, Franck
Roumy, and Mathias Schmoeckel (Norm und Struktur: Studien zum sozialen
Wandel in Mittelater und Früher Neuzeit 37.1. Köln-Weimar-Wien 2009), *Der
Einfluss der Kanonistik auf die europäische Rechtskultur, 3: Straf- und Strafprozessrecht,* ed. Condorelli, Roumy, Schmoekel (Norm und Struktur: Studien zum
sozialen Wandel in Mittelater und Früher Neuzeit 37.2. Köln-Weimar-Wien
2012), *Der Einfluss der Kanonistik auf die europäische Rechtskultur, 4: Prozessrecht,*
ed. Condorelli, Roumy, Schmoekel and Yves Mausen (Norm und Struktur:

Studien zum sozialen Wandel in Mittelater und Früher Neuzeit 37.4. Köln-Weimar-Wien 2014).

Fournier, *Officialités*   Paul Fournier, *Les offcialités au moyen âge: Étude sur l'organisation, la compétence et la procédure des tribunaux ecclésiastiques ordinaires en France de 1180 à 1328* (Paris, 1880; reprinted Aalen 1984).

Fowler-Magerl, *Ordo*   Linda Fowler-Magerl, *Ordo iudiciorum vel ordo iudiciarius: Begriff und Literaturgattung* (Ius commune Sonderheft 19; Frankfurt 1984).

Fowler-Magerl, 'Ordines'   Linda Fowler-Magerl, 'Ordines iudiciarii and Libelli de ordine iudiciorum: From the Middle of the Twelfth to the End of the Fifteenth Century', Typologie des sources du Moyen Age occidental (Fasc. 63; Turnhout 1993).

Geschichte des Kardinalats   *Geschichte des Kardinalats im Mittelalter*, ed. Jürgen. Dendorfer and R. Lützelschwab (Päpste und Papsttum 39; Stuttgart 2011).

Hartmann-Pennington *History*   *The History of Canon Law in the Classical Period, 1140–1234: From Gratian to the Decretals of Pope Gregory IX*, ed. Wilfried Hartmann and Kenneth Pennington (History of Medieval Canon Law; Washington, D.C.: 2008)

Kantorowicz, Gandinus 1, 2   Hermann U. Kantorowicz, *Albertus Gandinus und das Strafrecht der Scholastik, 1: Die Praxis, 2: Die Theorie* (2 vols. Berlin-Leipzig 1907–1926, reprinted 1978–1981).

Lefebvre-Teillard, *Officialités*   Anne Lefebvre-Teillard, *Les officialités à la veille du concile de Trente* (Bibliothèque d'histoire du droit et droit romain 19; Paris 1973).

Levillain, *Papacy*   Levillain, Philippe, ed. *The Papacy: An Encyclopedia* (3 vols. New York-London 2002).

Litewski, *Zivilprozeß*   Litweski, Wiesław, *Der römisch-kanonische Zivilprozeß nach den älteren ordines iudiciarii* (2 vols. Kraków1999).

Meijers, *Études*   Eduard M. Meijers, *Etudes d'histoire du droit, 3: Le droit romain au moyen age,* ed. Robert Feenstra and Herman F.W.D. Fischer (Leiden 1959).

Nörr, 'Literatur'   Knut Wolfgang Nörr, 'Die Literatur zum gemeinen Zivilprozess' *Handbuch der Quellen und Literatur der neueren europäischen Privatrechtsgeschichte 1: Mittelalter* (Munich 1973) 383–397.

Powicke-Cheney, *Councils*   Powicke, F. M., and C. R. Cheney, *Councils and Synods II: a.d. 1205–1313* (2 vols. Oxford 1964).

Proceedings Boston 1965   International Congresses of Medieval Canon Law will be referred to as *Proceedings Boston 1965, Proceedings Strassbourg 1968, Proceedings Toronto 1972,* etc.

Savigny, *Geschichte*   Friedrich C. von Savigny, *Geschichte des römischen Rechts im Mittelalter* (7 vols. Heidelberg 1850; repr. Bad Homberg 1961).

Schulte, *Geschichte*   Schulte, Johann Friedrich von. *Die Geschichte der Quellen und Literatur des canonischen Rechts von Gratian bis auf die Gegenwart, 1: Von Gratian bis auf Papst Gregor IX., 2: Von Papst Gregor IX. bis zum Concil von Trient, 3: Von der Mitte des 16. Jahrhunderts bis zur Gegenwart* (Stuttgart 1875, 1877, 1880, reprinted Graz 1956).

Stintzing, *Geschichte*   Roderich Stintzing, *Geschichte der populären Literatur des römisch-kanonischen Rechts in Deutschland am Ende des fünfzehnten und im Anfang des sechszehnten Jahrhunderts* (Leipzig 1867, reprinted Aalen 1959).

Wahrmund, *Quellen*   Ludwig Wahrmund, *Quellen zur Geschichte des römisch-kanonischen Processes im Mittelalter* (5 vols. Innsbruck and Heidelberg 1905–1931).

PART 1

Judicial Procedure and Practice in the
Medieval Church, 1100–1500

Introduction to the Courts

Kenneth Pennington

The essays in this volume deal with the courts of medieval and, by extension, early modern Europe. Barbara Deimling illustrates the places, public and otherwise, where courts were held. James Brundage discusses the education, training, and ethics of the judges, lawyers, and notaries who participated in trials. The rest of the essays, by Charles Donahue, Charles Duggan, Péter Cardinal Erdő, Antonio García y García, Richard Helmholz, Sara McDougall, Brigide Schwarz, and myself, deal with the organization and function of the courts within ecclesiastical and secular institutions.

A main focus of these essays is the terminology of procedure and norms of procedure in medieval ecclesiastical and secular courts. Furthermore, these essays illustrate the variety of practices that existed in different parts of Europe. Perhaps that variety is most striking in northwestern Europe, where ecclesiastical courts exercised their jurisdiction in ways that differed significantly from the secular courts.[1]

The essays also illuminate striking differences in the sources that we find in different parts of Europe. In northern Europe the sources are rich but do not always give us the details we need to understand a particular case. In Italy and Southern France the documentation is more detailed

---

1. See Richard Helmholz's article in this volume, 'Courts in England' (chap. 10) for an extended discussion.

than in other parts of Europe, but here too the archival records do not answer every question we might pose to them. In Spain, detailed documentation is strangely lacking, if not altogether absent. García y García consequently uses Iberian conciliar canons and tracts on procedure about practice in Spanish courts. As these essays demonstrate, scholars who want to peer into the medieval courtroom must also read a variety of sources: letters, papal decretals, chronicles, conciliar canons, and consilia to provide a nuanced and complete picture of what happened in the medieval courtroom. As these essays also make clear, however, many questions cannot be answered. Scholars should always remember that the sources almost never tell us what the judges who decided cases were thinking. It is always guesswork to read their minds. Consequently, those scholars who know norms that the jurists created in the jurisprudence of procedure have a much better chance of reading the sources correctly than those who do not.

It may be said that one may judge a society's sense of justice by examining its courts and procedure. In spite of the popular perceptions of torture, autos-da-fé, and brutal executions ('getting medieval' is Hollywood's phrase), medieval and early modern court procedure adhered to the principle of due process of law—that is, the rights of defendants—more firmly than modern American and most European courts. The term 'due process' entered the English language as an invention of fourteenth-century French jurists.[2] Medieval jurists who learned their law in schools expressed the idea in Latin as 'secundum ordinem iudiciarium' (according to the judicial order), or with similar phrasing.[3] The term 'secundum ordinem iudiciarium' did not mean that the rules of procedure in the courtroom were followed exactly, as it generally means today; it meant that the full rights of the defendant were respected by the court.[4] The rights of defendants—and plaintiffs—were of paramount importance in the medieval courtroom. Judges did not focus as much as they do today on whether evidence was admissible or not and on other rules that do not necessarily protect the rights of defendants.

The rules of procedure that the judges followed were contained in the Ius commune. Scholars and students must grapple with their ideas about procedure and its practice before they can understand a the full context

2. The earliest use of the term that I know is in a statute of Edward III, 28 Edward III, c.3 (1354): 'saunz estre mesne en respons par due process de lei', printed in Zechariah Chafee, *Documents on Fundamental Human Rights* (Cambridge, Mass. 1954) 246.

3. Kenneth Pennington, 'Law, Criminal Procedure,' *Dictionary of the Middle Ages: Supplement 1* (New York 2004) 309–320.

4. On the difference between due process in medieval and modern courts, see Kenneth Pennington, 'Innocent until Proven Guilty: The Origins of a Legal Maxim', *A Ennio Cortese* (3 vols. Roma 2001) 3.59–73 and revised and published in *The Jurist* 63 (2003) 106–124.

of a medieval or early- modern court case. The jurists called the jurisprudence that they taught in the law schools and that they interpreted in the commentaries they wrote on the 'libri legales' the Ius commune.[5] The Ius commune was a pan-European system of norms, principles, and practices.[6] I would not argue that medieval courts were models of justice. Medieval courts did violate principles of due process. Marginal people, especially heretics, the lower classes, and political enemies, could suffer miscarriages of justice. However, to know whether the sources reveal corrupt judges or document misguided court decisions, historians must know the rules of procedure in the jurisprudence of the Ius commune. It is one of the goals of this book to introduce students and scholars to the jurisprudence of procedure and its sources. My fellow authors and I would not argue that extra-legal considerations, human proclivities, and the interests of the powerful never influenced the outcomes of court cases or distorted its procedure yesterday, as they still do today. What we would argue, to adapt a very old maxim, is that the jurisprudence of procedure is the foundation upon which our understanding of the medieval and early modern court records must rest: 'periti sine iurisprudentia parum valent' (scholars who know no jurisprudence are not worth much). Scholars should always have one eye on the theory and another on how and whether a particular case adhered to jurisprudential principles and norms.[7]

There has been a recent trend among scholars studying the courts of medieval and early modern Europe to downplay the role of jurisprudential norms in the courts. Some scholars have concluded that the social, emotional, and political reasons compelling courts to subvert justice were more powerful than the norms that the jurists had created to dispense jus-

5. On the *libri legales* see Michael H. Hoeflich and Jasonne M. Grabher, 'The Establishment of Normative Legal Texts: The Beginnings of the Ius commune', *The History of Canon Law in the Classical Period, 1140-1234: From Gratian to the Decretals of Pope Gregory IX* (History of Medieval Canon Law; Washington, D.C. 2008) 1–21.

6. On the Ius commune, see Manlio Bellomo, *The Common Legal Past of Europe, 1000–1800* (Studies in Medieval and Early Modern Canon Law 4; Washington, D.C. 1995); also Kenneth Pennington, 'Learned Law, Droit Savant, Gelehrtes Recht: The Tyranny of a Concept', RIDC 5 (1994) 197–209, and most recently Pennington, 'Reform in 1215: *Magna Carta* and the Fourth Lateran Council', BMCL 32 (2015) 99–127, especially 125–127.

7. The three recent volumes of essays devoted to the jurisprudence of procedure in the medieval and early modern periods contain valuable essays and up-to-date bibliography. They will be cited in this volume with the short title *Einfluss der Kanonistik: Der Einfluss der Kanonistik auf die europäische Rechtskultur*, 1: *Zivil- und Zivilprozessrecht*, ed. Orazio Condorelli, Franck Roumy, and Mathias Schmoeckel (Norm und Struktur: Studien zum sozialen Wandel in Mittelater und Früher Neuzeit 37.1; Köln-Weimar-Wien 2009); *Der Einfluss der Kanonistik auf die europäische Rechtskultur, 3: Straf- und Strafprozessrecht*, ed. Orazio Condorelli, F. Roumy, and M. Schmoekel (Norm und Struktur: Studien zum sozialen Wandel in Mittelater und Früher Neuzeit 37.2; Köln-Weimar-Wien 2012); *Der Einfluss der Kanonistik auf die europäische Rechtskultur, 4: Prozessrecht*, ed. Orazio Condorelli, F. Roumy, M. Schmoekel, and Yves Mausen (Norm und Struktur: Studien zum sozialen Wandel in Mittelater und Früher Neuzeit 37.4; Köln-Weimar-Wien 2014).

tice. Other scholars have argued that the norms of procedure and the jurisprudence of the Ius commune had little influence on the development of courts.

This introduction is not the place to debate these approaches or to illustrate their shortcomings.[8] Readers will also notice that the authors in this volume differ on a number of issues. These differences mark areas where there is no consensus about how the procedure in medieval courts developed. Graduate students reading this book should note that these are topics that would be fruitful topics for further thought and research.

The goal of this chapter will be to illustrate how we should interpret court proceedings through the norms of procedure found in jurists' treatises. Theory can help us to understand practice. Although the evidence I present is limited, my interpretation of these sources assumes that the norms that we find in the writings of the proceduralists were generally followed in the courts. Although the two court cases that I will discuss below to describe the two most common methods of bringing a case to court are from a secular court, the same rules and procedures were followed in ecclesiastical courts. These two cases illustrate a crucial point that readers should constantly bear in mind as they read this book. The norms of courtroom procedure were developed primarily in canonical jurisprudence, but secular courts very quickly adopted the same norms and practices. Although this volume focuses on ecclesiastical courts, much of what is characteristic of church courts is also found in secular courts. In a third court case that I have taken from a papal decretal of Pope Innocent III, I try to show how this particular source poses problems but also provides insights into medieval juristic thought.

Hermann Kantorowicz pointed to the path that historians should take in order to understand medieval courts and their practices when he published a number of texts of complete late-thirteenth-century cases from the Bolognese archives. In addition he edited the works of Albertus Gandinus, a late-thirteenth-century proceduralist.[9] Albertus was not only

8. Examples of these approaches are: Laura Ikins Stern, *The Criminal Law System of Medieval and Renaissance Florence* (Johns Hopkins University Studies in Historical and Political Science, 112; Baltimore-London 1994); Chris Wickham, *Courts and Conflict in Twelfth-Century Tuscany* (Oxford 2003); Daniel Lord Smail, *The Consumption of Justice: Emotions, Publicity, and Legal Culture in Marseille 1264–1423* (Conjunctions of Religion and Power in the Medieval Past; Ithaca-London 2003); Sara Menzinger, *Giuristi e politica nei comuni di popolo: Siena, Perugia e Bologna, tre governi a confronto* (Ius nostrum, Studi e testi 34.; Roma 2006); Sarah Rubin Blanshei, *Politics and Justice in Late Medieval Bologna* (Medieval Law and Its Practice; Leiden-Boston 2010); Irene Fosi, *Papal Justice: Subjects and Courts in the Papal State, 1500–1750*, trans. Thomas V. Cohen (Washington, D.C. 2011); Massimo Vallerani, *Medieval Public Justice*, augmented edition, trans. Sarah Rubin Blanshei (Studies in Medieval and Early Modern Canon Law 9; Washington, D.C. 2012).

9. Kantorowicz, *Gandinus.*

a skilled interpreter of the law, but he was also a judge in Bologna who exercised jurisdiction through the authority of the Bolognese podestà.[10] Kantorowicz printed cases that illustrated all the procedural intricacies found in Italian courtrooms, especially those that brought the jurist in contact with the clamor of the courtroom. There were, after the twelfth century, two main ways that cases were brought to court, accusatorial and inquisitorial. The first mode of proof was through an accusation by a plaintiff (modus accusationis).[11] This mode of proof was the oldest, dating back to the procedure used in ancient Rome. The second mode of proof, inquisitorial proceedings, evolved in the last quarter of the twelfth century (modus inquisitionis). It was called inquisitorial because a judge could investigate a crime and summon a suspected wrongdoer to court. Inquisitorial procedure took its place alongside accusatorial, and both remained important for the next four centuries.

Inquisitorial procedure needed a strong governmental infrastructure to function. As will be discussed below in my essay on the 'ordines iudiciarii', inquisitorial procedure was born in ecclesiastical courts of the late twelfth century. Pope Innocent III's legislation at the Fourth Lateran Council established it as a mode of proof in ecclesiastical courts.[12] Inquisitorial procedure was quickly adopted by secular courts.[13] A Bolognese statute of 1252 sanctioned its use in the city's courts.[14] The slow but inexorable growth of governmental institutions in the city-states, principalities, and kingdoms ensured that inquisitorial procedure would gradually become pervasive throughout continental Europe.[15]

In the chapters of this volume there will be detailed discussions of

10. A few historians have misinterpreted Albertus's jurisprudence; see my remarks in 'Torture and Fear: Enemies of Justice', RIDC 19 (2008) 203–242 at 221–225.

11. Litewski, *Zivilprozeß* 1.37–43; Orazio Condorelli, 'Un contributo bolognese alla dottrina del processo romano-canonico: Il Tractatus de accusationibus et inquisitionibus di Bonincontro di Giovanni d'Andrea († 1350)', *Einfluss der Kanonistik* 4.65–90; also see my chapter 'Jurisprudence of Procedure' 146–147.

12. Ibid. 137–140 and passim.

13. André Gouron, 'Medieval Courts and Towns: Examples from Southern France', *Fundamina* 30 (1992) 30–46 at 39, reprinted in *Juristes et droits savants: Bologne et la France médiévale* (Selected Studies 679; Aldershot 2000) XIV. Gouron notes that inquisitorial procedure was incorporated into the consular statutes of Montpellier of 1223; on these statutes see Gouron, 'La *potestas statuendi* dans le droit coutumier montpelliérain du treizième siècle', *Diritto comune e diritti locali nella storia dell'Europa: Atti del Convegno di Varenna (12–15 June 1979)* (Milan 1980) 95–118; See also Donahue, 'Ecclesiastical Courts' 270.

14. *Statuti del comune di Bologna dall' anno 1245 all' anno 1267*, ed. Luigi Frati (Monumenti istorici pertenti alle provincie della Romagna, serie 1, Statuti, 1; Bologna 1869) 250: 'Placet quod si aliquis fuerit accusatus vel denuntiatus vel officio potestatis inquisitus de alliquo mallefitio, ex quod possit seu debeat personaliter puniri si haberi poterit non relaxetur pro securitate alliqua; set detineatur donec accusatio vel denuntiatio (denuntiabo *ed.*) vel inquisitio fuerit (*del.*ᴾᶜ) de eo facta fuerit terminata'.

15. Vallerani, *Medieval Public Justice* 47–52, 120–121, 230–233; Blanshei, *Politics and Justice* 314–315.

these two types of procedure. In order to set the stage for the essays that follow, I will give two examples from the court records of Bologna that Kantorowicz printed. The records that survive never provide enough information to answer all the questions that arise about the litigants, the court, the procedure, and the motives of the various players that we meet in the sources. The first two cases taken from Kantorowicz that I examine below, a case of attempted rape that ended in marriage and a criminal case that ended in a hanging, will introduce the courtroom, the accusatorial and inquisitorial procedure, the players, the people who applied and sought justice in medieval Europe, and how a medieval jurisprudence can illuminate what happened in the courtroom. The third case is taken from a papal decretal. With it I try to show what the decretals can and cannot tell us for our understanding of the courts. Finally, I will discuss the most misunderstood practice in the medieval courts: the summary procedure. It became important in the middle of the thirteenth century. There is probably no aspect of medieval and early modern procedure that has created more problems of interpretation for modern scholars.

Accusatorial Procedure

As the name implies, accusatorial procedure requires an accuser to begin a legal action. This principle was fundamental to medieval society's conception of justice until the end of the twelfth century.[16] Kantorowicz printed a text about a peasant woman, Bonavixina, and her accusation against her importunate suitor, Fulchitus. Bonavixina must have found an advocate to compose a 'libellus' that described her complaint and brought her case before the famous jurist Albertus Gandinus, who happened to be the sitting judge in Bologna. Normally the plaintiff had to bring her case to the ordinary judge who had jurisdiction over the defendant.[17] If this rule had been followed, then she must have accused Fulchitus in the municipal court, since he lived in Bologna.

The written record of the case is brief. We do not have detailed testimony of Fulchitus or Bonavixina. On June 11, 1289 she appeared before Gandinus.[18] Reciting the required formula, 'denunciare et accusare,' she

---

16. Tancred (ca. 1216), *Ordo iudiciarius*, ed. Fridericus Bergmann (Göttingen 1842) 158 and n. 80: 'Ad horum accusationem non admittitur nisi is, cuius interest, ut Dig. de privat. delict. 17.1', to which Accursius (ca. 1250) Glossa ordinaria (Venice 1494) fol. 101v to Dig. 17.1.3 s.v. *penam,* agreed and noted: 'numquid etiam extranei admittuntur ad huiusmodi accusationem de privatis delictis, cum criminalis sit? Respon. Non, quia privata est'.

17. Ibid. 127: 'Quis dicitur esse iudex ordinarius alicuius? Respondeo ille est iudex ordinarius rei, apud quem ipse reus domicilium habet'.

18. Kantorowicz, *Gandinus* 1.261–262; on Gandinus see Diego Quaglioni, 'Gandino, Alberto', DGI 1.942–944.

denounced and accused Fulchitus.[19] While she was tending her cattle, he had, she said, seized her with force and against her will and thrown her to the ground. He then attempted to 'know her carnally.' He wished to 'corrupt and violate' her. He struck her many times on different parts of her body because she would not surrender to him. She stated that he shouted, 'It is necessary that I take you and that you consent to obey my will. Otherwise I will kill you.'[20] People heard her cries and came to help her. If they had not arrived, he would have corrupted and violated her. She took the oath of calumny (iuramentum calumniae), gave securities in good faith (fide iussit pro eo de accusatione prosequenda)[21]—such an oath was given with the promise of a surety (fideiussor)—and was given a date for the continuation of her case. Taking an oath that confirmed that the accusation was true and not false was an important part of accusatorial procedure. The jurists described the purpose of the oath with a poem:[22]

> He swears that just is his accuse,
> And were he asked, the truth he would not confuse.

Gandinus gave Bonavixina and Fulchitus two days to think about their relationship. Two days later Bonavixina and Fulchitus appeared again before Gandinus. Bonavixina must have been carried away by Fulchitus's passion—or if one were skeptical of the laconic written record, she used the court to legalize his lust. Fulchitus told Gandinus that Bonavixina had accepted his proposal of marriage. When Gandinus asked Bonavixina if this claim were true, she replied that it was, with the added piece of information that she had consented to the marriage freely and of her free will.[23] She must have added this information at the insistence of her advocate. Free and willing consent was at the heart of the marriage contract by the end of the twelfth century. She added that these changed circumstances had caused her to withdraw her accusation.

---

19. Kantorowicz, *Gandinus* 1:261–262: 'Bonavixina . . . iurata, denuntiat et accusat . . .'

20. Ibid.: 'necesse est quod ego te habeam et quod tu consentias, tu michi faciendo meam voluntatem. Alioquin ego te occidam'.

21. On the oaths taken during the legal process, see Antonia Fiori, *Il giuramento di innocenza nel processo canonico medievale: Storia e disciplina della "purgatio canonica"* (Studien zur europäische Rechtsgeschichte 277; Frankurt am Main 2013); Tiziana Ferreri, *Ricerche sul crimen calumniae nella dottrina dei glossatori: Da Irnerio ad Azzone e da Graziano a Uguccione da Pisa* (Archivio per la storia del diritto medioevale e moderno, 15; Noceto 2010).

22. Tancred, *Ordo iudiciarius* 205: Illud iuretur, quod lis sibi iusta videtur, / Et cum quaeretur, verum non inficietur.

23. Kantorowicz, *Gandinus* 262: 'propria et spontanea voluntate'. Marriage could be contracted without a priest and outside a church if the couple exchanged vows of marriage in the present tense. See Charles J. Reid Jr., *Power over the Body, Equality in the Family: Rights and Domestic Relations in Medieval Canon Law* (Emory University Studies in Law and Religion; Grand Rapids, Mich.- Cambridge 2004) 28–29, 39–43, 55–58.

Fulchitus was not completely free. He was asked to deny Bonavixina's accusations. He did. He said that he had not done any of the things of which Bonavixina had accused him. Gandinus made Fulchitus deny his guilt in court because, just as today, guilt of sexual violence was not eradicated by the marriage bond. The court stipulated that if he were <later> condemned in any matter involving this case, he would resolve the matter with a fine of 100 Bolognese pounds. The court approved his marriage but <tacitly> reminded him that he must keep his promises to Bonavixina. Fulchitus also provided a surety for these promises.[24] Gandinus absolved him.

Inquisitorial Procedure

Kantorowicz printed several cases that illustrated the rules governing inquisitorial procedure.[25] A criminal case of theft is especially detailed.[26] In December 1299, Vecto, a criminal judge of Philip, podestà of Bologna, was delegated to begin an investigation of Mengho, son of Ugolino, and a certain Nicholas and Sandrolo.[27] As Kantorowicz points out, this text was written only after the conclusion of the case because the judge did not know who Mengho's accomplices were until after Mengho was tortured.[28]

Mengho's 'fama' led to an investigation.[29] The court declared that he and his accomplices were public and well-known robbers and receivers of thieves and stolen goods (publici et famosi latrones et furtorum receptatores).[30] In December 1299, Mengho was alleged to have broken into the store of the brothers Montanaro and Giovanni. He carried away many different colored skeins of silk. There were skeins of dark and light green silk that were worth 30 Bolognese pounds.

24. See Vallerani, *Medieval Public Justice* 143–146, for a good outline of the role of sureties.

25. Kantorowicz, *Gandinus* 1.203–235.

26. Ibid. 203–218. Litewski, *Zivilprozeß* 1.124–128; see the detailed ecclesiastical cases described by Donahue, 'Ecclesiastical Courts' 332–335; on the origins of the 'inquisitio', see my chapter 'Jurisprudence of Procedure' 138, with bibliography.

27. Kantorowicz, *Gandinus* 1.203: 'Hec est inquisitio que fit et fieri intenditur ex officio nobilis et potentis militis domini Phylippi de Vergiolensibus, honorabilis potestatis civitatis Bononie sub examine discreti et sapientis viri domini Vecti de Bonfilliolis'.

28. Ibid. 129.

29. On 'fama' and its role in the 'inquisitio', see my chapter 'Jurisprudence of Procedure' 146, and Vallerani, *Medieval Public Justice* 106–113, who misinterprets Gandinus's reasons for submitting a person to torture. A 'semiplena probatio' is not sufficient for torture but is only one piece of evidence that a judge can take into account. As Gandinus states a few sentences later, 'ut notatur infra de questionibus et tormentis' he will discuss there the evidence that a judge must have before submitting a defendant to torture; see Kantorowicz, *Gandinus* 1.155–177; also my 'Torture and Fear' 222–223.

30. Gero Dolezalek, *Das Imbreviaturbuch des erzbishöflichen Gerichtsnotars Hubaldus aus Pisa, Mai bis August 1230* (Forschungen zur neueren Privatrechtsgeschichte 13; Köln, 1969) 65–66, illustrates the role of 'fama' in procedure.

Vecto ordered a knight (miles) Lazario to conduct an investigation into the robbery. This step was an important part of the investigation (inquisitio). First, the investigation must be sanctioned by a public authority. Then the investigation must be recorded with a written record. On the 5th of December, Lazario supervised the testimony of nine witnesses and had their testimony recorded. The testimony of the witnesses was taken near the store and in the Chapel of San Bertolo. Justo of Pistoia was the notary.[31] The witnesses spoke Italian, but Justo translated their testimony into Latin. The document containing the accusation against Mengho was read to Jacobo Bonbolongini in Italian. Jacobo had a store near Montanaro's and Giovanni's. After swearing an oath to tell the truth, he said he knew nothing of the robbery but said that he believed Mengho to be a good man and not evil. Bartolomeo Benvenuti also had a store nearby. Like Jacobo, he had heard about the robbery but had no knowledge of Mengho. Ghisla, a neighbor, was questioned. She had heard the commotion that morning but had no knowledge of the robbery. She knew Mengho but knew nothing about his reputation (fama). Michele Ubertini also said that he heard the commotion and the accusations against Mengho, but he had no other knowledge. Lambertino Gherardi, another shopkeeper, stated that this morning, after attending Mass, he passed by the brothers' store. It was open. He asked whether there was damage. Montanaro responded, 'I don't think so'. Lambertinus told him to check his storage box. Montanaro did and told him that money was missing. Justo asked Lambertinus if he knew Mengho and his reputation. Lambertinus said he did and that Mengho had the reputation of a thief. Two more witnesses reported that Mengho was an evil denizen of the night but did not comment specifically on his reputation (fama).

On the same day Lazario and Justo went to Mengho's house with two armed retainers of the Bolognese podestà to search for the stolen goods.[32] They found dark green, light green, and red skeins of silk in the straw of a bed. They took the silk to one of the brothers, Giovanni, and asked him if he could identify the goods. He immediately said it was his and told them that he had bought them from Vanno Bonaventuri, a merchant from Lucca. Lazario and Justo with the retainers of the podestà went to see Vanno

---

31. On the role of notaries see Brundage, 'Practice' 56–59 and Donahue, 'Procedure' 113–118 and passim below. Dolezalek, *Das Imbreviaturbuch,* discovered and published a notary's notebook of Hubaldus's work in Pisa at the archepiscopal court in the year 1230. The document records the testimony of witnesses in a variety of cases and describes the actions of the court's response to papal letters. Hubaldus's records do not, however, let us understand the entire proceedings.

32. Kantorowicz, *Gandinus* 1.209.

to confirm Giovanni's story. He described the color of the silk. When he was shown the silk he could not identify it with certainty as the silk he had sold to Montanaro and Giovanni. A lot of silk is that color, he said. Vanno brought out his scales and weighed the silk. It weighed 5½ ounces.

On the same day, December 5th, Mengho was brought before Judge Vecto again. The results of the investigation were read to him in Italian. Mengho denied everything. Vecto asked Mengho whether he had bought silk within a month or maybe longer. Mengho said he did not know. He did remember that two months ago or so he had purchased a quantity of silk. Vecto asked whether Mengho normally stored silk in straw pillow. He said no. The colored silk was produced in court and shown to Mengho. Vecto explained that the silk was discovered in his bed by the nuncio of the podestà of Bologna, Pietro Partuccio, and his retainers. Mengho was quick to respond. A certain Pedecolo met him on the street that morning in a great rush and asked Mengho if he worked with silk. Mengho said yes. Pedecolo gave Mengho the silk and said, 'Hold this silk until I come back'. Mengho took the silk and put it in his bed.

Vecto asked Mengho whether he had asked Pedecolo where he got the silk. Mengho answered no. Mengho might have claimed that he accepted the silk under the unilateral contract of deposit,[33] but he destroyed that possibility when Vecto asked him what Pedecolo's status was. Mengho told the judge that he was a beggar, a thief, and an 'infamis' from robbery. Did Mengho give Pedecolo money for the silk, asked Vecto. No, responded Mengho. Vecto had one final question. Did Mengho know who took money from the Montanaro's store? Mengho claimed that he knew nothing about the robbery.

Vecto was confronted with a problem. How should he proceed? The investigation had produced no eyewitnesses and no certain evidence about Mengho's reputation. The silk found in his home was powerful but not conclusive evidence. Was Pedecolo the thief? Vanno's inability to identify the silk was troubling.

Vecto had two options. He could free Mengho for lack of evidence, or he could order him to be tortured. The Bolognese statutes of 1288 had placed restrictions on the use of torture, which conformed to the laws of other city-states.[34] The jurisprudence at this time dictated that a person could be tortured only if there were very compelling, but not conclusive,

33. Reinhard Zimmermann, *The Law of Obligations: Roman Foundations of the Civilian Tradition* (Oxford 1996) 205–216 and passim.

34. Partially printed by Kantorowicz, *Rechtshistorische Schriften,* ed. Helmut Coing and Gerhard Immel (Freiburger Rechts- und Staatswissenschaftliche Ablandlungen 30 (Karlsruhe 1970) 311–340 at 327.

presumptions of guilt (violentae praesumptiones). A judge must also take the status, age, and gender of the person into consideration when deciding on torture.[35] Some people were exempt from torture completely.[36]

There has been debate about the frequency of torture in European courts. Some historians have argued that it was frequently used and was the inevitable result of inquisitorial procedure. I have argued that it was used sparingly and only as a last resort to seek the truth.[37] I have also argued that there was a movement to abandon torture among the jurists long before the eighteenth century.[38] Vecto weighed his options, probably reflected upon and studied the jurisprudence, especially the recent Bolognese law of 1288 on the use of torture. A key phrase in the statute, 'public and notorious robbers', which Justo the notary had intentionally used several times in his depositions of witnesses, was most likely the legal reason that convinced Vecto that Mengho could be tortured.[39]

Torture was imposed on a defendant in a strictly orchestrated way that was established by statute. The Bolognese criminal statute of 1288 dictated that when a judge found compelling presumptions of guilt based on evidence, the defendant's testimony should be heard in the presence of four officials, of whom two must be judges.[40] No citizen of Bologna

35. Pennington, *The Prince and the Law, 1200–1600: Sovereignty and Rights in the Western Legal Tradition* (Berkeley-Los Angeles-London 1993) 157–160; see also my 'Torture and Fear', and my 'Women on the Rack: Torture and Gender in the Ius commune', *Recto ordine procedit magister: Liber amicorum E.C. Coppens*, ed. Jan Hallebeek, Louis Berkvens, Georges Martyn, and Paul Nève (Iuris Scripta Historica 28; Brussels 1212) 243–257.

36. Pennington, 'Torture and Fear' 216–218.

37. Ibid. 226–228. Here I point out that torture was used infrequently in criminal cases. It was far from being 'an integral part of due process' in the courts of the Ius commune, as stated by Blanshei, *Politics and Justice* 320. It was also not 'a basic part of inquisition procedure,' as Stern, *Criminal Law System* 211, would have it. Stern is also incorrect in stating that one cannot tell whether a confession was based on torture or not (ibid.). The records of Italian courts always recorded whether a confession was extracted by torture.

Some historians exaggerate the use of torture and write of it as if it were a daily occurrence, by plucking their evidence from chronicles and consilia in different cities and from different centuries. They do not try to understand the particular circumstances of why and how torture was used. See, for example, Trevor Dean, *Crime and Justice in Late Medieval Italy* (Cambridge 2007) 56–57, 107, especially 189–192, where he sensationalizes random evidence and departs from the sensible comments he had made on page 107 on the basis of the evidence of jurists in their legal consilia.

38. Mathias Schmoekel, *Humanität und Staatsraison: Die Abschaffung der Folter in Europa und die Entwicklung des gemeinen Strafprozeß- und Beweisrechts seit dem hohn Mittelalter* (Norm und Struktur: Studien zum sozialen Wandel in Mittelalter und Früher Neuzeit 14; Köln-Weimar-Wien 2000), has made the same argument.

39. Kantorowicz, *Rechtshistorische Schriften* 327: 'Ordinamus quod nullus possit vel debeat modo aliquo vel ingenio tormentari vel subici aliquibus tormentis tondoli vel tirelli vel cuiuscumque alterius generis tormentorum vel ei inferri mine alicuius vel aliquorum tormentorum nisi in casibus infrascriptis, videlicet publici et famosi latronis'.

40. Ibid.: 'Et in quolibet predictorum casuum, cum violente presumptiones invente fuerit, et tunc in presentia quatuor officialium, quorum duo sint iudices, audientium et intelligentium confessionem ipsius corum eorum presentia'.

or member of various guilds could be tortured or even threatened with torture without compelling presumptions and proven evidence.[41] The Captain of the People had to examine and approve each court order to torture. A notary must be present to record the proceedings. A member of the defendant's family and six 'anziani', or consuls, of the people must also be present.[42] These regulations must be exactly (praecise) observed.[43] The formal ceremony through which torture was administered was a significant limitation on judicial arbitrariness. Further, the ability of the family to accuse magistrates of malfeasance through the legal instrument of the 'sindacato' if these regulations were violated also limited judges who acted arbitrarily.[44] Jurists did complain that some judges resorted to torture too frequently. The evidence, however, seems to indicate that their complaints may have been about a small number of judges.

Vecto decided that Mengho could be tortured. Two days later, on the 7th of December, two judges, Arardo de Signorelli and Pietro Biterno, two knights (miles), and Pietro Bonfacio, a notary, accompanied Mengho to the room for torture. The record does not specify where the torture was carried out or how Mengho was tortured. The Bolognese records of the late thirteenth century used three words that seem to mean the same thing: 'tondolum', 'tirellum', and 'ad cordam' (La corda). These terms refer to the rope and pulley system of torture that remained popular for centuries. Defendants were hoisted into the air with a rope attached to their wrists with their arms held behind their backs. A large illumination in a Vatican Codex manuscript and a number of illuminations to Causa 15 in Gratian's Decretum illustrate 'la corda'.[45] Later, the length of time that

41. Ibid. 327–328: 'Salvo et reservato, quod nullus qui sit de societatibus artium vel armorum cambii vel merchadandie populi Bononie, vel intelligatur esse de populo Bononie ex forma alicuius privillegii, ordinamenti, statuti vel provisionis aut reformationis comunis vel populi Bononie, possit vel debeat modo aliquo vel ingenio tormentari vel subici aliquibus tormentis tondoli vel tirelli vel cuiuscunque generis tormentorum vel ei inferri mine alicuius tormenti vel aliquorum tormentorum nisi in premissis casibus superius anotatis'.

42. Ibid. 328: 'vel unius de sua familia et in praesentia sex ancianorum vel consulum'. On the establishment of the 'anziani et consules' in the mid-thirteenth century, see Blanshei, *Politics and Justice* 85.

43. Ibid.: 'Quod statutum in omnibus suis partibus sit precisum et precise debeat observari'.

44. Moritz Isenmann, 'From Rule of Law to Emergency Rule in Renaissance Florence', *The Politics of Law in Late Medieval and Renaissance Italy*, ed. Lawrin Armstrong and Julius Kirshner (Toronto Studies in Medieval Law 1; Toronto 2011) 55–76 at 58–59; 'sindacato' is also discussed in other essays in this volume. See also Susanne Lepsius, 'Summarischer Syndikatsprozeß: Einflüsse des kanonischen Rechts auf die städtische und kirchliche Gerichtspraxis des Spätmittelalters', *Church Law and the Origins of the Western Legal Tradition: A Tribute to Kenneth Pennington*, ed. Wolfgang Peter Müller and Mary E. Sommar (Washington, D.C. 2006) 252–274.

45. Biblioteca Apostolica Vaticana lat. 1430, fol. 179r, Justinian's Codex, Book 6, title 1 (*De fugitivis servis*), chapters 1–4, ca. 1325–1350; See also Maria Alessandra Biotti, *Le Décret de Gratien: Un manuscrit du XIVe siècle reconstitute* (Art de l'enluminure 24 [2008]) 10, 40–41, and Anthony Melni-

the defendant could be held aloft in that position was limited by the time needed to recite a short prayer such as the 'Ave Maria' or 'Pater noster'.[46] Court records of torture in the fifteenth and sixteenth centuries almost always listed the instruments of torture that were used.

Torture was carefully regulated. Albertus Gandinus was a judge in the Bolognese courts and a contemporary of Mengho who wrote about torture in great detail. Could a podestà torture a man who was accused of murder without any evidence of his guilt? And if he could, would the defendant's confession constitute a full and valid confession that would permit his condemnation? His answer was no.[47] 'What follows from an act lacking legitimacy cannot be valid'.[48] Albertus turned then to a more subtle question:

But I pose the question here: what of the confession made under the fear of torture? I think if <the facts of the case were>: the person to be tortured is led to the place of the torture, his hands are bound behind him, and the judge would say to him unless he confesses immediately he would torture him. In this case if he confesses the confession is not valid, unless he would persevere in his confession <in court>. The law holds such a confession extorted by fear to be the equivalent to one extracted by torture.[49]

Albertus imagined the defendant prepared for La corda. He next explored fear and torture. 'What if', he asked, 'the person were led to the torture chamber, but his hands were not bound behind him, <is his confession valid>? [i.e., he was not confronted with La corda]' Although there were differing opinions, he thought the confession was not admissible in court.[50] He posed another question to define exactly what constituted the fear in a reasonable man (homo constans):

---

kas, *The Corpus of Minatures in the Manuscripts of Decretum Gratiani* (SG 16–18; Rome 1975), illuminations to Causa 15 in volume 17.

46. See Pennington, 'Torture and Fear' 236.

47. Kantorowicz, *Gandinus* 2.167 lines 6–18.

48. Ibid. line 19: 'quo deficiente quicquid sequitur ex eo vel ob id non valet'.

49. Ibid. lines 24–30: 'Sed quero hic que confessio dicatur facta formidine tormentorum? Respondeo si torquendus ducatur ad pedem torture et legentur ei manus de retro et dicatur ei a iudice quod, nisi confiteatur quod in continenti subiiciet eum torture. In hoc casu si confiteatur non tenet talis confessio, nisi in confessione fuerit perseveratum, quia lex equiparat talem confessionem extortam formidine tormentorum confessioni facte in tormentis, ut C. quorum appellationes non recipiantur l.ii. (Cod. 7.65.2.1)'. The text of the Codex is from the Emperor Constantius (344 A.D.): 'Sicut enim haec ita observari disposuimus, ita aequum est testibus productis, instrumentis prolatis aliisque argumentis praestitis, si sententia contra eum lata sit et ipse, qui condemnatus est aut minime voce sua confessus sit aut formidine tormentorum tentus contra se aliquid dixerit, provocandi licentiam ei non denegari'. Albertus noted that Accursius, the ordinary glossator to the Codex (ca. 1230), s.v. *formidine tormentorum,* wrote that Constantius did not say 'fear in torture' but 'fear of torture'.

50. Ibid. 168 lines 10–18.

But what if outside the torture chamber the judge said, 'either you confess or I shall lead you to be tortured', trying to create as much terror in him as he could? The defendant confessed. Will it be said in this case that the confession was extorted by fear? I say no, because this was slight terror.... we ought to interpret terror or fear of torture as a present and immediate <threat of torture>.... Slight terror of torture outside the torture chamber is an illusory fact.[51]

Albertus tried to calibrate the amount of fear that constitutes torture. His solution was to distinguish between "an imminent and apparent danger" of torture, to use the terminology of current American criminal law, and the mere threat of torture.

The jurists had long noted that some defendants could endure much pain under torture. Others could not. Mengho confessed immediately. It was a long and detailed confession. Although the means of torture were not recorded and Mengho's screams of pain were left out of the account, Mengho confessed to crimes he committed years before. If the notary recorded his confession accurately, the first crime that he confessed was his most recent crime: that he stole the money from the store of Montanaro and Giovanni Bellecti. Mengho and his friend Pedecolo looked at the bag of money that Giovanni Bellecti carried into the store and decided to steal it during the night. They invited Sandrolo to join them. The notary wrote down Mengho's version of the conversation. Sandrolo had asked, 'What's the job?' Mengho and Pedecolo had told him about the money. Sandrolo had responded 'I'm in'.[52] Mengho went into the shop through a window and took the money from the locked box. He attempted to let Pedecolo and Sandrolo into the shop but made too much noise. Mengho exited through the window but also took the silk with him. Mengho went home. He buried the money and hid the silk in his bed, 'where it was found by Pietro Partuccio, the nuncio of the city'. Upon Mengho's confession, Lazario was sent to Mengho's house to see whether what he had confessed about the money was true. It was. Lazario found the money where Mengho had claimed he buried it.[53]

Once he had admitted to stealing the money and the silk, Mengho confessed to numerous other crimes over the years. Seven years earlier he had stolen from his teacher. Two years earlier he had stolen offerings

---

51. Ibid. lines 19–28: 'Sed quid si extra locum in quo homines torquentur iudex dixit "aut confitearis aut ducam te ad tormenta", inferendo sibi terrorem de hoc quantum poterat, et ille talis his auditis fuerit confessus. Numquid dicetur in hoc casu confessio facta formidine tormentorum? Dic quod non, quia levis territio.... Terrorem autem aut metum tormentorum debemus accipere presentem et instantem torture.... Levis enim territio tormentorum extra locum torture facta illusoria est, arg. ff. si cui plus quam per legem Falcidiam l. Hec satisdatio (Dig. 35.3.4)'.

52. Kantorowicz, *Gandinus* 1.212: 'Sandrolus dixit "ad quid faciendum"... "libenter eamus".'

53. Ibid. 214.

from the altar of Santa Maria del Monte.[54] Four months earlier, he and others whom he could not remember had stolen sacred objects from San Domenico. To these crimes Mengho added a number of others. Mengho 'persisted and persevered' in his confession, 'adding or subtracting nothing,' when he repeated it before the court, as was required by the norms governing the 'ordo iudiciarius'.[55]

After his confession, Judge Vecto set a date in three days for his defense. Vecto also ordered Justo to take Pedecolo and Sandrolo into custody. Justo reported to the judge that they could not be found anywhere in Bologna. On the 11th of December Alexander Jacobi, a nuncio of Bologna, was ordered to make a public proclamation before the homes of Pedecolo and Sandrolo summoning them to court. Alexander announced the summons day after day. Anyone could come before the court and present evidence in their defense. If Pedecolo and Sandrolo did not appear in court they would be banned.[56] On December 11 Vecto set aside the entire day for Mengho to receive the evidence against him and to do what he wished 'de iure' before the court and in public. Martino Bagnarolo, a public herald for the commune of Bologna, told Justo, the notary, on December 14th, that he had once again summoned Pedecolo and Sandrolo with public and loud declarations before their homes. On the same day, both men were publically banned with the consent of the Council of Eighty.[57] If the Podestà captured them they were condemned to be hanged. On the same day, Mengho confirmed his confessions before the court and judge Vecto. His confession 'added or subtracted nothing' to the written report submitted by the notary who had heard his confession. The stolen goods were returned to their owner. Mengho was condemned to the gallows and hanged.

This case illustrates many of the norms of inquisitorial criminal procedure in secular courts. The judge could order investigations on the author-

---

54. Santa Maria del Monte was founded in the twelfth century by Benedictines and is now part of the Villa Aldini; it lies just south of Bologna.

55. Kantorowicz, *Gandinus* I.216: 'Menghus suprascriptus constitutus coram dicto domino Vecto iudice malleficiorum dicti domini Potestatis, ad banchum malleficiorum comunis Bononie sub portichu palatii novi dicti comunis ante cameras iudicum Potestatis, dixit et perseveravit et confessus fuit omnia supra scripta, nil addens vel minuens suprascriptis confessionibus, sed in eis persistendo et perseverando'.

56. Peter Raymond Pazzaglini, *The Criminal Ban of the Sienese Commune 1225–1310* (Quaderni di 'Studi senesi' 45; Milan 1979).

57. Kantorowicz, *Gandinus* I.217–218: 'Thomaxius Iohannis, publicus preco comunis Bononie, in consilio octingenorum viorum comunis et populi Bononie, in palatio veteri dicti comunis voce preconia et ad sonum campanarum more solito congregato, ipso consilio bene audiente... magno sono tube premisso, gridavit et exbannivit et in banno comunis Bononie posuit predictos Niccholaum (Pedecolo) et Sandrolum'.

ity of his office. He had the power to conduct searches and to summon witnesses for interrogation. If there were grave presumptions of guilt and if a defendant refused to confess, the defendant could be tortured. Torture, however, should be used only as a last resort, when the evidence was almost but not quite conclusive, and when the defendant had a bad reputation. The Bolognese statutes of 1288 stated that no person who lived in Bologna and belonged to a guild could be tortured without legitimate proofs. The lord captain must examine each case and approve the use of torture in the presence of the defendant and six officials of the city. Four officials of the commune and a notary should hear the confession of the man being tortured. The defendant must, after confessing, be given an opportunity to produce witnesses or evidence in his defense. Other persons who were implicated in a criminal's confession must be given a chance to defend themselves in court. In Mengho's case the conflicting testimony of the witnesses was probably not sufficient for torture, but the discovery of the silk in Mengho's home created the required grave presumption of guilt. The norms of the Ius commune and the statutes of many Italian city states forbade indiscriminate and arbitrary torture. Further the jurists agreed that a confession extracted by torture must be repeated in court when the defendant was under no coercion. As Johannes Andreae noted several decades later, the statutes of the Italian cities prohibited torture unless there was a grave presumption of guilt. The Bolognese statute mandated that if torture was used in violation of the norms, the podestà would be condemned to a fine of 1,000 Bolognese pounds and excluded from the governance of the city.[58]

Papal Decretals as Evidence for Ecclesiastical Procedure

The papal appellate decisions that the canonists began to collect in the mid-twelfth century provide much evidence for how procedure was regulated in Rome and in the episcopal courts.[59] The richest collection of decretals, the *Decretals of Pope Gregory IX* (Liber Extra, or often cited with just a capital X), compiled by Raymond de Peñafort and promulgated in 1234 by Gregory, tells hundreds of stories and captures almost every human failing. Theft, robbery, adultery, incest, simony, clerical misconduct, and murder all appear again and again in its pages. Gregory's Decretals pre-

---

58. Kantorowicz, *Rechtshistorische Schriften* 328: 'Et si contra predicta vel aliquod predictorum fiat per dominum Potestatem vel aliquem de sua familia, ipso iure sit exclusus a regimine civitatis et condempnetur per dominum Capitaneum in mille libras bononenorum'.

59. Charles Duggan, 'Decretal Collections from Gratian's *Decretum* to the *Compilationes antiquae:* The Making of the New Case Law', *History*, ed. Hartmann and Pennington 246–292.

serves only a small proportion of the cases that were appealed to Rome. The papal registers contain thousands of cases that remain, in large part, still unexplored. I have selected a case from the early years of Pope Innocent III's pontificate to illustrate what can and what cannot be learned from them.

The first is an English marriage case from 1203. A certain W. from the diocese of Lincoln had an incestuous relationship with his wife's sister:

To Clement, the Prior of Oseney (Augustinian Priory, Diocese of Lincoln)

You have informed us in your letter that W., the bearer of your letter, had married a certain woman and after his marriage had fallen into an incestuous relationship with his wife's sister and, by doing so, had committed adultery. He wallowed in this filth for three years. The sister bore twins from this adulterous relationship, and the crime became known to the neighbors. W. has pleaded abject poverty in the presence of our penitentiary, and he asserts that he cannot make a pilgrimage to Jerusalem that had been imposed upon him. Since you can more fully determine his means, we are sending him back to you. We mandate by this apostolic letter that you should give him a penance that you deem appropriate.

You have also asked to be advised what you should do about his wife. We briefly respond that his wife should be enjoined diligently to be continent until her husband dies and to abstain completely from mingling her flesh with his on account of public honesty. Nonetheless if the wife refuses to obey because she fears to lapse from chastity, her husband may and ought render the conjugal debt to her with the fear of the Lord. The reason is that affinity iniquitously contracted after the marriage ought not to injure her since she was not a participant in the iniquity. Consequently the wife should not be deprived of her right without her fault [unde iure suo sine sua non debet culpa privari]. Notwithstanding whatever by certain of our predecessors had been decided in a similar case that either the adultery or incest was manifest or secret or, as others have maintained, whether the grade of consanguinity was close or remote, <the wife should not be deprived of her right>.

Pope Innocent III. Written at the Lateran on 24 February 1203 in the sixth year of our pontificate.[60]

A decretal can give us information about the procedure at the papal court and at the lower level ecclesiastical courts as well. It can also give us insight to the minds of the judges. It does not, however, answer all the questions that we would like to have resolved.

The social context of this case is difficult to understand completely—a common problem for scholars when they study papal decretals. W.—I will name him Walter—contracted a marriage with a woman. After the

---

60. *Die Register Innocenz' III. 6: 6. Pontifikatsjahr, 1203/1204, Texte und Indices*, ed. Othmar Hageneder, John C. Moore, and Andrea Sommerlechner, with Christoph Egger and Herwig Weigl (Publikationen des Historischen Instituts beim Österreichischen Kulturinstitut in Rom 2; Vienna 1995) 5–6.

marriage, Walter began to have an affair with his wife's sister that lasted three years. The sister bore twins. Neighbors began to talk. Although the decretal is silent about how the case came to the attention of ecclesiastical authorities, 'clamor' as reported by neighbors undoubtedly came to the attention of local ecclesiastical authorities. The statement that 'the crime became known to neighbors', which the curial judges included in their decision, is a clue that they assumed that Walter's wife and his wife's sister did not bring an accusation to the court. If accusers were not injured by Walter's crime, they could not bring an accusation against him.[61] This norm had always been widely accepted. Without an accuser to bring criminals to court, the moral and legal question was posed: should crimes for which accusers did not come forward remain unpunished?[62] The Fourth Lateran Council's *Qualiter et quando* canon 8 declared in 1215:

When a . . . matter reaches the ears of the superior through outcries and the rumor [clamor et fama] of many, not from enemies and slanderers, but from prudent and honest persons, not once only, but often.... If the quality of the evidence would demand it, canonical jurisdiction should be exercised over the accused, not as if the prelate were the accuser and the judge, but as if the judgments of many denounce the accused and the complaints making him obligated to exercise his duties.[63]

The text and the norms of canon 8 merely confirmed earlier procedural norms that had already been incorporated into canonical jurisprudence years before the Lateran Council. A decretal with the exact same wording as canon 8 was sent to the distinguished jurist Lotharius, bishop of Vercelli, in January 1206.[64] A short time later, Petrus Beneventanus included it in *Compilatio tertia*, 3 Comp. 5.1.4. The rules governing inquisitorial procedure were, in other words, well known long before the Fourth Lateran Council.[65]

---

61. Tancred (ca. 1216), *Ordo iudiciarius* 158; see n. 16 above.

62. Richard M. Fraher, 'The Theoretical Justification for the New Criminal Law of the High Middle Ages: Rei publicae interest ne crimina remaneant impunita', *University of Illinois Law Review* (1984) 557–595, argued that the legal maxim quoted in the title of his essay was a marker that led to inquisitorial procedure, torture, and the abandonment of accusation as a mode of proof. As research since then has demonstrated, the connections between theory and practice are much more complicated. I would particularly disagree that inquisitorial procedure led to the use of torture in the courts; see my essay 'Torture and Fear'.

63. Fourth Lateran Council c.8, ed. COD 171–172: 'Ex quibus auctoritatibus manifeste probatur, quod non solum cum subditus, verum etiam cum praelatus excedit, si per clamorem et famam ad aures superioris pervenerit, non quidem a malevolis et maledicis, sed a providis et honestis, nec semel tantum, sed saepe, quod clamor innuit et diffamatio manifestat, debet coram ecclesiae senioribus veritatem diligentius perscrutari'; based on the edition of Antonio García y García, *Constitutiones Concilii quarti Lateranensis una cum Commentariis glossatorum* (MIC Series A: Corpus Glossatorum 2; Vatican City 1981) 54–57.

64. On Lotharius, see my 'Lotharius of Cremona', BMCL 20 (1990) 43–50, reprinted in *Miscellanea Domenico Maffei dicata: Historia-Ius-Studium*, ed. Antonio García y García and Peter Weimar (4 vols; Goldbach 1995) 1.231–238; Luca Loschiavo, 'Lotario, Rosari da Cremona', DGI 2.1204.

65. See especially Lotte Kéry, 'Inquisitio—denunciatio—exceptio: Möglichkeiten der Ver-

The canonists linked clamor and fama in canon 8 to two biblical stories: when the Lord God reacted to the dreadful stories he heard about Sodom and Gomorrah by descending to earth to investigate (Gen 18:20), and when the master in the Gospel of Luke who, having heard the complaints about his steward, demanded that the steward justify his actions (Lk 16:1).[66] A half century earlier, Paucapalea had justified the new ordo iudiciarius with the story of the judgment of Adam and Eve (Gen 3:12–18).[67] The Bible also provided the jurists with powerful justifications for new inquisitorial methods in court procedure. St. Hugh, bishop of Lincoln, may have summoned Walter to explain how his wife's sister produced twins without a husband.[68] Walter must not have had a convincing answer. The case went to the monastery of Osney and its prior, Clement, who exercised his office, presumably, close to Walter's home. The jurists had always stipulated that defendants should not be summoned to distant courts.

We have very little evidence how a prelate (the bishop or, more likely, the archdeacon) would investigate Walter's crime. In a gloss written a few years before Lateran IV, Johannes Teutonicus thought that the members of the ecclesiastical court should go to an abbey to inquire about wrongdoing.[69] Presumably, Prior Clement went to Walter's home. His next step would have been to evaluate the credibility of the witnesses to Walter's crime. Johannes would not permit the testimony of Walter's enemies to be given in court. Further, these witnesses must take oaths that they are telling the truth.[70] The 'fama' should be, according to Johannes, enormous

---

fahrenseinleitung im Dekretalenrecht', ZRG Kan. Abt. 87 (2001) 226–268; and her *Gottesfurcht und irdische Strafe: Der Beitrag des mittelalterlichen Kirchenrechts zur Entstehung des öffentlichen Strafrechts* (Konflikt, Verbrechen und Sanktion in der Gesellschaft Alteuropas, 10; Köln-Weimar-Wien 2006) passim; see Pennington, 'Jurisprudence of Procedure' 141–142.

66. On some of the roots of 'clamor' and 'fama', see Gillian R. Evans, *Law and Theology in the Middle Ages* (London-New York 2002) v, vii, 23.

67. Pennington, 'Jurisprudence of Procedure' 137–139 and 142.

68. Hugh died in November 1200 but could have heard the case. It would have taken a long time for the appeal to reach Rome and for the Curia to render a decision. Alternatively, the See at Lincoln could have been vacant, which would explain why Prior Clement heard the case. On Hugh see *St. Hugh of Lincoln: Lectures Delivered at Oxford and Lincoln to Celebrate the Eighth Centenary of St. Hugh's Consecration as Bishop of Lincoln*, ed. Henry Mayr-Harting (Oxford 1987).

69. Johannes Teutonicus to 3 Comp. 5.1.4 s.v. *descendam*, Admont, Stiftsbibliothek 22, fol. 228r: 'Prelatus debet descendere cum canonicis suis, ut lxxxvi. di. Si quid (D.86 c.23) et xv. q. vii. Episcopus, et si inquiratur de excessu abbatis, tunc intererunt abbates eiusdem ordinis, ut xviii. q. ii. Si quis abbas. (C.18 q.2 c.15)'. On the canonistic commentaries and collections at this time, see Hartmann and Pennington, *History* 121–317.

70. Teutonicus to 3 Comp. 5.1.4, s.v. *a maliuolis*: 'Videtur ergo quod infamia orta ab inimicis non inducit suspitionem. xi. q. iii. In cunctis (C.11 q.3 c.52) et ii. q. v. Omnibus (C.2 q.5 c.19) et infra de purgat. canon. Cum in iuuentute 3 Comp. 5.17.3 (X 3.34.12), quod quidam admittunt, set quia difficile est probare ortum infamie, cum fama ab incerto auctore procedat. de. con. di. iiii. Sanctum (De con. D.4 c.36). Satis potest dici quod undecumque procedat infamia, sit indicenda purgatio, arg. infra de purgat. can. Accedens (3 Comp. 5.17.5 (X 5.34.14), infra de appostatis c. uno (3 Comp. 5.6.1 (X 5.9.3)'.

and intolerable. If the 'fama' continued to grow and an accuser did not come forward, the bishop should move forward with the senior members of his chapter and call witnesses.[71] We cannot know whether Prior Clement took these steps in the early thirteenth century when he investigated Walter's crime.

Walter either confessed to his crime or was convicted on the testimony of his neighbors. Prior Clement rendered a stiff penalty. Walter was obligated to take a penitential pilgrimage to Jerusalem. He appealed the decision to Rome. At the beginning of the thirteenth century, a pilgrimage to Jerusalem was a dangerous journey. The papal court was well aware that Christians captured by Muslims could be badly mistreated.[72] (Of course, Christians also mistreated Muslims.) Jerusalem was in Muslim hands since Saladin had conquered the city after the Battle of Hattin in October 1187. After the disastrous Third Crusade, Christians travelling to Jerusalem could expect not only the usual difficulties but also danger and threats to their safety.[73] Although there were critics of penitential pilgrimages, clerics continued to use them frequently, danger or not.[74]

Walter, however, did not appeal the decision on the basis of danger but on the grounds that he could not afford to go. His strategy is perplexing. Walter could afford to travel to Rome to appeal his case but did not have the money for a trip to Jerusalem? There may have been fundamental reasons for his decision of which we are not aware. It may be that any danger in penitential pilgrimages was thought to be part of the penance. Consequently, Walter may not have thought it wise to use that reason in his appeal. In any case, money, not danger, was the issue that Walter (and his advocate) chose for the appeal. Prior Clement had not sent the curia information about Walter's wealth. The judges in the curia sent the case back to Clement with the order to investigate his ability (facultas) to undertake a pilgrimage and to render a definitive decision through the authority of the pope (apostolica scripta mandantes). As is usually the case, we do not know whether Walter went to the Holy Land.

---

71. Ibid., s.v. *quod clamor*: 'Si uero accusator non apparet et mala fama crebrescit, tunc episcopus, uocatis ecclesie sue senioribus, procedet ad inquisitionem ut hic dicitur, et lxxxvi. di. Si quid uero (D.86 c.23), et ipsemet iudex potest inducere testes, ut xi. q. iii. Precipue, in fine (C.11 q.3 c.3), infra eodem, Cum oporteat (c.6) et ii. q. v. Presbyter (C.2 q.5 c.13)'.

72. Brenda Bolton and Constance M. Rousseau, 'Palmerius of Picciati: Innocent III meets his "Martin Guerre",' *Proceedings Syracuse 2001* 361–385 at 378–379.

73. On pilgrimage as penance, see Valerie I. J. Flint, 'Space and Discipline in Early Medieval Europe', *Medieval Practices of Space,* ed. Barbara A. Hanawalt and Michael Kobialka (Minneapolis 2000) 149–166 at 162–163; Jonathan Sumption, *The Age of Pilgrimage: The Medieval Journey to God* (Mahwah, N.J. 2003) 136–159; on the fall of Jerusalem, see Giorgio Albertini, *L'ultima battaglia dei Templari: Hattin e la caduta di Gerusalemme* (I volti della storia 226; Rome 2012).

74. See Sumption, *Age of Pilgrimage* passim.

Up to this point, the decretal provides information that, if the records existed, would have been similar to other court records discussed in this volume. The second part of the decretal permits us to peer into the minds of the curial judges. Other court records never or only rarely record what the judges thought. Papal decretals often do. In addition to whatever documentation Clement had sent to Rome about Walter's pilgrimage, he had added questions about the legal status of Walter's wife. Can Walter and his wife continue to live as man and wife, and does Walter's wife bear any guilt in his adultery? The judges' answer to the first question was that they could live together but without any sexual congress—unless the woman wanted it. They based their decision on their medical knowledge of a woman's body and her sexuality. Following Galen some medieval authors thought that if a woman did not have sexual intercourse, a 'semen' produced by the uterus would spoil and corrupt her blood. Her unsatisfied libido would lead to hysteria.[75] The judges in the papal curia would have also read about the sexual frailty of women in the canonistic commentaries.[76] Consequently, if his wife wanted to have intercourse, Walter was obligated to render the conjugal debt. They argued that the wife had incurred no guilt (culpa) in Walter's crime. One may justly ask, 'how was that possible?' The papal judges explained their decision. If the wife had knowingly participated in Walter's crime (e.g., by her tacit or verbal consent) she would have lost her conjugal rights. However, the judges quoted a maxim that was new to canonical jurisprudence but would remain a part of the Ius commune for centuries: 'Nemo non debet privari iure suo sine culpa' (No one may be deprived of her right without fault).[77] The papal court had used the maxim several years earlier in a German case that was similar to Walter's. Both decretals made the point that earlier decisions of Pope Alexander III got the jurisprudence wrong:[78] Walter's wife could not be guilty (culpa) if the crime were manifest (under the assumption that she must have known of Walter's crime even if she denied knowing) or if the consanguinity were close—using the same rea-

75. Pennington, 'A Note to Decameron 6.7: The Wit of Madonna Filippa', *Speculum* 52 (1977) 902–905 at 903–904.

76. James A. Brundage, *Law, Sex, and Christian Society in Medieval Europe* (Chicago-London 1987) 350–351, 426–428, 548–549, passim.

77. The maxim became part of the legal tradition for the first time in the canonical collection of Rainer of Pomposa, PL 216.1264, see Hartmann and Pennington, *History* 301–305; Petrus Beneventanus then placed it in 3 Comp. 4.9.1 (X 4.13.6); William of Ockham and others adopted the principle in non-legal works, e.g. *Opus nonaginta dierum* in *Opera politica*, ed. R. F. Bennett and H. S. Offler (Manchester 1963) 559.

78. See Atria A. Larson's discussion of this problem in *Master of Penance: Gratian and the Development of Penitential Thought and Law in the Twelfth Century* (Studies in Medieval and Early Modern Canon Law 11; Washington, D.C. 2014) 453–454, 477.

soning.[79] Rather, if the court had determined that she had not known or consented to the crime, she was innocent. Whether the crime was manifest or if there was close bond of consanguinity should not be decisive factors when determining her guilt. By this time the papal court had developed a doctrine of precedent (stare decisis), but only if the precedent was just and reasonable.[80] In this case, the curia decided Alexander's prior decisions were not.

Summary Procedure and Due Process

The rules and regulations that governed summary procedure have misled scholars who have tried to interpret court documents, court cases, or statutes.[81] Torture and its role in the courts have also been misunderstood. The development and origin of summary procedure bear a resemblance to the evolution of inquisitorial procedure.[82] Both first emerge in the practice of the courts and were later incorporated into the law of the church through legislation. The ecclesiastical and secular courts began to streamline some of the procedural rules in the courts early in the thirteenth century. The phrases that were used to indicate a shortened procedure were 'de plano et absque iudiciorum strepitu', 'simpliciter et de plano, ac sine strepitu et figura iudicii', and also 'simpliciter et de plano, ac sine advocatorum strepitu et figura iudicii'. There were other slight variations as well. Pope Gregory IX used 'de plano et absque iudiciorum strepitu' for the first time in a papal decretal between 1227 and 1234 dealing with the reform of a monastery in Rouen.[83] There is evidence dating to 1248 that the shortening of procedure in secular arbitration provided litigants with a quicker and less expensive way to deal with legal problems.[84] The application of

---

79. For the canonists' discussions of this maxim see *Glossa ordinaria* to D.22 c.6, s.v. *priusquam* and the *Glossa ordinaria* to X 1.2.2, s.v. *culpa caret*, and to X 4.13.11, s.v. *sine sua propria causa*.

80. 3 Comp. 2.18.9 (X 2.27.19).

81. See Blanshei, *Politics and Justice* 408, who writes that in Bolognese courts 'the grant of authority to the podestà and his judges usually specified they were to prosecute the trial "simply and plainly, without clamor and the normal forms of procedure," that is with the suspension of due process—by summary justice'. As we will see, that is not correct. The jurists never argued that the key elements of due process could be entirely omitted in summary procedure. Thomas A. Fudge, *The Trial of John Hus: Medieval Heresy and Criminal Procedure* (Oxford 2013) 91–96, misinterprets a number of papal decretals that deal with summary criminal procedure; the two most glaring examples are Boniface VIII's 'Statuta', VI 5.2.20, p. 93, and Innocent III's 'Veniens', X 5.1.15, p. 94, about which Fudge states that Boniface dictated that advocates could be barred from the courtroom (*advocatorum strepitu*) and that Innocent forbade advocates in criminal cases. I will deal with these issues and others in Fudge's work at another time.

82. See my essay below, 'Jurisprudence of Procedure' 141, and Brundage, *Medieval Origins* 449–451; Olivier Descamps, 'Aux origines de la procédure sommaire: Remarques sur la constitution Saepe contingit (Clem., V, 11, 2)', *Einfluss der Kanonistik* 4.45–64.

83. X 5.1.26 (Olim): 'in negotio de plano et absque iudiciorum strepitu procedentes'.

84. See a dispute over a land contract of 1248 printed by John Pryor, *Business Contracts of*

inquisitorial procedure to eradicate the scourge of heresy may have been another avenue on which the idea of streamlining the rules of procedure began.[85] Heresy was perceived to be a dangerous threat to society, and therefore heretics must be dealt with quickly and efficiently. The phrase reached the highest levels of society. In a contract of peace between King Alexander III of Scotland and King Magnus of Norway in 1266, all disputes in the future over the terms of the treaty were to be decided 'de plano et absque strepitu iudiciali'.[86] Although the origins of the phrase were earlier, the papacy laid down the rules for summary procedure in decretals of popes Boniface VIII and Clement V and at the Council of Vienne at the end of the thirteenth and the beginning of the fourteenth centuries. These rules were formulated by the papacy and the jurists of the Ius commune and adopted by secular and ecclesiastical courts.[87]

If the origins and early development of summary procedure remain murky, the legislative origins are well known.[88] A dispute between the Emperor Henry VII and Pope Clement V created the necessity of promulgating new legislation in the fourteenth century.[89] Henry had issued an imperial decree, *Ad reprimendum*, in which the emperor declared that he could dispense with many of the normal rules of procedure in the case of summary trials for serious crimes like treason, especially the norm that the defendant must be summoned and be given a public trial. Treason al-

---

Medieval Provence: Selected Notulae from the Cartulary of Giraud Amalric of Marseilles (Studies and Textes; Toronto 1981) 129: 'Et fuit de voluntate parcium predictarum actum in hoc compromisso quod dictus arbiter possit de plano absque strepitu et libelli oblatione dictas questiones... audire et diffinire'.

85. The phrase 'absque judicii et advocatorum strepitu' is found in a letter of Alexander IV in 1255, *Corpus documentorum inquisitionis haereticae pravitatis neerlandicae,* ed. Paul Fredericq (5 vols. Gent-'S Gravenhage 1889) 1.124. In addition, for summary procedure in English courts, see Donahue, 'Procedure' 116–117, and 'Ecclesiastical Courts' 284–287.

86. *The Acts of Alexander III King of Scots 1249–1286,* ed. Cynthia J. Neville and Grant Simpson, (Resgesta Regum Scottorum 4; Edinburgh 1213) 103; a few years earlier, in ca. 1251, Pope Innocent IV had used the phrase to describe how ecclesiastical cases in Scotland that involved clerics and their benefices should be handled, see *Annals of Scotland: From the Accession of Malcolm III Surnamed Canmore, to the Accession of Robert I,* ed. David Dalrymple (Edinburgh 1776) 342–346 at 346.

87. See Knut W. Nörr, 'Rechtsgeschichtliche Apostillen zur Clementine *Saepe*', *The Law's Delay: Essays on Undue Delay in Civil Litigation,* ed. C. H. van Rhee (Ius commune Europaeum 47; Antwerp-Groningen 2004) 203–215, reprinted in 'Panta rei': *Studi dedicati a Manlio Bellomo,* ed. Orazio Condorelli (5 vols. Roma 2004) 4.225–238, where he explores the sources for the various elements of the phrases; also see Nörr, 'Verzögert oder beschleunigt: Das Beispiel des römisch-kanonischen Prozessrechts', *Within a Reasonable Time: The History of Due and Undue Delay in Civil Litigation,* ed. C. H. van Rhee (Comparative Studies in Continental and Anglo-American Legal History 28; Berlin 2010) 93–104; Richard H. Helmholz, 'Due and Undue Delay in the English Ecclesiastical Courts (ca. 1300–1600)', *The Law's Delay* 131–39 at 135, and in *Within a Reasonable Time* 73–93.

88. See Litewski, *Zivilprozeß* 2.564–566.

89. On this dispute see my *Prince and the Law* 165–185; most recently Diego Quaglioni has examined the relationship between Dante's *Monarchia* and this dispute; he has discussed the papal and imperial legislation it produced in the 'Introduzione' to his edition of *Monarchia* in *Dante Alighieri Opere,* ed. Marco Santagata (Milan 2014) 841–858, and passim in the notes to his edition.

ways had its special rules and exceptions from ancient Roman law to the early fourteenth century. Henry or his jurists borrowed the idea that procedural short cuts could be taken from canon law. Canonical procedure had long recognized that certain serious matters should be handled swiftly and without delay. The canonists created summary judicial procedure that proceeded 'simpliciter et de plano, ac sine strepitu et figura iudicii' (simply and plainly, without clamor and the [normal] forms of procedure). Henry incorporated canonistic jurisprudence into *Ad reprimendum* and explicitly adopted it when he condemned Robert of Naples for treason in absentia.[90]

The result of these events and legislation must have led to confusion in the papal curia, the schools, and the courts. The Council of Vienne (1311–1312) had recently defined summary procedure with the canon *Dispendiosam*.[91] This canon had simply listed which cases could be treated summarily—benefices, tithes, marriage, and usury—but not how they were to be handled.[92] The jurists must have disagreed over exactly what could be omitted. Some may have thought that Henry could take procedural shortcuts during Robert's trial because the clause 'simpliciter et de plano, ac sine strepitu et figura iudicii' had never been carefully defined. They noticed the problem, and Johannes Andreae wrote he was responsible for pressing the lords and lawyers of the curia to define the words 'de plano sine strepitu et figura iudicii'.[93]

The result of Johannes's blandishments, the confusion, and, probably, the practical needs of judges was *Saepe contingit*.[94] It was a constitution, and Clement issued it 'proprio motu'—that is, the pope had no reason or motive other than that he wished to define practice. Its provisions conformed to the doctrine governing the judicial process developed by the jurists and established by another decretal of Clement V, *Pastoralis*, in which the pope had declared that a defendant's defense in court had been established by natural law.[95] In the *Clementines Pastoralis* was placed un-

90. *Constitutiones et acta publica imperatorum et regum*, 4.2: *Inde ab A. MCCXCVIII usque ad A. MCCCXIII*, ed. J. Schwalm (MGH, Legum sectio, 4; Hannover-Leipzig 1911) nr. 946, p. 989: 'alioquin tantundem camere nostre persolvant et ad id sine strepitu et figura iudicii conpellantur'.

91. C.6, later incorporated into Clem. 2.1.2; edited most recently by R. Saccenti COD 359–469 at 410.

92. Dolezalek, *Das Imbreviaturbuch* text 4, 89–93, is an extensive record of the testimony of witnesses in a case of usury before the Pisan archiepiscopal court, in which a loan of 20 denarii was paid off with 26 denarii, an interest payment of 30 percent.

93. Quoted by Stephan Kuttner, 'The Date of the Constitution "Saepe", the Vatican Manuscripts and the Roman Edition of the Clementines', *Mélanges Eugène Tisserant* (4 vols. Studi e Testi 234; Città del Vaticano 1964) 4.430: 'hanc contitutionem verborum blanditiis non egentem glossandam aggredior, de cuius causa impulsiva pars fui'. See Nörr, 'Apostillen', *Panta rei* 234, where Johannes's gloss is printed.

94. Nörr, 'Apostillen', *Panta rei* 232–237.

95. Pennington, *Prince and the Law* 187–188, included in Clem. 2.11.2.

der the title 'The significance of words' because, by defining the words 'de plano sine strepitu et figura iudicii,' it drew the boundaries of how abbreviated summary judicial procedure could be. Clement first specified the areas that a judge could trim from the judicial process: The *libellum* was not required; holidays must not be observed; objections, appeals, and witnesses could be limited. However, Clement insisted that a judge may not omit necessary proofs or legitimate defenses from the proceedings. A summons and an oath denying calumny could not be excluded.[96]

Lawyers, the jurists, and the courts still needed *Saepe* to be interpreted. Johannes Andreae, who wrote (ca. 1322) the Ordinary Gloss to the *Clementines*, the official collection of canon law that contained both *Pastoralis* and *Saepe*, underlined the significance of *Saepe* by glossing and lecturing on the new decretal soon after its promulgation, even before Pope John XXII issued the *Clementines* on November 1, 1317.[97]

Other canonists responding to the need were quick to gloss the *Clementines*. Johannes Andreae, Guillielmus de Monte Lauduno, Jesselin de Cassagnes, and Paulus de Liazariis all glossed the *Clementines* shortly after their promulgation and posed new questions about the rules of procedure and explored other areas of law that might be regulated by principles of due process based on natural law.[98]

The canonists did not treat, acknowledge, or cite Emperor Henry VII's constitution *Ad reprimendum* that contradicted papal legislation and canonistic commentaries on the necessity of due process in summary proceedings. In the mid-fourteenth century, the famous teacher of Roman law Bartolus of Sassoferrato wrote an extended commentary on Henry's decree ca. 1355. It became the Ordinary Gloss to the decree when *Ad reprimendum* was placed among the other medieval imperial decrees that were added to the body of Roman law.[99] The canonists may not have been willing to recognize Henry's constitution, but Bartolus knew the canonistic literature and interpreted *Ad reprimendum* through the procedural norms and rules that the canonists had created. His 'pro-papal' commentary on *Ad reprimendum* is surprising only if one would view a fourteenth-century

---

96. Clem. 5.11.2: 'Non sic tamen iudex litem abbreviet quin probationes necessariae et defensiones legitimae admittantur. Citationem vero ac praestationem iuramenti de calumnia vel malitia, sive de veritate dicenda, ne veritas occultetur, per commissionem huiusmodi intelligimus non excludi'. Oldradus de Ponte may have had a hand in the intellectual preparation of *Saepe* too. See his consilium treating the words 'sine strepitu iudicii et figura', nr. 115 in vulgate edition; nr. 34, Clm 5463, fol. 22r–22v.

97. Kuttner, 'Constitution "Saepe"' 430–432.

98. I have discussed their opinions in *Prince and the Law* 190–196.

99. Emilio Betti, 'La dottrina costruita da Bartolo sulla constitutio "Ad reprimendum",' *Bartolo da Sassoferrato: Studi e documenti per il VI centenario* (2 vols. Milan 1962) 2.37–47; see Susanne Lepsius, 'Bartolo da Sassoferrato', DGI 1.177–180.

civilian anachronistically: a jurist who put the interests of universal empire before national kingdoms, Italian city-states, or the Church. In his commentary on *Ad reprimendum*, Bartolus dealt not only with procedural norms but confronted the entire range of problems that jurists had raised about imperial and princely power for centuries.

Ad reprimendum had established two points: Emperor Henry VII could summon Robert of Naples to his court, and he could dispense with the normal rules of judicial procedure.[100] To the second point, Bartolus acknowledged that the constitution had to be interpreted through *Pastoralis* and *Saepe*. A judge is obligated to observe all the judicial norms that have been established by the law of nations and natural reason.[101] Bartolus discussed all those parts of the judicial process that he thought were essential. Although he seems to have held the view that actions themselves were part of the civil law,[102] a summons was necessary; God had, after all, called Adam to judgment.[103] Petitions, exceptions, delays, and proofs must also always be allowed because natural law had instituted them. Even the legal maxim that someone may not be judged twice for the same crime is a precept of natural law.[104] Therefore, although the significance of the words 'sine strepitu et figura iudicii' is that a judge's will is freed of the rules of the civil law, he must nevertheless preserve the equity and the norms of the law of nations and natural equity. The old question of the podestà is thus solved: the podestà may dispense with the solemnities of law, but he may not perpetrate an injustice.[105] Bartolus's reinterpretation of the key clauses

---

100. To the first point, see *Prince and the Law* 197–199.

101. Bartolus of Sassoferrato to *Ad reprimendum* (ed. 1472) fol. 11r, Munich, Staatsbibliothek Clm 6643, fol. 139v, s.v. *et figura iudicii*: 'Tu dic quod iudex per hec uerba releuatur ab omni forma et figura iudicii inducta a iure ciuili, et tenetur seruare omnem figuram formam iudicii inductam de iure gentium uel naturali ratione.... Quid ergo de sermone huius uerbi dicam: intellige idem si omnia coniungerentur. Quid hoc important per singulas partes iudicii prosequamur latius quam in dicto capitulo "Sepe" <Clem. 5.11.2>'.

102. Bartolus to Cod. 1.19.2 (Venice: 1476) unfoliated, Nürnberg, Stadtsbibliotek Cent. II 84, fol. 27r: '<potest tolli> quedam de iure ciuili, ut actiones; quedam de iure gentium, ut dominium <imperator non tolli potest>'.

103. Bartolus of Sassoferrato to *Ad reprimendum* (ed. 1472): 'Quero ergo an sit necesse ut pars citetur? Respondeo sic, ut infra in hac lege innuitur. Idem quia hoc est de iure naturali, nam primum hominem citauit Deus dicens "Adam, Adam, ubi es?" Hoc est probatur extra de re iud. Clem. Pastoralis <Clem. 2.11.2> ubi sententia domini imperatoris Henrici qui fecit hanc legem et postea condemnauit Robertum regem Iherusalem et Sicilie cassatur, ob hoc quod citatio non fuit facta legitime et probatur in dicto capitulo "Sepe".'

104. Ibid., ed. fol. 11v; Clm 6643, fol. 140r: 'Item an poterit opponi exceptio rei iudicate uel finite ad impediendum processum. Respondeo sic, quia de iure naturali est ne iudicetur bis in idipsum'.

105. Ibid., ed. fol. 12v, Clm 6643, fol. 141v, v. *iurisdictioni preest uidetur expedire*: 'Si uero per uerba significantia liberam uoluntatem tunc est liber a regulis iuris ciuilis, debet tamen seruare equitatem iuris gentium seu naturalem equitatem que idem est per dicta iura et est casus de re iud. in Clem. Pastoralis, nam imperator solutus est legibus et ex uigore sue potestatis tulit ibi sententiam, tamen quia in quibusdam fecit ibi contra naturalem equitatem ideo sententia cassatur.

of *Ad reprimendum* might be cited as another example of his willingness to subject imperial to papal prerogatives, in this case imperial law to papal. But one must recognize that his interpretation of *Ad reprimendum* reflected the jurisprudence of the Ius commune.

Bartolus's student, Baldus de Ubaldis, accepted the provisions of *Pastoralis* and *Saepe* completely. The prince was obligated by all parts of the judicial process. He could not deprive a defendant of his defense in court. The prince had an obligation to summon a defendant, because a summons is established by the law of nations. The prince must examine the truth in a courtroom because the search for truth is a mandate of the law of nations.[106]

Summary procedure was not a subversion of due process but only a shortening of some parts of the trial. Mengho, Pedecolo, Sandrolo and their successors, even the devil himself, must be given their full rights, without exception, in the courts of the Ius commune.[107] They generally, if not always, were. One should not, however, overlook the use of torture. It took some time before jurists and legislators recognized how torture violated the rights of defendants.

Et ideo patet quod in casu nostre legis ubi procedit absque figura iudicii, si committur iudici per uerba significantia, arbitrium boni uiri debet seruare regulas iurisgentium, quia hec uerba predicta "sine figura iudicii" important siue committantur per uerba significantia uoluntatem liberam. Et per hoc patet soluta questio quando Potestati datur liberum arbitrium an propter hoc poterit facere parti iniustitiam? Certe non, quia hoc est contra naturalem equitatem; set potest omittere solemnitates iuris ciuilis. De hoc per glossam in dicta Clem. Sepe, super uerbo "defensiones"; dixi de dona. l. Si <cum> filiusfamilias <Dig. 39.5.2>'.

106. Baldus to Cod. 1.14(17).11, ed. sine anno et loco (Hain *2279): 'Est et aliud speciale quia princeps non tenetur seruare ordinem iudiciorum in procedendo, ut not. Innoc. extra de re iud. c. In causis <X 2.27.19>. Debet tamen pars citari; alias ualet sententia principis, et potest opponi de nullitate, et textus est hic notabile cum sua glossa. Ideo enim pars est citanda ut possit se defendere, que defensio est de iure gentium seu naturali, et ideo non potest auferri, ut ff. de re milit. l.iii. Si ad diem <Dig. 49.16.3.7> et in c. Pastoralis, de re iud. in Clem. <Clem. 2.11.2> ff. de adopt. Adoptio per iura facta et l. Nam ita diuus, cum si. <Dig. 1.7.38 and 39> Item coram principe requiritur examinatio et uentilatio ueritatis, quia inquisitio ueritatis est de iure gentium. Vnde licet solemnitates legales non teneatur princeps obseruare, obseruantiam tamen iure gentium non debet deesse, quia pertinet ad naturalem equitatem, et hoc est quod uult littera dum dicit "cognitionaliter".'

107. See my chapter 'The Jurisprudence of Procedure' 146.

2

The Courtroom

From Church Portal to Town Hall

Barbara Deimling

From the time of Charlemagne to the fifteenth century, the sites of
the law courts in which legal activities were held in Italy and Germany
varied in number and location as much as the institutions claiming jurisdiction.[1] In his *Sachsenspiegel,* Eike of Repgow (c. 1180–c. 1233) maintained
that 'the judge may dispense justice at all places'.[2] Documentary evidence
shows that courts were held at natural and man-made landmarks, such as
at trees, rocks, hills, columns, crosses, statues, and bridges, as well as in
churches, palaces, and castles.[3] Convenience was one of the criteria for selecting a site. Law courts were often held where the crime had occurred,

1. For ease of reference, 'Italy' and 'Germany' will be used anachronistically to describe (in
rough outline) the regions north and south of the Alps that are called by those names today.

2. Eike of Repgow, *Der Sachsenspiegel: Landrecht* 1.62 § 10: 'in allen steden... dar die richtere
mit ordelen richtet'. See Klemens Klemmer, *Von der Linde über den Palast zu einem Haus des Rechts:
Katalog zur ständigen Ausstellung im Niedersächsischen Justizministerium* (Regensburg 1991); and
K. Klemmer, R. Wassermann, and T. M. Wessel, *Deutsche Gerichtsgebäude: Von der Dorflinde über
den Justizpalast zum Haus des Rechts* (Munich 1993).

3. For examples, see Jacob Grimm, *Deutsche Rechtsalterthümer* (4th ed. 2 vols. Leipzig 1899)
2.411–438; Johann Julius von Planck, *Das deutsche Gerichtsverfahren im Mittelalter, nach dem Sachsenspiegel und verwandten Rechtsquellen* (2 vols. Braunschweig 1879) 1.123–126; and the works by Karl

30

such as on public streets or in front of private houses.[4] Practical considerations were another criterion. Law courts were held preferably outside—if not directly under the open sky, then under the protecting roof of a porch, in case of unsuitable weather conditions.[5]

The location of courts outdoors ensured that people could gather and witness the judicial events.[6] In a society where writing was not widespread, witnesses were required to record legal transactions. Such witnessed memories provided the same permanent record as later the written word would. The broadcasting of the trial enhanced the enforcement of decisions. Each person witnessing the verdict became part of a public control system, which made it harder for the condemned to disrespect or even deny the judgment. Public dispensation of justice thus assured collective acceptance and commemoration of norms for behavior. It confirmed the leadership role of judicial powers in determining the rules and regulations according to which communities defined themselves.

The variety of locations for law courts and their outdoor settings in medieval Italy and Germany seem utterly at odds with the modern notion of the law court, the very words of which evoke a clear architectural structure describing both the courthouse, as an independent building, and the courtroom.[7] Today a courtroom is an interior space into the judge's bench and the witness boxes, the tables for the defense and the prosecution, and a bar separating the actors from the audience.[8] The following

---

Frölich: Frölich, *Alte Dorfplätze und andere Stätten bäuerlicher Rechtspflege* (Arbeiten zur rechtlichen Volkskunde 2; Tübingen 1938); Frölich, *Stätten mittelalterlicher Rechtspflege auf südwestdeutschem Boden, besonders in Hessen und den Nachbargebieten* (Arbeiten zur rechtlichen Volkskunde 1; Tübingen: 1938); Frölich, *Mittelalterliche Bauwerke als Rechtsdenkmäler* (Arbeiten zur rechtlichen Volkskunde 3; Tübingen: 1939); Frölich, *Denkmäler mittelalterlicher Strafrechtspflege in Ost- und Mitteldeutschland* (Arbeiten zur rechtlichen Volkskunde 5; Gießen 1946); Frölich, *Stätten mittelalterlicher Rechtspflege im niederdeutschen Bereich* (Arbeiten zur rechtlichen Volkskunde 4; Gießen 1946); Frölich, *Rechtsdenkmäler des deutschen Dorfs* (Gießener Beiträge zur deutschen Philologie 89; Gießen 1947).

4. See Grimm, *Deutsche Rechtsalterthümer* 2.430, 450, 460.

5. Ibid. 2.429. The edicts allowed for the construction of temporary shelters for protection of the courts from rain and hot sun.

6. For this and the following, see especially Bernard J. Hibbitts, '"Coming to our Senses": Communication and Legal Expression in Performance Cultures', *Emory Law Journal* 41 (1992) 874–960.

7. For a discussion of the buildings and spaces used for courtrooms in Florence, Italy during the twelfth, thirteenth, and fourteenth centuries, see Marie Ito, 'Orsanmichele—The Florentine Grain Market: Trade and Worship in the Later Middle Ages' (PhD diss., The Catholic University of America 2013) chapters 1 and 2; also André Gouron, 'Medieval Courts and Towns: Examples from Southern France', *Fundamina* 30 (1992) 30–46, reprinted in *Juristes et droits savants: Bologne et la France médiévale* (Selected Studies 679; Aldershot 2000) XIV, who discusses the establishment of town courts and their use of the *ordo iudiciarius*.

8. For the building typology of the courthouse, see Nikolaus Pevsner, *A History of Building*

study is but a partial archaeology of the modern courthouse, with no pretense of extending from Charlemagne to the present. It traces an early period in the architectural formalization of legal activities, reexamining Eike of Repgow's 'all places' less as a statement of fact, but as an assertion of spatial independence. The claim that courts could be held at any place implies, in fact, that they were not necessarily linked to a specific location. The imaginative rather than factual interpretation of Eike's statement is confirmed by documentary evidence. Although courts were indeed held at a variety of sites, many legal activities were associated with one particular structure—the church, and especially the church portal.

The first part of this essay will document the importance of the church portal as a locus of justice in the medieval community, the legal activities held there, and reasons, beyond those already mentioned, for medieval judges' selecting this site. The second part of the essay is concerned with changes in legal settings that occurred in the thirteenth and fourteenth centuries. Courts moved from church portals to town halls, and the legal and political bases for this movement were powerful enough to transform the topography and architecture of legal practice. Even so, throughout this process the architectural forms and imagery of the church portal persisted, sustaining religious legal imagery in a new secular context.

Before plunging into the past it is worth returning for one moment to the contemporary courtroom. I ask the reader to imagine possible prototypes for the placement of participants and audience in a trial. One might imagine the people on either side of a railing, with the public aligned in rows of seats divided by a central aisle, which would lead through a gate to the more open area occupied by the litigants. On an axis with this aisle and gate, a judge sits on a raised bench, isolated in the central position of room. Were one to rename the bar as the sanctuary rail or rood screen, the attorneys as deacons, and the witness box as the chancel for reading from texts witnessing religious events and doctrine, the image is easily transformed into the church nave and sanctuary, and the judge into bishop or priest. In modern democratic governments where there are varying but nonetheless clear divisions between church and state, this resemblance may be striking, but need not be disturbing. However, in the time of Charlemagne or Eike of Repgow, during a period of increasing conflict between sacred and secular authorities, one can easily imagine

Types (A. W. Mellon Lectures in the Fine Arts 19; Bollingen Series 35; Princeton 1976) 53–62. For a recent general overview, see Judith Resnik and Dennis E. Curtis, _Representing Justice: Invention, Controversy, and Rights in City-States and Democratic Courtrooms_ (Yale Law Library Series in Legal History and Reference; New Haven 2011).

that tensions inevitably arose between sustaining and severing the place of law not only from the physical site of the church, but also from the institution itself.

Factum ante Portam Ecclesiae: The Church Portal as a Judicial Site

Up to the thirteenth and fourteenth centuries, religious and secular rulers alike regularly chose the place in front of church entrances for their law courts, as is evident in many legal documents that were signed 'in galilea' (Perrecy-les-Forges, 1108),[9] 'sub portico' (Ferrara, 1140),[10] 'in atrio' (Regensburg, 1183),[11] 'ante portam' (Frankfurt, 1248),[12] 'ante minores fores Ecclesie' (Baar, Switzerland, 1274),[13] 'bi der kylchun' (Stans, 1300),[14] or 'uf die Grete' (Strasbourg, 1322).[15] The church door was the site of a wide variety of legal activities, which defined the meaning of the portal as the 'Porta Iustitiae' (Ps 117:19) for the medieval community, the place where justice was spoken, law enacted, and private actions legalized.[16]

Eike of Repgow's implicit downplaying of the legal primacy of the church portal should be seen in the context of a long-standing problem of spatially disassociating secular courts from the church since the time of Charlemagne. Charlemagne issued several decrees forbidding officials from holding law courts 'inside churches or in their atria,'[17] indicating that the custom was frequent enough to be perceived as a problem.

9. Peter C. Claussen, *Chartres-Studien: Zur Vorgeschichte, Funktion und Skulptur der Vorhallen* (Forschungen zur Kunstgeschichte und christlichen Archäologie 9; Wiesbaden 1975) 15 n. 114.

10. Christine Verzár Bornstein, *Portals and Politics in the Early Italian City State: The Sculpture of Nicholaus in Context* (Parma 1988) 104.

11. H. G. Evers, *Tod, Macht und Raum als Bereich der Architektur* (Munich 1939; 2nd rev. ed. Munich 1970) 182 n. 32.

12. *Codex Diplomaticus Moenofrancofurtanus: Urkundenbuch der Reichsstadt Frankfurt*, ed. Johann F. Böhmer, rev. Friedrich Lau (2 vols. Frankfurt 1901–1905, reprinted Glashütten im Taunus 1970) 1.73 no. 146.

13. *Urkunden zur Geschichte der eidgenössischen Bünde*, ed. Joseph E. Kopp (Lucerne 1835) 10.

14. Ibid. 108.

15. Adalbert Erler, *Das Straßburger Münster im Rechtsleben des Mittelalters* (Frankfurt 1954) 27.

16. See most recently Barbara Deimling, 'Ad Rufam Ianuam: Die rechtsgeschichtliche Bedeutung von roten Türen im Mittelalter', ZRG Germ. Abt. 115 (1998) 498–513; Deimling, 'Das mittelalterliche Kirchenportal in seiner rechtsgeschichtlichen Bedeutung', *Die Kunst der Romanik: Architektur, Skulptur, Malerei*, ed. R. Toman (Cologne 1996) 324–327 (English translation published in 1997); see also Peter Fergusson, 'The Greencourt Gatehouse at the Cathedral Monastery of Christchurch, Canterbury', *Das Bauwerk und die Stadt: Aufsätze für Eduard Sekler*, ed. W. Böhm (Vienna 1994) 87–97, dealing with monastic gatehouses in which legal ceremonies were held; Markus R. Ackermann, 'Mittelalterliche Kirchen als Gerichtsorte', ZRG Germ. Abt. 110 (1993) 530–545; Bornstein, *Portals and Politics* 39–42, 103–104; Adolf Reinle, 'Das Portal', *Zeichensprache der Architektur: Symbol, Darstellung und Brauch in der Baukunst des Mittelalters und der Neuzeit* (Zürich-Munich 1976) esp. 245–281; Claussen, *Chartres-Studien* 2–26; Evers, 'Zum romanischen Stufenportal', *Tod, Macht und Raum* 168–198; Grimm, *Deutsche Rechtsalterthümer* 2.426–429, 459–460.

17. 'Ut placita in domibus vel atriis ecclesiarum minime fiant', *Capitularia Regum Francorum*,

Hagen Keller has suggested that these prohibitive laws may reveal the policies of the early Carolingian emperors to empower the dukes as secular vassals in order to counterbalance the power of bishops and abbots. Secular law courts were to be held at places that were distant from church buildings, to demonstrate the independence of secular rulers from the church authorities.[18] Nevertheless, courts continued to be held inside churches and at church portals, as can be deduced from the need of late Carolingian emperors to repeat these prohibitive edicts.

The edicts are, surprisingly, contravened by the practice of the emperors themselves, particularly the Ottonians. Otto the Great, for instance, used the church portal as a place for his legal acts. On October 14, 1001, the emperor sat in judgment in a porch of his palace in Pavia, which was located in front of the palatine chapel of St. Maurice: 'in palatio domini imperatoris in laubia ipsius palacii, que extad ante capellam sancti Mauricii'.[19] Archeological evidence shows that the choice of this location was not unique. Excavations in front of the palatine chapel in Aachen have revealed that a permanent throne was set up in the hemicycle before the main entrance to the church. This throne has been attributed to Charlemagne;[20] however, there is no clear documentation before the tenth century.[21] Widukind of Corvey († ca. 975) tells us that, in 936, Otto the Great

---

ed. Alfred Boretius (MGH, LL 2; Hannover 1883) 1.174, no. 78, cap. 21; see also Jan F. Niermeyer, *Mediae Latinitatis Lexicon Minus* (Leiden 1984) 67 s.v. *atrium* with further examples; and Hagen Keller, 'Der Gerichtsort in oberitalienischen und toskanischen Städten: Untersuchungen zur Stellung der Stadt im Herrschaftssystem des Regnum Italicum vom 9. bis 11. Jahrhundert', QF 49 (1969) 1–72, esp. 37–38.

18. Keller, 'Gerichtsort', 36–38.

19. Cesare Manaresi, *I placiti del Regnum Italiae*, 2.1: A. 962–1002 (Fonti per la storia d'Italia 96; Rome 1957) no. 266, pp. 475–476; see also Helmut Beumann, 'Grab und Thron Karls des Großen zu Aachen', *Karl der Große*, 4: *Das Nachleben*, ed. Wolfgang Braunfels and P. E. Schramm (Düsseldorf 1967) 9–38, esp. 31–32.

20. Leo Hugot, 'Baugeschichtliches zum Grab Karls des Großen', *Aachener Kunstblätter* 52 (1984) 13–28; Roderich Schmidt, 'Zur Geschichte des fränkischen Königsthrons', *Frühmittelalterliche Studien* 2 (1968) 45–66; and Beumann, 'Grab und Thron'.

21. For a similar throne in Paderborn, see Wilhelm Winkelmann, 'Der Schauplatz', *Karolus Magnus et Leo Papa: Ein Paderborner Epos vom Jahre 799*, with contributions by Helmut Beumann, F. Brunhölzl, and W. Winkelmann (Paderborn 1966) 99–107; Winkelmann, 'Die Königspfalz und die Bischofspfalz des 11. und 12. Jahrhunderts in Paderborn', *Frühmittelalterliche Studien* 4 (1970) 398–415; and Winkelmann, 'Est Locus Insignis, quo Patra et Lippa Fluentant: Über die Ausgrabungen in den karolingischen und ottonischen Königspfalzen in Paderborn', *Beiträge zur Frühgeschichte Westfalens: Gesammelte Aufsätze* (Veröffentlichungen der Altertumskommission im Provinzialinstitut für westfälische Landes- und Volksforschung 8; Münster 1984) 118–128, reprint from *Études de castellologie médiévale* 5 (1972) 203–225. The throne has been connected with Charlemagne, and in particular with his famous meeting with Pope Leo III, as described in the *Paderborner Epos* from 799. This dating, however, has recently been called into doubt, and we will have to wait for the results presented at the forthcoming exhibition on this meeting in Paderborn (this information was obtained in private conversation with Matthias Wemhoff, director of the Westfälisches Museum für Archäologie, Museum in der Kaiserpfals, Paderborn).

was installed as king of the 'regnum Lotharii' and the 'imperium Francorum' on this throne in the atrium of the chapel in Aachen:[22]

And when they reached [the palace of Aachen], the dukes and the most distinguished princes together with other vassals came together. They installed the new ruler in the atrium of Charlemagne's church on the throne erected there.[23]

St. Maurice is the same place as where, in 1002, Konrad II 'governed the state excellently and ruled effectively according to divine and human law at public tribunals' and where 'general assemblies convened,' as we are told by Wipo († ca. 1046) in his *Gesta Chuonradi II Imperatoris*.[24] It was therefore not only the place of royal enthronement, but also the place where the ruler sat in judgment when governing the country. Helmut Beumann has shown that the throne in front of the Aachen palatine chapel—and not, as hitherto assumed, the throne on the gallery within the church—was the royal throne, the 'publicus thronus regalis' or the 'totius regni archisolium', as defined by Wipo.[25] Whoever was seated on this 'chair', as Eike of Repgow put it, held the royal 'potestas' and 'nomen'.[26] The location of the imperial throne in front of the church entrance indicates just how interlinked images of secular and religious authority were at this time. Secular or religious magistrates could only express the basis for their power through divine authority, and therefore, even in the Carolingians' attempts to separate secular law from church institutions, they and the Ottonians had no choice but to refer to religious imagery and even to the outlawed church portal sites when defining their own right to rule.

The strong association of justice with church portals was reinforced by the legal and regular practice of church law itself before, during, and

22. See Hans Constantin Faußner, 'Die Thronerhebung des deutschen Königs im Hochmittelalter und die Entstehung des Kurfürstenkollegiums', ZRG Germ. Abt. 108 (1991) 1–60, esp. 6. The newly installed king was acclaimed on the throne within the chapel at Aachen (see ibid. 7).

23. 'Cumque illo ventum esset, duces ac prefectorum principes cum caetera principum militum manu congregati in sixto basilicae Magni Karoli cohaerenti collocarunt novum ducem in solio ibidem constructo', Faußner, 'Thronerhebung' 4–5.

24. 'sedens excellentissime rem publicam ordinavit ibique publico placito et generali concilio habito divino at humana iura utiliter distribuebat', Beumann, 'Grab und Thron' 27. Faußner, 'Thronerhebung' 16, has argued that this reference does not indicate whether the enthronement in Aachen occurred in the atrium of the church or on the throne within the chapel. Hans Beumann, however, whom Faußner did not cite in his study, has rightly pointed out that it must have been the throne in the atrium, as a 'publicum placitum' could not have been held within the confined space of the church building. Beumann (p. 28), and Schmidt, 'Geschichte des fränkischen Königsthrons' 48–50, have shown that the throne in front of the entrance fell into disuse some time after the enthronement of Konrad III in 1138 and before that of Frederick Barbarossa in 1152. Beumann explains this as part of the trend of secularization in the election and coronation of German kings.

25. Beumann, 'Grab und Thron' 26.

26. Eike of Repgow, *Der Sachsenspiegel: Landrecht*, book 3, chapter 52, § 1.

after the Carolingians. At Werden in Westphalia, for instance, the now destroyed westwork in front of the main portal at the Church of the Savior was built, in 943, for the explicit purpose of housing ecclesiastical law courts: 'anything that pertains to the synod is to be held there'.[27] Trials by ordeal, which were administered by the bishop or another clergyman, with Christ invoked to serve as the actual judge, regularly took place in the atrium of the church, or simply 'ante ecclesiam'.[28] This custom lasted until the twelfth century, when the ordeal was replaced with trials according to the new rules established by the jurists in the 'ordines iudiciarii'.[29] Numerous documents from the ninth century show that the priest was supposed to indicate the place 'in atrio ecclesiae' where he had to light the fire over which the water was brought to a boil, or where the iron bars were made red-hot.[30] By the twelfth century, when many churches lacked atria, the trial took place in the narthex or in the porch of the church.[31] Don Denny has shown that the inscription of Gislebertus's Last Judgment tympanum at St. Lazare in Autun, describing the judicial power of Christ, alludes to trials by ordeal:[32] 'I alone dispose all things and crown the deserving. Those who are driven by crime, are curbed by punishment through my judgment'.[33]

Denny noted that the word 'dispose' (dispono) was taken from the ritual of ordeals, where Christ was invoked.[34] The placement of the inscrip-

27. 'quicquid ad synodalia pertinet, in ea exagitur': Wilhelm Effmann, *Die karolingisch-ottonischen Bauten zu Werden*, 1: *Stephanskirche, Salvatorskirche, Peterskirche* (Strasbourg 1899) 176.

28. Robert Bartlett, *Trial by Fire and Water: The Medieval Judicial Order* (Oxford 1986); Hermann Nottarp, *Gottesurteilstudien* (Bamberger Abhandlungen und Forschungen 2; Munich 1956); and Christine Leitmaier, *Die Kirche und die Gottesurteile: Eine rechtshistorische Studie* (Wiener rechtsgeschichtliche Arbeiten 2; Vienna 1953). For a recent attempt to explain the demise of the ordeal, see Finbarr McAuley, 'Canon Law and the End of the Ordeal', *Oxford Journal of Legal Studies* 26 (2006) 473–513. The most remarkable depiction of the ordeal in the medieval manuscripts is in a pontifical from the monastery of Lambach, Austria (Lambach, Stiftsbibliothek LXXIII, fol. 72r, see http://faculty.cua.edu/pennington/Law508/LambachLXXIII.htm).

29. See Kenneth Pennington, 'Due Process, Community, and the Prince in the Evolution of the Ordo iudiciarius', RIDC 9 (1998) 9–47; Pennington, 'Roman Law at the Papal Curia in the Early Twelfth Century', *Canon Law, Religion, and Politics: Liber Amicorum Robert Somerville*, ed. Uta-Renate Blumenthal, Anders Winroth, and Peter Landau (Washington, D.C. 2012) 233–252.

30. *Formulae Merowingici et Karolini Aevi, Accedunt Ordines Iudiciorum Dei*, ed. Karl Zeumer (MGH, LL 5; Hannover 1886) 609, 650, 674, 676–677, 682, 704.

31. Nottarp, *Gottesurteilstudien* 243–245.

32. Don Denny, 'The Last Judgment Tympanum at Autun: Its Sources and Meaning', *Speculum* 57 (1982) 532–547; Xenía Muratova, 'Il timpani della cattedrale di Saint-Lazare a Autun', *Alfa e omega: Il giudkzio universal tra Oriente e Occidente*, ed. Valentino Pace (Castel Bolognese 2006) 102–105.

33. 'Omnia Dispono Solus Meritosque Corono. Quos Scelus Exercet Me Judice Poena Coercet'.

34. Zeumer, *Formulae* 660: 'Domine Iesu Christe … qui regnas in celis et dominaris in omnibus locis, iudicans regna et disponens omnia secundum voluntatem tuam, tuum nomen suppliciter invocamus'. In the Lambach Pontifical (Stiftsbibliothek, fol 71v) the formula is 'Benedictio Dei, Patris et Filii et Spiritus Sancti descendat et maneat super hanc aquam ad discernendum uerum iudicium Dei'.

tion at the tympanum reflects the customary location of the trial in front of the church portal. The trial itself was seen as a warning of Christ's Last Judgment since there was little chance of clemency and no hope of appeal from the judgment of the ordeal. In a twelfth-century text of an ordeal rite from Vézelay, the condemned and the innocent are described as the 'damned' and the 'saved' thereby evoking their destinies on the day of the Last Judgment.[35] The tympanum at Autun expresses this link between the trial by ordeal and the Last Judgment not only in its inscription, but also visually, in the figure of Christ, which is much larger in relation to the whole composition than in any other representation of the Last Judgment at the time. The enormous scale of this figure reflects Christ's domination of the trial by ordeal, in which he serves as the only judge, just as on the Day of Judgment.

The powerful legal traditions of church portals made them fitting sites for a wide range of legal activities beyond court procedures. One such activity was the sanctioning and regulation of markets. With the increasing depersonalization of trade, as the economy shifted from a barter to a moneyed economy, merchants turned to ties of faith, rather than to feudal or kinship bonds, in order to assure the trustworthiness of clients or partners.[36] When signing contracts in front of church portals, Christ became the witness and, were one party to break the agreement, the implicit enforcer of justice. The many marketplaces in front of churches testify to this tradition.

The official weights and measures in use at the time were posted or incised near church portals, which indicates that they were also the site for formal market-regulatory institutions.[37] Freiburg cathedral offers one of the richest examples. One can still see at the buttresses of the porch tower in front of the main portal all different kinds of official measurements with the year of their enactment, including sizes for breads and rolls (dating from 1270, 1313, and 1320), and measurements for grain, wood, coal, and bricks.

The publication of the official weights and measures at church portals was paralleled by inscriptions announcing special laws, decrees, and privileges. There were pragmatic reasons for this: church portals, especially

35. Peter Browe, *De Ordaliis: In usum exercitationum et praelectionum academicarum, 2: Ordo et Rubricae: Acta et Facta: Sententiae theologorum et canonistarum* (Textus et documenta, Series theologica; Rome 1933) 48, no. 55; after Denny, 'Last Judgment' 544 n. 34.

36. Alick M. McLean, 'Sacred Space and Public Policy: The Establishment, Decline and Revival of Prato's Piazza della Pieve' (PhD diss., Princeton University 1993) 102–110.

37. See, for instance, A. Becker, 'Unheilige und heilige Längenmaße an Kirchen', *Blätter für pfälzische Kirchengeschichte* 11 (1935) 91–92.

where there were also markets, were highly visible to the entire public. Inscriptions, whether incised or hung at the entrances of church buildings, broadcast decrees and informed visitors and passers-by of legal enactments, and of the judicial authority within the community.[38] This is especially true for privileges that were granted to cities by feudal authorities, whether the emperor himself, the archbishop, or their vassals. Examples include the cathedrals in Speyer, with the privilege of Emperor Henry V from IIII engraved in golden letters above the main portal in the porch;[39] in Worms, with the privilege of Frederick Barbarossa from 1182 above the north portal;[40] and in Mainz, with the renewal of the tax and jurisdiction privileges by Archbishop Adalbert I from 1135 inscribed onto the bronze doors of Bishop Willigis, which open onto the market square.[41] The inscriptions were intended to last for a long time—they were chiseled in stone or cast in bronze. There are also examples of temporary messages that were affixed to the church door, written on impermanent, less expensive material, such as parchment. In Würzburg, for instance, the episcopal letter of safe-conduct for visitors of the annual mass of the patron saint Kilian was affixed to the main portal of the cathedral.[42]

The publication of permanent and temporary legal notices at church portals can only be partially explained by the utility of such a public location. Inscriptions, as well as official measurements, became associated with the same legal authority that was invested in these locations. Their reception was enhanced both by the actual and the implied presence of judicial and executive authorities to enforce them.[43] So long as the church portal functioned as a place for administering justice, it remained the preferred location for the placement of official inscriptions.

Up until now the portal's legal importance has been explained by extrinsic qualities: the rulers, courts, and legal activities associated with

---

38. See Frölich, *Mittelalterliche Bauwerke*, 29–32; Robert Favreau, 'Fonctions des inscriptions au moyen âge', *Cahiers de civilisation médiévale* 32 (1989) 203–232, esp. 210–214; Favreau, 'Le thème épigrahique de la porte', *Cahiers de civilisation médiévale* 34 (1991) 267–279; Favreau, 'L'apport des inscriptions à la compréhension des programmes iconographiques', *Lecturas de Historia del Arte* 3 (1992) 33–50.

39. *Die christlichen Inschriften der Rheinlande, 2: Die christlichen Inschriften der Rheinlande von der Mitte des achten bis zur Mitte des dreizehnten Jahrhunderts*, ed. Franz Xaver Kraus (Freiburg-Leipzig 1894) 70–73 n.152.

40. Rudolf Kautzsch, *Der Dom zu Worms* (3 vols. Berlin 1938) 3.122–123.

41. The original location of the bronze doors is uncertain; see Ursula Mende, *Die Türzieher des Mittelalters* (Denkmäler deutscher Kunst: Bronzegeräte des Mittelalters 2; Berlin 1981) 25–27, 133–134.

42. Friedrich Merzbacher, 'Der Kiliansdom als Rechtsdenkmal', *Ecclesia Cathedralis: Der Dom zu Würzburg*, ed. R. Schömig (Würzburg 1967) 69–82, esp. 76.

43. See Eberhard von Künßberg, *Rechtliche Volkskunde* (Grundriß der deutschen Volkskunde in Einzeldarstellungen 3; Halle 1936) 152–160; and Frölich, *Mittelalterliche Bauwerke* 29–32.

them. While the tradition of law at the church portal goes far to explain its persistence as a place of judgment, there are also specific architectural qualities inherent in the portal that helped to embed its legal role in both public and institutional imaginations. The thickness of the portal's threshold provides a physical and symbolic transition-point not just between inside and outside, but, by extension, between any two separated realms, whether the public and the private, the profane and the sacred, the vulnerable and the protected. Passing the threshold marks transition from one world to another, guarded by its gatekeepers.[44] The medieval church portal embodied the power of the gatekeepers to accept or reject the supplicant to the sacred precinct beyond. Its inherent meaning was that the just and the faithful could pass into the realm of the sacred, while those breaking the law would be denied access.

These intrinsic qualities of the church portal came to the fore in various forms of civil law associated with the portal, such as in the right of asylum, the taking of oaths, and in marriage ceremonies. The borders of the portal were an inviolable space for those who sought asylum. The church buildings had always possessed an apotropaic power to thwart evil.[45] In the same way portals, delineating the threshold between two realms, enclosed the inside protectively while shutting out evil from the outside.[46] The church door was therefore believed to have special, even sacred powers, which could be transmitted to any person touching it. Religious historians and anthropologists have designated objects that possess such protective power as *orenda*.[47] Ortwin Henssler has shown that, in many cultures throughout history, the right of asylum has been associated with touching these orenda.[48] Refugees were considered to be exempt and untouchable as long as they were holding onto an orenda or as long as they stayed in the sanctified area where the orenda was located, making harm to their persons taboo. The church door functioned as such an orenda for the medieval refugee.[49]

44. For this concept, see Arnold van Gennep, *The Rites of Passage*, trans. M. B. Vizedom and G. L. Caffee (Chicago 1960).

45. Chris Caple, 'The Apotropaic Symbolled Threshold to Nevern Castle—Castle Nanhyfer', *Archaeological Journal* 169 (2012) 422–452; and Deirdre E. Jackson, 'Shields of Faith: Apotropaic Images of the Virgin in Alfonso X's Cantigas de Santa Maria', *Racar* 24 (1997) 38–46.

46. See H. C. Trumbull, *The Threshold Covenant or the Beginning of Religious Rites* (New York 1896) 57–59.

47. The term was borrowed from the language of the Iroquois Indians of North America, who used it to describe a supernatural power believed to be present in all persons and objects. It was the spiritual force by which human accomplishment was attained or accounted for; see Rudolf Pfister, 'Orendismus', *Handwörterbuch des deutschen Aberglaubens*, ed. Hanns Bächtold-Stäubli (Berlin-Leipzig 1934–1935) 6.1294–1306.

48. Ortwin Henssler, *Formen des Asylrechts und ihre Verbreitung bei den Germanen* (Frankfurt 1954).

49. As early as the fourth century and thereafter, the Christian church offered asylum to anybody who entered a church building. In Merovingian times the right of asylum was extended

One of the earliest documented episodes of the church portal as an orenda in medieval Europe is the case of Philippe de Dreux, bishop of Beauvais, who was captured in Rouen in 1197 by his mortal enemy King Richard the Lionheart of England.[50] When in 1198 Philippe was led from his prison to the king's mother, the guardians had to walk him past the porch of a church. The contemporary chronicler Roger of Hoveden († after 1201) recounted the ensuing scene in his *Chronica*:

The aforementioned bishop ran as fast as he could to the door of the porch, although it was closed, quickly grasped the ring of the church and screamed in a loud voice, saying: 'I beg for the peace of God and the church'.[51]

Alas for Philippe, his plea for sanctuary was not respected. His guardians apprehended him and conveyed him back to the prison, from which he was released only after the king's death in 1199.

The role of the church in granting the right of asylum was limited over time by secular authorities. Communal governments eventually expropriated this power, arrogating the granting or denial of asylum exclusively to their own officials.[52] Instances of denying the right of asylum by simply pulling the refugee away from the door increased steadily. Between 1050 and 1190 no less than nine church councils had to remind the laity of the ecclesiastical right of asylum.[53] In many instances it was the members of

from the inner church to the adjacent atrium and to the boundaries of the building; see Hans Robert Hahnloser, 'Urkunden zur Bedeutung des Türrings', *Festschrift für Erich Meyer zum sechzigsten Geburtstag 29. Oktober 1957: Studien zu Werken in den Sammlungen des Museums für Kunst und Gewerbe Hamburg* (Hamburg 1959) 125–146, esp. 135. The right of asylum within church buildings was adopted from Roman culture, in which imperial temples, such as the Temple of Julius Caesar on the Forum Romanum, were used as places of asylum. The Romans were influenced by the Greeks, who allowed asylum in their temples; see P. Timbal Duclaux de Martin, *Le Droit d'Asile* (Paris 1939) 17–33. For the Merovingian use of the church atrium as a place of asylum, see, for example, the decree from King Chlodwig: 'Nullus latronem vel quemlibet culpabilem… de atrio ecclesiae extrahere praesumat. Quodsi sunt ecclesiae, quibus atriae clausae non sunt, ab utrasque partebus parietum terrae spacium aripennis pro atrio observetur'; or the Carolingian decree from 803: 'Si quis ad ecclesiam confugium fecerit, in atrio ipsius ecclesiae pacem habeat nec sit ei necesse ecclesiam ingredi, et nullus eum inde per vim abstrahere praesumat'; both citations taken from Niermeyer, *Mediae Latinitatis Lexicon*, s.v. *atrium*, 67. Most recently William Jordan, 'A Fresh Look at Medieval Sanctuary', *Law and the Illicit in Medieval Europe*, ed. Ruth Mazo Karras, Joel Kaye, and E. Ann Matter (The Middle Ages; Philadelphia 2008) 17–32.

50. For this example, see Hahnloser, 'Urkunden zur Bedeutung des Türrings' 136–137, who provides many examples of people seeking refuge at church doors in which the door ring had a crucial role.

51. 'Dum autem irent, contigit eos transitum facere per atrium cujusdam ecclesiae; ad cuius ostium, licet esset clausum, praefatus episcopus, ut potuit, cucurrit et, arrepto ecclesiae annullo, alta voce exclamavit, dicens: "Peto pacem Dei et Ecclesiae",' *Chronica Magistri Rogeri de Hovedene*, ed. William Stubbs (RS 51; London, 1871) 4.41; see also Hahnloser, 'Urkunden zur Bedeutung des Türrings' 136–137, 145.

52. See Paul Frauenstädt, *Blutrache und Todtschlagsühne im deutschen Mittelalter: Studien zur deutschen Kultur- und Rechtsgeschichte* (Leipzig 1881) 51–87, esp. 53–54; and Hahnloser, 'Urkunden zur Bedeutung des Türrings' 136.

53. Ibid. 137.

the city council themselves who did not respect this right. That was the case in Goslar, when in 1313 the senate of the city ordered a criminal to be dragged from his place of asylum, the Church of Sts. Simon, Judas, and Matthias (later destroyed), whereupon the whole city was punished with excommunication.[54]

The touching of the church door was also an important element in the act of swearing oaths. The swearing of oaths was employed in the private sphere, as a means to resolve personal disputes, and in trials, where witnesses swore to the truthfulness of their testimony.[55] In northern Europe particularly, oaths were sworn 'on the threshold' or 'ad portam ecclesiae'.[56] When no Bible was at hand for such oaths, the oath taker would touch the doorpost or the door ring.[57] One of the earliest references to an oath sworn on the door ring can be found in the *Miracula Sancti Germani Episcopi Autissiodorensis,* written by Hericus from Auxerre between 877 and 880.[58] Hericus claimed that anybody who committed perjury at the door rings would be avenged immediately by the forfeit of his property or by corporal punishment.

The custom of choosing the church portal for swearing oaths is also documented in a literary passage, in the *Legend of the Ring* from around 1200.[59] When the two queens Kriemhilde and Brünhilde failed to resolve their argument as to which of them was superior in feudal ranking, they agreed to meet in front of the cathedral portal of Worms:

54. 'Erat e fece hominum nescio quis, qui gravi se delicto polluerat, justamque Senatus nostri promeruerat animadversionem. Sed homuncio, vitae suae timens, fugaque in curiam quandam claustralem se proripiens, lictorum insequentium celeritatem elusit. Ideo Senatus sceleris ultor reum e curia extrahi jussit. Graviter ea res commovit Canonicorum Capitulum, forte quod se imprudentibus id factum fuerat. Hinc litem movit senatui, prolatisque Pontificum, Caesarumque privilegiis, quibus de plena securitate ecclesiae cautum fuerat, ostendit, civitatem re ipsa excommunicationis sententiam incidisse'; Johann M. Heineccius, *Antiquitates Goslariensium et Vicinarum Regionum* (Frankfurt 1707) 329; see also Frauenstädt, *Blutrache und Todtschlagsühne* 54 n. 4.

55. If insufficient proof was available to determine guilt or innocence, the court resorted to the trial of ordeal, as a form of divine presentation of the case, most often used in cases of theft, treason, or adultery, as in Bartlett, *Trial by Fire* 24–25. For a contrary understanding of the ordeal, see Paul R. Hyams, 'Trial by Ordeal: The Key to Proof in Early Common Law', *On the Laws and Customs of England: Essays in Honor of Samuel E. Thorne,* ed. Morris S. Arnold et al. (Chapel Hill 1981) 90–126. For the connection of ordeals and oaths, see also John M. Roberts, 'Oaths, Autonomic Ordeals, and Power', *American Anthropologist* 67 (1965) 186–212.

56. See the fundamental study by Hahnloser, 'Urkunden zur Bedeutung des Türrings' 130–131; also Grimm, *Deutsche Rechtsalterthümer* 1.242–243 and 2.556–557.

57. Grimm, *Deutsche Rechtsalterthümer* 2.557.

58. 'Nam si quis aut cupiditatis illectu, aut animi pertinacis impulsu, mendacio patrocinari definiens, saltem in armilla januae jus jurandum explere presumpserit, hunc quod sit reus perjurii, tum rei familiaris dispendio, tum corporeae damno valetudinis'. The full document is printed in Hahnloser, 'Urkunden zur Bedeutung des Türrings' 143 no. 3 and 130.

59. Mentioned in Evers, *Tod, Macht und Raum* 180.

They met before the church. The wife of noble Gunther (full of hate was she) very angrily bade the Lady Kriemhild not to walk ahead. . . . 'It is not allowed for a bondmaid to go before a queen', she said. After having heard mass, they returned to the portal only to resume their dispute. They called to witness their husbands, Siegfried and Gunther, and Siegfried offered to take an oath at the threshold: Now I have no objection to swearing solemnly in front of all your followers.[60]

This literary evidence corroborates the broad acceptance of the church portal's judicial importance more than any single legal document could. Just as the litigants transcend their specific identities to become universal tragic heroines and heroes, so the portal becomes an archetype, transcending the specificity of the Worms portal to become a universal mythic representation of the judicial character of the church threshold.

A particular oath sworn at the church door occurred at the celebration of weddings, when the bride and groom swore fidelity to each other. It is well established that weddings took place in front of the church door.[61] The designation of many a church portal as the 'bridal door' provides evidence of this widespread tradition.[62] As Jean-Baptiste Molin and Protais Mutembe have shown in their fundamental study on marriage rituals, the beginnings of this custom can be traced back to Anglo-Norman practice, recorded in pontificals and missals from Brittany, Normandy, and England at the turn of the eleventh and twelfth centuries.[63] The pontifical of Lire from the early twelfth century ordered, 'Before all else let those who are to be joined in marriage come in front of the doors of the church before very many witnesses'. The contemporaneous *Ordo* in the missal of Rennes stipulated similarly, 'First let the priest come in front of the door of the church'.[64]

One literary source for this custom is the poem *Lohengrin*, written in

60. *The Nibelungenlied*, translated from the German and with an introduction by R. Lichtenstein (Studies in German Language and Literature 9; Lewiston 1991) 86, canto 14, verse 838 and 88, canto 14, verse 858.

61. See Trumbull, *Threshold Covenant* 138–140; Jean-Baptiste Molin and Protais Mutembe, *Le Rituel du mariage en France du XIIe au XVIe siècle* (Théologie historique 26; Paris 1974) 32–40; Christine Klapisch-Zuber, 'Zacharias, or the Ousted Father: Nuptial Rites in Tuscany between Giotto and the Council of Trent', *Women, Family, and Ritual in Renaissance Italy*, trans. Lydia G. Cochrane (Chicago 1985) 178–212, esp. 202–203; and Christopher N. L. Brooke, *The Medieval Idea of Marriage* (Oxford 1989) 248–257; see also Francesco Brandileone, *Saggi sulla storia della celebrazione del matrimonio in Italia* (Milan 1906) 6.78–79, 90–91 n. 3, with examples from medieval Italy. The church, however, did not have to solemnize the wedding to validate it, and many marriages were held at home; see Brooke, *Medieval Idea* 250–253.

62. Friedrich Zoepfl, 'Brauttüre', *Reallexikon zur deutschen Kunstgeschichte*, ed. O. Schmitt (Stuttgart 1948) 2.1134–1137. Brooke, *Medieval Idea* 253–257, suggests that the provision of porches at churches can be seen as a reflection of the marriage rituals performed there.

63. Molin and Mutembe, *Rituel du mariage* 34–37, 284–290.

64. Lire: 'Ante omnia veniant ad januas ecclesiae sub testimonio plurimorum, qui thoro maritali conjungendi sunt'; Molin and Mutembe, *Rituel du mariage* 286. Rennes: 'In primis veniat sacerdos ante ostium ecclesiae', ibid. 285; translation taken from Brooke, *Medieval Idea* 249.

southern Germany by Nouhuwius between 1283 and 1286. When King Henry's daughter was promised to the lord of Lorraine, the marriage was solemnized by the bishop of Mainz in front of the portal of the cathedral: 'So they convened in front of the cathedral. In the presence of the bishop of Mainz, they promised each other in marriage at the front of the door of the church'.[65] The poet clearly separated this part of the wedding from the following Mass within the church building, into which the newly married couple was led by the bishop of Mainz.[66] The split between the two parts of the wedding in this poetic text echoes the spatial division implicit in the portal. Whether with the marriage vows, the oath, or the right of asylum, the portal represented a threshold between two realms, the passage of which was guarded: the just and faithful could pass into the realm of the sacred, while those breaking oaths, vows, or sacred law were denied access.

Sculptural imagery reinforced this fundamental meaning of portals as thresholds. The entrances were guarded by gatekeepers, who had the power to allow passage or deny it. One of the most popular demarcations was the imagery of two lions, whether carved in stone flanking the entrances of churches, or cast in metal with door rings affixed to them.[67] The meaning of the lion is multifold.[68] The image of the lion was thought to have apotropaic power because of that animal's strength, vigilance, and dignity. Paired lions appeared therefore as guardians at city gates, palaces and thrones, temples, sanctuaries and burial chambers, or at entrances of churches, preventing evil from penetrating the holy precincts.

In the Middle Ages, the symbolic resonance of the lion went beyond the power to protect from evil: he also symbolized judicial power, in his association with King Solomon, the exemplary judge of the Old Testament, and with the Christ of the Last Judgment.[69] The Old and New Tes-

65. 'Alsô quâmens vür daz tuom. der ê nû anderweide veriâhens vor des münsters tür dem bischòf von Mênze', Thomas Cramer, *Lohengrin: Edition und Untersuchungen* (Munich 1971) 531, strophe 684, verses 6837–6838.

66. '[der] bischòf von Mênze, der sie nû hin vür brâht in den kôr.... Nû wart diu messe rîlich erhaben, Cramer', *Lohengrin* 531, strophe 684, verses 6839–6840; and 532, strophe 686, verse 6851.

67. Lion sculptures flanking church portals appeared first in southern Italy at the end of the eleventh century (Bornstein, *Portals and Politics* 32–34), while bronze lion rings seem to have been part of an unbroken tradition since antiquity (Mende, *Türzieher* 128–129). The lions decorating the tombs constructed for King Roger II of Sicily are magnificent evocations of their power; see Jószf Deér, *The Dynastic Porphyry Tombs of the Norman Period in Sicily*, trans. G. A. Gillhoff (Dumbarton Oaks Studies 5; Cambridge 1959), and Gianfilippo Villari, *Il sarcofago dell'imperatore: Studi, ricerche e indagini sulla tomba di Federico II nella Cattedrale di Palermo, 1994–1999* (Palermo 2002). The tomb can be seen at http://faculty.cua.edu/pennington/Haskins%20Lecture/Cefalu4.htm.

68. Of the vast literature, see Mende, *Türzieher* 140–142, 142 n. 87, with further bibliography.

69. For this aspect, see in particular Isa Ragusa, 'Terror Demonum and Terror Inimicorum: The Two Lions of the Throne of Solomon and the Open Door of Paradise', *Zeitschrift für Kunstgeschichte* 40 (1977) 93–114.

tament symbolism of paired lions at the church door demonstrated their capacity to reinforce both earthly and ultimate justice. The French monk Pierre Bersuire reported in his 1362 *Repertorium Morale* a moralizing interpretation of the world:

[Solomon] is associated with two lions… which are located at various stairs, flanking many entrances. They make passage difficult, and for this reason they are seated there where officials make judgments to incarcerate avaricious and rapacious men.[70]

This judicial custom is also indicated by documents that record judgments made 'inter duos leones'.[71] At the Church of St. Nicholas in Werden in Westphalia (erected in 1047 and later destroyed), lions surmounted two freestanding pillars in front of the staircase leading to the church's main portal.[72] The pillars also served as an allusion to King Solomon, evoking the two columns, named Iachim and Booz, in front of his temple (1 Kings 7:15–22; 1 Chron 3:15–17).[73] The abbot of Werden pronounced his judgments while seated between the two pillars of St. Nicholas, thus equating himself with Solomon.

The columns of the twelfth-century porches in northern Italy, which are supported by paired lions, can be interpreted in a similar way. As Christine Verzár Bornstein has shown, the columns and the lions represented a visual symbolic allusion to Solomon, who was thereby evoked as a role model for officials as they performed legal transactions at these entrances.[74] We know, for instance, that in the 1140s, the canons performed legal transactions *sub portico* at the cathedral of Ferrara.[75] In the same place, in

70. 'Est a duobus leonibus associatus. … Ibi sunt diversi gradus et ostia multa intermedia per quae transire oportet, qui faciunt aditus difficultatem, et hoc quia ibi sedent leunculi, id officiales ballivi, qui avariciam diligunt, et rapacitatem', P. Bersuire, 'Reductorium Morale super Totam Bibliam', *Dictionarii sev Repertorii Moralis* (Venice 1583) 3.133; paraphrased in Ragusa, 'Terror Demonum' 105–106.

71. Grimm, *Deutsche Rechtsalterthümer* 2.428.

72. Effmann, *Karolingisch-ottonischen Bauten* 387 nn. 3 and 2; *Clemenskirche, Luciuskirche, Nikolauskirche*, ed. E. Hohmann (Berlin 1922) 61–62; see also Rudolf Kötzschke, 'Das Gericht Werden im späteren Mittelalter Ausübung der Landesgewalt im Stiftsgebiet', *Beiträge zur Geschichte des Stiftes Werden* 10 (1904) 70–126, esp. 106.

73. For the Solomonic columns in Romanesque art, see Walter Cahn, 'Solomonic Elements in Romanesque Art', *The Temple of Solomon: Archaeological Facts and Medieval Tradition in Christian, Islamic and Jewish Art*, ed. J. Gutmann (Missoula 1976) 45–72, esp. 50–56.

74. Bornstein, *Portals and Politics* 35 and 39–42, 91–93.

75. Ibid. 92, 104. The site is mentioned in the documents as being 'sub portico canonice Sancti Georgi' and 'sub portice canonice'. It is not clear whether this refers to the entrance of the main facade or to the portal on the south side, opening onto the market square, the Porta dei Mesi. In each case two lions flank the entrance, supporting two columns of the porch. It seems more probable that the portal on the south side was used for the legal actions, as it was known as the Portal of Justice; see Adriano Franceschini, *I frammenti epigrafici degli statuti di Ferrara del 1173 venuti in luci nella cattedrale* (Ferrara 1969) 11–12.

1173, the commune of Ferrara set up their statutes, as visual expressions of the judicial authority that was invested in the church door before their own town hall was erected.[76]

The columns alone appear to have been sufficient to remind the viewer of Solomon's temple. The south portal of the church at Langenhorst in Westphalia, functioning as the main entrance, is flanked by two engaged columns that serve no architectural function. They are purely symbolical, alluding to the Temple of King Solomon. This reference becomes even more convincing in light of the judicial use of this door. From 1203 onward, the archdeacon sat in judgment in front of this portal.[77]

Depictions of King Solomon himself were also common at church portals, marking portals as places of adjudication. This was the case at León, where at the porch of the cathedral, below the enthroned figure of King Solomon, the inscription 'Locus Apellacionis' (Place of Appeal) was incised on a column. While the epigraphy is from the eleventh century, the heraldic engraving with the arms of Castile and León dates to the thirteenth century, indicating that royal justice was dispensed from this place, at least from the 1200s onward.[78] Strasbourg cathedral is another example. On the central pillar between the two doorways of the south portal is a thirteenth-century sculpture of King Solomon, crowned and seated, with his sword laid across his knees.[79] It was here that the city council of Strasbourg administered justice until they erected their new town hall around 1321, and the figure of Solomon served to symbolize and support their judicial activities.[80]

The lions, King Solomon, or Christ in Judgment were the gate-keepers, controlling the passage over the threshold. At the portal of Autun, for instance, the over-large image of Christ is a visual expression of the Savior's

76. The statues are now hidden behind the shops that were erected along the south wall; see Bornstein, *Portals and Politics* 103–104. The construction of the communal palace of Ferrara, the Palazzo della Ragione, was not started until 1324–1325, after a revolt against the signoria of the Este family, whose rule was established in 1208; see Jürgen Paul, 'Die mittelalterlichen Kommunalpaläste in Italien' (PhD diss., Albert-Ludwigs-Universität Freiburg 1963) 142–144.

77. Georg Dehio, *Handbuch der deutschen Kunstdenkmäler: Nordrhein-Westfalen*, 2: *Westfalen*, ed. Dorothea Kluge and Wilfried Hansmann (Munich-Berlin 1977) 276.

78. F. B. Deknatel, 'The Thirteenth Century Gothic Sculpture of the Cathedrals of Burgos and León', *Art Bulletin* 17 (1935) 243–389, esp. 339–340.

79. See Erler, *Straßburger Münster* 2–3, 17–18. The sculpture there now is a nineteenth-century copy of the original. The portal was destroyed during the French Revolution. Of the thirteenth-century decoration of the two portals, only the depictions of 'Synagogue' and 'Ecclesia' and the reliefs with stories of the Virgin Mary in the tympanums have survived. However, a 1617 print by Isaac Brun allows us to reconstruct the portal's original appearance. It shows that the figure of King Solomon and of Christ above him follow this original model, while the reliefs on the consoles of 'Ecclesia,' 'Synagogue,' and 'Solomon' were replaced in a rather free manner; the apostles in the jambs of the portals were never replaced.

80. Ibid. Also S. Tipton, *'Res Publica Bene Ordinata': Regentenspiel und Bilder vom guten Regiment: Rathausdekorationen in der frühen Neuzeit* (Hildesheim-Zürich-New York 1996) 409ff.

function as the gatekeeper of the entrance to Paradise: 'I am the door, by me if any man enter in, he shall be saved' (Jn 10:9). In his judicial authority, Christ has the power to open or close the doors, allowing passage to those who led a just life, as is made clear in the Psalm text: 'Open to me the gate of righteousness.... This is the gate of the Lord; the righteous shall enter through it' (Ps 117:19–20).

This imagery of granting or denial of access to salvation animated the setting of courts held before church portals and thereby reinforced the power of legal magistrates, and in fact written records from the fifth to the fifteenth centuries linked the image of Christ in Judgment to earthly judges.[81] The Constantinopolitan patriarch John Chrysostom († 407) expounded in his homily on Matthew:

Just as the servants draw back the curtains to reveal the judge at a public court to all beholders, so it will be on the day of the Last Judgment; all will see the enthroned Christ, all mankind will appear before Him, and He himself will begin to speak.[82]

The metaphor of John Chrysostom eventually became an explicit association between earthly judges and Christ.

One of the first examples is a gloss to the Saxonian compendium of laws, the *Sächsisches Weichbildrecht*, written between 1330 and 1386:

Wherever the judge is located to dispense justice, God will sit in divine judgment over judge and jurors at the same place and at the same time. Every magistrate should paint therefore in his town hall the stern judgment of Our Lord, so that he be reminded of His judgment and remember that he shall be the judge of the people.[83]

The analogy between the two courts of justice was made even more explicit by depicting the Last Judgment directly above an earthly court. There are other pictorial examples that combine the divine judgment

81. See, in particular, Jérôme Baschet, *Les Justices de l'au-delà: Les Représentation de l'enfer en France et en Italie (XIIe–XVe siècle)* (Rome 1993).

82. 'Nam sicut cum judices publice sententiam prolutari sunt, qui adstant remotis velis, sic illos omnibus conscipiendos prebent: ita et tunc omnes illum sedentem videbunt, et tota humana natura sistetur, ipseque per se illis respondebit; atque aliis dicet', John Chrysostom, 'Homiliarum in Matthaeum—continuatio', PG 58.554–555 cap. 16, ver. 28; see also Beat Brenk, *Tradition und Neuerung in der christlichen Kunst des ersten Jahrtausends: Studien zur Geschichte des Weltgerichtsbildes* (Vienna 1966) 28; and Wolfgang Schild, 'Gott als Richter', and 'Gerechtigkeitsbilder', *Recht und Gerechtigkeit im Spiegel der europäischen Kunst*, ed. Wolfgang Pleister and W. Schild (Cologne 1988) 44–171, esp. 70–72.

83. 'wenn wo der richter mit orteiln richtit, in der selbien stat, unde in der selbien stunde sizit got in sinem gotlichen gerichte obir den richter, unde obir die schepphen; unde dorum sulde eyn izlichir richter in dem rathuse lazin molen daz gestrenge gerichte unsers herren; unde ist dorumme daz er gedenken sal an daz gerichte, daz das unsers herren sy; unde daz er ouch gedenke, daz er richter sal sien des volkes', cited from Georg Troescher, 'Weltgerichtsbilder in Rathäusern und Gerichtsstätten', *Wallraf-Richartz-Jahrbuch* 11 (1939) 139–214, esp. 148.

with a secular law court. In a miniature in the book of laws from Hamburg, dated 1497, for example, the judge, two assessors and the clerk of the court sit in judgment below a painting of the Apocalyptic Christ, which hangs on the wall of the loggia.[84] Inscriptions on scrolls held by the hands of God explicate the painting's meaning. On the left are the words from the Sermon on the Mount: 'With the judgment you pronounce you will be judged, and the measure you give will be the measure you get' (Mt 7:2). The words on the right are cited from the exhortation of Josaphat to the judges: 'Consider what you do, for you judge not for man but for the Lord; he is with you in judgment' (2 Chron 19:6).

The parallels between earthly and divine judgment reflect the situation at the medieval church portal, where the local judge was seated below the figure of Christ, to dispense justice and to remind the participants of the Last Judgment. This was more than a parallel, and even more than a divine source of power. Visual and spatial association of the earthly judge to Christ in Judgment extended the authority of the judge from the temporal domain to the afterlife, suggesting that even crimes undiscovered would be punished.

From Church Portal to Town Hall: The Rise of the Communes

Given the mass of evidence, tradition, and imagery of the church portal as a judicial site, it comes as a surprise that, between the thirteenth and fifteenth centuries, first in Italy and then in Germany, the church portal was used less and less frequently as the site for law courts. This decline in the use of church portals is directly proportional to the growth of lay civic institutions. During the rapid rise of the Italian communes in the eleventh and twelfth centuries, the tensions between secular and religious judicial authority that had plagued the Carolingians resurfaced. Early civic governments erected independent town halls for their administration and law courts, but then located these structures beside or opposite churches. While some communes eventually separated their town halls from the church buildings, they were never fully able to split themselves from the church. Religious imagery remained a tool in the expression of independence of the communes, since the civil authorities used the same portal architecture and sacred figures in their town halls. From the thirteenth century, the same transference took

84. See Hans Fehr, *Das Recht im Bilde* (Munich-Leipzig 1923) 44–45 no. 28; and *Die Bilderhandschrift des Hamburgischen Stadtrechts von 1497,* annotations by H. Reincke, newly ed. J. Bolland (Veröffentlichungen aus dem Staatsarchiv der Freien und Hansestadt Hamburg 10; Hamburg 1968) 47, 174–175.

place in German free cities. The result characterizes the paradoxical process of secular institutions splitting from sacred authority: the persistence of church portal architecture and imagery at town halls indicates that, though lay governments could separate themselves from the institutions of local rulers, they could not split themselves from the power of the church.

Medieval communal institutions simultaneously broke from and remained linked to the church in their civic architecture, and they did this in a variety of ways. At first the earliest civic governments continued the tradition of locating their legal activities at or within churches, revealing their need to base civic rule on divine justice. This practice can be documented for many cities throughout northern and central Italy.[85] The construction of the first town halls shows a break with this tradition, revealing a stronger desire for civic autonomy by building an independent structure for civic administration and legal procedures. However, the placing of these buildings within the urban setting and their architectural forms reveal a dependency on religious structures. The earliest extant town hall in Italy is the Palazzo della Ragione in Bergamo, built in 1198.[86] Its construction postdated by around 90 years the establishment of a lay consular government, which replaced the bishop's rule. The Palazzo della Ragione is located in front of the church of Santa Maria Maggiore, and beside the cathedral of San Vicenzo, emphasizing the role of bishop's judicial authority. The architectural details also reveal a reference to religious structures. The ground-floor loggia of the palace and the articulation of the pier capitals and upper-level windows derive from the cathedral itself and from regional religious architecture. The most telling of these references is the loggia. In its siting and its triple arches it bears a strong resemblance to monastic gatehouses, such as at Lorsch, and to the entrance to the atrium of Old St. Peter's in Rome. Although it was an independent structure for an independent institution, the town hall remained spatially and typologically linked to the cathedral and to the institution of the church.

Other Lombard town halls follow the same models. Como's town hall, from 1215, shares the same loggia and religious architectural articulation, and it adjoins the cathedral.[87] Milan's Palazzo della Ragione, begun in 1228, has the same ground-floor loggia, this time five bays, but is separated from

85. See Paul, *Mittelalterlichen Kommunalpaläste* 37; for specific instances, see Paul's historical survey of individual communal palaces (122–124). Also Areli Marina, *The Italian Piazza Transformed: Parma in the Communal Age* (University Park, Pa. 2012) for a detailed study of a commune.

86. For this building, see R. D. Russell, '*Vox Civitatis*: Aspects of Thirteenth-Century Communal Architecture in Lombardy' (PhD diss., Princeton University 1988).

87. See Russell, '*Vox Civitatis*' 175–195; see also Maureen C. Miller, 'From Episcopal to Communal Palaces: Places and Power in Northern Italy (1000–1250)', *Journal of the Society of Architectural*

the cathedral and from its local architectural precedent, Sant'Ambrogio.[88] The mixture of brickwork and limestone for the ground-floor arches, the 'opus mixtum' arch extradoi, and particularly the loggia itself are directly copied from Sant'Ambrogio.[89] The fact that the latter had served as one of the city's most important judicial sites shows that even with the construction of an independent governing structure away from the church, the communal authorities relied on an ecclesiastical model.[90] The most telling connection, however, is in the equestrian relief from 1233 between the arches of the fourth and third bays, showing the podestà Oldrado da Trissino. While his position on horseback links him to imperial equestrian figures, specifically to the statue of Marcus Aurelius on Rome's Capitoline, its meaning is more ambiguous. At the time the image was sculpted, the Marcus Aurelius was known as Constantine the Great. The statue's strong ties to Christian imperial rule, rather than to the pagan Roman emperor, were reinforced by its location at the Lateran complex, the site of the pope in his role as bishop of Rome. Constantine was not only the first Christian emperor, but also the first to crusade in the name of Christ. Oldrado clearly took this crusading heritage to heart as much in his actions as in his equestrian self-representation. The inscription beneath his image, 'He burnt Cathars as he ought to', makes it clear that despite the fact that he was a secular ruler situated in a secular structure posing as a Roman emperor, he wanted to be remembered as having used his temporal power to enforce the orthodoxy, and therefore the authority, of the church.[91]

There were tensions between secular and religious authorities—over site, architecture, and imagery of judicial power—in communes not only in Italy but also in Germany. A case in point is the city of Worms. The origins of the commune go back as early as 1073, when the citizens expelled the bishop, and acknowledged instead Emperor Henry IV as their ruler.[92] Henry's successor, Henry V, supported the civic movement, granting the citizens in 1114 important privileges. He was followed by Frederick Barbarossa in 1184. The citizens initially chose the space in front of the north portal of the cathedral as the site for their legal activities.[93] It faced

---

Historians 54 (1995) 175–185, and Miller, *The Bishop's Palace: Architecture and Authority in Medieval Italy* (Ithaca-London 2000).

88. See Russell, 'Vox Civitatis' 195–210; and A. Grimoldi, *Il Palazzo della Ragione* (Milan 1983).

89. For this and the following, see Alick M. McLean, 'Romanesque Architecture in Italy', *Romanesque: Architecture, Sculpture, Painting*, ed. R. Toman (Cologne 1997) 74–117, esp. 114–117.

90. Keller, 'Gerichtsort' 28–30.

91. 'catharos ut debuit uxit'.

92. For this and the following, see Hans Planitz, 'Die deutsche Stadtgemeinde: Forschungen zur Stadtverfassungsgeschichte', ZRG Germ. Abt. 64 (1944) 1–85, esp. 23–25.

93. Georg von Below, *Das ältere deutsche Städtewesen und Bürgertum* (Bielefeld-Leipizg 1898) 43–45.

the bishop's court, including the bishop's palace, thus continuing the legal tradition invested in this place. Around 1200, the meeting place was to be formalized with the construction of a porch; one can still see traces of the stonework on either side of the entry, where the privileges from Frederick Barbarossa were displayed.[94] The townspeople soon decided, however, to erect an independent city hall—far from the portal of the cathedral and against the explicit will of Bishop Henry II (1217–1234)—thus asserting their independence from traditional ecclesiastical authority.[95]

The shift in location of judicial activities, whether in Germany or in Italy, was undoubtedly sparked by the rise of the communes. The transfer had several implications. Law courts were now held increasingly inside, rather than outside. The move from outdoor to inner spaces of legal activities supported a general tendency during this period that paralleled the revival of Roman law, namely the process of rationalizing judicial processes, which culminated in the formulation of procedures. Trials by ordeal were replaced by law courts following clearly laid-out procedures. Rule by law began to supersede rule by men willfully asserting divine right and supported by divine judgments.

However, as is clear from the examples provided above, the architecture of this new form of justice and rule was not always a simple affair. Even in cities such as Siena or Cologne, where enduring civic governments were established, the imagery of divine authority persisted, with Simone Martini and Stephan Lochner's monumental representations of the Virgin in Majesty situated in the council chambers of their respective city halls. Such images, together with depictions of the Last Judgment, which became the most popular imagery in town halls, were adopted by civic authorities as potent symbols of establishing their spatial and institutional independence.[96] By displacing and rationalizing the place and procedures of justice from the church portal to the town hall, Italian and German communes may have been successful in wresting authority from local secular and religious rulers but never completely separated their courts from the foundation of legal authority in Christ and from the ultimate court of appeal: the Last Judgment. One need only to contemplate the architecture of the modern courtroom, or the religious text upon which witnesses must lay their hands when they swear to speak the truth, to understand the power of this tradition on the setting, if not practice, of western justice.

94. Claussen, *Chartres-Studien* 16–17.

95. The existence of a town hall is first mentioned in 1232; see Planitz, 'Deutsche Stadtgemeinde' 25.

96. For examples, see the study by Troescher, 'Weltgerichtsbilder'.

3

The Practice of Canon Law

James A. Brundage

Trained jurists began practicing law during the first half of the twelfth century.[1] During the second half of the twelfth century, references to individuals who furnished legal advice to litigants in the ecclesiastical courts and spoke on behalf of the parties in contentious proceedings appear with increasing frequency in contemporary records.[2] In 1149, for example, St. Bernard of Clairvaux (1090–1153) cautioned Pope Eugene III (1145–1153) to beware of the cunning and convoluted snares set by the lawyers who infested the papal curia. Bernard admonished the pope that it was altogether inappropriate for him to spend days and hours upon end listening to the arguments that curial lawyers concocted in order to pervert the

1. Johannes Fried's doctoral dissertation at the University of Heidelberg, later published as *Die Entstehung des Juristenstandes im 12. Jahrhundert: Zur sozialen Stellung und politischen Bedeutung gelehrter Juristen in Bologna und Modena* (Forschungen zur neueren Privatrechtsgeschichte 21; Cologne-Vienna 1974), was a groundbreaking work for describing the emergence of jurists and their education during the twelfth century.

2. Brundage, *Medieval Origins* 407–465. Thus we hear e.g. of Master Robert Blund, a busy ecclesiastical advocate who journeyed between Paris, Lincoln, and Oxford, arguing cases in the 1150s; see Peter of Blois, *Epistolae* 62, PL 207.184–186. Likewise Gerald of Wales mentions the advocates he engaged to press his claims against Hubert Walter; see Gerald's *Opera*, ed. J. S. Brewer, J. F. Dimock, and G. F. Warner (RS 21; London 1861–1891) 3.228. Again, we learn of the fees charged by canonical advocates in the well-known case of *Anstey c. Francheville*; see P. M. Barnes, 'The Anstey Case', *A Medieval Miscellany for Doris Mary Stenton*, ed. P. M. Barnes and C. F. Slade (London 1962) 1–23.

course of ecclesiastical justice.[3] Three years later the pope heard similar warnings from Gerhoch of Reichersberg (1093–1169), who echoed St. Bernard's concern about the influence of lawyers at the curia.[4] For a time the papacy contemplated forbidding the clergy, particularly monks, to attend law schools.[5] Over the course of the next half century reformers commonly complained about the sinister ascendency within the church of men trained in law. Critics as diverse as Peter the Chanter (d. 1197) and Walter of Châtillon (ca. 1135–1202/1203), Jacques de Vitry (ca. 1160/70–1240), and Peter of Blois (d. after 1181), deplored the growing numbers of lawyers and their mounting influence in church courts throughout the Christian world.[6]

Not all references to practitioners in the canonical courts during the second half of the twelfth century were critical or disparaging. The number of ecclesiastical lawyers increased during this period, and their services were highly valued. Participants in weighty matters increasingly depended on legal experts to secure their rights, safeguard their property, and defend their honor. Monasteries, such as the Benedictine abbey of Evesham, might employ a battery of experienced legal practitioners to protect themselves against grasping bishops.[7] Well-to-do laymen, such as

3. Bernard of Clairvaux, *De consideratione ad Eugenium papam tertiam libri quinque* 1.3.4–1.4.5, 1.10.13, 1.11.14 (*Sancti Bernardi Opera*, ed. Jean Leclercq, C. H. Talbot, H. M. Rochais, et al.; Rome 1957–1977) 3.397–399, 408–410; see also the English translation, *Five Books on Consideration: Advice to a Pope*, trans. J. D. Anderson and Elizabeth T. Kennan (Cistercian Fathers Series 37; Kalamazoo 1976) 29–32, 44–46. On this topic, see further Brundage, 'St. Bernard and the Jurists', *The Second Crusade*, ed. Michael Gervers (New York 1992) 25–33.

4. Karl F. Morrison, 'The Church as Play: Gerhoch of Reichersberg's Call for Reform', *Popes, Teachers, and Canon Law in the Middle Ages*, ed. James R. Sweeney and Stanley Chodorow (Ithaca, N.Y. 1989) 115.

5. See Robert Somerville, 'Pope Innocent II and the Study of Roman Law', *Revue des Études islamiques* 44 (1976) 105–114, reprinted in *Papacy, Councils and Canon Law in the 11th–12th Centuries* (Collected Studies 312; Aldershot 1990), as well as Kenneth Pennington, 'Roman Law at the Papal Curia in the Early Twelfth Century', *Canon Law, Religion, and Politics: Liber Amicorum Robert Somerville*, ed. Uta-Renate Blumenthal, Anders Winroth, and Peter Landau (Washington, D.C. 2012) 233–252.

6. Peter the Chanter, *Verbum abbreviatum* 52, PL 105.161–162; L. Eldridge, 'Walter of Châtillon and the Decretum of Gratian: An Analysis of *Propter Sion non tacebo*', *Studies in Medieval Culture* 3 (1970) 64; Jacques de Vitry, *Die Exempla aus den Sermones feriales et communes* 83, ed. J. Greven (Sammlung mittellateinischer Texte 9; Heidelberg 1914) 50; Peter of Blois, 'Epistola ad socium,' *Chartularium universitatis Parisiensis* 27, ed. Heinrich Denifle and É. Chatelain (Paris 1889–1897, reprinted Brussels 1964) 1:33; and see generally John W. Baldwin, 'Critics of the Legal Profession: Peter the Chanter and His Circle', *Proceedings Boston 1965* 249–259, as well as Brundage, 'Ethics of the Legal Profession: Medieval Canonists and Their Clients', *The Jurist* 33 (1973) 237–248; and Brundage, 'Professional Canonists and Their Clients: Problems in Legal Ethics', *Proceedings Washington 2004* 857–874; and Brundage, 'Legal Ethics: A Medieval Ghost Story', *Law and the Illicit in Medieval Europe*, ed. Ruth Mazo Karras, Joel Kaye, and E. Ann Matter (Philadelphia 2008) 47–56.

7. Or at least so the monks saw things; the bishop of Worcester doubtless had a different view; *Chronicon abbatiae de Evesham ad annum 1418*, ed. W. D. Macray (RS 29; London 1863) 152–53, 164, 168, 184.

Richard of Anstey, found it advisable to pay for the services of canonical counsel to defend the legitimacy of a marriage which would secure their right to succeed to a handsome estate.[8]

Prior to 1200, however, there is little evidence that the lawyers who habitually worked in the ecclesiastical courts thought of themselves as professional specialists, nor is there much sign that they had developed widely shared standards of professional ethics or exercised formal control over admission to practice. It seems appropriate, therefore, to classify canonical practitioners of that period as proto-professionals and to reserve the term 'professional canonist' to describe practitioners in the later stages of occupational development, when mechanisms for control of admission, explicit standards of conduct, and conscious self-identification began to appear.

Practitioners with substantial formal training in canon law first appear to have developed a conscious professional identity around the turn of the thirteenth century.[9] Although canonists of Gratian's period (ca. 1140) and the generations that immediately followed showed scant sign of the other characteristics that we associate with professionalism in the modern world. The meanings of 'profession' and related terms have been hotly debated, especially in the abundant literature on the sociology of the professions. In ordinary usage 'profession' can be taken to mean a full-time occupation that enjoys high social esteem and confers privileges and prestige upon its practitioners. Professional prestige rests largely upon the mastery of esoteric knowledge and skills not generally available to non-professionals. Members of a profession normally acquire their special knowledge through formal training, usually at a university or similar institution, and typically require prospective practitioners to demonstrate some minimal level of academic preparation as a condition of admission to practice. It is further characteristic of professions that their members seek to secure a monopoly over the practice of their craft and attempt to control admissions to their ranks as a means of maintaining that monopoly.[10]

By the canonist Huguccio's generation in the 1180s and 1190s, the practice of law was for some canonists their principal occupation. Within the next generation a good many teachers and practitioners of canon

---

8. Christopher R. Cheney, *From Becket to Langton: English Church Government, 1170–1213* (Manchester 1956) 54–58; as well as Barnes, 'The Anstey Case'.

9. On the form and content of that training see below.

10. See generally Brundage, *Medieval Origins* 1–2 and 488–492; Roscoe Pound, 'What Is a Profession? The Rise of the Legal Profession in Antiquity', *Notre Dame Lawyer* 19 (1944) 203–228; A. P. Chroust, 'The Emergence of Professional Standards and the Rise of the Legal Profession', *Boston University Law Review* 36 (1956): 587–98; R. L. Abel and P. S. C. Lewis, eds., *Lawyers in Society: The Common Law World* (Berkeley and Los Angeles 1988–1989).

law showed an awareness that as advocates, jurists, and procurators they shared a common identity.[11]

By about 1200, the language describing the canonists suggests that they were seen as a distinct group, both functionally and socially, by others and by themselves. Canonists in this period began to refer to their occupation in terms similar to those commonly employed for the priesthood or the monastic life. Canonical advocates, for example, boasted that they exercised a 'ministerium' or an 'officium' and characterized their functions as a 'professio'.[12] Others also used these and similar terms when speaking of the canonists: thus, for example, the Franciscan preacher, Guibert of Tournai (ca. 1210–1284) referred to the 'ministerium' of advocates and proctors, called them an 'ordo', and styled their functions an 'officium'.[13]

One clear sign of the dawn of conscious professional identity is the emergence of attempts to control admission to practice. By the 1230s a process for the formal admission of canonical advocates had begun to appear in a few places. From the beginning, admission centered on the swearing of an oath of office.[14] Requirements that canonical practitioners swear such an oath first occurred in the canons of local ecclesiastical councils.[15] A generation later, the Second Council of Lyon (1274), on the initiative of William Durandus (1231–1296), adopted a constitution that required practitioners in canonical courts throughout Christendom to take

11. On the problems that detecting such an awareness raise for historians, see especially Pierre Michaud-Quantin, 'La conscience d'être membre d'une universitas', *Beiträge zum Berufsbewusstsein des mittelalterlichen Menschen*, ed. P. Wilpert (Miscellanea mediaevalia 3; Berlin 1964) 1–14.

12. These terms appear as early as the eleventh century in medieval sources dealing with lawyers and occur occasionally in this context even earlier; M. G. Merello Altea, *Scienza e professione legale nel secolo XI: Ricerche e appunti* (Università di Trieste, Facoltà di scienze politiche 16; Milan 1979) 45; cf. Cod. 2.7.24 pr. and Cod. 3.13.7; John of Caen, *Abbreviatio Decreti* to C.3 q.7 c.2, in BL, Cotton Claud. A.IV, fol. 138vb; Frederick II, in J. L. A. Huillard-Bréholles, ed. *Historia diplomatica Friderici secundi* (Paris 1852–1861; reprinted Turin 1963) 2.1.450.

13. Guibert of Tournai, *Sermones ad status de nouo correcti et emendati* (Ad iudices et aduocatos 1; Lyon 1511) fol. 105va, 106vb; I am grateful to Penny Cole for bringing these sermons to my attention. For similar descriptions, see Nikolaus Paulus, 'Die Wertung der weltlichen Berufe im Mittelalter', HJb 32 (1911) 725–755, and 'Zur Geschichte des "Wortes Beruf"', HJb 45 (1925) 308–16; Jacques Le Goff, 'Métier et profession d'après les manuels de confesseurs du moyen âge', *Beiträge zum Berufsbewusstsein*, ed. P. Wilpert (Miscellanea mediaevalia 3; Berlin 1964) 57; on the implications of these terms see also M.-D. Chenu, '*Officium*: Théologiens et canonistes', *Études d'histoire de droit canonique dédiées à Gabriel Le Bras* (Paris 1965) 2.835–839; Antony Black, *Guilds and Civil Society in European Political Thought from the Twelfth Century to the Present* (Ithaca, N.Y. 1984) 15, 21.

14. Bernard of Pavia, writing in the 1190s, referred to an oath that advocates had to take, but it is not clear that this was specifically an admissions oath; *Summa decretalium*, ed. Theodore Laspeyres (Graz 1956) 52; see also *Summa Elegantius in iure diuino seu Coloniensis* (4 vols. MIC Ser. A; New York-Città del Vaticano 1969–1990) 2.112–113.

15. The earliest clear enunciation of a requirement that ecclesiastical advocates swear an admissions oath appears in two Norman councils of 1231: the Council of Château-Gontier, c.36, in Mansi 23.240–241, and the Council of Rouen, c.35, in Mansi 23.218–219. In 1237 the papal legate, Cardinal Otto da Tonengo, required an admissions oath from ecclesiastical advocates in England; Legatine Council of London, c.29, Powicke and Cheney, *Councils* 1.258–259.

such an oath when they commenced to appear regularly in the courts.[16]

Litigants never lost the right to present their cases in person, and continued to exercise it, especially in the lower courts, throughout the medieval period. By the beginning of the thirteenth century, however, parties who appeared on their own behalf began to seem at a disadvantage in contentious proceedings.[17] Certainly at the papal curia, and in appellate proceedings elsewhere, advocates and proctors learned in the law and experienced in the practices and usages of the courts were well-established, and litigants commonly employed them in these courts long before 1200.

University-trained canonists appeared in the church courts in three distinct roles. Some functioned as advocates, some as legal counselors, and some as proctors. At different times, the same individual might appear in each of these capacities, and the boundaries between these functions were seldom as rigid in practice as academic theory made them out to be.

Advocates were qualified legal experts; they constituted the most highly trained, the best paid, and consequently the most esteemed branch of the profession. Bishops and archdeacons, and high-ranking administrative functionaries of the church, as well as consistory and commissary judges, often came from their ranks. The advocate was an officer of the court. His function was to advise both litigants and judges concerning the law, to furnish them with legal analysis of the issues that a case presented, and to supply the arguments that related the particular issues of an individual problem to the general provisions of the law.[18] A substantial part of an advocate's work thus consisted of what we would call legal analysis and research. The advocate had to identify the legal issues that a problem presented, find the law relevant to those issues, and show how the abstract propositions of the law applied to the specific situation at hand.

A legal counsellor, or 'iurisperitus' (who was often an advocate as well)

16. II Lyon (1274), c.9, in COD 317–322. This canon so offended the curial advocates with its suggestion that their fees should be placed under judicial control that it was omitted from the *Liber sextus*. Its provisions were soon revived, however, by subsequent reforming popes; Charles Lefebvre, 'La constitution *Properandum* et les avocats de la curie à la fin du XIIIe siècle', *1274: Anné charnière; mutations et continuités* (Paris 1977) 525–531.

17. Some courts, however, insisted on professional representation in serious matters: thus at Reims, a reform decree of March 1267, quoted in the *Privilegia curie Remensis archiepiscopi* of 1269, required the use of advocates in all matters in which the sum of 100 solidi or more was at issue; *Archives législatives de Reims*, ed. P. Varin (Paris 1839–1853) 1.13; and see below.

18. Bulgarus, *Excerpta legum*, Wahrmund, *Quellen* 4.1, pp. 2–3; William of Drogheda, *Summa aurea* § 33, Wahrmund, *Quellen* 2.2, pp. 36–37; Lefebvre, 'La constitution *Properandum*' 525–531; Winfried Trusen, 'Advocatus—Zu den Anfängen der gelehrten Anwaltschaft in Deutschland und ihren rechtlichen Grundlagen', *Um Recht und Freiheit: Festschrift für Friedrich August Freiherr von der Heydte zur Vollendung des 70. Lebensjahres*, ed. H. Kipp, F. Mayer, and A. Steinkamm (Berlin 1977) 1235–1248; W. Engelmann, *Die Wiedergeburt der Rechtskultur in Italien durch die wissenschaftliche Lehre: Eine Darlegung der Entfaltung des gemeinen italienischen Rechts und seiner Justizkultur im Mittelalter* (Leipzig 1938) 338.

might be asked to supply either the judge or an individual litigant with a formal written opinion, or *consilium*, in which he set forth his analysis and conclusions for the guidance of his client.[19] Counsellors were also employed during the course of litigation to analyze the testimony of witnesses and other evidence, to supply the legal arguments, or 'allegationes', that supported the view of the matter that their clients wished the court to adopt, and to present their clients' view of the case to the judges, both orally and in writing. Practicing advocates and counsellors were thus key players in the litigation process and in consequence could command premium fees. Their earnings, as well as their perceived capacity to influence the outcome of litigation, in turn, reinforced the social and professional prestige that their skill and learning secured for them.

It is also apparent, however, that advocates sometimes fell a good deal short of the level of training and expertise that theory said they ought to have. In England, for example, Archbishop John Pecham, at the provincial council of Lambeth in 1281, complained bitterly about poorly trained advocates who arrogate to themselves the office of pleading publicly in ecclesiastical suits when all they have studied, and that barely, is half a book of law. And because of their ignorance of the truth of the law, they indulge in horrible frauds which impede the judicial process. The council accordingly required that thenceforth advocates must have studied civil and canon law for a minimum of three years before admission to practice.[20]

Proctors were less expert in law, but often more experienced in practical courtroom technicalities, than advocates or iurisperiti. Since their skills were less theoretical and more practical, proctors commanded less esteem than advocates. Proctors were essentially litigation agents, who assisted and advised litigants in the management of their cases and often appeared in place of, as well as on behalf of, the parties whom they represented.[21] Litigants appointed proctors through a formal contract, called

19. Peter Riesenberg, 'The Consilia Literature: A Prospectus', *Manuscripta* 6 (1962) 3–22; Guido Kisch, *Consilia: Eine Bibliographie der juristischen Konsiliensammlungen* (Basel 1970); Mario Ascheri, *I consilia dei giuristi medievali: Per un repertorio-incipitario computerizzato* (Siena 1982); Engelmann, *Wiedergeburt* 243–255.

20. Council of Lambeth, c. 26 in Powicke and Cheney, *Councils* 2.917–918; *The Early Oxford Schools*, ed. J. I. Catto and Leonard Boyle (The History of the University of Oxford 1; Oxford 1984) 1.549.

21. Proctors might also be appointed as business agents to perform commercial and other transactions for their clients, but we are not here concerned with those activities of proctors. For more detail see Brundage, *Medieval Origins* 334–338, 354–360, 477–487 and passim. See also generally the seminal article by Rudolf von Heckel, 'Das Aufkommen der ständigen Prokuratoren an der päpstlichen Kurie im 13. Jahrhundert', *Miscellanea Francesco Ehrle: Scritti di storia e paleografia* (Studi e testi 37–42; Vatican City 1924) 2.290–321, as well as Peter Herde, *Beiträge zum päpstlichen Kanzlei- und Urkundenwesen im dreizehnten Jahrhundert* (2nd ed. Münchener historische Studien, Abteilung Geschichtlichen Hilfswissenschaften 1; Kallmünz 1967) 125–148; Robert Brentano, *Two Churches:*

a mandate. Because the mandate authorized the proctor to appear not merely on behalf of, but actually instead of the litigant, the notaries who kept court records habitually recorded when a mandate was submitted or when a proctor appeared. The names of proctors accordingly occur quite regularly in litigation records, as do entries concerning the actions they performed for their clients.

The lesser level of prestige that proctors enjoyed reflected their more modest learning, for their expertise was primarily pragmatic. Although they often had some academic training in law, it is uncommon to find proctors holding the doctorate, or indeed any university degree. Most proctors seem to have learned their craft through apprenticeship, and some became proctors after first having qualified as notaries.[22] It was the proctor's job to make routine appearances for his client, to see that the proper motions were entered at the required times, that necessary documents were submitted in the appropriate form, that witnesses appeared to testify when needed, and in general to attend to the bewildering mass of technical formalities that litigation entailed.[23]

Other legal functionaries complemented the activities of these practitioners. Canonical judges who held permanent (or at least long-term) appointments, such as the auditors of the Roman Rota or the officials-principal who served as judges in the consistory courts of bishops, were often drawn from the ranks of practicing advocates. Many cases, even quite important ones, however, were delegated to ad hoc judges, who might have little or no formal training in the law. Thus canonical judges never acquired a distinct professional identity, although many of them held academic degrees in canon law, and some had long experience as advocates prior to their appointment to the bench.[24]

England and Italy in the Thirteenth Century (Princeton 1968, reprinted Berkeley-Los Angeles 1988) 38–56; Peter Linehan, 'Spanish Litigants and Their Agents at the Thirteenth-Century Papal Curia', *Proceedings Salamanca 1976* 487–501; Jane E. Sayers, 'Canterbury Proctors at the Court of the "audiencia litterarum contradictarum",' *Traditio* 22 (1966) 311–345; Sayers, 'Proctors Representing British Interests at the Papal Court, 1198–1415,' *Proceedings Strasbourg 1968* (Città del Vaticano 1971) 143–163; Winfried Stelzer, 'Beiträge zur Geschichte der Kurienprokuratoren im 13. Jahrhundert', AHP 8 (1970) 113–138; Patrick N. R. Zutshi, 'Petitioners, Popes, Proctors: The Development of Curial Institutions, c. 1150–1250', *Pensiero e sperimentazioni istituzionali nella societas Christiana (1046–1250): Atti della sedicesima Settimana internazionale di studio, Mendola 26–31 agosto 2004*, ed. Giancarlo Andenna (Milan 2007) 265–293.

22. A notable example is Master Johannes de Sancto Germano, a papal notary who also served as a proctor at the curia and even occasionally as a curial auditor between 1245 and 1257; Winfried Stelzer, 'Aus der päpstlichen Kanzlei des 13. Jahrhunderts: Magister Johannes de Sancto Germano, Kurienprokurator und päpstlicher Notar', RHM 11 (1969) 210–221.

23. Inst. 4.10; Dig. 3.3.1 pr. Albericus de Rosate, *Vocabularius* s.v. *Procurator* (Paris 1525), fol. 189ra–189va; Heckel, 'Aufkommen' 2.290–321.

24. Dieter Girgensohn, 'Wie wird man Kardinal? Kuriale und außerkuriale Karrieren an der Wende des 14. zum 15. Jahrhundert', QF 57 (1977) 138–162.

Notaries were another important group of legal professionals who performed skilled tasks that were essential, but ancillary, to the work of advocates, proctors, and judges. Unlike judges, the notaries did enjoy a well-defined professional identity, but separate from that of the advocates and proctors. Despite the close relationship between the notaries' functions and those of the advocates and proctors, the notaries remained a subordinate and inferior to the more elite legal occupations. Notaries occupied a subsidiary but vital niche in this hierarchy of legal functionaries. They specialized in drafting and copying legal documents of all kinds. They drew up contracts and wills for private clients; produced official records of witnesses' testimony and court proceedings; maintained the act books of courts and judges; drafted laws, decrees, proclamations, and other public documents; kept minutes of the actions of governmental bodies and public officials; and in general were employed wherever and whenever an authentic public record of an action or agreement was required.[25] Documents produced by a notary were presumed to be genuine and reliable records of the actions that they recorded, although that presumption might be rebutted if defects in the document could be demonstrated to the satisfaction of a judge. The burden of proving defects fell upon the party who attacked the document, however, and judges were reluctant to rule a notarial document spurious unless substantial evidence of forgery or alteration could be shown.[26] The presumption of authenticity, accordingly, made notarial records highly desirable for all important transactions.

The training of notaries was a technical business. While some notaries had studied law, and a few even held law degrees,[27] most notaries qualified

25. See Brundage, *Medieval Origins* 396–404 and passim; Litewski, *Zivilprozeß* 420–426; A. Pratesi, 'Il notariato latino nel mezzogiorno medievale d'Italia', *Scuole diritto e società nel mezzogiorno medievale d'Italia*, ed. M. Bellomo (Catania 1985) 137–168. Cf. Sarah Rubin Blanshei, *Politics and Justice in Late Medieval Bologna* (Medieval Law and Its Practice; Leiden-Boston 2010) 306–309; Armin Wolf, 'Das öffentliche Notariat', Coing, *Handbuch* 1.505–514; Martin Bertram, 'I manoscritti delle opere di Rolandino conservati nelle biblioteche italiane e nella Biblioteca Vaticana', *Rolandino e l'ars notaria da Bologna all'Europa: Atti del Convegno Nazionale di Studi Storici sulla figura e l'opera di Rolandino*, ed. Giorgio Tamba (Milan 2002) 683–718.

26. *Glossa ordinaria* to C.1 q.7 c.4 s.v. *convenientibus*; *Glossa ordinaria* to X 2.19.9 s.v. *duos viros*; Tilmann Schmidt, 'Der ungetreue Notar', *Fälschungen im Mittelalter: Internationaler Kongress der Monumenta Germaniae Historica* (MGH Schriften 33; Hannover 1988) 2.691–711; Peter Herde, 'Römisches und kanonisches Recht bei der Verfolgung des Fälschungsdelikt im Mittelalter', *Traditio* 21 (1965) 291–362. *Glossa ordinaria* to C.1 q.7 c.4 s.v. *convenientibus*; *Glossa ordinaria* to X 2.19.9 s.v. *duos viros*; Tilmann Schmidt, 'Der ungetreue Notar', *Fälschungen im Mittelalter: Internationaler Kongress der Monumenta Germaniae Historica* (MGH Schriften 33; Hannover 1988) 2.691–711; Peter Herde, 'Römisches und kanonisches Recht bei der Verfolgung des Fälschungsdelikt im Mittelalter', *Traditio* 21 (1965) 291–362.

27. For example, Master Heinrich von Kirchberg, the *notarius civium* at Erfurt, was also a *doctor decretorum*; G. May, *Die geistliche Gerichtsbarkeit des Erzbischofs von Mainz* (Leipzig 1956) 267.

for their appointments through some combination of academic study of the 'ars notariae' (which dealt with the forms and contents of legal documents) and apprenticeship, either in the service of an established private practitioner, in a bishop's chancery, on the staff of the registrar of a court, or as assistant to a judge's clerk.[28] Formally qualified notaries were numerous and they, in turn, stood at the apex of a much larger mass of scribes, scriveners, and copyists, who lacked the power to authenticate documents and the qualifications to draft them. Such scribes were employed, much as modern clerks or typists are, principally to copy what was dictated or put before them by a notary or a private employer.[29]

Notaries were admitted to practice through a formal appointment, made by a properly empowered authority and attested in a notarial document. A few great public authorities, most notably the Holy Roman emperor and the pope, were universally acknowledged to have the power to create notaries. They in turn could, and routinely did, delegate to other powerful officials, such as dukes, counts-palatine, archbishops, and bishops, the right to appoint a limited number of notaries. Some other authorities and public bodies, such as the Italian podestà and communal councils, also claimed (and exercised) the right to create notaries. In some places notaries were required to pass an examination prior to admission; moreover, cities, especially in Italy, often required as a condition of practice that notaries within their jurisdiction must be accepted as members of a local notaries' guild. These guilds commonly limited their active members to a fixed number and were thus able to restrain competition for the available business. Ecclesiastical authorities sometimes placed limits on the numbers of notaries who might be authorized to practice in a particular region; at Reims a decree of March 1267 limited the number of practicing notaries there to seventy.[30]

Advocates and proctors, unlike notaries, were admitted by the judges of the courts in which they practiced. A formal admission process began to develop in several different regions during the second quarter of the thirteenth century. Admission usually required certification that the candidate had met the minimum educational standards established by the

---

28. Gianfranco Orlandelli, '"Studio" e scuola di notariato', *Atti del convegno internazionale di studi accursiani*, ed. G. Rossi (Milan 1968) 1.71–95, and his 'La scuola di notariato fra VIII e IX Centenario dello Studio bolognese', *Studio bolognese e formazione del notariato, Convegno organizzato dal Consiglio notarile di Bologna col patrocinio della Università degli Studi di Bologna (Bologna, 6 maggio 1989, Palazzo dei Notai)* (Studi storici sul notariato 9; Milan 1992) 23–59.

29. Christopher R. Cheney, *Notaries Public in England in the Thirteenth and Fourteenth Centuries* (Oxford 1972).

30. Varin, *Archives législatives* 1.12.

court—typically three to six years' study of law were demanded for advocates—and that he was of good moral character.[31] Some courts, especially in northern Italy, also required prospective advocates and proctors to pass an examination, and a few courts (mainly in Italy) required as a further condition for eligibility that candidates be members of a local guild or association of men trained in law.[32]

Records of professional associations occur earliest and most abundantly in Italy, especially in the northern Italian cities, where civic life and associations were particularly well developed by the second half of the thirteenth century. The proliferation of professional and trade associations that began in this period formed part of a larger pattern of social restructuring evident throughout Europe.[33]

These developments also reflected the more immediate and pressing concern of canon lawyers to secure control of the right to appear before the ecclesiastical courts, especially in the face of competition from men experienced in the usage and practices of civil courts. The canonists' success in gaining a monopoly on practice in the church courts apparently varied considerably from one region to another. Where that monopoly was likely to be challenged, professional associations emerged early; where competition was rare, professional associations appeared much later.

In Italy, especially in northern Italy, the supply of men trained in the Ius commune was more ample than it was elsewhere; hence professional associations emerged there early and in considerable numbers. Canonists often appeared alongside civil lawyers on the rolls of legal guilds through-

---

31. Trusen, 'Gelehrte Gerichtsbarkeit', Coing, *Handbuch* 1.477.

32. Fried, *Entstehung des Juristenstandes,* as well as his 'Vermögensbildung der bologneser Juristen im 12. und 13. Jahrhundert', *Università e società nei secoli XII–XVI* (Pistoia 1982) 27–59; Norbert Horn, 'Bologneser Doctores und Iudices im 12. Jahrhundert und die Rezeption der studierten Berufsjuristen', *Zeitschrift für historische Forschung* 3 (1976) 221–232; Ennio Cortese, 'Legisti, canonisti e feudisti: La formazione di un ceto medievale', *Università e società nei secoli XII–XVI,* 195–284, and his 'Scienza di giudici e scienza di professori tra XII e XIII secolo', *Legge, giudici, giuristi: Atti del convegno tenuto a Cagliari* (Università di Cagliari, Pubblicazioni della Facoltà di Giurisprudenza 26; Milan 1982) 93–148; Trusen, 'Advocatus'; Engelmann, *Wiedergeburt* 47–48. Fried, *Entstehung des Juristenstandes,* as well as his 'Vermögensbildung der bologneser Juristen im 12. und 13. Jahrhundert', *Università e società nei secoli XII–XVI* (Pistoia 1982) 27–59; Norbert Horn, 'Bologneser Doctores und Iudices im 12. Jahrhundert und die Rezeption der studierten Berufsjuristen', *Zeitschrift für historische Forschung* 3 (1976) 221–232; Ennio Cortese, 'Legisti, canonisti e feudisti: La formazione di un ceto medievale', *Università e società nei secoli XII–XVI,* 195–284, and his 'Scienza di giudici e scienza di professori tra XII e XIII secolo', *Legge, giudici, giuristi: Atti del convegno tenuto a Cagliari* (Università di Cagliari, Pubblicazioni della Facoltà di Giurisprudenza 26; Milan 1982) 93–148; Trusen, 'Advocatus'; Engelmann, *Wiedergeburt* 47–48.

33. Black, *Guilds and Civil Society* 6–11; Jacques Le Goff, 'Quelle conscience l'université médiévale a-t-elle d'elle-même?' *Beiträge zum Bewußtsein,* ed. Wilpert, 15–29; Weimar, 'Zur Doktorwürde' 429–435. Black, *Guilds and Civil Society* 6–11; Jacques Le Goff, 'Quelle conscience l'université médiévale a-t-elle d'elle-même?' *Beiträge zum Bewußtsein,* ed. Wilpert, 15–29; Weimar, 'Zur Doktorwürde' 429–435.

out northern Italy and many of them probably practiced simultaneously in ecclesiastical and civil tribunals. The composition of professional associations varied greatly. A few towns restricted membership in their legal guild to doctors of civil or canon law, as was the case, for example, at Modena.[34] More often, practitioners qualified as advocates and judges belonged to the same guild, which was the pattern at Bologna,[35] while elsewhere, for example at Florence, the lawyers' guild also included notaries.[36] Regardless of local variations in structure, the Italian pattern of guild organization brought together men with formal training in the two laws in order to assert and protect their joint interest in limiting appearance before both the local civil and ecclesiastical courts to guild members. Lawyers' guilds in Italian cities, however, sometimes admitted laymen trained in canon law but barred clerics from membership.[37] They seem to have sought to protect their turf against other would-be practitioners who lacked training in the Ius commune, that is, against those with expertise in local customary law.

The pattern of professional associations in France resembled in part the Italian model. In Paris, to take the best-documented example, the principal organization of legal practitioners was the Confraternity of St. Nicholas, composed of advocates (canonists as well as civilians) who practiced at the Parlement de Paris, the principal law court of the French Crown. Although organized as a religious confraternity, the association was for practical purposes virtually identical with a guild.[38] Membership became obligatory from the reign of Philip VI (1328–1350), and thenceforth only those who belonged to this confraternity could practice at the Parlement. Although the Parlement was a crown court, a substantial number of its practitioners were clerics —indeed, they constituted a majority up to the mid-fifteenth century—and many advocates, laymen as well as clerics, held degrees in canon law.[39] Unlike the Italian practice, however, canonists at the Court of the Official of the bishop of Paris also created a separate confraternity of their own, which was in existence by the reign of St.

34. Fried, *Entstehung* 212; cf. Brundage, *Medieval Origins* 365–370.

35. Ibid. 44.

36. Lauro Martines, *Lawyers and Statecraft in Renaissance Florence* (Princeton 1968) 14, 28–29, 41.

37. *Statuta civitatis Parmae*, 2.34 (Parma, 1494) fol. 75r. Whether clerical canonists in these or other Italian cities created separate organizations of their own is an interesting question to which there is no answer.

38. See Black, *Guilds and Civil Society* 4–5.

39. Charles Bataillard, *Les origines de l'histoire des procureurs et des avoués depuis le Ve siècle jusqu'au XVe (422?–1453)* (Paris 1868) 142–143, 151–152; Roland Delachenal, *Histoire des avocats au Parlement de Paris, 1300–1600* (Paris 1885) 24–36; Joseph H. Shennan, *The Parlement of Paris* (Ithaca, N.Y. 1968) 14–15, 46–48, 81–82, 110–111; Michael P. Fitzsimmons, *The Parisian Order of Barristers and the French Revolution* (Harvard Historical Monographs 74; Cambridge, Mass. 1987) 2–4.

Louis (1226–1270).[40] Although little is known of the history of this group, memberships in the two legal confraternities almost certainly overlapped.[41]

In England, by way of contrast, the leading professional organization of canonists was Doctors' Commons, an association of advocates and proctors who practiced in London at the Court of Arches, the canonical appeals court for the whole ecclesiastical province of Canterbury. Although these men had emerged as an identifiable group by the mid-thirteenth century, they did not create a corporate structure for themselves until the mid-fifteenth century.[42] The two-century gap between appearance and formal organization suggests that, unlike their counterparts in France and Italy, English ecclesiastical lawyers at St. Mary le Bow did not feel seriously threatened by competition from the common lawyers in Chancery Lane. Their confidence seems to have been justified, at least in the short run. Members of Doctors' Commons managed to maintain their organization, their identity, and much of their monopoly for nearly half a millennium, right through the Reformation and the upheavals of the Puritan Revolution, the Restoration, and the dynastic changes of the seventeenth and eighteenth centuries.[43] In the long term, however, the common lawyers ultimately did win out: Doctors' Commons dissolved itself in the years 1861 to 1862, and common lawyers absorbed what little was left by that point of the business that had occupied the old ecclesiastical courts.[44]

The relationship between competition and the organization is even more evident north of the Tweed. In thirteenth-century Scotland, canonists appeared in virtually every weighty and important civil dispute, for they were better equipped than those acquainted only with Scots customary law to deal with intricate and complex issues. Roman and canon law

40. Louis Carolus-Barré, 'L'organisation de la juridiction gracieuse à Paris dans le dernier tiers du XIIIe siècle: L'Officialité et le Châtelet', *Moyen Âge* 69 (1963) 421; Oliver Guyotjeannin, 'Juridiction gracieuse ecclésiastique et naissance de l'officialité à Beauvais (1175–1220)', *À propos des actes d'évêques: Hommage à Lucie Fossiet,* ed. Michel Parisse (Nancy 1991) 295–310.

41. It would be interesting to know more about associations of canonists and other legal professionals in some of the French provincial cities, especially in the 'pays de droit écrit', such as Toulouse, for example, where a provincial Parlement coexisted with canonical tribunals.

42. Archbishop Robert Kilwardby formulated regulations for the advocates and proctors of the Court of Arches between 1272 and 1278; 'Constitutio Roberti de Kilwardby', *Concilia Magnae Britanniae et Hiberniae,* ed. D. Wilkins (London 1737, reprinted Bruxelles 1964) 2.27; Brian Woodcock, *Medieval Ecclesiastical Courts in the Diocese of Canterbury* (Oxford Historical Series; London 1952) 7, 10–11; See M. D. Slatter, 'The Records of the Court of Arches', JEH 4 (1953) 139–153. Irene J. Churchill, *Canterbury Administration: The Administrative Machinery of the Archbishopric of Canterbury Illustrated from Original Records* (Church Historical Society Publications 15; London 1933) 1.425–426, 431–432, 441–442, 450–452; 2.206–210.

43. Richard H. Helmholz, *Roman Canon Law in Reformation England* (Cambridge 1990).

44. George D. Squibb, *Doctors' Commons: A History of the College of Advocates and Doctors of Law* (Oxford 1977) 1–22, 102–109.

consequently played a leading role in shaping the very structure of Scottish jurisprudence. The *Regiam maiestatem,* one of the fundamental sources of Scottish law, was compiled by a canonist, who larded his treatment of Scots custom with ideas and practices that he had learned from the books of such canonists as Hostiensis (ca. 1200–1271) and Geoffrey of Trani (d. 1245).[45] Since competition remained so sparse for so long, Scots canonists apparently felt no need to form an organization to protect their interests.

By the mid-sixteenth century, when civilians and canonists practicing in Scotland finally did create the College of Advocates, formal academic training in canon law was no longer available in Great Britain, as Henry VIII in 1535 had put an end to the granting of university degrees in canon law.[46] The college, accordingly, was (and for that matter continues to be) dominated by men trained in the civilian tradition, although since the Act of Union (1706), and especially during the past century, Common Law has secured a steadily increasing grip on Scottish legal practice.[47]

The history of professional associations among canonists and civilians thus reflects both the opportunities and apprehensions that practitioners faced in different regions and different periods of the Middle Ages. It also testifies to the pervasiveness and importance of canonical courts and the relative uniformity of the law that they applied. Jurists with essentially identical training practiced throughout Western Europe, from the Mediterranean shores to the Baltic coasts, from Reykjavik to Jerusalem. Training in canon law was thus a highly portable skill, and able practitioners might find profitable employment almost anywhere in Latin Christendom.

Virtually everywhere by the second half of the thirteenth century, advocates and proctors in ecclesiastical courts were required to swear an oath of admission, in which they bound themselves to observe certain minimal standards of professional ethics. These oaths, which seem to have been modeled upon the calumny oath (iuramentum de calumnia) prescribed in Roman civil procedure, required the advocate or proctor to promise that he would accept only worthy and well-founded cases, that he

45. Peter G. Stein, 'The Source of the Romano-canonical Part of Regiam Maiestatem', *Scottish Historical Review* 48 (1969) 107–123; John G. H. Hudson, 'Regiam Maiestatem', LMA 7.572–573.

46. Nan Wilson, 'The Scottish Bar: The Evolution of the Faculty of Advocates in Its Historical Setting', *Louisiana Law Review* 28 (1968) 235–295; G. Donaldson, 'The Legal Profession in Scottish Society in the Sixteenth and Seventeenth Centuries', *Lawyers in Their Social Setting,* ed. D. N. MacCormick (Edinburgh 1976) 154–155. On the royal injunctions of 1535 and the suppression of the teaching of canon law, see F. Donald Logan, 'The First Royal Visitation of the English Universities, 1535', EHR 106 (1991) 861–888. For the post-Reformation practice of canon law, see Helmholz, *Roman Canon Law.*

47. A. A. Paterson, 'The Legal Profession in Scotland: An Endangered Species or a Problem Case for Market Theory?' *Lawyers in Society,* ed. R. L. Abel and P. S. C. Lewis (Berkeley-Los Angeles 1988) 1.77–89.

would present his client's case diligently and in lawful form, that he would neither suborn perjury nor instruct his client or witnesses to give false testimony, and that, should he discover his client's case to be groundless, he would at once abandon the client and inform the court.[48] The swearing of the oath of admission was the central element of the admissions ritual and the names of those who had taken it were often enrolled in a register or other formal record of the court in which they practiced.[49]

The appearance of an admissions ritual that involved an oath to observe basic standards of ethical behavior, in conjunction with requirements for some minimum legal education, implies that by the 1230s advocates and proctors had begun to see themselves and to be seen by others as a distinct occupational group with special skills and knowledge. Evidence that they also attempted to restrict the right of audience before canonical courts to formally recognized and admitted practitioners further reinforces this perception. The legatine constitutions that Cardinal Otto da Tonengo promulgated in London in 1237 clearly enunciated all of these ideas. Cardinal Otto decreed that an advocate who had failed to take the admissions oath

will not be admitted to participate in marriage or election cases, unless he shall swear such an oath in every case; nor may an advocate who has not taken the prescribed oath participate in other cases before an ecclesiastical judge for more than three [legal] terms,[50] unless he is pleading on behalf of his own church, his lord, a close friend, a pauper, a foreigner, or a disadvantaged person.[51]

48. Council of Rouen (1231), c.45, and Council of Château-Gontier (1231), c.36, in Mansi 23:218–219, 240–241; Legatine Council of London (1237), c.29, in Powicke and Cheney, *Councils* 1.258–259; M. Tangl, ed., *Päpstlichen Kanzleiordnungen von 1200–1500* (Innsbruck 1894, reprinted Aalen 1959) 46–47. See also J. A. Brundage, 'Perceptions of Propriety: The Discipline of the Canonical Bar in Late Medieval England', *Die Reaktion der Normalen* (Frankfurt a/M. 1989) 122–154; and Brundage, 'The Calumny Oath and the Ethical Ideals of Canonical Advocates', *Proceedings Munich 1992* 793–805, reprinted in *The Profession and Practice of Medieval Canon Law* (Collected Studies 797; Aldershot 2004) IV.

49. The requirement that advocates and proctors take such an oath was adopted for ecclesiastical courts throughout Christendom by the Second Council of Lyon (1274), c.9, in COD 317–322. See Lefebvre, 'La constitution *Properandum* et les avocats de la curie' 525–531; and Stephan Kuttner, 'Conciliar Law in the Making: The Lyonese Constitutions (1274) of Gregory X in a Manuscript of Washington', *Miscellanea Pio Paschini* (Roma 1949) 2.42–43.

50. Legal 'terms' presumably referred to subdivisions of the annual court calendar, running respectively from September to Christmas, from mid-January to Easter, and from Easter to the beginning of August. A scheme roughly of this sort was practiced in some English church courts by the fourteenth century; see Hamo Hethe, Bishop of Rochester, *Registrum*, ed. C. Johnson (Canterbury and York Society, Publications 48–49; Oxford 1948) 2.911; Christopher R. Cheney, *Handbook of Dates for Students of English History* (London 1961) 73–74; Brian L. Woodcock, *Medieval Ecclesiastical Courts in the Diocese of Canterbury* (Oxford Historical Series; London 1952) 31–34; Colin Morris, 'A Consistory Court in the Middle Ages', JEH 14 (1963) 155–156. Such a calendar may even have begun to emerge as early as the first half of the thirteenth century; see Adams/Donahue, *Canterbury Cases*, 'Introduction' 17–18.

51. Legatine Council of London (1237), c.29, in Powicke and Cheney, *Councils* 1.258–259: 'Alias

This constitution and similar documents from the mid and later thirteenth century make it clear that, by this period, litigants in the church courts not only had ready access to trained and experienced advocates and proctors, but also that parties regularly sought expert assistance and advice in litigation.[52]

Even before the appearance of admissions oaths and the other appurtenances of an organized ecclesiastical bar, litigants who lacked access to expert legal advice or to assistance in pursuing their claims were commonly deemed to be at a disadvantage. Thus, for example, Master Thomas of Marlborough recounted with evident relish how his opponent in Evesham's lawsuit against the bishop of Worcester complained that Thomas had engaged all the best advocates in Rome for his side, and how Pope Innocent III (1198–1216) had grinned as he brushed aside that complaint, saying, 'There's never any shortage of advocates at the Roman curia'.[53]

While access to counsel posed little problem for the well-to-do, impoverished litigants found it difficult to secure adequate representation and advice and thus were unable to pursue their just claims or to defend themselves against affluent adversaries, who might in fact engage the services of every advocate locally available, leaving their opponents bereft of skilled legal advice.[54] Consequently Pope Honorius III (1216–1227) authorized judges in ecclesiastical courts to appoint advocates to assist

---

autem non admittatur in causis matrimonialibus et electionibus nisi iuramentum simile velit prestare singulariter in eisdem, sed nec in aliis causis coram ecclesiastico iudice ultra tres terminos absque iuramento huiusmodi admittatur, nisi pro ecclesia sua vel domino vel amico notorio seu paupere vel extraneo vel persona miserabili duxerit forsitan postulandum'. The exceptions listed in the final clause here correspond to the canonical list of exceptional situations in which (contrary to general rule) a cleric might properly appear on behalf of a client in courts of secular jurisdiction; D.86 c.6; C.21 q.3 c.1; X 1.37.1 (3 Lateran Council, c.12); X 3.50.1; J. A. Brundage, 'The Monk as Lawyer', *The Jurist* 39 (1979) 423–436; L. Charvet, 'Accession des clercs aux fonctions d'avocat', *Bulletin de littérature ecclésiastique* 67 (1966) 287–298. Also Gérard D. Guyon, 'L'avocat dans le procédure des anciennes coutumes médievales bordelaises', RHD 86 (2008) 21–38; and André Gouron, 'Le rôle de l'avocat selon la doctrine romaniste du douzieme siècle', *L'Assistance dans la résolution des conflits* (Recueils de la Société Jean Bodin pour l'Histoire Comparative des Institutions 65; Brussels 1998) 7–19, reprinted in *Conflicts Pionniers du droit occidental au Moyen Âge* (Collected Studies 865; Aldershot 2006) XV.

52. Thus Azo († 1220), *Summa super Codicem* (Torino 1578; reprinted Torino 1966) to Cod. 2.6 fol. 28, observed that the wealthy had no difficulty in securing legal assistance—they and their money, he declared, could readily find all the advocates they needed. Cf. Goffredus de Trano, *Summa super titulos* to X.1.37 *De postulando* § 1 (Lyon 1519, reprinted Aalen 1968) 126; Hostiensis († 1270), *Summa aurea*, lib.1, *De postulando* § 2 (Lyon 1537, reprinted Aalen 1562) fol. 62ra–62rb.

53. *Chronicon abbatiae de Evesham*, s.a. 1205, 153. *Chronicon abbatiae de Evesham*, s.a. 1205, 153.

54. Raymond of Penyafort, *Summa de penitentia* 2.5.39, ed. Xavier Ochoa and A. Diez, Universa bibliotheca iuris 1.B (Roma 1976) col. 518. Gerald of Wales alleges, for example, that in his litigation over the see of St. David's, his opponent hired all the experienced advocates in Oxford, leaving him with only one timid beginner, newly arrived from overseas and of untested mettle; *De jure et statu Menevensis ecclesiae* in Gerald of Wales, *Opera*, ed. Brewer et al., 3.228.

those who otherwise would be unable to secure them.[55] Honorius's decretal formalized and made mandatory what evidently had been for some time a common practice.[56] Honorius failed to make clear, however, how court-appointed counsel should be paid. He may well have assumed, as later commentators sometimes did, that advocates appointed in this way would charge no fee for their services, or, in other words that the lawyers would, in effect, finance legal aid by contributing their services without charge when called upon to do so.[57] That assumption was, for obvious reasons, less than popular with canonical advocates and proctors, who felt that use of their skill and effort entitled them to collect fees, even when helping poor clients, and that in such cases the court itself should bear the costs of the services that it ordered them to provide.[58] Theologians and moral writers were not notably sympathetic to the lawyers' claims, although they conceded that it would be burdensome if advocates were obliged to give free advice to every poor person who might need it. Moralists were prepared to allow lawyers to limit the number of cases that they accepted without remuneration.[59]

These references to fees make it clear that substantial numbers of trained legal advisers were available by the late twelfth century, but only for a price: they expected to be rewarded for their services. Contemporary observers, to be sure, showed some ambivalence about the morality of lawyers' fees. An ancient Roman aristocratic tradition had maintained that advocates ought to make their services available without charge, as a civic obligation.[60] Medieval canonists did not subscribe to this patrician tradi-

---

55. X 1.32.1. This policy had ancient precedents, both in Roman law and in the early church, as medieval commentators were well aware. For Roman law and medieval civilian commentary see e.g. Cod.2.6.7; Dig.3.1.1.4; Accursius, *Glossa ordinaria* to Dig. 9.27.5(4) s.v. *synopsin*. In canon law, see Council of Chalcedon (451), c.3, in Gratian, D.86 c.26, as well as D.87 c.8 (4 Toledo, 633) and D.88 c.1 (Pseudo-Melchiades). See further J. A. Brundage, 'Legal Aid for the Poor and the Professionalization of Law in the Middle Ages', *Journal of Legal History* 9 (1988) 169–179; and Brundage, *Medieval Origins* 188–191; and Franck Roumy, 'Le développement du système de l'avocat commis d'office dans la procédure romano-canonique (XIIe–XIVe)', TRG 71 (2003) 359–386.

56. Bernard of Pavia, *Summa decretalium* 1.28.4, p. 23.

57. Ibid. 1.28.3, p. 23; Raymond of Penyafort, *Summa de penitentia* 2.5.39, p. 518.

58. Brian Tierney, *Medieval Poor Law: A Sketch of Canonical Theory and Its Application in England* (Berkeley and Los Angeles 1959) 14.

59. Thomas Aquinas, *Summa theologiae* II-II, q.71, a.4, ad 1; on fees for advocates see Brundage, *Medieval Origins* 192–203.

60. The *Lex Cincia* (204 B.C.E.) had explicitly forbidden advocates in Republican Rome to accept fees or gifts from clients. It is not clear whether the terms of this plebiscite were ever widely observed, although the classical jurist, Paul, took it seriously enough to write a commentary on it, a fragment of which survives in Dig.1.3.19. Pliny the Younger mentions one case in which the *Lex Cincia* was invoked as a secondary issue, and Tacitus reports a call for its enforcement; Pliny, *Epistolae* 5.14; Tacitus, *Annales* 11.5–6. Certainly the Cincian Law was often circumvented, and legislators finally adjusted legislation to reality by the *Senatusconsultum Claudianum* of 47 C.E., which established a maximum fee (10,000 sesterces) that an advocate might take for his services;

tion of gratuitous service, however, and they further rejected the charge, sometimes leveled by theologians and other critics, that an advocate who accepted fees was selling justice, which ought to be freely available to all. In reply to their critics, canonists cited the distinction, hallowed by St. Augustine's authority, between legal representation or advice, on the one hand, and justice on the other. Advocates, the canonists contended, were not paid to deliver justice, but rather for their skilled assistance in avoiding or resolving conflicts.[61] Canonists likewise rejected the notion that they were in the business of marketing knowledge, which was a gift of the Holy Spirit. Rather, they maintained, they simply made their time, skill, and labor available to clients, and for this they were entitled to a reward.[62]

Although they conceded that the access to legal counsel should not depend solely upon ability to pay, jurists nonetheless insisted that they were entitled to compensation for their services.[63] Advocates, they pointed out, were not so constituted that they could live on air alone, nor would good reputation and civic-mindedness fill an empty belly. Or, as Pope Innocent III put it, no one should be expected to fight for another at his own expense.[64]

Legal fees were in principle supposed to vary according to the nature of the case, the circumstances of the client, and the custom of the courts involved.[65] In reality the client's affluence seems to have been the primary factor in determining fee levels—rich clients paid more than poor ones for essentially similar services.[66] Monasteries, prelates, and powerful individu-

---

Tacitus, *Annales* 11.7. By the time of Ulpian, the maximum fee for an advocate had been set at 100 *aurei*; Dig. 50.13.1.12. See generally Károly Visky, 'Retribuzioni per il lavoro giuridico nelle fonti del diritto romano', *Iura* 15 (1964) 1–31; and J. A. Brundage, 'The Profits of the Law: Legal Fees of University-Trained Advocates', AJLH 32 (1988) 1–15.

61. Gratian, C.11 q.3 c.71 and C.14 q.5 c.15, as well as Johannes Teutonicus, *Glossa ordinaria* s.v. *patrocinium*; similarly, gloss to Extrav. comm. 5.10.1 s.v. *sub generalia*.

62. On this argument, see especially Gaines Post, K. Giocarinis, and Richard Kay, 'The Medieval Heritage of a Humanistic Ideal: "Scientia donum dei est, unde vendi non potest",' *Traditio* 11 (1955) 195–234 at 200–201, 208–209.

63. Dig. 50.13.4, as well as Dig. 1.16.6.3, cited by Johannes Teutonicus in *Glossa ordinaria* to C.11 q.3 c.71, s.v. *iustum* and to C.1 q.3 c.11, s.v. *retributionis*; likewise *The Summa Parisiensis on the Decretum Gratiani*, ed. Terence P. McLaughlin (Toronto 1952) to C.14 q.5 c.15, p. 171.

64. X 2.26.16, paraphrasing 1 Cor 9:13–14; cf. Tacitus, *Annales* 11.7.

65. Dig. 50.13.1.10; Johannes Teutonicus, *Glossa ordinaria* to C.11 q.3 c.71, v. *iustum*; Azo, *Summa* to Cod.2.6; Accursius, *Glossa ordinaria* to Cod.2.6.3, s.v. *certum modum*; Raymond of Peñafort, *Summa de pen.* 2.5.39, p. 517; Goffredus de Trano, *Summa* to X.1.37 § 8 at 128. Some Italian cities set sliding scales of maximum fees that advocates and proctors could charge; e.g. *Lucensis civitatis statuta nuperrime castigata* 5.51 (Lucca 1539) fol. 296v–298r; *Reformationes et decreta civitatis Vrbiueteris super mercedibus officialium* 2.7 (Rome 1581) 101–102; *Statuta et decreta civitatis Placentiae* 4.71 (Brescia 1495; unfoliated). Separate fee schedules for *consilia* are also common; e.g. *Statuti di Bologna dell'anno 1288*, ed. G. Fasoli and P. Sella (Studi e testi 73; Vatican City 1937–1939) 2.16–18; Lucca, *Statuta* 5.52 (1539 ed.), fol. 298r–298v; Piacenza, *Statuta* 4.74 (1495 ed., unfoliated).

66. Accursius, *Glossa ordinaria* to Cod.2.6.6, s.v. *habeat*; Tangl, *Päpstlichen Kanzleiordnungen* 123;

als often paid advocates and proctors periodic retainers in order to assure that their services would be available when required.[67]

The obligation to pay the advocate or proctor fell upon the party whom he advised or represented.[68] If several advocates participated in a matter, they normally received a global fee, which they then divided among themselves, rather than making the client pay a full individual fee to each legal adviser.[69] Canon law from the late twelfth century as a rule required the losing party in litigation to pay the victor's legal costs as well as his own, a policy that continues to the present day in many jurisdictions, where it is justified on the grounds that it deters frivolous litigation.[70]

The fees of clerics who functioned as advocates or proctors raised special policy issues. Although the canons taught that clerics in general, and beneficed clergymen in particular, should in principle furnish legal assistance without charge to anyone who needed it, clerical lawyers normally expected to be paid, just as laymen did. Gratian noted that the church tolerated this custom, even though it violated the canons.[71]

How much income medieval canonists typically realized from professional practice is not easy to determine. A few advocates undoubtedly made substantial fortunes from the law. Successful practitioners sometimes became landowners on a large scale, and a few were able to move into the ranks of the landed nobility.[72] Even modestly successful local advocates were able to command daily fees in a range roughly between eight and twelve times the daily wages of skilled craftsmen, such as carpenters or masons. Proctors' fees were usually smaller than those of advocates, but they were still by no means insubstantial.[73]

The unit of account for advocates and proctors was the case, and their fees (at least in principle) varied with the amount of time and the level

---

Bernard Guenée, *Tribunaux et gens de justice dans le bailliage de Senlis à la fin du moyen âge (vers 1380–vers 1550)* (Publications de la Faculté des Lettres de l'Université de Strasbourg 144; Strasbourg 1963) 199.

67. Bernard of Parma, *Glossa ordinaria* to X 1.391 s.v. *generaliter*; William of Drogheda, *Summa aurea* §§ 148–149, Wahrmund, *Quellen* 2.2, pp. 177–778.

68. *Glos. ord.* to C.3 q.7 c.2 s.v. *ut par*.

69. Johannes Teutonicus, *Glossa ordinaria* to C.3 q.7 c.2 s.v. *ut par*.

70. X 5.37.4; *Decisiones Rotae Romanae* (Mainz 1477), no.534. This had been the rule in Roman law at least since the time of Justinian—see Cod. 3.1.13.6, as well as Bartolus of Sassoferrato, *Commentaria* to Cod. 2.7.10, in his *Opera omnia* (Venezia, 1575–1585) vol. 7, fol. 63r.

71. Gratian, C.15 q.2 d.p.c. un.; *Summa Parisiensis* to C.14 q.5 s.v. *sed non qui contra*, p. 172; Hostiensis, *Summa aurea*, X 1.37 tit. *De postulando* § 6 (1537 ed.), fol. 62vb.

72. Guenée, *Tribunaux et gens de justice* 366; Martines, *Lawyers and Statecraft* 366.

73. Richard H. Helmholz, 'Ethical Standards for Advocates and Proctors in Theory and Practice', *Proceedings Toronto 1972* 28, reprinted in *Canon Law and the Law of England* (London 1987) 46. See also E. F. Jacob, 'To and From the Court of Rome in the Early Fifteenth Century', *Essays in Later Medieval History* (Manchester 1968) 69–70.

of skill that a particular matter demanded. The notaries' unit of account, on the other hand, was the individual document, and their fees were accordingly based on its length and type.[74] From the client's point of view, therefore, the costs of litigation included not only the fees of the advocate and proctor involved, but also the notarial charges for all the documents required, in addition to the party's own travel expenses to attend hearings, as well as the travel and lodging costs of witnesses, and a multitude of other expenses, such as the fees of the apparitors who served summonses, the court registrar's fees for enrolling judgments in the court records, and miscellaneous customary gifts and presents to the judges and their clerks. Litigation, then as now, was an expensive enterprise that must have stretched the resources of many people and exceeded the means of a great many others.[75] Even relatively prosperous institutions, such as the monastery of Evesham or the cathedral chapter of Wells, for example, found that litigation costs ate heavily into their resources. Despite the monastery of Evesham's sacrifices, which included sequestering the funds normally used to buy wine and repair the fabric of the church, scrimping on the monks' diet, and restricting charitable expenditures, Evesham's proctor, Thomas of Marlborough, eventually had to slip away from Rome secretly at night in order to evade creditors whose bills he was unable to meet.[76]

The relationship between client and legal adviser was delicate and complicated by potentially conflicting interests. Authors of manuals of profes-

---

74. Thus e.g. Bologna, *Statuti* 6.48, ed. Fasoli and Sella, 2.38–41; *Statuta magnificae communitatis Regii* 8.5 (Reggio Emilia 1582), fol. 317v–321v; Richard Trexler, *Synodal Law in Florence and Fiesole, 1306–1518* (Studi e testi 268; Vatican City 1972) 345.

75. Detailed expense accounts for one well-known case, *Anstey c. Francheville* (1159–1162), which cost the plaintiff a total of about £143, were first printed by F. Palgrave, *The Rise and Progress of the English Commonwealth* (London 1831–1832) 2.v–xxvii, lxxv–lxxxvii; but see now the full texts and translation in *English Lawsuits from William I to Richard I*, ed. Raoul C. Van Caenegem (Selden Society Publications 106–107; London 1990–1991) 2.387–404; a partial English translation also appears in *English Historical Documents*, ed. D. C. Douglas and G. W. Greenaway (2nd ed. London-New York 1981) 2.488–90. See also on this case, Cheney, *From Becket to Langton* 54–56, 67; Barnes, 'The Anstey Case'; Paul A. Brand, 'New Light on the Anstey Case', *Essex Archaeology and History* 15 (1983) 68–83. For litigation expenses in some less notorious cases, see Gero Dolezalek, *Das Imbreviaturbuch des erzbischöflichen Gerichtsnotars Hubaldus aus Pisa, Mai bis August 1230* (Forschungen zur neueren Privatrechtsgeschichte 13; Cologne 1969) 41–43; E. F. Jacob, 'To and From the Court of Rome' 66–67; and Richard H. Helmholz, *Marriage Litigation in Medieval England* (Cambridge Studies in English Legal History; Cambridge 1974) 161.

76. *Chronicon abbatiae de Evesham* 121–122, 200. On the litigation costs over a disputed election at Wells, see Jane E. Sayers, *Papal Judges Delegate in the Province of Canterbury, 1198–1254: A Study in Ecclesiastical Jurisdiction and Administration* (Oxford Historical Monographs; Oxford 1971) 267. Another costly lawsuit was the bitter struggle between the monks of Canterbury and their archbishop, on which see Christopher R. Cheney, *Hubert Walter* (London 1967) 134–157. For the costs of more ordinary kinds of cases see Dorothy M. Owen, 'Ecclesiastical Jurisdiction in England, 1300–1550: The Records and Their Interpretation', *Studies in Church History* 11 (1975) 199–221; as well as Helmholz, *Marriage Litigation* 161; and Dolezalek, *Imbreviaturbuch* 41–43.

sional advice for practitioners, such as Bagarottus († 1246), Johannes de Deo (1189/91–1267), and Bonaguida d'Arezzo (fl. 1249–1263),[77] cautioned advocates that prospective clients might try to induce them to take on unworthy causes or, even worse, hopeless ones. The practitioner had to be careful to accept only clients who were trustworthy and who would give him written instructions, so that there would be no misunderstanding. The advocate should never take the client's word about his proofs, but should examine them critically and test them as thoroughly as he could.[78] Toward fellow-practitioners, especially those representing his client's adversary, the practitioner ought to adopt a respectful attitude; above all, he should refrain from insulting his opponent, although it was perfectly acceptable to needle him and to attempt to make him lose his temper.[79] Toward the judge, the practitioner was advised to adopt a deferential, even fawning, attitude. Durandus suggested the sort of tone that judges liked to hear from advocates in a sample speech of the sort calculated to put a judge into a benevolent frame of mind:

Oh, Lord our God, how admirable is your wisdom! How brightly glows your eloquence, in which your servant delights! I rejoice in your words like one who has found a great treasure. Your speech is sweeter in my throat than honey in my mouth. Your word is a lamp for my feet and a light for my path. Your justice is like unto the mountains of God and unto the great abyss.[80]

But no matter how well-disposed the judge might become, the astute advocate also made sure that his opponent never remained alone with him.[81]

Throughout his handling of a case, the practitioner was cautioned to be economical with his words: not only did over-much verbiage drag out proceedings, but the lawyer who introduced extraneous issues might be called upon by his adversary to prove his statements, which could be embarrassing to the advocate and costly to his client.[82]

Writers on professional conduct repeatedly admonished practitioners to deal honestly with their clients and warned against allowing themselves to be drawn into situations where conflicts of interest might arise. Notions of professional ethics, naturally enough, forbade advocates and

---

77. Emanuele Conte, 'Bagarotto (Bagarottus de Coradis)', DGI 1.142–143, António de Sousa Costa, *Doutrina penitencial do canonista João de Deus* (Braga 1956), and his *Um mestre português em Bolonha no século XIII, João de Deus: Vida e obras* (Braga 1957); Martino Semeraro, 'Bonaguida d'Arezzo', DGI 1.282.

78. Bonaguida, *Summa* 1.3, pp. ed. Wunderlich, 154–155, 157, 159.

79. Ibid. 156; Durandus, *Speculum* 1.4, De advocato §4 (Frankfurt 1592) 258–259.

80. Durandus, *Speculum* 1.4, De advocato §5, 259–260. For another specimen of this sort of ritual flattery, see William of Drogheda, *Summa aurea* § 37, pp. 39–40.

81. Ibid. §8.5, 269.

82. Bonaguida, *Summa introductoria* 1.3, pp. 160–161.

proctors to betray private information that clients had confided to them. Accordingly the advocate who advised one party in litigation must not subsequently be engaged by the other in the same matter. The situation became especially tricky if, for example, the advocate who supported the plaintiff in a court of first instance was then approached to handle his opponent's case on appeal, and writers on professional ethics differed about how to handle such a predicament.[83] Likewise the lawyer who became a judge was supposed to recuse himself from hearing cases in which he had previously been an advocate.[84] Above all, the practitioner must not become a party to a case by entering into an agreement whereby he shared in the proceeds of the judgment or settlement that his client received should the action succeed (in other words, what would now be called a contingent fee arrangement). Such agreements were generally regarded as both immoral and illegal, although a few writers indicated that they might be permitted so long as the lawyer's share did not exceed one-half of the amount at issue.[85] Advocates and proctors were discouraged from taking advantage of their clients in other ways as well. Thus, for example, writers on professional conduct admonished advocates not to press for their fees while litigation was in progress, on the theory that the client's apprehensions about the outcome of the matter might induce him to promise more than was appropriate.[86]

The timing of fee payments was a delicate matter. Gratia of Arezzo, a thirteenth-century canonist, advised practitioners that, although they should not demand payment before arguments in a case had been concluded, they should make certain to get their money before judgment had been pronounced. During the interval between closing argument and judgment, Gratia observed, litigants tend to be optimistic and sure that they will win; hence they will pay more cheerfully at this point than at any other.[87]

Enforcement of the standards of professional responsibility lay in the hands of public authorities and injured clients. The client had the right to bring an action for damages against an advocate or proctor who failed to

---

83. Cf. the position adopted by Durandus in *Speculum* 1.3, *De advocato* § 3.10–13, with the comments of Johannes Andreae in his *Additiones* to Durandus's text (p. 257).

84. This was the rule set forth in Cod. 2.6.6 pr.; but see the dispute between Martinus and Bulgarus, cited by Guido Rossi, *Consilium sapientis iudiciale: Studi e ricerche per la storia del processo romano-canonico* (Università di Bologna, Seminario giuridico, Pubblicazione 18; Milan 1958) 86–87. Cf. Brundage, *Medieval Origins* 325–338.

85. Azo, *Summa* to Cod.2.6; Accursius, *Glossa ordinaria* to Cod.2.6.5, s.v. *immensa*; *Glossa ordinaria* to Dig.2.14.53 s.v. *datum*; Gratian, C.3 q.7 c.7, paraphrasing Cod.2.6.5.

86. Accursius, *Glossa ordinaria* to Cod.2.6.6 s.v. *contractum ineat*.

87. Gratia Aretinus, *Summa de iudiciario ordine* 2.9, ed. F.C. Bergmann, *Pillius, Tancredus, Gratia libri de iudiciorum ordine* (Göttingen 1842, reprinted Aalen 1965) 378–379.

conduct his case properly. Alternatively, a judge could initiate charges about violations of the standards of professional propriety that he had observed. Such charges, if proved, carried sanctions such as fines, restitution, temporary suspension from practice, or in extreme cases permanent disbarment.

Occasional examples of disciplinary proceedings appear in the records of church courts, but they are rare and widely scattered. Virtually every such action that I have encountered seems to have originated with a dissatisfied client, rather than with judges or fellow-lawyers. This fact might mean that medieval advocates, proctors, and notaries were so exemplary and law-abiding that deviations from the rules of conduct were in fact exceedingly uncommon. A second possible interpretation of the evidence might be that judges and other members of the canonical bar preferred to employ informal disciplinary mechanisms that never found their way into the record, so that they could sanction delinquents without creating public scandal. Or, alternatively, one might infer that canonical disciplinary mechanisms were inefficient and that many delinquents either escaped detection or went unpunished.

Each explanation, no doubt, applied in some places and at some times. Still, the available evidence, such as it is, about the character and reputation of advocates and proctors in medieval society might well be thought to make the third explanation seem most often the most probable. Records of the ecclesiastical bar at the local level, such as, for example, those of the visitation of the Exeter Consistory Court in 1322–1323, paint a picture of a body of judges who were not over-vigilant and lawyers not greatly distinguished for scrupulous adherence to the prescribed standards of conduct. Similarly the career of Hugh Candlesby, proctor of the consistory court and registrar of the archdeacon's court in the diocese of Ely a generation later, lends further credibility to the caricatures of poets and the complaints of critics who described lawyers in the church courts in generally unflattering terms. Complaints by such authorities as church councils and papal legates about the failure of advocates and proctors to adhere to prescribed standards of conduct further reinforce the impression that compliance with ethical prescriptions was often at a low level.[88]

Men trained in canon law—and increasingly after 1300, men who held degrees in civil law—stood near the center of civic affairs, not only in Ita-

---

88. See W. Stapeldon, *Register of Walter de Stapeldon, Bishop of Exeter (A.D. 1307–1326)*, ed. F. C. Hingeston-Randolph (London 1892) 115–119; and Tangl, *Päpstlichen Kanzleiordnungen* 364–365; Legatine Councils of London (1237), c.29 and (1268), c.26, in Powicke and Cheney, *Councils* 1.258 and 2.773. For a more benevolent view of the evidence, see Helmholz, 'Ethical Standards', *Canon Law and the Law of England* 43–57; or *Proceedings Toronto 1972* 185–199. In general see Brundage, *Medieval Origins* 28–33, 181–191, 295–305, 317–318, 476–487.

ly and the French Midi, where the Romano-canonical legal tradition was especially pervasive, but also in northern France, Spain, Germany, England, and other regions of northern and central Europe, where customary practices held sway. The emergence of the continental Ius commune, grounded in concepts, categories, and practices that were fully intelligible only to those with a grasp of the Romano-canonical tradition, guaranteed that men trained in that tradition could find gainful employment almost everywhere. Even in England, whose Common Law remained aloof from the legal practices of the Continent, canonists and civilians found opportunities to exercise their professional skills not only in the courts of the church, but also in the service of monarchs who were deeply (if often disastrously) involved in continental affairs.[89]

The demand for informed legal advice was already great by 1250 and in most places continued to grow through the next two centuries. The supply of students, teachers, and practitioners responded by expanding as well. Needless to say, supply and demand fluctuated from one region to another and from one decade to the next. In a world of imperfect markets, the two were invariably out of phase with one another at times, resulting in cyclic shortages of trained lawyers, each soon followed by a surplus a few decades later. Nevertheless the secular trend was clearly one of expansion in the market for legal services, and a corresponding growth in the ranks of legal professionals persisted through the later Middle Ages and well into the early modern period.

Canon law thus had certainly become a profession in the rigor of the term by about 1250 and arguably was already approaching professional status as early as 1200. Its teachers and practitioners were recognized as a distinctive social group, characterized by their familiarity with a substantial body of important but esoteric knowledge and skills not available to everyone, bound together by a common intellectual formation in the schools of law, commanding social prestige and institutional authority by virtue of their ability to manipulate the levers of power. Often honored, but harshly criticized as well, the canonists increasingly filled the upper ranks of church administration and government, as indeed they have continued to dominate the institutional structure of Roman Catholicism into modern times. Theirs was almost certainly the earliest profession to take shape in medieval Europe, and the pattern that they set provided a model that other aspiring professions have ever since flattered by imitation.

---

89. Ralph V. Turner, 'Clerical Judges in English Secular Courts: The Ideal versus the Reality', *Medievalia et humanistica* 3 (1972) 75–98.

4

Procedure in the Courts of the Ius commune

Charles Donahue Jr.

There are two general chapters in this book on procedure and an introduction that also deals generally with the topic. Perhaps the easiest explanation for this proliferation is that the topic is too important to be left to one treatment. Pennington's 'Introduction' is an overview of the three main ways in which courts dealt with criminal defendants: accusatorial, inquisitorial, and summary procedure. Pennington's essay on the 'Jurisprudence of Procedure' is written from the point of view of writers about procedure, treating those writers as creating coherent body of literature. It focuses quite heavily on criminal procedure. The present essay deals with writing about procedure in order to introduce the procedure actually followed by the courts, particularly the ecclesiastical courts. It is principally concerned with what modern lawyers call 'civil procedure', procedure in cases between parties in which the plaintiff seeks a remedy for him- or herself. It says relatively little about criminal procedure. It focuses on the law of proof, particularly that about witness testimony, both as an example of the way in which Romano-canonical procedure developed and because this is probably the most important of its innovations. All three treatments assume that the reader has a basic familiarity with the stages of Romano-canonical procedure as they existed in the later Middle Ages.[1]

Why is procedure important? According to Oliver Wendell Holmes Jr.: '[F]or legal purposes a right is only the hypostasis of a prophecy—the imagination of a substance supporting the fact that the public force will be brought to bear upon those who do things said to contravene it'.[2] Although Holmes can be regarded as a legal realist only in an extended sense, his predictive theory of the law became an article of faith among the American legal realists.[3] It is also an article of faith among American legal academics today, including those who are far from the tradition of legal realism, notably the members of the 'law-and-economics school.'

Some would protest a bit. Law probably does affect behavior outside of the mechanisms of its enforcement. People may obey what they think is the law simply because it is the law, whether it can or will be enforced. Many societies have mechanisms of enforcement of the law, various forms of social pressure and/or various types of policing that will lead those not otherwise inclined to obey the law to obey it, even when no courts are involved. For a long time, however, in western societies the ultimate mechanism of enforcement of the law has been the courts. Hence, it seems reasonable to adopt the predictive theory of the law, even if we adopt it in a somewhat weaker form than that implied by Holmes's aphorism.

If we accept the predictive theory of law, even in its weaker forms, we cannot separate substantive law from procedure. The most obvious illustration of this proposition is in the area of remedy. It is not just that public force will be brought to bear; it is what public force will do that defines the right. In most instances in the West today, if you do not perform your lawful contract with me, you will be compelled, by an elaborate procedure that goes under the heading 'execution of judgments', to pay me the money. The amout will be what I can show that I have lost as a result of your failure to perform. A contractual right, then, is not a right to have the contract performed, it is a right either to have the contract performed or to obtain money damages, frequently qualified by what in Anglo-American law is often called 'the duty to mitigate', and the choice between the two rests with the obligor. If, by contrast, you take possession of land that I

1. For the reader who is unfamiliar with these stages Donahue, 'The Ecclesiastical Courts: An Introduction' 276–282, offers a brief introduction. Pennington's 'Introduction' at the beginning of the book also provides some examples drawn from thirteenth-century cases.

2. Oliver Wendell Holmes Jr., 'Natural Law', *Harvard Law Review* 32 (1918) 42. The following paragraphs are derived from Charles Donahue, '"The Hypostasis of Prophecy": Legal Realism and Legal History', *Law and Legal Process: Substantive Law and Procedure in English Legal History*, ed. Matthew Dyson and David Ibbetson (Cambridge 2013) 1–16.

3. For legal realism generally, see William W. Fisher, Morton J. Horwitz, and Thomas Reed, eds., *American Legal Realism* (New York 1993).

am entitled immediately to possess, public force will frequently be brought to bear to put you off the land and put me back on it. Hence, my right to immediate possession of my land allows me, in most circumstances, to employ the procedure of execution, to have an officer of the state remove someone who does not have my permission to be on the land.

The two rights are really quite different, and, at least from the point of view of the predictive theory of law, the difference does not principally lie in the fact that the contractual right is sometimes called a personal right and the property right a real one. Both rights, as I have described them, only arise when I am prepared to take someone to court, and at this stage of the proceedings both rights are eminently personal. What differentiates the two rights is that one is a right to money damages calculated in a particular way, and the other is a right to have an officer of the state do something physically to someone who is on the land. We can argue about how important this difference is. It probably is quite important. We can certainly argue about whether this difference should exist. There are those who have argued that it should not.[4] The point, however, is that until one sees the difference, one cannot even ask the normative question.

If one adopts the predictive theory of law, it is not only the remedy that must be incorporated into the statement of substantive rights and duties, it is the entire procedural system. Even if we confine ourselves, as Holmes did, to law enforced by courts, we need to know how cases are brought into those courts. What are the rules in the various courts about personal and subject-matter jurisdiction? What are the rules about pleading and proof? What types of evidence may be produced before the court? What are the mechanisms of review, if any? And, of course, what are the procedures for execution of judgments? In short, rather than imagining that the law consists of abstract rights and duties that apply to the world outside the institutions of the legal system, we should imagine that the abstract rights and duties only apply once the legal system has come to the conclusion on the basis of what it has determined by employing its procedures that public force will be brought to bear. That process, of course, may or may not accurately reflect what happened in the world outside of the system.

But if we go this far, why should we confine ourselves just to the institutions as they are conceived and the rules of procedure as they are stated? If I am going to make a prediction that public force will be brought to bear, should I not also consider factors that are not explicitly recognized

---

4. Guido Calabresi and A. Douglas Malamed, 'Property Rules and Liability Rules: One View of the Cathedral', *Harvard Law Review* 85 (1972) 1089–1128.

by the system but that likely, are going to affect the result? Rather than raising here the thorny issue of the role that politics, broadly conceived, plays in the operations of the legal system, let me mention one such factor that we can probably all agree plays a role in the actual results: cost. If the way that costs are structured in the system is such that only some members of the society can afford to use the system, then our definition of a right must be qualified. It is a prediction that public force will be brought to bear only on behalf of someone who can afford it if that person can demonstrate in accordance with the procedural system that something has been done to contravene the right. That statement of the aphorism is, of course, far less elegant than Holmes's, but it is more realistic in both the technical and the non-technical senses of the word 'realistic'.

Whether we accept the predictive theory of law as a philosophical matter or not, there can be little doubt that in any professionalized system of law, prediction is a large part of what lawyers do. If a client comes to me and asks what the law is and how it applies to his or her situation, I immediately begin to ask myself what will happen if this situation is presented to a court. Is there a procedure that allows it to be presented to a court? Does the client have the type of evidence that the court will allow? If the case is presented to a court, what is the likely result, not only in terms of win or loss but also in terms of remedy? And will it be worth the cost? Of course, most disputes in most societies are not presented to courts. The society would grind to a halt if they were. But those disputes that are presented to lawyers, and perhaps even those that are not, are settled on the basis of predictions of what would happen if they were to go to court.[5]

Granted how important procedure is for any predictive theory of law and granted how much prediction is a part of every lawyer's equipment, how is it that procedure is sometimes forgotten? How is it that legal discourse, particularly in the academy, frequently focuses on substantive rights and duties and ignores procedure? Ignoring procedure in favor of substantive rights and duties happens less often in the American legal academy than it does in England, and less often in England than it does on the Continent of Europe, but the substance/procedure distinction exists in all three places. How did this distinction come about?

I recently sought to answer that question elsewhere.[6] In the context of this essay, that would take us too far afield, for it depends, not exclusively, but substantially, on developments that postdate the Middle Ages. For

---

5. See Robert Mnookin and Lewis Kornhauser, 'Bargaining in the Shadow of the Law', *Yale Law Journal* 88 (1979) 950–997.

6. Donahue, 'The Hypostasis of a Prophecy'.

the purposes of this essay, we should ask a related but somewhat different question: to what extent is the predictive theory of law evident in our sources up to and including the Middle Ages, and to what extent is it useful in explaining those sources even if it is not evident in them?

Procedure in Roman Law

The first Roman civil law of which we have the text states: 'If the plaintiff calls the defendant to court, let him go'. It then goes on to say what is to happen if he does not go.[7] The Romans of 450 BC were legal realists. When did they stop being legal realists? I am not sure that they ever did. What did happen was that the Roman jurists of the middle and late classical periods, roughly 100 to 230 of our era, developed a method of teaching law that distinguished among the law of persons, the law of things (roughly the substantive rights and duties of the civil law), and the law of actions. This last body of law we can call procedure without too much anachronism. We first see these distinctions operating in the teaching program in Gaius's *Institutes* of roughly 160 AD. Gaius's *Institutes* formed the backbone of Justinian's *Institutes,* and from there they passed on to the medieval and modern West.

What must be emphasized is that this tripartite division of 'all law' may have been how the Roman jurists organized the curriculum, at least for the beginners, but they did not observe it when they did their jobs. The fundamental question that juristic casuistic literature asks is what form of action is available granted that this is what has happened. A large part of the commentary literature is devoted to explicating word-by-word the edicts of the judicial magistrates, particularly the urban praetor. Those edicts are built around a series of promises by the magistrate, that if such-and-such has happened, 'I will give an action'. Even the commentaries on the civil law generally are built around the actions available at civil law.[8]

It must be admitted that this juristic focus on what could be expected of the Roman judicial magistrate, particularly the urban praetor, is not quite a focus—in Holmes's words—on prophecies that public force will be brought to bear, for two reasons. The first is probably the more important: Classical Roman civil procedure came, for the most part, in two parts, proceedings before the magistrate, called proceedings 'in ius', and proceedings before the judge, called proceedings 'apud iudicem'. The

---

7. *XII Tables* (c. 450 BC), Table 1.1, in *Fontes iuris romani ante-iustiniani*, ed. Salvatore Riccobono (2nd ed. Firenze 1941) 1.26 (my trans.): 'Si in ius vocat, [ito.] Ni it, antestamino: igitur em capito'.

8. For these distinctions among types of juristic literature, see Fritz Schulz, *History of Roman Legal Science* (Oxford 1953).

plaintiff's claim and the defenses were incorporated in a written formula that was sent to the judge, who was not a state official, for what we would call trial: 'If you find these facts, condemn the defendant; if you do not, absolve'. The decision of the judge was final; there was no appeal. The professional competence of the Roman jurists did not extend to proceedings 'apud iudicem'. Proceedings 'apud iudicem' were the responsibility of orators, not jurists. As a result there was little law about proceedings 'apud iudicem' other than the law contained in the formula. There were no rules of evidence. Proceedings 'apud iudicem' were a kind of black box. The judge came up with an answer following whatever procedure he chose to adopt. The judge's motives for his judgment were inscrutable.[9]

The second reason why the work of the Roman jurists does not quite fit the model of prophecies of when public force will be brought to bear is that classical Roman law seems to have made relatively little use of public force in civil proceedings. All civil judgments were, ultimately, money judgments, and if the defendant did not pay, the ultimate sanction was an authorization from the praetor to the successful plaintiff to seize the defendant's goods. How the plaintiff accomplished this if the defendant was a strong man whose goods were well guarded, we do not know. That we do not know is quite amazing. The question would occur to anyone who has even mild tendencies in the direction of legal realism.[10]

Before we conclude, however, that the Roman juristic enterprise was not a realistic one, we should remember that the principal source of our knowledge of what the jurists wrote is Justinian's *Digest,* which was compiled some three centuries after the death of the last classical jurist. Shortly after the death of the last classical jurist around 240 AD, the procedural system changed.[11] There were no longer separate proceedings 'apud iudicem'. The entire civil process was conducted before a state-appointed judge. The formulae were no longer used, and appeal was possible.[12] Quite understandably, the compilers of the *Digest* tended to leave out material in their sources that dealt with problems that were unique to the classical formulary procedure. Indeed, they left out so much that it was not until the discovery of an almost complete text of Gaius's *Institutes* in the early

9. For an introduction to classical Roman civil procedure, see Herbert Felix Jolowicz and Barry Nicholas, *Historical Introduction to the Study of Roman Law* (3rd ed. Cambridge 1972) 191–232.

10. A question trenchantly raised in John Maurice Kelly, *Roman Litigation* (Oxford 1966).

11. Like all such changes, the change from the formulary system about which the classical jurists largely wrote and the 'extraordinaria cognitio', the system in effect in the later empire, was gradual. It would seem, however, that by about the year 300 AD, the 'extraordinaria cognitio' had totally replaced the formulary system.

12. On this procedure, the 'extraordinaria cognitio', see Jolowicz and Nicholas, *Historical Introduction* 395–404, 439–50.

nineteenth century that we understood many of the basics of how the classical formulary system worked.

The state of our sources about Roman law thus combines with the undeniable fact that the classical institutional treatises make a sharp distinction between substance and procedure to give the impression that such a distinction is inevitable. The compilers probably took as much procedure out of the *Digest* as they could. They were interested in the classical substance, not classical procedure. What the *Corpus Iuris Civilis* says about the later procedure—and it is not nearly enough—is, for the most part, in the *Code* and the *Novels,* not in the *Digest.* Thus, to exaggerate, the *Corpus Iuris Civilis* offers us substance without procedure for the classical period and procedure without substance for the post-classical period. For a legal realist, separating the two is incoherent. For the western jurist trying to make sense of the *Corpus* in a later age, the message is that procedure and substance are in two different worlds.

The 'Revival of Jurisprudence'

The history of Western law next went into a long period that begins with the 'barbarian codes' of the sixth and later centuries and ends with the 'revival of jurisprudence' in the twelfth century. The sources for this long period are thin, diverse, and quite intractable. It is obviously difficult to generalize about them. We have to say something about them, however, because the main argument in this section is that what happened in the twelfth century was quite different and that what happened set western procedural law on a course that it was to follow throughout the Middle Ages, and, indeed, on to where we are today.

There is some procedural material in the early sources, particularly in the documents that record transactions. We hear of inquests, accusers and witnesses, oaths and battles and ordeals. One can construct a model of early medieval procedure, even if one cannot be sure how much of it may have been in effect in various places at various times.[13] It is striking, however, how much of the legal material from this period consists of casuistic or apodictic statements shorn of procedure. Except for remedies, of which we hear a great deal, there is, for example, no procedure at all in the first English law, Aethelbert's Code, of the late sixth or early seventh century.[14]

The laws of the Anglo-Saxon kings constitute a particularly remarkable

13. For a recent, and remarkably successful, attempt to do so with regard to methods of proof, see Mike McNair, 'Vicinage and the Antecedents of the Jury', LHR 17 (1999) 537–571.

14. The most recent, and by far the best, edition: Lisi Oliver, *The Beginnings of English Law* (Toronto 2002) 60–81.

series. Beginning with Aethelbert, various English kings, up to and including Cnut in the eleventh century, promulgated a large body of law with numerous substantive provisions about what was to be done in particular cases. The late Patrick Wormald put together a compendium of all the known records of Anglo-Saxon cases, approximately two hundred.[15] Not a single one of them cites any provision of the Anglo-Saxon codes, even where there is a provision that is obviously relevant to the case and could have been known to the participants in the case. A few cases can be shown to reach results contrary to what the relevant code provision dictates. The predictive theory of law may or may not work in such a context, but it is pretty obvious that the written law would not be a good basis for making the prediction.

This situation obviously causes problems for anyone who has even mild tendencies to positivism. If what purports to be a law is not enforced by the state, is it law? The problem goes deeper than that. If we are speaking of Aethelbert's Kent or Cnut's England, what is the state? If one takes the view that it is illegitimate to speak of the territorial nation state before the sixteenth century, then the problem will continue, even after the major change that we will argue occurred in the twelfth century. I cannot solve the problem of the committed positivist. If your definition of law is that it must be enforced by the state, then you are going to have to find another word to describe the Anglo-Saxon laws. But the Anglo-Saxon laws certainly look like what we call law, and there is evidence, at least in some periods, that people were manipulating them in ways that we typically associate with law.[16] The Anglo-Saxons do not, however, seem to have applied their laws to actual disputes.

As we have already seen in the case of Rome, we need to modify Holmes's definition of law, if we are to apply it to much of history. We need to take out the word 'public'. The Romans had a distinction between public and private, but they do not seem to have made much use of their public force in the area of civil law. The Anglo-Saxons did not have an express distinction between public and private, and the distinction between public and private force took a long time to work out. It was certainly not clearly present in the twelfth century.[17] If we wish, we can substitute 'le-

15. Patrick Wormald, 'A Handlist of Anglo-Saxon Lawsuits', *Anglo-Saxon England*, 17 (1988) 247–281.

16. For pursuit of this argument over a rather wide expanse of history, see Charles Donahue, 'Private Law without the State and during its Formation', *American Journal of Comparative Law* 56 (2008) 541–566, reprinted in *Beyond the State: Rethinking Private Law*, ed. Nils Jansen and Ralf Michaels (Tübingen 2008) 121–143.

17. See most recently Thomas N. Bisson, *The Crisis of the Twelfth Century: Power, Lordship, and the Origins of European Government* (Princeton 2009).

gitimate' for 'public' in the definition, so long as we remember that for a long period what was legitimate force was controversial.

What was new in the twelfth century was a renewed commitment to the proposition that what was stated in the law should determine the results in cases. This commitment is evident whether we are talking about the development of the central royal courts in England or the remarkable revival of legal studies, both canonic and civilian, that is traditionally associated with Bologna. Our concern here is with Bologna. It seems to be a bit earlier than England, and it had far more effect on medieval canon law.

Many would trace the beginnings of the modern European legal professions to the glossators of Roman and canon law of the twelfth century.[18] By the end of the thirteenth century, if not before, there were lawyers in every area of Western Europe who were making their living by advising clients and representing them in courts. As I suggested earlier, if one is going to advise clients and represent them in court, one has to make predictions as to what the courts are going to do, and such predictions must include the relevant procedure.

Perhaps the most remarkable achievement of the twelfth- and thirteenth-century glossators was the development of Romano-canonical procedure, both civil and criminal. It was an achievement in which both canonists and civilians participated.

The material on this topic that the glossators had from the past was singularly unhelpful. In the case of Roman law, as we have already seen, the texts in the *Corpus Iuris Civilis* are deficient as to both the procedure in effect at the time of the jurists and that in effect at the time of the compilers. In the case of canon law, it seems reasonably clear that no one had ever tried to create a specifically canonic procedure. The church had taken procedure as it found it and had engrafted on it some basic ideas that were of concern. There are some examples of this engrafting in the mid-eleventh century canonical *Collection in Seventy-Four Titles* ('74T').[19] A particularly dramatic example in 74T is the Pseudo-Isidorean decretal that says: 'A prelate shall not be condemned except with seventy-two witnesses'.[20] Overall, if a cleric, particularly a bishop, was to be tried, there ought to be legitimate accusers and legitimate witnesses. Defendants ought to have notice and an opportunity to be heard, and so forth. Many of the basics of

---

18. A point made quite powerfully in James A. Brundage, *The Medieval Origins of the Legal Profession: Canonists, Civilians, and Courts* (Chicago 2008).

19. *Diversorum patrum sententiae; sive, Collectio in LXXIV titulos digesta*, ed. John T. Gilchrist (MIC B:1; Città del Vaticano 1973), conveniently translated and annotated in John T. Gilchrist, *The Collection in Seventy-four Titles: A Canon Law Manual of the Gregorian Reform* (Toronto 1980) ['74T'].

20. 74T, c. 69, tit. 7; cf. c. 84.

what we call due process can be found in this tendentious work. There is, however, no evidence that the system of procedure described in 74T was ever implemented. Indeed, it is hard to imagine how it could have been; 74T is not a how-to-do-it book.

It seems relatively clear that the impetus for creating a useable procedural system came from the church, and specifically from the great increase in appeals to the papacy that occurred in the twelfth century. As will be explained more fully in Pennington's 'Jurisprudence of Procedure', the first 'ordo iudiciarius', a description of the entire course of procedure from initial summons to appeal, was written by Bulgarus de Bulgarinis, the earliest of the four civilian doctors, sometime between 1123 and 1141, at the request of Emery, the chancellor of the Roman church. The most comprehensive 'ordo' was compiled by Guillelmus Durantis at the end of the thirteenth century. In between Bulgarus and Durantis, some forty treatises, many of them still unedited, were written on the whole course of procedure. The number of surviving manuscripts shows that this was a popular form of literature. There were also countless treatises on pieces of the procedure, like witnesses, or accusations, or libels (roughly the equivalent of the Anglo-American complaint). At least in the twelfth century it is quite clear that the literature proceeds in tandem with the development of the papal court and papal decretal letters, as can be seen by the extensive citations of this type of source in the surviving 'ordines'. Procedural writing is particularly extensive in the Anglo-Norman school of canonists.[21]

Tancred and the Law of Witnesses

The most popular 'ordo', to judge by the number of surviving manuscripts and the fact that it was later translated into both French and German, is Tancred's.[22] The original version of the work can be dated from just before or just after 1215, and extensive additions were made to it, perhaps not by Tancred, to update the citations and to incorporate material found only in the *Liber extra* of 1234. The work is divided into four parts: Part 1, 'Persons'; Part 2, 'From summons to *litis contestatio*' (including the exceptions that can, and in some cases must, be raised before we get to the proof stage);[23] Part 3, 'Proof'; and Part 4, 'Sentences,' or, as we would say, 'judgments'.

21. A survey of the 'ordines', many of which are still in manuscript, may be found in Fowler-Magerl, *Ordo*. See most recently Peter Landau, 'Die Anfänge der Prozessrechtswissenschaft in der Kanonistik des 12. Jahrhunderts', *Einfluss der Kanonistik* 1.7–23.

22. Described more fully in Pennington, 'Jurisprudence of Procedure' 144–148; see Andrea Bettetini, 'Tancredi da Bologna', DGI 2.1930–1931.

23. For American lawyers, these are roughly equivalent to Rule 12b motions.

To illustrate how Tancred proceeds, let us take as an example his treatment of the law of witnesses.[24] The form Tancred gives for the admission, examination, and reprover of witnesses is part of the standard overall form for the course of judgment in Romano-canonic civil procedure. The case is introduced by a summons and a libel on behalf of the plaintiff and then a joinder of issue (litis contestatio). The plaintiff is then assigned a number of terms (three was standard; a fourth was given as an exceptional matter) to produce witnesses to discharge his burden of proof on his case in chief.[25]

Once produced, the witnesses are to take an oath to tell the whole truth and to tell the truth for both parties. They are also to swear that they have not come to bear testimony for a price or out of friendship, or for private hate, or for any benefit they might receive. After they have taken the oath, the witnesses are to be examined separately and in secret, after the model of Daniel's questioning of the elders in the Biblical story of Susanna (Dn 13). What the witnesses say is written down, normally by a notary, in the form of written depositions.

When all the witnesses have been examined, the judge is to order the publication of the witnesses' depositions. The defendant now has an opportunity to except to the testimony of the witnesses. He may except to their persons, if he reserved the right to do so when they were produced, or he may seek to demonstrate that their testimony is false in some respect. The defendant may also at this point raise what we now call affirmative defenses, which are also called exceptions. They would concede, at least for the sake of argument, the validity of the plaintiff's claim but argue that the plaintiff should nonetheless not recover: 'Perhaps I did exchange words of marital consent with this woman, but I still cannot marry her because I was already married to someone else', or 'because we are too closely related'. The defendant would then be assigned terms to prove his or her side of the case.

The proceduralists not only outline the form by which witnesses are to be admitted, examined, and reproved; they also elaborate some basic

24. The following paragraphs are derived from Charles Donahue, 'Proof by Witnesses in the Church Courts of Medieval England: An Imperfect Reception of the Learned Law', *On the Laws and Customs of England: Essays in Honor of Samuel E. Thorne*, ed. Morris S. Arnold et al. (Chapel Hill, N.C. 1981) 127–158.

25. For this and what follows, see Tancred, *Ordo* 3.8–10, in *Pillii, Tancredi, Gratiae Libri De iudiciorum ordine*, ed. Friedrich Bergmann (Göttingen 1842) 230–245. For similar doctrines in the context of many 'ordines', see Litewski, *Zivilprozeß* 2.353–445; see most recently and comprehensively, with examples drawn largely from the French secular courts, Yves Maussen, *Veritatis adiutor: La procédure du témoignage dans le droit savant et la pratique française (xiie – xive siècles)* (Università degli studi di Milano, Facoltà di giurisprudenza, Pubblicazioni dell' Istituto di storia del diritto medievale e moderno 35; Milano 2006).

principles of their system of proof by witnesses. At the core of that system are three propositions: First, the character of each witness is to be examined: certain witnesses are not to be heard because of their status, and others' testimony is to be regarded as suspicious because of their status or mores or their relationship to one or the other of the parties. Second, witnesses are to be examined carefully to determine if they are telling the truth about events they saw and heard themselves. Third, on the basis of the written depositions and what has been demonstrated about the character of the witnesses, the judge is to determine whether the standard of proof fixed by law has been met.

As a general matter, Tancred tells us, two witnesses make a full proof.[26] But not everyone may be a witness. Slaves, women (in certain circumstances), those below the age of fourteen, the insane, the infamous, paupers (although Tancred has some doubts about whether paupers should automatically be excluded), and infidels may not be witnesses. Criminals may not be witnesses. No one may be a witness in his own cause. Judges, advocates, and executors may not be witnesses in cases in which they have performed their official duties. Children may not testify on behalf of their parents, nor parents on behalf of their children, with certain exceptions. Familiars and domestics of the producing party and those who are enemies of the party against whom they are produced may not be witnesses.[27] These conditions are all summed up in a dreadful mnemonic poem:[28]

> Condition, gender, age, and discretion,
> Fame and fortune and truth,
> If these are lacking,
> Without the court's backing,
> From witnessing hold 'em aloof.

Witnesses are to be questioned, Tancred continues, about all the details of what they have seen or heard, for only then can it be determined whether they are consistent. They are to be asked about the matter, the people, the place, the time, perhaps even what the weather was like, what the people were wearing, who was consul, and so forth. In only a few instances, such as computing the remoter degrees of kinship in incest cases, would hearsay testimony be accepted.[29]

If a witness contradicts himself, Tancred concludes, then his testimony should be rejected. If the witnesses agree, and their 'dicta' seem to conform to the nature of the case, then their 'dicta' are to be followed. If the

---

26. Tancred, *Ordo* 3.7, p. 228.   27. Ibid. 3.6, pp. 223–228.

28. The Latin is no better as poetry: 'Conditio, sexus, aetas, discretio, fama / Et fortuna, fides, in testibus ista requires' (p. 225).

29. Ibid. 3.9.2, pp. 238–240.

witnesses on one side disagree among themselves, then the judge must be-lieve those statements that best fit the nature of the matter at hand and are the least suspicious. If the witnesses on one side conflict with those on the other, then the judge ought to attempt to reconcile their statements if he can. If he cannot, then he ought to follow those who are most trustworthy, the freeborn rather than the freedman, the older rather than the younger, the man of more honorable estate rather than the inferior, the noble rather than the ignoble, the man rather than the woman. Further, the truth-teller is to be believed rather than the liar, the man of pure life rather than the man who lives in vice, the rich man rather than the poor, anyone other than a great friend of the person for whom he testifies or an enemy of him against whom he testifies. If the witnesses are all of the same dignity, then the judge should stand with the side that has the greatest number of witnesses. If they are of the same number and dignity, then absolve the de-fendant.[30] The basic principle, then, is 'onus probandi incumbit ei qui dicit' (the burden of proof rests upon the person who asserts).

When the Bolognese glossators began writing, the standard methods for proof in the secular courts included ordeal, battle, and compurgation; and compurgation was also used in the church courts, and, occasionally, ordeal.[31] Asking questions of those who knew or could find out about the case was not unknown, but it was clearly not the only method of proof. To put the proposition more affirmatively: though witnesses in various forms were used, appeal to the divine through the ordeal, and perhaps through battle or even oath, was still quite common. Now there is nothing about ordeal or battle or compurgation in the classical texts of Roman law, to which the early glossators addressed themselves,[32] although some of the ancient canonic texts did deal with these methods of proof.[33] The Roman-law texts deal exclusively, and the canon-law texts principally, with proofs by witnesses and written instruments. The discovery that 'the law' called for proof by 'rational' methods—witnesses and writings—rather than 'ir-rational' methods—ordeal, battle, and compurgation—was among the causes of the intellectuals' attacks on the irrational methods of proof.[34] It was not the only argument that was made. Perhaps the most powerful

---

30. Ibid. 3.12, pp. 245–248.

31. See generally *La preuve*, vol. 2 (Receuils de la Société Jean Bodin 17; Bruxelles 1965).

32. A few Roman texts deal with what a later age would call the 'decisory oath'.

33. See especially the texts collected in C.2 q.5.

34. See Jean-Phillipe Lévy, *La hierarchie des preuves dans le droit savant du moyen âge* (Annales de l'université de Lyon, 3e sér., droit, fasc. 5; Paris 1935) 131–135; John Baldwin, 'The Intellectual Preparation for the Canon of 1215 Against Ordeals', *Speculum* 36 (1961) 613–636; Paul Hyams, 'Trial by Ordeal: The Key to Proof in the Early Common Law', *On the Laws and Customs* 90–126; Robert Bartlett, *Trial by Fire and Water: The Medieval Judicial Ordeal* (Oxford 1986).

theological argument was based on the text 'Thou shalt not tempt the Lord thy God'.[35] You should not ask for a miracle about something that you can find out by human effort.

We find some reflections of this hostility to the irrational methods of proof in the writings of the early proceduralists.[36] The attitude reflected in an anonymous *Summula de testibus* of the late twelfth century, perhaps by an Anglo-Norman canonist, is typical. The *Summula* repeats an injunction found in C.2 q.1 c.2 of Gratian's *Concordance of Discordant Canons:* a bishop is not to be judged unless he himself confesses or unless he is regularly convicted by innocent witnesses canonically examined. 'Regularly convicted by innocent witnesses canonically examined' means, the jurist notes, 'not in single combat nor in [the trial of] hot iron, nor of cold or hot water, nor of lashes, but of oath alone'.[37] Few proceduralists address themselves as specifically to the issue of irrational methods of proof, but many emphasize that witnesses are the best method of proof, better than written instruments, and, by implication, far better than ordeal or battle.[38]

As is well known, the church withdrew its support for the ordeal at the Fourth Lateran Council in 1215.[39] The development of an alternative system of proof was the work of the Romano-canonical proceduralists up to and including Tancred.

Relatively little innovation occurs after Tancred's time in the basic system of Romano-canonical procedure. The doctrinal development prior to Tancred, however, is considerable. For example, Gratian's original text had little or nothing on the topic of the qualifications of witnesses; his students added a long list from Roman law, far too long a list, full of anachronistic and bizarre social categories (herewith of publicans, decurions, and hermaphrodites).[40] The first treatise on witnesses, written by Albericus de Porta Ravennate sometime in the 1170s, is also derived solely from Roman law, has a much shorter but still anachronistic list of possible exceptions against the persons of witnesses, mentions the two-witness rule but does not go into the question of how the witnesses are to be examined, and contains no advice at all on how to resolve conflicts among the witnesses.[41]

35. Mt 4:7, Lk 4:12, derived from Dt 6:16.

36. There is considerably more material of relevance to this debate in the decretists. See Baldwin, 'Intellectual Preparation' 619–626.

37. Cambridge, Trinity College o.40.70, fol. 182v: 'Non in monomachiam necque [examinacionem] candentis ferri necque acque frigide necque verberum sed solius iuramenti'.

38. For the controversy on the witnesses versus instrument point and its ultimate resolution in favor of witnesses, see Lévy, *Hiérarchie* 84–105, and sources cited.

39. Lateran IV (1215), c. 18, COD 177 (=X 3.50.9); cf. X 5.35.3.

40. C.2 q.1 c.2.

41. Erich Genzmer edited the text in '*Summula de testibus ab Alberico de Porta Ravennate composita*', *Studi di storia e diritto in onore di Enrico Besta* (Milano 1939) 1.491–510.

In the development of practical advice on questioning and on balancing discordant testimony, papal decretal law played a considerable role, as the numerous citations to the *Compilationes Antiquae* in Tancred indicate.[42] Perhaps of equal importance, however, was the work of the proceduralists in the generation preceding Tancred. The first extended discussion I have found of how to question a witness is in an anonymous *Summula de testibus*, dating from around 1200.[43] There are, however, hints of what is to be the later approach as early as 1171 in the French canonist 'ordo' 'In principio'.[44] By far the most elaborate treatment of how to evaluate conflicting testimony is to be found in Pillius's *Summula* on witnesses, which probably dates from sometime between 1185 and 1195.[45] Pillius's rule-laden treatment of the issue stands in marked contrast to that of the earlier anonymous 'ordo' 'Si quis de quacumque re':[46]

In sum, respect should never be paid to the multitude of witness but to the sincere faith of the testimony and to the testimony that the light of truth rather aids, because the judge, once he has examined what is said in the constitutions and responses of the jurists on these matters, can know more than the discipline of law can teach or permanently define.

Similar statements, derived from a long dictum in Gratian's *Causa* 4 (C.4 q.3 d.p. c.2–3), may be found in the French 'ordo' 'Tractaturi de judiciis' of about 1165 and the ?Irish 'ordo' 'Quia judiciorum' of about 1185.[47]

42. See Knut Wolfgang Nörr, 'Päpstliche Dekretalen in den ordines iudiciorum der friihen Legistik', Ius Commune 3 (1970) 1–9; and his 'Päpstliche Dekretalen und römisch-kanonischer Zivilprozess', *Studien zur europäischen Rechtsgeschichte* [fiir Helmut Coing], ed. Walter Wilhelm (Frankfurt 1972) 53–65.

43. Erich Genzmer edited the text in 'Eine anonyme Kleinschrift de testibus aus der Zeit urn 1200', *Festschrift Paul Koschaker* (3 vols. Weimar 1939, reprinted Leipzig 1977) 3.399–401.

44. Friedrich Kunstmann edited the text in 'Über den altesten *Ordo judiciarius*', *Kritische Überschau der deutschen Gesetzgebung und Rechtswissenschaft* 2 (1855) 17–29 at 19; see Landau, 'Anfänge' 17.

45. Pillius, '*Quoniam in iuditiis frequentissime*', edited by Yves Mausen in 2008 on the basis of five manuscripts, http://fhi.rg.mpg.de/zitat/0805mausen.htm. For the date, see Stephan Kuttner, '*Analecta iuridica vaticana*', *Collectanea vaticana in honorem Anselmi card. Albareda* (Studi e Testi 219; Città del Vaticano 1962) 430, modified in Fowler-Magerl, *Ordo* 224–225. On Pillius, see Ennio Cortese, 'Pillio da Medicina', DGI 2.1587–1590.

46. Edited by Nicolaus Rhodius, as Bk. 4 of *Placentini iurisconsulti vetustissimi de varietate actionum libri sex* (Mainz 1530) 4.17 (p. 105): 'In summa nequamque ad testium multitudinem respici opportet, sed ad synceram testimoniorum fidem et testimonia, quibus potius lux veritatis adsistit [citations]. Quod iudex, discussis omnibus quae in responsis et constitutionibus de his caventur magis scire poterit, quam ulla iuris possit disciplina doceri vel in perpetuum definiet'. For the work, see Knut Wolfgang Nörr, 'Die Literatur des gemeinen Zivilprozeß', *Handbuch der Quellen und Literatur der neueren eupropäischen Privatrechtsgeschichte. 1: Mittelalter (1100–1500)*, ed. Helmut Coing (München 1973) 365–397 at 387; Landau, 'Anfänge' 12–13.

47. 'Tractaturi de judiciis', ed. Carl Gross, in *Incerti auctoris ordo judiciarius* (lnnsbruck 1870) 13.3 (pp. 120–121): 'Si vero alter litigantium multos habeat testes, alter paucos, non pluralitati credendum est, immo conversatio et vita et fides illorum et istorum consideranda est et secundum hoc judicandum est'. For the work, see Nörr, 'Literatur' 388; Landau, 'Anfänge' 14. 'Ordo iudicio-

In marked contrast to the Roman texts and some of the earlier canonists, the mainstream Bolognese jurists in this period focused on limiting the discretion of the judge. Over the course of the middle ages more room was opened up for judicial discretion in evaluating testimony.

Why the mainstream Bolognese jurists focused on limiting the discretion of the judge is controverted. Perhaps the best explanation for this, at least so far as the canonists are concerned, is that they were seeking to separate the role of confessor from that of judge: 'iudex secundum allegata nec secundum conscientiam iudicat' (the judge judges according to the things alleged and not according to his conscience) is a maxim found often in their writing.[48] An alternative explanation, not inconsistent with this one, is that in seeking to substitute human judgment for appeals to the divine they needed to convince people that the judge would render decisions somewhat mechanically, according to rules, and not according his social position or connections.[49]

There is some evidence that by Tancred's time the proceduralists may have realized that they had gone too far. Perhaps the best evidence that they may have realized this as a general matter is at the very beginning of Tancred's section on witnesses: 'Everyone can be a witness who is not prohibited, because the edict about witnesses, like that about proctors, is prohibitory; all, therefore, who are not prohibited can be admitted. [Dig. 22.5.1.1]'.[50] The cited passage comes from the monograph of Arcadius Charisius, an obscure jurist of the late third or early fourth century, considerably after the classical period: 'Witnesses can be called not only in criminal cases but, when appropriate, in money suits, if not forbidden to testify nor excused from testimony by any statute'.[51]

Tancred's move is important. Arcadius Charisius seems to be making a

---

rum', ed. Johann Friedrich von Schulte, in 'Der *Ordo judiciarius* des Codex Bambergensis P.I.11', *Sb. Akad. Vienna*, 70 (1872) 285–326 at 310. For the work, see Nörr, 'Literatur' 387; Fowler-Magerl, *Ordo* 105–106; Landau, 'Anfänge' 18–19.

48. See Knut Wolfgang Nörr, *Zur Stellung des Richters im gelehrten Prozess der Frühzeit, iudex secundum allegata non secundum conscientiam iudicat* (München 1967). For an interesting argument about the role that conscience might have played in the whole development, see James Q. Whitman, *The Origins of Reasonable Doubt: Theological Roots of the Criminal Trial* (New Haven 2008).

49. See John Langbein, *Torture and the Law of Proof: Europe and England in the Ancien Régime* (2nd ed. Chicago 2006) 6–7.

50. Tancred, *Ordo* 3.6, p. 223: 'Testes possunt esse omnes, qui non probibentur, quoniam edictum de testibus, sicut de procuratoribus, prohibitorium est; omnes enim, qui non prohibentur, admitti possunt. ut Dig. de testib. 22, 5. l. 1. §. i.'.

51. Dig. 22.5.1.1 (*Aurelius Arcadius Charisius magister libellorum libro singulari de testibus*): 'Adhiberi quoque testes possunt non solum in criminalibus causis, sed etiam in pecuniariis litibus sicubi res postulat, ex his quibus non interdicitur testimonium nec ulla lege a dicendo testimonio excusantur'. For Arcadius Charisius, see Adolf Berger, *Encyclopedic Dictionary of Roman Law* (Transactions of the American Philosophical Society, new series 43.2; Philadephia 1953) 388.

negative inference: because there are statutes that prohibit certain people from testifying in certain cases; therefore, anyone who is not covered by the statutes can testify in any case. The logic of such arguments is false, but Tancred seizes on the argument, because it creates a presumption in favor of admitting the witness. If you want to exclude someone, you have to find a specific authority that says that this witness ought to be excluded. This limitation puts a cap on any future development of exclusionary rules. It is a quite typical move, where the glossators thought that the past had gone too far. They did the same thing in the case of incest. The first step was to put a cap on future expansion of the incest prohibition. They then went to work on cutting it back.

In virtually all cases, except perhaps for infidels, the insane, and the feeble-minded, Tancred cuts back on what could have been a complete exclusion.[52] What he has to say about paupers is particularly interesting because he has no authority for the limitation that he suggests but simply his own argument based on what we would call 'policy':[53]

Paupers are prohibited from testimony, both by the law of the forum and by the law of heaven [C.2 q.1 c.7 s.3, c.14; Nov. 90.1]. And some say this only obtains in criminal cases, and [others] that it generally obtains of any pauper who has less then fifty aurei. To me it seems that this is said only of those paupers who are presumed to suppress the truth upon receiving money, for if the witness is honest, so that there is no presumption against him that he would lie for money, he ought not be excluded from testimony; otherwise you would have to say that many holy and religious men, and even the apostles themselves, ought to be excluded, for they were paupers, having nothing.

Tancred deals with the exclusion of criminals in two different places. In the first, he seems to exclude all criminals from giving testimony, but then seems to back off that proposition for something called 'excepted crimes'.[54] The second passage, five paragraphs later on, seems to preclude enemies and those that are suspected of enmity against the party against whom they are produced, but once more qualifies what it has to say, dis-

---

52. He does this, for example, on the topic of women as witnesses. For a full discussion, see Giovanni Minnucci, *La capacità processuale della donna nel pensiero canonistico classico, 2: Dalle scuole d'oltralpe a S. Raimondo di Pennaforte* (Quaderni di 'Studi senesi' 79; Milano 1994) 177–193 and passim.

53. Tancred, *Ordo* 3.6, p. 225: 'Prohibentur etiam pauperes a testimonio, tam iure fori, quam iure poli. ut C. 2. q. 1. c. inprimis. 7. (§.3.) et l. prohibetur. (c. 14.) et in Auth. de testib. §.1. (Nov. 90. c. 1.) Et dicunt quidam, hoc obtinere in criminalibus causis dumtaxat, et generaliter obtinere de quibuslibet pauperibus, qui minus quam quinquaginta aureos habent. Mihi videtur hoc dictum esse de his pauperibus tantum, qui obtentu pecuniae praesumuntur supprimere veritatem; quoniam si testis est honestus, ita quod nulla praesumtio sit contra eum, ut pro pecunia mentiatur, licet pauper sit, non est repellendus a testimonio; alioquin enim oporteret dici multos sanctos et viros religiosos et etiam ipsos apostolos a testimonio repellendos, qui pauperes sunt nihil habentes'.

54. Ibid. 3.6, p. 226.

tinguishing between enemies because of criminal litigation and enemies because of pecuniary litigation.[55] Let us take a look at the first passage:[56]

Again, all criminals are prohibited from testimony, whether they were previously convicted of the crime or not, so long as they are convicted by way of exception, the crime being stated and proved [1 Comp. 2.13.13, 12; 2 Comp. 2.11.1; 3 Comp. 2.4.1]. And this is true in every case, according to the canons, except in excepted crimes [3 Comp. 5.2.3, 4]. What excepted crimes are and what the law is when they are tried is fully noted above in the title on crimes [Tancred, *Ordo* 2.7.6]. And this is the reason why all criminals are excluded from testimony, because they are infamous by canonical infamy [C.6 q.1 c.3, c.4].

Obviously, the citations to the *Complatio tertia*, which are citations to decretals of Innocent III exactly contemporary with Tancred, are important. In particular, one of them, 3 Comp. 5.2.3 (= X 5.3.31, *Licet Heli*) is cited before the mnenomic poem in support of the proposition that the infamous may testify in the case of excepted crimes; *Licet Heli* is cited again here; and it is cited for a third time in support of the proposition that capital enemies and conspirators are to be heard in no situation.[57]

The decretal *Licet Heli* was issued by Innocent III in 1199, in the case of the abbot of Pomposa, who was accused, among other things, of simony.[58] The decretal is famous because it says that simony could be dealt with by a new form of procedure, an inquisitorial process, in which the judge of his own motion questions those who know about the incident and proceeds to make a ruling. The judge does not have to wait until someone makes a formal accusation, nor is he bound by the elaborate set of procedural rules that limit those who can make such an accusation and those who can testify about it. The decretal contains two biblical references, the only authorities cited in it: 'Although Eli, the high priest, was himself a good man', the decretal begins, 'nonetheless because he did

55. Ibid. 3.6, p. 228.

56. Ibid. 3.6, p. 226: 'Item prohibentur a testimonio omnes criminosi, sive antea fuerint convicti de illo crimine, sive non, dummodo convincantur in modum·exceptionis opposito crimine et probato. ut X. 1. de testib. 2, 13. c. porro. 13. c. super eo. 12. X. 2. de except. 2, 11. c. denique. 1. X. 3. de ord. cogn. 2, 4. c. cum 5 dilectus. 1. in f. Et habet hoc locum in omni causa, secundum canones, nisi in criminibus exceptis. ut X. 3. de simon. 5, 2. c. licet Heli. 3. c. per tuas. Quae autem sint excepta crimina et quid iuris sit, cum de his agitur, plene notatum est supra in titulo de criminibus. Et haec est causa, quare omnes criminosi repelluntur a testimonio, quia sunt infames infamia canonica. ut C. 6. q. 1. c. illi qui. 3. c. omnes. 4'.

57. Ibid. 3.6, pp. 224–225, 226, 228.

58. This paragraph is derived from Charles Donahue, 'Malchus's Ear: Reflections on Classical Canon Law as a Religious Legal System', *Lex et Romanitas: Essays for Alan Watson* (Berkeley 2000) 109–110. For the background of the decretal, see Richard Fraher, 'IV Lateran's Revolution in Criminal Procedure', *Studia in honorem eminentissimi cardinalis Alphonsi M. Stickler*, ed. R. Castillo Lara (Roma 1992) 97–111; and his 'The Theoretical Justification for the New Criminal Law of the High Middle Ages', *University of Illinois Law Review* (1984) 557–595. See further Pennington, 'Jurisprudence of Procedure' 141–142.

not effectively punish the wickedness of his sons, he brought down the rod of divine judgment both on them and on himself' (referring to 1 Sm 2:12–4:18).[59] That a pastor has the obligation to discipline his flock is a fundamental principle of canon law, and one does not need to cite Old Testament examples to show it.[60] 'I will go down', the decretal later says, quoting words that Genesis 18:21 ascribes to God in the context of Sodom, 'and see whether they have done in fact what is reported to me'.[61] This biblical reference is a little closer to the real issue, because it suggests that reports of crimes must be investigated. But the quotation raises more issues than it settles: Is the pope really arrogating to himself the power of divine judgment? How is the pope to know what God knows? In particular, is there anything about the story of Sodom that suggests that it is appropriate for the pope to set aside the ancient canonical requirements about accusers and witnesses? It would seem, then, that the Bible is being used here more for its rhetorical effect (no one who heard these words would miss the implicit verbal equation of simony and sodomy) than it is for the guidance that it provides for the resolution of the issue at hand.

Innocent reports the arguments in the case as follows:[62]

And because simony in many ways seemed to have been proven by witnesses against the same abbot, he opposed many exceptions against the witnesses, on which there was a great dispute on both sides, some asserting that in the crime of simony as in the crime of treason ['laesa maiestas'] all indifferently, both infamous and criminals were to be admitted not only to accusation but also to testifying, others replying to the contrary that although these two crimes are deemed as equal with regard to accusation, they differ in many ways, since one penalty is imposed for one and another penalty for the other, and there is a distinction between the person of the accuser and the person of the witness, since crimes are proved not by accusers but by witnesses, many reasons and arguments being brought forth about this.

59. X 5.3.31: 'Licet Heli summus sacerdos in se ipso bonus existeret, quia tamen filiorum excessus efficaciter non corripuit, et in se pariter, et in ipsis animadversionis divinae vindictam excepit'.

60. The *locus classicus* for this requirement is 1 Tim 3:4–5: 'He [the bishop] must manage his household well, keeping his children submissive and respectful in every way—for if someone does not know how to manage his own household, how can he take care of God's church?' See e.g. D.47 d.p.c.8 (with a long string of biblical examples, including Eli).

61. X 5.3.31: '"Descendam," inquit Dominus, "et videbo utrum clamorem, qui venit ad me, opere compleverint".'

62. Ibid.: 'Et quia per testes simonia multis modis contra ipsum abbatem videbatur esse probata, ipse contra testes multas exceptiones opposuit, super quibus utrinque fuit multipliciter disputatum, aliis asserentibus in crimine simoniae, sicut [et] in crimine laesae maiestatis, omnes indifferenter, tam infames quam criminosos, non solum ad accusandum, sed etiam ad testificandum admittendos, quum ad instar publici criminis et laesae maiestatis procedat accusatio simoniae, multis super hoc et legibus et canonibus allegatis; aliis e contrario respondentibus, quod, licet haec duo crimina quantum ad accusationem quasi paria iudicentur, differunt tamen in multis; quum et alia poena pro uno, et alia pro altero inferatur, et inter personas accusatorum et testium sit utique distinguendum, quum non per accusatores, sed per testes crimina comprobentur, multis nihilominus super hoc citationibus et argumentis inductis'.

The glossators had had their effect; these are not only classic glossatorial arguments, but the method of distinction is classically glossatorial.

Innocent concludes:[63]

Lest either the purity of innocence fall confounded or the evil of simony escape unpunished, we, weighing equity, deemed that not all the exceptions proposed against the witnesses be admitted, nor all repelled, but admitted to proof those exceptions that seem to prove that they [the witnesses] proceeded not from the zeal for justice but the tinder of malignity, to wit, conspiracies and capital enmities. We deem that the other opposed objections, like theft and adultery, because of the pervasiveness of the heresy of simony, in comparison with which all crimes are like nothing, are to be rejected, for even if they weaken the confidence in the witness in some measure, they do not totally remove it, especially when other indications ['adminicula'] support.

There has obviously been a change here from the procedural rules outlined in 74T. Why did this change happen? It seems pretty clear that if you follow the rules laid out in 74T, you are not going to convict many criminals. Perhaps we might say, as did some of the authors of the thirteenth century: 'rei publicae interest ne maleficia maneant impunita' (it is of interest to the republic that crimes not go unpunished).[64]

Despite Innocent's move in the direction of opening up the possibility of discretion, at least for himself as a judge, the drive, in Tancred's work, is for clear rules as opposed to discretion. He accepts Innocent's distinction in the case of excepted crimes, but does not carry it any further. Tancred's desire to find clear, but quite rigid, rules is in part dictated by the nature of the work: it is eminently a how-to-do-it book. But, as we have suggested, other things are at stake as well. The proceduralists, as we have noted, wanted to separate the role of the confessor from that of the judge. They also wanted to convince people that judges would judge according to rules, not whim.

A comparison of Guillelmus Durantis's great work on procedure at the end of the thirteenth century and Tancred's work is instructive.[65] The na-

63. Ibid.: 'Ne vero vel innocentiae puritas confusa succumberet, vel simoniae pravitas effugeret impunita, nos, aequitate pensata, nec omnes exceptiones contra testes oppositas duximus admittendas, nec repellendas duximus universas, sed illas duntaxat exceptiones oppositas probandas admisimus, quae forte probatae non de zelo iustitiae, sed de malignitatis fomite procedere viderentur, conspirationes scilicet et inimicitias capitales, ceteras autem obiectiones oppositas ut furti et adulterii propter immanitatem haeresis simoniacae, ad cuius comparationem omnia crimina quasi pro nihilo reputantur, duximus repellendas, quoniam et si fidem testium debilitarent in aliquo, non tamen evacuarent ex toto, praesertim quum alia contigerit adminicula suffragari'.

64. Cf. X 5.39.35 (Innocent III); see Fraher, 'Theoretical Justification'. The ideas behind the phrase would seem to go back to the twelfth centuy. See Peter Landau, 'Ne crimina maneant impunita: Zur Entstehung des öffentlichen Strafanspruchs in der Rechtswissenschaft des 12. Jahrhunderts', Einfluss der Kanonistik 3:23–35; Pennington, 'Jurisprudence of Procedure' 141–142.

65. On Durantis see Pennington, 'Jurisprudence of Procedure' 139, 147, 148, 151–153, and Jean Gaudemet, 'Durand (Durant, Durante), Guillaume (Guglielmo), Detto Lo Speculatore', DBI 42 (1993) 82–87.

ture of Durantis's work suggests that this drive for clear rules may have changed by the late thirteenth century. Whereas Tancred is crisp and to the point, Durantis is prolix. His work is a compilation of various procedural works with remarkable inconsistencies. Perhaps, however, by the end of the thirteenth century this was what the lawyers needed. They knew the basics. What they wanted was support for arguments when they wanted to get around the basics.[66]

The Impact of Romano-Canonical Procedure

As has been suggested,[67] the creation of Romano-canonical procedure was a precondition for the abolition of the ordeal. It had never been common in the ecclesiastical courts, and after 1215 it disappeared from them virtually without a trace. This disappearance does not mean that all cases were decided on the basis of the testimony of witnesses. The use of compurgation remained very common, even in the ecclesiastical courts.[68] The ordeal also disappeared in the secular courts, even where Romano-canonical procedure was not adopted or not fully adopted. In the secular courts in England, the ordeal disappeared shortly after 1215, replaced by the petty jury in criminal cases, though trial by battle remained a possibility in some criminal cases and in certain types of civil cases. The ordeal also disappeared in France, though it took somewhat longer to happen. Louis IX of France, who died in 1270, promulgated an ordinance, in which he seems to have attempted to abolish trial by battle in the royal domain and replace it with proof by witnesses.[69] By this time the ordeal was probably not being used generally in France. A recent attempt to argue that the ordeal was very long in dying out in Europe is flawed, at least in my view, by the fact that it attempts to count the number of ordeals recorded in the thirteenth and early fourteenth centuries.[70] The statistics are skewed by the fact that we have records from a large number of cases from Hungary in the early fourteenth century, where the ordeal was still being used. Hungary in this period was pretty far out of the main stream.[71]

The development of Romano-canonical procedure is important for

66. I owe this argument to Richard Fraher in a private conversation many years ago.

67. See 87.

68. See Antonia Fiori, *Il giuramento di innocenza nel processo canonico medievale: Storia e disciplina della 'purgatio canonica'* (Studien zur europäische Rechtsgeschichte 277; Frankurt am Main 2013).

69. *Ordonnances des rois de France de la troisième race...* (Paris 1723) 1.86–93. The editor, who seems for this volume to have been Eusèbe Laurière, dates the ordinance to 1260, but the evidence that he presents for this dating is not particularly powerful.

70. Bartlett, *Trial by Fire and Water.*

71. For this collection of case records, the so-called *Registrum Varadinense,* see Erdő, 'Eastern Central Europe' 432–433.

more reasons than that it was a precondition or harbinger of the abolition of the ordeal. I would suggest at least three more reasons for its importance: First, those who were attempting in this period to apply the law as they understood it to specific cases realized that they had to have a procedural system in which to do it. It is not by chance that the pressure to develop this system came first from the papacy, because the papacy was the first institution in this period to move in the direction of law-application in individual cases. Second, because the testimony of the witnesses is part of the record of the case in Romano-canonical procedure, it became possible to develop law tailored to specific facts. An exchange of present consent, for example, between a man and a woman capable of marriage makes a valid marriage. That rule could have been developed without knowing the facts of individual cases. Once they did see the facts of individual cases, however, the canonists were able to consider at some length just what constituted present consent. Third, Romano-canonical procedure was basically an integrated system of procedure. It was not quite one-size-fits all. There were, for example, some important differences between criminal procedure and civil, including a higher standard proof in the former. But the similarities between Romano-canonical civil procedure and Romano-canonical criminal procedure are far greater than the differences.

This integrated character of Romano-canonical procedure had the tendency to separate procedure from substance. Romano-canonical procedure could be thought of as a unitary body of law separated from substance. This made it possible for it to be adapted by courts that were not following either substantive Roman law or substantive canon law. We can already see this happening in Beaumanoir's treatise on law of the Beauvaisis written in the latter part of the thirteenth century. The adoption of Romano-canonical procedure in Beaumanoir is far from complete but its influence is unmistakable.[72] In the seventeenth century Jean-Baptiste Colbert was able to promulgate a comprehensive ordinance on civil procedure and insist that it be applied in all the courts of the kingdom of France without regard to the substantive rules that they were following.[73]

One does not have to be an unreconstructed realist to realize that the adoption of Romano-canonical procedure, or any new procedural system, by a court is going to have a substantive effect. It will become possible to think about questions that were previously hidden from view, as in

72. For example, Philippe de Beaumanoir, *Coutumes de Beauvaisis,* ed. Amédée Salmon (2 vols. Paris 1900, reprinted Paris 1970) c. 39, §§ 1170–1223.

73. Ordonnance du Roi pour la procédure civile (1667), in *Recueil des grandes ordonnances, édits et déclarations des rois de France* (Toulouse 1786) 428–90.

the case of my example about words used to express present consent to marry. It may also suppress the consideration of questions that previously could be asked. If the defendant in a land action is no longer allowed to assert his right by waging battle, then he had better have witnesses or a written instrument. If he does not, then he has no right in the realistic sense. These changes in substance will not, however, be immediately seen. The law-giver can claim that no substantive change is implied by a change in the procedural system.

The Acceptance of Romano-Canonical Procedure in Secular Courts

What happened, as a general matter, on the Continent with regard to the adoption of Romano-canonical procedure did not happen in England, probably for the reason suggested by Raul van Caenegem some time ago. By the time that Romano-canonical procedure had developed to the point where it could be adopted by courts that were not already committed to it—probably early in the thirteenth century—England already had a central royal court with its own procedures.[74] We can argue how much that was already happening in the realm of Romano-canonical procedure influenced the precocious development of the English central royal court. The late John Barton suggested that the author of *Glanvill* had the early 'ordines iudiciarii' in mind when he structured a large part of the treatise on the course of an action on a writ of right.[75] Be that as it may be, what the central royal courts ended up with was quite different from Romano-canonical procedure. In marked contrast to the unitary nature of Romano-canonical procedure, English procedure varied depending on the type of action that was brought. Also, in marked contrast to Romano-canonical procedure, England employed a largely inscrutable decision-maker at the proof stage, normally some form of jury or oath-helper.

It is generally thought that there was more acceptance of Romano-canonical procedure by the secular courts on the Continent than there was in England. We have already mentioned that there are clear indications of its influence in Beaumanoir's *Coutumes de Beauvaisis*. We are hampered, however, in pursuit of an answer to this question by the spotty survival of secular court records on the Continent even as late as the late thirteenth century.

There are some hints of such a development in *Usatges de Barcelona*. The *Usatges* purports to have been promulgated by the count of Barcelona,

---

74. Raul C. van Caenegem, *The Birth of the English Common Law* (2nd ed. Cambridge 1988).
75. John L. Barton, *Roman Law in England* (IRMÆ 5.13a; Milano 1971) 9–10.

Raymond Berenger I and his wife Almodis, and a twelfth-century chronicle gives the date as 1068. Most scholars now believe that earliest portions of the version that we have date from the middle of the twelfth century, though older elements may be incorporated in it, and that there are many additions that are later than the mid-twelfth century.[76] The work begins:[77]

1. [1] Before the *Usatges* were issued, so that all misdeeds might always be emended if they could not be ignored, the judges used to judge by oath, or by battle, or by cold or hot water, by saying thus: 'I (name) swear to you (name) by Jesus God and these four holy gospels that the evil that I have done to you I have done by my right and your wrong ['a mon dret et a ton tort']; and I would stand to battle about this or to one of the above-said judgments, of cold or hot water'.

The implication that could be drawn from this text—that judges pronounce this oath—is probably not what was intended. This is almost certainly a traditional form of the defendant's oath. The parallels, even the linguistic parallels, to counts or defenses from as far away as French-speaking England are striking.[78] What concerns us here is the inference that our mid-twelfth-century author seems to want us to draw: that the *Usatges* did away with 'oath, battle, and hot or cold water'. They did not. Chapter 112 [88] tells us that if a husband accuses his wife of adultery she is to purge herself by a champion by oath and by battle, and the wife of a peasant by her own hand in the cauldron.[79] But our mid-twelfth-century author seems to want us to believe that these forms of proof were on the way out and that the abolition of such forms of proof was desirable. Such views are quite common in this period, particularly among clerics

The provisions about witnesses in the *Usatges* suggest a gradual acceptance of the Romano-canonical scheme. The beginning is clearly in c.57

76. The earliest manuscript dates from the late thirteenth century. In the early fifteenth century an 'official' version of the *Usatges* was adopted. The work exists in both Catalan and Latin versions, of which the Latin seems to be the older. The translations in what follows are mine, based on the Latin (and as much of the Catalan as I can handle) from the edition of Ramón D'Abadal i Vanyals and Ferràn Valls Taberner, *Usatges de Barcelona* (Textes de Dret Català 1; Barcelona 1913). A more recent edition by Joan Bastardas, *Usatges de Barcelona: El Codi a mitjan segle XII* (Barcelona 1984), does not differ greatly in the substance of the items quoted, though it uses a somewhat different numbering system, which is given in square brackets. The full translation of Bastardas's text by Donald Kagay, *The Usatges of Barcelona: The Fundamental Law of Catalonia* (Philadelphia 1994), should be used with caution.

77. *Usatges* 1: 'Antequam usatici fuissent missi soleba[n]t judices judicare ut cuncta malefacta fuissent omni tempore emendata, si non potuerint esse neglecta, per sacramentum, vel per batalliam, vel per aquam frigidam sive calidam, ita dicendo: Juro ego talis tibi tali quod hec malefacta, que tibi habeo facta, sic ea tibi feci ad meum directum et in tuo neglecto, quod ego tibi illa emendar[e] non debeo, per Deum Ihesum et hec sancta quatuor evangelia; et inde stetissem ad bellum vel ad unum ex supra dictis judici[i]s, scilicet aque frigide vel calide'.

78. See *Brevia Placitata*, ed. George J. Turner and Theodore F. T. Plucknett (Selden Society 66; London 1947).

79. *Usatges* 50.

[54] where witnesses are being used instead of battle in disputes about land in which the tenant, it would seem, is not in possession:[80]

57 [54]. Fees which knights hold, if their lords deny that they have given them to them, they shall aver them by oath and by battle and shall have them. Those which they do not hold but[81] claim, they shall either prove by witnesses or by writing that they acquired them from their lords, or they shall abandon them.

Even here we must be careful. Witness procedure is mentioned in the Visigothic Code, and Catalan documents earlier than the mid-twelfth century mention them. What is interesting about this provision is that witnesses or writing seem to be the only method of proof available in the situation where the tenant is not in possession. (If he is, he may wage battle.) This provision is the only one about witnesses that the most recent editor includes in his edition of the base (mid–twelfth-century) text.

Chapters 85 through 89 [B2–B6] suggest a further development. They state, among other things, the following rules: 'Witnesses… shall be separated from each other and examined singly (c. 85).'[82] 'Faith shall be placed on more honest rather than more vile witnesses. The testimony of one, however splendid and suitable a person he might seem, shall never be heard (c. 86)'.[83] 'Two or three suitable witnesses suffice to prove all matters. The testimony of one is disapproved by the laws and the canons (c. 87)'.[84] 'No one shall ever presume to be at once accuser, judge and witness, since in every judgment it is necessary that four persons be present, i.e., a chosen judge, suitable accusers, appropriate defenders, and legitimate witnesses (c. 88)'.[85] 'An unoffended affect ['inoffensus effectus'] is to be sought in accusers and witnesses, not a suspect one (c. 89)'.[86]

The substance of chapters 85 through 88 can be found in eleventh-

---

80. *Usatges* 22: 'Feuos quos tenuerint milites, si seniores eorum negaverint non eos illis dedisse, averent per sacramentum et per batalliam et habeant illos. Illos autem quos non tenuerint et exclamaverint, aut probent per testes, vel per scripturas, eos a senioribus eorum adquisivisse, aut dimittant eos'.

81. The 'et' in the original must be taken in an adversative sense in order for the passage to make sense.

82. *Usatges* 88: 'Precipimus ut perjuria caveantur, nec admittantur testes ad juramentum antequam discuciantur; et si aliter discuti non possunt, separentur ad invicem, et singulariter inquirantur'.

83. Ibid.89: 'Hoc etiam jubemus ut honestioribus magis quam vilioribus testibus [rectius: honestiores magis quam viliores testes] ad fidem pocius admittantur; unius autem testimonium, quamvis splendida et idonea videatur esse persona, nullatenus audiendum'.

84. Ibid.: 'Duo vel tres ydeonei testes ad omnia negocia probanda sufficiunt. Unius testimonium legibus et canonibus improbatur'.

85. Ibid.: 'Nullus unquam presumat accusator simul esse et judex et testis, quoniam in omni judicio quatuor personas necesse sunt semper·adesse; id est judex electus, accusatores idonei, defensores congrui, atque testes legitimi'.

86. Ibid.: '[I]noffensus ergo accusatorum et testium effectus querendus est, non suspectus'.

century canonical collections, and they are largely drawn from Pseudo-Isidore.[87] Chapter 89 probably requires a more profound knowledge of Roman law, though it could be by way of proceduralists like Tancred. It is possible that these provisions date from the mid-twelfth century, but it seems unlikely, both because they are not in all the early manuscripts and because the effort that would have been necessary to put them together from existing sources in the mid-twelfth century is probably beyond what the people who were putting this material together were capable of. I think that they probably date from the thirteenth century, though not necessarily very far into that century.

Chapters 143 through 144,[88] which deal with perjury and frivolous appeals, respectively, are interesting because they are so clearly legislative. In order to follow the form of legislation used here, one probably needs to have either Justinian's Code or papal decretal letters or both. The concern with the corruption and falsity of witnesses in chapter 143 is, at least to me, some indication of thirteenth-century origins. 'The slipperiness of witnesses' ['testium facilitate'], a phrase the occurs in this chapter, is the incipit of a well-known thirteenth-century treatise on witnesses,[89] though the phrase also occurs in the Digest. Chapter 144 reminds one of the increasing efforts of the papacy from the time of Alexander III onwards, but particularly in the pontificate of Innocent IV, to limit frivolous appeals. When this evidence of later origin is combined with the fact that these texts are in none of the early manuscripts, we pretty clearly have reached another stage of development.

With care and some guesswork, it is possible to construct stages of the reception of at least the formal law of Romano-canonical procedure in Barcelona. To what extent this reception was reflected in the courts is a question that might be answered (the Aragonese archives are rich), but no one seems to have done the work yet.

The Acceptance of Romano-Canonical Procedure in the Ecclesiastical Courts

Beginnings

If the acceptance of Romano-canonical procedure in the secular courts on the Continent seems, on the basis of the knowledge that we have, to

---

87. Charles Poumarède, 'Les Usages de Barcelone' (thèse; Toulouse 1920), suggests parallels for all the provisions in the *Usatges*.

88. Bastardas omits these chapters because they are not in his early manuscripts.

89. Discussed below, text at 112–114.

have been a fairly gradual process, we can be more certain that its adoption by the ecclesiastical courts was more rapid and more complete.[90]

We must, however, be careful about the term 'ecclesiastical court'. As will be argued in later chapters, there were no 'ecclesiastical courts', as we understand the term 'court', until the mid-thirteenth century. From the mid-twelfth century onwards, however, there were plenty of ecclesiastical proceedings, sometimes conducted by a bishop or a lesser ecclesiastical official, sometimes by the delegates of these persons, sometimes by delegates of the pope.

The chance deposit at Canterbury of some ninety documents relating to church court cases from the last years of Archbishop Hubert Walter's pontificate († July 13, 1205) allows us to see something of the process of adoption of Romano-canonical procedure before the publication of Tancred's *Ordo* and before the Fourth Lateran Council. These documents are important because most of them do not concern papal delegations, but they confirm what the studies of papal delegations show, that the ecclesiastical courts, at least at the higher level, were well on their way to becoming courts of Romano-canonical procedure by the year 1200.

Most of these documents are correspondence: letters from Walter to commissioners to hear all or part of a case, letters from commissioners to Walter, and letters from parties (including early forms of proxies) also addressed to the archbishop.[91] There are some twenty-two sets of depositions among these documents, two sets of pleadings (three documents in all—they are not quite formal enough to call them 'libelli'), and four compositions or arbitration awards.[92] These documents together constitute the earliest records of an English church court (as opposed to records of ecclesiastical litigation preserved by a party to the case, normally in a cartulary). Indeed, they may be the earliest such records which have survived anywhere, for English church court records, like English secular court records, are notable for their antiquity and fullness.

The procedure of the 'curia Cantuariensis' in Hubert Walter's time was not as formal as that of the later Court of Canterbury, but the documents, despite their informal and relatively undifferentiated character, show that proceedings were already following the basic steps outlined in the 'ordines'.

---

90. See further Pennington, 'Jurisprudence of Procedure' 134–137; for the acceptance of the 'ordo iudiciarius' in the courts north of the Alps, see Othmar Hageneder, *Die Geistliche Gerichtsbarkeit in Ober- und Niederösterreich von den Anfängen bis zum Beginn des 15. Jahrhunderts* (Forschungen zur Geschichte Oberösterrerichs 10; Graz 1967) chapters 1–4.

91. These are calendared in Adams and Donahue, *Canterbury Cases*, App. I, pp. *104–114*. The following paragraphs are derived from the introduction to that book, *10–12*.

92. Depositions: ibid., App. I, nos. 4, 40, 47–48, 51–55, 71–88; pleadings: nos. 22, 65–66; compositions or arbitration awards: nos. 56, 62, 67, 69.

Particularly revealing are the accounts by delegates of the steps they have taken in a case and the accounts given in commissions to delegates of the steps already taken. For example, papal judges delegate, seeking the aid of the archbishop in executing their sentence, recite their commission from Innocent III to hear the case and then describe the proceedings held before them as follows:[93]

By the authority of this mandate [of Innocent III], therefore, the parties having been constituted before us and issue at length having been joined on a peremptory day, we admitted witnesses. And when each party had enjoyed a three-fold production and a fourth production had been granted to the defendant with the solemnity of law, the attestations of the same witnesses were lawfully published. And when there had been a dispute about the same witnesses and [their] testimony for many days, it was plainly apparent to us from the proof and assertion of the witnesses produced on both sides that the claim of the aforesaid [plaintiff] had been proven. We, moreover, by the apostolic authority which we were exercising, having heard the merits of the case on each side, having observed the solemnity of the law in all things, adjudged the possession of the tithes and of the entire parochial right in the fee of Robert de Weston to the aforesaid [plaintiff] and his church of Portisham, two sheaves from the demesne excepted.

Similar stages of proceeding were being followed in cases that had no reference to the papal curia. For example, a commission by the archbishop to the priors of Sherborne and Andover describes the procedure before the archbishop as follows:[94]

When a case of bastardy, which was pending between... on the one side, and... on the other, was brought by appeal from the audience of the bishop of Winchester to us, the parties constituted before us, it was proposed on behalf of [the plaintiff] that .... The opposing party replied, on the other hand .... Issue having been joined in this manner... we think fit to be examined by you and before you the witnesses which either party shall cause to be produced. Wherefore we command... that having called the parties together, you admit [the witnesses] and examine them sworn... on all the annexed articles. Having examined them, sign what the witnesses say faithfully with your seals and transmit it to us on... setting the same day for the parties by peremptory edict, on which [day] they should appear before us to receive what the reason of law might require.

93. Canterbury, Cathedral Archives, Ch. Ant. P46; Adams and Donahue, *Canterbury Cases,* App. I, no. 64: 'Huius ergo auctoritate mandati, partibus coram nobis constitutis, die demum peremptorio lite contestata, testes admissimus. Cumque pars utraque trina esset productione gavisa, quarta etiam productione reo indulta cum iuris solempnitate, attestaciones eorundem testium legittime fuerunt puplicate. Cumque super eisdem testibus et testificatis per plures dies esset disputatum, tandem nobis ex probacione et assercione testium ex utraque parte productorum liquido constitit super intencione predicti H. probata. Nos autem auctoritate apostolica qua fungimur, auditis meritis cause utriusque partis, iuris solempnitate in omnibus observata, predicto H. et ecclesie sue de Portech' possessionem decimarum et tocius iuris parochialis de feodo Roberti de Weston, exceptis duabus garbis de dominico, adiudicavimus'.

94. Ibid. no. A.1, p. 1.

Here we have not only the steps of the case (claim, answer, and joinder of issue; admission, swearing, and examination of witnesses; publication of the written testimony, dispute, and sentence), but the very terms which are used in the 'ordines' and the later court acta ('causa que vertitur'; 'ex parte una', 'ex altera'; 'constitutis coram nobis partibus'; 'in iure fuit propositum'; 'lite contestata'; 'testes quos uterque duxerit producendos'; 'admittatis et iuratos super omnibus annexis articulis examinetis'; 'dicta testium'; 'diem partibus edicto peremptorio prefigentes quo coram nobis compareant quod iuris racio exigerit recapture').

But the fact is that we do not have any court acta, and although there is at least one reference to a 'processus', no processus has yet come to light.[95] Further, the form of the documents is primitive when compared with the sophisticated and highly differentiated types of documents which survive from the latter part of the thirteenth century.[96] The surviving proxies contain no recitation of the powers of the proctor; indeed they are only beginning to be differentiated from a simple letter in which the writer excuses himself from appearing on a given court day.[97] The depositions are terse, at times to the point of obscurity.[98] Of the three pleadings which have come to light, one is a list of 'gravamina', the second a rhetorical outburst more suitable for a chronicle than a court of law, while the third, ascribed to Peter of Blois, begins to show the style that characterizes the later pleadings.[99] No articles have come to light; we have not found even a mention of interrogatories, and the sentences which we have found show nothing of the form of later sentences, perhaps because they all seem to be the result of arbitration proceedings or compromises.[100]

In Hubert Walter's time, in addition to the proof by witnesses and written instruments authorized in the academic writing, we find traces of older or different methods.[101] For example, the petition of Peter of Blois, which, as we noted above, is quite advanced in form, asks not that he be

---

95. Ibid. App. I, no. 5. The first surviving 'processus' (summary of the steps taken in the case and the relevant documents at each stage) of which I am aware is in a judgment of Stephen Langton (29 November, 1223). *Acta Stephani Langton*, ed. Kathleen Major (Canterbury and York Society 50; Oxford 1950) no. 61, pp. 78–83. For a 'processus' transmitted from a lower court to a higher upon appeal, we have to wait until the 1270 vacancy in the see of Canterbury. For example, Adams and Donahue, *Canterbury Cases* C.1, C.2, C.6.

96. See Adams and Donahue, *Canterbury Cases* 37–72.

97. For example, ibid. App. I, nos. 17, 31, 33–36.

98. For example, ibid. no. A.3 (on the question what are 'spiritualia'), no. A.6 (on the nature of the underlying dispute).

99. Ibid. pp. 47–48 (no. A.15); pp. 41–46; App. I, no. 22.

100. Ibid. App. I, nos. 56, 62, 67, 69. The same tendency to arbitration or compromise forms can be noted in Langton's surviving acta. For example, *Acta Langton*, nos. 20, 26, 32, 33, 42–43, 76, 82, 125, pp. 27–28, 32–33, 43–44, 56–60, 95–96, 101–102, 140–41.

101. See Donahue, 'Proof by Witnesses'.

admitted to prove his case by witnesses but that an inquisition be made by twelve of the 'more lawful parishioners of the church by their oath' ('per legaliores parochianos ecclesie per iuramentum eorum') to determine his rights.[102]

It would seem, then, that the reception of Romano-canonical procedure was not quite complete in Hubert Walter's time and that the capacity of Hubert Walter's court and of the parties and their advisers who were appearing before it to express in writing the procedure that they were employing had not quite kept up with advances in the procedure itself. The requirement laid down by the Fourth Lateran Council that written records be kept of all ecclesiastical court proceedings must have contributed to greater sophistication in written records, but the council did not meet until ten years after Walter's death.[103]

In attempting a general conclusion about these records in 1978, Norma Adams and I wrote:[104]

[T]he lack of sophistication of the records of Walter's time casts some doubt on our conclusion that the procedure the courts were employing was already well-advanced along Romano-canonical lines; any definitive assessment must await further work with this remarkable group of documents. We offer the view, however, at least as a tentative hypothesis, that despite the simplicity of its machinery and the relatively crude nature of its documents, the jurisdiction and procedure of the *curia Cantuariensis* of Hubert Walter's time was well on the way to becoming that of the Court of Canterbury of the 1270s.

Despite the publication of all the Canterbury episcopal acta and those of many of the other English dioceses, the work that we called for in 1978 still has not been done. Professor Adams is no longer with us, but looking back on what we said in 1978, and until that further work is done, I would probably emphasize more than we did then the experimental nature of what was happening around 1200, for example, the quite gradual separation of witnesses from jurors. I would probably also emphasize more than we did the importance of the development of professionalized courts in mid-century as the catalyst for locking in the Romano-canonical form of procedure. I see no reason, however, to alter the basic conclusion.

---

102. Adams and Donahue, *Canterbury Cases* App. I, no. 22. For a German case (X 4.1.3, referenced in Hageneder, *Gerichtsbarkeit* 15–16, and nn. 45–46) in which Innocent III disapproves of a custom in which 'litterati et illitterati, sapientes et insipientes' render sentence, see Pennington, 'Due Process, Community, and the Prince in the Evolution of the Ordo iudiciarius', RIDC 9 (1998) 9–47 at 16 n. 25.

103. Lateran IV (1215), c. 38 (= X 2.19.11), in COD 185.

104. Adams and Donahue, *Canterbury Cases* p. 12.

The Later Thirteenth Century

The next extensive group of English church court records are also Canterbury records; they date from the vacancy of the archiepiscopal see between the death of Boniface of Savoy in July 1270 and the consecration of Robert Kilwardby in February 1273. These records are also quite early as records of church courts go. Most English and Continental medieval church court records date from the fourteenth or fifteenth centuries. Professor Adams and I published a selection of these records in *Select Canterbury Cases* and devoted a considerable part of the introduction to outlining the procedure that they revealed.[105] There is no question that the procedure is Romano-canonical. Most of its elements can be tracked in the 'ordines'. There are a few local variations, such as tuitorial appeals (appeals to the court of Rome and for the 'protection' of the Court of Canterbury), that are quite compatible with the procedure outlined in the 'ordines'.

For a full account of this procedure, I must refer the reader to *Select Canterbury Cases*.[106] We can, however, get a taste of this procedure by looking at the processus in a relatively straightforward marriage case that was appealed to the Court of Canterbury from the official of the bishop of Salisbury. The record quoted below is that of the Salisbury proceedings:[107]

A.D. 1271, Friday after the feast of the translation of St. Thomas, martyr [July 10], Alice of Winterbourne Stoke appeared against William Smith saying against him that he contracted marriage with her, wherefore she asked that he be adjudged her husband by sentence; she says this, etc. [not committing herself to proving each and every element in her libel but insofar as she proves so far may she obtain].

Winterbourne Stoke is about eleven miles northwest of Salisbury. For the last two centuries it has had a population of about two hundred, and is unlikely to have been larger in the thirteenth century, and was probably smaller. Salisbury, on the other hand, had, and still has, one of the most impressive of England's Gothic cathedrals, and it is here that the court sat. By 1271, the bishop of Salisbury had a regularly sitting consistory court. That court's jurisdiction over matters concerning the formation of marriage was not contested, nor was its jurisdiction over the parties. The record does not mention that Alice had a lawyer, and it almost certainly

---

105. Ibid. 37–72; 49–337.

106. There is a compressed version in Donahue, 'Ecclesiastical Courts' 276–283.

107. Adams and Donahue, *Canterbury Cases*, no. C.6, p. 128: 'Anno domini M CC lxx primo, die veneris proximo post festum translacionis Sancti Thome martiris conparuit Alicia de Wynterburn' Stok' contra Willelmum Fabrum dicens contra eundem quod contraxit cum ea matrimonium, quare petit ipsum in virum sibi sentencialiter adiudicari, hoc dicit, etc.'.

would have if one had appeared for her. She may have gotten more informal advice from a lawyer as to how to formulate her libel, or the clerk
may have helped her because it is totally standard in form, including the
'etc.', which I have filled in from other records. The processus continues:[108]

The man, joining issue, denies the contract; the parties sworn to tell the truth say
the same thing as before. The reception and examination of witnesses is committed to the dean of Amesbury.

William denied the charge, in what we are expressly told was a *litis contestatio.* The parties take the oath *de veritate dicenda* (the oath *de calumpnia*
is not mentioned), and swear to what they have just said. Alice was told
to produce her witnesses before the rural dean of Amesbury, a town a
couple of miles from Winterbourne Stoke:[109]

Thursday next after the feast of St. Peter in chains [July 30], the parties appeared
personally and the woman asked for a second production and got it. Wednesday
next after the feast of St. Matthew the apostle [September 23], the parties appeared personally; the woman renounced further production; the attestations
were published with the consent of the parties; the parties were given a copy; a
day was given for sentencing if it was clear. The woman constituted her brother
Roger her proctor in the acts to hear the definitive sentence.

Alice could have gotten three terms to produce her witnesses as a matter of right, but she only took two. In late September, after the summer
recess, the depositions of what we later learn were three witnesses were
published in open court:[110]

Monday next after the feast of the apostles Simon and Jude [October 26], the parties appeared personally; the man under interrogation confessed in court that he
had carnal knowledge of the said Alice a half a year ago. The same man proposed

108. Ibid.: 'Vir litem contestando negat contractum; partes iurate de veritate dicenda idem
dicunt quod prius. Commissa est recepcio testium et eorundem examinacio .. decano de Ambr'.'
109. Ibid. 128–29: 'Die iovis proximo ante festum beati Petri quod dicitur "ad vincula" comparuerunt partes personaliter et mulier peciit secundam produccionem et optinuit. Die mercurii
proximo post festum Sancti Mathei apostoli conparuerunt partes personaliter; mulier renunciavit
ulteriori produccioni; publicatis attestacionibus de consensu parcium, oblata partibus copia, datus est dies ad sentenciandum si liqueat; mulier constituit Rogerum fratrem suum procuratorem
suum apud acta ad audiendam sentenciam diffinitivam'.
110. Ibid. 129: 'Die lune proximo ante festum apostolorum Symonis et Jude comparuerunt
partes personaliter; vir interrogatus confessus est in iudicio se cognovisse dictam Aliciam car-
naliter infra dimidium annum retro. Idem vir excepcionem proposuit in forma subscripta. "Coram vobis, domine iudex, ego Willelmus de Wynterburn Stok' peremptorie excipiendo propono
contra testes Alicie Dolling quod falsum deponunt ex eo quod ab hora nona diei quo testes sui
deponunt se contraxisse matrimonium cum eadem usque ad horam primam diei subsequentis
steti apud Bulteford continue, ita quod inpossibile esset quod secum eadem hora de qua testes sui
deponunt apud Wynterburn'[? Place-name, as before] contraxisse matrimonium, quod me offero
probaturum". Commissa est recepcio testium et eorundem examinacio ex parte viri super sua
excepcione producendorum .. decano de Ambr'.'

an exception in the following form: 'Before you, sir judge, I, William of Winterbourne Stoke, peremptorily excepting propose against the witnesses of Alice Dolling that they depose falsely because from the ninth hour of the day on which her witnesses depose that I contracted marriage with her until the first hour of the subsequent day I was continuously at Bulford, so that it would have been impossible for me at the hour about which the witnesses depose to have contracted marriage at Winterbourne Stoke. And this I offer to prove'. The reception of the witnesses produced by the man on his exception and their examination is committed to the dean of Amesbury.

The 'ex officio' interrogation of the defendant is not a required part of the procedure, but it seems to have been authorized by it. In October, William confessed that he had had intercourse with Alice but denied that they had contracted marriage, claiming that he had been in another town on what we learn from the depositions was St. Stephen's day [December 26], almost three years previously, the day on which Alice's witnesses testified that she and William had exchanged words of marital consent. The dean of Amesbury was to examine William's witnesses. The form of William's exception is standard. Once more, no lawyer is mentioned, but it is inconceivable that he did not get legal advice on how to formulate it:[111]

Wednesday next before the feast of St. Edmund, king and martyr [October 28, two days later], the parties appeared personally; the woman made a replication of presence; let the woman produce her witnesses before the rectors of Berwick and Orcheston [towns quite near to Winterbourne Stoke], however many she wishes to produce before the next consistory; let the man also produce however many witnesses he wishes to produce about his absence before the said dean and the chaplain of Amesbury before the next consistory. Tuesday after the feast of St. Lucy the virgin [December 15, 1271, there may be an intervening entry missing here], the parties appeared personally; the woman excepting proposed that it was not her fault that her witnesses had not been examined and asked that they be admitted in court; they were sworn, their examination committed to the dean of Amesbury and Richard de Rodbourne, and the way of further production precluded for her. On the same day the attestations both of absence and presence were published with the consent of the parties [the dean and Richard were apparently in Salisbury that day]; copies of the attestations were offered to and obtained by the parties, and a day was given for doing what law shall dictate.

111. Ibid.: 'Die mercurii proximo ante festum Sancti Eadmundi regis et martiris conparuerunt partes personaliter; mulier replicavit de presencia; producat mulier testes suos coram rectoribus de Berwyk' et de Orcheston' quot quod voluerit producere citra proximum consistorium; producat eciam vir testes suos super sua absencia coram dicto decano et capellano de Ambr' citra proximum consistorium quot quod intendit producere. Die martis proximo post festum Sancte Lucie virginis comparuerunt partes personaliter; mulier excipiendo proposuit per ipsam non stetisse quo minus testes sui fuerunt examinati et peciit ipsos in iudicio admitti; quibus iuratis, statim fuit commissa examinacio eorundem .. decano de Ambr' et Ricardo de Rokeburn' et preclusa est ei via ulterius producendi; eodem die publicate fuerunt attestaciones tam super absencia quam presencia de consensu parcium; oblata partibus copia eorum attestacionum et optenta, datus est dies ad faciendum quod ius dictabit'.

We learn from the depositions that William's ten witnesses testified that he had been in Bulford all day on St. Stephen's day in 1268, and Alice's four witnesses testified that they had seen William in Winterbourne Stoke that day:[112]

Wednesday next after the octave of St. Hilary [January 27, 1271/72], the parties appeared personally, and when there had been some dispute among the parties about the attestations of the parties, a day was given for sentencing if it was clear. The day after St. Scholastica the virgin [February 11, 1271/2] the parties appeared personally. It was decreed that the aforesaid W. produce in the next consistory all his witnesses whom he had previously produced on his exception so that it might be inquired more fully about the continuity of absence . . . . Tuesday after the feast of St. Mathias the apostle, continued until Wednesday, Thursday, Friday, Saturday next following [March 1–5, 1271–1272], the parties appeared personally. The same man alleged that he could not produce his witnesses before us because some of them did not exist in the nature of things and some of them had left the province for a pilgrimage and for other necessary cause. And when the parties had disputed for a while about the processus, the same William demanded that a copy of the entire processus be made for him [this may have been preparatory to the appeal that William eventually took], which decreed and obtained, a day was given for doing what law shall dictate in the next consistory after Easter.[113]

After William's depositions had been published, the official asked him to produce his witnesses again, but he said that he could not, citing what seem to be formulaic excuses:

Wednesday after 'Misericordia' Sunday [May 11], A.D. 1272, the parties appeared personally and concluding the case asked that sentence be given. We the official of Salisbury proceeded to definitive sentence in this way: 'In the name of the Father, amen. We the official of Salisbury having examined the merits of the aforesaid cause and having gone over the acts of court carefully, because we find the

112. Ibid. 129, 132: 'Die mercurii proximo post octabas Sancti Hyllarii conparuerunt partes personaliter et cum aliquantulum super attestacionibus parcium inter partes esset disputatum, datus est dies ad sentenciandum si liqueat. In crastino Sancte Scolastice virginis conparuerunt partes personaliter. Decretum est quod predictus W. producat omnes testes suos quos prius produxerat super sua excepcione in proximo consistorio ut super continuitate absencie plenius requiri possint. . . . Die martis proximo post festum Sancti Mathie apostoli usque ad diem mercurii, iovis, veneris, sabbati proximo sequentem continuata conparuerunt partes personaliter. Idem vir allegavit se testes suos coram nobis producere non posse quia quidam illorum in rerum natura non existunt et quidam illorum causa peregrinacionis et ob aliam causam necessariam a provincia recesserunt. Et cum super processu aliquantulum inter partes esset disputatum idem Willelmus copiam tocius processus instanter sibi fieri postulavit, qua decreta et optenta, datus est dies ad faciendum quod ius dictabit in proximo consistorio post pascha'.

113. Ibid. 132: 'Die mercurii proximo post dominicam qua cantatur "Misericordia Domini", anno gracie M CC lxx secundo, conparuerunt partes personaliter et concludentes in causa sentenciam instanter ferri postulantes unde nos officialis Sarr' ad sentenciam diffinitivam processimus in hunc modum: "In nomine patris amen. Nos officialis Sarr' examinatis cause meritis predicte et actis tocius iudicii cum diligentia recensitis, quia intencionem dicte Alicie sufficienter probatam comperimus, non obstante excepcione ex parte ipsius Willelmi proposita, que in sua forma non probatur liquide, ut oportet, ipsum Willelmum eidem Alicie in virum legitimum sentencialiter et diffinitive adiudicamus"'.'

claim of the said Alice sufficiently proven, notwithstanding the exception proposed on the part of William, which is not proved clearly in its form, as it ought to be, adjudge William by sentence and definitively to be husband to the same Alice'.

Hence, in May 1272, the official rendered sentence for Alice declaring that William was her lawful husband.

This is the 'ordo iudiciarius' as Tancred defines it. It also seems to be quite efficient. The case was begun in July 1271; final judgment in the lower court was rendered in May 1272. The defendant, who lost in the original court, appealed, and the appellate court reversed the judgment of the Salisbury court in October 1272. Trial and appeal took a little more than a year. Many modern courts could not do as well as that.

The three sets of depositions are included in the record transmitted from the court of Salisbury,[114] and they are of some interest: Alice first produced three witnesses, all women. The first testified that on December 26 two years previously she was present in the house of one John le Ankere in Winterbourne Stoke at nightfall, in front of the bed that she and Alice shared. William and Alice were sitting, probably on a bench in front of the bed. He was dressed in a black tunic of Irish homespun with an overtunic and hood of russet; she was dressed in a white tunic with a blue hood and wore shoes with laces. William took her by the hand and said: 'I, William, will have thee, Alice, as wife so long as we both shall live and to this I pledge my troth'. Alice replied: 'And I, Alice, will have thee as husband and to this I pledge thee my troth'. Asked why William had come there, she said to have carnal knowledge of Alice if he could. Asked if she had ever seen them having intercourse, she said no, but she did see them lying together naked in the same bed. The second witness called herself the sister of the first, and basically agreed with the first's testimony, though she said that William's tunic, overtunic, and hood were all gray. She never saw them lying together. The third witness had a slightly different version of the words exchanged: William said: 'I, William, take thee, Alice, as my wife if holy church allow it, and to this I pledge thee my troth'. She said: 'I, Alice, will have thee as husband and will hold thee as husband'.

William's ten witnesses, all men, tell a different story. William was in Bulford, four miles away, on St. Stephen's day two years previously. They give a vivid description of an all-day ale-feast, held by the parish guild. William was serving at the feast and could not possibly have been in Winterbourne that day.

114. Ibid. 129–132.

Alice's four replication witnesses, all women, say that they saw William in Winterbourne that day, where he is described as leading around a crowd of women or going hand-in-hand with a woman.

What are we to make of all this?

In the first place, someone was clearly lying. William could not have been at Winterbourne exchanging consent with Alice and at Bulford attending an all-day guild feast at the same time. (Of course, it is logically possible that no one was telling the truth.) Second, two of Alice's witnesses on the principal case and one of her replication witnesses seem to have been related to her: they were probably her half-sisters. Third, the witnesses on the principal case are not completely clear about what words were exchanged: two of them seem to testify to 'verba de futuro', one of them to 'verba de presenti'—but the tense of the verbs should make no difference when intercourse is conceded. Fourth, the three sets of witnesses are not completely certain about their dates, though this may be the result of scribal error rather than any confusion on the witnesses' part.

None of the observations that I just made is new. In fact, they are all made in a remarkable document that survives from the case on appeal.[115] The judge of the provincial court of Canterbury asked the examiners of the court to look at the processus below and evaluate it for him. They committed their evaluation to parchment, and this evaluation has, by chance, survived. In the end the examiners suggest that there are too many inconsistencies in Alice's story, and, besides, ten witnesses are better than seven. The judge of the provincial court seems to have agreed; he reversed the official of Salisbury's decision. He, like the examiners, seems to have followed Tancred's advice about how to evaluate witnesses' testimony.

Other than the examiners' report, the record on appeal is less interesting. It is probably significant that Alice never appears in the proceedings at Canterbury. The court says that it made considerable effort to get her to come, but ultimately it renders its decision without her.

There are many such cases in the medieval records, and they raise three pretty obvious questions: First, how should such cases affect our understanding of the substantive law of marriage in the Middle Ages? Second, how did such cases affect the social institution of medieval marriage? Third, ultimately, was justice done? All three questions have been the subject of considerable discussion elsewhere.[116] Our concern here is

---

115. Ibid. 134–136.

116. See Charles Donahue Jr., *Law, Marriage, and Society in the Later Middle Ages* (New York 2007), with references to previous literature.

with how the procedure affects all three. To begin with an obvious point: the substantive law may be that parties capable of marriage (which these parties were) become married by exchanging words of present consent or exchanging words of future consent and following that consent with sexual intercourse. There was no solemnity requirement; the presence of witnesses was not part of the substantive law. But if one of the parties denied the charge, then the party claiming the marriage had to prove it, and in the absence of written documents (which are very rare in such cases), there had to be witnesses to the exchange of consent.

A more subtle point: William was able to mount a defense that ultimately proved to be successful because he knew the specifics of what it was that he had to rebut: that on December 26, 1268, he had exchanged words of marital consent with Alice. The temptation to suborn the perjured testimony of ten of his friends that he was in Bulford all that day must have been strong. That seems to have been what he did, and the official of Salisbury seems to have thought that he did so. That he could not produce the witnesses again at Salisbury because all of them had either died or gone on a pilgrimage seems quite incredible. The writers on procedure were well aware of the opportunity for perjury in this type of situation, and for this reason they devised a rule that once the testimony had been published, no one could produce further testimony on the same article.[117] That rule is why William's exception of absence is technically not an exception of absence; it is an exception that Alice's witnesses are perjurers. They perjured themselves when they said that he was in Winterbourne Stoke, because he was actually in Bulford.

In practice, exceptions of absence of this sort are allowed routinely. We can have some sympathy for the judges who allowed them. If William had to prove the negative, that at no time had he ever exchanged words of marital consent with Alice, such a proof would have been impossible. The structure of Romano-canonical procedure is that proof appears in stages, ever narrowing the issue until the key point is reached. Faced with a choice of giving the defendant an impossible burden to rebut and running the risk that he or she would suborn perjury, the courts chose the latter course.

Perhaps an even more subtle point: however much Tancred and the other writers of the 'ordines' wanted to limit the discretion of the judge, there was no way that they could eliminate it if the outcome of the case

---

117. See Adams and Donahue, *Canterbury Cases* 51–52; Donahue, 'Proof by Witnesses' 144. The topic deserves more treatment than it has received, so far as I am aware, in the literature. The basics with references are given in Maussen, *Veritatis adiutor* 56–65.

depended on the evaluation of witnesses' testimony. It seems fairly obvious that the official of Salisbury did not believe the testimony of William's witnesses, and thought that there was enough to what Alice's witnesses had said, particularly when William confessed that he had had intercourse with her, that he could render sentence for Alice. The appellate court, which did not have the benefit of hearing Alice, focused on the deficiencies in her witnesses' testimony. If we do not believe them, then it makes no difference whether William's witnesses were lying or not. The procedural rules may favor the conclusion that the appellate court reached, but they certainly do not dictate it. Both courts exercised discretion.

Procedure in the Period of the Post-Glossators

Treatises

The post-glossators on the topic of procedure generally are a bit of a puzzle. A considerable amount of material in the style of the commentators, though here by way of treatise rather than by way of commentary on ancient texts, was produced in the second half of the thirteenth century. Guillelmus Durantis's great *Speculum iudiciale* collected most of this material at the end of the century. Johannes Andreae wrote *additiones* to Durantis's text in the first half of the fourteenth century, and Baldus wrote some in the second half of that century.[118] These *additiones* ensured the survival of Durantis's work. The next major treatise on procedure was by Robertus Maranta, who says he completed his work around 1525.[119] Panormitanus had a considerable interest in procedure. His commentaries on the second book of the *Liber extra* are quite detailed.[120] But I think it is fair to say that writing about procedure was not a principal focus of those writing about law in the fourteenth and fifteenth centuries.

When we looked at Tancred on witnesses it seemed that the key issue was what types of witnesses were going to be excluded from testifying. This is also the key focus of Durantis's treatment of the topic. Maranta, though he cites a number of works on the topic of exclusion of certain kinds of witnesses, works that had been written closer to his time, devotes very little space to that topic. Though the evidence is certainly not all in, it would seem that between the early fourteenth century and

118. See Pennington, 'Jurisprudence of Procedure' 150.

119. Robertus Maranta, *Speculum aureum* (Venezia, 1574) 481; on the date, see Marco Nicola Miletti, 'Maranta, Roberto', DGI, 2.1269–71 at 1269b.

120. See Kenneth Pennington, 'Nicholaus de Tudeschis (Panormantus)', *Niccolò Tedeschi (Abbas Panormitanus) e i suoi Commentaria in Decretales,* ed. Orazio Condorelli (Libri di Erice 25; Rome 2000) 9–36. Whether he also wrote a *Practica,* an 'ordo iudiciarius' that appears in a number of the printed editions of his works, is a question that needs further exploration.

the early sixteenth century when Maranta wrote, the courts, in practice, ceased to follow the rules that even in Tancred's hands were rather rigid. The judges were, of course, well aware of the possibility of bias, bribery, and lying, but they wanted to listen to the testimony anyway and make up their own minds as to whether it should be believed. Let us turn to this problem more specifically.

There is a treatise in a number of manuscripts and early printed editions with the incipit 'Testium facilitate et varietate', of which Durantis made considerable use. Who wrote it? Jacobus Balduini, a student of the well-known Bolognese jurist Azo, who died in 1235? Bagarotus, who was roughly Jacobus's contemporary, a writer on procedural matters exclusively? Jacobus Aegidii de Viterbo, prior Ameliensis, who cannot be dated, but the second half of thirteenth-century is plausible, unless he is a contemporary of Bartolus as Diplovatatius, an early sixteenth-century humanist, seems to say? Bartolus? There are manuscripts that support each of these attributions.[121] All of them may, is some sense, be right. The most doubtful attribution is to Bartolus; much of the treatise has to have been in existence by the end of the thirteenth century, because Durantis used it. But Bartolus may have made some additions. Baldus's brother, Angelus de Ubaldis, wrote some additions that are so marked. We are dealing with a 'living text', a work that is the product of a number of authors. The summary that precedes the printed text reads:[122]

In the name of the lord Jesus Christ and his glorious virgin mother Mary, amen. Here begins the treatise of sir Bartolus de Sassoferrato for reproving witnesses, and in the first place are reproved, to wit, the infamous, slaves, rectors of churches, or a monk, abbot, etc., friars minor or preachers, and representatives of corporations [oeconomi], women, minors, madmen, paupers, infidels and excommunicates, domestics, those who do not swear, those in their own case, concerning the debtor, concerning the seller, concerning the surety, concerning the tutor curator, concerning the 'negotiorum gestor', concerning the judge, concerning the advocate and proctor, if they are single, if in a common cause, if participants and partners, if they are obscure, if the witnesses return to the judge, if they do not say the reason

121. The variety of the manuscript attributions can most easily be seen by expanding the titles that appear after searching for the Incipit 'testium' at http://manuscripts.rg.mpg.de/search/. Which of these are actually in the manuscripts, however, and which are the product of later cataloguers can only be seen by looking at the manuscripts themselves. See also Fowler-Magerl, *Ordo* 239. Maussen, *Veritatis adiutor* 792, assigns the treatise to Iacobus Aegidius and dates it to the middle of the 14th century, but does not seem to have gone behind the printed text in the *Tractatus* of Venice of 1584. For an attempt to come to some resolution of the issue, see http://amesfoundation.law.harvard.edu/digital/TUI1584/TUI1584Metadata_v4.html, item 18, and the hyperlinked 'notes'.

122. Bartolus, '*De reprobatione testium*', *Tractatus de testibus*, ed. Giovanni Battista Ziletti (Venezia 1574) 83–106 at 83–84. I have used the digital edition of the Bavarian State Library: http://www.mdz-nbn-resolving.de/urn/resolver.pl?urn=urn:nbn:de:bvb:12-bsb10163569-8.

for their statement, if the judge does not interrogate them, if they are enemies or a criminal case is pending between them, if they say one thing for another, if they speak having been corrupted, if they don't speak the truth, if they don't give testimony close to the matter that is being inquired about, if they give a premeditated and single speech. Notaries are reproved who do not write out the saying of the witness in full. If one speaks about one thing and another about another. If one speaks about one person and another of another. If they do not well compute the grade of consanguinity. If they are in discord about the place. If they are in discord about the time. If they are in discord about the matter. If someone speaks about my thing for you and your things for me. When they don't speak to the matter, because they speak false things and various things. If they are usurers. Even suspect judges are reproved. Concerning the recusal of judges. If they are received again. If they are otherwise false or were so. If they have testified against you and you want to produce them for you. If they have learned what they testify. If they do not say their saying secretly. If they are not received by the judge. If they lack the required number when a certain number is required. If articles are not made for the case. If they depose beyond what is claimed. If they are interrogated about their crimes. If the multitude of them is great. If their sayings are not reduced to public form. If witnesses or instruments are thought to be brought in against themselves. Who are compelled though unwilling and who are not. Pimps and tax-collectors [proxenetae et censuales] are reproved, hermaphrodites, parents and mothers infinitum. Concerning children. Concerning those who are in mortal sin. If they do not speak from sight but from credulity and hearing. Whether allowed witnesses [testes dati] are reproved, and how, and which are not. [123]

One might think that this text is no improvement on Tancred. In place of Tancred's neat listing of the relevant disqualifying factors for witnesses, we have a bed-sheet list. Hermaphrodites have returned. As suggested previously, it may be that this text *is* an improvement on Tancred. Once you know the basics, you want to know the details, particularly if you are looking for arguments to 'reprove' witnesses. This is the way that Durantis operates too. He gives you all that you might possibly want to know and then some. Who knows? You might have a case involving an hermaphrodite. The lawyer is even given a blatant piece of sexism to use against women:[124]

> Femina fallere falsaque dicere quando carebit?
> Beccharia piscibus et mare fluctibus tuncque carebit.

> [When will woman cease to deceive and speak falsehood?
> When the fishmonger ceases to have fish and the sea, waves, then will
>   she cease.]

---

123. The meaning of this last sentence is unclear, and the full text has nothing that corresponds to it. There is a passage that corresponds to it in Bartolus, *Opera Omnia* (Venezia 1596) vol. 10, fol. 169rb. It has all the hallmarks of an afterthought.

124. *Tractatus de testibus* (Venezia, 1574), no. 5, at 87 (my trans.). It is not a particularly good

What is interesting about Maranta's 'ordo' is that around 1525 the question of what kinds of witnesses can be repelled is referred to other authors. What kinds of witnesses can be repelled is simply not something that you need to tell people about in a basic treatise. What you need to tell them is: (1) the order in which witnesses are introduced, (2) how the witnesses are to depose, (3) when they can be produced, (4) how to protest in such a way as to give rise to the right of repulsion, (5) that you cannot repel witnesses whom you have produced, and (6) that you cannot reprove witnesses on appeal. On most of these matters, local rules have been introduced, and the local rules have a tendency to cut down on opportunities for delay, by, for example, limiting the number of witnesses to seven or ten as opposed to the canonic forty.[125]

Cases

What is driving these changes is interesting, but we cannot see it in the treatises. Let us examine a decision of the Rota Romana in a case about marriage from Lisbon in 1574, which shows rather nicely the intersection of the problem of rigid rules on witnesses and 'arbitrium', which seems in this context to be roughly equivalent to our 'discretion'. We are dealing with two witnesses in a case brought by one donna Maria and one don Pedro, who seems to be her father, against an unnamed man, and both witnesses are testifying on behalf of donna Maria that a marriage was formed.[126] The fact that this is 1574 makes it unclear whether the pre-Tridentine rules about marriage were still being applied, but I suspect that they were; that is, that the alleged marriage occurred before the decree of the council of Trent of 1563 that required the presence of a priest and two witnesses for the validity of the exchange of marital consent, or at least before that decree became effective in Portugal.

The two witnesses produced in the case raise slightly different issues. One witness, Helena, is a slave, probably the half-sister of the plaintiff. A large collection of material is brought to bear on the proposition that she is a slave. She is the daughter of a woman who is a slave and offspring follows the womb. The testimony that she was treated like a slave, was regarded as one both inside the home and outside, that she acted as a

---

verse. If I have it right, a 'beccaria' is a butcher-shop, though a fishmonger is probably meant here, unless it is an in-joke about a person of that name.

125. Maranta, *Speculum Aureum*, pars 6, tit. *De testium productione*, tit. *De repulsa testium* (Venezia 1574) 345–47, 384–86.

126. Caesar de Grassis [Cesare Grassi], *Decisiones Sacrae Rotae* (Roma 1590) 79–80. (Published with and frequently bound with the *Decisiones* of his brother Achilles de Grassis, 1498–1555; see Stefano Tabacchi, 'Grassi, Achille', DBI 58 [2002] 591–595 at 594.)

slave and was called a slave is all admissible for the purpose of drawing the inference that she is a slave. That she was well treated and was said to be Maria's half-sister is irrelevant. The fact that it is said that Maria's father freed Helena in his testament is also irrelevant, because the father is still alive, and testaments do not take effect until the death of the testator. Nor is it relevant that Helena is the slave of Maria's father and not of his daughter, because 'since she is a slave or freedwoman of the father, she is also the slave or freedwoman of the daughter'.[127] She was also said to be a 'nanny'. And nannies must beware of bawdry, the status of being a bawd being another reason for excluding testimony.[128]

Catharina, the other witness brought by the plaintiffs, is a woman of higher status, but she was Maria's nurse, and emphasis is laid on the proposition that she is still a servant in the household, or, at least, that she still lives there. She favors the marriage, which some authorities regard as grounds for excluding her testimony. Her testimony is also inconsistent, but that could be explained by the fact that a considerable amount of time elapsed between her first and second depositions.

With all these difficulties, one would think that both witnesses would be excluded. That does not seem to be what happened, however. The clearest statement of the holding comes at the beginning: 'The lords [of the Rota] said that diminished faith, at the discretion [arbitrio] of the lords, was to be given to Helena de Conto and Catharina Gundisalvi, witnesses examined for donna Maria'. 'Some of the lords', we are told, 'thought that absolutely no faith was to be given to the aforesaid Helena'. 'On the part of some', we are later told, 'it seemed that she ought to be repelled entirely'. This may well have been the position of the reporter. On the one hand, 'some said that she ought not be entirely repelled, since some of the witnesses seemed to depose of her reputation and of a certain sort of treatment as free, and since the matter is favorable. When there is a case about proof of marriage, in the proof of it witnesses not greater than any exception seem to be admitted'. For this proposition there seemed to be a considerable amount of academic support. But, we are told, 'Even those who felt this way agreed that her faith should be reserved for discretion, with not a little diminution'. There seems to have been more agreement about Catharina: 'The lords wanted equally to reserve her faith also for discretion with considerable diminution'.[129]

127. De Grassis, *Decisiones Sacrae Rotae* 80a: 'ex quo est serva vel liberta patris est etiam serva vel liberta filiae et sic etiam Mariae'.

128. Ibid.: 'Praeterea dicitur esse aya sive cuitos. Unde de suo magno interesse agi videtur ne lenocinium exercuisse dicatur, quo casu testis repellitur'.

129. Ibid. 79b: 'Domini dixerunt tam Helenae Conto quam Catharinae Gundisalvi, testibus

We do not know how the case came out. We noted in *Smith c. Dolling* that the Salisbury court ignored the inconsistencies in Alice's witnesses and their possible bias, whereas the appellate court at Canterbury paid much more attention to the rules about consistency and bias. It is possible that the further away the court is from the parties, the more likely it is that it decide on the basis of the rules rather than on the basis of the facts as it sees them. What is remarkable here is that a court in Rome, a long way from Lisbon, is also preserving, for the most part, its discretion. The exclusion of the testimony of slaves, except when tortured in a criminal case, is one of the brightest of the bright-line rules about the exclusion of witnesses. Even here, if we have it right, the majority of the Roman Rota in 1574 wanted to exercise its discretion, though 'with considerable diminution'.

Summary Procedure

There is a major development in the law of procedure in this period, normally associated with the decretals *Dispendiosam* (Clem. 2.1.2) and *Saepe contingit* (Clem. 5.11.2): the use of a 'summary' form of the 'ordo' in place of the 'long-form' procedure described in the 'ordines'.[130] The language used in both decretals speaks of proceeding 'de plano, et sine strepitu et figura iudicii'. Although *Saepe contingit* has more detail than does *Dispendiosam*, neither is particularly detailed, especially if one is asking the question of just what can be omitted. It also seems to be the case that at least some courts were experimenting with ways to cut down the length of the procedure even before these decretals were issued, probably in 1312. For example, the Court of Canterbury in the late thirteenth century was making use of a pleading known as a 'factum contrarium seu exclusorium' in tuitorial appeals, in which the defendant was required to present all his defenses at one time, and witnesses were heard on all of them together.[131]

---

examinatis pro donna Maria, diminutam fidem esse adhibendam arbitrio Dominorum. Et aliqui ex Dominis existimabant predictae Helenae nullam prorsus fidem fore adhibendam'. At 80a: '[V]isa est aliquibus ex Dominis repellenda in totum.... Aliqui enim dicebant quod omnino non esset repellenda, cum aliqui testes videantur deponere de reputatione et quodam quasi tractatu ut liberae, et cum materia sit favorabilis, cum agatur de probatione matrimonii in quo probando aliquando testes non omni exceptione maiores admitti videntur [citations omitted]. Coveniebant tamen etiam ita sentientes quod eius fides reservaretur arbitrio cum non modica diminutione'. At 80b: 'eius [Catharinae] etiam fidem Domini voluerunt reservare arbitrio cum considerabili diminutione'.

130. See Nörr, 'Literatur' 396–397; Olivier Descamps, 'Aux origines de la procédure sommaire: Remarques sur la constitution Saepe contingit (Clem., V, 11, 2)', *Einfluss der Kanonistik* 4.45–64, with an up-to-date bibliography; Brundage, *Medieval Origins* 449–51; Pennington, 'Introduction' 24–29; and Donahue, 'Ecclesiastical Courts' 284–287.

131. See Adams and Donahue, *Canterbury Cases 70–71*.

Granted how few court records survive from before 1312, it is easier to see the later uses of more summary forms of procedure than it is to tell how many of them were in existence before the decretals that officially authorized it were issued. It was, for example, regular practice in the consistory court of York in the fourteenth century and beyond to combine the plaintiff's articles on his libel—the propositions that the witnesses were to be asked about—with the positions—specific propositions that the plaintiff wanted the defendant to confess or deny. More radically shortened forms of procedure could be used when the parties requested it.[132] In a number of cases before the consistory court of Ely in the years 1374 to 1382, the parties specifically ask to proceed 'de plano, et sine strepitu et figura iudicii', a pretty obvious reference to *Dispendiosam* and *Saepe contingit,* even if they are not specifically cited, which they sometimes are.[133] Choosing to proceed this way does seem to shorten the normal procedure considerably, but it seems to have been employed only when the parties agreed to it.

Whether, as is sometimes said, *Dispendiosam* and *Saepe contingit* are responsible for the quite radically shortened form of procedure that emerged in routine criminal cases in the church courts in the later Middle Ages is a matter about which we may have more doubt. *Dispendiosam* seems to be dealing with what we would call civil cases, and *Saepe contingit* concerns the interpretation of the phrase 'de plano, et sine strepitu et figura iudicii' in delegations, which did not normally happen in routine criminal cases. Be that as it may, most routine criminal cases in church courts in the later Middle Ages seem to have been handled in one or two sessions. A couple, or one of them, was charged 'ex officio' with, let us say, fornication. The record, if it says this much, says that the charge arose 'fama publica referente', leaving us to guess how it is that the judge found out about it. The judge asks the defendant(s) what it is that they have to say about the charge. If they confess, they are given a penance. If they deny, they are ordered to undergo compurgation. Some of them succeed; some of them fail to come up with the requisite number of oath-helpers, the number and quality of which seems to have been within the discretion of the judge. In either event, the procedure normally takes one or two sessions of court.[134]

<hr>

132. For example, York, Borthwick Institute, C.P.E. 181.1 [item 3] (1390), http://dlibcausepapers.york. ac.uk/yodl/app/image/detail?id=yorkcp%3a85878183&ref=search.

133. For example, Cambridge, University Library, EDR D2/1, fol. 37r (1376), http://amesfoundation.law.harvard.edu/ElyAB/images/068%20fol%2037r.jpg.

134. For example, ibid. fol. 140r (1380) (a case of spousal abuse), http://amesfoundation.law.harvard.edu/ElyAB/images/276%20fol%20140r.jpg.

Procedure in the Church Courts of the Later Middle Ages

In the later Middle Ages, the episcopal courts, and to a lesser but still significant extent, the ecclesiastical courts below the episcopal level, were thoroughly professionalized. A rather large body of officers of these courts maintained a tradition of that court; and most of them seem to have had a number of lawyers who regularly practiced before them.[135] Such a situation might have led to a gradual divergence of the procedure of these courts from the pattern established by the basic norms of Romano-canonical procedure, but such does not seem to have been the case. The common university training of at least the higher officers of these courts and of some of the lawyers, particularly those styled as 'advocates', helped to ensure that these courts followed the basic norms, as did the fact that these courts were subject to appellate review, in some cases going all the way to the court of Rome.

There were, however, local variations.[136] Any court that does a large amount business, as some of these courts did, will establish routines for handling matters of detail that are not specifically treated in the general law. Notaries and proctors who draft the documents will settle on a style that is not required by the 'ordo' but is consistent with it. The procedural move may be the same as one authorized or required by the 'ordo', but the way in which it is expressed will not look the same in, say, France, as it does in England. For purposes of instruction and in order to ensure that those practicing before a court or working for it produce something that can be easily recognized for what it is, court officers will sometimes issue what we might call 'local rules'. These will be called the 'stylus curie X' or the 'consuetudines curie X'. The bishop may use his legislative authority to issue statutes dealing with the practice in his court. Proctors and notaries will make up formularies for their own practices, some of which will then come to circulate among other proctors and notaries. A rather large number of all of these formularies have survived, although relatively little attention has been paid to them.

Recently, Donald Logan has published a collection of such material concerning the Court of Canterbury (the Court of Arches, the appellate

---

135. More on this topic will be found in part 2 of this book.

136. García, 'Spain' 417–424, contains a list of treatises on procedure written in the Iberian Peninsula. While some of these treatises seem to deal with the common procedure, others, particularly those written in Castilian, seem to be more directed to local practice. They deserve more attention than they have received.

court for the southern province of England) in the later Middle Ages.[137] A number of archbishops of Canterbury, notably Archbishops Winchelsey (1292–1313) and Stratford (1333–1348), issued statutes governing the practice of the court. The court kept an official copy of these statutes, although there were some that circulated outside of the official collection. The court had a collection of *consuetudines,* which Professor Logan suggests had statutory authority. There were also several treatises on procedure in the court, one of which is quite large (seventy-five pages in the printed edition). This is a learned work that seems never to have been put together in final form. It demands further study, but a preliminary analysis suggests that a busy court, just below the court of Rome in the hierarchy of courts, could develop quite elaborate procedures on its own that, while not departing from the basic principles, made the Romano-canonical system work in the context of this court. Still unpublished are a number of formularies, which were made up of records used in the court.[138] These are valuable, particularly because the records of the court, except for the thirteenth-century records from vacancies that we have already discussed, have been lost.

One of the reasons why the basic principles of Romano-canonical procedure survived was that they were flexible. They could be bent to make them fit different types of cases without breaking them. To illustrate this point let us turn to France, and to the only surviving medieval record of the officiality of the bishop of Paris. Our record is a register, or act book, as are most of the late medieval records of the church courts, covering the years 1384 to 1387. We lack the accompanying documents, if there were any. Our surviving register is described as a 'civil' register, and there may have been other registers of criminal cases that have not survived, and probably a register of formal sentences, only one quire of which has survived. Both criminal cases and non-contentious material are contained in this 'civil' register, and the procedure gives us relatively little evidence of the differences among them. Let us examine the work of the court in one folio of the register, which partially covers one day, Monday, January 2, 1385.[139]

In the first contentious matter recorded, Thomas Domont 'proposes'

137. F. Donald Logan, *The Medieval Court of Arches* (Canterbury and York Society 95; Woodbridge, Suffolk 2005).

138. Donahue, *Records 2* II/01b/3/4.

139. *Registre des causes civiles de l'officialité de Paris, 1384–1387,* ed. Joseph Petit and Paul Marichal (Collection des documents inédits sur l'histoire de France; Paris 1919) 22 (references are to column numbers). A bit more about this register will be found in Donahue and McDougall, 'France' 310 and 331. What follows describes only those cases recorded on fol. 8 *ter* r of the register. Similar entries for the same day appear on fols. 8 *bis* v and 8 *ter* v; ibid. 21, 23.

against Perette la Cousine 'sponsalia de futuro re integra' (a promise of marriage not followed by intercourse). Perette replies that Thomas asked her to be his wife, that she had said that she would do nothing unless it pleased her father, and that her father was not pleased. Thomas is required to take the oath of calumny.[140] The case is set down for the following week 'to propose once and for all', and a cryptic note suggests that the costs of the session were set at 4 *deniers*. There is no mention of a libel and no indication in the later entries that one was ever filed. The term 'ad proponendum omnia' is known from the procedure of other officialities, but it normally comes at the end of the case, not the beginning.[141] What we have here is the beginning of a highly truncated (summary) procedure that will be conducted, so far as we can tell, orally.

The subsequent entries in the same case confirm this impression. Nothing is reported on the next date set (there may have been a further elaboration of the pleadings that the notary neglected to record), but the case reappears in the third week of January, and is set for five days later.[142] Costs are fixed at 8 *deniers,* though it is not clear whether these are cumulative or individual. The former seems more likely. Five days later the case is set for a week later for the publication of a witness whom a commissary is to examine in the interim. Costs are now 12 *deniers.*[143] In the fifth week the case is set for the following week for the same publication, the 'rea' being present and consenting that someone else (not named) be examined in the interim.[144] In the sixth week the witnesses are published (their depositions are unfortunately not given), and the case is set to the following week for the 'rea' to speak against the witnesses for the first time.[145] That session is postponed from the seventh week to the eighth, where there is a note that the case was concluded, a day given in the following week to hear the judgment, and a 'conference' (collatio) is ordered on the intervening Sunday.[146] At this point the case disappears from view.

Obviously there is much more that we would like to know about this case and about how it was conducted, but the record does tell us quite a bit. Elements of the long-form 'ordo' are there. The case begins with a claim and a defense. A more elaborate procedure would have called for Perette to deny the claim generally and then introduce her substantive defense by way of exception. There is no indication, however, that she was represented by counsel, and she simply tells her story at the start.

---

140. On the oath of calumny, see Litewski, *Zivilprozeß* 335–344.
141. See Adams and Donahue, *Canterbury Cases* 52–53 and references.
142. Petit, *Registre* 31.   143. Ibid. 35.
144. Ibid. 42.   145. Ibid. 46.
146. Ibid. 53, 58.

In long-form procedure Thomas would have been entitled to three terms
to produce his witnesses on the principal. He apparently gets one term,
though this is extended, with Perette's consent, so that he ultimately in-
troduces two witnesses. The testimony is published (the only indication
that we get that anything other than the record itself was written down),
and Perette is given a term 'for speaking against the witnesses for the first
time', implying that she might be entitled to more such terms. When that
term finally comes, however, the case is concluded, perhaps, although the
record does not say so, with Perette's consent, and the case is set down
for sentencing. But no sentence will be recorded in the register, though
one may have been recorded in a separate register of sentences. It is also
possible that the 'conference' set for the intervening Sunday (emphatically
not a 'court day') resulted in a settlement of the case, probably unfavorable to Thomas.[147]

The next case recorded on January 2, 1385, had begun before the Christmas recess.[148] Jean Bichot, who is suing on behalf of his daughter who is
not otherwise named, against one Robin Radulphi, clerk, produces Master Alain Forestarii as a witness, and a day a week later is set for the third
production of witnesses. From this we may infer that Jean has already had
one term for the production of witnesses and that this is the second.[149] On
January 11 (one wonders what happened on January 9), Jean apparently
produces no further witnesses, and January 18 is set for publication of the
witnesses. Costs are assessed at 4 *deniers.*[150] On January 18, the testimony of the witnesses is published; Jean produces a piece of documentary
evidence (registrum); Robin acknowledges the seal on the document but
does not approve its contents; the case is set for February 1 for Robin to
speak against the witnesses for the first time, and costs are assessed at 8
deniers.[151] The term for speaking against the witnesses for the first time is
postponed from February 1 to February 10, then to February 17, and then
to February 23, and on February 17 costs are assessed at 4 *deniers.*[152] On
February 23, a new term is set for March 9 to speak against the witnesses

147. See Donahue, *Law, Marriage* 335–36, and T&C no. 624.

148. Donahue, *Law, Marriage* 4, 10.

149. Petit, *Registre* 22. In the last previously recorded entry (ibid. 17 [December 23]), Jean had
produced six witnesses, including Master Jean Meleti, who regularly served as commissary for
examining witnesses and who is also described as 'promotor curie Parisiensis', and the writer
of the document, Jean de Villemaden, a notary who describes himself elsewhere as 'scriba curie
Parisiensis', and their examination was committed to Hervé Dulcis, who regularly served as commissary for this purpose and who is also described as 'promotor curie Parisiensis'. Master Alain
Forestarii, who is produced as a witness on January 2, also regularly served as a commissary for
examining witnesses for the court.

150. Ibid. 28.   151. Ibid. 32.

152. Ibid. 44, 51, 55.

for the second time, and costs are again assessed at 4 *deniers*.[153] On March 9, March 16 is set for Robin to reduce to writing the things that he proposed against the witnesses orally.[154] On March 18 a term is set for March 24 to proceed according to law on the objections filed (rationibus traditis) against the witnesses.[155] On March 24, the case is set for April 12, to make an interlocutory sentence on the things filed by Robin and to proceed with filing every five days, and first on behalf of Jean ('ad interloquendum super traditis ex parte rei et tradendis de quinque in quinque et primo ex parte actoris').[156] No further entries have been found in the case. The long gap between March 24 and April 12 may be explained by the fact that Easter fell on April 2 in 1385, and as in the preceding case, one suspects that in the intervening time the case was settled.

For the social historian or the historian of substantive law, this is a singularly frustrating record. Why was Jean suing the clerk on his daughter's behalf? Was a promise of marriage involved? What was contained in the 'register,' the seal of which Robin acknowledged but the contents of which he did not? What was contained in the testimony of the two Parisian masters and the notary who testified on Jean's behalf? What were Robin's objections to the witnesses?[157]

From the point of view of the historian of procedure, however, this case tells us quite bit. It tells us that the Paris court was prepared to follow the basic outlines of long-form Romano-canonical procedure in an appropriate case, one in which the defendant is a clerk, where two Parisian masters and a notary testify, and where written documents form part of the proof. Proctors and an advocate are mentioned on Robin's side; it is hard to imagine that this process was not being conducted by professionals on both sides.[158] (The redaction of the objections to the testimony to writing, for example, must have been done by a professional.) The case also tells us that even where the long-form 'ordo' was being followed, the practice of the Paris court was to expedite it at every turn. Thus, the 'terms' (the word is never used) for producing witnesses and speaking against them

153. Ibid. 61.

154. Ibid. 72.

155. Ibid. 80.

156. Ibid. 88. This entry is so cryptic as to be almost incomprehensible, but I think what it means is that the court will render an interlocutory sentence on the objections that the defendant has filed against the witnesses and that the parties are to come back every five days thereafter to file material about the about the witnesses, beginning the plaintiff's arguments in support of the witnesses, then the defendant's counterarguments and so on, until a definitive issue is finally reached.

157. The identifications of the witnesses suggests that the issue in the case concerned a previous case, perhaps one between Jean's daughter and Robin, to which Jean had not been a party.

158. Petit, *Registre* 4, 10, 17.

are short.[159] It would seem that the ideal was one week per term, though the court would grant extensions for reasons that the record does not state. There is no separate term for the production of documentary evidence. Rather, it is produced on the same day on which the plaintiff's depositions are published. While we do not have the complete record, it is hard to imagine that the whole process from initial complaint until the matter is finally dropped took much more than five months, and those months included both the Christmas and Easter vacations.

Opportunities for delay did exist in the Paris court, but they were limited. The next case on the record for January 2, 1385, is the fourth entry in a separation case: Jeanne, wife of Jean Ferrebouc, king's clerk, having already obtained a separation of goods from her husband, sues him for separation from bed.[160] Jean replies that he wants to contest the case and is given nine days to make a 'litis contestatio' in writing. He defaults on the 11th of January and is given another ten days. On the 21st of January he asks for extra time to instruct his advocate. On the 30th of January, the advocate does not appear. On the 13th of February, however, a written 'litis contestatio' is filed, and the case is set to proceed in the following week. It does not, and the social historian wonders whether it was compromised and how it might have been compromised extrajudicially. The historian of procedure notes, however, that even where the defendant is a king's clerk and is recalcitrant, six weeks may well have been the maximum that a case could be delayed without incurring serious consequences.[161]

Not only were the cases that called for multiple court days handled quite expeditiously, but the norm in the Paris court was not to have multiple court days. Four of the entries on our sample folio for January 2, 1385, involved matters that were handled in one session:

The first entry on our sample folio is a confession of debt.[162] Jean Alexandri confesses ('confitetur') that he owes Noël Fillette 6 *francs*, 8 *sous*, 6 *deniers*, for a loan (mutuum). There is nothing in this entry to suggest that this was a contentious matter. This entry and others like it suggest strongly that the court was being used as a registry for recognizances of debts. The procedure was a common one, and it survives well into the sixteenth century. What procedures would be followed if the debt were

159. The same may be said of the term for making positions 'once and for all', which seems to have been combined with the term for producing witnesses for the first time. Ibid. 10, 17.

160. Ibid. 22; in previous entries in December, Jeanne had constituted proctors. The case is discussed further in Donahue, *Law, Marriage* 535, and T&C no. 1088.

161. The argument is based on the inference from the record, confirmed by other cases, that one default by the party and one by his advocate would be excused, but that after that relatively serious penalties for contumacy would ensue.

162. Petit, *Registre* 22.

not paid varied from court to court and time to time. The whole topic is in need of a more thorough treatment than it has received.[163]

The three remaining entries on our sample folio were also handled in one session.[164] The court commissioned Master Hervé Dulcis to tax the salary of a notary and a servant of the priory of Saint-Éloi, who had drawn up an inventory of the goods of Jean de Moy, alias de Sulli, deceased. While the administration of Jean's estate probably occupied more than one court session, this entry gives a glimpse into an administrative procedure that was taking place outside of direct supervision of the court.[165] On the same day, two church wardens were created for the parish of Fontenay-aux-Roses (dép. Seine), on the oath of the chaplain and nine witnesses. The wardens took their oath, paid a fee of 2 *sous* and departed. Finally, what is probably a marriage case is begun by Jean de Bosco against Jacquette la Hocherone, but Jean defaults, and the case is dismissed.

A reading of the rest of register supports the conclusion that January 2, 1385, was a typical day in Paris episcopal officiality. While it would be dangerous to draw firm conclusions about the nature of the court and its procedure from one record covering a bit more than three years, this record certainly suggests a blending of long-form and more summary procedures and a mixture of contentious and non-contentious matters. Criminal cases are almost, but not quite totally, absent.[166] Whether there was a separate register for criminal cases we do not know. In the fifteenth century, the French officialities, at least those in the north, turned much more to criminal procedure. But that is a topic for Donahue and McDougall in our chapter on France.

What our fourteenth-century record does show is that Romano-canonical procedure was flexible. As we have said, it could be bent to meet the requirements of the circumstances without breaking. The principles of the system have proved to be long lasting. They are the basis of both the civil and the criminal procedure of Continental European courts today, and, through the medium of chancery procedure, they form a significant part of the modern law of procedure in Anglo-American jurisdictions as well. That its principles could be adapted to changing circumstances without breaking is almost certainly one of the reasons why they lasted so long.

---

163. Initial accounts may be found in Lefebvre-Teillard, *Officialités* 222–250; J. Bréban, 'Registre de l'officialité épiscopale de Troyes, 1389–1396 (Archives de l'Aube G 4170)' (thèse [droit], typescript; Paris 1954) 58–77.

164. Petit, *Registre* 22.

165. No other mention of the deceased appears in the index to the register. The probate may have occurred before the official of the exempt jurisdiction of Saint-Éloi. Ibid. 22 n. 1.

166. See Charles Donahue, '*Ex officio* Cases in the Officiality of Paris, 1384–1387', *Mélanges en l'honneur d'Anne Lefebvre-Teillard,* ed. Bernard d'Alteroche et al. (Paris 2009) 393–412.

5

The Jurisprudence of Procedure

Kenneth Pennington

During the past thirty years legal historians have studied the establishment of the Romano-canonical procedure, the 'ordo iudiciarius' or 'ordo iudiciorum', in ecclesiastical and secular courts throughout Europe and have illuminated how and why it replaced older modes of proof.[1] They have come to understand that the transition from the ordeal to the 'ordo iudiciarius' occurred long before canon 18 of the Fourth Lateran Council (1215 A.D.), which forbade clerical participation in the ordeal.[2] From at least 1150 on, when the evidence becomes plentiful, church courts all over Europe had almost completely abandoned the ordeal as a mode of proof for deciding ecclesiastical cases. Secular courts quickly followed. This fact is attested for ecclesiastical courts by the vast number of twelfth-century

---

1. The difference in terminology has been overemphasized in the literature. *Ordo iudiciorum* was used rarely in Justinian's codification, in the title of Cod. 3.9 and Cod. 7.45.4. 'ordo iudiciarius' became the standard terminology when the jurist referred to the legal process. The term dates back to pre-Justinian Roman law. The use of the term in the medieval sources does not signify an adherence to Roman law or canon law sources. See Knut W. Nörr, 'Ordo iudiciorum und ordo iudiciarius', *Collectana Stephan Kuttner* (SG 11; Bologna 1967) 327–344; and Linda Fowler-Magerl, 'Ordines' 19–24.

2. With some exceptions, e.g. Herbert A. Johnson, Nancy Travis Volfe, and Mark Jones, *History of Criminal Justice* (4th ed. Newark 2008) 56: 'The absence of records makes it impossible to determine why the ordeal procedure became a matter of pressing concern to Innocent III just one year before his death'.

papal decretals that describe implicitly and sometimes explicitly the procedures of the 'ordo iudiciarius' that were, by the second half of the twelfth century, well established.[3] The documentation for secular courts is not as rich.

In the early Middle Ages courts dealt with evidence of many kinds and decided cases in many different ways. Roman legal procedural rules still circulated widely.[4] There was, however, no commonly accepted mode of proof or rules governing how a court case should be handled. The centralization of papal legislative and judicial power in the eleventh century had altered the procedure in ecclesiastical courts. The *Dictatus papae* of Pope Gregory VII stipulated that 'no one shall dare to condemn one who appeals to the apostolic chair' (D.P. 20). This papal maxim called into question a central mode of proof in ecclesiastical and secular courts, the ordeal. Appeal from the decision of an ordeal—the judgment of God— was logically impossible. The inexorable logic of the pope's dictum demanded that the Germanic ordeal not be used. As the papal court became the court of highest appellate court within the church, ecclesiastical procedure had to adapt to a system of proof that was based on written and oral evidence. Papal letters of the early twelfth century pullulate with references to witnesses and their testimony.

The rebirth of Roman law in the late eleventh and early twelfth centuries was a crucial moment in the transformation of the procedure in the courts.[5] Roman law had entered into the courtroom, but an intricate question confronted the judges and officials in the courtroom: what were the rules of procedure according to Justinian's codification?[6] The citation

3. Some have argued for the longevity of the ordeal, first asserted by Robert Bartlett, *Trial by Fire and Water: The Medieval Judicial Ordeal* (Oxford 1986); and most recently, following Bartlett, Scott L. Taylor, 'Survival of Customary Justice', *Crime and Punishment in the Middle Ages and the Early Modern Age*, ed. Albrecht Classen and Connie Scarborough (Fundamentals of Medieval and Early Modern Culture 11; Berlin-New York 2012) 109–130 at 114–115.

4. Luca Loschiavo, 'Isidoro di Siviglia e il suo contributo *all'ordo iudiciarius* medievale', *Einfluss der Kanonistik* 4.1–19; I am not sure that we can discount Isidore's knowledge of law (ibid. 18–19).

5. Since Linda Fowler-Magerl published her study of the manuscripts of the *ordines*, her work has been the starting point of scholarship on medieval court procedure. Although this chapter differs somewhat from some of her conclusions, her book is the foundation of this chapter; see her fundamental study, *Ordo,* and her more synthetic 'Ordines'. Still useful is Alfons M. Stickler, 'Ordines judiciarii', DDC 6.1132–1143.

6. Julius Ficker was the first to attempt a survey of Roman law in ecclesiastical and secular courts. He published 531 court cases that he excavated from manuscripts in European archives and from printed sources. The earliest case citing Roman law dated to 776; see *Forschungen zur Reichs- und Rechtsgeschichte Italiens* (4 vols. Innsbruck 1868–1874, reprinted Aalen 1961). Antonio Padoa Schioppa surveyed the use of Roman law in the eleventh and twelfth centuries, basing his study on four of Ficker's cases. Justinian's *Codex, Digest,* and the *Institutes* were cited in these court cases, which chronologically extend from 1060 to 1107. As Padoa Schioppa points out, a case from 1107 in Rome reached a new stage for the role of juridical learning in legal practice. That juridical learning could not have existed without the law school in Bologna and, possibly, in other

of texts taken from Justinian's *Codex* and *Digest* in the courtroom prepared the way for seeking procedural rules in Roman law.[7] Although the ecclesiastical and secular courts began to rely on Roman law and concepts for settling disputes, the rules of procedure were not easily excavated from Justinian's massive set of texts. Ferreting out principles and rules from Justinian's codification for instruments such as contracts was much easier than understanding how Roman courts functioned.

Because the papal court in Rome had already incorporated significant amounts of Roman law into its proceedings, it is not surprising that Rome looked north to the School of Roman law in Bologna for answers. The papal chancellor under Pope Innocent II (1130–1143), Haimeric, wrote to his friend Bulgarus, the most important teacher of Roman law in Bologna, and asked him to write a treatise that summarized the rules of procedure.[8] Fowler-Magerl has observed that Bulgarus's treatise was not an ordo, but a letter, and that the second 'part' has nothing to do with procedure.[9] Her comment ignores the manuscript evidence that the second part was almost undoubtedly not in the original letter to Haimeric. Only three manuscripts combine the tracts. Bulgarus's treatise is found by itself in six manuscripts.[10] Fowler-Magerl has also argued that an earlier ordo found on the flyleaf of a Cologne manuscript predates Bulgarus's letter.[11] Ennio Cortese has not found her argument persuasive.[12] Furthermore, the Cologne text, even if one could date it to the late eleventh century, did not circulate and had no influence. Bulgarus's treaty was the first.

With the centralization of judicial procedure in the Church, Haimeric's request to Bulgarus was inevitable. If not Haimeric, some other court official in some other court would have requested a treatise on court procedure in the 1130s. The practical needs of judges demanded theoretical and practical solutions. Bulgarus did not write to Haimeric for an academic treatise. He wrote to address the practical needs of the papal courtroom, not to satisfy his intellectual curiosity.[13]

---

places. See Antonio Padoa Schioppa, 'Il ruolo della cultura giuridica in alcuni atti giudiziari italiani dei secoli XI e XII', *Nuova rivista storica* 64 (1980) 265–289.

7. Kenneth Pennington, 'Roman Law at the Papal Curia in the Early Twelfth Century', *Canon Law, Religion, and Politics: Liber Amicorum Robert Somerville*, ed. Uta-Renate Blumenthal, Anders Winroth, and Peter Landau (Washington, D.C. 2012) 233–252.

8. Luca Loschiavo, 'Bulgaro', DGI 1.357–359; Hermann Lange, *Römisches Recht im Mittelalter*, 1: *Die Glossatoren* (München 1997) 162–170 at 167–168.

9. Fowler-Magerl, 'Ordines' 24. See Bruce C. Brasington, *Order in the Court: Medieval Procedural Treatises in Translation* (Medieval Law and Practice 21; Leiden 2016) 86–111.

10. Fowler-Magerl, *Ordo* 35–36   11. Ibid. 33–35.

12. Ennio Cortese, *Le grandi linee della storia giuridica medievale* (Rome 2000) 237–238.

13. I emphasize this point because some social historians are still unconvinced that jurisprudence had any practical importance; e.g. Chris Wickham, *Courts and Conflict in Twelfth-Century Tuscany* (Oxford 2003) 4: Roman law was 'as divorced from practical knowledge as any Parisian

Bulgarus probably sent his little treatise to Rome in the early 1130s, since it was quoted in two papal letters around 1133 to 1138. The first letter can be dated 1133 to 1136. Bulgarus's tract was exactly what the papal and other courts needed. It circulated widely from England to Spain.[14] The Vatican lat. 8782 manuscript containing the letter was glossed with citations to Justinian's *Digest* and the *Codex*: these glosses explained exactly, line by line, from where in Justinian's codification Bulgarus's text was drawn. The manuscript dates from the middle of the twelfth century.[15] It offers substantial proof that Bulgarus's treatise was not a simple treatise for practitioners; they had no need to know the Roman law sources that Bulgarus used. The Vatican manuscript is very good evidence that teachers of law also found it useful for directing their students to the sections of Justinian's codification that dealt with procedure.[16] They and their students also needed a framework for discussing procedure. Bulgarus gave them a teaching tool and a handbook.

Although we do not have Haimeric's letter to Bulgarus, he must have asked Bulgarus a series of questions about court procedure. The first question must have been that Bulgarus should explain the difference between the rules governing an arbitration between the litigants and a suit brought before a judge in a court. The legal sources of the early twelfth century provide evidence for Haimeric's interest in arbitration. It was a very important part of the legal landscape. If we can judge from the surviving court records, perhaps half of all litigation in the courts was arbitrated. The importance of arbitration did not diminish as ecclesiastical and secular courts evolved. Gratian discussed arbitration in some detail, the decretal collections devoted a title to arbitration, and the later procedural tracts all discussed arbitration, like Bulgarus, at the beginning of

---

theological treatise'. Wickham's understanding reflects the state of the question in the scholarship of the 1960s but not in the twenty-first century.

14. Fowler-Magerl, *Ordo* 35–37. Paris, BNF 14517, fol. 78r–81v, described by Gunnar Teske, 'Ein neuer Text des Bulgarus-Briefes an den römischen Kanzler Haimerich: Zugleich ein Beitrag zum Verhältnis von Saint-Victor in Paris zur Kurie,' *Vinculum societatis: Joachim Wollasch zum 60. Geburtstag*, ed. F. Neske et al. (Sigmaringendorf 1991) 302–313. For a contrary opinion, see André Gouron, 'Innocent II, Bulgarus et Gratien', *Vetera novis augere: Mélanges offerts au professeur Wacław Uruszczak*, ed. Stanisław Grodziski et al. (2 vols. Kraków 2010) 1.255–260. Cf. Emanuele Conte, '*Ordo iudicii* et *Regula iuris*: Bulgarus et les origines de la culture juridique (XIIᵉ siècle)', *Frontières des savoirs en Italie á l'époque des premières universités (XIIe–XVe)*, ed. Joël Chandelier et A. Robert (Collection de l'École française de Rome 505; Rome 2015) 157–176 at 161–162.

15. Kenneth Pennington, 'The Constitutiones of King Roger II of Sicily in Vat. lat. 8782', RIDC 21 (2010) 35–54.

16. Bulgarus's text in Cambridge, Trinity College, O.7.40, fol. 248r–254r, also contains a set of glosses. It remains to be explored whether the Vatican and Cambridge glosses are similar. I have posted the first Vatican glosses at http://faculty.cua.edu/pennington/Law508/BulgarusDeArbitris .htm, with a photo of the first folio of Bulgarus text at http://faculty.cua.edu/pennington/ Law508/RomanLawAssizes6.htm.

their tracts on procedure.[17] Issues about arbitration still swirled around in the late thirteenth century. Pope Boniface VIII rendered a decision that if one arbiter out of three disputed the decision of the other two, the two could render a valid decision.[18]

Bulgarus distinguished between the public authority of a judge to whom judicial jurisdiction had been granted and an arbiter whom the litigants selected by mutual agreement. Arbiters could not decide criminal cases or cases in which the legal status of a person could be decided; that is, arbiters could not decide whether a person was free or a slave.[19]

Haimeric's next question was a request to explain the role of lawyers in the courtroom. Advocates or patrons, Bulgarus wrote, should enter the courtroom to provide help to the litigants. At the end of a trial they had to swear an oath that they had done everything possible to assist their clients. The judge could supply what the advocates omitted. The judgment of the court must be accepted by them as truth.

In the next section Bulgarus turned to the 'actor' (plaintiff) and 'reus' (defendant). The actor must present proofs. If the actor did not prove his case, the reus was victorious, because the court should be more favorable to the reus than the actor. Justice and equity (iura) must be inclined to absolve rather than to condemn.[20] Bulgarus made the important point that when the reus made an objection (*exceptio*) to the accusation of the actor, the reus became the actor and must, therefore, provide proof. The reus benefited from the exceptio, and the actor from the reply to the exceptio (*replicatio*). Bulgarus also listed the persons who were not permitted to bring suit in court: women, children, *infames*, persons who have taken money to accuse or to not accuse, and those who have rendered false witness, among others.

Witnesses were the next topic. They could be forced to testify by the court, but they could also be excused for many reasons: old age, sickness, and criminal convictions. Sometimes judges could refuse to admit

---

17. Dig. 4.8 presented the jurists with the Roman jurisprudence of arbitration; Gratian in C.2 q.6 dictum post c.33 had a brief treatment of arbitration. The papal court rendered decisions on arbitration, and these decisions were collected by the canonists: 1 Comp. 1.34(33), 2 Comp. 1.20, 3 Comp. 1.25, 4 Comp. 1.18, 5 Comp. 1.24, X 1.43 (14 decretals), Liber sextus 1.22.

18. Liber Sextus 1.22.2. Boniface made a text included in X 1.43.1 more precise.

19. Agathon Wunderlich, *Anecdota quae processum civilem spectat* (Göttingen 1841) 13–26, at 13–15. Wahrmund, *Quellen* 4.1 (1925). Wunderlich printed the first of two parts that circulated under Bulgarus's name. Wahrmund edited both sections. In the first part Bulgarus discussed only procedure. I think there is good reason to believe that this section constituted the letter to Haimeric and that the second section was attached to the letter only later in the manuscripts.

20. Wunderlich, *Anecdota* 16–17, Vat. lat. 8782, fol. 95r: 'Iura promptiora [procliviora, ed. Wunderlich] sunt ad absoluendum quam ad condempnandum.' The gloss in Vat. lat. 8782 cited Dig. 50.17.125, which reads, 'Favorabiliores rei potius quam actores habentur'.

the willing and bring the unwilling into court. Litigants could object to witnesses for several reasons. Witnesses must be held to a high standard of honesty and respectability. An enemy can never testify against a litigant.[21]

Bulgarus then turned to the principal actors in the court room and formulated a maxim for the courtroom that has reverberated through the jurisprudential literature for centuries: 'Iudicium accipitur actus ad minus trium personarum, actoris, intendentis, rei intentionem evitantis, iudicis in medio cognoscentis'.[22] Although the statement may at first glance be unsophisticated and simple, it is not. Later jurists embraced it.[23] The maxim quickly found its way into the literature. Bracton picked it up for his treatise on English law.[24] The procedural literature of the Ius commune repeated it again and again. Although the maxim may seem a simple statement of fact, its implications are profound and would not be fully worked out in the jurisprudence of the Ius commune until the end of the thirteenth century.[25] The inexorable logic of Bulgarus's maxim is that none of the three participants can be omitted for any reason (that is not to say that he recognized this logic). What today we call due process must be observed. The maxim seems to have been Bulgarus's creation. It is not found in Roman law. His treatise was far from a slavish pastiche of texts drawn from his sources.[26]

The last topics that Bulgarus covered were appeals and the importance of jurists for determining whether appeals from court decisions should be considered. A litigant could appeal because the court had rendered a judgment that violated equity or the rights of the litigant. An appeal could not be made because of a norm or principle in a statute. A jurist determined through a *consultatio* whether the decision of the court could be appealed and whether the case had been well decided.[27]

Bulgarus added a final warning to all judges at the end of his treatise.[28]

---

21. Wunderlich, *Anecdota* 19–20.

22. Ibid. 20–21.

23. Knut Wolfgang Nörr, *Iudicium est actus trium personarum: Beiträge zur Geschichte des Zivilprozessrechts in Europa* (Biblioteca eruditorom 4; Goldbach 1993); and more generally, his *Zur Stellung des Richters im gelehrten Prozeß der Frühzeit: Iudex secundum allegata non secundum conscientiam iudicat* (Münchener Universitätsschriften, Reihe der Juristischen Fakultät 2; München 1967).

24. Bracton, *De legibus et consuetudinibus Angliae,* ed. Samuel Thorne (4 vols. Cambridge 1968) 2.302: 'Iudicium est in qualibet actione trinus actus trium personarum iudicis, videlicet, actoris et rei'.

25. Kenneth Pennington, 'Due Process, Community, and the Prince in the Evolution of the Ordo iudiciarius', RIDC 9 (1998) 9–47.

26. Cf. Fowler-Magerl, *Ordo* 37–38.

27. Wunderlich, *Anecdota* 22–23. Bulgarus emphasized the necessity of litigants' obtaining legal advice. This marks the beginning of a 'class of jurists'. See Johannes Fried, *Die Entstehung des Juristenstandes im 12. Jahrhundert: Zur sozialen Stellung und politischen Bedeutung gelehrter Juristen in Bologna und Modena* (Forschungen zur neueren Privatrechtsgeschichte 21; Cologne-Vienna 1974).

28. A final admonition, if my supposition is correct that Bulgarus's letter to Haimeric ended

A judge who rendered a decision because he had been bribed or because he favored one of the litigants would be punished. If the judge rendered an unjust decision because of ignorance, his punishment was left to his superior judge.[29] Bulgarus's last two admonitions influenced the final two statutes in King Roger II's *Constitutiones* a few years later (1140).[30]

Bulgarus may not have written the first ordo, but he undoubtedly wrote the most influential early ordo.[31] Although one can divide the ordines into categories, we should approach them as attempts to understand the judicial process and as reflections of a particular jurist's special interests. Other ordines were written in Italy and Southern France in the last half of the eleventh or the first half of the twelfth century.[32] Bulgarus's letter to Haimeric was a part of a widespread effort of the jurists to understand the Roman *cognitio extraordinaria* and bring it into European courtrooms. However, as I will attempt to show in this chapter, the evolution of the jurisprudence governing procedure must be traced in several juridical literary genres. The ordines are significant guideposts, but the jurists' commentaries on the *libri legales* of the Ius commune are of equal and perhaps even more importance.[33]

In the first half of the twelfth century, Gratian, the Father of Canon Law, devoted much thought and space to court procedure in his *Decretum*.[34] He expanded Bulgarus's discussion considerably when he posed a series of questions to the hypothetical cases in causae 2 to 6 of his collection of canon law, which had rapidly become the most widespread and central source of canonical jurisprudence in the 1130s. There is no proof that he knew Bulgarus's tract, but he could have had it at his elbow as he created questions drawn from his cases.[35] The first question of Causa 2

here and that the section on the rules of law was not in the original letter. Cf. Fowler-Magerl, *Ordo* 38–39, and 'Ordines', 24.

29. Fowler-Magerl, 'Ordines' 26.

30. Pennington, '*Constitutiones* of King Roger' 47–51.

31. Fowler-Magerl, *Ordo* 38, and 'Ordines' 25, argues that Bulgarus's letter was not an ordo because it was a letter, and none of the manuscripts called it an ordo. I do not find these reasons convincing.

32. Fowler-Magerl, *Ordo* 33–34 (Northern Italy), 41–44 (?), 160–165 (Northern Italy), 165–167 (Southern France or Northern Italy). The early ordines are extremely difficult to localize and date. Peter Landau, 'Dei Anfänge der Prozessrechtswissenschaft in der Kanonistik des 12. Jahrhunderts', *Einfluss der Kanonistik*, 1.7–23, has localized a number of twelfth-century ordines.

33. On the *Libri legales* and their role in the law schools, see the chapter of Michael H. Hofflich and Jasonne M. Grabher, 'The Establishment of Normative Legal Texts: The Beginnings of the *Ius commune*', *History*, ed. Hartmann and Pennington 1–21.

34. See Landau's chapter on Gratian in Hartmann and Pennington, *History*; and Anders Winroth, *The Making of Gratian's Decretum* (Cambridge Studies in Medieval Life and Thought, 4th Series, 49; Cambridge 2000). Also Orazio Condorelli, 'Graziano', DGI 1.1058–1061, who gives an excellent summary of current research and the scholarly debates.

35. Gratian did explicitly cite Bulgarus's *De ignorantia iuris*; see C.1 q.4 d.p.c.12. The relation-

was central to the status of the 'ordo iudiciarius' in the courts: must the 'ordo iudiciarius' be used for notorious crimes?[36] After citing texts from the canonistic tradition, Gratian decided that judges could omit the 'ordo iudicarius' for notorious crimes. Early on the jurists attempted to draw distinctions between those crimes that required a trial and those that did not. Later canonists refined Gratian's conclusions.[37] In the end, however, the jurists commonly agreed that under certain circumstances, usually when a crime was heinous and notorious, a judge could render a decision against a defendant without a trial.

The question was not just theoretical. It had already surfaced during the great conflict between Pope Gregory VII and Emperor Henry IV. At the papal Lenten Synod of 1076 in Rome, Pope Gregory VII excommunicated the German bishops who had taken part in the Synod at Worms.[38] Gregory's summary action led to an exchange of letters among Bernoldus, Adelbertus of Constance, and Bernhardus of Hildesheim. Bernhardus insisted that Gregory did not have the right to excommunicate the bishops without a trial, although he conceded that if the bishops had been summoned, but refused to appear, their condemnation would have been justified. Bernoldus insisted, however, that the pope could excommunicate criminals without a trial if their crimes were public and they were contumacious. Petrus Crassus raised the same issue when he defended Henry IV in 1084. Citing texts from Roman and canon law, Petrus insisted that since Gregory had refused to hear the king's advocates and had condemned him in absentia, his sentence was not just.

In spite of objections, the pope's right to render a sentence without granting due process became well established. In the middle of the thirteenth century, the distinguished canonist and cardinal, Henricus de Segusio (Hostiensis), defended Pope Innocent IV's deposition of Frederick II at the First Council of Lyons in 1245 effortlessly.[39] Notorious crimes, he con-

---

ship was first noted by Hermann Kantorwicz and William W. Buckland, *Studies in the Glossators of the Roman Law: Newly Discovered Writings of the Twelfth Century*, ed. Peter Weimar (Aalen 1969) 77–80 at 80; Kantorwicz edited the tract pp. 244–246. cf. Winroth, *Making of Gratian's Decretum* 160–161.

36. Gratian, Decretum C.2 q.1 dictum ante c.1: 'Hic primum queritur an in manifestis iudiciarius ordo sit requirendus?'

37. Following paragraphs are based on Pennington, 'Due Process, Community, and the Prince', 17–37. Fowler-Magerl, *Ordo* 13–28, treats this problem in juristic thought from the early Middle Ages to the twelfth century. See also Richard M. Fraher, 'Ut nullus describatur reus prius quam convincatur: Presumption of Innocence in Medieval Canon Law', *Proceedings Berkeley 1980* 493–506.

38. Georg Gresser, *Die Synoden und Konzilien in der Zeit des Reformpapsttums in Deutschland und Italien von Leo IX. bis Calixt II. 1049–1123* (Konziliengeschichte, Reihe A: Darstellungen; Paderborn-München-Wien-Zürich 2006) 149–156.

39. Kenneth Pennington, 'Enrico da Susa', DBI 42 (1993) 758a–763b; and 'Enrico da Susa, cardinale Ostiense', DGI 1.795–98.

cluded, particularly those committed against the church, need no examination. The papacy granted exceptions to the normal rules of due process for lesser crimes as well. By the beginning of the fourteenth century, ecclesiastical courts employed a shortened, summary procedure in cases that ranged from marriage to ecclesiastical benefices. It should be emphasized that this shortened procedure could not eliminate a defendant's fundamental right of due process.[40]

Gratian then asked whether the court could recognize a plaintiff who had been despoiled before his property or rights had been restored. Next he asked what punishment a plaintiff should receive if he had made an accusation he could not prove (C.2 q.2–3). In the following question he posed a problem that jurists would struggle with for centuries: how many witnesses were required to constitute a proof? In question six Gratian grappled with the rules governing appeals. Up to this point in his discussion he relied on canonical sources, but to resolve many of the issues surrounding appeals he had to open his Roman law books. The rest of the question pullulated with texts from the *Codex, Digest, Authenticum,* and other sources. One intriguing and very long, complicated text that Gratian had already included in his first recension was a novel that Justinian had promulgated in 536 and included in his *Novellae.*[41] In question eight, Gratian established that a plaintiff had to present his complaint to a judge in writing.

In causae three, four, five, and six, Gratian raised many further questions about the rules of procedure. C.3 q.1: Must a plaintiff be restored to his property before a trial? Q.5: Can witnesses be from the household of defendants or can they be the defendant's enemies? Q.11: Can a defendant turn himself into a plaintiff during a trial? C.4 q.2: May someone younger than 14 testify? C.5 q.1: What punishment should be bestowed upon a plaintiff who has libeled someone secretly? Q.6: What punishment should a plaintiff who has not proven his case receive?

Finally Gratian broached a central principle of procedure at the end of C.6 q.5: Must a defendant prove his innocence if his accuser's proof fails? His conclusion was one that did not change from what may be the earliest version of his text until his final pen stroke. Gratian noted that normally a

---

40. Kenneth Pennington, *The Prince and the Law: Sovereignty and Rights in the Western Legal Tradition* (Berkeley-Los Angeles-London 1993) 186–201, especially 186–190; and Brundage, *Medieval Origins* 449–451; Olivier Descamps, 'Aux origines de la procédure sommaire: Remarques sur la constitution Saepe contingit (Clem., V, 11, 2)', *Einfluss der Kanonistik* 4.45–64; in this volume, see Donahue's chapter 'Ecclesiastical Courts' 284–287, and my remarks in 'Introduction' 94–96.

41. C.2 q.6 c.28 (Novella 23 [= Authenticum 4.2]). See Winroth, *Making of Gratian's Decretum* 146–148. Winroth does not attempt to explain how Gratian might have known this text.

defendant was completely exonerated when his accusers could not prove his case. However, if the question before the court were an issue of public notoriety, then the defendant had to prove his innocence through oaths of compurgation.[42]

The jurists did not like Gratian's conclusion, and the early manuscripts of his text reflect their objections. They interpolated a sentence that purported to be Gratian's words (*dictum*) in which he explained that a defendant had only to prove exceptions and not his innocence.[43] They also added a text taken from Justinian's Codex to make clear that a defendant was not encumbered if a plaintiff had not proven his case.[44] This example is a good piece of evidence that Gratian did not understand the full ramifications of replacing Germanic modes of proofs, like compurgation, with the ordo iudiciarius. He still found older ideas of justice attractive and did not fully accept the Roman jurisprudence that regulated procedure. In his defense, the jurisprudence of procedure was still in its infancy.[45]

The new procedure was not immediately or universally accepted. Procedural norms die hard in human society. In England, for example, ecclesiastical courts used the ordo, but the secular courts did not. There the ordeal flourished until 1215. Further, we are not well informed about the evolution of secular procedure of the twelfth century under the influence of the new jurisprudence of the Ius commune. Some secular courts, especially in Southern Europe, seem to have adopted the rules of the 'ordo iudiciarius' before the courts in Northern Europe.[46] But since the court proceedings were oral and were rarely recorded, we cannot follow the story of how the rules and assumptions of the new system may have conflicted with those of the old. One source—papal letters—provides a window, albeit a very small one, into twelfth-century courtrooms and a glimpse of the new practices and rules supplanting customary procedural norms. Litigants and institutions obtained letters from the papacy that guaran-

---

42. Antonia Fiori, *Il giuramento di innocenza nel processo canonico medievale: Storia e disciplina della 'purgatio canonica'* (Studien zur Europäischen Rechtsgeschichte 277; Frankfurt am Main 2012).

43. 'Accusatus non negationem sed exceptionem probare debet.' On this textual problem see Kenneth Pennington, 'Gratian and Compurgation', BMCL 31 (2014) 253–256 at 256.

44. Gratian, C.6 q.4, attached to the end of c.7: 'Actor quod asseuerat profitendo se probare non posse, reum necessitate monstrandi contrarium non astringit, cum per rerum naturam factum negantis probatio nulla sit'. Brendan McManus reported on another similar addition to Gratian's vulgate text: Brendan J. McManus, 'An interpolation at D.12 c.6', BMCL 18 (1988) 55–57.

45. Franck Roumy, 'Les origines pénales et canoniques de l'idée moderne d'ordre judiciaire', *Einfluss der Kanonistik* 2.313–349 at 335–342, where he lists a number of papal letters in which the term 'ordo iudiciarius' indicated the procedure used in the case or the idea that the norms of the ordo should be followed, i.e., due process of law in English. For more examples, see my 'Due Process, Community, and the Prince' 12–15.

46. See the reflections of Donahue, 'Procedure' 95–99.

teed that their cases would be heard according to the ordo iudiciarius, a clear indication that they wished to protect themselves from other forms of proof—the ordeal—or other forms of procedure that violated the principles of the ordo iudiciarius.[47]

If one judges from the extant papal letters of the twelfth century, the pontificate of Alexander III (1159–1181) was of crucial importance for this development. For example, Alexander granted the abbey of Holcultram the right to have their disputes involving their possessions heard before the bishops of Glasgow and Whithorn according to the 'ordo iudiciarius'. On no account, the pope ordered, should these cases be heard in secular forum or in secular courts.[48] He also ordered the archbishops, bishops, and archdeacons who exercised jurisdiction where houses of the order of Sempringham were situated not to permit laymen to disturb them 'outside the "ordo iuris".'[49] One cannot always discover what facts lie behind a papal mandate, but when Alexander prohibited the abbot and monks of Clairmarais from disturbing the rights of another monastery 'outside the "ordo iuris",' because their actions would injure their religious vocation, we may, perhaps, presume that the abbot was using the procedure of customary secular courts to claim his rights.[50] This interpretation of the letter is reinforced by Alexander's conclusion that if the monks wished to litigate, they should do so before an elected judge and according to the ordo iudiciarius.[51]

Sometimes a papal letter is explicit enough to allow a brief glimpse of the struggle between the rules of the new ordo and the customary law of proof and contract. An English example described in two letters of Alex-

47. See the examples published by Charles Duggan and Stanley Chodorow in *Decretales ineditae saeculi XII, from the Papers of Walther Holtzmann* (MIC, Series B, 4; Vatican City 1982) 137: 'nec eum super eadem molestari sine ordine iudiciario permittatis'. Other examples in letters 17 (p. 31), 35 (p. 58), 46 (p. 81), 65 (p. 112).

48. *Scotia pontificia: Papal Letters to Scotland before the Pontificate of Innocent III*, ed. Robert Somerville (Oxford 1982) no. 98, pp. 94–95: 'Verum si qui adversus illos super hiis agere forte voluerint, sub examine vestro secum exinde iudiciario ordine experiantur, nec eos super aliquibus possessionibus suis sibi aut monasterio suo pia devotione collatis extra curiam ecclesiasticam ad seculare forum aliqua ratione trahi permittatis aut eius iudicium quoquo modo subire'. The date of this letter is 1175–1181.

49. *Papsturkunden in England, 1: Bibliotheken und Archive in London*, ed. Walther Holtzmann (Abhandlungen der Akademie der Wissenschaften in Göttingen, phil.-historische Klasse 25; Berlin 1931) 1, no. 185 (1159–1181), p. 455: 'ne canonicos aut moniales... a quolibet contra iuris ordinem fatigari'.

50. *Papsturkunden in Frankreich, 3: Artois*, ed. Johannes Ramackers (Abhandlungen der Gesellschaft der Wissenschaften zu Göttingen 23; Göttingen 1940) no. 63 (1173), p. 123: 'quatinus iura et possessiones... eis in pace et quiete dimittatis nec... per uos aut per alios indebite molestare aut quolibet modo uexare contra iuris ordinem presumatis. Si enim eos exinde minus rationabiliter grauare presumpseritis, religionem uestram plurimum dedecebit'.

51. Ibid.: 'Ceterum si aduersus iamdictos abbatem et fratres de iustitia uestra confidentes agere uolueritis, coram iudice ab utraque parte communiter electo ordine iudiciario experiamini'.

ander III illuminates the situation in the late 1160s. In the first, Alexander mandated that Roger, the archbishop of York, and Hugo, the bishop of Durham, should not permit laymen in their dioceses to obtain possession of the lands of the abbey of Rievaulx (Helmsley, Yorkshire) through the secular courts. Their parishioners were accustomed to occupy the abbey's lands 'by whatever means' and then to vindicate their rights to the property by means of 'a certain customary contract that they call gage' in a secular court. Consequently, the abbot and the monks frequently were unjustly despoiled of their property without the benefit of the ordo iudiciarius.[52] In a second letter to the same recipients, Alexander issued a general mandate that all cases involving the abbey's possessions should be heard in ecclesiastical courts according to the ordo iudiciarius.[53] The formula of prohibition in the depository section of the letter is exactly the same as that of the abbey of Holcultram, but in this case we are informed, if only sketchily, about the background of the complaint. If we knew more about English procedure and law of gage at this time, we could better understand the situation at Rievaulx.[54] Ecclesiastics quickly found that their own system of justice more equitable than that offered by secular courts, and they appealed to Rome for help when their right to litigate according to the norms of the 'ordo iudiciarius' was violated. These papal letters reveal that the wishes of the papal curia and the local clergy were in harmony.

The new procedure took root slowly in some parts of Europe. Although jurists produced scores of treatises that described the rules and procedures of the ordo iudiciarius, old local customs were often resistant to change. In a letter from the first year of his pontificate (1199), Pope Innocent III (1198–1216) ordered Wolfger, the bishop of Passau, not to consult the community when deciding ecclesiastical cases. Local custom, it seems, permitted the bishop to use 'literate and illiterate, knowledgeable and ignorant', men to hear the evidence presented in the episcopal court and to render decisions.[55] The letter does not indicate whether the men

---

52. *Papsturkunden in England*, ed. Holtzmann, 1, no. 105, p. 370 (1167–1169): 'Ad aures nostras peruenisse noscatis, quod cum aliqui parrochiani uestri sibi quamlibet possessionem abbatis et fratrum de Rieualle uendicare uoluerint, eam quoquo modo occupare consueuerunt et deinde, postquam ipsam qualitercumque intrauerint, se ius suum sicut mos est seculari curia euicturos sub cuiusdam consuetudinis obligatione quam guagium uocant soliti sunt offerre, unde frequenter contingit, quod iamdicti abbas et fratres suis possessionibus iniuste et absque ordine iudiciario spoliantur'.

53. Ibid. no. 107 p. 371.

54. On gage, see Frederick Pollock and Frederic Maitland, *The History of English Law before the Time of Edward I*, ed. S. F. C. Milsom (2 vols. Cambridge 1968) 2.117–124.

55. *Die Register Innocenz' III.*, 1. *Pontifikatsjahr: Texte*, ed. O. Hageneder and A. Haidacher (Graz-Köln 1964), no. 565 (571), p. 824: 'quod in tua diocesi etiam in causis ecclesiasticis consuetudo minus rationabilis habeatur, quod cum aliqua causa tractatur ibidem, allegationibus et querelis utriusque partis auditis a presentibus, litteratis et illitteratis, sapientibus et insipientibus, quid

were clerical or lay. From what we know about the function of ecclesiastical courts and synods during the twelfth century, they were probably a mixed group containing both. These men may have been the 'iurati' of Germanic customary law.

These men, fumed Innocent, rendered judgments in ecclesiastical cases, and even their counsel (consilium) was accepted as rendering a judgment. This procedure, he continued, was an 'irrational' custom because it obviated canon law and rendered judgments on defendants by judges 'who were not their own'. This argument is clever and revealing. Innocent conceived of the episcopal court and his diocese as being under the jurisdiction of the bishop alone. Just as the pope was the ordinary judge of the entire church, the bishop was the ordinary judge of his diocese, and only he could render judicial decisions for those who were subject to him. A group of laymen and clerics did not represent the corporate church; only the bishop did. Innocent admonished Wolfger that 'he should deliver judgments for his subjects after having considered the issues of the cases, as the 'ordo' of reason demands'.[56]

As the ordo was established as the sole, legitimate mode of proof in ecclesiastical tribunals, jurists in the second half of the twelfth century needed to justify its substitution for other modes of proof. Although they might have pointed to its use by the ancient Romans, they preferred to cite biblical examples. Their reliance on the Bible is another example of its importance for the jurisprudence of the Ius commune.[57] They found their inspiration in the Old Testament and ingeniously traced the origins of the 'ordo iudiciarius' to God's judgment of Adam and Eve in paradise. By doing so, they created a powerful myth justifying the ordo that retained its explanatory force until the sixteenth century.

Around 1150 Paucapalea was the first canonist to connect the form of procedure used in ecclesiastical courts with a biblical model.[58] The Bible provided evidence of the ordo iudiciarius's antiquity and its legitimacy. He

---

iuris sit queritur, et quod illi dictaverint vel aliquis eorum presentium consilio requisito, pro sententia teneatur'.

56. Ibid.: 'Nos igitur attendentes quod consuetudo que canonicis obviat institutis, nullius debeat esse momenti, cum sententia a non suo iudice lata nullam obtineat firmitatem, ut in causis ecclesiasticis subiectorum tuorum, postquam tibi de meritis earum constiterit, sententiam proferre valeas, sicut ordo postulat rationis'.

57. On the importance of the Bible for juristic thought, see the remarks of Jean Gaudemet, *Les naissances du droit: Le temps, le pouvoir et la science au service du droit* (Domat droit public; Paris 1997) 7–9; Ernst Kantorowicz, *The King's Two Bodies: A Study in Mediaeval Political Theology* (Princeton 1957) 116–122; and Walter Ullmann's fundamental study in 'The Bible and Principles of Government in the Middle Ages', *Settimane di studio del Centro Italiano di Studi sull'Alto Medioevo* 10 (1963) 183–227.

58. Antonia Fiori, 'Paucapalea', DGI 2.1525–1526.

noted that the ordo originated in paradise when Adam pleaded innocent to the Lord's accusation. When Adam complained to God—'My wife, whom You gave to me, gave [the apple] to me, and I ate it'—he responded to God's summons: 'Adam ubi es?' 'Adam, where are you?' Although Paucapalea may not have been aware of the implications of Adam's cheeky reply to God, Adam came dangerously close to accusing the Lord of 'entrapment', a term in Anglo-American law used to describe a situation in which a government agent induces a person to commit a crime. If the Lord realized that Adam's reply was subversive and perhaps even blasphemous, he overlooked it.

Paucapalea's main point was subtle but would not be lost on later jurists: even though God is omniscient, He too must summon defendants and hear their pleas. Besides the text from Genesis, Paucapalea cited a passage from Deuteronomy in which Moses decreed that the truth could be found in the testimony of two or three witnesses. Since the rules of the 'ordo iudiciarius' also required two or more witnesses, Deuteronomy was further proof of the procedure's antiquity.[59] Two principles emerge from this gloss that do not enter English common law until centuries later. The first is that every accusation requires at least two witnesses or proofs to the crime; the second, that defendants have the right to testify in their own defense.

A few years later (ca. 1165) Stephen of Tournai further dissected the 'trial' of Adam and Eve, finding even more evidence that this event marked the establishment of the ordo iudiciarius. He pointed out that each part of the story conformed to the stages of a trial in the ordo and labeled each part with the appropriate technical term. He noted that Adam raised, as it were, a formal objection (exceptio), to the Lord God's complaint (actio) and shifted the blame to his wife or to the serpent.[60] As we have seen from Bulgarus's tract, 'exceptio' and 'actio' were technical terms taken from

---

59. Paucapalea, Prologue to *Summa*, ed. Johann F. von Schulte (Giessen 1890; reprinted Aalen 1965) 1: 'Quoniam in omnibus rebus animadvertitur, id esse perfectum, quod his omnibus ex partibus constat, exordium vero cuiusque rei potentissima pars est, ideoque mihi videtur, agendarum causarum formam ecclesiastici iuris originem eiusque processum non esse inutile ignorantibus reserare.... Placitandi forma in paradiso primum videtur inventa, dum prothoplastus de inobedientiae crimine ibidem a domino interrogatus criminis relatione sive remotione usus culpam in coniugem removisse autumat dicens, "mulier, quam dedisti, dedit mihi et comedi" (Gen 3:12). Deinde in veteri lege nobis tradita, dum Moyses in lege sua ait: "In ore duorum vel trium testium stabit omne verbum" (Deut. 19.15).'

60. Stephen of Tournai, Prologue to Summa, printed by Herbert Kalb, *Studien zur Summa Stephans von Tournai: Ein Beitrag zur kanonistischen Wissenshaftsgeschichte des späten 12. Jahrhunderts* (Forschungen zur Rechts- und Kulturgeschichte 12; Innsbruck 1983) 114; and Fowler-Magerl, *Ordo* 1 n. 1: 'Cum enim Adam de inobedientia argueretur a Domino, quasi actioni exceptionem obiciens relationem criminis in coniugem'.

Roman law that had become essential parts of the 'ordo iudiciarius'. Stephen was the first jurist to define the 'ordo iudiciarius':

The defendant shall be summoned before his own judge and be legitimately called by three edicts or one peremptory edict. He must be permitted to have legitimate delays. The accusation must be formally presented in writing. Legitimate witnesses must be produced. A decision may be rendered only after someone has been convicted or has confessed. The decision must be in writing.[61]

This litany of admonitions indicates that by the second half of the twelfth century, the jurists were conscious of a defendant's right to a trial and of his right to have a trial conducted according to the rules of the ordo iudiciarius. The story of Adam and Eve's trial in the Book of Genesis provided a historical, theological, and judicial justification for Romano-canonical procedure. Guillelmus Durantis († 1296) copied the remarks of Paucapalea and Stephen in the *Proemium* of his great treatise on procedure at the end of the thirteenth century. There the story lived on in the minds of European jurists for centuries.[62]

A key issue in the jurisprudence building around the 'ordo iudiciarius' became whether a person had a right to a trial. Twelfth-century jurists inherited a vague sense of a right to a trial from Roman law. The term 'actio' could mean the particular formulary of Roman procedure by which the plaintiff brought suit, the whole judicial proceedings, or, as a passage in Justinian's *Institutes* put it, 'the right of an individual to sue in a trial for what is due to him'.[63] In this last sense, 'actio' meant 'ius', or right. Only after the jurists concluded that parts of the judicial process were protected by natural law did they clearly articulate a subjective, almost inalienable, right of a defendant to have his day in court.

We must not imagine that the early Middle Ages was bereft of any conception of this right just because no one ever expressed the idea in 'The Age without Jurists'. We find some evidence in twelfth-century literature that the right to a trial was not foreign to the world of the ordeal. A man (or a woman) had the right to prove his innocence. In the *Romance of Tristan*, after King Mark condemned Tristan and Isolt to death without a trial when they were caught in 'flagrante delicto', the people of the King-

---

61. Stephen of Tournai to C.2 q.1, s.v. *an in manifestis*, printed by Fowler-Magerl, *Ordo* 27–28 n. 76: 'Videndum quod ordo iudiciarius dicitur, ut apud suum iudicem quid conveniatur, ut legitime vocetur ad causam tribus edictis vel uno peremptorio pro omnibus, ut vocato legitime prestentur inducie, ut accusatio sollempniter et in scriptis fiat, ut testes legitimi producantur, ut nonnisi in convictum vel confessum feratur <sententia>; que sententia nonnisi in scriptis fieri debet, nisi sint breves lites et maxime vilium'.

62. Guillelmus Durantis, *Speculum iudiciale* (4 vols. Nürenberg 1486) 1 fol. 3ra. Jean Gaudemet, 'Durand (Durant, Durante), Guillaume (Guglielmo), Detto Lo Speculatore', DBI 42 (1993) 82–87.

63. Inst. 4.6 pr.: 'Actio autem nihil aliud est quam ius persequendi iudicio quod sibi debetur'.

dom cried out: 'King, you would do them too great a wrong if they were not first brought to trial. Afterwards put them to death'. Although the people's plea might seem to be a simple cry for fair play, notorious crimes presented a key difficulty for jurists. They did not find it easy to justify a right to a trial for a defendant who had been caught in the act of committing the crime. King Mark, Tristan's judge, had seen the crime. Why was a trial necessary? The jurist struggled with that issue for a long time. It was only at the end of the thirteenth century that the jurists concurred that a defendant had an absolute right to mount a defense in a court according to the rules of the ordo iudiciarius.[64]

In the beginning the jurists assumed that every defendant, like Adam, should have the benefit of confronting his accuser. This expectation has deep roots in ancient and medieval procedure. In the second half of the twelfth century, the jurists began to see that a purely accusatorial system of proof had flaws. There has been scholarly debate about when the doctrine and practice of inquisitorial procedure was established. Most scholars have concluded that Pope Innocent III brought this procedure into existence. The lack of sources makes it difficult to know exactly when this significant change occurred in European courts, but it is more likely that Innocent was responsible for shaping and promulgating the rules governing this procedure rather than inventing it. The most recent scholarship has demonstrated that prelates had been ordered to investigate (inquisitio veritatis) since the pontificate of Pope Alexander III. No one, however, denies that by the end of Innocent III's pontificate the obligation and the duty of bishops to prosecute clerical crimes had become firmly established as an important part of ecclesiastical procedure.[65]

A signpost of this development is the birth of an important maxim of criminal law: 'publicae utilitatis intersit ne crimina remaneant impunita' (it is in the interest of the public good that crimes do not remain unpunished). 'Ne crimina remaneant impunita' became a standard maxim of the Ius commune in the later Middle Ages. It was used by the jurists to express their conviction that princes and judges had the duty to prosecute crime. Like many of the rules of law that became part of medieval juris-

---

64. See Pennington, *The Prince and the Law* 119–164, for the development of rights of due process in the Ius commune. Also my 'Innocent until Proven Guilty: The Origins of a Legal Maxim', *The Jurist* 63 (2003) 106–124.

65. The following paragraphs are based on Kenneth Pennington, 'Law, Criminal Procedure', DMA: Supplement 1 (New York 2004) 309–320 at 312; see especially Lotte Kéry, 'Inquisitio—denunciatio—exceptio: Möglichkeiten der Verfahrenseinleitung im Dekretalenrecht', ZRG Kan. Abt. 87 (2001) 226–268; and her *Gottesfurcht und irdische Strafe: Der Beitrag des mittelalterlichen Kirchenrechts zur Entstehung des öffentlichen Strafrechts* (Konflikt, Verbrechen und Sanktion in der Gesellschaft Alteuropas 10; Köln-Weimar-Wien 2006) passim.

prudence, elements of the maxim had its origins in Roman law, but its final form was shaped by the medieval jurists of the Ius commune.

Some scholars have argued that the adoption of the maxim in the jurisprudence of the Ius commune began to undermine the presumption of a defendant's innocence in European courts.[66] Others have even speculated that the penetration of the maxim into the minds of the jurists inclined them to accept torture as an acceptable institution for obtaining evidence. A careful study of the medieval jurists' writings reveals that the presumption of innocence evolved into an absolute right by the end of the thirteenth century. The jurists did not find the idea that crimes should be punished as being incompatible with a presumption of a defendant's innocence.[67] These two powerful norms existed side by side in the jurisprudence of the Ius commune for centuries. They still exist in one form or another in every legal system's legal thought.

'Ne crimina' was born in the Roman chancellery during the first years of Innocent III's pontificate.[68] In a letter to the king of Hungary, Innocent demanded that the king take action against the criminals who had committed crimes against the Church and used 'ne crimina remaneant impunita' to urge the king to act. A few years later the pope used the maxim again in a decretal to the archbishop of Lund (Sweden) in 1203. The bishop had asked Innocent two questions: first, whether he could imprison incorrigible clerics who persistently committed crimes; second, if he could give judicial orders to laymen instructing them to seize criminal clerics, even violently, without suffering the penalty of automatic excommunication that was normally imposed on laymen who perpetrated violence on clerics. In the name of law and order, Innocent permitted prelates in Sweden to jail clerics who persistently committed violence. They could also delegate the task of forcibly apprehending these criminals to laymen because 'publice utilitatis intersit ne crimina remaneant impunita'. The jurists quickly adopted the maxim as a fundamental principle of medieval criminal law. By 1210 Tancred of Bologna began his important tract

66. Takashi Shogimen, *Ockham and Political Discourse in the Late Middle Ages* (Cambridge 2007) 147–148.

67. Pennington, *The Prince and the Law* 119–164; and Pennington, 'Innocent until Proven Guilty' 106–124.

68. On the origins of the maxim 'ne crimina remaneant impunita,' see Kenneth Pennington, 'Innocent III and the Ius commune', *Grundlagen des Rechts: Festschrift für Peter Landau zum 65. Geburtstag*, ed. Richard Helmholz, Paul Mikat, Jörg Müller, and Michael Stolleis (Rechts- und Staatswissenschaftliche Veröffentlichungen der Görres-Gesellschaft, NF 91; Paderborn 2000) 352–354. The birth of the exact wording of the maxim took place in Innocent III's curia; the ideas behind the maxim evolved in the thought of the canonists during the second half of the twelfth century; see Peter Landau, '*Ne crimina maneant impunita*: Zur Entstehung des öffentlichen Strafanspruchs in der Rechtswissenschaft des 12. Jahrhunderts', *Einfluss der Kanonistik* 2.23–35.

on criminal law with the words 'Quoniam rei publice interest ut crimina non remaneant impunita', and the maxim's career was established.[69] More importantly the maxim signaled that the church would no longer depend upon the accusatorial procedure to bring criminal clerics to justice. Prelates had a duty to prosecute crimes for the public good.

At the end of his pontificate, Innocent III promulgated a decree at the Fourth Lateran Council (1215) that laid down extensive rules about how and when an ecclesiastical judge could prosecute criminals under his jurisdiction. This conciliar canon, *Qualiter et quando* (c.8), established basic rules for ecclesiastical judges to investigate and punish criminal clerics. Its provisions were based on a number of earlier decretal letters that Innocent's curia had sent in answer to questions that judges had posed about the rules governing court procedure. The rules of procedure for the accusatorial procedure had been well established. When one party brought suit against another and the judges sat as arbiters in the proceedings, the judges were disinterested parties when they applied the rules governing and protecting the rights of each litigant. However, when judges had initiated a prosecution, their role and their relationship to the defendant changed significantly. From the first year of Innocent's pontificate, judges from various parts of Christendom asked the Roman curia for guidance about these issues. Their questions and Innocent's responses to them were not, most likely, the creation of a new procedure, but rather the gradual resolution of procedural questions raised by ecclesiastical judges who were beginning to play a more active role in prosecuting crime.

Consequently at the end of his pontificate, Innocent issued *Qualiter et quando*, in which he summed up the rules that were scattered among his decretals.[70] The first and most important point that Innocent made was that prelates had the right and the duty to prosecute criminal clerics. Just as jurists had used the biblical story of Adam and Eve to justify the accusatorial procedure a half century earlier, Innocent cited the Bible and quoted two passages, one from Genesis (18:21) and the other from the Gospel of Luke (16:2) to justify the inquisitorial mode of proof. The first passage quoted God's words to Abraham before he rendered judgment on Sodom and Gomorrah: 'I must go down to see for myself whether they have mer-

69. Richard Fraher, 'Tancred's "Summula de criminibus": A New Text and a Key to the Ordo iudiciarius', BMCL 9 (1979) 29–35; Andrea Bettetini, 'Tancredi da Bologna', DGI 2.1930–1931.

70. On *Qualiter et quando* and the other canons Innocent III promulgated at the Fourth Lateran Council see Kenneth Pennington, 'Fourth Lateran Council, Its Legislation, and the Development of Legal Procedure', *Texts and Contexts in Legal History: Essays in Honor of Charles Donahue*, ed. John Witte Jr., Sara McDougall, Anna di Robilant (Robbins Collection; Berkeley 2016) 167–186.

ited their reputation'. The second was a proverb of the rich man who had heard that his steward had mismanaged his affairs. 'What do I hear about you? Either you must explain your actions or you can no longer exercise your office'. Innocent had first used these biblical passages years earlier in a previous decretal letter. These biblical passages became powerful justifications for inquisitorial procedure.

The Fourth Lateran canon gave judges the authority to investigate and prosecute clerics whose crimes were well known. Innocent noted that the accusatorial procedure was not being replaced but that ecclesiastical judges should not have any scruples when they opened an investigation of clerical misdeeds. The pope insisted that all the procedural protections that were granted to defendants in accusatorial procedure were also given in this procedure. Defendants had the right to defend themselves with testimony, witnesses, and exceptions as well as replications (judicial replies to specific charges). The defendant should also be present at the trial.

The jurists defined the jurisdiction of a judge who investigated a criminal as being based on his office (*ex officio suo*). The judge would summon witnesses and make a defendant swear that he would respond to questions but not, as is often asserted, that he must tell the truth. If the witnesses produced incomplete proofs, then the defendant could clear his name by taking the oath of canonical purgation. If oath-takers declared the defendant innocent, he was freed without any penalty or infamy. The jurists who first commented on the conciliar canon thought that the only new element in the procedure was that the defendant had to be present at the hearing. The question arose because in the accusatorial procedure litigants were often represented in courts by proctors. Later jurists and legislation concluded that defendants could be represented by proctors when the accusation was not serious.

In their commentaries the jurists developed principles of procedure for the accusatorial and inquisitorial mode of proof that would remain firmly imbedded in the jurisprudence of the Ius commune for centuries. They also continued to write tracts on the 'ordo iudiciarius' in the tradition of Bulgarus. These tracts can be difficult to attribute to individual jurists and to localize. The manuscripts can be frustratingly silent or misleading or just wrong. The same is true of printed editions. Early modern printers were keen to attribute tracts to famous jurists of the past. Their names sold books.[71] Sometimes, however, the printers were misled by the manu-

---

71. Domenico Maffei, *Giuristi medievali e falsificazioni editoriali del primo cinquecento* (Ius commune, Sonderhefte 10; Frankfurt am Main 1979).

scripts, not by their greed. I will focus on the major ordines for this essay. The less important ordines have been catalogued and their influence assessed in the work of Linda Fowler-Magerl.[72]

If one were to judge on the basis of the extant manuscripts, none of the ordines written in the twelfth century became accepted throughout the dominions of the Ius commune as standard works. Some of the most important were anonymous or at least from the manuscript evidence difficult to ascribe to a particular jurist. The early thirteenth-century ordo with the incipit *Antequam dicatur de processu iudicii* is a striking example. *Antequam* exists in scores of manuscripts, was printed in the sixteenth century under the name of Johannes Andreae, and has been printed in several modern editions.[73] From the manuscript and printed texts, jurists found it a useful text until well into the early modern period. Other texts had similar fates. *Ad summariam notitiam* is ascribed to and found among the works attributed to Petrus Hispanus.

In the thirteenth century, procedural literature reached its maturity. A number of Italian jurists composed comprehensive and important treatises on procedure that soon supplanted the twelfth-century texts.[74] Tancred of Bologna wrote the most copied, the most revised, and the most influential treatise.[75] The timing of Tancred's text is not serendipitous. The new inquisitorial procedure and other emerging norms of procedure had to be incorporated into the ordo iudiciarius. Tancred's *Ordo* had immediate and long lasting success. It is preserved in several hundred manuscripts. It was revised by Bartholomaeus Brixiensis and other anonymous

72. Fowler-Magerl, *Ordo* passim, and 'Ordines' 56–78. She also treats the major ordines, as my notes will indicate.

73. Fowler-Magerl, *Ordo* 151–153. Pirmin Spiess, 'Ordo iudiciarius antequam', *Palatia Historica: Festschrift für Ludwig Anton Doll zum 75. Geburtstag*, ed. P. Spiess (Quellen und Abhandlungen zur mittelrheinischen Kirchengeschichte 75; Mainz 1994) 155–226.

74. Bettetini, 'Tancredi da Bologna' 2.1930–1931. Litewski, *Zivilprozeß*, has written the most thorough description of the norms and rules established by the jurists for the 'ordo iudiciarius'. He based his analysis on the ordines published by Friedrich Bergmann, ed., *Pillii, Tancredi, Gratiae Libri De iudiciorum ordine* (Göttingen 1842). The most recent attempt to describe the theoretical foundations and the various parts of the 'ordo iudiciarius' is Knut Wolfgang Nörr, *Romanisch-kanonisches Prozessrecht: Erkenntnisverfahren erster Instanz in civilibus* (Enzyklopädie der Rechts- und Staatswissenschaft, Abteilung Rechtswissenschaft; Berlin-Heidelberg-New York 2012). For an excellent synthesis of the rules of procedure that focuses on English ecclesiastical courts, see Richard Helmholz, *The Canon Law and Ecclesiastical Jurisdiction from 597 to the 1640s* (Oxford History of the Laws of England 1; Oxford-New York 2004) 311–353 and 599–642. Thomas Wetzstein, *Heilige vor Gericht: Das Kanonisationverfahren im europäischen Spätmittelalter* (Forschungen zur Kirchlichen Rechtsgeschichte und zum Kirchenrecht 28; Köln-Weimar-Wien 2004), has an excellent chapter on procedure. Peter Landau has gathered his essays on procedure in *Europäische Rechtsgeschichte und kanonisches Recht im Mittelalter* (Badenweiler 2013) 539–631.

75. Easily accessible manuscripts of Tancred's original text are Klagenfurt ML XXIX.a.10, fol. 135ra–150rb; Lisbon BN 371, fol. 81–94; Madrid BN 823, fol. 1r–12va; Vat. Borgh. 261, fol. 53ra–68va; Vat. Pal. lat. 656, fol. 175ra–186rb; Vat. Reg. lat. 1126, fol. 1r–10r; Vienna ÖNB 2080, fol. 127ra–134rb.

jurists.[76] Tancred cited three canons from the Fourth Lateran Council of 1215 as canons of the council and not from the canonical collection, *Compilatio quarta*, through which they entered canon law.[77] These texts cannot be a sure guide to dating the first version of Tancred's *Ordo,* since controversy surrounded Johannes Teutonicus's compilation, and some canonists refused to use it.[78] However, since Tancred referred to these important procedural canons sparingly and to *Qualiter et quando* (c.8) only once, we might assume he finished his text shortly after 1215.[79] The other two canons Tancred cited, *Ut debitus* (c.35, On appeals) and *Quoniam contra falsam* (c.38, On false accusations) were cited only in the later parts of his *Ordo,* which could be another piece of evidence that Tancred finished his text in the shadow of the Fourth Lateran Council.

In his prologue, Tancred mentioned two of his predecessors who influenced his work, Ricardus Anglicus and Pillius.[80] He highlighted the differences between Pillius's and his own work. Pillius concentrated on Roman law texts, cited only a few texts from canon law, and wrote his treatise in the form of a 'summa'. Tancred declares that he will follow Pillius's style of writing, but he will pay much more attention to canonical sources.[81] He did this not just because he was a canonist. He must have understood that papal decretals and the writings of the canonists had been crucial for shaping the norms of the 'ordo iudiciarius'. At the beginning of his treatise, Tancred gives a summary of the entire judicial process:

The competent judge is chosen, the defendant is summoned through a document or through a summoner. The complaint (libellus) is given to the defendant. At that point he may ask for delays. The petition for a trial (litis contestatio) is made, oaths that promised the accusation is not false are taken (iuramentum calumniae), the defendant and the plaintiff are questioned by the judge; witnesses and documents are produced. Finally, a sentence is rendered. The entire proceedings are then written down.[82]

76. Fowler-Magerl, *Ordo* 128–130.

77. Kenneth Pennington, 'Decretal Collections 1190–1234', Hartmann and Pennington, *History* 293–317.

78. Ibid. 314–315.

79. Tancred, *Ordo,* ed. Bergmann, 154, 183, 249, 267, 291, 298, 299, 301. The clustering of citations after part 1 and especially in part 4 may indicate a rough time frame for the completion of his treatise.

80. Ennio Cortese, 'Pillio da Medicina', DGI 2.1587–1590, at 1588b–1589a. Fowler-Magerl, *Ordo* 115–119 (Ricardus), and the ordo *Invocato Christi nomine,* attributed to Pillius in almost all the extant manuscripts; Fowler-Magerl prefers not to accept his authorship, *Ordo* 120–121. In any case, at the very least, Pillius's thought influenced the tract. See Stephan Kuttner, 'Ricardus Anglicus (Richard de Mores ou de Morins)', DDC 7 (1965) 676–681. See also Mario Caravale, 'Bencivenne da Siena', DBI 8 (1966) 215–216; and Lange, *Römisches Recht* 226–236.

81. Tancred, ed. Bergmann, 89. The treatise that Tancred probably assumed was that of Pillius did cite canonical texts sparingly. Tancred referred to Gratian a dozen times and to decretals of popes Lucius III, Alexander III, and Celestine III.

82. Ibid. 90.

He then outlined the contents of his treatise. It was, he noted, divided into four parts: the first part dealt with the court; the second with the plaintiff and the defendant; the third considered the trial itself; and the fourth examined court judgments, their execution, and appeals.[83] It is noteworthy that Tancred did not mention the new inquisitorial procedure contained in *Qualiter et quando* at the beginning of his treatise. He reserved the inquisitorial procedure for criminal offences and discussed it in the second part of his book.

In the panoply of rights that the jurists established for defendants, the summons (*citatio*) was the most important. Tancred began by describing the various ways that a defendant should be summoned. Tancred did not cite *Qualiter et quando*, but he took his description of criminal summons from Innocent III: 'We may be silent about how to summon a defendant in notorious crimes; [a defendant is summoned] through a denunciation, an inquisition, an exception and accusation'.[84]

Although Tancred used the conciliar canon's wording, part of it did not fit his purpose, and he made an important clarification to the three modes of proof. Innocent did not mention notorious crimes, but Tancred did. Although he had declared that he would not discuss notorious crimes, he immediately plunged into the thicket of contradictory norms that swirled around that issue.

I have said that I would not treat notorious crimes because neither an accusation nor witnesses are necessary. Notorious crimes can be punished without them.... Nevertheless, certain parts of the 'ordo iudiciarius' must be observed in notorious criminal cases.... The defendant ought to be summoned and interrogated. He ought to have a sentence rendered whether he is present or contumaciously absent... because, if he would not be cited, the sentence would not hold.... Anyone whose crime is notorious can be punished by a judge from the power of his office, although the defendant does not appear before him and is not convicted with witnesses.[85]

I have mentioned that Gratian accepted the principle of rendering a judgment on a defendant without a trial in the case of a notorious crime. By the early thirteenth century the jurists questioned Gratian's conclusions. Tancred's comments reflect a stage in the evolution of the jurists' thought. They would eventually conclude that no one may be condemned without a trial to which the defendant had been summoned and in which he

---

83. Ibid. 90–91.

84. Ibid. 150–151: 'Ut etiam de notoriis taceatur in modum denuntiationis, inquisitionis, exceptionis et accusationis'. 4 Lat. c.8: 'Contra quos, ut de notoriis excessibus taceatur, etsi tribus modis possit procedi, per accusationem videlicet, denunciationem et inquisitionem ipsorum'. COD 238.

85. Ibid. 151–152.

participated. Even the defendant who had committed the most heinous crime had an absolute right to have a trial. To use the maxim that Guillelmus Durantis created in his great tract on procedure, which we will discuss below, even the devil had a right to have his day in court.[86]

After discussing notorious cases, Tancred returned to the forms of summons that were permitted in a criminal trial. In a denunciation, a written document (*libellus inscriptionis*) was not necessary, and every denunciation should be preceded by a charitable warning that the wrongdoer should do penance and 'retreat from evil' (a malo recedat).[87] If his accuser does not give a warning the denunciation is not valid. If the accuser was a criminal, 'infamis', or an enemy, his denunciations will be rejected.[88] Tancred clearly considered this category of crimes to be sins, rather than serious crimes. 'The punishment for the accusation by denunciation is mild, because a penance ought be imposed on the defendant for the crime'.[89] However, if the crime was one that would require the defendant to be deposed from his office, such as simony, the judge must proceed differently. A simoniac cleric can perform penance for his crime but cannot retain his ecclesiastical office.

The judge exercised inquisitorial procedure entirely from the authority and jurisdiction of his office. He can appoint an investigator (prosecutor or exsecutor) to uncover or examine the evidence. 'Fama' should always precede an inquisition.[90] Innocent III had emphasized the importance of fama in *Qualiter et quando*, but Tancred limited the scope of an inquisition. The fama cannot be singular but must be repeated and must come from good and worthy men. Otherwise, an inquisition ought not to be made.[91]

The last method Tancred discussed, and the oldest, was accusatorial (modus accusationis). Any accusation against a cleric or a layman required a written accusation (libellus inscriptionis). If his suit failed, the accuser

---

86. Guillelmus Durantis, *Speculum iudiciale*, 4 vols. (Strassburg 1473) vol. 3, part 3, De inquisitione § Ultimo, fol. 15ra: 'et etiam diabolo si in iudicio adesset non negaretur'. Guillelmus's striking statement had a long and illustrious life in procedural literature.

87. Yves Mausen, 'Accusation et dénonciation: Au sujet de l'éthique de l'action pénale', *Einfluss der Kanonistik* 2.411–426.

88. Durantis, *Speculum* 152–153.

89. Ibid. 153: 'Poena huius processus est mitis quia debet penitentia ei imponi pro illo crimine'.

90. On 'fama' is the fundamental work of Francesco Migliorino, *Fama e infamia: Problemi della società medievale nel pensiero giuridico nei secoli XII e XIII* (Catania 1985). Most recently, with full bibliography, Antonia Fiori, '*Quasi denunciante fama*: Note sull'introduzione del processo tra rito accusatorio e inquisitorio', *Einfluss der Kanonistik* 2.351–67, who still adheres to Trusen's thesis that Pope Innocent III 'introduced' inquisitorial procedure into ecclesiastical courts, even though she cites Lotte Kéry's work. See n. 65 above. Also the essays by Wickham and Kuehn in *Fama: The Politics of Talk and Reputation in Medieval Europe*, ed. Thelma Fenster and Daniel Lord Smail (Ithaca-London 2003) 15–46.

91. Tancred, ed. Bergmann, 153–154.

was subject to the 'poena talionis' (a penalty equivalent to that which the defendant would suffer if found guilty).[92] The 'lex talionis' had a long tradition in the history of law and by the thirteenth century must have been a deterrent to any plaintiff who wished to accuse someone instead of leaving the accusation to the court.[93] As generations of jurists before him, Tancred found the poena talionis to be an appropriate protection for the defendant. Juristic opinion and custom, however, began to find fault. Egidius de Fuscarariis, the first layman to teach canon law in Bologna, wrote that ecclesiastical courts and secular courts no longer obligated a plaintiff to the poena talionis. Bolognese custom had rejected the poena talionis in ecclesiastical and secular courts. The ecclesiastical courts had abandoned it completely. The secular courts stipulated that a plaintiff should make a deposit. If his case failed, he must pay twenty Bolognese solidi. Egidius did not approve of this departure from the norms of the Ius commune in the courts of the *Ius proprium*. The Bolognese custom, he argued, was an invitation to calumny and many injustices.[94] What he did not consider was the impediment to justice that this ancient institution created. Other jurists were already moving to abandon it. Goffredus de Trano offered a long series of exceptions to the requirement that a plaintiff must obligate himself to the poena talionis.[95]

Guillelmus Durantis concluded that the customs of many regions permitted that a libellus inscriptionis no longer be required for a criminal summons.[96] That was all he wrote about the issue. Baldus de Ubaldis († 1400) understood that the triumph of custom over the Ius commune had to be defended. He added a long 'additio' to Guillelmus's text.

This custom, nevertheless, continues to be observed in Italy that although laymen present 'libelli accusatorii' when they make an accusation, they do not make an inscriptio or an obligation to render the poena talionis.... Egidius disapproved of the custom. He argued that the custom invited accusers to make false accusations that oppressed defendants in lands where persons who are accused of serious crimes must spend a month in prison.... Guido of Suzzara approved this

---

92. Ibid. 157: 'Est inscriptio necessaria et accusator se obligare tenetur ad poena talionis... si non probaverit.'

93. An adequate general history of the *Lex talionis* has not been written; see, for example, Adrianus Petrus van Deinse, *Dissertatio Juridica Inauguralis de poena talionis apud varias gentes, praesertim apud Romanos* (Leiden 1822, reprinted Charleston, S.C. 2011).

94. Egidius de Fuscarariis, *Ordo iudiciarius*, Wahrmund, *Quellen* 3.152–153. On Egidius, see Cristina Bukowska Gorgoni, 'Foscarari (Foscherari), Egidio', DBI 49 (1997) 277–280; and Sara Menzinger, 'Foscarari, Egidio (Egidius, Gilius de Foscarariis, Fuscarariis)', DGI 1.893–894.

95. Goffredus de Trano (Tranensis), *Summa* (1491), fol. 70va (Book 5, titie1) (ed. Lyon 1519, reprinted Aalen 1968), fol. 196va. Martin Bertram, 'Goffredo da Trani', DGI 1.1038–1039.

96. Guillelmus Durantis, *Speculum iudiciale*, vol. 1, title de accusatore, fol. 84rb: 'Hodie tamen de consuetudine multarum regionum non fiunt inscriptiones'.

custom because crimes would remain unpunished because of accusers' fear of the poena talionis. A valid accusation can easily fail because a full proof was not made, either because witnesses were rejected or because advocates were incompetent. [For these reasons] men are fearful of submitting to the poena talionis.[97]

Guido of Suzzara († ca. 1291) was an extraordinarily creative thinker who had a great influence on later jurists, especially on their conceptions of justice.[98] This reference to his thought is one more example of his importance. It is also an example that provides evidence of why Guillelmus's treatise had a long run as the most important procedural tract of the later Middle Ages and was still used widely in the sixteenth century.

Besides Baldus, the most important canonist of the fourteenth century, Johannes Andreae († 1348) wrote 'additiones' to Guillelmus's text.[99] Together they updated Guillelmus's text and incorporated the significant changes in the jurisprudence of procedure that had evolved between the second half of the thirteenth and the first half of the fourteenth century.[100]

Egidius's prologue gives us some insight into the mind of a professor of law in the mid-thirteenth century (following the Bamberg manuscript):

I, Egidius de Fuscarariis, citizen of Bologna and unworthy doctor of canon law, at the urging of some of my friends and for the education of new advocates working in canon law, who, although learned in jurisprudence, do not know how to deal with cases, I have written the present work for them, in which I shall demonstrate how civil, spiritual, and criminal cases ought to be dealt with and concluded.[101]

I have followed the Bamberg manuscript's readings to show how not having good editions of a text may distort our understanding of a jurist's

97. Ibid.: 'Hanc autem consuetudinem improbat Egidius dicens quod per illiam invitantur homines ad calamniandum et ad gravandos reos maxime in illis locis quibus de certis gravibus criminibus accusati per mensem carcerati tenentur. Guido de Suzzara in l. Qui crimen, C. qui accus. non poss. (Cod. 9.1.3) commendat illiam quia timore talionis remanebant crimina impunita quia in vera accusatione posset agens facile deficere ut quia non plene probat, vel propter repulsam testium vel propter imperitiam advocati, propter que nolunt se homines submittere periculo talionis'.

98. Pennington, *Prince and the Law* 93–96 and 103–106. Giuseppe Mazzanti, 'Guido da Suzzara', DBI 61 (2004) 421–426; and Corrado Benatti, 'Guido da Suzzara', DGI 1.1093–1094.

99. Giorgio Tamba, 'Giovanni d'Andrea', DBI 55 (2001) 667–672; Andrea Bartocci, 'Giovanni d'Andrea (Johannes Andreae de Bononia)', DGI 1.1008–1012.

100. See Pennington, *Prince and the Law*, especially chapters 4 and 5.

101. Egidius de Fuscarariis, *Ordo iudiciarius*, ed. Wahrmund, *Quellen* 3.1–2: 'Ego Egidius de Fuscariis, civis Bononiae, doctor decretorum licet indignus, ad instantiam quorundam meorum scolarium (amicorum Bamberg MS) et ad eruditionem novorum advocatorum militantium in iure canonico, qui licet periti in iure existant, ignorantes tamen practicam (ignorantes practicam *om.* B) causas nesciunt ordinare, et etiam ad instructionem iudicum et notariorum (et etiam—notariorum *om.* Bamberg) aggredior praesens opus, in quo qualiter causae tam civiles quam spirituales ac etiam criminales secundum ordinem iuris et laudabilem consuetudinem civitatis Bononiae (secundum—Bononiae *om.* Bamberg) tractari debeant et finiri'.

purpose. Wahrmund used six manuscripts to establish his edition of the almost four score known to him. If we follow his edition of Egidius's prologue, he wrote for students who were ignorant of how the courts worked and for judges and advocates, who presumably knew how the courts functioned but, perhaps, had no legal training. In any case, Wahrmund's edition of Egidius's prologue presents a muddled mélange of his purpose and has led scholars to denigrate the high quality of his text. Egidius did include examples of the legal documents that an advocate needed to present to the court during a trial, which has led scholars to think that his text had a purely practical purpose and that he had no sophisticated understanding of the jurisprudence of procedure.[102]

I have already discussed Egidius's discussion of the poena talionis. Although later jurists rejected his opinion, which was the common opinion of the jurists when he wrote, it is possible to begin reading his *Ordo* at almost any point to see the sophisticated understanding of procedure he possessed. For example, when he discussed courts, he made the point that a defendant could be summoned to courts outside his local jurisdiction:

It should be noted that the defendant is forced to submit to the jurisdiction of another court for these reasons, namely: reason of the wrong, disputes of possession and contract, an accusation in another forum, questions of residence, by mutual consent, a reconvening of a trial, to deny wrong doing, for a will, administrative misdeeds, professional wrongs, forum dictated by a constitution, questions of origins, disputes of free status, summons during military service, questions of status, and of marriage. Any defendant can be summoned to Rome because Rome is the common homeland of all men.[103]

Egidius's list had evolved in the Ius commune over the previous century and could never have been understood by someone who had not had legal training. The question of where a defendant could be summoned was a difficult question that took a long time for the jurists to solve. Local defendants and their advocates did not give up their rights to have their disputes heard in local courts easily.[104]

---

102. Bethmann-Hollweg, *Der Civilprozeß* 6.138–139: Egidius's tract had an 'oberflächlich praktische Richtung' and demonstrated a 'schlechtere Methode in der zweiten Hälfte des dreizehnten Jahrhunderts auch unter den Kanonisten herrschend wurde'; cited by Wahrmund, pp. xxxvii–xxxviii.

103. Egidius, *Ordo iudiciarius,* ed. Wahrmund, 78: 'Set notandum est, quod reus forum non suum cogitur subire, his de causis videlicet: ratione delicti, possessionis, contractus, accusationis, domicilii, consensus, reconventionis, negationis, ultime voluntatis, amministrationis, professionis, constitutionis, originis, manumissionis, militie, temporis, dignitatis et matrimonii. Rome tamen quilibet potest conveniri, cum sit communis hominum patria.'

104. Kenneth Pennington, 'Johannes Teutonicus and Papal Legates', AHP 21 (1983) 183–194, for an example. Richard H. Helmholz, *The Spirit of Classical Canon Law* (The Spirit of the Laws; Athens-London 1996), has described some of the principles of canonical procedure in chapters 4 and 11.

Guillelmus Durantis was the greatest and most influential procedural-ist of the thirteenth century.[105] He wrote his *Speculum iudiciale* in the last quarter of the thirteenth century. It is disputed whether he wrote two ver-sions.[106] At the beginning of the *Speculum* he gave a list of all the treatises on procedure he knew:[107]

Pillius,[108] Bagarottus,[109] Tancred,[110] Roffredus Beneventanus,[111] Ubertus de Bob-bio,[112] Ubertus de Bonaccurso,[113] Johannes de Deo Gratia,[114] Bonaguida Aretti-nus,[115] Johannes de Blanosco,[116] and Egidius Bononensis.[117]

---

105. Gaudemet, 'Durand' 82–87. Hermann Lange and Maximiliane Kriechbaum, *Römisches Recht im Mittelalter*, 2: *Die Kommentatoren* (München 2007) 477–87 at 483–486; Knut W. Nörr, 'A Propos du Speculum Iudiciale de Guilaume Durand', *Guilaume Durand: Évêque de Mende (vers 1230–1296): Canoniste, legiste et homme politique*, ed. P. M. Gy (Actes de la Table Ronde de CNRS. Mende, 24–27 Mai 1990; Paris 1992) 63–67. See also Vincenzo Colli's three essays reprinted in *Giuristi me-dievali e produzione libraria: Manoscritti, autografi* (Stockstadt am Main 2005), and a few additional comments and bibliography that Martin Bertram added in *Kanonisten und ihre Texte (1234 bis Mitte 14. Jh.): 18 Aufsätze und 14 Exkurse* (Education and Society in the Middle Ages and Renaissance 43; Leiden-Boston 2013) 508.

106. Easily obtained manuscripts of the text are Berlin SB lat. fol. 300, fol. 1r–374 and Savigny 5, fol. 1r–329; Klosterneuburg ML 122, fol. 1ra–332ra and 123, fol. 62ra–337vb; Munich BSB Clm 6601 and 6602, 9502, 10241, 15705, 18047, 19511, 21630; Paris BNF lat. 4254, fol. 5r–302r, 4255, 4256, 4257, 4258, 4259, 8038, 14333, 15417; Vat. lat. 2339, fol. 4ra–128vb, 130ra–365ra, lat. 2340 fol. 1ra–287vb, lat. 2341 fol. 18ra–191vb and fol. 212ra–308rb (with addditions of Johannes Andreae in the margins), lat. 2547 fol. 54ra–402va, lat. 2627 fol. 1ra–282vb, lat. 2628 fol. 1ra–304vb, lat. 2629 fol. 1ra–316rb, lat. 2630 fol. 1ra–259vb, lat. 2631 fol. 4ra–385rb, lat. 2635 fol. 1ra–281ra (first and second parts of *Speculum* with additions of Johannes Andreae added after each section), lat. 2636 fol. 1ra–208ra (third and fourth parts of *Speculum* with additions of Johannes Andreae added after each section); Vienna ÖNB 2048 and 2049.

107. Guillelmus Durantis, *Speculum iudiciale* (1473), vol. 1, prologue fol. 1vb.

108. Cortese, 'Pillio da Medicina', DGI 2.1587–1590.

109. Roberto Abbondanza, 'Bagarotto (Bagarotto dei Corradi)', DBI 5 (1963) 170–174; and En-nio Cortese, 'Bagarotto', DGI 1.142–143.

110. Bettetini, 'Tancredi da Bologna', DGI 2.1930–1931.

111. Ingrid Baumgärtner, 'Was muß ein Legist vom Kirchenrecht wissen? Roffredus Beneven-tanus und seine "Libelli de iure canonico",' *Proceedings Cambridge 1984* 223–245. Manlio Bellomo, 'Intorno a Roffredo Beneventano: Professore a Roma?' *Scuole, diritto e società nel mezzogiorno medi-evale d Italia* (Catania 1985) 1.135–181. Daniela Novarese, 'Roffredo da Benevento', *Federico II: Enci-clopedia Fridericiana* (Rome 2005) 578–580. Ennio Cortese, 'Roffredo Epifani (Epifanius, Epifandes) da Benevento', DGI 2.1712–1715.

112. Nicoletta Sarti, 'Uberto da Bobbio', DGI 2.1989–1990.

113. Isidoro Soffietti, 'Uberto di Bonaccorso', DGI 2.1991.

114. On the contested name and origin of this jurist and his work, see Andrea Padovani, 'Gra-zia', DBI 58 (2002) 780–793; and 'Prime ricerche sul ms. "Bologna, Collegio di Spagna, 210": L'*Ordo iudiciarius di Grazia aretino*', *La filosofia del diritto dei giuristi*, ed. Bernardo Pieri and Antonino Rotolo (2 vols. Bologna 2003) 33–51.

115. Severino Caprioli, 'Bonaguida d'Arezzo (de Aretio si dice egli stesso; Aretinus, de Areti-nis)', DBI 11 (1969) 512–513. Martino Semeraro, 'Bonaguida d'Arezzo', DGI 1.282.

116. Lange and Kriechbaum, *Römisches Recht* 461–468 at 466–467.

117. See Fowler-Magerl, *Ordo*, for information about jurists not mentioned earlier in this chap-ter: Bagarottus, 186–193, 223–229, 231–236; Ubertus de Bobbio, 215–216; Ubertus de Bonaccursio, 185–210; Johannes de Deo, 198, 215–216. See also Stephan Kuttner, 'Analecta iuridica Vaticana (Vat. lat. 2343)', *Collectanea Vaticana in honorem Anselmi M. Card. Albareda a Biblioteca Apostolica edita* (Stu-di e Testi 219–220; Vatican City 1962) 1.415–452, who discusses several of these works.

To which he added, 'and many others'. Those jurists were, however, his predecessors upon whom he most relied. Johannes Andreae later added much more information in a long addition to Guillelmus's text about these jurists and also added details about a large number of other proceduralists whom Guillelmus did not mention. A few very early incunabula editions do not have Johannes's additions (nor do they have Baldus's).[118] Guillelmus recorded the most important writers; Johannes, as was his inclination in all of his works, cited every jurist about whom he had information.[119]

The *Speculum iudiciale* is a massive work, especially with the additions of Johannes and Baldus, and defies any easy summary of its contents. Its structure is more easily described. Guillelmus divided the work into four parts. In the first he deals with the persons involved in any court case, in the second with the civil procedure, in the third with criminal procedure, and in the fourth part he gave examples of the documents necessary for legal proceedings. He also included examples of documents in the first three parts. For the most part he followed the organization of his material established by the decretal collections since the time of Bernard of Pavia.[120]

In his Prologue, he dedicated his work to Cardinal Deacon Ottobonus de Fieschi, who was elected Pope Adrian V in 1276.[121] (Ottobonus was a member of the Fieschi family, which had produced Pope Innocent IV.) Guillelmus told once again Paucapalea's story that the 'ordo iudiciarius' had its origins in paradise.[122] He wrote his book for judges, advocates, tabelliones (notaries), litigants, and witnesses so that they could function in extraordinary and ordinary trials, both civil and criminal. He boldly asserted that anyone who used this book, no matter how inexpert, whether a judge, lawyer, or notary, would become learned.[123] Guillelmus could not have known how true his boast was. The extensive additions of Johannes Andreae and Baldus de Ubaldis gave his text an extraordinarily long life in the literature of procedure. Without those additions, Guillelmus's book

118. I have used Strassburg 1473. Baldus's additions were printed separately in Rome 1473. All the later editions of the *Speculum iudiciale* contain both sets of additions.

119. Guido Rossi, 'Contributi alla biografia del canonista Giovanni d'Andrea', *Rivista trimestrale di diritto e procedura civile* 11 (1957) 145–152.

120. Pennington, 'Decretal Collections' 295–300.

121. Agostino Paravicini Bagliani, *Cardinali di curia e 'familiae' cardinalizie dal 1227 al 1254* (Italia Sacra 18–19; Padua 1972) 2:358–365; Brenda M. Bolton, 'Ottobuono [Ottobuono or Ottobono Fieschi; later Adrian V] (c.1205–1276)', *Oxford Dictionary of National Biography*, online ed. (Oxford 2004).

122. Guillelmus Durantis, *Speculum iudiciale* (1473), fol. 2ra.

123. Ibid. fol. 2ra–2rb: 'Hoc autem solum assero audacter quod huius sollers inspectio quemvis quantumlibet inexpertum peritum, iudicem cautum causidicum et tabularium efficiet eruditum'.

would have become outdated by the first half of the fourteenth century.[124]

Treatises on procedure continued to be an important genre of legal writing in the Ius commune until the end of the seventeenth century. In the late Middle Ages and early modern period, criminal procedure and monographic studies on parts of the 'ordo iudiciarius' became a central focus for the jurists.[125] The only early-modern literary genre that surpassed procedural treatises were 'consilia'. The work of these proceduralists has been neglected by legal historians. Two sixteenth-century jurists are particularly significant for the development of the jurisprudence of procedure: Giacomo Menochio (1532–1607) and Giuseppe Mascardi (1540–1587). Their work was very influential in the late sixteenth century and well into the seventeenth century.

Menochio studied law at Pavia and received his law degree in 1556.[126] He married shortly after having finished his studies and eventually fathered eleven children. In 1561 Duke Emanuele Filiberto of Savoy offered him a chair in canon law at the new university in Mondovì, which the prince had founded in the previous year.[127] Shortly afterwards Menochio moved to the University of Pavia. His career was not without controversy. In 1596 the Archbishop Federico Borromeo of Milan excommunicated him for his views on the boundaries between secular and ecclesiastical jurisdictions.

Menochio discussed procedure in all of his works, but his most important and influential treatise was *De praesumptionibus, coniecturis, signis et indiciis* in three books.[128] He was prolific. During his career he wrote over 1000 consilia, which were printed in twelve volumes. The last edition was published in Frankfurt am Main in 1676. In his treatise on presumptions he began by observing that although it may lack other parts, no trial can be held without proof. He then went on to pose 100 questions about proof and the presumptions that justified a proof. In the second part of his work he dealt with specific problems in 96 presumptions. For example, Presumption 90: When one granted a greater presumption to the defendant than for the plaintiff. Menochio listed twenty-six cases in which the defendant was presumed to be favored over the plaintiff.[129] His discussion centered on the maxim 'In dubio pro reo' (in doubt the defendant should

124. The edition of the *Speculum iudiciale (iuris)* that is available in most libraries is the Basel 1574 edition, reprinted Aalen 1975 and Frankfurt am Main 2009.

125. Maria Gigliola di Renzo Villata, 'Alle origini di una scienza criminalistica laica matura: L'apporto dei canonisti quattrocenteschi: Riflessioni brevi', *Einfluss der Kanonistik* 2.1–21.

126. Chiara Valsecchi, 'Menochio, Giacomo (Jacopo)', DBI 73 (2009) 521–24; and Valsecchi, 'Menochio, Jacopo', DGI 2.1328–1330.

127. Gioachino Grassi, *Dell'università degli studi in Mondovì dissertazione* (Mondovì 1804) 7–22.

128. Printed in Cologne 1587 and Lyon 1588.

129. Menochio, *De praesumptionibus* (Cologne 1587) fol. 466r–470r.

be favored), which governed how the courts had evaluated evidence for centuries.[130] Menochio's book filled a need. It was reprinted many times. The last edition seems to have been printed in Geneva in 1724.

The monographic procedural literature in the sixteenth century is varied and rich. In this essay I can point only to a few significant examples. Another jurist whose work had a long-lasting influence on later jurists was Giuseppe Mascardi.[131] He was born in Sarzana around 1540 into an aristocratic family with a tradition of working in law. He received his law degree at Pisa in 1565. After a brief stay in Rome, he went to Milan to join the court of Archbishop Carlo Borromeo. Later he worked in several Italian cities. He had become a cleric early on. When he published the first two volumes of his *Conclusiones probationum omnium quae in utroque foro* in 1584, he dedicated his work to Pope Gregory XIII. Like Menochio's work, it was printed many times until the end of the seventeenth century. Also like Menochio, he structured his text around questions. After posing nineteen questions, he gave 1428 conclusions. It was, however, a far more extensive and thorough treatment of proof and presumption than Menochio's. Gian Luigi Riccio and Bartolomeo Negro provided additiones to the work after Mascardi's death. The last edition of the work was published in Cologne 1751. It was the last word on presumption in the Ius commune.

Mascardi began his discussion of criminal procedure by stating a principle that was embedded in the jurisprudence of procedure since the twelfth century: a defendant could not be convicted by the testimony of one witness, even if the witness was of spotless reputation.[132] The reason was that in criminal cases proofs must have even greater clarity than the midday sun.[133] A defendant cannot be convicted with imperfect proofs.[134] In civil cases a judgment may be rendered against a defendant on the basis of presumptions but never in a criminal accusation.[135] Mascardi limited the principle that a full proof required more than one witness with a second

---

130. Dig. 50.17.125, and Bernard d'Alteroche, 'De l'interprétation favorable du doute à l'interprétation favorable de la loi pénale: Recherche sur les origines canoniques d'un principe', *Einfluss der Kanonistik* 2.135–168.

131. Lorenzo Sinisi, 'Mascardi, Giuseppe', DBI 71 (2008) 538–541; and Sinisi, 'Mascardi, Giuseppe', DGI 2.1298–1299.

132. Mascardi, *Conclusiones* (Frankfurt am Main 1593), fol. 284r: 'In criminalibus unum testem coniunctum cum fama non probare', to which he added a long list of jurists who endorsed the principle.

133. Ibid. fol. 284va: 'quia in criminalibus debent esse probationes luce meridiana clariores'.

134. Ibid.: 'etiam in criminalibus probationes imperfectae non coniunguntur ad faciendam plenam probationem'.

135. Ibid.: 'Et licet in civilibus ex praesumptionibus quis damnari possit, ut supra multis in locis diximus, tamen secus est in criminalibus'.

principle that if there were other evidence that was very convincing, then even in criminal cases one witness was sufficient.[136] The jurists commonly used two words to describe evidence that was produced by sources other than witnesses: 'indicia' and 'coniecturae'. They would attach the adjective 'indubitata' or 'vehementes' to such evidence that was conclusive and convincing. Mascardi defined both in his treatise and noted that 'coniecturae' and 'indicia' are closely related.[137] The jurists often seemed to write as if the words meant the same thing. Mascardi placed two more limitations on the principle that a criminal conviction needed two witnesses: if the penalty is monetary, only more general presumptions are necessary; and if lucidly clear proofs cannot be had in a criminal case, then 'most urgent' presumptions can be used to render a judgment.[138] I have written elsewhere that from the thirteenth century on, medieval proceduralists and jurists were not bound by the archaic principle that a criminal trial required two witnesses for a conviction. They fully recognized circumstantial evidence that was 'vehemens' and 'indubitata' as being probative. Most importantly for modern scholarship, if two witnesses were not required for a full proof, then the argument put forward by many scholars that this rigid principle led to the frequent use of torture in the medieval courts loses its force. This fact also undercuts the argument that the evolution of extraordinary punishments (poenae extraordinariae) was due to the courts not using torture in the sixteenth century.[139]

The most important criminal lawyer of the medieval and early modern period was undoubtedly Prospero Farinacci (1544–1618).[140] He was prob-

136. Ibid. fol. 284vb: 'Limita quod dictum est supra unum testem cum fama plene non probare, ut non procedat, si adsint aliae coniecturae vehementes, etenim tunc etiam in criminalibus per unum testem plena probatio habetur'.

137. Ibid. fol. 23r–25r at fol. 24va: 'Coniecturae proxima sunt indicia de quorum natura nunc a nobis strictim videndum est'.

138. Ibid. fol. 284rb: 'quod dixi supra in criminalibus requiri probationes luce clariores, nec satis esse praesumptiones, ut hoc tantum verum sit, quando ageretur de poena corporali, secus si de poena pecuniaria, tunc enim huiusmodi praesumptiones sufficiunt… quando sumus in casu in quo clarae probationes haberi non possunt <in criminalibus>, tunc nempe ex urgentissimis praesumptionibus potest procedi et condemnari'.

139. Kenneth Pennington, 'Torture and Fear: Enemies of Justice', RIDC 19 (2008) 213, 216–217, 236, and passim. Cf. John H. Langbein, *Torture and the Law of Proof: Europe and England in the Ancien Régime* (Chicago-London 2006) 47–69 and passim.

140. The following paragraphs are based on ibid. 203–242.

141. Aldo Mazzacane, 'Farinacci, Prospero', DBI 45 (1995) 1–5; Mazzacane, 'Farinacci, Prospero', DGI 1.822–825; and Mazzacane, 'Farinacci, Prospero (1544–1618)', *Juristen: Ein biographisches Lexikon von der Antike bis zum 20. Jahrhundert*, ed. Michael Stolleis (München 1995) 199–200; Niccolò Del Re, 'Prospero Farinacci giureconsulto romano (1544–1618)', *Archivio della Società Romana di Storia Patria*, 3rd series, 28 (1975) 135–220. Mazzacane writes that Farinacci completed it in 1614, but an edition of *Praxis et theoricae criminalis* was published in Venice ('apud Georgium Variscum, 1603 [in fine 1601]'), which is described as the third edition, with additions made by the author to the first and second editions; see *Antichi testi giuridici (secoli XV–XVIII) dell'Istituto di Storia del*

ably educated in Perugia and quickly gained experience on both sides of the bench. In 1567 he became the general commissioner in the service of the Orsini of Bracciano; the next year he took up residence in Rome as a member of the papal 'camera'. However, in 1570 he was imprisoned for an unknown crime. Legal problems hounded him for the rest of his life. He lost an eye in a fight, was stripped of his positions, and was even accused of sodomy. In spite of his difficulties, Pope Clement VIII reinstated him to the papal court in 1596. He began his most important work, *Praxis et theoria criminalis,* in 1581 and put the finishing touches on it by 1601.[141]

One of Farinacci's most important contributions to the jurisprudence of procedure is his detailed discussion of torture. He summed up the three centuries of jurisprudence governing the use of torture by judges in the courtroom. He repeated the standard norm that the evidence establishing the judge's right to torture a person must be legitimate, probable, grave, and sufficient. The judge must be almost certain of the person's guilt before he can order torture. Farinacci repeated the condemnation of many earlier jurists that judges are too ready to torture. 'Princes', he proclaimed, 'should not tolerate those evil judges'.[142] The proofs necessary to torture should be grave, urgent, certain, clear, but even clearer than the light at midday. The judge should be almost certain (quasi certus) of the defendant's guilt that nothing is lacking except a confession.[143] Without substantial evidence the judge is very limited in what he can do to a defendant. He cannot torture the defendant. He cannot even frighten him. Fear of torture is, he argued, the same as torture. If the defendant is bound or stripped as if to be tortured, that threat is torture. If a judge acted contrary to the rules, the defendant's confession was not valid.[144] If a man were wise and accustomed to prison the judge could terrorize him outside the courtroom, but if the defendant were base and timid and not accustomed to prison, then the judge could not.[145] A judge who violated the rights of defendants without legitimate evidence or who tortured defendants savagely will be liable for judgment and must be punished.[146] If a judge decided that defendants should be tortured, he must permit them to provide a defense. They must be given the evidence against them.[147] Judges who thought that the evidence was sufficient to torture must ren-

---

Diritto Italiano, ed. Giuliana Sapori (Università degli Studi di Milano, Pubblicazioni dell'Istituto di Storia del Diritto Italiano 7; Milan 1977) 1.242, no. 1162.

142. Prospero Farinacci (Prosperus Farinacius), *Praxis et theoricae criminalis libri duo in quinque titulos distributi* (Frankfurt 1606) book 1, title 5, quaestio 37, p. 575. For the Latin texts here and in the following notes, see my essay 'Torture and Fear.'

143. Farinacci, *Praxis* 576.   144. Ibid. 587.

145. Ibid. 588.   146. Ibid. 589.

147. Ibid. book 1, title 5, quaestio 38, p. 602.

der an interlocutory judgment, from which the defendant could appeal. Farinacci condemned those bloodthirsty judges who did not render the interlocutory sentence in order to proceed directly to the torture chamber. The judge must include all the reasons why he thought the evidence was sufficient for torturing the defendant.[148] The defendant could appeal from a decree of torture and even from the threat of torture. After an appeal from his decree or threat of torture, the judge's hands were bound. He could do nothing.[149] A confession extorted from a defendant by torture after an appeal was invalid.[150] Finally, Farinacci defined three grades of torture: (1) judge-created fear of torture; (2) the defendant is bound and raised (la corda); and (3) the defendant is bound, raised, and beaten.[151]

Perhaps the most misunderstood norm of inquisitorial procedure is when and whether torture was used in the court. As we have seen, the jurists thought that a person could be tortured only if the evidence was, as Farinacci put it, almost certain (quasi certus). A number of scholars have put forward the theory that inquisitorial judges were forced to torture in cases when the defendant had not confessed because a confession was necessary for a full proof if there had not been two witnesses.[152] Baldus had rejected that idea two centuries before; it is no surprise that Farinacci also firmly rejected the idea that a judge could torture a defendant even when he had indisputable evidence of guilt.[153]

There had been a long tradition in the Ius commune that some people were exempt from torture, especially knights, minors, pregnant women, and nobles. Farinacci repeated the traditional teaching.[154] However, the nobility could be tortured with the permission of the prince. Nonetheless, even with his 'absolute power', the prince could not permit judges to torture people without adequate proofs of guilt.[155] Just as the prince could not take away a defendant's rights of due process, Farinacci argued that the prince's 'absolute power' would not permit him to violate the norm that defendants cannot be tortured without sufficient proofs. If judges were to obey princely orders to torture without having sufficient proofs, they will be brought to trial for their crime.[156] Even the pope was limited by these norms of the Ius commune.

148. Ibid. 603.

149. Ibid. 604.

150. Ibid.

151. Ibid. 606–607.

152. Richard M. Fraher, 'Conviction according to Conscience: The Medieval Jurists' Debate concerning Judicial Discretion and the Law of Proof', *Law and History Review* 7 (1989) 23–88, at 80 n. 201.

153. Farinacci, *Praxis*, book 1, title 5, quaestio 38, p. 602.

154. Ibid. 603.

155. Pennington, 'Due Process, Community, and the Prince' 9–47; and Pennington, 'Innocent until Proven Guilty' 106–124.

156. On the jurists' understanding of 'potestas absoluta', see Pennington, *Prince and the Law* 106–118 and passim.

By 1600, jurists and theologians were beginning to question torture's morality and legality. Mathias Schmoeckel has recently constructed a Column of Honor for those who began to condemn torture in the early modern world, long before Beccaria and Verri.[157] He ordains Juan Luis Vives (1493–1540) as the first to speak out against the use of torture in his *Epistola to Erasmus*. Later in the century, Michel de Montaigne (1533–1592) was inscribed on the Column.[158] In the seventeenth century, Johannes Grevius (de Greve, ca. 1580–1630),[159] Friedrich von Spee (1632),[160] and Augustin Nicolas (1682) raised their voices in protest.[161]

There might be yet another story about the gradual revulsion against torture. Lisa Silverman has studied the court records in Toulouse and found that from 1600 to 1780 the Parlement of Toulouse used torture less and less frequently.[162] Judges might have also been voting against the use of torture with their feet. In any case, more work on the records of the courts must be done to know whether courts began to abandon torture before legislatures and princes began to ban torture from the courtroom and from their states in the eighteenth century.

The jurists after Farinacci insisted that torture was inhumane, and, most importantly, did not produce reliable evidence. Beginning in the fifteenth century they began to argue for its abolishment. The success that Cesare Beccaria (1738–1794), Pietro Verri (1728–1797), and others had in the eighteenth century when they battled for the abolition of torture was prepared by centuries of debate in the classroom, in the treatises on procedure, in the courtroom, and in the chambers of parliaments.[163]

The procedural literature of the medieval and early modern jurists is daunting. In conclusion I would like to stress several points. The first and most important is that the purpose of the early tracts written in the twelfth century was primarily practical. It may be argued that the many

157. Mathias Schmoeckel, *Humanität und Staatsraison: Die Abschaffung der Folter in Europa und die Entwicklung des gemeinen Strafprozeß- und Beweisrechts seit dem hohen Mittelalter* (Norm und Struktur: Studien zum sozialen Wandel in Mittelalter und Früher Neuzeit 14; Köln-Weimar-Wien 2000) 93–186.

158. Montaigne, *Essays* 1.22; 2.5, 11.

159. Johannes Grevius, *Tribunal reformatum* (Hamburg 1624).

160. [Friedrich von Spee], *Cautio criminalis seu de processibus contra sagas liber* (Frankfurt am Main 1632), published anonymously.

161. Augustin Nicolas, *Si la torture est un moyen seur a verifier les crimes secrets: Dissertation morale et juridique* (Amsterdam 1682).

162. Lisa Silverman, *Tortured Subjects: Pain, Truth, and the Body in Early Modern France* (Chicago-London 2001) 71–84.

163. [Cesare Beccaria], *Dei delitti e delle pene* (Monaco [Livorno?] 1764), published anonymously. Pietro Verri, *Osservazioni sulla tortura: E singolarmente sugli effetti che produsse all'occasione delle unzioni malefiche, alle quali si attribuì la pestilenza che devastò Milano l'anno 1630* (Milan 1804), published posthumously.

treatises composed during the twelfth and early thirteenth century were not very sophisticated. As I have stated earlier, these tracts were written more for practice and not so much for teaching. However, these early tracts had very little or no influence on the development of procedural jurisprudence and thought. The tracts that I have discussed in this essay were in an entirely different category. They filled a large hole in the books of the Ius commune. Nowhere in the libri legales can the rules and principles governing the 'ordo iudiciarius' as they had been elaborated in the commentaries of the jurists be found presented in a systematic way. Tancred, Egidius, Guillelmus, and their early modern successors filled that void. With great success.

6

The Roman Curia

(until about 1300)

Brigide Schwarz

The history of the Roman Curia[1] that I will write will not be the usual one that deals with papal 'bureaucracy' (avant la lettre, at least for the earlier periods), but rather that of a medieval court that was admittedly sui generis.[2]

This chapter is organized according to the various phases of papal and

I am greatly indebted to Dr. Brigitte Flug, now at the University of Bochum, for her generous help with the translation.

1. A definition of the Roman Curia will be given below. There is no history of the 'curia' that is more than a mere history of the organization of curial bureaucracy. My own article is a first attempt: see Brigide Schwarz, 'Die römische Kurie, Teil Mittelalter', TRE 20 (1990) 343–347. Written from different angles are the articles of Agostino Paravicini Bagliani on the history of the Roman curia from 1054 to 1274 in several chapters of volume 5 of the *Histoire du christianisme des origines à nos jours: Apogée de la papauté et expansion de la chrétienté (1054–1274)*, ed. A. Vauchez et al. (Paris 1993) sections 1.2.II, 2.1.VI, 2.1.XI, 4.1.IV,V; Paravicini Bagliani, Il *papato nel secolo XIII: Cent'anni di bibliografia (1875–2009)* (Millennio medievale 83, Strumenti e studi 23; Florence 2010). Brigide Schwarz, 'Die Erforschung der mittelalterlichen römischen Kurie von Ludwig Quidde bis heute', *Friedensnobelpreis und Grundlagenforschung: Ludwig Quidde und die Erschließung der kurialen Registerüberlieferung*, ed. Michael Matheus (BDHI 124; Berlin-New York 2012) 415–439.

2. Of the literature on the currently fashionable theme of 'court', the following works can be cited: H. Patze and W. Paravicini, ed. *Fürstliche Residenzen im spätmittelalterlichen Europa* (Vorträge und Forschungen 36; Sigmaringen 1991); ed. H. Ragotzky and H. Wenzel, *Höfische Repräsentation: Das Zeremoniell und die Zeichen* (Tübingen 1990); *Feste und Feiern im Mittelalter*, ed. D. Altenburg et al. (Sigmaringen 1991).

curial history, though it has been necessary on occasion to pursue the history of a particular institution beyond the chronological limits of this essay, because the phases of development of each part of the curia did not occur concurrently with that of the curia as a whole.

'Pre-history' and the Beginning

Since the days of early Christianity, the bishops of Rome have had a permanent entourage of clerics and secular servitors, in order to fulfil their obligations in liturgy and ceremonial, jurisdiction, administration of possessions, and the care of the poor.[3] However, their see was not referred to as the 'curia Romana' until the era of the reform popes, from about 1090. This new term indicates a significant change in structures, so that it has become customary to speak of the 'emergence of the Roman curia' in this period.[4]

To be sure, the reform popes did not create something entirely new ex nihilo. Any interpretation of the 'structural change'[5] in the history of the papal entourage as the 'emergence' of an institution should not overlook the fact that there were naturally elements of continuity.[6] In this section I shall describe some of the traditional structures derived from the older history of the papal court, that is, from the 'pre-history' of the curia Romana, as well as the situation of the papal court as the first reform popes encountered it, and their reform ideas and measures which were important for the 'emergence of the Roman curia.'[7]

3. For the time leading up to the alliance with the Franks, see Jeffrey Richards, *The Popes and the Papacy in the Early Middle Ages, 476–752* (London-Boston-Henley 1979) esp. 287–323; for the period following, see Karl Jordan, 'Die päpstliche Verwaltung im Zeitalter Gregors VII.', *Studi Gregoriani* 1 (1947) 111–135, reprinted in *Ausgewählte Aufsätze zur Geschichte des Mittelalters* (Kieler Historische Studien 29; Stuttgart 1980) 129–153, with updating 348–349; and Edith Pásztor, 'La curia romana', *Le istituzioni ecclesiastiche della 'societas christiana' dei secoli XI–XII: Papato, cardinalato ed episcopato: Atti della quinta settimana internazionale di studio, Mendola, 26–31 agosto 1971* (Miscellanea del Centro di Studi Medioevali 7; Milan 1974) 490–504.

4. Karl Jordan, 'Die Entstehung der römischen Kurie: Ein Versuch', ZRG Kan. Abt. 28 (1939) 97–152, reprinted as a book, Darmstadt 1962; the later edition is used in what follows. Also Étienne Humbert, 'Curia: Origin to Gregory the Great', Levillain, *Papacy* 1.444–446.

5. Jordan, *Entstehung* 7.

6. Jordan, 'Die päpstliche Verwaltung' 129; Pásztor, 'Curia romana' 491.

7. It is common to see the curia as subject to continual development, despite the break constituted by the reform papacy, cf. Pásztor, 'Curia romana', which divides the 'pre-history' of the curia into three phases: era of the *episcopium* (5th–6th centuries), the *patriarchium Lateranense* (7th–8th centuries); the *sacrum palatium Lateranense* (9th–10th centuries).

The Offices and Titles of Office
in the Early Curia

The offices and titles of office (sometimes with altered or obsolete functions)[8] and traditions[9] often survived into a new era from very distant times. Offices were renewed by reverting to earlier traditions, often with altered functions (see below). The basic structures derived from earlier times were

1. the conception of the office as an institution with a constant sphere of responsibilities which survive the individual office-holder ('objective perpetuity' according to Max Weber);[10]

2. the organization of office-holders in colleges of persons who were equal in principle (according to seniority);[11]

3. the recruitment of the entourage of the pope[12] from celibate clerics:[13] hence no development of heritability of office;

4. the granting of higher ranking offices only to clerics with higher grades of ordination, and the employment of the entire papal entourage as liturgical assistants;

8. (Cardinal-)deacons and subdeacons, acolytes, notaries, cubicularies, *hostiarii*, legates, and rectors. Later, old titles of office were used to show off, as the occasional use of *sacellarius, maiordomus,* and *annona* shows.

9. It appears that the offices of 'prosecutor for the crown' of the *Romana ecclesia* (in antiquity the *defensor,* in the Middle Ages the *procurator fiscalis*) and the official in charge of petitioners (in antiquity the *nomenculator* and in the Middle Ages the *referendarius*) were such traditional functions. In the same way, some organizational principles were reassumed, such as the division of the financial office and the central treasury, as well as that of the central treasury and the privy treasury of the pope. On the other hand, there might have been practical reasons as well.

10. 'Objektive Perpetuität' and 'subjektive Perpetuität' (holding an office for lifetime) are key terms of 'bürokratische Herrschaft' (bureaucratic government) in Max Weber, *Wirtschaft und Gesellschaft* (5th ed. *Tübingen* 1976; trans. Keith Tribe, *Economy and Society: The Final Version,* ed. Sam Whimster (London 2008).

11. On the *scholae* organization, see Emmanuel Pierre Rodocanachi, *Les corporations ouvrières à Rome: Depuis la chute de l'empire romain* (2 vols. Paris 1894) i.viii. Such old colleges survived, at least in part, in ceremonial: see Bernhard Schimmelpfennig, 'Die Bedeutung Roms im päpstlichen Zeremoniell', *Rom im hohen Mittelalter: Studien zu den Romvorstellungen und zur Rompolitik vom 10. bis zum 12. Jahrhundert: Reinhard Elze zur Vollendung seines siebzigsten Lebensjahres gewidmet,* ed. B. Schimmelpfennig and Ludwig Schmugge (Sigmaringen 1992) 47–61, esp. 59.

12. In line with Tellenbach's example, every effort shall be made in what follows to avoid speaking of 'the papacy' and 'the pope', since one can speak of an institutionalized papacy only from the High Middle Ages onward; Gerd Tellenbach, *Die westliche Kirche vom 10. bis zum frühen 12. Jahrhundert* (Die Kirche in ihrer Geschichte 2, F1; Göttingen 1988) 152–153; in English: *The Church in Western Europe from the Tenth to the Early Twelfth Century,* trans. Timothy Reuter (Cambridge Medieval Textbooks; Cambridge 1993); Michael Borgolte, *Die mittelalterliche Kirche* (Enzyklopädie deutscher Geschichte 17; Munich: 1992) 89.

13. Usually from lower orders, which did not exclude marriage; Bernhard Schimmelpfennig, *Das Papsttum: Von der Antike bis zur Renaissance* (6th ed. Darmstadt 2009) 68–69; in English: *The Papacy,* trans. James Sievert (New York 1992). The only laymen who were the pope's legal advisors; Richards, *Popes and the Papacy* 299. Attempts by Gregory I to replace them by monks provoked a harsh reaction within the higher Roman clergy (ibid. 268, 289).

5. the appointment to most offices of the entourage for life (subjective perpetuity).

Another significant feature was that most of the office-holders were protégés of the former pope, which gave rise to a typical situation that a newly elected pope was confronted by a circle of persons he could not rely on, and hence he had to try to form a new clientele for himself by giving trusted persons, especially close male relatives (nepotes), special commissions and appointing them to lifetime positions if any became vacant during his pontificate. The new pope would also draw upon as many of the clients inherited from his predecessors as possible into his own clientele. Nepotism and clientelism are constants in this history of the curia.

Ever since antiquity, but reaching new heights in Carolingian times, the popes adopted forms of princely, particularly imperial, ceremonial.[14]

The Curia in the Eleventh Century

With the accession of Leo IX in 1049, the age of the popes selected from the Roman nobility[15] came to an end, and that of the reform popes began. Under the rule of the popes from the Roman nobility, the papacy had lost power and prestige within the church. On the other hand, these popes had further intensified their own 'imitatio imperii' as they had copied the ceremonial practices and vocabulary of the Western Empire.

The permanent residence[16] of the popes was now the Lateran, thought to have once been an imperial palace and now called the 'sacrum palatium', after the example of the imperial court.[17] The 'iudices sacri palatii' were court officials modelled after the 'supreme court officials' of the emperor of the same name. (There were seven of them at the papal court, following the number of the 'scholae' of late antiquity; they were also called the iudices de clero.) Older offices lived on in 'iudices de clero': primicerius and secundicerius notariorum; primicerius defensorum; 'ar-

14. Percy E. Schramm, 'Sacerdotium und Regnum im Austausch ihrer Vorrechte: "Imitatio imperii" und "imitatio sacerdotii",' *Kaiser, Könige und Päpste* (4 vols. Stuttgart 1968–1971) 4.1.57–106; Schramm, 'Die Imitatio Imperii in der Zeit des Reformpapsttums' (first published 1956), *Kaiser, Könige und Päpste* 4.1.180–191. Horst Fuhrmann, 'Papst Gregor VII. und das Kirchenrecht: Zum Problem des Dictatus Papae', *Studi Gregoriani* 13 (1989) 123–149.

15. Klaus-Jürgen Herrmann, *Das Tuskulaner-Papsttum, 1012–1046* (Päpste und Papsttum 4; Stuttgart 1973). Agostino Paravicini Bagliani, 'Curia: 11th to 13th Centuries', Levillain, *Papacy* 1.448–455.

16. Ingo Herklotz, *Gli eredi di Costantino: Il papato, il Laterano e la propaganda visiva nel XII secolo* (La corte dei papi 6; Rome 2000) 41–94; Hans Belting, 'Die beiden Palastaulen Leos III. im Lateran und die Entstehung einer päpstlichen Programmkunst', *Frühmittelalterliche Studien* 12 (1978) 55–83.

17. Previously called the *patriarchum*; Reinhard Elze, 'Das Sacrum "Palatium Lateranense" im 10. und 11. Jahrhundert', *Studi Gregoriani* 4 (1952) 27–54, reprinted in Elze, *Päpste – Kaiser - Könige und die mittelalterliche Herrschaftssymbolik* (Variorum reprints, Collected Studies 152; London 1982) no. I.

carius'; 'sacellarius'; 'nomenculator' and 'protoscriniarius', with somewhat altered functions. They also formed a schola, led by the 'primicerius notariorum'. The 'iudices de clero' increasingly fell into the hands of Roman noble families in the course of the tenth century, becoming honorary offices in the ceremonial.[18] It was not only in the liturgy in the Lateran Basilica,[19] but also on ceremonial occasions[20] in the 'sacrum palatium',[21] that the pope was assisted not only by the palace clergy—the seven (cardinal)[22] deacons,[23] the cardinal sub-deacons as well as other 'cardinales clerici' and (undefined) 'clerici Lateranenses'[24]—but also by the high Roman clergy,[25] among whom were the seven (cardinal) bishops of neighboring (suburbicarian) bishoprics.[26]

The circle of persons responsible for papal correspondence was now called the 'chancery', following the imperial model, which also influenced the external form and 'dictamen' of the documents.[27]

The fact that this splendid court was more a matter of appearance than reality around 1050, insofar as the scarcity of sources permits an evaluation here, can be seen by a closer look: the offices of the iudices de clero had long become hereditary and honorary offices in Roman ceremonial.[28]

18. These older offices did retain some jurisdictional duties in the city of Rome; Jordan, 'Die päpstliche Verwaltung' 133–134; Pásztor, 'Curia romana' 492–493.

19. Sible de Blaauw, *Cultus et décor: Liturgie en architectuur in laatantiek en middeleeuws Rome* (Delft 1987); in Italian: *Cultus et décor: Liturgia e architettura nella Roma tardoantica e medievale*, trans. Maria B. Annis (Studi e Testi 355–356; Vatican City 1994).

20. Herklotz, *Eredi di Costantino* 41–57; Schimmelpfennig, 'Bedeutung Roms', esp. 58 on the 'festival crownings' and the 'wearing of the crown' in the ceremonial of the pope.

21. Herklotz, *Eredi di Costantino* 41–57, 159–209.

22. On the concept of cardinal: the adjective 'cardinalis' derives from the noun 'cardo', originally meaning 'hinge', applied to the cathedral as the turning point of a diocese. 'Cardinales' in Rome, but also in other great sees, signifies those clergy standing particularly close to the bishop or assisting him in his liturgical duties; Stephan Kuttner, '"Cardinalis": The History of a Canonical Concept', *Traditio* 3 (1945) 160–163, reprinted in Kuttner, *The History of Ideas and Doctrines of Canon Law in the Middle Ages* (Variorum reprints, Collected Studies 113; London 1980) no. IX, with additional thoughts.

23. These are the six *diaconi palatini* plus the archdeacon. At the start of the eleventh century the archdeaconry was united with the office of the *vicedominus*. On the novel use of the office of archdeacon by Hildebrand, see Jürgen Sydow, 'Untersuchungen zur kurialen Verwaltungsgeschichte im Zeitalter des Reformpapsttums', DA 11 (1954) 18–73, esp. 23–27.

24. Elze, 'Sacrum Palatium' 46.

25. Ibid. 40–46.

26. At first sight, this list seems to show the high medieval structure, lacking only the cardinal priests presiding over the titular churches of the city of Rome. The cardinal priests, however, did not belong to the papal entourage until the later eleventh century.

27. Elze, 'Sacrum Palatium', 36–37; see also Harry Bresslau, *Handbuch der Urkundenlehre für Deutschland und Italien* (2nd ed. Leipzig 1912) 1.240; in Italian: *Manuale di diplomatica per la Germania e l'Italia*, trans. Anna Maria Voci-Roth (Pubblicazioni degli Archivi di Stato, Sussidi 10; Rome 1998); Leo Santifaller, *Saggio di un elenco dei funzionari, impiegati e scrittori della cancellaria pontificia dall'inizio all'anno 1099* (2 vols. BISM 56–57; Rome 1940).

28. See above n. 18.

The chancery, which is by far the best-documented institution, consisted of a 'cancellarius' (also 'bibliothecarius'),[29] and, in theory, the 'notarii et scriniarii sacri palatii', who had to write the engrossments (mundum). But as these officials could scarcely support themselves on the commissions from the chancery, they, together with other notaries, had long become part of an urban professional class from which the drafters and writers of papal documents were drawn.[30] This demonstrates that the demand for papal settlements of dispute and interventions had decreased considerably, not only in terms of quantity but of quality:[31] letters of protection,[32] confirmations of possession, and settlements of disputes constituted the bulk of 'manifestations of the will of the pope'. In contrast to earlier centuries, papal legates were usually sent in response to the initiative of interested parties. When filling administrative offices far from Rome, the popes could no longer prevail upon office-holders living there (such as bishops). They had to rely on persons from the city of Rome and its environs, mostly on (low-ranking) clients. The popes' area of control had shrunk to a central region around Rome, and the structures of 'clientela' considerably exceeded the institutional ones[33] in importance and had begun to replace them.

The 'Reform' Curia

The reform popes, who no longer came from the local nobility and who sought a fundamental and comprehensive reform of conditions within

29. The 'cancellarius' appears to have originally been a subordinate of the librarian; then the two offices were united, and, from the middle of the eleventh century, given to a cardinal deacon or priest; Paulius Rabikauskas, 'Kanzlei, päpstliche', LMA 5.921–22; and 'Chancery, Papal', Levillain, *Papacy* 1.289–294. While earlier the bibliothecarius had been a bishop to emphasize the dignity of the office, that rank became sheer necessity in the tenth through eleventh centuries in order to protect the office against power struggles within the Roman nobility. In the reform era, the office was hence given to an experienced cardinal who was trusted by the reform group.

30. Elze, 'Sacrum Palatium' 38. See also Paulius Rabikauskas, *Die römische Kuriale in der päpstlichen Kanzlei* (Miscellanea Historiae Pontificiae 20; Rome 1958) 28–33, 65–71, 90–100; Cristina Carbonetti Vendittelli, 'Tabellioni e scriniari a Roma tra IX e XI secolo', *Archivio della Società romana di storia patria* 102 (1979) 77–156.

31. Heinrich Fichtenau, 'Vom Ansehen des Papsttums im 10. Jahrhundert', *Aus Kirche und Reich: Studien zu Theologie, Politik und Recht im Mittelalter: Festschrift Friedrich Kempf,* ed. Hubert Mordek (Sigmaringen 1983) 117–124.

32. Jean-François Lemarignier, 'L'exemption monastique et les origines de la réforme grégorienne', *A Cluny: Congrès scientifique* (Dijon 1950) 288–340; Heinrich Appelt, 'Die Anfänge des päpstlichen Schutzes', MIÖG 62 (1954) 101–111; Johannes Fried, *Der päpstliche Schutz für Laienfürsten: Die politische Geschichte des päpstlichen Schutzprivilegs für Laien (11.–13. Jahrhundert)* (Abh. Akad. Heidelberg 1; Heidelberg 1980). On the development of privileges of protection for monasteries until Alexander III, see Ian Stuart Robinson, *The Papacy 1073–1198: Continuity and Innovation* (Cambridge 1990) 223–234.

33. Tellenbach, *Die westliche Kirche* 66–67.

the church,[34] could at first[35] make only few alterations to those conditions; their position in the city of Rome was too precarious for that. At first they were only able to hold their own in certain parts of Rome, if at all. Long vacancies of the throne, successful Roman 'anti-popes', and their own financial calamity restricted their freedom of action even further. Insofar as the reform popes placed their own adherents in high offices,[36] or gave to them important political functions without the offices traditionally linked to them,[37] they continued the policies of their immediate predecessors. The difference now was that, wherever possible, they favored reformers, who were in most cases non-Romans. The tradition was also continued in as much as (in addition to their difficulties) the reformers had to rely on clans of Roman nobles.

Still, the reform popes laid the foundations for decisive change:

1. They tried to bring the concept of 'Christianitas' (Christendom) which their predecessors had developed in the confrontation with Islam,[38] to life in a Europe that was segmented in small regions hardly in contact with each other or with the pope.[39]

2. They searched everywhere for the 'tradition of the Romana eccle-

34. Rudolf Schieffer, '*Motu proprio*: Über die papstgeschichtliche Wende im 11. Jahrhundert', HJb 122 (2002) 27–41. The new conception can already be traced in the pontificate of Leo IX: see Felicitas Schmieder, 'Peripherie und Zentrum Europas: Der nordalpine Raum in der Politik Papst Leos IX (1049–1054)', *Kurie und Region: Festschrift Brigide Schwarz*, ed. Brigitte Flug et al. (Geschichtliche Landeskunde 59; Stuttgart 2005) 359–369.

35. Sydow, 'Untersuchungen' 19–38; Pasztor, 'La curia romana' 500–502.

36. Particularly the cardinal bishops; see Edith Pásztor, 'Riforma della chiesa nel secolo XI e l'origine del collegio dei cardinali', *Studi sul Medioevo Christiano, offerti a Raffaello Morghen: Per il 90. anniversario dell'Istituto storico italiano (1883–1973)* (2 vols. Studi Storici fasc. 88–92; Rome 1974) 2.609–625; Pásztor, 'San Pier Damiani, il cardinalato e la formazione della curia romana', *Studi Gregoriani* 10 (1975) 317–339; Claudia Zey, 'Entstehung und erste Konsolidierung: Das Kardinalskollegium zwischen 1049 und 1143', *Geschichte des Kardinalats im Mittelalter*, ed. J. Dendorfer and R. Lützelschwab (Päpste und Papsttum 39; Stuttgart 2011) 63–94, at 63–76.

37. Cf. Pásztor, 'La curia romana' 500–501.

38. Raoul Manselli, 'La republica christiana e l'Islam', *L'Occidente e l'Islam nell'Alto Medioevo* (Atti delle Settimane di Studio del Centro Italiano di Studi sull' Alto Medioevo 12; Spoleto 1965) 1.115–147; Friedrich Kempf, 'Das Problem der Christianitas im 12.–13. Jahrhundert', HJb 79 (1960) 104–123.

39. *Römisches Zentrum und kirchliche Peripherie: Das universale Papsttum als Bezugspunkt der Kirchen von den Reformpäpsten bis zu Innozenz III.* ed. Jochen Johrendt and Harald Müller (Abh. Akad. Göttingen, Neue Folge 2; Berlin 2008), which includes these essays: Harald Müller, 'Zentrum und Peripherie. Prozesse des Austausches, der Durchdringung und der Zentralisierung in der lateinischen Kirche des hohen Mittelalters' 1–16; Müller, 'Entscheidung auf Nachfrage: Die delegierten Richter als Verbindungsglieder zwischen Kurie und Region sowie als Gradmesser päpstlicher Autorität' 109–131; Thomas Wetzstein, 'Wie die *urbs* zum *orbis* wurde: Der Beitrag des Papsttums zur Entstehung neuer Kommunikationsräume im europäischen Hochmittelalter' 47–75; Lotte Kéry, 'Dekretalenrecht zwischen Zentrale und Peripherie' 19–45; Lotte Kéry, 'Klosterfreiheit und päpstliche Organisationsgewalt. Exemtion als Herrschaftsinstrument des Papsttums?' *Rom und die Regionen: Die Homogenisierung der lateinischen Kirche im Hochmittelalter*, ed. J. Johrendt and H. Müller (Abh. Akad. Göttingen, Neue Folge 19; Berlin 2012) 71–130.

sia', of which they had a preconceived idea, and they interpreted what they found (or invented) according to their idea. The preferred medium through which they propagated their vision, especially on their travels, was that of liturgical[40] and ceremonial acts,[41] so effective and influential in the Middle Ages.

3. They particularly sought the 'old, incorrupted law of the "Romana ecclesia"'[42] in order to support their concept of her significance in the history of salvation, an idea which was to have great influence in the years to come. The evocation of the great popes of the past also becomes evident in the stilus of the chancery.[43]

4. However, the most important prerequisite for change which the reformers created was the new concept of the pope as monarchical head of the whole church,[44] a concept through which he gradually came to resemble the secular rulers of his time in theory and in ceremonial practice.

The new conception of the office of the pope found its expression in changes in the formulary but also in the external appearance of papal char-

40. On the renewal of the stationary liturgy: see Elze, 'Sacrum Palatium' 49–50, 53; Hans-Walter Klewitz, 'Die Krönung des Papstes' ZRG Kan. Abt. 30 (1941) 96–130, esp. 118; Herklotz, *Gli eredi di Costantino* 45–48. See also Gerd Althoff, 'Demonstration und Inszenierung: Zur Funktion von Zeichen, Reden und Ritualen im Mittelalter', *Frühmittelalterliche Studien* 27 (1993) 27–50.

41. Herklotz, *Gli eredi di Costantino* 41–45. In what was believed to be the revival of old tradition, 'a new type of papal "laudes" was developed on the analogy of the "laudes of rulers", but fashioned only to the person of the pope'; see Reinhard Elze, 'Die Herrscherlaudes im Mittelalter', ZRG Kan. Abt. 40 (1954) 201–223, reprinted in *Päpste - Kaiser - Könige* no. X, 206, 216. The reformers also sought to follow tradition in their burials, by being buried in St. Peter's Basilica. However, this was only accomplished for two of them (Leo IX and Urban II), while two others were buried by the Lateran canons they had supported (Alexander II, Paschal II). In all other cases, the principal Roman churches were too distant, so that the popes were interred in their old episcopal churches or religious houses; Michael Borgolte, *Petrusnachfolge und Kaiserimitation: Die Grablegen der Päpste, ihre Genese und Traditionsbildung* (Veröffentlichungen des Max-Planck-Instituts für Geschichte 95; Göttingen 1989) 146–147. It is only with Calixtus II that a fundamental change takes place.

42. On the attempts of the reformers to revive the old Roman legal tradition in the sense in which they understood it, see John T. Gilchrist, *Canon Law in the Age of Reform, 11th and 12th Centuries* (Variorum reprints, Collected Studies 406; Aldershot 1993); Uta-Renate Blumenthal, 'Conciliar Canons and Manuscripts: The Implications of their Transmission in the Eleventh Century', *Proceedings Munich 1992*, ed. P. Landau and J. Müller 357–379, reprinted in Blumenthal, *Papal Reform and Canon Law in the 11th and 12th Centuries* (Variorum reprints, Collected Studies 18; Aldershot 1998) no. VII.

43. As when Gregory VII refers back to Gregory I: see Sydow, 'Untersuchungen' 23.

44. Yves M.-J. Congar, 'Der Platz des Papsttums in der Kirchenfrömmigkeit der Reformer des 11. Jahrhunderts', *Sentire Ecclesiam: Das Bewusstein von der Kirche als gestaltende Kraft der Frömmigkeit*, ed. J. Daniélou and H. Vorgrimler (Freiburg i. B. 1961) 196–217; Colin Morris, *Papal Monarchy: The Western Church from 1050 to 1250* (Oxford History of the Christian Church; Oxford 1989). On the development of the idea of 'episcopus universalis ecclesiae', see Georg May, *Ego N.N. Catholicae Ecclesiae Episcopus: Entstehung, Entwicklung und Bedeutung einer Unterschriftsformel im Hinblick auf den Universalepiskopat des Papstes* (Kanonistische Studien und Texte 43; Berlin 1995); Matthias Schrör, *Metropolitangewalt und papstgeschichtliche Wende* (Historische Studien 494; Husum 2009).

ters: Leo IX invented the Rota as part of the papal subscription. The design of this disc was understood by contemporaries as that of the orbis (face of the earth), for whose salvation the pope was responsible.[45] At the same time the iconogaphy of the papal seal began to borrow from that of the emperors.[46]

Two interdependent structural changes important for the development of the papacy and the papal court were introduced or initiated in this period, namely, the new regulation of papal election and the transformation of the position of the cardinals.

The papal electorial decree of 1059[47] regulated papal elections until 1179, although it was ignored in many specific instances.[48] It distinguishes between a 'preliminary election' by the cardinal bishops and eventually by the other cardinal clergy[49] and the subsequent acts of confirmation by the clergy and people of Rome. The constitutive act is the preliminary election, which determines the candidate, and reduces all further acts to subordinate ones in a series.[50] The intention behind this becomes clear when one considers that the popes themselves had strong rights in nominating the cardinal bishops:[51] by investing the right of papal election in a circle of persons whose composition was largely determined by the popes, the reformers had assured themselves a monopoly on the papacy. The affir-

45. Joachim Dahlhaus, 'Aufkommen und Bedeutung der Rota in den Urkunden des Papstes Leo IX.' AHP 27 (1989) 7–84; Leo Santifaller, 'Über die Neugestaltung der äußeren Form der Papstprivilegien unter Leo IX.' *Festschrift Hermann Wiesflecker zum 60. Geburtstag,* ed. Alexander Novotny and O. Pickl (Graz 1973) 29–38.

46. Ingo Herklotz, 'Zur Ikonographie der *Papstsiegel* im 11. und 12. Jahrhundert', *Für irdischen Ruhm und himmlischen Lohn: Stifter und Auftraggeber in der mittelalterlichen Kunst,* ed. H.-R. Meier and C. Jäggi (Berlin 1995) 116–130, esp. 120. The same change seems to appear in the coins of this pope; Phillip Grierson, 'HENRICUS IMP or ALBRICUS PRINCEPS: A Note on the Supposed Denaro of Pope Leo IX (1049–54) and Henry III', *Numismatiska meddelanden* 30 (1965) 51–56, reprinted in Grierson, *Dark Age Numismatics* (Variorum reprints, Collected Studies 96; London 1979) no. XXXIX.

47. Detlev Jasper, *Das Papstwahldekret von 1059: Überlieferung und Textgestalt* (Beiträge zur Geschichte und Quellenkunde des Mittelalters 12; Sigmaringen 1986). In addition, Hans-Georg Krause, 'Die Bedeutung der neuentdeckten handschriftlichen Überlieferung des Papstwahldekrets von 1059: Bemerkungen zu einem neuen Buch' ZRG Kan. Abt. 76 (1990) 89–134.

48. Rudolf Schieffer, 'Rechtstexte des Reformpapsttums und ihre zeitgenössische Resonanz', *Überlieferung und Geltung normativer Texte des frühen und hohen Mittelalters,* ed. H. Mordek (Quellen und Forschungen zum Recht im Mittelalter 4; Sigmaringen 1986) 51–69, esp. 51–56.

49. Jasper, *Das Papstwahldekret von 1059*: 'imprimis cardinales episcopi diligentissima simul consideratione tractantes, mox sibi clericos cardinales adhibeant, sicque reliquus clerus et populus ad consensum nove electionis accedant' (101–102). The passage is carefully formulated so as to be imprecise. It only regulates unequivocally that the cardinals should have the primary role (*nova electio*), but it leaves open what roles the 'cardinales clerici' were to play: is it left to the cardinal bishops whom they call in and at what point in the procedure?

50. Cf. Heinrich Mitteis, *Die deutsche Königswahl: Ihre Rechtsgrundlagen bis zur Goldenen Bulle* (2nd ed. Brünn-Munich-Vienna 1944, reprinted Darmstadt 1965) 75–81.

51. He had a traditional right of nomination, and he alone was the competent consecrator.

mation of the 'clergy and people of Rome' continued to be necessary in principle, as well as in practice, if the pope wished to rule in Rome.

The independence de jure from Rome was laid down in the disposition that the papal election could take place outside the city of Rome, and the pope so elected could begin his rule without an installation ceremony in Rome. However, these regulations were only to be applied in case of necessity, since the usual solemn acts of elevation—taking possession of the Lateran, benediction in St. Peter's Basilica (after his consecration as bishop, if that was necessary) and coronation (since 1099 at the latest), and finally the solemn procession back to the Lateran[52] —remained necessary. These acts were now clericalized and spiritualized, in keeping with the transformed conception of the papal office.[53]

By the eleventh century, in a process that is hard to trace in any detail, the cardinals had become the most important liturgical assistants of the pope.[54]

The seven suburbicarian bishops and the Lateran clergy assisted in the particularly extensive papal liturgy in the Lateran (on all Sundays).[55] The cardinal bishops alone could take the place of the pope at the services on the other days (work days and specific festivals) as well as in the four other principal basilicas, where they served in a weekly cycle. Here they were assisted by seven cardinal priests from the twenty-eight titular churches, who also took weekly turns. There was a corresponding regulation for the twelve 'cardinales diaconi regionarii', who assisted in a lower function. The three ordines of the cardinal clergy—cardinal bishops, car-

---

52. Schimmelpfennig, 'Bedeutung Roms', 58; see Schimmelpfennig, 'Die Krönung des Papstes im Mittelalter, dargestellt am Beispiel der Krönung Pius' II. (3.IX.1458)', QF 54 (1974) 192–270; Eduard Eichmann, *Weihe und Krönung des Papstes im Mittelalter: Aus dem Nachlass herausgegeben von Klaus Mörsdorf* (Münchner Theologische Studien 3, Kanonistische Abt. 1; Munich 1951); Nikolaus Gussone, *Thron und Inthronisation des Papstes von den Anfängen bis zum 12. Jahrhundert: Zur Beziehung von Herrschaftszeichen und bildhaften Begriffen, Recht, Liturgie im christlichen Verständnis von Wort und Wirklichkeit* (Bonner Historische Forschungen 41; Bonn 1978).

53. While the city still did homage to the pope as its Lord in the *possesso* in the ninth century, from the start of the twelfth century it was conceived that only the cardinals and other clerics would submit to the pope as the Successor to the apostles and Lord of the palace. The homage of the city only took place during his procession through the city. Correspondingly, the crowning of the pope, which took place after consecration in St. Peter's, was altered: now the pope was crowned with the *phrygium* by the archdeacon, instead of by the 'prior stabuli', who could only present the crown; Schimmelpfennig, 'Bedeutung Roms' 58; Schimmelpfennnig, 'Ein bisher unbekannter Text zur Wahl, Konsekration und Krönung des Papstes im 12. Jahrhundert', AHP 6 (1968) 43–70, esp. 61.

54. For the cardinals from 1049 to 1143 see Zey, 'Entstehung und erste Konsolidierung' 63–94; Kuttner, 'Cardinalis' 129–214, 160–163. Ancient ideas and antique forms play a role in the gradual closing together of the cardinals to form a body among others.

55. Jean Gaudemet, 'Suburbicarian Italy', Levillain, *Papacy* 3.1464–1467; Kristina Sessa, *The Formation of Papal Authority in Late Antique Italy: Roman Bishops and the Domestic Sphere* (Cambridge 2012) 25–29 and passim.

dinal priests, and cardinal deacons—assisted in the Roman stationary liturgy, which was held throughout the entire ecclesiastical year at various churches, the so-called station churches.[56]

Assistance in the papal liturgy was certainly honorable, but for the cardinals their tie with their titular church took precedence. This only changed when the reform popes started filling the positions of cardinal bishops with reformers; by 1059 they had succeeded in establishing five cardinal bishops, four cardinal priests, and three cardinal deacons out of their own circle.[57]

In these years the position of the cardinals changed profoundly. Most obviously, the cardinal bishops now became assistants of the popes, a concept whose theological foundations were laid down by Peter Damian,[58] who saw them as participants in the primatial mission of the successor of St. Peter, sharing the pope's commitment to reform the church. Their most important new function in this context has already been mentioned: the (preliminary) election of the pope. The signatures under the Papal Election Decree, which was passed at the Easter Synod of 1059, demonstrate the recognition by the 'ecclesiastical hierarchy' that the cardinals had a particular rank.[59] The signatures are not arranged according to the date of ordination, as was traditional: instead, now the diaconi cardinales were ranked even above archbishops.

During the following decades, more cardinal positions were filled with reformers, who increasingly did not come from Rome. This, combined with the repeated absence of the papal court from Rome for years, loosened the ties between these Roman supreme liturgists and the city of Rome itself. The preferential use of reform cardinals as advisors, legates, and officials fulfilling other functions (see below) led to their gradually growing into a group, despite their division into three ordines. Yet it took the entire twelfth century for all of the 28 cardinal priests and 18 cardinal

56. In addition to the twelve regional deacons, there were also the seven (later six) Lateran deacons.

57. According to the list of subscriptions to the papal election decree. The cardinals who did not sign were not all on the side of the 'anti-pope' Benedict X; a considerable number probably remained neutral. Hildebrand's nomination as archdeacon in the Lateran was also decisive in their success.

58. *Die Briefe des Petrus Damiani,* ed. K. Reindel (MGH Briefe der deutschen Kaiserzeit 4.2; Munich 1988) 2.52–61, no. 48. The fact that the cardinal bishops participated in the liturgy at the papal altar in the Lateran plays a great role in Peter Damian; Sible de Blaauw, 'The Solitary Celebration of the Supreme Pontiff: The Lateran Basilica as the New Temple in the Medieval Liturgy of Maundy Thursday', *Omnes circumadstantes: Contributions towards a History of the Role of the People in the Liturgy,* ed. Charles Caspers and M. Schneiders (Kampen 1990) 120–143.

59. Deusdedit charged that these were not 'the hierarchy', but rather a narrow party of papalists: see Uta-Renate Blumenthal, 'Rom in der Kanonistik', *Rom im hohen Mittelalter* 1–19, reprinted in *Papal Reform and Canon Law,* no. V, 29–39, esp. 32.

deacons to complete the change from an orientation toward their titular churches and diaconates to a focus on serving the pope, and for internal homogeneity and coherence to develop to such an extent that a college of cardinals could be formed.[60]

The 'Emergence of the Roman Curia' (from about 1090 to 1130)

This section discusses the term 'curia' around 1100 and its applicability to the papal court.[61] The term curia[62] for the court of the pope first appears in 1089 in a papal treaty[63] applied to a city of the Patrimony (Velletri). It is certainly no accident that this was a treaty of feudal content, and that Urban II (1088–1099), who as a Frenchman and former prior of Cluny was well acquainted with feudalism, concluded it.

The curia of a ruler in those days meant (1) in a personal sense, the household of the prince, which moved with him as he travelled;[64] (2) in an institutional sense, the solemn court which the prince held together with his confidantes, ministers, and courtiers, as well as with the magnates of

60. How little the papalist interpretation of the mission of the Romana ecclesia was recognized in the city of Rome, even among the lower ordines of the cardinals, is shown by the interpretation of *Deusdedit* by Blumenthal, 'Rom in der Kanonistik'. Until the time of Alexander III, cardinal priests and deacons gave up their positions as cardinals when they were promoted to bishoprics somewhere. From the time of Clement III, they remained 'honorary cardinals'; Klaus Ganzer, 'Das römische Kardinalskollegium', *Le istituzioni ecclesiastiche della 'societas christiana' dei secoli XI–XII* 153–181, esp. 179–180; Werner Maleczek, *Papst und Kardinalskolleg von 1191–1216: Die Kardinäle unter Coelestin III. und Innozenz III.* (Publikationen des Historischen Instituts beim Österreichischen Kulturinstitut in Rom I.6; Vienna 1984) 251–252.

61. Fundamental on this is Jordan, 'Die Entstehung'. The caesura caused by the defection of the whole curia of Gregory VII to the anti-pope Clement III (who preserved the Roman tradition), the long vacancy of the Holy See, and the short pontificate of Victor III is also stressed by Sydow, 'Untersuchungen' 18, 22–23, 37–39. The reformers purposefully established new institutions that were meant to terminate the dependency on the Roman nobility; ibid. 41.

62. On the history of the concept of 'curia', see Jordan, 'Die Entstehung' 18–32; Thomas Zotz, 'Curia regis', LMA 3.373–375. From the first half of the eleventh century the notion of curia replaced terms such as 'palatium' and 'curtis', since the concept of the house as the center of princely lordship had given way to 'lordship with the counsel of the magnates'.

63. See *Italia Pontificia*, ed. P. F. Kehr (10 vols. Berlin 1906–1978) 2.104 n. 2. This is the first instance of the court offices being mentioned (see below, 174). Certainly one must be very careful with such terms, since they are often creations by analogy, used either by outsiders applying something they know to something actually or only apparently similar, or they are used by those concerned who seek to make themselves understood; see Sydow, 'Untersuchungen' 41. In the term 'curia' as a self-description of the Roman curia, vague memories of the curia of the ancient Roman Senate (with which the cardinals loved to equate themselves) merged with contemporary meanings of holding court, court assembly, and judicial court; see Jordan, 'Die päpstliche Verwaltung' 152. In secular realms, 'curia' is preferred to older terms such as 'palatium' when the consultation with the princes became the distinctive element (see the previous note). The Roman curia for a long time preferred to describe itself with other terms.

64. In the twelfth century the term long vacillated between holding court and juridical court; Jordan, 'Die päpstliche Verwaltung' 152.

his realm at central places of that realm (usually on high ecclesiastical festivals) for the purpose of common counsel and decision, jurisdiction, the granting of privileges, and the like;[65] and (3) the prince's judicial court.

Corresponding phenomena are to be found with the popes of this period: (1) the entourage (Hofstaat) that was often forced to move about with him; (2) the solemn papal synod, more and more replaced by the consistory;[66] and (3) the papal judicial court.

These are not simply external analogies. 'Curia' is a fitting self-description for the entourage of the pope after the structural changes initiated by the reform popes: the monarchical conception of the papacy, the development of the cardinals into the most important collaborators of the pope, and a loosening of the ties to the city of Rome (see above). The papacy developed similar structures as similar solutions for similar problems, besides simply adopting institutions of secular courts. There were naturally differences arising from the fundamental dissimilarity of the functions of the head of Christendom, at once supreme hierarch and liturgist on the one hand and ruler of a secular principality (Herrschaftsverband) on the other. The pope had functions that had no equivalent in the secular realm (such as penance and liturgy). Correspondingly, the composition of the curia was considerably different from that of secular courts (with an overwhelmingly clerical,[67] international[68] recruitment), and liturgy[69] and ceremonial[70] not only played a much larger role, but also differed considerably from what was usual at princely courts.

The Curia in a Personal Sense: The Composition of the Court of the Pope

The court of a ruler as a Personenverband (association of persons) can be divided into the following groups of persons:

65. Or at least of the area affected; how seldom assemblies corresponded to this ideal is shown by the study of Wolfgang Petke, *Kanzlei, Kapelle und königliche Kurie unter Lothar III. (1125–1137)* (Beihefte zu J. F. Böhmer, Regesta imperii 5; Cologne-Vienna 1985).

66. On these innovations by the reform popes, see 182.

67. Which was only one element at secular courts, though an important one. The fact that there were phases at the curia when there was a relatively large lay element was a result of the dependence on the favor of Roman families. These also participated in decisions that, in the strict sense, were spiritual; Jordan, 'Die Entstehung' 45–49; Sydow, 'Untersuchungen' 63.

68. In keeping with the concept of universal sovereignty, which the popes claimed at least in matters of jurisdiction, the composition of the court personnel is international, compared with the other courts; see 225.

69. In contrast to secular courts, the liturgy at the papal court did not bow to local traditions, and, when travelling, the curia always placed its own liturgy over that of the place of its sojourn.

70. Papal ceremonial developed according to its own Roman traditions. Until Innocent III, for instance, the old palace personnel of the Lateran had a higher rank in the ceremonial than the originally non-papal prelates such as cardinal bishops and cardinal priests; Schimmelpfennig, *Papsttum* 155–156, 182–184.

• the person of the prince, together with his closest relatives and friends, forming the core;

• the holders of court offices (and their subordinates), who are responsible for maintaining the court according to the estate of the prince, for appearance appropriate to a ruler, and for military defense;[71]

• a group of clerics who celebrate the court liturgy and serve as experts in jurisdiction, administration, and particularly the issuing of charters (court chapel);[72]

• a group, with changing composition, of magnates who are tied to the prince by blood relation, service, and/or office; they also form a juridical court with the prince at its head; depending on the subject and the situation, this council can also be augmented by persons from the lower ranks;

• in addition, petitioners and litigants in extremely varying number and composition.

These persons lived together as a court, which followed the strict rules established and sanctioned by tradition, and they participated in court liturgy and ceremonial, where their place was determined partly by their status, partly by the favor of the prince. They formed a commemorative fraternity for the dead members of the court[73] as well as a community exempt from the spheres of law of the place where they took temporary residence.

The court of the pope can be divided into the following groups by analogy:

I. The person of the pope with his closest confidants who form the head of his familia (see below); to the familia belonged the following two groups: (1) the court officials and (2) the clerics of the papal chapel.

(1) The court officials. These played a smaller role at the curia than at secular courts, since they lacked the usual representational duties.[74] In the

71. Werner Rösener, 'Hofämter', LMA 5.67–68. They derived from a time when the concept of the house (*domus, palatium*) of the ruler as the central element of his lordship was predominant.

72. The classic study on this is Josef Fleckenstein, *Die Hofkapelle der deutschen Könige* (MGH Schriften 16.1–2; Stuttgart 1959–1966).

73. The commemorial confraternity of the pope and the cardinals is first documented in the thirteenth century: Alexander IV decrees regulations on the celebration of the *commemoratio* of all hitherto deceased popes and cardinals as well as for the future death of each pope and cardinal; Raynaldus, *Annales Ecclesiastici*, appendix ad an. 1261 § 7; see *Le Liber censuum de l'Église Romaine*, ed. P. Fabre, L. Duchesne, et al. (3 vols. Paris 1910–1952) 1.584–585; *De Rome en Avignon ou le cérémonial de Jacques Stephaneschi*, ed. Marc Dykmans (Le cérémonial papal de la fin du Moyen Age à la Renaissance 2, Bibliothèque de l'Institut Historique Belge de Rome 25; Brussels-Rome 1981) 205–206, 411–412.

74. Karl Jordan, 'Das Eindringen des Lehnswesens in das Rechtsleben der römischen Kurie', *Archiv für Urkundungforschung* 12 (1931): 13–110; Jordan, 'Die päpstliche Verwaltung' 150; Pierre Tou-

document of 1089 quoted above, the steward and the cupbearer[75] appear for the first time, whereas the marshal first appears in the middle of the twelfth century, though the office must be much older. The first chamberlain known to us was a monk of Cluny, who had obviously been brought along by Urban II. In the course of the next two centuries, the offices of steward and cupbearer vanished, with only the sub-offices necessary for the purposes of the pope's household in a stricter sense remaining: the 'buticularia',[76] (out of the cupbearer's office) and the 'panetaria' and 'coquina' (from the office of the steward) survived. The seneschal, formerly in all likelihood a subordinate of the chamberlain, became the head of these offices. The marshal increasingly was in charge of the military and police functions of the court (see below) and lost a part of his original functions (preparing quarters, provisioning) to the chamberlain; the office was always held by a layman. The two constables,[77] who since the time of Gregory IX were usually monks, were in charge of the mounts of the curia. The chamberlain and his closest collaborators always belonged to the chapel and will therefore be dealt with in that context.

(2) The clerics of the papal chapel. They were more important for the papal court than their counterparts in secular courts, though it should be borne in mind that they were adopted from secular courts.[78] The per-

---

bert, *Les structures du Latium médiéval: Le Latium méridional et la Sabine du IXe siècle à la fin du XIIe siècle* (2 vols. Bibliothèque des Écoles Françaises d'Athènes et de Rome 332; Rome 1973) 2.1038–1052, 1089–1102.

75. The 'emissarius' of the treaty of 1089 cited above (n. 63) is probably the *buticularius* and not, as Jordan, 'Die Entstehung' 38 n. 2, believes, an envoy who was sent along with the steward, since what is being talked about here is the commission which was negotiating, on the pope's behalf, the obligations of the town of Velletri in providing hospitality to the papal court. To this delegation probably belonged, other than the person responsible for the food, the one responsible for the drink; similarly Sydow, 'Untersuchungen' 48. The offices of steward and chamberlain had much in common. In the middle of the twelfth century the office of steward was replaced by that of seneschal; Jordan, 'Die päpstliche Verwaltung' 150. Under Paschal II in 1118 a *thesaurarius* is recorded who did not belong to the camera; Sydow, 'Untersuchungen' 56.

76. Agostino Paravicini Bagliani, *La vita quotidiana alla corte dei papi nel Duecento* (Rome 1996); in French: *La cour des Papes au XIIIe siècle* (Paris 1995), 64–65, 99–102. It was not uncommon for the heads of the court offices, even the head cooks, to be monks. On the 'coquina', see Borwin Rusch, *Die Behörden und Hofbeamten der päpstlichen Kurie des 13. Jahrhunderts* (Schriften der Albertus-Universität, Geisteswissenschaftliche Reihe 3; Königsberg 1936) 112–117 (in the last third of the thirteenth century, a 'coquina parva' was separated off from the 'coquina magna'). On the 'panetaria', see ibid., 118–119; on the *buticularia*, see 120–122.

77. Rusch, *Die Behörden und Hofbeamten* 122–127. They took over some of the functions of the old marshal. For the pope's travels, they were in part responsible for the packing of all movable goods of the apostolic camera, the wardrobe of the pope (camera papae), and the papal treasure, as well as for their transport, and for preparing quarters. They further had the superintendence of the prisons of the 'camera'. In the thirteenth century there were two stables, the so-called 'white' stable (in which the white palfreys and mules of the pope were kept) and a larger, 'black' stable.

78. Fundamental is Reinhard Elze, 'Die päpstliche Kapelle', ZRG Kan. Abt. 36 (1950) 145–204; reprinted in *Päpste - Kaiser - Könige* no. II. See also Sydow, 'Untersuchungen' 49; the attempt by

sonnel belonging to the chapel cannot be distinguished clearly until the twelfth century, because the sources use only the ambiguous term 'subdiaconi' for the chaplains.[79] As there were also subdiaconi in Rome who did not belong to the chapel, it is often not possible to determine with complete certainty whether or not the term refers to a papal chaplain. Even the term 'subdiaconus Romanae ecclesiae' and the term 'subdiaconus papae', which came into use in the middle of the twelfth century, do not provide definite indications, since the latter can mean a cleric who was merely ordained by the pope himself. From the time of the reform, on the basis of their universal episcopacy,[80] the popes have claimed the right to consecrate clerics from all dioceses.

The papal subdiaconi enjoyed a high rank in ceremonial; were, according to canon law, exempt from the ordinary ecclesiastical jurisdiction; and were entitled to provision by the pope (even with benefices). For that reason it was an attractive and sought-after honor to be consecrated as a subdiaconus by the popes on their travels, even when the ordained remained in partibus, for example as a canon (see below on these 'external chaplains'). Those subdiaconi who actually were papal chaplains had important functions in the Roman stationary liturgy, and they participated in the daily divine service in the papal chapel.[81] Otherwise, they appear in a situation similar to the cardinals, though lower in rank, particularly in the chancery,[82] in the judicial court or as envoys.[83] Many of the chaplains later became cardinals, bishops, or prelates.[84]

Siegfried Haider, 'Zu den Anfängen der päpstlichen Kapelle', MIÖG 87 (1979) 38–70, to set the beginnings of the papal chapel at a significantly earlier date does not appear convincing. The 'chaplains' 'found' by him in the entourage of popes earlier than Urban II prove little about a functioning chapel in the sense of the court of the emperor or of bishops.

79. Elze, 'Kapelle' 157, explains why the title of 'subdiaconus' was preferred to that of 'capellanus': while 'capellanus papae' meant an actual servant of the pope, the 'subdiaconi' were a rank of high prestige within the Roman church and represented the Roman tradition. The same problem arose in the thirteenth century, since chaplains who held another curial office were referred to by the title of that office, so that even now the size of the chapel cannot be fully determined. The model of the imperial chapel is still showing through in the thirteenth century; Elze, 'Kapelle' 204.

80. Thomas Wetzstein, 'Die Welt als Sprengel: Der päpstliche Universalepiskopat zwischen 1050 und 1215', *Die Ordnung der Kommunikation und die Kommunikation der Ordnungen im mittelalterlichen Europa, 2: Zentralität: Papsttum und Orden im Europa des 12. und 13. Jahrhunderts*, ed. Cristina K. Andenna et al. (Aurora; Stuttgart 2013) 169–190.

81. Elze, 'Kapelle' 154; Paravicini Bagliani, *La vita* 55–56. Their participation in stationary liturgy was now restricted to the two principal basilicas. The normal papal divine service took place in Rome in the Lateran in the papal chapel of St. Nicholas (although the chapel of St. Lawrence was the proper private chapel of the pope; such exclusive altars included the high altar of the Lateran basilica as well as that of St. Peter's in the Vatican).

82. Elze, 'Kapelle' 158–160.

83. Ibid. 154. On the duties of a chaplain, see the telling treatment by Godfrey of Viterbo, MGH SS 22.105.

84. Elze, 'Kapelle' 164–168.

Also belonging to or deriving from the chapel were (a) the chamberlain and (b) the chancellor and their collaborators. One may speak of 'administrative departments' even in a medieval sense only after the institutional solidification around 1200.

(a) The office of chamberlain was apparently introduced by Urban II to raise financial resources in the desperate situation in which he found himself at the time.[85] In the period before 1082 (when Gregory VII had been abandoned by almost his entire entourage), the reform popes had succeeded—especially through the determined efforts of Hildebrand first as an archidiaconus, and later as Pope Gregory VII—in opening up new sources of income beyond the traditional revenue from the city of Rome and the Patrimony,[86] drawing upon Christendom as a whole (particularly from the lands on the periphery):[87] (1) census payments from churches and religious houses in return for papal protection; (2) census payments from secular princes deriving from feudal obligations or the privilege of papal protection; and (3) Peter's Pence.[88] In order to collect these dues, papal envoys and local prelates were used.[89] What these incomes had in common is that they were basically voluntary contributions. They were the only ones that Urban II, with a great deal of effort, was able to mobilize for himself, and they were by far not enough. Hence the pope and the growing curia were compelled to try all sorts of expedients (support by churches or princes who had a close relationship to the papacy;[90] 'taxing' visitors to the curia;[91] raising loans).

Not only did the first chamberlain[92] and his immediate successor come from Cluny,[93] but the institution of the camera[94] was obviously also

85. Karl Jordan, 'Zur päpstlichen Finanzgeschichte im 11. und 12. Jahrhundert', QF 25 (1933–1934): 61–104, reprinted in *Ausgewählte Aufsätze* 85–128, with updating 347–348; Jordan, 'Die päpstliche Verwaltung' 146–150; Robinson, *Papacy* 244–291.

86. On the feudal transformation of the Patrimony, see Jordan, 'Die päpstliche Verwaltung' 141–142; Sydow, 'Untersuchungen' 62.

87. Sydow, 'Untersuchungen' 24–31. Robinson, *Papacy* 269–275, demonstrates this also for the first two of these types of payment of dues. Thomas Wetzstein, '*Noverca omnium ecclesiarum*: Der römische Universalepiskopat des Hochmittelalters im Spiegel der päpstlichen Finanzgeschichte', *Rom und die Regionen* 11–52.

88. Peter's Pence, hitherto seen as an offering (*oblatio*), which was presented on the altar of St. Peter's, was now claimed exclusively for the pope and interpreted and collected as a tax.

89. Sydow, 'Untersuchungen' 32.

90. Even the papal synods (see below) were instruments of fundraising; Robinson, *Papacy* 268.

91. Ibid. 262–265, using mainly the example of the very high *pallium* charges, demonstrates how earlier voluntary donations gradually became taxes. In addition, there were 'gifts' that the officials of the curia demanded; ibid. 265–266.

92. Robinson, *Papacy* 249–252; Jordan, 'Die päpstliche Verwaltung' 146.

93. Jordan, 'Finanzgeschichte'; Jürgen Sydow, 'Cluny und die Anfänge der Apostolischen Kammer: Studie zur Geschichte der päpstlichen Finanzverwaltung im 11. und 12. Jahrhundert', *Studien und Mitteilungen des Benediktinerordens und seiner Zweige* 63 (1951) 45–66, reprinted in Sydow, *Cum omni mensura et ratione: Ausgewählte Aufsätze: Festgabe zu seinem 70. Geburtstag*, ed. Helmut Maurer (Sigmaringen 1991) 31–53; Sydow, 'Untersuchungen' 42–44, 55–59.

94. Robinson, *Papacy* 244–291.

brought from there by Urban II. He and his successors until Calixtus II used Cluny as the 'papal house bank': to borrow money and, using Cluny's connections, to raise dues or transfer money. Until 1130, the camerarii all had a close personal relationship to 'their' pope. This can also be deduced from the fact that, unlike the other curials, the chamberlain[95] was referred to as the 'camerarius domini papae' (and not sanctae Romanae ecclesiae) from the beginning, and the office-holders changed with each pope.[96] Despite their subordinate rank, individual chamberlains obviously wielded considerable influence.[97]

(b) The papal chancery was thoroughly reorganised after 1082 as well, according to the model of western princely courts. The new cancellarius, Johannes of Gaeta, was a monk from Montecassino, who first became acting head of the chancery, then cardinal deacon and chancellor.[98] It is under him that there was a thorough renewal of the production of charters (dating, chancery style, writing).[99] The charters were now drawn up by palace notaries, who accompanied the popes on their travels.[100] It was out of the

95. In general, Rusch, *Die Behörden und Hofbeamten* 20–38.

96. 'The "Lateranense palatium" continues to figure in papal documents as the collecting place for payments to the curia.' Sydow, 'Untersuchungen' 58.

97. Robinson, *Papacy* 252. The office of chamberlain had absorbed that of the archdeacon (who remained only as a liturgical figure), as well as the early medieval offices of the arcarius and sacellarius.

98. On Johannes of Gaeta, see Dietrich Lohrmann, 'Die Jugendwerke des Johannes von Gaeta', QF 47 (1967) 355–445; Lohrmann, *Das Register Papst Johannes' VIII. (872–882): Neue Studien zur Abschrift Reg. Vat. I, zum verlorenen Originalregister und zum Diktat der Briefe* (BDHI 30; Tübingen 1968) 80–94; Robinson, *Papacy* 213–214. The chancellor of Alexander II, Gregory VII, and Wibert—Petrus, cardinal of S. Grisogono—and another collaborator in the chancery—Leo, later cardinal deacon of SS. Vitus and Modestus—also came from Montecassino; the Roman *dépendance* of Montecassino was actually a sub-archive of the papal chancery; Hans-Walter Klewitz, 'Montecassino in Rom' QF 28 (1937–1938) 36–47, esp. 45.

99. A lot of research has been done recently on the products and the production of the papal chancery of this time: besides Dahlhaus, 'Aufkommen und Bedeutung' see Gudrun Bromm, *Die Entwicklung der Grossbuchstaben im Kontext hochmittelalterlicher Papsturkunden* (Elementa diplomatica 3; Marburg-Lahn 1995); Frank M. Bischoff, *Urkundenformate im Mittelalter: Größe, Format und Proportionen von Papsturkunden in Zeiten expandierender Schriftlichkeit (11. – 13. Jahrhundert)* (Elementa diplomatica 5; Marburg-Lahn 1996); Beate Kruska, 'Zeilen, Ränder und Initiale—Zur Normierung des Layouts hochmittelalterlicher Papsturkunden [1050–1250]', *Mabillons Spur: Zweiundzwanzig Miszellen aus dem Fachgebiet für Historisches Hilfswissenschaften: Zum 80. Geburtstag von Walter Heinemeyer*, ed. Peter Rück (Marburg-Lahn 1992) 231–245. Rudolf Hiestand, 'Die Leistungsfähigkeit der päpstlichen Kanzlei im 12. Jahrhundert mit einem Blick auf den lateinischen Osten', *Papsturkunde und europäisches Urkundenwesen: Studien zu ihrer formalen und rechtlichen Kohärenz vom 11. bis 15. Jahrhundert*, ed. Peter Herde and H. Jakobs (Cologne 1999) 1–26; Stefan Hirschmann, *Die päpstliche Kanzlei und ihre Urkundenproduktion (1141–1159)* (Peter Lang, Reihe 3: Geschichte und ihre Hilfswissenschaften 913; Frankfurt am Main 2001). Przemysław Nowak, 'Die Urkundenproduktion der päpstlichen Kanzlei 1181–1187', *Archiv für Diplomatik* 49 (2003) 91–122. Since from Alexander III onward privileges became rare, I prefer to talk of letters as products of the chancery.

100. Paulius Rabikauskas, *Diplomatica pontificia: Praelectionum lineamenta* (4th ed. Rome 1980) 35–41. See also Andreas Meyer, 'Die päpstliche Kanzlei im Mittelalter – ein Versuch', *Archiv für Diplomatik* 61 (2015) 291–342, and see an abbreviated version of this essay in *A Companion to the Medieval Papacy*, ed. Keith Sisson and Atria Larson (Brill's Companions to the Christian Tradition

chapel (and the court offices) that the central curial offices developed in the thirteenth century (see below).

II. The grandees. These were part of the papal court insofar as they travelled with the pope, and they were primarily cardinals and other high-ranking persons (see below).

III. The group of those who were part of the papal court only temporarily: this group was much more numerous than at other courts and had an entirely different composition: (1) prelates on a visit (visitatio liminum)[101] and clerics who wished to be ordained at the curia;[102] (2) petitioners for papal favors, as well as penitents; (3) litigants; (4) legal experts (notaries, proctors, advocates), whose knowledge and services were indispensible[103] for petitioners as well as parties to litigation because of the formal canon-law process at the curia (that had to be put down in writing). These 'iurisperiti' remained at the curia for some time, but they were not formally in service there. The legal status of all these persons 'Romanam curiam sequentes' presented special problems.

The Hofstaat (Max Weber's Court) and the Person of the Pope

Like that of secular rulers, the 'Hofstaat' of the pope from now on consisted in large part of members bound to his person, belonging to his 'familia'. This group was dissolved at the death of the pope, and the familiars lost their functions. For that reason, a vacancy of the throne now had a more disintegrating effect than before and than at the secular courts, where the princely dynasty provided an element of continuity which obviously did not exist in the case of the celibate elective monarchy that was the papacy.[104]

70; Leiden 2016) as well as the other chapters on the papal curia in the volume; Thomas Frenz, *Papsturkunden des Mittelalters und der Neuzeit* (Historische Grundwissenschaften in Einzeldarstellungen 2; 2nd rev. ed. Stuttgart 2000), is rather specialized on the later Middle Ages. This is the period of the development of the new curial minuscule, with which papal documentary practice left the Roman tradition and fell in line with that of other chanceries; Sydow, 'Untersuchungen', 50–51, 63. See note above.

101. Johann B. Sägmüller, 'Die Visitatio liminum ss. apostolorum bis Bonifaz VIII', *Theologische Quartalschrift* 82 (1900) 69–117; Januarius Pater, *Die bischöfliche Visitatio liminum ss. Apostolorum: Eine historisch-kanonistische Studie* (Görres-Gesellschaft: Veröffentlichungen der Sektion für Rechts- und Sozialwissenschaften 19; Paderborn 1914).

102. See above n. 80.

103. Sydow, 'Untersuchungen' 63. Patrick Zutshi, 'Petitioners, Popes, Proctors: The Development of Curial Institutions, c. 1150–1250', *Pensiero e sperimentazioni istituzionali nella 'Societas Christiana' (1046–1250)*, ed. Giancarlo Andenna (Atti della sedicesima Settimana internazionale di studio; Milan 2007) 265–293.

104. But the college of cardinals, which resided continuously at the curia and from which the popes were almost always chosen, in a certain sense developed into an *Ersatz* of a dynasty; see 191.

With the death of the pope, the normal functions of the curia came to a halt.[105] The fact that the often lengthy vacancies of the throne, which repeatedly placed the survival of the reform papacy in question, did not lead to complete crippling of the institution, can be explained by the fact that at least a part of the curials considered themselves to be representatives (officeholders) of the Roman church and believed that that church remained alive in them even when the pope died. Here we find the first traces of an ecclesiology of the cardinalate, whose final articulation still lay far into the future.[106]

Now the temporary absence of the pope from Rome no longer created overwhelming difficulties. After it had been established that Rome was where the pope was ('ubi papa ibi Roma'),[107] the regulation which had previously existed for representation in Rome whenever the pope was absent from the city was no longer necessary.[108]

The Papal Hofstaat as a Travelling Court

The fact that the Hofstaat of the popes of this period was at most times an itinerant one is yet another characteristic shared with contemporary secular princes. However, there were different reasons for these travels. For the princes, they were a necessary instrument of governance (Reiseherrschaft, itinerant lordship),[109] while for the popes of our period travel was one of the few means to contact their followers and demonstrate their programm;[110] at times it was simply necessary, because they were seldom able to hold themselves in the city of Rome.[111]

It was more important to the popes to reside in Rome, since this was

---

105. On the death of the pope in the Middle Ages, see 190.

106. Zey, 'Entstehung und erste Konsolidierung' 87–90.

107. Thus the title of an essay by Michele Maccarone, 'Ubi est papa, ibi est Roma', *Aus Kirche und Reich* 371–382.

108. Jordan, 'Die päpstliche Verwaltung' 139.

109. Hans Conrad Peyer, 'Das Reisekönigtum des Mittelalters', *Vierteljahrschrift für Sozial- und Wirtschaftsgeschichte* 54 (1964) 1–21; John W. Bernhardt, *Itinerant Kingship and Royal Monasteries in Early Medieval Germany, c. 936–1075* (Cambridge Studies in Medieval Life and Thought, 4th series, 21; Cambridge 1993); Eckhard Müller-Mertens, 'Reich und Hauptorte der Salier: Probleme und Fragen', *Die Salier und das Reich, 1: Salier, Adel und Reichsverfassung,* ed. St. Weinfurter et al. (Sigmaringen 1991) 139–158. On the orientation of the itineraries towards the high festivals, see Hans Martin Schaller, 'Der heilige Tag als Termin mittelalterlicher Staatsakte', DA 30 (1974) 1–24.

110. Currently a fashionable theme: Jochen Johrendt, 'Die Reisen der frühen Reformpäpste – Ihre Ursachen und Funktionen', RQ 96 (2001) 57–94; André Graboïs, 'Les séjours des papes en France au XIIᵉ siècle et leur rapports avec le développement de la fiscalité pontificale', *Revue d'histoire de l'église de France* 49 (1963) 5–18, reprinted in Grabois, *Civilisation et société dans l'occident médiéval* (Variorum reprints, Collected Studies 174; London 1983) no. I; Agostino Paravicini Bagliani, 'Der Papst auf Reisen im Mittelalter', *Feste und Feiern* 501–514.

111. Werner Maleczek, 'Rombeherrschung und Romerneuerung durch das Papsttum', *Rom im hohen Mittelalter* 15–27.

one proof of their legitimacy, even if juristically it was not necessary.[112] The reform popes, who often met with opposition, naturally were glad to make use of the opportunities presented by their travels to promote themselves and their cause. The popes practiced an itinerant lordship in the manner of a secular prince within their Patrimony from the twelfth century onwards.[113] From the thirteenth century, their residence changed at half-yearly intervals: they spent the cool season in the capital, while during the warm one practicing itinerant lordship in the Patrimony of St. Peter.[114]

In their manifestations the itinerant courts of the princes had much in common with that of the pope. The secular ruler showed himself in his territory, adorned by the insignia of his office and surrounded by his court on special occasions: on high ecclesiastical festivals and at the court assemblies, which often followed. Even the solemn entry into a town (adventus) and solemn departure from it[115] offered occasions for self-representation.

The manifestations of the papal court were quite similar; the popes even adopted the practice of festival crownings.[116] They also held a kind of court assembly. Solemn entries are documented since the end of the reform era;[117] they were also a right of the papal legates.[118] A difference ex-

112. The loosening of the ties to Rome was not intended: every connection to the city of Rome was exploited by later reform popes to demonstrate the legitimacy of their claim. For that reason, Roman officeholders were admitted, although they did not fit into the new policy; Sydow, 'Untersuchungen' 54.

113. Robinson, *Papacy* 29–32; *Itineranza pontificia: La mobilità della Curia papale nel Lazio (secoli XII–XIII)*, ed. Sandro Carocci (Nuovi studi storici 61; Rome 2003).

114. Agostino Paravicini Bagliani, 'La mobilità della Curia Romana nel secolo XIII: Riflessi locali', *Società e istituzioni dell'Italia comunale: L'esempio di Perugia (secoli XII–XIV)* (Perugia 1988) 155–278; the appendix (225–253) includes an itinerary of the popes from 1181 to 1304. On the *alternatio* introduced by Innocent III between the city of Rome, where he spent winter and spring, with their liturgical high points, and the summer rulership (villegiatura) and itinerant lordship, see ibid. 168. The curia in Avignon followed the same usage, as did later the popes from Martin V onward. Itinerant lordship outside the Patrimony between the time of Innocent III and the Renaissance only occurred due to extraordinary circumstances (as in the cases of Innocent IV, Gregory X, Urban V, Gregory XI, Eugene IV, and Pius II) or schisms (the Great Schism until the return of Martin V to Rome).

115. Paravicini Bagliani, 'Papst auf Reisen' 511–514; Theo Kölzer, 'Adventus regis', LMA 1.170–171; Susan Twyman, *Papal Ceremonial at Rome in the Twelfth Century* (Henry Bradshaw Society, Subsidia 4; London 2002) passim. On the tradition, see Joachim Lehnen, *Adventus principis: Untersuchungen zu Sinngehalt und Zeremoniell der Kaiserankunft in den Städten des Imperium Romanum* (Prismata 7; Frankfurt am Main 1997); and Gerrit Jasper Schenk, *Zeremoniell und Politik: Herrschereinzüge im spätmittelalterlichen Reich* (Beihefte zu J. F. Böhmer Regesta Imperii 21; Köln-Weimar-Wien 2003). On the flags of the Roman Church carried on travels, see Carl Erdmann, 'Das Wappen und die Fahne der römischen Kirche', QF 22 (1930–1931) 227–255. This papal symbol of lordship also derived from imperial ceremonial; ibid. 231.

116. Robinson, *Papacy* 20–22.

117. As in other cases, it is Calixtus II who founds a tradition (cf. JL 7457 and elsewhere), see n. 41 above.

118. The cathedral clergy of Tours refused to receive the legates of Gregory VII 'processuali-

isted in the form of the liturgy of high festivals. While the princely courts celebrated the liturgy of the church they were in, the Roman court always celebrated the Roman stationary liturgy,[119] insofar as the host town or church[120] could accommodate it, to demonstrate by this liturgical action that one stood within the Roman tradition.

The lodging and feeding of the itinerant court depended on the dues from the areas being visited. Similarly to secular princes, Urban II and other popes demanded a tax to support their itinerant court, which was apparently considered the equivalent of the compensation of a visiting bishop, the 'procuratio canonica'.[121] But this claim appears to have met with little success, as is demonstrated by the fact that until the middle of the twelfth century the popes chose as their hosts primarily churches and lordships with whom there was already a treaty of papal protection—so that their contributions could be interpreted as arising from this relationship—or bishoprics of the French crown, which the king had conceded to the popes for joint use. The popes attempted to compensate their hosts with privileges, but preferably by consecrating churches and altars, which, like the celebration of the grand Roman liturgy, drew an audience and thus donations in favor of these churches.[122] Consideration for the hosts forced the sojourns to be brief.

Financing changed with Alexander III: he demanded and received a 'subsidium' from the entire ecclesiastical province to relieve the hosts.[123]

---

ter'. It cited its privilege that it had to receive only the pope himself and (once in his life) the king of France and the archbishop of Bordeaux (JL 5620 = Migne PL 151.449–450 § 177).

119. The curia continued to take the responsibility of the pope as supreme liturgist of the city of Rome very seriously. The 'ordines' of the twelfth century assumed the presence of the pope in Rome, although that really only applied for 1140–1143 and from 1179 on. The curia defined in the 'ordines' corresponds to developments before the emergence of the reform papacy; see Schimmelpfennig, *Papsttum* 155–156, 182–184.

120. During longer stays, especially in the thirteenth century, certain churches and the papal palace (or parts thereof) were equated with Roman 'stationes'. For Avignon see Bernhard Schimmelpfennig, 'Die Funktion des Papstpalastes und der kurialen Gesellschaft vor und während des Großen Schismas', *Génèse et débuts du Grand Schisme d'Occident (1362–1394)* (Paris 1980) 317–328, esp. 319–320.

121. Cf. Robinson, *Papacy* 283–284; Carlrichard Brühl, 'Zur Geschichte der procuratio canonica vornehmlich im 11. und 12. Jahrhundert', *Le istituzioni ecclesiastiche della 'societas christiana' dei secoli XI–XII* 419–431, reprinted in Brühl, *Aus Mittelalter und Diplomatik* (3 vols. Hildesheim 1989) 1.323-335. On the corresponding difficulties of secular princes, see Brühl, *Fodrum, Gistum, Servitium regis: Studien zu den wirtschaftlichen Grundlagen des Königtums* (Kölner Historische Abhandlungen 14.1–2; Cologne-Graz 1968). Travels outside the Patrimony became an increasingly delicate matter in the course of the twelfth century, since the princes no longer wanted to cede their rights in the places where the curia was sojourning; Graboïs, 'Les séjours des papes' 13, 16.

122. Graboïs, 'Les séjours des papes' 10–12; Robinson, *Papacy* 288. On the consecration of altars and churches in this period, see also Cyriakus Heinrich Brakel, 'Die vom Reformpapsttum geförderten Heiligenkulte', *Studi Gregoriani* 9 (1972) 241–311.

123. This was dictated by precaution. The travels of the popes could be compared to the visitation travels of bishops only by a great stretch of the imagination; those of the legates were more comparable; see 184.

In addition, he 'asked' individual churches to provide for curials by giving them benefices (provision).[124]

The Curia in an Institutional Sense

The papal synod had been introduced by the first reform popes using elements of the old Roman provincial synods (the place of assembly, that is, the Lateran; the time of meeting, that is, normally at Easter, or later Lent; the ceremonial) and elements of the Imperial councils of the past and present (being convened and presided over by the 'monarchical' pope).[125] Even bishops from outside Italy and the Empire were summoned to these papal synods, particularly those competent for the cases in question. Universal validity was claimed for resolutions. The synods were juridical bodies for trying the offences of highly-placed clerics and laymen (even princes), and they were also assemblies for issuing reform decrees. In the former case, the participants acted as the court assessors, while in the latter they passed resolutions by majority vote. The pope had the right to veto these decisions or to make them law through his consent.

In this epoch, the character of the papal synod was transformed, particularly under Urban II and Calixtus II.[126] Synods were now also (and predominantly) held when the popes were travelling, abandoning the traditional place and time of assembly, and some synods had a much larger circle of participants than even those of Gregory VII had ever had.[127] On the whole, the majority of participants would be those from the country being visited, particularly those from the immediate vicinity, and those who were visiting the curia in order to pursue their own interests, especially in legal disputes.

The traditional procedure at the synod—debate and formulation of decrees by the participants—also underwent a change: (1) While the 'causae maiores' continued to be negotiated at synods at least in part, it was the pope who decided the case, after deliberation (de consilio) with the high curials he consulted, particularly the cardinals, who held an elevated po-

---

124. Robinson, *Papacy* 289–291.

125. Georg Gresser, *Die Synoden und Konzilien in der Zeit des Reformpapsttums in Deutschland und Italien von Leo IX. bis Calixt II. 1049–1123* (Konziliengeschichte, Reihe A; Paderborn 2006); Gresser, 'Sanctorum patrum auctoritate: Zum Wandel der Rolle des Papstes im Kirchenrecht auf den päpstlichen Synoden in der Zeit der Gregorianischen Reform', ZRG Kan. Abt. 91 (2005) 59–73. Franz-Josef Schmale, 'Synodus - synodale concilium - concilium', AHC 8 (1976) 80–102; and Atria Larson, 'Early Stages of Gratian's *Decretum* and the Second Lateran Council: A Reconsideration', BMCL 27 (2007) 21–56 at 27–36.

126. Robinson, *Papacy* 124–135

127. On the dominant role of the cardinals at the synods, see Maleczek, *Papst und Kardinalskolleg* 304, 307. They prepared the synods, and at the synods they constituted a kind of standing committee, since the other participants continually came and went.

sition (in the literal sense as well) at the synod. The plenum was given the part of the 'people' in the announcement of the verdict or decision.[128] (2) Legal disputes that participants brought before the synod were only received there, while the actual negotiations took place outside the synod in the consistory. (3) The plenum no longer voted on measures for reform, although it might still debate them. It became common practice for the synod only to acclaim proposals made and formulated by the pope. From the time of Calixtus II on, the decrees were published in the form of papal decretals.

In this way the synods lost importance both for the popes and for the participants. They became correspondingly less frequent, and they were now only called when the pope sought the advice and help of the entire church in questions of fundamental importance, such as resolving a schism or fighting heresy. The synod, now regularly referred to as 'concilium generale', between 1130 and 1179 developed into the legislative assembly that it was in the high Middle Ages.[129]

Since Urban II, the popes, in addition to the synods, which in form and function came to resemble the great diets of princes, also held solemn court assemblies (called by contemporaries 'curiae solemnes'), which were celebrated on high festivals at ecclesiastical centers of the country visited. They only differed from the synods in the restriction of the circle of participants and the limitation of matters to be dealt with to less important, usually regional, problems. In addition, as at the princely courts, court assemblies without any special solemnity became more frequent, with an even more restricted number of participants (besides the cardinals, there were other curials, high-ranking ecclesiastical visitors, and occasionally Roman nobles). This body, which was called the consistorium from about 1130, gradually took over almost all the functions of the synods and solemn court meetings and became the council of the pope in all questions touching the Roman church and the government of the universal church.[130]

128. The synods continued to consult participants as experts. A judgment could be passed after the synod.

129. With participants of the whole church and a claim to orthodoxy (which are the two original senses of *generalis*); see Horst Fuhrmann, 'Ecclesia Romana – Ecclesia Universalis', *Rom im hohen Mittelalter* 41–45.

130. 'Consistory' in the narrower sense meant the promulgation and rendering of judgments. In the case of legal disputes between third parties, it also included the proceedings before a juridical court, also called the 'audientia publica'. The term derives from a hall of this name in the Lateran in which the curial judicial sessions were held by preference; Jürgen Sydow, 'Il "consistorium" dopo lo scisma del 1130', RSCI 9 (1955) 165–176, reprinted in *Cum omni mensura* 53–64; and 'Untersuchungen' 52–55; Maleczek, *Papst und Kardinalskolleg* 297–302; Robinson, *Papacy* 188–190.

The Connection between the Curia and the Periphery: Papal Legates

The institution of legates made it possible for the popes to keep up a more intensive contact with the periphery than contemporary secular princes were able to establish. The use of legates to achieve the claims of primacy and to enforce reform decrees goes back to Gregory VII. He and his successors until about 1120 used special representatives with temporary commissions, and also commissioned local bishops and archbishops for the duration of the pontificate with full deputy powers. (Both categories of representatives were usually called 'vicarii' at first.) They were assigned a specific defined district. To carry out their mission, they convened legatine synods. During their legation in the specific district, they held a rank superior to the episcopate.[131] So far as they were acting in an official capacity, they had a claim on the procuratio[132] for themselves and their suite.[133]

From about 1120 the legal status of the legates was differentiated and more clearly defined:[134]

(1) Full representation of the pope—which was also expressed in ceremonial—was held only by those now technically called 'legati a latere'.[135] Their mission was limited not only with regard to time and space, but also with regard to subject.[136] Increasingly, only cardinals were named legati a latere, and they usually were cardinal bishops.

131. Based on the edition by Stefan Weiß, *Die Urkunden der päpstlichen Legaten von Leo IX. bis zu Coelestin III. (1049–1198)* (Cologne 1995); see Claudia Zey, 'Die Augen des Papstes: Zu Eigenschaften und Vollmachten päpstlicher Legaten', *Römisches Zentrum und kirchliche Peripherie* 77–108; and Zey, 'Gleiches Recht für alle? Konfliktlösung und Rechtsprechung durch päpstliche Legaten im 11. und 12. Jahrhundert', *Rechtsverständnis und Konfliktbewältigung: Gerichtliche und außergerichtliche Strategien im Mittelalter*, ed. S. Esders (Cologne-Weimar-Vienna 2007) 93–119; Zey, *Die päpstliche Legatenpolitik im 11. und 12. Jh.* (forthcoming).

132. Demanded from the time of Gregory VII onward; see Brühl, 'Zur Geschichte der procuratio canonica' 427. On procurations for legates and nuncios (later especially collectors), see also William Edward Lunt, *Financial Relations of the Papacy with England to 1327* (Studies in Anglo-Papal Relations during the Middle Ages 1; Cambridge, Mass. 1939) 1.532–570.

133. The costs of the legates' entourages were a notorious point of complaint; see Hans Ollendiek, *Die päpstlichen Legaten im deutschen Reichsgebiet von 1261 bis zum Ende des Interregnums* (Historische Schriften der Universität Freiburg 3; Freiburg, Switzerland 1976) 125–127; Robinson, *Papacy* 162–163.

134. Robinson, *Papacy* 146–78; bibliography of historical studies in Maleczek, *Papst und Kardinalskolleg* 336 n. 94.

135. See Lunt, *Financial Relations* 1.534–541, where one finds documentation for the early period. Real 'ordines' for legates are only known from the later Middle Ages, composed by Guillelmus Durandi: *Le pontifical de Guillaume Durand*, ed. M. Andrieu (Le pontifical Romain 3, Studi e testi 88; Vatican City 1940) 627–629; Jacopo Stephaneschi, *De Rome en Avignon* 496–502 (1334), 245–247; see also Franz Wasner, 'Fifteenth Century Texts on the Ceremonial of the Papal "Legatus a latere",' *Traditio* 14 (1958) 295–358, and 16 (1960) 405–416 (with a collection of evidence from earlier times).

136. An exception were legates called 'vicarii' with long-term commissions, installed in northern Italy and in France. They had personal relations to their geographical areas. See Robinson, *Papacy* 164–166.

(2) Besides the legati a latere, until the end of the twelfth century the popes continued to use other representatives. These legates were drawn from the lower ranks (mainly papal chaplains) and had special missions, usually without a specific area of competence and without a special title and status (the later 'nuntii').[137]

(3) There were archbishops who were named in partibus as permanent legates for the duration of a pontificate, usually based on a personal relationship of trust (to be distinguished from the later 'legati nati'). They were definitely secondary to the legati a latere. Their function was increasingly (particularly since Alexander III) to stem the flow of litigation, which flooded the curia.

In the thirteenth century the decretalists developed a system of legation that was binding for the future.[138] They distinguished the following: (1) legatus a latere; (2) legatus missus (cardinal legate with restricted powers) and nuntius (legate of non-cardinal rank); (3) legatus natus (the status of legate dependent on the episcopal see, not the person, with restricted powers).[139]

The iudices delegati

Another official link between the curia and the periphery, and because of their sheer numbers probably an even more important link, were the 'iudices delegati'.[140] These were local clerics, usually prelates, who—ignor-

137. Elze, 'Kapelle' 181–183.

138. Paul Hinschius, *Das System des katholischen Kirchenrechts mit besonderer Rücksicht auf Deutschland* (Berlin 1869) 1.103–115; Karl Ruess, *Die rechtliche Stellung der päpstlichen Legaten bis Bonifaz VIII* (Görresgesellschaft zur Pflege der Wissenschaft im katholischen Deutschland: Veröffentlichungen der Sektion für Rechts- und Sozialwissenschaften 13; Paderborn 1912); see the various studies by Robert C. Figueira, 'Papal Reserved Powers and the Limitation of Legatine Authority', *Popes, Teachers and Canon Law in the Middle Ages,* ed. James R. Sweeney and S. Chodorow (Ithaca-London 1989) 191–211, and 'The Medieval Papal Legate and His Province: Geographical Limits of Jurisdiction', *Apollinaris* 16 (1988) 817–860; and by Clifford Jan Kyer, 'The Legation of Cardinal Latinus and William Duranti's "Speculum legatorum",' BMCL 10 (1980) 56–62, 'Legate and Nuntius as Used to Denote Papal Envoys 1245–1378', *Mediaeval Studies* 40 (1978) 473–477,and 'The Papal Legate and the "Solemn" Papal Nuncio, 1243–1378: The Changing Pattern of Papal Representation' (PhD Diss. Toronto 1979).

139. There were also rulers who claimed the legation for their own realms; see Jószef Deér, 'Der Anspruch der Herrscher des 12. Jahrhunderts auf die apostolische Legation', AHP 2 (1964) 117–186.

140. For the literature (historical and pragmatic), see Harald Müller, *Päpstliche Delegationsgerichtsbarkeit in der Normandie (12. und frühes 13. Jahrhundert)* (Studien und Dokumente zur Gallia Pontificia 4.1 and 2; Bonn 1997); and Müller, 'Gesandte mit beschränkter Handlungsvollmacht: Zu Struktur und Praxis päpstlich delegierter Gerichtsbarkeit', *Aus der Frühzeit europäischer Diplomatie: Zum geistlichen und weltlichen Gesandtschaftswesen vom 12. bis zum 15. Jahrhundert,* ed. Claudia Märtl and C. Zey (Zürich 2008) 41–65; Jane E. Sayers, *Papal Judges Delegate in the Province of Canterbury 1198–1254* (Oxford Historical Monographs; Oxford 1971). Canonistic literature: Richard A. Schmutz, 'Medieval Papal Representatives: Legates, Nuncios and Judges-Delegate', *Collectanea Stephan Kuttner* (SG 15; Bologna 1972) 441–463; George Pavloff, *Papal Judges Delegate at the time of*

ing the hierarchy—had been commissioned by the pope to investigate, in partibus, individual cases pending at the curia. Brought into being in the 1130s, the iudices delegati served, as did the archbishop-legates, to reduce the burden on the curia, particularly from Alexander III onward.

The Connections between the Curia and the Periphery through Networks

The envoys (legates or nuntii) represented the popes in the periphery.[141] Since they were usually chosen because they already had contacts in their districts, and added further contacts during their stay, on their return to the curia they were regarded as representatives of (and not just as experts on) their region at the curia.[142] The connections of other curials functioned in a similar way: their contacts with the periphery on the basis of such factors as family, local connections, common educational background or professional activity, or in some cases monastic association, were exploited in both directions, but more by the periphery toward the curia than vice versa. Since there were only a few institutions that could afford a representative of their own at the curia (such as, for a time, reform houses and orders), the net of personal ties of curial officials was, from the beginning, very important for the connections of the pope with the periphery.

Moreover, there are signs of first efforts on the part of the curia to develop institutions through which the relations to the periphery could be systematically maintained: important prelates in partibus received the title of cardinal or of papal chaplain, with the honorary rights tied to it. These 'external' cardinals and chaplains did not reside at the curia and were its exponents in partibus.[143] In this way, the reform papacy began to create a

---

the Corpus Iuris Canonici (The Catholic University of America Canon Law Studies 426; Washington, D.C. 1963); Richard H. Helmholz, 'Canonists and Standards of Impartiality for Papal Judges Delegate', Traditio 25 (1969) 386–404. A variant of the iudex delegatus is the conservator; see Charles Lefebvre, 'La concession des conservateurs apostoliques au temps d'Innocent IV (1234–1254)', Ephemerides Juris Canonici 31 (1975) 116–135; various studies by Henri Hénaff in RDC 27 (1977) 243–272, RDC 35 (1985) 194–221, RDC 36 (1986) 3–26, RDC 47 (1997) 71–88, RDC 50 (2000) 283–308.

141. The concept of networks is currently a fashionable theme: see Zentrum und Netzwerk: Kirchliche Kommunikationen und Raumstrukturen im Mittelalter, ed. Gisela Drossbach and H.-J. Schmidt (Scrinium Friburgense 22; Berlin-New York 2008); see also the essays in the volume by Claudia Zey, 'Handlungsspielräume - Handlungsinitiativen. Aspekte der päpstlichen Legatenpolitik im 12. Jahrhundert' 63–92; and Wetzstein, 'Kommunikationsgeschichtliche Bedeutung der Kirchenversammlungen des hohen Mittelalters' 247–297. Robert Gramsch, 'Kommunikation als Lebensform: Kuriale in Thüringen vom 13. bis zum 16. Jahrhundert', Kurie und Region 417–434.

142. Experts for the region and also protectors; Sydow, 'Untersuchungen' 70.

143. Klaus Ganzer, Die Entwicklung des auswärtigen Kardinalats im hohen Mittelalter. Ein Beitrag zur Geschichte des Kardinalskollegiums vom 11. bis 13. Jahrhundert (BDHI 26; Tübingen 1963). The subdiaconi consecrated by the pope took positions in partibus as honorary papal chaplains, with ceremonial precedence over the clergy of their church, notwithstanding the superior ordination of

net of client relationships without which no medieval lordship could survive.

Years of Peril and Consolidation (1130–1198)

The outbreak of the schism of 1130, on the one hand, and the accession of Innocent III, on the other, demarcate an epoch in curial history.[144] The two schisms, that of 1130 to 1138 and particularly that of 1159 to 1180, rudely interrupted the consolidation of the curia, cutting the popes off from the Patrimony once more. Again there followed years of unsettled travelling, extreme financial need, and improvisation. On the other hand, this is a period of strong and increasing demand for papal interpretation of the law in cases of doubt, and for settlement by the pope in disputed cases, as well as for papal dispensation and absolution.[145] Such demand came particularly from the culturally advanced areas of Northern Italy and France, which belonged to the obedience of Popes Innocent II and Alexander III and where they repeatedly resided. The curia, which became increasingly dependent on consent, had to adapt to this demand and had to organize the chancery.

The most striking change in diplomatic affairs was in the external appearance of papal charters. Since the schism of 1130 the signatures of the cardinals were found on all charters of a specific type (particularly confirmations of possession) in three columns below that of the pope, according to their ordination date. Previously, charters had only carried signatures when they seemed called for in keeping with the content of the charter, and then not only those of cardinals but also of others.[146]

The courts and the penitentiary were also reorganized accordingly, a

the latter. This, as well as their exemption (and possibly their claim to provision by the pope with benefices in partibus) created increasing tensions with the bishops. They could receive higher degrees of ordination only at the curia. Hence the popes from the end of the twelfth century onward tended increasingly to appoint chaplains instead, which also had the advantage that one could choose clerics who already had higher degrees of ordination; Elze, 'Kapelle' 156, 177. See 175.

144. Werner Maleczek, 'Das Kardinalskolleg unter Innocenz II. und Anaklet II.' AHP 19 (1981) 27–78.

145. On censures imposed by iudices delegati, see 185–186.

146. On the 'rationalization measures' undertaken at the chancery due to the great demand, see below. Also see Maleczek, *Papst und Kardinalskolleg* 320–321. This change is to be understood (1) as a propaganda measure: presenting one's own high-ranking cardinals is meant to demonstrate the better claim to the papal throne; (2) as a fiscal accomodation, since it provided the cardinals with fees from the pockets of solvent petitioners. The second change in diplomatics was an adaptation of the cursus to the practice of northwestern chanceries, completing the process begun by the reform popes of separating the chancery from the city of Rome; see 177.

change which was reflected in the recruitment of the curia.[147] In a certain sense the pontificate of Clement III (1187–1191) constitutes another break in the history of the curia, because he achieved a lasting reconciliation with the Romans, which had considerable impact on the recruiting of curial personnel.[148] Yet a truly new era was marked later by the pontificate of Innocent III, who systematically reorganized the curia.[149]

Altered Conception of the Papacy

The development of the pope into a monarch of the hierarchically organized clerical church went forward. Parallel to this, to the same extent that his position as the head of christianitas was strengthened, he became alienated from the city of Rome.[150]

These changes were expressed in the fashioning of the papal residence after the return to the city of Rome in 1120: as a sign of the victorious ending of the investiture contest, Calixtus II triumphally enlarged and transformed the Lateran palace, creating a quasi-imperial residence.[151] Following the example of the emperors, the popes collected the most holy relics in the chapel of their palace—not in the Lateran church. This was designated by nearly all the popes of that time as their place of burial.[152] Although they were often compelled to leave Rome, the popes held fast

147. In the twelfth century the centralization of the penitential system of the church initially only led to the appointment of one cardinal as penitentiary; Emil Göller, *Die päpstliche Pönitentiarie von ihrem Ursprung bis zu ihrer Umgestaltung unter Pius V.* (2 vols. Bibliothek des königlich Preussischen Historischen Instituts in Rom 3–4, 7–8; Rome 1907, 1911) 1.75–81.

148. See on this point Maleczek, *Papst und Kardinalskolleg* 241, 291. Clement's cardinals were less educated than those of both his predecessors and his successors. See also note 167.

149. See Maleczek, *Papst und Kardinalskolleg* 331–333, 336, concerning the use of chaplains as auditors; on the use of lower-ranking curials and extra-curial persons as legates, see ibid. 338–341, and in the Papal States, ibid. 345–346; on other innovations of Innocent (in ceremonial, in his itinerant rulership, in the chapel, chancery, penitentiary, and in the position of the procurators), see below.

150. Gerhart B. Ladner, 'The Concept of "Ecclesia" and "Christianitas" and Their Relation to the Idea of Papal "Plenitudo Potestatis" from Gregory VII to Boniface VIII', *Sacerdocio e Regno da Gregorio VII a Bonifacio VIII* (Miscellanea Historiae Pontificiae 18; Rome 1954) 1.49–77, reprinted in *Images and Ideas in the Middle Ages* (Storia e Letteratura 156; Rome 1983) 2.487–515; Walter Ullmann, *The Growth of Papal Government in the Middle Ages: A Study in the Ideological Relation of Clerical to Lay Power* (London 1955) passim; Michael Wilks, *The Problem of Sovereignty in the Later Middle Ages: The Papal Monarchy with Augustinus Triumphus and the Publicists* (Cambridge Studies in Medieval Life and Thought, 2nd series, 9; Cambridge 1964).

151. On the 'imitatio imperii' in Roman churches in the twelfth century, see Dorothy F. Glass, 'Papal Patronage in the Early Twelfth Century: Notes on the Iconography of Cosmatesque Pavements', *Journal of the Warburg and Courtaulds Institutes* 32 (1969) 386–390. See also Peter Cornelius Claussen, 'Renovatio Romae: Erneuerungsphasen römischer Architektur im 11. und 12. Jahrhundert', *Rom im hohen Mittelalter* 67–125.

152. Borgolte, *Petrusnachfolge und Kaiserimitation*, chapter 5: 'Papstgräber als Herrschermonumente' 151–178. In the thirteenth century, the graves of the 'universales pontifices' lay scattered across the Papal States; ibid. 179–213.

to the Lateran as their residence until 1188. After their permanent return, however, they resided at various places within Rome.

Corresponding tendencies can be seen in the ceremonial, which, at the papal court, includes the liturgy.[153] In this period a special curial ritual (mos Romanae curiae) developed for the liturgical celebration of the ecclesiastical year, which differed significantly from previous Roman practice.[154] This was maintained even after the permanent return to Rome in 1188.[155] The Roman ritual, to which the popes had attached such importance during their exile, sank to the level of a local special liturgy in the following period.

A comparison of the ordines for the papal processions of about 1100 and about 1200 shows the change in self-portrayal from the pope as 'Lord of the Lateran palace and of the City of Rome' to 'Leader of the Universal Church'.[156]

The partly spiritual, partly secular ceremonies for bestowing the Golden Rose (on Laetare Sunday),[157] and for distributing to court society candles (on Mary Candlemas), palms (on Palm Sunday), and the Agnus dei tablet (on the Saturday after Easter) were typical opportunities for displaying the court ceremonial, with the positions of participants being determined by the official order of rank on the one hand, and the favor of the pope on the other.

Similar to secular courts, a special ceremony was developed at the curia to receive visitors of rank, secular or clerical, which included solemn adventus or reception in the papal palace, and entertainment.[158] The dif-

153. Bernhard Schimmelpfennig, *Die Zeremonienbücher der römischen Kurie im Mittelalter* (BDHI 40; Tübingen 1973) 381–382, Konkordanz.

154. Codified ca. 1200 in liturgical regulations, called ordines; see Schimmelpfennig, *Zeremonienbücher* 6–35; *Le pontifical romain au Moyen Age, 1: Le pontifical romain au XIIe siècle, 2: Le pontifical de la curie romaine au XIIIe siècle, 4: Index*, ed. M. Andrieu (Studi e testi 86–87; Vatican City 1938–1941); Pierre-Marie Gy, 'La papauté et le droit liturgique aux XIIe et XIIIe siècles', *The Religious Roles of the Papacy: Ideals and Realities 1150–1330* (Pontifical Institute of Mediaeval Studies, Papers in Mediaeval Studies 8; Toronto 1989) 229–245.

155. Schimmelpfennig, 'Die Bedeutung Roms' 47, and 'Päpstliche Liturgie und päpstliches Zeremoniell im 12. Jahrhundert', *Das Papsttum in der Welt des 12. Jahrhunderts*, ed. E.-D. Hehl et al. (Mittelalter-Forschungen 6; Stuttgart 2002) 263–272.

156. Citation from Schimmelpfennig, 'Die Bedeutung Roms' 60; on the same subject, his essay 'Krönung' 219–229.

157. Elisabeth Garms-Cornides, *Rose und Schwert im päpstlichen Zeremoniell von den Anfängen bis zum Pontifikat Gregors XIII.* (Wiener Dissertationen aus dem Gebiete der Geschichte 9; Vienna 1967); Paravicini Bagliani, *La vita* 216–231. For documentation of the practice of the popes to honor hosts and protectors on their travels in this way, see Robinson, *Papacy* 22.

158. A systematic study of the pope's reception is lacking. On the ritual of receiving an emperor in Rome see Achim Thomas Hack, *Das Empfangszeremoniell bei mittelalterlichen Papst - Kaiser - Treffen* (Forschungen zur Kaiser- und Papstgeschichte des Mittelalters 18; Cologne 1999) 271–367. The popes at Avignon developed a very fine gradation of courtoisie: for example, the pope received only very high-ranking persons, whom he fed at his own table, in his camera secreta, while

ferences in detail in this procedure showed how much the curia valued a guest.

The ceremonial after the death of the pope was significantly different from that observed with secular princes. While in the case of secular rulers, the mourning and burial developed into an apotheosis of princedom,[159] the pope was buried 'ut homo ante apostolatum'.[160] But even this simple manner of burial was not always assured; it was not unusual for the dead pope to be plundered,[161] since his relatives and clients, chiefly responsible for the care of the corpse, scattered quickly after his death.[162]

Status and Tasks of the College of Cardinals

Pope Gregory VII had been the first to claim the prerogatives of the Roman senate for the cardinals.[163] It is only in our period that the differences between the three ordines diminish to such an extent that the cardinals are referred to as a collegium, from about 1150.[164] From Alexander III onwards, the cardinals had a common purse, which is always an indica-

those of lower rank had to be content with a group reception, and they would be fed in a chamber far from the arcanum and with different company; see Stefan Weiß, *Die Versorgung des päpstlichen Hofes in Avignon mit Lebensmitteln (1316–1378): Studien zur Sozial- und Wirtschaftsgeschichte eines mittelalterlichen Hofes* (Berlin 2002) 226–264.

159. Ernst H. Kantorowicz, *The King's Two Bodies: A Study in Mediaeval Political Theology* (Princeton 1957) 409–413, 419–427; Ralph E. Giesey, *The Royal Funeral Ceremony in Renaissance France* (Travaux d'humanisme et Renaissance 37; Geneva 1960); Elizabeth M. Hallam, 'Royal Burial and the Cult of Kingship in France and England 1060–1330', JMH 8 (1982) 359–380.

160. Formulation by Johannes Burchard: 'quia in eo quod homo est moritur et desinit esse major hominum, ideo ut homo ante apostolatum sepeliri debet'; *Liber notarum,* ed. E. Celani (Muratori, RIS² 32.1–2; Città di Castello 1910–1942) 1.16, lines 28–29.

161. Reinhard Elze, 'Sic transit gloria mundi: Zum Tode des Papstes im Mittelalter', DA 34 (1978) 1–18, reprinted in *Päpste - Kaiser - Könige* no. IV. Agostino Paravicini Bagliani, *Il corpo del papa* (Torino 1994) 183. The suite, as well as the conclave cell of the newly elected pope, was pillaged. Cardinals were also robbed; Paravacini Bagliani, 'Die Polemik der Bettelorden um den Tod des Kardinals Peter von Collemezzo (1253)', *Aus Kirche und Reich* 355–362, esp. 357–358.

162. Burial was a family obligation in the case of secular princes. Here, as well, looting is known in cases when the prince died far away from his family; Elze, 'Sic transit gloria mundi'.

163. Prosopographical studies on subsequent cardinals, chronologically (though with gaps), are: Rudolf Hüls, *Kardinäle, Klerus und Kirchen 1049–1130* (BDHI 48; Tübingen 1977); Barbara Zenker, *Die Mitglieder des Kardinalskollegiums von 1130–1159* (Würzburg 1964); the two works of Maleczek, *Papst und Kardinalskolleg* (1191–1216) and 'Das Kardinalskolleg unter Innocenz II.' (1130–1143, revising Zenker); Robinson, *Papacy*; as well as the works of Paravicini Bagliani, *Cardinali di curia e 'familiae' cardinalizie dal 1227 al 1254* (2 vols. Italia Sacra 18–19; Padua 1972), and *I testamenti dei cardinali del Duecento* (Miscellanea della Società Romana di Storia Patria 25; Rome 1980). The biographies of all known cardinals in the Middle Ages will be treated in the forthcoming volume 2 of *Geschichte des Kardinalats im Mittelalter,* see above note 36.

164. For a long time to come, 'translatio' to a higher ordo was a step up in a career; Zenker, *Mitglieder* 227. Further, as is the case today with chairs at prestigious universities, there seem to have been titular churches particularly distinguished by preeminent occupants; Michael Horn, *Studien zur Geschichte Papst Eugens III. 1145–1153* (Europäische Hochschulschriften 3.508; Frankfurt am Main 1992) 191–192.

tor of a tighter corporate organization. Gradually the view developed by analogy that the college of cardinals together with the pope represented the Roman church, just as contemporary cathedral chapters together with the bishop constituted a particular church.[165]

The decretal *Licet de vitanda* of 1179 on papal election was important for this development;[166] it had been promulgated because of two schisms, and it ruled that the person elected by two-thirds of the cardinals became pope, establishing the election as the constitutional foundation of the papal office. The cardinals of all three ordines were established as the legitimate electoral body. The canon excluded all other electors. Since the cardinals de facto were almost the only ones to be eligible, the college of cardinals was comparable in some respects to the dynastic arrangements at secular courts. As was the case in the first phase, the recruiting of the cardinals[167] remained international until the end of the twelfth century, though a significant proportion of them was Roman. The criteria for selection continued to include expertise and experience in administration (particularly in the papal chapel) and connection to the centers of reform[168] as well as political considerations (particularly that of securing the Patrimony).[169] Like the magnates in secular principalities, the cardinals were also representatives of the centers and the princes who were important for the popes. With the growing importance of jurisprudence at the curia, the proportionate number of cardinals who had an academic education in law increased. The total number of cardinals declined towards the end of the twelfth century.

Tasks and Responsibilities

The primary task of the cardinals was electing the pope. In our period further special tasks and responsibilities of the cardinals developed. The most important of them was that of participating in the consistory. The consistory from about 1130 was the solemn public assembly of the cardi-

---

165. See Rudolf Schieffer, *Die Entstehung von Domkapiteln in Deutschland* (Bonner Historische Forschungen 43; Bonn 1982).

166. 3 Lat. c. 1 (1 Comp. 1.4.15(11) = X 1.6.6).

167. Robinson, *Papacy*: the role of reform orders, 209–218, 222–223; of the reform monasteries and chapters, 218–220, 223–226; of learned centers, 220–222. Werner Maleczek, 'Die Kardinäle von 1143 bis 1216: Exklusive Papstwähler und erste Agenten der päpstlichen *plenitudo potestatis*', *Geschichte des Kardinalats* 95–154 at 99–110.

168. Maleczek, *Papst und Kardinalskolleg* 251. The pontificate of Clement III marks a caesura: Clement sought reconciliation with the Romans by receiving sons and nepotes of the leading families, thus dividing the college; ibid. 352.

169. In the twelfth century the cardinals were primarily from Italy, but from central and northern Italy with their communes. France was represented by a few but important cardinals (learned members of orders); Maleczek, *Papst und Kardinalskolleg* 251.

nals presided over by the pope, meeting to deliberate and decide matters of great significance.[170]

In our period it still had no competence to make decisions. It was simply a consulting body whose composition was determined from case to case by the pope himself, with the cardinals predominating.[171] The pope also determined those matters in which he desired counsel. The course of the sessions did not yet follow any set rule, which is why Maleczek,[172] among others, would rather speak of a council of cardinals, although the term consistorium is the usual one from our era onwards.[173] Matters dealt with at these assemblies included questions of general importance: particularly political matters and questions of doctrine, planning of legatine missions,[174] administration of the Patrimonium Petri,[175] creation of new cardinals, legislation, and canonizations.[176]

Jurisdictional issues took up most of the time. From about 1100 the consistory was the supreme court of the curia. Since Urban II, causae maiores were handled here. For other cases the consistory was primarily a court of appeal, though toward the end of the twelfth century it was also a court of first instance in certain cases. The sheer number of cases pending gave the papal curia the appearance of a judicial court, to a considerably larger extent than was the case with secular courts. Because of this, the curia was criticized as growing worldly.[177]

In the judicial proceedings, the pope presided, while the other members of the consistory acted as assessors, and were complemented when necessary by persons who were regarded as qualified. To reduce the bur-

170. Robinson, *Papacy* 99–102, with literature. The institution was juristically developed only in the second half of the thirteenth century (causae consistoriales); Maleczek, *Papst und Kardinalskolleg* 297–302.

171. The composition varied according to what was being treated and according to external circumstances. For the consultation of chaplains, prelates, monks, nobles, and permanent non-Roman judges, see Sydow, 'Untersuchungen' 50; Theodor Hirschfeld, 'Das Gerichtswesen der Stadt Rom vom 8. bis 12. Jahrhundert wesentlich nach stadttrömischen Urkunden', *Archiv für Urkundenforschung* 4 (1912) 419–562, esp. 491, 537–538; Sayers, *Papal Judges Delegate*; Johannes Fried, 'Die römische Kurie und die Anfänge der Prozeßliteratur', ZRG Kan. Abt. 59 (1973) 151–174.

172. Maleczek, *Papst und Kardinalskolleg* 302–312; Maleczek, 'Kardinäle' 124–126.

173. Maleczek, *Papst und Kardinalskolleg* 302. See Maleczek, 'Das Kardinalskolleg unter Innozenz II.' 52.

174. Maleczek, *Papst und Kardinalskolleg* 236.

175. Ibid. 312 and 318. From the time of the reform papacy the Patrimony was no longer conceived of as a patrimonial possession but as the "state" of the popes; that state had to be bound to the court of the prince through personal ties, which was one of the reasons for the composition of the curia; Toubert, *Les structures du Latium médiéval* 2.1051–1068, 1083–1084.

176. On the development of a process of canonization and on the attitude of the popes towards the cult of saints, see Thomas Wetzstein, *Heilige vor Gericht: Das Kanonisationsverfahren im europäischen Spätmittelalter* (Forschungen zur kirchlichen Rechtsgeschichte und zum Kirchenrecht 28; Köln-Weimar-Wien 2004) 212–243.

177. Maleczek, *Papst und Kardinalskolleg* 225, 256; Maleczek, 'Kardinäle' 132–133; Robinson, *Papacy* 198.

den on the court, the pope increasingly commissioned a few cardinals or even a single cardinal to hear the cases (hence the term 'auditores') and to write a final report, which formed the basis for the judgment. In some cases they were even commissioned to render the sentence.[178] Sometimes before decisions the pope withdrew with the cardinals into the secretum; in this case he pronounced the sentence 'de consilio fratrum'.[179]

Besides participation in the consistory, the tasks and responsibilities of the cardinals included leading the important offices at the curia as head of the penitentiary, the 'vicarius urbis' (deputy of the pope in the city of Rome), and the chancellor (usually cardinals from the lower ordines).[180] In contrast, the chamberlains were not of cardinal rank, and if they were promoted to cardinals, they usually did not remain in office for long after their promotion (see below).

Legations of political significance became almost the monopoly of cardinals because, as ambassadors, only they could claim the same ceremonial as the pope, and thus represent him visibly. Cardinals also took on special assignments, particularly in the Patrimony (for instance as rectors).

One may discern the specific position of trust held by a cardinal in the eyes of the pope from the type and frequency of missions received but not from the bestowal of a high office.

Further Development of the 'Bureaucracy': The Chamber

Although there had been chamberlains from the time of Urban II (see above), their office and functions[181] were not yet institutionalized, as is shown by the crises starting in 1130, 1143, and 1159. Two prominent personalities were crucial: both were active in the phases when the city of Rome could be recovered and the recuperation of the Patrimony could be taken in hand. Both seemed too powerful to the following pope to be left in office: Boso (1154–1159)[182] and Cencius Savelli (1188–1198); Cencius then became chamberlain of the college of cardinals.[183]

---

178. The burdens of the consistory were reduced by the chancery; see below.

179. If the curial sources, on which we mostly have to rely, emphasize the participation of the cardinals or name them alone, this arises out of the desire of the popes to present their decisions as those of the 'Romana ecclesia'.

180. His council and court in a certain sense constitute a small version of the consistory, to which probably all the cardinals who were present in Rome belonged; Sydow, 'Untersuchungen' 73; Peter Classen, 'Zur Geschichte Papst Anastasius' IV.' QF 48 (1968) 36–63. For a list (though incomplete) of the 'vicarii Urbis' from 1207 to 1555, see Konrad Eubel, 'Kleinere Mitteilungen', RQ 8 (1894) 494–499.

181. Robinson, *Papacy* 252–254. There were temporarily also two chamberlains, whose functions cannot be distinguished clearly; ibid.

182. Werner Maleczek, 'Boso', LMA 2.478–479; Fritz Geisthardt, *Der Kämmerer Boso* (Historische Studien 293; Berlin 1936) 77–81.

183. Robinson, *Papacy* 253. A biography of Cencius, later Pope Honorius III, is lacking. Cf.

In times of crisis, the nascent institutionalization of an orderly financial administration collapsed, and the popes were once more left with the situation described above.[184] The Templars, with their center in Paris, under Alexander III played a role similar to that played by Cluny under Urban II.[185] Only the final return to Rome permitted the papal finances to be consolidated. An important means for this consolidation was the *Liber Censuum*, whose compilation had begun under Boso, but it was Cencius who transformed the book into a serviceable tool.[186] It is to Cencius, the dominant figure at the end of the twelfth century, that the office of chamberlain owes its reputation and competences.[187] (1) The chamberlain stood at the head of the papal household. As was the case with the seneschal in secular courts, it was the obligation of the chamberlain to establish the death of the pope formally. Only gradually did the theory develop that the chamberlain, as the head of the curia, should continue conducting routine business even after the death of the pope, including the burial of the dead pope and the preparation for a new election. His functions ended only with the proclamation of the new pope. This is evident for the first time with Boso.[188] (2) The chamberlain had the supervision of the papal treasury;[189] (3) he was responsible for the administration of the papal finances;[190] (4) he was the supreme representative of the secular power of the pope in the city of Rome and in the Patrimony.

Jane E. Sayers, *Papal Government and England during the Pontificate of Honorius III (1216–1227)* (Cambridge Studies in Medieval Life and Thought, 3rd Series, 21; Cambridge 1984).

184. The expedients the curia was compelled to try included loans from Jewish and Italian "banks"; Robinson, *Papacy* 259. On the accomodations of the curia of Urban II, see 176.

185. Jordan, 'Finanzgeschichte' 77 n. 3; Robinson, *Papacy* 257–258.

186. On this see also Tilmann Schmidt, 'Die älteste Überlieferung von Cencius' "Ordo Romanus",' QF 60 (1980) 513–522.

187. Elze, "Kapelle," 194–197; see also Maleczek, *Papst und Kardinalskolleg* 112, 349. The functions of the chamberlain as head of the household were those held by the queen in secular courts. See Heinrich Fichtenau, *Lebensordnungen des 10. Jahrhunderts: Studien über Denkart und Existenz im einstigen Karolingerreich* (Monographien zur Geschichte des Mittelalters 30; Stuttgart 1984) 1.239–243. Later the chamberlain passed these duties partly to the treasurer, partly to the almoner, and partly to the marshal (see 214–219 and also 198).

188. See Geisthardt, *Der Kämmerer Boso* 61–62. In the long vacancy of the Apostolic See from 1268 to 1271, the responsibilities of the chamberlain were so clear that if he had died in the meantime, the cardinals would have elected another; Rusch, *Die Behörden und Hofbeamten* 41; Andreas Fischer, *Kardinäle im Konklave: Die lange Sedisvakanz der Jahre 1268 bis 1271* (BDHI 118; Tübingen 2008) 305–309, 334–338; cf. Const. Clem. 1.3.2.

189. In the twelfth century this included the archive and the library; Bresslau, *Handbuch* 1.156 n. 1.

190. The collection of documentary material, the assembly of a register of dues to the Roman curia which was the basis of the later *Liber censuum*; on this point, see Tilmann Schmidt, 'Liber censuum Ecclesiae Romanae', LMA 5.1941, with literature.

The Chancery

Although the chancery was more firmly consolidated as an institution than the chamber, individuals were crucial for the development of the office of chancellor as well.[191] Besides the previously mentioned Johannes of Gaeta (later Pope Gelasius II), these individuals were Haimerich (1123–1141) and the chancellors and later popes Gerard (1141–1144, Lucius II), Roland Bandinelli (1153–1159, Alexander III), Albert of Morra (1178–1187, Gregory VIII) as well as the chamberlains Boso and Cencius, who for a time led the chancery as well (1149–1152 and 1194–1198), though in both cases without bearing the title of chancellor. Each of these chancellors held an outstanding position in the curia in his own time.[192]

The functions of the chancellor which appear in the sources consist of the following:

(1) Advising the pope, especially in juristic questions;

(2) Being head of the chancery, which was a group of notaries and scribes; in this function the chancellor was responsible for (almost) all documents issued by the curia on behalf of the pope, and for the registers;

(3) Functions in jurisdiction, though only documented sporadically in our period. They consist of receiving pleas and deciding their further handling, and pronouncing sentences in the consistory.[193] New demands on the chancery[194] now arose not only from the amount of business, but also from the fact that the juristic essentials of the 'litterae de gratia' and 'litterae de iustitia'[195] had been defined (by the development of the system of judges delegate, see above). The new amount of business was met by increasing the personnel and creating the first formularies. In addition, an examination of the letters and other documents by the notaries before

191. Robinson, *Papacy* 93–96.

192. The interruption of the series of chancellors between 1159 and 1178 and after 1187 is explained by Robinson, *Papacy* 97, as due to the popes' fears that the chancellor might become too powerful. To me this assertion appears unprovable.

193. Ernst Müller, 'Der Bericht des Abtes Hariulf von Oudenburg über seine Prozeßverhandlungen an der römischen Kurie i. J. 1141', NA 48 (1930) 101–111.

194. Fundamental on this point: Robinson, *Papacy* 179–208.

195. Brigitte Meduna, *Studien zum Formular der päpstlichen Justizbriefe von Alexander III. bis Innozenz III. (1159–1216): Die non obstantibus-Formel* (SB Wien Phil.-hist. Klasse 536; Vienna 1989). On the clause 'salva sedis apostolicae auctoritate' since Celestine II, see Horst Fuhrmann, 'Das Reformpapsttum und die Rechtswissenschaft', *Investiturstreit und Reichsverfassung*, ed. J. Fleckenstein (Vorträge und Forschungen 17; Sigmaringen 1973) 175–203, esp. 191–192. From Innocent II on, the arenga of letters of protection for religious houses reflect the new claims of the pope to be supreme judge, 'judex ordinarius omnium'; Robinson, *Papacy* 206, 232. On the development of the formula 'plenitudo potestatis', see ibid. 92, and Robert L. Benson, '*Plenitudo potestatis*: Evolution of a Formula from Gregory IV to Gratian', *Collectana Stephan Kuttner* (SG 14; Bologna 1968) 195–217.

they were presented to the pope (and eventually also the cardinals) was introduced. Finally, the assertions of the parties were inserted into the dictamen of the letter, and it was left to the petitioner to produce evidence of the correctness of his assertions (veritas precum) in partibus, rather than to investigate the case at the curia.

The Great Century of the Roman Papacy, from Innocent III to Boniface VIII (1198–1303)

The pontificate of Innocent III constitutes a caesura in the history of the curia. This has already been shown in the treatment of the ceremonial, which demonstrated the altered conception of the papal monarchy, whose theoretical development now reached new heights.[196] Innocent reformed and reorganized the curia, concerned for its renown, but also striving for a more effective administration. A new phase of papal history as well as curial history began with the Avignonese papacy (1305–1378).

The density and quality of sources for the research on the history of the Roman curia in the thirteenth century are much better than for the twelfth century.[197] From Innocent III onwards, the papal registers have survived, though with considerable losses, and have been published.[198] From Boniface VIII onwards the same is true for the books of the camera.[199] Now there are also sources from which the composition and internal organization of the curia can be reconstructed: (1) treaties with communes of the Papal States about the reception of the papal court;[200] (2) so-called

196. Othmar Hageneder, 'Weltherrschaft im Mittelalter', MIÖG 93 (1985) 257–278 (with literature).

197. Paravicini Bagliani, *La vita*. On the biographies of the popes of the thirteenth century, see Paravicini Bagliani, 'La storiografia pontificia del secolo XIII. Prospettive di ricerca', RHM 18 (1976) 45–54.

198. All papal registers from Gregory IX onward are being published by the *Bibliothèque des Écoles Françaises d'Athènes et de Rome*, 2nd series (thirteenth century); 3rd series (fourteenth century). With the exception of the registers of Innocent III, which are being edited by the Institut für Österreichische Geschichtsforschung (at present 12 volumes), all volumes (those of Honorius III included) are now available in the database 'ut per litteras apostolicas' at http://www.brepolis. net/. The editions of the École Française include the few registers of the camera that survived (Urban IV, Clement IV, Nicholas IV, and Boniface VIII), but not that of Martin IV; see *Das Kammerregister Papst Martins IV. (Reg. Vat. 42)*, ed. G. Rudolph (Littera antiqua 14; Vatican City 2007).

199. Editions: *Libri rationum camerae Bonifatii Papae VIII*, ASV Collect. 446 necnon Intr. et Ex. 5, ed. T. Schmidt (Littera antiqua 2; Vatican City 1984); *Les recettes et les dépenses de la Chambre apostolique pour la quatrième année du pontificat de Clément V (1308–1309) (Introitus et exitus 75)*, ed. B. Guillemain (Collection de l'École Française de Rome 39; Rome 1978); *Die Ausgaben der Kammer unter Johannes XXII., nebst Jahresbilanzen von 1316–1375* and *Die Ausgaben der Kammer unter Benedikt XII., Klemens VI. und Innozenz VI. (1335–1362)* and *Die Ausgaben der Kammer unter den Päpsten Urban V. und Gregor XI. (1362–1378)* ed. K. H. Schäfer (Vatikanische Quellen zur Geschichte der päpstlichen Hof- und Finanzverwaltung 2, 3, 6; Paderborn 1911, 1914, 1937).

200. Three such treaties are known; Paravicini Bagliani, 'Mobilità' 198, with appendix III, 272–278.

court ordinances;[201] (3) lists of 'officials';[202] (4) lists on the distribution of special rations by the camera.[203]

The Papal Retinue: The Papal Familia

When one speaks of the papal familia, it is not the family or clan from which the current pope descends and which supports him in his rule (nepotism, see below), but the association of those personally dependent on him and committed to his service, whom he protects and supports.[204] In the sources, the terms 'familia' and 'familiaris' sporadically appear from the later twelfth century onwards,[205] but the institution itself must have existed as early as the end of the eleventh century.[206] We have no precise knowledge of its composition; it is certain that the chaplains belonged to

201. A list of the recipients of the rations of the camera ('assiszie continentes nomina omnium illorum qui percipiunt prebendas a curia') has survived from May 1278 (the beginning of the pontificate of Nicholas III), and has been edited by Friedrich Baethgen, 'Quellen und Untersuchungen zur Geschichte der päpstlichen Hof- und Finanzverwaltung unter Bonifaz VIII.' QF 20 (1928–29) 114–237, Beilage I, 195–206. Further, two records of similar content survive: (1) an instruction for the chamberlain of the new pope, and (2) an instruction by the chamberlain for the new pope. On the first, a 'court ordinance' from 1306, that has been edited by Amato P. Frutaz, 'La famiglia pontificia in un documento dell'inizio del sec. XIV', *Palaeografica diplomatica et archivistica studi in onore di Giulio Battelli* (2 vols. Rome 1979) 2.277–323, esp. 284–323, see Paravicini Bagliani, 'Papst auf Reisen' 507; on older layers of this text (from the middle of the thirteenth century), see Schimmelpfennig, *Zeremonienbücher* 46–47. On the second, notes dated from July 4, 1409, probably compiled by the chamberlain François de Conzié, have been edited in *Les textes avignonnais jusque à la fin du Grand Schisme d'Occident*, ed. M. Dykmans (Le cérémonial papal de la fin du Moyen Age à la Renaissance 3, Bibliothèque de l'Institut Historique Belge de Rome 26; Rome 1983) 420–445. A list of 'ministeria et officia domus pontificalis' of 1460 has a different character, since it deals with how many familiars a particular 'officialis' is allowed to have; printed in G. Marini, Degli Archiatri pontifici (Rome 1784) 2.152–156. The later 'ruoli di famiglia' are similar.

202. *Libri officialium* survive only from later times, the earliest from the Avignon pope Clement VII (Vat. Archive, Collect. 457). That of Martin V is printed in F.-C. Uginet, Le 'Liber officialium' de Martin V (Rome 1975). The series of the *libri officialium* and the *libri officiorum* in the Vatican registers has not yet been systematically studied.

203. For example, portions of the 'presbyteria', of the altar cover, of the 'fees' for consecration at the curia, of the small 'servitia'; see Elze, 'Kapelle' 173–174.

204. A study of the familia of the pope is a desideratum of research, as was established by Paravicini, 'Cardinali di curia', 2.462–463, see also below n. 256. The article J. Deshusses, 'familiers du pape', DDC 5.810–814, cannot be used for our purposes. On the fourteenth century, see Bernard Guillemain, *La cour pontificale d'Avignon 1309–1376: Étude d'une société* (Bibliothèque des Écoles Françaises d'Athènes et de Rome 201; Paris 1962, reprinted 1966) 39–48, 493. On the 'familia' as a model for the court, see Fichtenau, *Lebensordnungen* 175. The 'court ordinance' from 1306 (above n. 200) contains a 'modus' for the distribution of the small 'servitia' among the pope's familiars (omitting those of the cardinals); ibid. 317–319.

205. See *Liber censuum* 1.296; *Gesta Innocentii III* (Migne PL 214.ccxii–ccxv § cxlvii = James M. Powell, *The Deeds of Pope Innocent III by an Anonymous Author* (Washington, D.C. 2004) 265–266. As in the case of the chapel, the silence of the sources may be caused by the fact that traditional designations relating to the 'Romana ecclesia' long continued to be used. A genre of sources which throws light on the composition of the 'familia' of cardinals is that of the testaments, which survive in great numbers (see the studies of Paravicini Bagliani); unfortunately, of the papal testaments, only those of Honorius IV and Clement V survive.

206. This is the only way the source from 1089 quoted above (n. 65) can be understood, according to which the laymen of the town had to provide housing and food for 'the curia' while

it.[207] Only the sources of the thirteenth century allow us a clearer view of the institution.

After his accession, every pope created his familia, whose core was usually the familia from his time as a cardinal. The number of papal familiars increased so much in the course of time that a familia in a more restricted sense was separated from it:[208] only to the latter was the pope obliged to provide full support. A treaty with the commune of Viterbo in 1278[209] contains the stipulation that the commune only had to provide quarters for the 'familia domestica et commensalis' of the pope, and an additional list of the categories of persons belonging to the familia: camera and chancery,[210] which each had its own household (see below); the three monastic households of the penitentiaries, bullaria, and almonry;[211] the entire personnel of the papal house ('domus', now primarily called 'palatium')[212] from the seneschal (or maiordomus) down to the last servant; the marshal of justice or marshal of the curia,[213] who also had a household of his own. Lastly, the close confidantes of the pope are listed: his physicians, the house bankers, the 'capellani [veri] commensales' and an unidentified remnant of cetera domestica familia papae, which may have included the personal chamberlains, the confessor, and the like. (Naturally the households cited above as well as the higher-placed papal familiars, but also members of the curial staff down to the scribes had in turn their own familiares. These were normally not counted as part of the familia of the pope, any more than the familia of the cardinals).

---

the clergy had to provide for 'the pope'. The term 'the pope' in this document must refer to a group of persons as numerous as the circle that constitutes the Grandees of the curia with their retainers ('the curia').

207. As a rule the chaplains residing at the court must be considered members of the pope's 'familia', an inference by Elze, 'Kapelle' 180, 196.

208. The number of persons receiving food rations from the camera in 1278 was 341, according to the list of Baethgen, 'Quellen und Untersuchungen'; for 1299 it was 194, according to Paravicini, "Papst auf Reisen" 507; for 1309 the count was 192 according to Guillemain, *La cour pontificale* 493; for John XXII, about 270, etc.

209. Treaty of May 1, 1278, newly edited by Paravicini, 'Mobilità' 271–274, supplemented by promises of the commune to the camera on May 20, 1278; ibid. 275–278.

210. See *Die päpstlichen Kanzleiordnungen von 1200–1500*, ed. M. Tangl (Innsbruck 1894, reprinted Aalen 1959) 65 § 4; here, the chancery was obviously fighting for its old status.

211. First documented under Innocent III; Rusch, *Die Behörden und Hofbeamten* 64–69; Guillemain, *La cour pontificale* 409–417. As further welfare institutions, the curia sustained the 'hospitale S. Spiritus in Saxia de Urbe' and the 'hospitale portatile s. Antonii', which travelled with the curia; Rusch, *Die Behörden und Hofbeamten* 70–74. Offices not dealt with in what follows will be dealt with elsewhere.

212. In Avignon, according to the usage of this time, it was called hospitium, or hôtel. On the term palatium/maison/ hôtel in the era of Avignon, see Guillemain, *La cour pontificale* 357–417.

213. Not to be confused with the heads of the papal stables, who were always clerics, often monks.

Further familiares with a right to draw certain traditional rations (servitia minuta) are named in a list[214] from the end of the thirteenth century:[215] the colleges of the pages (domicelli),[216] the sergeants at arms (servientes armorum),[217] the runners (cursores),[218] the two (or three) classes of doorkeepers (ostiarii),[219] and certain others.[220]

Although they are not named in the two sources, there were other persons whose membership in (later) papal familiae is certain: those chaplains who were no longer constant table companions of the pope, at this time the 'auditor camerae', the 'magister palatii' (or 'magister theologiae'),[221] the chancery notaries, as well as probably most of the auditores of

214. Modus for the distribution of the small servitia from the end of the century (Frutaz, 'La famiglia pontificia', see above n. 201). Another classification of the curials is found in the treaty of Viterbo in 1266, M. Dykmans, 'Les transferts de la curie romaine du XIIIe au XVe siècle', *Archivio della Società romana di storia patria* 103 (1980) 91–116, esp. 113–116, and in the treaty of 1278.

215. This list divides those with a claim to receive into five equal sections. The fifth part went to the familiars of the cardinals, while the first four went to the familia papae, which was divided into four groups. Each of these was in various ways divided into subgroups, whose portion was determined by a special key. From this key, the rank of the various offices may be deduced, for which age was a significant determinant.

216. There is evidence of noble pages at the curia from the twelfth century onward. They formed the suite of the pope when he went riding; Rusch, *Die Behörden und Hofbeamten* 96–97. See also Paravicini Bagliani, *La vita* III.6.

217. Like the other familiares named below, the 'servientes armorum' were successors of old 'scholae' of the Lateran who functioned until Innocent III. All were organised in a sort of guild with a 'senescalcus' as chief. Little is known about the sergeants at arms till the court ordinance of 1278 (see above n. 201). They were clad uniformly and carried a mace. According to the court ordinance from 1306 (see above n. 201; § 44, cf. § 41) they had the right to (1) accompany the chamberlain; (2) prepare the public appearances of the pope in liturgy and ceremonial and assist him thereby; (3) keep watch of the precious objects used on these occasions, especially when on travel; (4) be jailer of prisoners for the marshal of the curia; Rusch, *Die Behörden und Hofbeamten* 97–99.

218. Brigide Schwarz, 'Im Auftrag des Papstes: Die päpstlichen Kursoren von ca. 1200 bis 1470', *Päpste, Pilger, Pönitentarie: Festschrift Ludwig Schmugge zum 65. Geburtstag*, ed. A. Meyer et al. (Tübingen 2004) 49–71; Schwarz, 'Les courriers pontificaux du XIIIe au XVe siècle (vers 1200–vers 1470)' *Offices et papauté (XIVe–XVIIe siècle). Charges, hommes, destins*, ed. A. Jamme and O. Poncet (Collection de l'Ecole Française de Rome 334; Rome: 2005) 647–650. Like the sergeants at arms, the runners had the papal coat of arms on their clothing and carried a mace; they also assisted in ceremonies and performed watch duty in the palace. The main element of their duties was the forwarding of *de curia* mail and the delivery of court documents to all parts of the world, while at the seat of the curia the elders officiated as beadles of the different courts.

219. Rusch, *Die Behörden und Hofbeamten* 99–106. The three ranks developing from the middle of the thirteenth century corresponded to their various obligations: (a) the 'magistri hostiarii' were responsible for standing guard over the person of the pope, for accompanying him on various public appearances, and for controlling admission to audiences; accordingly, some were monks and some noble laymen; (b) the 'hostiarii minores' were the watch for the hall of the consistory and its beadles; (c) the simple doorkeepers guarded the external gates of the palace. All three ranks were sharply criticized in the sources because they exploited their 'access to the wielder of power' (see below n. 239) for the purpose of extortion.

220. See above n. 215.

221. Raymond Creytens, 'Le Studium Romanae curiae et le Maître du Sacré Palais', AFP 12 (1942) 1–83; on the 'Magister sacri palatii' see Brigide Schwarz, *Kurienuniversität und stadtrömische Universität von ca. 1300 bis 1471* (Education and Society 46; Leiden-Boston 2013) 253–263. For the studium Romane curiae, see 220.

the Rota. Besides these persons, there was a steadily growing number of honorary chaplains and honorary familiars.[222]

Clerics were clearly in the majority in the papal familia. Besides being committed to 'obsequium' and 'fidelitas', familiars were obliged to fulfil the duties of the office they were charged with. Obsequium was expressed in various ways, such as accompanying the pope on public appearances.[223] In exchange for this service, besides support, the pope owed his familiars (as demonstrated above only to a part of them, on travels only to a part of this part, the 'parva' or 'stricta familia papae'),[224] advancement. Advancement was granted especially through provision with benefices (see below)[225] or support in the acquisition and possession of benefices by the granting of privileges (prerogatives), and concession of other material advantages.[226] From the end of the thirteenth century, the popes used the bestowal of the status of familiars to distinguish persons they trusted or to win them over, and they did this for great numbers, since such designations caused no significant obligations for the pope (they received only a claim on the prerogatives of familiars). On the other hand, these appointments did not provoke as much resentment in partibus as was the case with 'external' chaplains,[227] with their ceremonial prerogatives. In this the

222. Elze, 'Kapelle' 190; Karl Heinrich Schäfer, 'Päpstliche Ehrenkapläne aus deutschen Diözesen im 14. Jahrhundert', RQ 21 (1907) 97–113; Bernard Guillemain, 'Les chapelains d'honneur des papes d'Avignon', *Mélanges d'archéologie et d'histoire* 64 (1952) 217–228; Charles Burns, 'Vatican Sources and the Honorary Papal Chaplains of the Fourteenth Century', *Römische Kurie: Kirchliche Finanzen: Vatikanisches Archiv: Studien zu Ehren von Hermann Hoberg*, ed. Erwin Gatz (Miscellanea Historiae Pontificiae 45–46; Rome 1979) 1.65–98. In the fourteenth century certain officials were also 'familiares papae' because of their office, for example, the scribes of the chancery.

223. Short-term contracts were signed with knights and squires for the period of their service in papal livery. At least from the beginning of the Avignonese period the familiars appear to have worn the colors of the current pope; see *Acta Aragonensia: Quellen zur deutschen, italienischen, französischen, spanischen, zur Kirchen- und Kulturgeschichte aus der diplomatischen Korrespondenz*, ed. H. Finke (Münster-Berlin 1908–1923, reprinted Aalen 1968) 1.490, no. 326. In times of need they would have to serve as creditors of the pope. Charles Victor Langlois, 'Notices et documents relatifs à l'histoire du XIII° et du XIV° siècle: Nova Curie', *Revue Historique* 87 (1905) 55–79, esp. 62–63; for the later Middle Ages, see Brigide Schwarz, 'Die römische Kurie im Zeitalter des Schismas und der Reformkonzilien', *Institutionen und Geschichte. Theoretische Aspekte und mittelalterliche Befunde*, ed. G. Melville (Norm und Struktur: Studien zum sozialen Wandel in Mittelalter und früher Neuzeit 1; Cologne-Weimar-Vienna 1992) 231–258, esp. 239–240.

224. Thus the key to the distribution of 'servitia' in the 'Modus'; Frutaz, 'La famiglia pontificia' (above n. 201), and Guillemain, *La cour pontificale* 39–48.

225. Pietas toward the familia is a virtue which 'singulis virtutibus iustitiae annexa sit'. Thomas Aquinas, *Summa Theologiae* II–II, q.101 (Rome 1903), see below n. 388. Honorius III expressed it thus: 'provisio clericorum opus in se continet pietatis'. *Regesta Honorii papae III*, ed. Petrus Pressutti, vols. 1–2 (Rome 1888–1895, reprinted Hildesheim 1978) no. 1146.

226. The *Gesta Innocentii III*, Migne PL 214.ccxii–ccxv § cxlvii (= Powell, 265–266), stresses this duty. See Klaus Ganzer, *Papsttum und Bistumsbesetzungen in der Zeit von Gregor IX. bis Bonifaz VIII.* (Forschungen zur kirchlichen Rechtsgeschichte und zum Kirchenrecht 9; Graz-Cologne 1968) passim.

227. Elze, 'Kapelle' 189–191. In the fourteenth century the 'external' chaplains were replaced by the *capellani honoris*; ibid.

popes had an instrument with which to improve their net of client relationships,[228] which now was much larger and reached much deeper into
the social ranks than before.

The Papal Chapel

With time, several bureaus grew out of the papal chapel and established their own seperate households (see below). From the time of Innocent IV, who dramatically increased the number of chaplains, a distinction
developed between 'capellani commensales', who constituted the chapel
in a stricter sense,[229] and the many papal chaplains both within and outside
the curia. Innocent III had intervened in the chapel to reform it as well,
with the decree of a new ordinance for divine service (ordinarium) for
the papal chapel.[230] Chaplains assisted the pope in daily divine services in
the chapel of the papal palace, as well as at important extraordinary ceremonies (such as the ever more frequent consecrations at the curia), and
when the pope was absent they celebrated the curial liturgy without him.
They guarded the capella, with its collection of liturgical implements and
books, which they took along on travels.

The chaplains led a common life (vita communis) in chambers called
the 'capellania'.[231] The size of the rations supplied by the 'camera' to support the chaplains as well as to support the bureaus which had developed
out of the chapel,[232] indicates that they belonged to the upper stratum of
the curia. Just like the courts of the cardinals (see below), the papal chapel
was also a cultural center to which scholars and artists belonged.[233] From
about 1260 the chapel[234] had servants, which is more evidence of the high
status of its members.

228. A glance at the index volume of Norbert Kamp, *Kirche und Monarchie im staufischen König-
reich Sizilien, 1: Prosopographische Grundlegung: Bistümer und Bischöfe des Königreiches 1194–1266* (4
vols. Münstersche Mittelalterschriften 1–4; Münster 1973–1975, 1982) 4.1487–1489, will show the
network of clients in the kingdom of Sicily from Gregory IX. See also the reference in Agostino
Paravicini Bagliani, 'Pour une approche prosopographique de la cour pontificale du XIIIe siècle.
Problèmes de méthode', *Medieval Lives and the Historian: Studies in Medieval Prosopography*, ed. N.
Bulst and J.-Ph. Genet (Proceedings of the First International Interdisciplinary Conference on
Medieval Prosopography; Kalamazoo, Mich. 1986) 113–121, esp. 116.

229. Elze, 'Kapelle' 172–174; Bernhard Schimmelpfennig, 'Die Organisation der päpstlichen
Kapelle in Avignon', QF 50 (1971) 80–111, esp. 83–88; Schimmelpfennig, *Papsttum* 215–216.

230. *The Ordinal of the Papal Court from Innocent III to Boniface VIII and Related Documents*, ed. S.
J. P. Van Dijk and J. Hazelden Walker (Fribourg, Switzerland 1975) 87–483.

231. See n. 283 below. This practice was not maintained in Avignon; Schimmelpfennig, *Papsttum* 87.

232. On social recruitment, see Elze, 'Kapelle' 192–194.

233. Antonio Paravicini Bagliani, 'Il personale della Curia romana preavignoncse: Bilancio e
prospettive di ricerca', *Proceedings Berkeley 1980* 391–410, esp. 407–410.

234. A *clericus capellae*, a sort of keeper (*ostiarius*) as well as a cleaner (*portitor aquae*).

The Nucleus of the Confidantes of the Pope

Although, as has been said, every pope formed his own 'familia', both for reasons of continuity in curial work[235] and in view of the power constellations present at the curia,[236] he had to take on a considerable part of the familia of his predecessor, or consider them when he was recruiting new members.[237] For that reason, it was important for the new pope to have reliable support in the really important positions and—often in unofficial roles—in his intimate surroundings. Who these reliable persons were is shown by the reports of the proctors from the curia,[238] who strove for the intervention of those curials, often little distinguished, at least on the outside, from their fellows of the same status. Besides nepotes and cardinals, clients often sought the favor of persons who had 'access to the wielder of power',[239] such as confessor fathers, secretaries, clerics assigned to deal with certain cases (referendarii), almoners, privy chamberlains,[240] chamber servants (cubicularii),[241] doorkeepers,[242] and even simple servants. The positions of the chamberlain and the marshal of the curia always required the trust of the pope.

235. Continuity became so important that a large portion of the familiars of the dead pope continued in office during the vacancy of the Apostolic See; see the 'court ordinance' of 1306, cited above n. 201.

236. Fundamental on Roman noble clans at the curia: Robert Brentano, *Rome before Avignon: A Social History of Thirteenth-Century Rome* (London 1974) 174–209; Andreas Rehberg, *Kirche und Macht im römischen Trecento: Die Colonna und ihre Klientel auf dem kurialen Pfründenmarkt (1278–1378)* (BDHI 88; Tübingen 1999); Rehberg, 'Familien aus Rom und die Colonna auf dem kurialen Pfründenmarkt (1278–1348/78)', in 2 parts: QF 78 (1998) 1–122, and QF 79 (1999) 99–214. On the Fieschi, see Thérèse Boespflug Montecchi, 'Les stratégies parentales du pontificat d'Innocent IV' (unpublished conference manuscript, Lyon 1996), and articles in DBI 46.

237. On the accession to the throne of Boniface VIII, see Heinz Göring, 'Die Beamten der Kurie unter Bonifaz VIII.' (PhD diss., Königsberg 1934) 90–91; Thérèse Boespflug, *La curie au temps de Boniface VIII: Étude prosopographique* (Bonifaciana 1; Rome 2005).

238. There is no survey of the known and published proctor's reports. Of those from the period around 1300, the *Acta Aragonensia* are famous.

239. Term coined by Carl Schmitt, *Gespräch über die Macht und den Zugang zum Machthaber* (Pfullingen 1954; reprinted Stuttgart 2008). In Avignon they were called the 'clerici intrinseci'; Schimmelpfennig, *Päpstliche Kapelle* 89–92. On their composition under Boniface VIII, see Göring, *Die Beamten der Kurie* 31–32. In Avignon, there was a papal hôtel in the strict sense of the term, that is, those who actually dined with the pope; see Guillemain, *La cour pontificale* 357–391.

240. From the middle of the thirteenth century onwards; Rusch, *Die Behörden und Hofbeamten* 59.

241. The 'cubicularii' were almost always monks or brothers from the crusading orders, as was the case with doorkeepers (see next note). Under Boniface VIII they were Knights Templar. They were highly placed in ceremonies because of their important duties; see Rusch, *Die Behörden und Hofbeamten* 95–96; Göring, *Die Beamten der Kurie* 31; Emil Göller, 'Die Kubikulare im Dienst der päpstlichen Hofverwaltung vom XII. bis XV. Jahrhundert', *Papsttum und Kaisertum: Forschungen zur politischen Geschichte und Geisteskultur des Mittelalters: Paul Kehr zum 65. Geburtstag*, ed. Albert Brackmann (Munich 1926) 622–647.

242. In the 'Modus' for the distribution of the small 'servitia' (Frutaz, 'La famiglia pontificia',

The Development of Cardinals into Princes of the Church

In the pontificates of Gregory IX and Innocent IV the college of cardinals underwent a profound transformation. Only now had the prestige of the cardinals grown so high that the cardinalate was incompatible with high offices in the hierarchy (see above).[243] The de facto participation of the cardinals in leading the ecclesia universalis had become a right to take part in the decisions that was exercised in the consistory (see above).[244] Their number had now been reduced for practical and also particularly for financial reasons: only thus could they maintain themselves on their income in the style of life they regarded as fitting. The prestige and power of the cardinals had grown to such an extent[245] that popes ceased to bestow on them offices that carried political weight. At the curia this is the case with the chancellor and the chamberlain, and only the great penitentiary remains a cardinal. In partibus the powers granted to the legates a latere are restricted (see above).

The Cardinals' Camera

An expression of the new relationship between the pope and the cardinals is the division of certain incomes between them. Now a common purse of the cardinals was institutionalized: the cardinals' camera.[246] It

---

see above n. 201), it is still assumed that the doorkeepers for the chamber of the pope would be monks. From Innocent IV onwards they often were Theotonic knights; Robert Gramsch, 'Juristenschelte und Juristenleben. Nikolaus von Bibra und Heinrich von Kirchberg', *Zeitschrift des Vereins für Thüringische Geschichte* 56 (2002) 133–168, esp. 145–146. The continuing importance of the great abbeys, and, from 1130 on, the reform houses and great chapters, has been investigated by Robinson, *Papacy* 209–243 (with literature), for cardinals in the eleventh and twelfth centuries, but not for the simpler curials. Here one must pursue occasional references, such as to Casamari at the time of Innocent III and Honorius III; Falko Neininger, *Konrad von Urach († 1227): Zähringer, Zisterzienser, Kardinallegat* (Quellen und Forschungen aus dem Gebiet der Geschichte, 2nd series, 17; Paderborn 1994) 157–158.

243. Only at this point does the office of cardinal become incompatible with that of an archbishop. On the position of cardinals after the second half of the thirteenth century, see Andreas Fischer, 'Die Kardinäle von 1216 bis 1304: Zwischen eigenständigem Handeln und päpstlicher Autorität', *Geschichte des Kardinalats* 193–203, 210–217; see also Brian Tierney, *Foundations of the Conciliar Theory: The Contribution of the Medieval Canonists from Gratian to the Great Schism* (Cambridge 1955; reprinted with additonal material Leiden-New York-Köln 1998) 68–84; Wilks, *The Problem of Sovereignty in the Later Middle Ages* 455–62.

244. John A. Watt, 'The Constitutional Law of the College of Cardinals: Hostiensis to Johannes Andreae', *Mediaeval Studies* 33 (1971) 127–157; Brian Tierney, 'Hostiensis and Collegiality', *Proceedings Toronto 1972* 401–409, responded to Watt's arguments. See Roberto Grison, 'Il problema del cardinalato nell'Ostiense', AHP 30 (1992) 125–157, who shows the evolution of Hostiensis's thought with the evidence from Oxford, New College 205. See also Norman Zacour, 'The Cardinals' View of the Papacy', *The Religious Roles of the Papacy* 413–38.

245. Paravicini Bagliani, 'Cardinali di curia' 2.473.

246. Johann Peter Kirsch, *Die Finanzverwaltung des Kardinalkollegiums im 13. und 14. Jahrhundert*

was presided over by a cardinal chamberlain[247] (not to be confused with the Apostolic chamberlain), who served in this office for life, with some clerics as professional personnel.[248] This 'camera' was also used by the cardinals (and the pope) as a bank.

The incomes of the cardinals have to be distinguished as follows: (a) those divided between the pope and the cardinals, and (b) those that went directly to the individual cardinals.

On type (a): the 'servitia communia'[249] (traditional gifts due from a prelate on his promotion, which became a fee),[250] the fees on the occasion of the 'visitationes liminum'; the census from feudal principalities, incomes from the Patrimony and other territories of the Roman church,[251] Peter's Pence and the census for the protection of churches immediately subject to Rome. In addition, there were extraordinary incomes, gifts of the pope on the occasion of his election, other gifts (from outsiders as well), and fines. These incomes were collected and calculated by different institutions (esp. Apostolic camera), and the sums due to the cardinals transferred to the cardinal's bank. These incomes were divided by the camera of the cardinals according to rules similar to those in a collegiate church.[252]

On type (b): so-called propinae for the presentation (positio) of a provision by a cardinal in the consistory;[253] fees for placing his signature on

(Kirchengeschichtliche Studien 2.4; Münster in Westfalen 1895); Paul Maria Baumgarten, *Untersuchungen und Urkunden über die Camera Collegii Cardinalium für die Zeit von 1295–1437* (Leipzig 1898, reprinted Hildesheim 1982). According to Robinson, *Papacy* 253, the cardinals had a chamberlain of their own, possibly as early as 1123, but probably only at the end of the twelfth century. The camera of the cardinals experienced its full expansion, as was the case with so many bureaus, under John XXII. There was a reorganization under Eugenius IV.

247. His nomination, as well as that of his deputy, is a matter for the consistory. A list of chamberlains of the cardinals is found in Kirsch, *Die Finanzverwaltung* 44–46; Baumgarten, *Untersuchungen und Urkunden* lxxxix–xciv, 266–283 (alphabetical); additions in *Hierarchia Catholica Medii Aevi, sive summorum pontificum, S.R.E. cardinalium, ecclesiarum antistitum series ab a. 1198*, ed. K. Eubel (2nd ed. Münster 1913, reprinted Padova 1960) 2.57–58, 68, and 3.81–84.

248. In the fourteenth century, as was the case in the camera, there were clerici, servitores, and scribes. The camera of the cardinals, like the camera itself, had a procurator who defended their rights; this task was later taken over by the clerici. The clerics of the camera of the cardinals always automatically became familiares of the current cardinal chamberlain, hence the concept that each bureau constitutes a domus is found here as well; cf. Baumgarten, *Untersuchungen und Urkunden* lviii–lxxviiii.

249. And this applied also to a certain degree to the 'servitia minuta' (see below n. 360), of which a portion went to the familiares of the cardinals. A list of the servitia paid by English prelates in the thirteenth century is in Lunt, *Financial Relations* 1.677–681.

250. Cf. William Edward Lunt, *Papal Revenues in the Middle Ages* (2 vols. Records of Civilization: Sources and Studies 19; New York 1934, reprinted 1965).

251. Later the counties of Venaissin and Ferrara.

252. The very designation 'distributiones' derives from this sphere. Only those cardinals who were present profited from this distribution, a practice that was weakened by exceptions here and there.

253. Lunt, *Financial Relations* 1.474–475. In the thirteenth century this was still a 'gift' ensured

a privilegium, that is, a solemn chancery charter;[254] lastly incomes from protections,[255] and especially incomes from benefices.[256]

The Formation of 'Minor' Courts at the Curia: The Courts of the Cardinals and other Grandees

Just like the pope, individual cardinals[257] at an early date had their own chaplains assisting them.[258] They conducted a lively correspondence and had their own seals.[259] An institutionalization of the suites of cardinals becomes evident in the sources only in the last third of the twelfth century. Their courts were small-scale images of the curia:[260] the cardinal resided in an autonomous close ('domus librata', later 'hospitium'),[261] which carried his own coat of arms and which was subject only to his own jurisdiction. It was a place in which he was surrounded by his own 'familia'.[262]

by customary law, later a tax; 'propinae' sometimes were also given to familiares of the cardinal; Adrien Clergeac, 'La curie et les bénéfices consistoriaux: Étude sur les communs et menus services, 1300–1600' (PhD diss., Paris 1911) 188–190. On the consistorial provisions, see also Lajos Pásztor, 'Le cedole concistoriali', AHP 11 (1973) 209–268.

254. Maleczek, *Papst und Kardinalskolleg* 320–322.

255. Robert Brentano, *Two Churches: England and Italy in the 13th Century* (Princeton, N.J. 1968) 49–50. On the assumption of their compatriots that the cardinals were their natural protectors, even when the cardinals did not see themselves as such, see Brentano, *Rome before Avignon* 191; Johannes Vincke, 'Der Kampf Jakobs II. und Alfons' IV. um einen Landeskardinal', ZRG Kan. Abt. 21 (1932) 1–20. On protections of religious orders see Kathleen Walsh, 'Kardinalprotektor', LMA 5.951–952 (with literature).

256. This form of maintenance grew to such a degree that in Avignon some cardinals employed several clerics (called proctors) in their suite to administer their benefices; Anne-Lise Rey-Courtel, 'Les clientèles des cardinaux limousins en 1378', *Mélanges de l'École Française de Rome: Moyen Age, Temps modernes* 89 (1977) 889–944, esp. 894.

257. The fundamental studies on the courts of the cardinals are the two works of Paravicini Bagliani, *Cardinali di curia* and his *I testamenti dei cardinali*. See also Olaf Müller, 'Die Familien der Kardinäle 1254–1268: 'Prosopographische Untersuchung zur Geschichte der Römischen Kurie' (unpublished MA thesis, Göttingen 1996).

258. Paravicini Bagliani, *Cardinali di curia* 2.445–516, esp. 480.

259. Werner Maleczek, 'Die Siegel der Kardinäle: Von den Anfängen bis zum Beginn des 13. Jahrhunderts', MIÖG 112 (2004) 177–203; Maleczek, 'Die Brüder des Papstes: Kardinäle und Schriftgut der Kardinäle', *Das Papsttum und das vielgestaltige Italien: Hundert Jahre Italia Pontificia*, ed. K. Herbers and J. Johrendt (Abh. Akad. Göttingen, NF 5; Berlin-New York 2009) 331–372.

260. Sources for the familiae are, on the one hand, the testaments of cardinals, which deal primarily with the secular members of their suites (Paravicini Bagliani, *Cardinali di curia* 2.457), and on the other hand, the (rare) rolls of supplications of cardinals on behalf of their familiars, containing only clerics. Of importance for the familia was the development of the servitia into a tax around 1260; ibid. 473; see above n. 201 and below n. 360.

261. On areas of immunity, see Guillaume Mollat, 'Contribution à l'étude du Sacré Collège de Clément V à Eugène IV', RHE 46 (1951): 22–112, 566–594, esp. 50–57, 76–77; Pierre Pansier, *Les palais cardinalices d'Avignon au XIVe et XVe siècles* (3 vols. Avignon 1926–1932); supplemented by Marc Dykmans, 'Les palais cardinalices d'Avignon', *Mélanges de l'École Française de Rome: Moyen Age, Temps modernes* 83 (1971) 389–438.

262. It is only in the course of the thirteenth century that 'familia' meant especially the clerical members of the 'domus'; Paravicini Bagliani, *Cardinali di curia* 2.462. The clergy of the cardinal's church did not belong to the 'familia'. Naturally there was also a marked courtly life at the courts of the cardinals, documented in Maleczek, *Papst und Kardinalskolleg* 259.

This 'familia' supported him in his duties and accompanied him on his public appearances (in the later Middle Ages the retinue was augmented also by further clients, clad in the cardinal's colors).[263] The suites of the cardinals also became autonomous de jure.[264]

Despite all differences[265] in size and composition, one may imagine a typical cardinal's familia in the thirteenth century: it comprised between twenty and thirty persons, perhaps half of them clerics, making up the cardinal's chapel. The suite was internally differentiated according to function (auditor; camera;[266] chancery;[267] chapel;[268] watch and escort, partly by nobles; sergeants—and also the four courtly offices[269]) and ac-

263. There were repeated papal ordinances to reduce these suites, such as the restriction to twenty mounted 'familiares' by Martin V in his reform decrees of 13 April and 16 May 1425: *Materialien zur Geschichte des 15. und 16. Jahrhunderts: Beiträge zur politischen, kirchlichen und Cultur-Geschichte der 6 letzten Jahrhunderte*, ed. Johann Josef Ignaz Döllinger (Regensburg 1863) 2.335–344, esp. 336–337; excerpts in Tangl, *Die päpstlichen Kanzleiordnungen* 162–165, who shows that the pomp displayed by clerics gave offence. Some cardinals had enormous suites, such as Hannibal of Ceccano around 1340; Marc Dykmans, 'Le cardinal Annibal de Ceccano (vers 1282–1350): Étude biographique et testament du 17 juin 1348', *Bulletin de l'Institut Historique Belge de Rome* 43 (1973) 145–344. Banquets given there by rich cardinals were notorious, such as that of Annibaldo de Ceccano for Clement VI in 1343; ibid. 216; Georges de Loye, 'Réception du pape Clément VI par des cardinaux Annibal Ceccano et Pedro Gomez à Gentilly et Montfavet (30 avril–1er mai 1343) d'après une relation anonyme contemporaine', *Avignon au Moyen Âge: Textes et documents*, ed. Hervé Aliquot (Institut de recherches et d'études du bas Moyen Âge avignonnais; Avignon 1988) 81–92.

264. They were under the immediate jurisdiction of the cardinal, who questioned the extensive rights of the papal chamberlain and the marshal of the curia; *Acta concilii Constanciensis*, ed. H. Finke et al. (4 vols. Münster im Westfalen 1896–1928) 2.102–103, 114, 3.73. They were also autonomous as to the care of souls (they had their own penitentiary; Paravicini Bagliani, *Cardinali de Curia* 2.494–495). As far as possible (that is, if they were cardinal-bishops) the cardinal consecrated his own people.

265. For instance, a Cistercian cardinal at the time of Innocent III was allowed, like a bishop of the order, to have two monks and three 'conversi' as a suite; Neininger, *Konrad von Urach* 147. Later even cardinals who were monks succumbed to the usage of keeping a grand house; Paravicini Bagliani, *Testamenti* 321–355; Paravicini Bagliani, 'Il personale' 396. The great variation in income among the individual cardinals can be deduced from the taxes imposed on them on February 22, 1372; A. Segre, 'I dispacci di Christoforo da Piacenza, procuratore Mantovano alla Corte pontificia (1371–1383)', *Archivio Storico Italiano*, seria 5, 43 (1909) 27–95, esp. 44, 48; and 44 (1909) 253–326.

266. Paravicini Bagliani, *Cardinali de Curia* 2.472–474. Every suite also had a library; ibid. 470.

267. In earlier times the chancery was made up of chaplains who, as was the case with papal chaplains, took over all administrative duties that came their way; and later secretaries and scribal personnel; Paravicini Bagliani, *Cardinali de Curia* 2.474–478.

268. Paravicini Bagliani, *Cardinali de Curia* 2.478–493. Formal nomination; ibid. 455–459. Formularies survive since about 1300; Geoffrey Barraclough, *Public Notaries and the Papal Curia: A Calendar and Study of a Formularium notariorum curie from the Early Years of the Fourteenth Century* (London 1934) 171–174, § 78–105, differentiated according to estate. The chamberlain of the household kept records of the familiares, Mollat, 'Sacré Collège' 550. Somewhat later, the chapel of the cardinals underwent the same development as the papal chapel, becoming a musical chapel.

269. Paravicini Bagliani, *Cardinali di curia* 2.463–469: on the community of the table (mensa) in the livery, hence 'familiaris commensalis' was a designation of membership of the innermost core. Two late-medieval court ordinances for a cardinal's court are published: (a) for a 'domus cardinalis' in 1336, composed by the 'camerarius' of a suite, by Norman Zacour, 'Papal Regulations of Cardinals' Households in the 14th Century', *Speculum* 50 (1975) 434–455, esp. 449–453; and (b) from c. 1409–1417, Dykmans, *Les textes avignonnais jusque à la fin du Grand Schisme d'Occident* 446–461.

cording to estate[270] (nobles and prelates naturally ranked first). Cardinals furthered the advancement of artists and scholars in their suites before the popes did.[271] Besides these persons, who lived in the suites of the cardinals, there were other familiares who lived primarily in partibus.[272] Guests were often lodged in the suites of cardinals,[273] and clients came and went. The spheres of influence of the cardinal as a patron can be deduced from the origin and connections of his familiares: they were determined by his own origin, his legations,[274] and his political options.[275] The so much more widely spread client networks of the cardinals[276] supplemented that of the current pope.

Like the pope, the cardinals not only had to provide sustenance for their familiares, but they also owed their familiares advancement in exchange for their service and loyalty.[277] For the clerics among them, this

270. On the composition of the suites of cardinals of Avignonese popes, see Pierre Jugie, 'Les familiae cardinalices et leur organisation interne au temps de la papautè d'Avignon: Esquisse d'un bilan', *Le fonctionnement administratif de la papauté d'Avignon: Actes de la table ronde 1988* (Collection de l'École Française de Rome 138; Rome 1990) 41–59, with further literature.

271. Paravicini Bagliani, 'Il personale' 409. On the advancement of art and science by wealthy cardinals and popes, who competed in thoroughly transforming the city of Rome and Latium in the second half of the thirteeenth century, see Richard Krautheimer, *Rome: Profile of a City, 312–1308* (Princeton 1980) 207–228; and the various works by Julian Gardner, especially 'Patterns of Papal Patronage, ca. 1260–ca. 1300', *The Religious Roles of the Papacy* 439–456. Well-known jurists belonging to cardinals' 'familiae' were Albertus Azarii, Cognoscens, Godfrey of Trani, Guido de Baysio, Hugh of Atrio Dei, John of Monchy, Peter de Salinis, and Raymond of Peñaforte; see Paravicini Bagliani, *Cardinali de Curia* 2.492; and Schimmelpfennig, *Papsttum* 197.

272. Even for contemporaries it was hard to tell if and when someone belonged to a 'familia', and to what class of 'familiaris.' For that reason there were attempts at classification, such as are to be found in the cardinals' testaments around 1300 (Paravicini Bagliani, *Testamenti* cxvi–cxxii): (1) 'familiares commensales, qui habent officia in hospicio'; (2) 'domicelli vel armigeri, in domo sua continue commorantes'; (3) 'servientes' in the wardrobe, kitchen, camera, and stables; (4) further servants; (5) 'clerici de capella' after the dissolution of the original chapel. Like those of the pope, the number of honorary familiars of the cardinals also grew constantly. At the council of Constance, for example, every cardinal was granted prerogatives for thirty 'familiares', and then for sixty more who did not necessarily have to have the status of a familiar, all of them clerics.

273. Bishops presented problems in the thirteenth century when the patron was not a cardinal bishop; in the fourteenth century, however, this situation became normal; Paravicini Bagliani, *Cardinali di curia* 2.501–502.

274. These were people who knew the country and were sometimes chosen by the pope as well because of this; Geisthardt, *Der Kämmerer Boso* 20–21.

275. Many cardinals' suites included familiars who were also familiars of the pope and of princes; Paravicini Bagliani, *Cardinali di curia* 2.496, 498. These then served as diplomatic representatives (procuratores) of the other court. There was also an exchange between the suites, or takeovers of one suite by another cardinal. In case of promotion of a cardinal to the papal throne, he normally retained his old suite; ibid. 498–499.

276. Paravicini Bagliani, *Cardinali di curia* 2.505; Guillemain, *La cour pontificale*, map 6. The entirely distinct pattern of recruitment for the cardinals themselves is interesting; ibid. map 5; Guillemain, 'Cardinaux et société curiale aux origines de la double élection de 1378', *Génèse et débuts du Grand Schisme* 19–30, esp. 21 and passim. An informative study of the relation between a region and the curia is Johannes Vincke, 'Krone, Kardinal und Kirchenpfründe in Aragón zu Beginn des 14. Jahrhunderts', RQ 51 (1956) 34–53.

277. On the promotion of cardinals' 'familiares', see also Paravicini Bagliani, 'Approche proso-

meant provision with benefices,[278] prelacies if possible.[279] Cardinals treated benefices once won for a familiaris as their own property and disposed of them according to their whim to support their clientele.[280]

The Development of Bureaus out of the Papal Chapel

In the course of the twelfth century, the responsibilities of various officeholders and circles of personnel became more clearly defined. At the beginning of the thirteenth century there was a great 'push toward bureaucratization':[281] specialization and definition of competence reached a higher degree through the formation of individual departments with their own 'ressorts' under a head of the 'ressort'; these were the camera, chancery, penitentiary, and the various courts. For each of them, Innocent III erected a 'house' of its own, creating household communities including the higher officials and their familiares.[282] The head of the ressort had disciplinary powers over these collaborators as well as over those who were not members of the common household. Some of the heads and the higher collaborators held 'officia perpetua', which is to say they remained in office even when the pope changed.

---

pographique' 115–116. A telling poem on life as a familiar in the suite of a cardinal in the first half of the fourteenth century has been published by Norman Zacour, 'Petrus de Braco and His "repudium ambitionis",' *Mediaeval Studies* 41 (1979) 1–29. See the clientele of a cardinal in the reform decrees of Martin V in Döllinger, *Materialien zur Geschichte* 336.

278. On drawing income from a benefice *in absentia* for chaplains of cardinals, see Barraclough, *Public Notaries* 145, § 18, 18a, 18b. The number given of twenty 'familiares' in the constitution of John XXII, 'Dat vivendi normam' of 1316, means only that those prerogatives were given to that number of the 'familiares commensales' of each cardinal; it was not a ruling concerning the size or quantity of their actual suites. Zacour has a different view in 'Regulations' 436–449; see the corresponding constitution by Innocent VI, *Ad honorem* of 1352; ibid. 453–455. Other attempts to differentiate between cardinals' familiares according to their functions: preferential treatment of the 'auditores' or the 'camerarii'—see 'regulae cancellariae' of John XXII, § 44, in Andreas Meyer, Päpstliche Kanzleiregeln im Spätmittelalter, database, http://www.uni-marburg .de/fb06/forschung/webpubl/magpubl/paepstlkanzl.

279. Paravicini Bagliani, *Cardinali di curia* 2.500–502.

280. Designated as 'reservatio cardinalis' by Paravicini Bagliani, *Cardinali di curia* 2.504. The popes legalized this concept in the fifteenth century; see Brigide Schwarz, 'Patronage und Klientel in der spätmittelalterlichen Kirche', QF 68 (1988) 284–310, esp. 302–303.

281. Innocent III had the following buildings constructed in his palace near St. Peter's, among others: (1) capellania; (2) camera et capella; (3) panetaria; (4) buti[cu]laria; (5) coquina; (6) mareschalia; further, houses of their own for the (7) cancellarius; (8) camerarius; (9) elemosinarius. The entire complex was surrounded by walls and towers; *Gesta Innocentii III* (to 1208) (Migne PL 214.ccxi–ccxii, § cxlvi); reprint of the passage in Franz Ehrle and H. Egger, *Der Vaticanische Palast in seiner Entwicklung bis zur Mitte des 15. Jahrhunderts* (Vatican City 1935) 33–34; English translation by Powell, *Deeds of Pope Innocent III* 265. A new edition of the *Gesta Innocentii III* is being prepared by Jochen Johrendt (MGH-Project).

282. Where they were supplied with all necessary items by the 'camera'; see below.

The Chancery

The papal chancery was fundamentally reformed by Innocent III.[283] In the place of the cardinal chancellor, he introduced a collegiate leadership of the chancery by a vice-chancellor and seven chancery notaries.[284] Further innovations were the 'audientia litterarum contradictarum',[285] the corrector and the bullaria; he gave official status to the scribes of the chancery, and he regulated that of permanent proctors (see below). The leading members of the chancery inherited their high rank in ceremonial from the chancellors of the twelfth century: the vice-chancellor, the chancery notaries, the 'auditor litterarum contradictarum' and the corrector ranked below the cardinals and above the archbishops.

The major function of the chancery was not actually to issue manifestations of the sovereign will of the pope—those played a marginal role— but to issue documents of favors requested from the pope (or deriving from the handling of litigation at the curia).[286] The organization corresponded to this function, a fact that can best be demonstrated by illustrating the procedure: The petitioner had to present a petition that had to be in keeping with the 'stilus curiae'. For this, he needed assistance in formulation, which was provided by the 'petitionarii',[287] independent persons working at the residence of the curia who had specialized in drawing up such documents. Alternatively, he might use a representative (procurator, proctor) at the curia who promoted his cause, even when he did not visit the curia himself. The petitions were presented at the 'data communis' (an appointed time and place) or transmitted to the notary appointed to deal with them; if necessary they were reformulated, and if admitted organized by subject before being presented to the vice-chancellor and/or a

---

283. Peter Herde, *Beiträge zum päpstlichen Kanzlei- und Urkundenwesen im 13. Jahrhundert* (Münchener Historische Studien, Abteilung Geschichtliche Hilfswissenschaften 1; 2nd ed. Kallmünz 1967); *Letters of Pope Innocent III (1198–1216) concerning England and Wales*, ed. Christopher R. and Mary Cheney (Oxford 1967) xi–xviii; Patrick N. R. Zutshi, 'Innocent III and the Reform of the Papal Chancery', *Innocenzo III: Urbs et Orbis*, ed. Andrea Sommerlechner (Rome 2003) 1.84–101. Gerd F. Nüske, 'Untersuchungen über das Personal der päpstlichen Kanzlei 1254–1304', *Archiv für Diplomatik* 20 (1974) 39–240 (part 1); and 21 (1975) 249–431 (part 2), with prosopographic studies.

284. On the chancery in the thirteenth century, see Bresslau, *Handbuch* 1.248–255; Herde, *Beiträge zum päpstlichen Kanzlei- und Urkundenwesen* passim. At the end of the thirteenth century the vice-chancellor was once more normally a cardinal.

285. Geoffrey Barraclough, DDC 1.1387–1399, assumes a connection between the development of the 'audientia litterarum contradictarum' and the systematization of the institution of the 'iudices delegati' by Alexander III, first documented under Innocent III.

286. See Brigide Schwarz, 'Supplik', LThK² 9.1136–1137. On the documents, see Sayers, *Papal Government* 94–122.

287. Geoffrey Barraclough, 'Formulare für Suppliken der ersten Hälfte des 13. Jahrhunderts', AKKR 115 (1935) 435–456, esp. 455; Zutshi, *Petitioners, popes, proctors* 272–274.

chancery notary. These petitions were then either rejected or accepted (either fully or in part) by the vice-chancellor, and the more important ones were presented to the pope for approval through a 'referendarius'. According to his reply, the petition was converted into a draft (minute) (by abbreviators), from which the engrossment (mundum) was prepared (by the 'scriptores litterarum apostolicarum'). Both the draft and the engrossment were compared with its earlier forms and accompanying documents and checked for correctness in form and content. All letters touching the rights of third parties (so-called 'litterae communes') had to be read out in the audientia publica, where there was an opportunity for objection. If they passed without objection, they were expedited by the pope and/or by 'the chancery', the assembly of the notaries and the corrector, presided over by the vice-chancellor. The last step was the attachment of the bull and the registration. A simplified express procedure was developed toward the end of the thirteenth century for simple petitions with standard formularies: approval of the petition by the vice-chancellor, the draft being unnecessary here, then engrossment in keeping with a formulary, reading in the audientia, and expedition by the corrector. During the many stages of procedure, the petitioners or their proctors had to seek out the officials concerned to make sure that the case was treated according to the regular procedure, and to secure its reaching the next stages by paying the fees and tips.

The vice-chancellor supervised the procedure of issuing the papal letters.[288] This included checking the qualifications of those on whom the pope had bestowed an expectation to a benefice or a notariate auctoritate apostolica,[289] provided they were at the curia, as to their professional expertise and their character. For the responsibilities of the vice-chancellor in the consistory see above. As with other heads of department, he exercised disciplinary jurisdiction over the entire personnel of the chancery, as well as over the personnel of the Rota.[290] Under Innocent III the entire higher chancery personnel (including the auditor litterarum contradictarum and the corrector) seems to have belonged to the household of the vicechancellor; later only the chancery notaries and, toward the end of the

---

288. Hence he was also responsible for the prosecution of forgeries, which is why he had an auditor of his own in the fourteenth century; Emil Göller, 'Zur Geschichte der Kriminaljustiz und des Gefängniswesens am päpstlichen Hof in Avignon', RQ 19 (1905) part 2, 190–193.

289. Paul Maria Baumgarten, *Von der apostolischen Kanzlei: Untersuchungen über die päpstlichen Tabellionen und die Vizekanzler der Hl. Römischen Kirche im 13., 14. und 15. Jahrhundert* (Veröffentlichungen der Sektion für Rechts- und Sozialwissenschaften 4; Cologne 1908) 13–15; Barraclough, *Public notaries* 13; Guilio Battelli, 'L'esame dei notai pubblici apostolica auctoritate nel duecento', *Forschungen zur Reichs-, Papst- und Landesgeschichte: Peter Herde zum 65. Geburtstag*, ed. Karl Borchardt and Enno Bünz (2 vols. Stuttgart 1998) 1.255–263, who covers Innocent IV to Boniface VIII.

290. See below n. 328.

century, only his private servitors (particularly the abbreviators) did. The 'vicecancellaria' had the usual household personnel. Among these the seneschal[291] of the vicecancellaria was important, because he controlled contacts with the public. Among the vice-chancellors of the thirteenth century were several well-known jurists.[292]

The 'notarii domini papae', like the vice-chancellor, emerged from the papal chapel.[293] They were organized by Innocent III into a college of seven, on the model of early medieval notaries, ranked according to time in office (see above). Towards the end of the thirteenth century they were more and more reduced to the issuing of the simpler letters (primarily the so-called letters of justice), subject to the simplified procedure described above, which did not require specially trained personnel. However, since the office possessed a high ceremonial rank (see above), the popes increasingly gave it as an honorary position to deserving men, a process which had been completed by the fourteenth century.[294] The actual work of the notarii domini papae was done by others. Both the vice-chancellor and the notaries called in abbreviators, who in the beginning were only their private assistants, but who later became 'officiales' of the chancery in their own right.[295]

The 'auditor litterarum contradictarum'[296] was responsible for reviewing any objections raised in the 'audientia publica'.[297] His position and

291. Rusch, *Die Behörden und Hofbeamten* 10; later he was also called 'custos', and at the end of the fourteenth century he was always 'scriptor' of the chancery and 'abbreviator' as well; Brigide Schwarz, *Die Organisation kurialer Schreiberkollegien von ihrer Entstehung bis zur Mitte des 15. Jahrhunderts* (BDHI 37; Tübingen 1972) 109.

292. In the thirteenth century: Johannes Monachus, Jordanus de Terracina, Marinus of Eboli, Petrus Peregrossus, Richard of Siena, and, of course, Sinibaldus Fieschi; Bresslau, *Handbuch* 1.248–255; Nüske, 'Untersuchungen über das Personal' 2.396.

293. Elze, 'Kapelle' 175–180; Nüske, 'Untersuchungen über das Personal' 1.94–133, 2.397–406.

294. Patrick Zutshi, 'The Office of Notary in the Papal Chancery in the Mid-Fourteenth Century', *Forschungen zur Reichs-, Papst- und Landesgeschichte* 2.665–683, esp. 668–669. Chancery notaries frequently were members of great Roman families; juristic training can frequently be proven, but there are no noted scholars among them.

295. Schwarz, *Schreiberkollegien* 21–22. In the course of the later Middle Ages, the abbreviators of the vice-chancellor replaced the notaries in the expedition of letters in the chancery; Brigide Schwarz, '*Abbreviature officium est assistere vicecancellario in expeditione litterarum apostolicarum:* Zur Entwicklung des Abbreviatorenamtes vom Großen Schisma bis zur Gründung des Vakabilistenkollegs der Abbreviatoren durch Pius II.', *Römische Kurie, Kirchliche Finanzen, Vatikanisches Archiv* 2.789–823.

296. Fundamental is Peter Herde, *Audientia litterarum contradictarum: Untersuchungen über die päpstlichen Justizbriefe und die päpstliche Delegationsgerichtsbarkeit vom 13. bis zum Beginn des 16. Jahrhunderts*, 2 vols. (BDHI 31–32; Tübingen 1970); and Herde, 'Audientia litterarum contradictarum (audientia publica)', LMA 1.1192–1193.

297. Herde, *Beiträge* 213–215; Winfried Stelzer, 'Über Vermerke der beiden Audientiae auf Papsturkunden in der 2. Hälfte des 13. Jahrhunderts', MIÖG 78 (1970) 308–322; Jane Sayers, 'The Court of *Audientia litterarum contradictarum* revisited', *Forschungen zur Reichs-, Papst- und Landesgeschichte* 1.411–427.

his prestige grew, partly due to the qualifications of the office-holders: well-known jurists held this office. At the end of the thirteenth century,[298] the 'auditor litterarum contradictarum' left the household of the chancery and was granted his own household. He had disciplinary authority over the proctors accredited to his court, as well as over the lectors active there and over the notary. It was in the 'audientia publica' (later the 'audientia litterarum contradictarum') that all matters of the curia which had to be published were announced.

Somewhat in the shadow of the 'auditor litterarum contradictarum' stood the corrector (corrector litterarum apostolicarum). Originally it was his responsibility to see that all the letters that left the chancery should correspond to the 'stilus curiae', that is, that they should be formulated in a juristically correct manner. The greater portion of the 'litterae'[299] to be checked by him were those read out in the 'audientia'; it was for this reason that he participated in the proceedings of the 'audientia litterarum contradictarum'.[300] Towards the end of the thirteenth century the corrector, like the notaries, was reduced more and more to dealing with letters of justice. Here, however, he continued to play a decisive role (the later expeditio per correctoriam).[301]

The scribes of the chancery[302] prepared the engrossments of the letters (see above). Their number was very large even at an early date, and they organized themselves in the course of the thirteenth century into a corporation on the model of the 'official notaries' of the Northern Italian communes. They gradually took some tasks of examination and distribution into their own hands (distribution, 'auscultatio', reading out in the 'audientia litterarum contradictarum').[303] Their organization (and that of the

---

298. In the thirteenth century: Gerard of Parma, Godfrey of Trani, Guy of Baysio, Guy of Sexto, OP, James the canon of Bologna decr. doct., and naturally Sinibaldus Fieschi; see Bresslau, *Handbuch* 1:284 n. 1; Herde, *Audientia* 1.74–78; Nüske, 'Untersuchungen über das Personal' 1.133–142, 2.406–408.

299. When he was no longer responsible for the examination of the formal parts of the letters, this task was taken over by auxiliaries who were delegated by the college of the scribes; Schwarz, 'Der corrector' (see below n. 300), 152–154, 178–180; on the intricacies of writing papal letters correctly, see Tom Graber, 'Ein Spurium auf Papst Gregor X. für das Zisterzienserinnenkloster zu Leipzig', *Diplomatische Forschungen in Mitteldeutschland*, ed. T. Graber (Schriften zur sächsischen Geschichte und Volkskunde 12; Leipzig 2005) 89–144.

300. For this reason the corrector could take the place of the auditor; see Nüske, 'Untersuchungen über das Personal' 1.140–141.

301. In about 1370 he succeeded in placing himself at the head of the abbreviators of the vice-chancellor; Brigide Schwarz, 'Der corrector litterarum apostolicarum: Entwicklung des Korrektorenamtes der päpstlichen Kanzlei von Innozenz III. bis Martin V.' QF 54 (1974) 122–191; Schwarz, 'Corrector litterarum apostolicarum', LMA 3.278–279.

302. Bernard Barbiche, 'Diplomatique et histoire sociale: Les "scriptores" de la chancellerie apostolique au XIIIᵉ siècle', *Annali della Scuola Speciale per Archivisti e Bibliotecari dell'Università di Roma* 12 (1972) 117–129.

303. Schwarz, *Schreiberkollegien* 100–102. On the official notaries, see Andreas Meyer, *Felix et*

scribes of the penitentiary) at the end of the fourteenth century became a precondition for the development of the venality of offices at the curia.[304]

In a wider sense, the bullaria also belonged to the chancery, in which two to four monastic 'conversi' fastened the lead bulls to the letters that had been expedited.[305] The 'bullaria' constituted another modest household of its own. The vice-chancellor had the right to give instructions to the servitors of the register,[306] which still belonged to the camera. Fees for bulling and registration went to the 'camera'.

Only loosely attached to the chancery were the proctors, some of whom kept the process of issuing the letters going (procuratores ad agendum), while others were accredited to the 'audientia litterarum contradictarum'.[307] There were also proctors at the papal juridical courts and the cursors,[308] who were both mail couriers and court beadles.

The Camera

The close relationship of the chamberlain to the current pope continued for a long time,[309] as can also be seen from the fact that he and his household and several further servants of the camera were always kept in the immediate vicinity of the pope.[310] Like the heads of the other great offices, the chamberlain maintained his own household from the thirteenth century on, with the usual personnel.[311] Some popes felt it necessary to have an entirely personal (privy) chamberlain as well, whom they chose from among the personnel of their bedchamber (cubiculum).[312] Com-

---

inclitus notarius: Studien zum italienischen Notariat vom 7. bis 13. Jahrhundert (BDHI 92; Tübingen 2000) 155, 321–327, 333.

304. Brigide Schwarz, 'Die Ämterkäuflichkeit an der römischen Kurie: Voraussetzungen und Entwicklung bis 1463', *Proceedings Berkeley 1980* 451–463.

305. Paul Maria Baumgarten, *Aus Kanzei und Kammer: Erörterungen zur kurialen Hof- und Verwaltungsgeschichte im XIII., XIV. und XV. Jahrhundert* (Freiburg im Breislau 1907) 78–91.

306. On the papal registers of the twelfth and thirteenth centuries, see Sayers, *Papal Government* 65–93. In the thirteenth century there were no offices specifically for register scribes; the duty was taken over by chancery scribes; Nüske, 'Untersuchungen über das Personal' 2.393.

307. The proctors of the 'audientia litterarum contradictarum' later underwent a development of their own. On their work, see Sayers, 'The Court of *Audientia litterarum contradictarum* revisited', *Forschungen zur Reichs-, Papst- und Landesgeschichte* 1.412–415.

308. See below nn. 339–342 (procuratores ad agendum et defendendum) and above n. 217 (cursores).

309. A list of the chamberlains of the twelfth and thirteenth centuries is in Rusch, *Die Behörden und Hofbeamten* 138–141.

310. The best survey of the camera is Rusch, *Die Behörden und Hofbeamten* 20–38; Maurice Michaud, 'Chambre apostolique', DDC 3.388–431. Beyond the literature in n. 85 above, see also Adolf Gottlob, *Aus der camera apostolica des 15. Jahrhunderts: Ein Beitrag zur Geschichte des päpstlichen Finanzwesens und des endenden Mittelalters* (Innsbruck 1889).

311. Rusch, *Die Behörden und Hofbeamten* 28; 'court ordinance' from 1306, in Frutaz, 'La famiglia pontificia' 284–288. On the information about the 'camera' given in the lists of payments, it must be remembered that the 'camera' partly covered its costs out of its own income.

312. Rusch, *Die Behörden und Hofbeamten* 31; Gerd Tellenbach, 'Beiträge zur kurialen Verwal-

214   Brigide Schwarz

pared with the chamberlains of the twelfth century (see above), the chamberlain of the thirteenth century had gained further functions,[313] which were increasingly delegated to other officials. He now was head of the whole of curial administration, he decided disputes between departments over competences, and he was the principal of all curials, if they had no other. His jurisdiction gradually extended beyond the papal familia to all curials and 'curiam sequentes', insofar as they were clerics. Further, as the representative of the pope, the chamberlain was Lord of the Papal States. He thus became the supreme official at the papal court.

Supporting the chamberlain in the camera in a stricter sense were the clerics of the camera, who also represented him on occasion—in particular, they dealt with the correspondence of the camera, were responsible for bookkeeping and dealing with ban, and by the fourteenth century at the latest they took down the proceedings in the consistory (see below). In addition, there were two treasurers who had control over the treasury from the thirteenth century on;[314] the treasury, which had also once been considered part of the papal chapel, gradually became the central cashbox of the camera.[315]

A division of its own within the camera was the cameral court, headed by the cameral judge[316] as the sole judge. It was the court competent for the possessions and rights of the Romana ecclesia. The cameral judge represented the chamberlain in his function as judge over the curials and curiam sequentes. From the time of Nicholas III (1277–1280), the 'procurator Romanae ecclesiae' or 'procurator fiscalis' belonged to the cameral court. He was a sort of 'prosecutor for the crown' of the Roman church, who also represented the rights of the curials ex officio. At the end of the thirteenth century, there were cameral advocates proper, who represented the 'camera' before other courts and served as its legal advisors.[317]

The higher officials of the 'camera' (domini de camera) assembled for common consultation under the presidency of the chamberlain, and occa-

tungsgeschichte im 14. Jahrhundert: Camera papae', QF 24 (1932–1933) 150–187, esp. 150–151; reprinted in Tellenbach, *Ausgewählte Abhandlungen und Aufsätze* 1.144–181, esp. 144–145.

313. There is no satisfactory study of the development of the office of chamberlain.

314. Which also included the archive as well as the rich library of the popes; see Franz Ehrle, *Historia Bibliothecae Romanorum Pontificum tum Bonifatianae tum Avenionensis* (Biblioteca dell'Academia storicogiuridica 7; Rome 1890).

315. Rusch, *Die Behörden und Hofbeamten* 35.

316. Emil Göller, 'Der Gerichtshof der päpstlichen Kammer und die Entstehung des Amtes des procurator fiscalis im kirchlichen Prozeßverfahren', AKKR 94 (1914) 605–19; Guillaume Mollat, 'Contribution à la Chambre apostolique au XIVe siècle', RHE 45 (1950) 82–94; Daniel Williman, 'Summary Justice in the Avignonese Camera', *Proceedings Berkeley 1980* 437–450.

317. 'Court ordinance' from 1306 in Frutaz, 'La famiglia pontificia' § 36, 305 (see above n. 201).

sionally formed a jurisdictional body to settle legal questions. (This body must not be confused with the cameral court!)[318]

These persons were papal chaplains and also belonged to the closer papal familia. On the other hand, the other persons active in the camera were only officiales, without the status of a familiaris. This was the case with the notaries of the camera, who took down the proceedings of the camera and of the cameral court, kept the books, dispatched the correspondence, etc.[319] The cameral bankers were firmly accredited to the camera, representing particular Italian banks;[320] they mainly transferred the money gathered by the collectors to the curia.

The *Sacra Poenitentiaria*

The penitentiary[321] was a kind of juridical court for matters of conscience (forum conscientiae) as well as a court of grace (forum gratiae). The development of the doctrine of the plenitude of papal power in the twelfth century made it necessary to establish the penitentiary. Its primary competence was absolution of those sins and ecclesiastical censures that were now reserved to the pope ('reserved cases'), the concession of indulgences and letters of confession, and dispensation from ecclesiastical laws.

While the popes in the twelfth century had delegated such matters to individual cardinals on a case-by-case basis, under Innocent III the practice developed of appointing to the charge of great penitentiary (poenitentiarius domini papae) a cardinal, who often was a monk.[322] In the thir-

318. See Gottlob, *Aus der camera* 117–118.

319. See Norbert Kamp, 'Una fonte poco nota sul conclave del 1268–1271: I protocolli del notaio Basso della Camera apostolica', *Atti del Convegno di studio VII Centenario del 1° conclave (1268–1271)* (Viterbo 1975) 62–68; Stephan Reinke, *Kurie - Kammer - Kollektoren: Die Magister Albertus de Parma und Sinitius als päpstliche Kuriale und Nuntien im 13. Jahrhundert* (Regesta Imperii; Beihefte: Forschungen zur Kaiser- und Papstgeschichte des Mittelalters 30; Cologne 2011).

320. Édouard Jordan, *De mercatoribus Camerae apostolicae saeculi XIII* (Rennes 1909); Lunt, *Financial Relations* 1.599–603; Bruno Dini, 'I mercanti-banchieri e la sede apostolica (XIII—prima metà del XIV secolo)', *Gli spazi economici della chiesa nell'occidente (secoli XII—metà XIV)* (Centro Italiano di Studi di Storia e d'Arte 16; Pistoia 1999) 43–62; also in Dini, *Manifattura, commercio e banca nella Firenze medievale* (Florence 2001) 67–81. For the beginning of the thirteenth century, see Marco Vendittelli, 'Mercanti romani del primo Duecento "in Urbe potentes",' *Roma nei secoli XIII–XIV: Cinque saggi,* ed. É. Hubert (Rome 1993) 87–135; Maria Pia Alberzoni, 'I "mercatores romani" nel registro di Innocenzo III', *Le storie e la memoria: In onore di Arnold Esch* (Firenze 2002) 91–108. For the end, see Ivana Ait, 'I mercatores Camere Bonifacii pape octavi', *Dante e il Giubileo,* ed. E. Esposito (Città di Castello 2000) 55–68.

321. Fundamental for understanding the penitentiary are Göller, *Die päpstliche Pönitentiarie*; Rusch, *Die Behörden und Hofbeamten* 38–45; Andreas Meyer, 'Quellen zur Geschichte der päpstlichen Pönitentiarie aus Luccheser Imbreviaturen des 13. Jahrhunderts', *Päpste, Pilger, Pönitentiarie* 317–351.

322. The lists of great penitentiaries in Göller, *Die päpstliche Pönitentiarie* 1.86–96, and in Filippo Tamburini, 'Per la storia dei cardinali penitenzieri maggiori e dell'archivio della penitenzieria apostolica: Il trattato "de antiquitate cardinalis poenitentiarii maioris" di G. B. Coccino († 1641)', RSCI 36 (1982) 322–380, esp. 359–380, are incomplete.

teenth century the tenure of the great penitentiary still terminated with the death of the pope. Unlike the chamberlain and vice-chancellor, the great penitentiary did not have a domus because of his office, but rather he supplemented his bureau with people from his court as a cardinal.

Besides the competences mentioned above, he was father confessor of all higher curials and curiam sequentes. His competences in foro interno and in foro externo were summarized and systematized in the course of the thirteenth century in 'faculties.' In the fourteenth century an auditor poenitentiariae assisted him with difficult cases.

A portion of the power of the great penitentiary was subdelegated to the 'poenitentiarii minores'. They seem to have been another creation of Innocent III. They were part of the familia papae; it is probable that all penitentiaries were also chaplains. Since their primary task was hearing the confessions of penitential pilgrims, the offices were given almost exclusively to monks, particularly mendicants who had developed a new concept of the sacrament of confession and practiced it. Because of the various linguistic skills required, they came from all parts of Christendom, making the penitentiary the sole 'department' of the curia, which was always truly international. Like the chancery notaries, they were often used as 'nuntii'.[323] They lived in a house of their own in a 'vita communis', and unlike any other 'bureau', they received their support from the almonry of the pope, not from the 'camera'. There were also several clerics to assist them in their tasks.

In the course of the thirteenth century, the penitentiary developed its own chancery. The procedure of issuing the 'litterae sacrae poenitentiariae'[324] was much simpler than for the letters in the chancery, with a similar distinction between a simplified course for letters according to a fixed formula (officium minus), which were part of the responsibilities of the poenitentiarii minores, and one for the more complicated ones (officium maius). To compose the latter, there were proctors also at the penitentiary, but no abbreviators. The engrossing was a monopoly of the scribes of the penitentiary, who—like the scribes in the chancery—took the examination and the distribution of some of their tasks into their own hands. Drawn from this college at a later time were the two correctores,[325] who performed all corrections. The scribes of the penitentiary were organized according to the model of the scribes of the chancery.[326]

---

323. Elze, 'Kapelle' 180.

324. Schwarz, *Schreiberkollegien* 115–125.

325. Schwarz, 'Der corrector' 187–190.

326. See 212.

The Curial Courts

Like the other 'departments', the best-known curial court, the 'audientia sacri palatii', also called the Rota in the fourteenth century,[327] emerged from the chapel. Besides the Rota, there was a series of other curial courts, whose competence was also clarified in the thirteenth century.[328]

The consistory was the competent court[329] for all cases brought to the curia concerning the appointment to prelacies and other causae maiores (see above). The representatives who were admitted to the consistory,[330] the consistorial advocates and proctors, had to be accredited in the chancery; they were subject to the disciplinary authority of the vice-chancellor, who played an important role in the proceedings. Chancery notaries, later cameral clerics,[331] kept the minutes. The consistory had to approve all petitions of importance.[332]

The cardinal courts,[333] formed by individual cardinals, were increasingly given the same matters as the Rota. For the preparation of the proceedings, there were special auditors in the suites of the cardinals.[334]

327. Charles Lefebvre, 'Rote romaine', DDC 8.742–771; Gero Dolezalek, 'Audientia sacri palatii', LMA 1.1193–1194; Dolezalek, 'Rota', HRG 4.1318–1319. For the research on the medieval Rota, see Thomas Woelki, *Lodovico Pontano (ca. 1409–1439): Eine Juristenkarriere an Universität, Fürstenhof, Kurie und Konzil* (Education and Society 38; (Leiden-Boston 2011) 100–103; and Ferdinando Treggiari, 'Pontano, Ludovico', DGI 2.1615–1617.

328. A comprehensive investigation of the curial courts, though only of the Avignonese period, is offered by Guillaume Mollat, *Les papes d'Avignon (1305–1378)* (10th ed. Paris 1964) 482–494; see Bernard Guillemain, 'Les *tribunaux* de la cour pontificale d'Avignon', *L'Eglise et le droit dans le Midi (XIIIe–XIVe siècles)* (Cahiers de Fanjeaux 29; Toulouse 1994) 339–360.

329. Charles Lefebvre, 'La constitution "Properandum" et les avocats de la curie à la fin du XIIIᵉ siécle', *1274: Année charnière: Mutations et continuités* (Colloques internationales du Centre Nationale de la Recherche Scientifique. Sciences humaines 558; Paris 1977) 525–531. On the material dealt with in the consistory, see Tangl, *Die päpstlichen Kanzleiordnungen* 119, 122, § 3 and 21.

330. Thorough information on the representatives of parties is contained in the constitution 'Properandum' of 4 June 1274; Norman P. Tanner, *Decrees of the Ecumenical Councils* (2 vols. Washington D.C. 1990) 1.324 c.19 COD 2.1, p. 317–322, c.9 , which was modified by the constitution 'Decens et necessarium' of Benedict XII of October 27, 1340 for the consistory and the cardinals' judicial courts: Tangl, *Die päpstlichen Kanzleiordnungen* 118–124. One may doubt whether these had the desired outcome. The consistorial advocates had a loosely collegial organization at an early date. This was foreshadowed in the constitution of Benedict XII. See Schwarz, *Kurienuniversität und stadtrömische Universität* 404–412.

331. The history of the consistory has not been investigated. See Tellenbach, 'Beiträge zur kurialen Verwaltungsgeschichte' 155–161, reprinted in Tellenbach, *Ausgewählte Abhandlungen und Aufsätze* 1.149–155; and Helmut Schröder, 'Die Protokollbücher der päpstlichen Kammerkleriker 1329–1347', *Archiv für Kulturgeschichte* 27 (1937) 121–286.

332. In the dispatch of consistorial letters, the conditions of the twelfth and thirteenth centuries continued into the fifteenth century. The chancery notaries had the right to abbreviate these letters, and the corrector had the right of correction; see Schwarz, 'Der corrector' 157–158; Zutshi, 'The Office of Notary' 671–676.

333. Maleczek, 'Kardinäle von 1143 bis 1216', *Geschichte des Kardinalats* 137–139; and Fischer, 'Die Kardinäle von 1216 bis 1304' 180–181.

334. See above on the composition of cardinals' courts.

From the end of the thirteenth century, there was a 'iudex appellationum'[335] who served as a court of appeal for the courts of the Papal States.

The marshal of the curia in the thirteenth century had jurisdiction[336]
over almost all curials and curiam sequentes who were laymen;[337] he was
also the commander of the papal troops in Rome and in the Papal States[338]
as well as chief of the watch and security personnel of the curia.

Further, one has to mention the various 'iudicaturae', sessions of the
responsible members of all departments dealing with the issuing of documents (the chancery, the penitentiary, the camera, and the consistory) as
courts, where the documents were checked for their usus curiae and the
stilus of each particular department before they were dispatched. (In the
chancery a letter had to pass a iudicatura several times.)

On the cameral court and the court of the camera, and on the 'audientia litterarum contradictarum', see above.

The Proctors

Representatives of parties who had vastly different responsibilities and
status are designated by the terms 'procuratores', 'sollicatores', and such-
like in the sources.[339]

The *procuratores ad impetrandum*

As early as the end of the twelfth century, petitioners thought it necessary to make use of the expertise of curials to get their request impetrated
and their letters issued.[340] It was only with Innocent III, however, that pe-

335. Competent for penal jurisdiction, he, like the curial marshal, was a layman. Benedict XII
also introduced a court for civil pleas; Rusch, *Die Behörden und Hofbeamten* 61–62.

336. Rusch, *Die Behörden und Hofbeamten* 59. Armand Jamme, 'Formes dissociées ou polyva-
lence de l'office curial? La cité du pape et le maréchal du siège apostolique (XIIIe–XVe siècle)',
Offices, écrit et papauté (XIIIe–XVIIe Siècle), ed. A. Jamme and O. Poncet (Collection de l'École Française de Rome 386; Rome 2007) 313–392.

337. The reorganization of Benedict XII in 1336 was a turning point in the history of this office; see Bernhard Schimmelpfennig, *Zisterzienserideal und Kirchenreform: Benedikt XII. (1334–42) als
Reformpapst* (Zisterzienser-Studien 3; Berlin 1976) 11–43, esp. 24.

338. On this, see Daniel Waley, *The Papal State in the Thirteenth Century* (London 1961).

339. Fundamental is Winfried Stelzer, 'Beiträge zur Geschichte der Kurienprokuratoren im 13.
Jahrhundert', AHP 8 (1970) 113–138; Herde, *Beiträge* 125–133; Jane Sayers, 'Canterbury Proctors at the
Court of the Audientia litterarum contradictarum', *Traditio* 22 (1966) 311–345; Stelzer, 'Proctors rep-
resenting British Interests at the Papal Court, 1198–1415', *Proceedings Strasbourg 1968*, 143–163; Peter
Linehan, 'Proctors representing Spanish Interests at the Papal Court, 1216–1303', AHP 17 (1979) 69–
123; Linehan, 'Spanish Litigants and Their Agents at the Thirteenth-Century Papal Curia', *Proceedings
Salamanca 1976* 487–501. On the various types of proctors, see Zutshi, 'Petitioners, Popes, Proctors'
279–283. On the world of the proctors in the thirteenth century, see Brentano, *Two Churches* 20–29.

340. On the *procuratores ad impetrandum* see Rudolf von Heckel, 'Das Aufkommen der ständigen Prokuratoren an der päpstlichen Kurie im 13. Jahrhundert', *Miscellanea Francesco Ehrle* (Studi
e testi 8; Vatican City 1924) 2.290–321; Herde, *Beiträge* 125–129; Winfried Stelzer, 'Die Anfänge der
Petentenvertretung an der päpstlichen Kurie unter Innozenz III.', *Annali della Scuola Speciale per
Archivisti e Bibliotecari dell'Università di Roma* 12 (1972) 130–139.

titioners were allowed to be represented. From that time on, there were 'resident proctors' as a professional estate who took on such commissions, alongside those proctors who were sent to the curia by parties (procuratores principales) but who were also glad to make use of the help of the professional proctors practicing there. In addition, there were certain curials, particularly from the chancery, who offered this and other services as a sideline.[341] Prosopographical studies of the professional 'procuratores ad impetrandum' are possible, because they had to endorse their names on the back of letters entrusted to them.[342] Among them, one group gradually specialized in the 'audientia litterarum contradictarum', obtaining a monopoly and developing on its own as a curial college.

The *procuratores ad agendum et defendendum*

Besides the representatives mentioned above in the chanceries of the curia, there were also a great number of proctors who represented parties before the various courts (the two functions not being mutually exclusive). Unlike the advocates, the proctors in the courts never managed to establish a permanent monopoly.

Curials and Others as Permanent Representatives of Parties

Many parties gave proctors a permanent commission and 'supported' curials[343] so that they would watch over their interests. They provided their representatives with general powers of attorney which would enable them to act on their client's/principal's behalf wherever necessary. Special proctors general were maintained by religious orders, by some princes, and by cities. The reports of these proctors general from the curia, as well as the accounts of other 'procuratores'[344] of this sort are among the

341. These might be the discharging of sums, giving bail, procuring witnesses, protesting before or laying claims at a court, brokerage of benefices, recommending proctors and supervizing them, helping in formulation, advising on the best way to operate tactically, etc. In addition there was the gathering of current information and its transmission (such as on benefices vacant at the curia); see above n. 239.

342. See the lists of the volumes that have appeared in the series *Index actorum Romanorum pontificum ab Innocentio III ad Martinum V electum*. A survey in Frenz, *Papsturkunden* § 170, and Schwarz, 'Die Erforschung'; see above n. 1.

343. On cardinal protectors, see n. 255 above.

344. Famous are the *Acta Aragonensia*; the reports of Andreas Sapiti (*Il registro di Andrea Sapiti, procuratore alla curia avignonese*, ed. Barbara Bombi [Ricerche dell'Istituto Storico Germanico di Roma 1; Rome 2007]); the reports and litigation acts of the Hamburg trial of 1338–1355 (*Rat und Domkapitel von Hamburg um die Mitte des 14. Jahrhunderts*, ed. R. Salomon and J. Reetz [Veröffentlichungen des Staatsarchivs der Freien und Hansestadt Hamburg 9, 1–3; Hamburg 1968, 1975, 1980]; *Die Rechnungsbücher der hamburgischen Gesandten in Avignon 1338–1355*, ed. Th. Schrader [Hamburg-Leipzig 1907]; *Das Formelbuch des Heinrich Bucglant: An die päpstliche Kurie in Avignon gerichtete Suppliken aus der ersten Hälfte des 14. Jahrhunderts*, ed. J. Schwalm [Hamburg 1910]); as well as the records edited by Kurt Forstreuter, *Berichte der Generalprokuratoren des Deutschen Ordens an der Kurie, 1: Die Geschichte der Generalprokuratoren von den Anfängen bis 1403* (Veröffentlichungen der Nieder-

most important sources for curial history. In the later Middle Ages, these proctors general developed into diplomatic representatives[345] of individual powers at the curia.

The Curials in the Broader Sense

In comparison with the twelfth century, the number of curiam sequentes continued to grow dramatically. In addition to the judicial personnel mentioned above (proctors, advocates, notaries), whose number had also increased, and to visitors of the curia,[346] there were also (1) prelates who could not reside at their churches, particularly the large number of expelled missionary bishops,[347] (2) lectors and students of the curial university,[348] (3) the (itinerant) convents of the proctors general including a *studium curiae* of the great mendicant orders,[349] and (4) the court suppliers, the bankers, traders and craftsmen who had exclusive contracts with the curia and travelled with it.[350] At the end of the thirteenth century, the curia had grown so large that the number of curials and Romanam curiam sequentes amounted to more than 1000 persons.[351]

Maintenance and Status of Curials

Maintenance of Curials   Only members of the papal familia had a claim on being housed, fed, and even to some degree clothed by the camera.[352]

---

sächsischen Archivverwaltung 12; Göttingen 1961). On further reports, letters and other material from the curia, see the bibliography in Guillemain, *La cour pontificale* 14–15, and n. 238 above.

345. See Heinrich Finke, 'Gesandtschaftswesen und diplomatische Berichte z. Z. Jaymes II.', *Acta Aragonensia* 1.cxxiii–clxxvi.

346. See 178.

347. See Bernard Guillemain, 'Le personnel de la cour de Clément V', *Mélanges d'archéologie et d'histoire* 63 (1951) 139–181, esp. 178. These prelates earned extra income to support themselves at the curia by granting indulgences; Christopher R. Cheney, 'Illustrated Collective Indulgences from Avignon', *Paleografica diplomatica et Archivistica* 353–373, esp. 356–357, reprinted in *The Papacy and England, 12th–14th centuries: Historical and Legal Studies* (Variorum reprints, Collected Studies 154; London 1982) no. XVI; Alexander Seibold, *Sammelindulgenzen: Ablaßurkunden des Spätmittelalters und der Frühneuzeit* (Archiv für Diplomatik, Beiheft 8; Cologne-Weimar-Vienna 2001) 207–216.

348. Innocent IV founded the university of the Roman curia, and Boniface VIII reorganized it completely; see Agostino Paravicini Bagliani, 'La fondazione dello "Studium Curiae": Una rilettura critica', *Luoghi e metodi di insegnamento nell' Italia medioevale (secoli XII–XIV)*, ed. Luciano Gargan and O. Limone (Galatina 1989) 57–81; reprinted in Paravicini, *Medicina e scienze della natura alla corte dei papi nel Duecento* (Biblioteca di 'Medioevo latino' 4; Spoleto 1991) 363–390; Brigide Schwarz, 'Die beiden römischen Universitäten: Das *studium Romanae curiae* und das *studium Urbis* (14. und 15. Jahrhundert)', *Über Mobilität von Studenten und Gelehrten zwischen dem Reich und Italien (1400–1600): Della mobilità degli studiosi e eruditi fra il regno e l'Italia (1400–1600)*, ed. S. Andresen and R.C. Schwinges (Repertorium Academicum Germanicum [RAG]—Forschungen 1; Zürich 2011, e-book) 141–161; Schwarz, *Kurienuniversität und stadtrömische Universität* 80–87.

349. Schwarz, *Kurienuniversität und stadtrömische Universität* 351–363.

350. 'Court ordinance' from 1306 in Frutaz, 'La famiglia pontifia' § 19–22, 51, pp. 296, 311.

351. Paravicini Bagliani, 'Il personale' 403.

352. Sometimes the pope's care extended even further, as in the case of illness or feast days; see Baethgen, 'Quellen und Untersuchungen' 146.

Procuring these goods and distributing them in rations (called the 'vadia') depending on the rank of the familiars was the principal task of the court offices;[353] in Avignon these supplies were replaced by monetary payments.[354] The expenses for familiars constituted the largest item of the papal budget in the thirteenth century.[355]

As at other courts, the curials, from the pope through the cardinals and down to the last 'serviens', were also financed by 'gifts' presented by petitioners, who thus showed their recognition of favors obtained or their expectation to obtain them. This, as long as it remained within customary limits and followed certain forms, did not offend contemporaries, but was seen on the contrary as a right of curials. We have evidence for gifts being rejected as not honorable enough, either for the giver or the receiver.[356] Petitioners competed in their exercise of the high art of promoting one's own cause (or the cause of a client) through a gift well-chosen and well-placed with curials regarded as influential. (Only those who lost in the competition or zealots called this practice 'venality'.)[357] Valuable gifts, pensions, and other advantages could fall to the highly placed or those who had 'access to the wielder of power'. Complaints were directed particularly against the attempts of such persons at extortion.[358]

Besides these 'free' gifts, there were also, on certain occasions, gratuities, which had become fixed fees: 'presbyteria',[359] 'servitia minuta',[360] 'sa-

---

353. It is to this fact that we owe the court ordinances from 1278 and from 1306, mentioned above (n. 200). See for the fourteenth century, Schäfer, *Ausgaben* 1.544–602, 603–620. The higher placed familiars needed higher 'vadia' to support their own 'familia'. By no means small compensation for persons in court offices were the waste products from their work, such as hides or hair. A graphic illustration of this is in the court ordinance from 1306 (Frutaz, 'La famiglia pontificia').

354. Weiß, *Die Versorgung des päpstlichen Hofes* 76–77.

355. Baethgen, 'Quellen und Untersuchungen' 128.

356. Lunt, *Financial Relations* 1.180–181; Emmy Heller, 'Der kuriale Geschäftsgang in den Briefen des Thomas von Capua', *Archiv für Urkundenforschung* 13 (1935) 198–318, esp. 234–238.

357. There is a long literary tradition of satire/invective on the corruption of the curia as part of the criticism of Rome; see Josef Benzinger, *Invectiva in Romam: Romkritik im Mittelalter vom 9. bis zum 12. Jahrhundert* (Historische Studien 404; Lübeck 1968); Helga Schüppert, *Kirchenkritik in der lateinischen Lyrik des 12. und 13. Jahrhunderts* (Medium aevum 23; (Munich 1972) 75–90; John A. Yunck, *The Lineage of Lady Meed: The Development of Mediaeval Venality-Satire* (Publications in Medieval Studies 17; Notre Dame 1963) 85–117; Thomas Haye, *Päpste und Poeten: Die mittelalterliche Kurie als Objekt und Förderer panegyrischer Dichtung* (Berlin 2009) 81–84, 210–218.

358. See above n. 219.

359. Monetary gifts of the pope to curials and other clerics at high festivals (Schimmelpfennig, *Zeremonienbücher* 381). The 'liberalitas' of individual popes on these occasions is stressed in the *Liber censuum*, in Johannes B. Sägmüller, *Die Thätigkeit und Stellung der Cardinäle bis Bonifaz VIII.* (Freiburg im Breisgau 1896) 186–187.

360. The lively discussion on the 'servitia minuta' see Karl Henrik Karlsson, 'Die Berechnungsart der servitia minuta', MIÖG 18 (1897) 582–587; Adolf Gottlob, *Die Servitientaxe im 13. Jahrhundert: Eine Studie zur Geschichte des päpstlichen Gebührenwesens* (Kirchenrechtliche Abhandlungen 2; Stuttgart 1903; reprinted Amsterdam 1962) 101–118; Clergeac, *La curie et les bénéfices consistoriaux*, was finished by Emil Göller, in his "Introduction" to *Die Einnahmen Johannes XXII.*, ed. Göller

cra' and the like.[361] The circle of those entitled to receive such gratuities was determined early. They were usually distributed within the group of functionaries according to a set formula. The primary reason why these groups organized as colleges with a common purse was to collect and distribute these incomes.

Since the repeated attempts of the popes to support their curials as befitted their station by asking the churches to grant them certain prebends[362] were rejected by the churches—in one instance with the significant explanation that the prevailing system, through which one could cultivate 'friends' at the curia, was preferred[363]—the popes set about exploiting these means of support through subterfuge, so to speak. At first the popes 'recommended' to certain churches the provision of a client (or granted 'expectatives' on the next open position) and increasingly turned this recommendation into a command. The papal claim to the prerogative to dispense prebends was successfully realized by the general reservation of benefices, that is, when benefices became vacant for specific reasons (such as death at the curia, the death of a curial, entering a monastery, etc.) or special reservation, as when the pope reserved to himself the appointment to a particular benefice on the grounds of the 'best of that particular church', suspending the normal collation 'hac vice'.[364] Benefices

---

(Vatikanische Quellen zur Geschichte der päpstlichen Hof- und Finanzverwaltung 1; Paderborn 1910) 47*–52*.

361. On the 'sacra', that is, acquital from spoliation, see Schimmelpfennig, *Zeremonienbücher* 196–197. In the course of the fourteenth and fifteenth centuries, other fees were added, in which the various groups of officials had various shares: 'pallia' (Clergeac, *La curie et les bénéfices consistoriaux* 208–213); 'jocalia' on being nominated (to honorary chaplain, for example), on being sworn in, on recieving honors, etc.

362. Hermann Baier, *Päpstliche Provisionen für niedere Pfründen bis zum Jahre, 1304* (Vorreformationsgeschichtliche Studien 7; Münster in Westfalen 1911); Sigrid Seifert, 'Die Provisionen für niedere Pfründen an Mitglieder der Kurie im 13. Jahrhundert' (PhD diss., Berlin 1945); Geoffrey Barraclough, *Papal Provisions: Aspects of Church History, Constitutional, Legal, and Administrative in the Later Middle Ages* (Oxford 1935, reprinted 1971). Prerogatives for 'familiares' of cardinals in the acquisition of benefices were regulated in the papal chancery rules; see Andreas Meyer, Päpstliche Kanzleiregeln passim.

363. Lunt, *Financial Relations* 1.178–186. There were protests that the system of 'papal benefices' at the local churches, as suggested by the popes, would lead to the permanent installation of papal collectors, resulting in additional costs and a disturbance of the traditional order.

364. A good survey of the development of the papal rights of benefice is in Andreas Meyer, *Zürich und Rom: Ordentliche Kollatur und päpstliche Provisionen am Frau- und Großmünster 1316–1523* (BDHI 64; Tübingen 1986) 25–49; Kerstin Hitzbleck, *Exekutoren: Die außerordentliche Kollatur von Benefizien im Pontifikat Johannes' XXII.* (Spätmittelalter, Humanismus und Reformation 48; Tübingen 2009). On the difficulties of making a papal provision work, see Hitzbleck, 'Veri et legitimi vicarii et procuratores: Beobachtungen zu Provisionswesen und Stellvertretung an der päpstlichen Kurie von Avignon', QF 86 (2006) 208–251. On the use made of papal provisions in a region, see Brigitte Hotz, *Päpstliche Stellenvergabe am Konstanzer Domkapitel: Die avignonesische Periode (1316–1378) und die Domherrengemeinschaft beim Übergang zum Schisma 1378* (Vorträge und Forschungen, Sonderband 49; Ostfildern 2005).

only became the principal source of income for the majority of curials in the Avignonese period.[365]

A relevant number of the officiales, such as the notaries in the courts, the scribes in the chancery and penitentiary, etc., were entitled to 'sportula' (fees). The popes from Innocent III introduced fixed rates in almost all officia for each individual act. Since these rates, like all medieval fixed amounts, were regarded as unchangable, (moderate) violations by the invention of new incidental fees were tolerated. It was regarded as a matter of course that one had to promote the activity of every officialis as well as the qualitiy and speed of his work by giving tips—which was a part of the know-how of the proctors.

The Status of Curials

All members of the familia of the pope, of grandees, or of other curials were regarded as curials. Further, officeholders (officiales), that is, all those who took an oath of office, were also curials.[366] Curials were exempt from spiritual and secular jurisdiction,[367] which applied both to their person and to their benefices in partibus. The extent to which this immunity applied to the 'curiam sequentes' was gradually clarified by curial jurisprudence.[368] Obviously for this purpose, in the Avignonese period lists of curials were kept in the camera and with the marshal of justice. (On the juridical status of curials at the curia, see below.) All curials were obliged to follow the curia when it moved.[369] If they wanted to depart from the curia they needed a 'leave'. On the death of curials, their benefices were

365. In the thirteenth century the higher-ranking secular curials were compensated with fiefs and leaseholds; Baethgen, 'Quellen und Untersuchungen' 143–144.

366. On the oath register in the camera, see Oskar F. von Mitis, 'Curiale Eidregister: Zwei Amtsbücher aus der Kammer Martins V.' MIÖG, Supplemental vol. 6 (1901) 413–448, which also deals with earlier registers.

367. There are various papal constitutions on this: Boniface VIII, *Presenti* VI 3.4.34; John XXII, *Cum Matheus* of December 21, 1327, *Extrav. comm.* 5.4.3, Benedict XII, *Olim nonnulli Romani, Vitae Paparum Avenionensium* [1305–1394], ed. Stephanus Baluzius (new edition by Guillaume Mollat [Paris 1921] 3.483–486); expanded by Clement VI to even more 'familiares et officiales' in *Dudum felicis recordationis* of August 1, 1349, edited by Tellenbach, 'Beiträge' 180–181, reprinted *Ausgewählte Abhandlungen und Aufsätze* 1.174–175; repealed by Innocent VI, see Tangl, *Die päpstlichen Kanzleiordnungen* 126; expanded and systematized by Eugenius IV, *Divina in eminenti* of March 8, 1432, *Bullarium Romanum Editio Taurinensis* 5 (Turin 1860), no. 5, pp. 10–11. One could also be banned from the curia, which was a penalty inflicted by curial courts; see e.g. Göller, 'Kriminaljustiz' 192.

368. *Regulae Cancellariae Apostolicae: Die päpstlichen Kanzleiregeln von Johannes XXII. bis Nikolaus V.* ed. Emil von Ottenthal, (Innsbruck 1888, reprinted Aalen 1968), Martin V. § 125, 217–218; see also Meyer, Päpstliche Kanzleiregeln; everyone who spent six uninterrupted months at the curia was a 'curialis' in the broader sense; see Christiane Schuchard, *Die Deutschen an der päpstlichen Kurie im späten Mittelalter (1378–1447)* (BDHI 65; Tübingen 1987) 42–43; Guillemain, *La cour pontificale* 561–591, 653–673.

369. Schäfer, *Ausgaben* 3.33; otherwise they risked their positions.

reserved to the pope, which meant reappointment to them 'hac vice'. Their estates also fell to the pope.[370]

The curia distinguished two categories of 'officiales', as can be seen from their oath of office. The upper ranks swore comprehensive loyalty to the Holy See as well as correct administration of office[371] (a 'civil servant's' oath), while the others, such as the scribes, abbreviators, advocates, proctors and notaries accredited to the Rota as well as to the 'audientia litterarum contradictarum', only swore the latter.[372] The 'civil servant's' oath was also sworn by the honorary curials, by 'external' chaplains and familiars, and increasingly also by the nominal bearers of high-ranking offices such as chancery notaries and cubiculars.[373]

As shown above, all those papal familiars and curials as well as 'curiam sequentes' who were clerics were subject to the jurisdiction of the chamberlain,[374] with the exception of those directly subject to the pope.[375] The laymen, on the other hand, in most cases were under the jurisdiction of the marshal of the curia. In principle, the chamberlain was also the superior of all officiales, so long as no other regulation existed for their service (see above).

This jurisdictional exemption was the curials' most important privilege. Further privileges were assistance in finding quarters, reduced rents—where quarters were not provided free of charge anyway—and the duty-free purchase of goods. Prerogatives concerning acquiring and keeping benefices, such as the dispensation from the obligation to reside at the site of the benefice, became increasingly important for the clerics among the curials in the fourteenth and fifteenth centuries, the golden age of the benefice market.

---

370. See the criticism by Andreas Meyer of Daniel Williman, *The Right of Spoil of the Popes of Avignon 1316–1415* (Transactions of the American Philosophical Society 78, 6; Philadelphia 1988), in 'Das päpstliche Spolienrecht im Spätmittelalter und die licentia testandi: Anmerkungen zu einer Neuerscheinung', ZRG Kan. Abt. 77 (1991) 399–405, esp. 403: this is not a further unwarranted presumption on the part of the popes, as Williman believes, but rather a measure to secure the portion of the deceased's estate derived from the curial office.

371. In the chancerybook oaths are preserved for the vice-chancellor, the corrector, the chancery notaries, the Rota judges, the penitentiaries, the secretaries, and the *custos cancellariae*; Schwarz, *Schreiberkollegien* 72.

372. These were sworn in anew every year. The familiars of the vice-chancellor and the charges of the two scribal colleges also gave an oath of service; Schwarz, *Schreiberkollegien* 72–73.

373. Children are not infrequently mentioned among the higher personnel; see Schäfer, *Ausgaben* 3.ix–x.

374. The papal palace in Avignon naturally had a prison, under the superintendence of the chamberlain; Göller, *Kriminaljustiz*.

375. Rusch, *Die Behörden und Hofbeamten* 56.

The Social Networks of Curials

The Recruitment of Curials

Accomplishment and formal qualifications were certainly important for a curial career, but a determining factor was protection by influential patrons.[376] This can be seen by the regional origin of curials, which is documented best in the sources: from the twelfth century, most curials no longer had Roman origins. Insofar as we can say anything (for the cardinals, chaplains, and the chancery personnel) they came primarily from Italy in the twelfth and thirteenth centuries,[377] while in this period, as later in Avignon, the familiars of the cardinals and other grandees were already recruited from the whole of Europe.[378] The advocates and permanent proctors were almost exclusively Italians. In contrast, the benefices of the higher curials were increasingly not situated in the regions they came from or in which they had influence, but rather in regions of 'fat' benefices: France, south-eastern England, and northwest Germany.[379]

The offices at the curia were always avidly sought. Except for those offices held by his familiares, the pope filled few offices himself; the others were filled by the heads of departments. These department heads and other protectors strove to win further positions for their clients, while lower-ranking curials tried to bring in their own 'friends' ('roped teams'). The social networks surrounding the curia developed into complex patterns. The most common ones were those constituted by compatriots,[380] while the most important ones in the thirteenth century were blocks formed by Roman noble clans.[381]

To be accepted in the higher ranks of curials in the eleventh and twelfth centuries, it helped to belong to reform orders or houses, and from the

376. Wolfgang Reinhard, 'Herkunft und Karriere der Päpste 1417–1963: Beiträge zu einer historischen Soziologie der römischen Kurie', *Mededelingen van het Nederlands Institut te Rome* 38 (1976) 87–108.

377. Paravicini Bagliani, 'Il personale' 402, with literature on individual regions. On the cardinals, see 186; on the chaplains, see 200. In the second half of the thirteenth century, there were surprising differences among chancery personnel as to origin, the benefices they held, and career, between the "upper class" of the chancery and the scribes; the latter were recruited primarily from the Papal States; Nüske, 'Untersuchungen über das Personal' part 2.

378. See the works of Paravicini Bagliani.

379. See Nüske, 'Untersuchungen über das Personal' 2.405–408, for the higher chancery personnel.

380. These groups could become dominating: 'landsmanschaftliche Blockbildung' is the term used by Arnold Esch, 'Das Papsttum unter der Herrschaft der Neapolitaner: Die führende Gruppe Neapolitaner Familien an der Kurie während des Schismas 1378–1415', *Festschrift für Hermann Heimpel zum 70. Geburtstag am 19. September 1971* (3 vols. Veröffentlichungen des Max-Planck-Instituts für Geschichte 36; Göttingen 1972) 2.798.

381. Brentano, *Rome* 174–209; Paravicini Bagliani, 'Il personale' 403.

end of the twelfth century it helped increasingly to have an education, particularly legal training.[382]

The Connections between the Curia and the Periphery through the Curials

A systematic study of the social network of curials only exists for the fifteenth century.[383] For the earlier period, there are only case studies on the connections of particular churches or regions with the curia, and more are in the making.[384] Still, some trends can be recognised: Curials only spent a part of their lives at the curia. They brought with them their social ties: their social and regional origins, the contacts they had made at the churches and the other institutions (particularly orders and schools) to which they belonged. On the other hand, they could use relationships formed at the curia (see above on the proctors) to make a career or to gain a living for themselves in partibus, even when they had finally left the curia. Their most pressing interest was to obtain an endowment of benefices they considered suitable to their station.[385] Since this acquisition took place according to set social rules and is documented best, it offers the best opportunity for an investigation of the social networking of curials. Via these networks, interested parties came into contact with the curia and transacted their business through them.

Nepotism was a feature of networking with its own very particular characteristics. The promotion of relatives[386] was a necessity for every

382. This was recognized early by the great Roman families, who accordingly sent their sons to the centers of education to be trained; Paravicini Bagliani, 'Il personale' 406. Cf. Peter Classen, 'La Curia romana e le scuole di Francia nel secolo XIII', *Le istituzioni ecclesiastiche della 'societas christiana' dei secoli XI–XII* 432–436.

383. Schuchard, *Die Deutschen an der päpstlichen Kurie*, continued in Schuchard, 'Deutsche an der päpstlichen Kurie im 15. und frühen 16. Jahrhundert', RQ 86 (1991) 78–97. Guillemain, *La cour pontificale*, barely investigates this aspect.

384. Exemplary is Charles McCurry, '"Utilia Metensia": Local Benefices for the Papal Curia, 1212–ca. 1370', *Law, Church and Society: Essays in Honor of Stephan Kuttner* (Philadelphia 1977) 311–323; Gerhard Fouquet, *Das Speyrer Domkapitel im späten Mittelalter (ca. 1350–1540): Adelige Freundschaft, fürstliche Patronage und päpstliche Klientel* (2 vols. Quellen und Abhandlungen zur mittelrheinischen Kirchengeschichte 57; Mainz 1987). See Rehberg, *Kirche und Macht*, and Rehberg, 'Familien aus Rom und die Colonna'; Gramsch, 'Kommunikation als Lebensform'; as well as Meyer, *Zürich und Rom* and Hotz, *Stellenvergabe*. On the curia as marketplace for German benefices and curial networking, see Brigide Schwarz, 'Römische Kurie und Pfründenmarkt im Spätmittelalter', *Zeitschrift für historische Forschung* 20 (1993) 129–152, esp. 130, 133 and n. 21; Schwartz, 'Das Repertorium Germanicum: Eine Einführung', *Vierteljahrschrift für Sozial- und Wirtschaftsgeschichte* 90 (2003) 429–440, esp. 436–439 with bibliography.

385. On the possession of benefices by chancery personnel, see Nüske, 'Untersuchungen über das Personal' 2.405–408, 426–427; and especially Barbiche, 'Scriptores'.

386. Wolfgang Reinhard, 'Nepotismus: Der Funktionswandel einer papstgeschichtlichen Konstante', ZKG 86 (1975) 145–185; Reinhard, 'Papa pius: Prolegomena zu einer Sozialgeschichte des Papsttums', *Von Konstanz nach Trient: Beiträge zur Geschichte der Kirche von den Reformkonzilien bis*

pope who wished to exercise effective rule, for the institutional structure of the church was still relatively loose. Rule was still founded on personal ties.[387] And family bonds constituted the strongest social tie in the Middle Ages: only with relatives did the pope find reliability and an interest in his well-being. Hence the really important offices of the curia went mostly to clerics who were relatives, and the popes used their growing prerogative of dispensing benefices to provide for their clerical relatives. Nepotism was an obvious duty of 'pietas' of every pope. As a result, medieval criticism of the curia never turned against nepotism in principle, only against offences against discretion,[388] as was the case with gifts. Medieval popes invented many ways to promote and distinguish their relatives.[389] The shape of papal nepotism changed profoundly during the Middle Ages, as Wolfgang Reinhard has shown. Until the middle of the thirteenth century the popes had to bring all the means and influence of their families to bear to keep the city of Rome and later the Patrimony under their control;[390] from then on, with the growing prerogatives to dispense benefices, nepotism as a system to provide for relatives—always a latent function—gained equal importance: the popes used ecclesiastical benefices to a vast extent to provide for relatives as befitted their station, and to raise the position of their families.[391]

On the offices to which clerics who were relatives were typically appointed, see above. These clerics are always to be found in the intimate vicinity of the pope, in the college of cardinals, in the camera, and—de-

---

zum Tridentinum: Festgabe für August Franzen, ed. Remigius Bäumer (Munich-Paderborn-Vienna 1972) 261–299. To Alexander III was attributed the proverb, 'Deus abstulit nobis filios, et diabolus dedit nobis nepotes'; Petrus Cantor, Migne PL 205.211D § 71. Innocent III also warned of the perils of nepotism, *De miseria humanae conditionis*, ed. Michele Maccarrone (Lucca 1955) lib. 2, § 27, p. 60.

387. Reinhard, 'Nepotismus' 153. For this principle of medieval rulership see Robert Gramsch, *Das Reich als Netzwerk der Fürsten: Politische Strukturen unter dem Doppelkönigtum Friedrichs II. und Heinrichs (VII.) 1225–1235* (Mittelalter-Forschungen 40; Ostfildern 2013).

388. See on this Alexander of Hales, *Glossa in 4 libros sententiarum* (Quaracchi 1951) 7*–24*, 68*; Alexander of Hales, *Summa theologica* (Quaracchi 1930) III, 379–380, 805; Thomas Aquinas, *Summa theologica* 2.2 q.63 a. 2, ad 1, and q.100 a.5 ad 2.

389. Possibilities for creating connections in this way were (1) concerning persons (besides marital ties, which were also common with secular rulers): conferment of the pope's own cardinal titular church, consecration by the pope himself, standing as godfather, dubbing to knighthood; (2) concerning institutions: establishing pious foundations, and granting privileges and indulgences. Great popes such as Innocent III set an example; see Michele Maccarrone, *Studi su Innocenzo III* (Italia Sacra 17; Padova 1972) passim.

390. Their control was always unstable; Waley, *The Papal State* 9–29; Toubert, *Les structures du Latium médiéval* 2.1068–1081 and 1314–1348; Maleczek, 'Rombeherrschung und Romerneuerung durch das Papsttum'.

391. On the various kinds of nepotism in the later Middle Ages, see Reinhard, 'Nepotismus'; and for the Avignon popes, see Ralf Lützelschwab, 'Die Kardinäle des Avignonesischen Papsttums (1305–1378): Kreaturen des Papstes, Sachwalter partikularer Interessen', *Geschichte des Kardinalats 227–228*.

creasingly—in the chancery. These clerics, however, are only the head of the clientele, which every pope had to create at the curia in competition with the net of patronage and clientele of his own grandees. Up until recently, modern historiography has continued to neglect these social relationships in favor of the official ones of service. Even though research into social ties, which are very hard to prove at the curia in the thirteenth century,[392] is still in its preliminary stages, one may still say that these relationships are as important as official relationships, and in the later Middle Ages, the social ties even came to overshadow the others.

392. Hitzbleck, *Exekutoren,* part 3, showed that it is possible (if you know how) to use the executors in letters of provision (who were mostly proposed by the petitioners) as indicators of the working of curial networks.

7

Judges Delegate

Charles Duggan†

From their inception, the decretal collections reflected the evolution of papal jurisdictional authority and recorded its application through the office of delegated judges. With the exception of recent conciliar legislation, the collections were compiled very largely from commissions to judges delegate. Almost every commission related in some way to canonical doctrine and procedure. In some cases the decision contains an analytical exposition of points of law or judicial procedure. The preponderance of such commissions to English judges delegate or to English prelates and canonists in the Anglo-Norman territories has been discussed in another volume.[1]

In contrast with the 'paleae' inserted in Gratian manuscripts and appendices to the *Decretum,* the contents of decretal collections record the current state of law and its evolving formulation. Gratian's *Decretum* had provided the legal and procedural foundation for the development of an appellate process; the increasing activity of reforming popes and reforming councils provided the impetus; and the emergence of the law schools in Bologna, Oxford/Lincoln, Padua, and elsewhere—where Justinian's *Corpus iuris civilis* and Gratian's *Decretum* were studied side-by-side—provided the forum for the formation of an international system of ecclesiastical law, characterized

---

1. Charles Duggan, 'Decretal Collections from Gratian's *Decretum* to the *Compilationes antiquae*: The Making of the New Case Law', Hartmann and Pennington *History* 246–292.

by consistent procedure and appeal to the papal curia. In the course of the twelfth century, a Europe-wide system of canon law came into existence, based on uniform process and a single Ius commune, whose twin agencies were the papal decretal and the office of papal judge delegate.[2]

The Growth of the Appellate Jurisdiction of the Papacy

Gratian himself had proclaimed the universality of papal appellate jurisdiction in his proclamation of the pope as 'judge of all, but judged by none' (iudex omnium, papa a nemine est iudicandus); moreover in a series of chapters in Causa 2, quaestio 6, all four of which were in the pre-Vulgate *Decretum*, he had stated the universal right of appeal.[3] Then, in the Vulgate version, he inserted three form letters into his pre-Vulgate dictum following c.31 (C.2 q.6 d.p.c.31), which illustrated different types of appeal: an appeal against oppression by a metropolitan, an appeal of an unjust decision, and a collective appeal by agents (syndics) of a collegiate church.

In the first, a bishop, claiming 'oppression', requests letters dimissory from his archbishop: 'The form of appeal is this: I, Adelmus, unworthy minister of the holy church of Reggio (Emilia), feeling myself oppressed by the lord Gualterius, archbishop of the holy church of Ravenna, appeal to the Roman see, and request *apostoli*'.[4] Both prelates were in office in the early twelfth century: Gualterius was bishop of Ravenna from 1119 to February 1144 and Adelmus was bishop of Reggio from 1130 to 1139.

In the second, a bishop, claiming unjust judgment, seeks letters dimissory from his archbishop: 'The form of appeal after sentence will be: I, Adelmus, unworthy minister of the holy church of Reggio, appeal to the Roman see against the sentence of lord Gualterius, archbishop of the holy church of Ravenna, unjustly laid on me on Wednesday, 30 April, in the year of the Lord 1105,[5] and request *apostoli*'.[6]

2. Stephan Kuttner, 'The Revival of Jurisprudence', *Renaissance and Renewal in the Twelfth Century*, ed. R. L. Benson and Giles Constable (Cambridge, Mass. 1982) 299–323. Anne J. Duggan, 'Making Law or Not? The Function of Papal Decretals in the Twelfth Century', *Proceedings Esztergom 2008* 41–70.

3. Gratian, *Decretum*, C.2 q.6 c. 6, 8, 12 and 21.

4. Ibid. C.2 q.6 d.p.c.31, Florence, BN Conventi soppressi A.1.402, fol. 125r (Supplement), Admont, ML, fol. 132v (Supplement). Biberach, Spitalarchiv B.3515, fol. 106v, Bremen, SB und Universitätsbibliothek a.142, fol. s.n. Florence, Biblioteca Laurenziana 1.sin.1, fol. 122rb, Munich, BSB 28161, fol. 96r, Salzburg, ML a.xi.9, fol. s.n, St. Gall, ML 673, p. 55a–b: 'Forma vero appellationis hæc est: Ego Adelmus[a] sanctæ Reginæ[b] æcclesiæ minister indignus sentiens me pregravari a domino Walterio[c] sanctæ Ravennatis æcclesiæ archiepiscopo romanam sedem appello et apostolos peto. [[a] Lanfrancus: St. Gall, Adelinus: Admont [b] sancte Parmensis: St. Gall [c]Walterio: Admont Gualterio]'

5. As many scholars have observed, this date is clearly incorrect.

6. Ibid.: 'Si vero post datam sententiam appellare voluerit, hic erit ei modus appellandi: Ego

In the third, a plurality of appellants, in this case procurators acting for a collegiate church, seek letters dimissory either before or after sentence has been given: 'If one or two wish to appeal on behalf of several, they shall appeal in this form: 'We, G. and P., acting for the canons of the holy church of B(ologna), feeling ourselves oppressed, or, against the sentence, etc., appeal to the Roman see, and request *apostoli*'.[7]

Finally, as he revised his *Decretum* for the last time, Gratian added an example of the letters dimissory, called *apostoli,* which a bishop must issue to a cleric who has appealed his judgment: 'The form of apostoli is this: I, Henricus, bishop of the holy church of Bologna, with these apostoli, send you Roland, priest and chaplain of San Apollinare, to the apostolic see, to which you appealed from the observance of my judgment'.[8]

The Bishop Henricus whom Gratian named here was undoubtedly bishop of Bologna from 1129 to July 1145. Rolandus cannot be identified. The presence of these personal and regional names in the early manuscripts strongly supports the argument that Gratian was teaching in Bologna and was active in the region during that time.

In most instances, cases so appealed, or referred directly by the plaintiff, to Rome were not tried in the Curia but referred back to reliable and well-regarded ecclesiastics in the locality from which the appeal arose. This practice had the advantage of drawing local bishops, deans, archdeacons, abbots, and priors into the web of papal jurisdiction; it also had the great merit of

---

Adelmus[d] sanctæ Reginæ æcclesiæ minister licet indignus contra sententiam domini Gualterii[e] sanctæ ravennatis æcclesiæ archiepiscopi iniuste in me illatam pridie Mai[f] anno incarnationis domini mill. c.v.[g] feria iiii. romanam sedem appello et apostolos peto. [[d]A. Paris: Munich, L. St. Gall [e]Walterii: Admont, Munich [f] Aug.: St. Gall [g] c.xlvi. St. Gall]' On the St. Gall manuscript and this dictum of Gratian, see Carlos Larrainzar, 'El borrador de la "Concordia" de Graciano: Sankt Gallen, ML 673 (=Sg)', *Ius ecclesiae* 11 (1999) 593–666 at 636–645, who discusses the text and prints an edition of the dictum from pre-Vulgate manuscripts. Lanfrancus was bishop of Parma from ca. 1139 to 1162.

7. Decretum, C.2 q.6 d.p.c.31, Florence, BN Conventi soppressi A.1.402, fol. 125r (Supplement), Admont, ML, fol. 132v (Supplement). Biberach, Spitalarchiv B.3515, fol. 106v, Bremen,SB und Universitätsbibliothek a.142, fol. s.n. Florence, Biblioteca Laurenziana 1.sin.1, fol. 122rb, Munich, BSB 28161, fol. 96r, Salzburg, ML a.xi.9, fol. s.n, St. Gall, ML 673, p. 55b: 'Si autem unus vel duo pro pluribus appellare voluerit sic appellabunt: Ego G. et P. sindici[a] canonicorum s.b.e. (sanctae bononiensis ecclesiae) sentientes nos pregravari vel contra sententiam etc. romanam sedem appellamus et apostolos postulamus. [[a]idest defensores *add.* Munich.]' The sentence 'Ego G. et P. — apostolos' is omitted by St. Gall.

8. This text is not in the pre-Vulgate Decretum manuscripts. Florence, BN Conventi soppressi A.1.402, fol. 125r (Supplement), Admont, ML, fol. s.n (Supplement). Biberach, Spitalarchiv B.3515, fol. 106v, Bremen, SB und Universitätsbibliothek a.142, fol. s.n. Florence, Biblioteca Laurenziana 1.sin.1, fol. 122rb, Munich, BSB 28161, fol. 96r, Salzburg, ML a.xi.9, fol. s.n.: 'Forma apostolorum hæc est: Ego Henricus[a] sanctæ bononiensis æcclesiæ episcopus te presbyterum Rolandum capellanum[b] ecclesiæ sancti Apollinaris ad apostolicam sedem quam appellasti ab observatione mei iudicii, his apostolis[c] dimitto. [[a] Henricus: Admont, Bremen, Enricus Salzburg, Florence Laurenziana[rc]; H.: Florence, Biberach, Munich [b] cappellanum *om.* Florence [c] appł Florence]'

placing responsibility for trial, judgment, and execution in the hands of men of experience familiar with local conditions.[9] By the second half of the twelfth century, the exercise of delegated jurisdiction had become a significant part of episcopal and abbatial activities.[10] Indeed, from the early thirteenth century, it became customary for plaintiffs to nominate appropriate judges (and the practice may have been established even earlier).[11] Nomination by the plaintiff or his proctor had its risks, but the defendant could refuse the jurisdiction of anyone suspect to him on grounds of ignorance of the law, bias, relationship, or other comparable grounds. Recusal was a basic defense of the defendant.[12]

Although Stephen of Orléans (ca. 1160–1170), later bishop of Tournai, defined the decretal letter as 'a papal rescript to any bishop or ecclesiastical judge, who has consulted the Roman Church on any doubtful matter',[13] judge-

9. Harald Müller, 'Entscheidung auf Nachfrage: Die delegierten Richter als Verbindungsglieder zwischen Kurie und Region sowie als Gradmesser päpstlicher Autorität', *Römisches Zentrum und kirchliche Peripherie: Das universale Papsttum als Bezugspunkt der Kirchen von den Reformpäpsten bis zu Innozenz III.*, ed. Jochen Johrendt and Harald Müller (Abh. Akad. Göttingen 2; Berlin 2008) 109–131; and the same author's 'Gesandte mit beschränkter Handlungsvollmacht: Zu Struktur und Praxis päpstlich delegierter Gerichtsbarkeit', *Aus der Frühzeit europäischer Diplomatie: Zum geistlichen und weltlichen Gesandtschaftswesen vom 12. bis zum 15. Jahrhundert,* ed. Claudia Märtl and C. Zey (Zürich 2008) 41–65; Peter Herde, 'Zur päpstlichen Delegationsgerichtsbarkeit im Mittelalter und in der Frühen Neuzeit', ZRG Kan. Abt. 119 (2002) 20–43; Richard A. Schmutz, 'Medieval Papal Representatives: Legates, Nuncios and Judges-Delegate', SG 15 (Bologna 1972) 441–463; for more literature, see Schwarz, 'Roman Curia' above.

10. See, for example, Dom Adrian Morey, *Bartholomew of Exeter: Bishop and Canonist* (Cambridge 1937) 44–78; and his work with Christopher N. L. Brooke, *Gilbert Foliot and his Letters* (Cambridge 1965) 230–424; Mary G. Cheney, *Roger, Bishop of Worcester, 1164–79* (Oxford 1980) 113–212; *Papal Decretals Relating to the Diocese of Lincoln in the Twelfth Century*, ed. Walther Holtzmann and E. W. Kemp (Lincoln Record Society 47; Hereford 1954); Wacław Uruszczak, 'Les juges délégués du pape et la procédure romano-canonique à Reims dans la seconde moitié du xiie siècle', TRG 53 (1985) 27–41; Ludwig Falkenstein, 'Appellationen an den Papst und Delegationsgerichtsbarkeit am Beispiel Alexanders III. und Heinrichs von Frankreich', ZKG 97 (1986) 36–65. For a short overall survey, see G. G. Pavloff, *Papal Judges Delegate at the Time of the Corpus Iuris Canonici* (The Catholic University of America, Canon Law Studies 42; Washington, D.C. 1963); Jane E. Sayers, *Papal Judges Delegate in the Province of Canterbury 1198–1254* (Oxford 1971) 114–118; Charles Duggan, *Twelfth-Century Decretal Collections and Their Importance in English History* (University of London Historical Studies 12; London 1963) passim; and Duggan, 'Decretal Letters to Hungary', *Folia Theologica* 3 (1992) 5–31.

11. Sayers, *Papal Judges Delegate* 109–118.

12. For a full discussion of the development of the procedure of 'recusatio iudicis', see Linda Fowler-Magerl, 'Recusatio Iudicis in Civilian and Canonist Thought', SG 15 (Bologna 1972) 719–785; cf. Richard H. Helmholz, 'Canonists and Standards of Impartiality for Papal Judges Delegate', *Canon Law and the Law of England* (London-Ronceverte 1987) 21–39. For the legal basis of recusation, see Gratian's *Decretum*, C.3 q.5 c.15 § 4: 'Licet ei, qui suspectum sibi iudicem putat, antequam lis inchoetur, eum recusare, ut ad alium recurratur'; cf. Rufinus, *Summa decretorum*, ed. Heinrich Singer (Paderborn 1902, reprinted Aalen 1963), 267; cf. Tancred (1214–1216), *Ordo iudiciarius, Pillius, Tancredus, Gratia, Libri de iudiciorum ordine,* ed. Friedrich Christian Bergmann (Göttingen 1842, reprinted Aalen 1965) 87–316, tit. 6, pp. 146–150, esp. 6.1: 'Recusatio est audientiae vel iurisdictionis declinatio, per exceptionem suspicionis oppositam'; 6.6: 'Causa recusationis unica est, scilicet suspicio… puta, si inimicus eius, qui convenitur'. See Litewski, *Zivilprozeß* 102–113, 136–137.

13. *Die Summa des Stephanus Tornacensis über das Decretum Gratiani*, ed. Johann F. von Schulte

delegate commissions were treated as decretals, in the sense that they contained authoritative papal directions. Whether as consultations or as commissions, decretals became the essential link in the chain of papal jurisdiction. In its simplest form, a decretal commissioned one, two, or more local judges to hear and conclude a case which had been referred to the pope's jurisdiction, as in the following example, where Pope Alexander III delegated a patronage case to Bishops Bartholomew of Exeter and Roger of Worcester, 'the twin lights of the English Church',[14] between 1164 and 1179:

> We commit the case which is in process between the noble Fr. de The<lwall> and R. de Bic<kerton> concerning the right of patronage over the church of Walton to your experience, to be heard and brought to an appropriate conclusion, and command you to summon the parties to your presence, when you are required, and, having heard the arguments advanced on both sides, to conclude the case either by agreement or by your judgment.... Moreover, if either party having been summoned disdains to appear and obey your judgment, you are to compel that party by ecclesiastical censure without leave of appeal. But if either of you cannot participate, either one of you may proceed to hear the case, without appeal.[15]

Since such 'simple letters of justice' were issued as a matter of course at the request of the plaintiff or his legal representative (proctor), there was ample opportunity for the dishonest litigant to secure judicial mandates based on false allegations or suppression of the truth. Such surreption would probably have been revealed once the case was brought before local judges in the presence of the defendant; but it could undermine the whole process. For this reason, the papal chancery, at least from Innocent III's pontificate, adopted the practice of formally reading such letters 'in publica audientia', so that if defendants were present in person or through a representative they could enter a challenge either to the statement of the case or to the proposed judges. If a challenge were entered, the question was referred to the 'audientia litterarum contradictarum', where the audi-

---

(Giessen 1891) 2: 'Decretalis epistola est, quam dominus apostolicus aliquo episcopo vel alio iudice ecclesiastico super aliqua causa dubitante et ecclesiam Romanam consulente rescribit et ei transmittit'.

14. Giraldus Cambrensis, *Opera*, ed. J. S. Brewer, J. F. Dimock and G. F. Warner (8 vols. RS 21; London 1861–1891) 7, 57.

15. Latin text printed in *Decretales ineditae saeculi XII*, ed. et rev. Stanley Chodorow and Charles Duggan (MIC Series B: Corpus Collectionum 4; Vatican City 1982) 98, no. 55; Charles Duggan, 'Decretals of Alexander III to England', *Miscellanea Rolando Bandinelli, Papa Alessandro III*, ed. F. Liotta (Accademia Senesi degli Intronati; Siena 1986) 85–151. For a valuable and comprehensive treatment of papal rescripts and the canonists, see H. Dondorp, 'Review of Papal Rescripts in the Canonists' Teaching', ZRG Kan.Abt. 76 (1990) 172–253, and 77 (1991) 32–109; cf. Brigitte Meduna, *Studien zum Formular der päpstlichen Justizbriefe von Alexander III. bis Innocenz III. (1159–1216): Die non obstantibus-Formel* (Sb Vienna 536; Vienna 1989).

tor or a deputy decided to suppress or alter the letter in the light of the defendant's submissions.[16]

The Office of a Judge Delegate

Setting aside the difficulties that judges might encounter when their cases involved eminent ecclesiastics and powerful secular interests, the short decretal quoted above illustrates the essential elements of delegated jurisdiction.[17] The judge delegate acted in the pope's name; he could summon litigants and witnesses under ecclesiastical censure; he could reach an amicable settlement between the parties. (In fact, in many cases, as in the example above, the first instruction was to reach a compromise; only when the parties failed to agree, was the judge to proceed 'judicialiter'.) He could impose sentence, and instruct the local bishop to execute the mandate. Yet, although certain ecclesiastics were regularly nominated, they did not form a local papal magistracy. Every commission was individual and specific: it nominated judges to act in a particular case between named parties, and the judges' authority terminated with the conclusion of the case.[18] While it lasted, however, the delegate's authority was a reflection of papal jurisdictional supremacy. As Alexander III declared to John of Salisbury, bishop of Chartres (1176–1180), 'a judge delegated by us exercises our authority', and this judge took precedence over bishops and even over papal legates in the conduct of the case committed to him.[19]

The normal practice was to appoint two or three judges simultaneously, with the proviso that where one could not act the other was empowered to conclude the case—'but if either of you cannot participate, either one of you may proceed to hear the case'. It was also possible for one of the principal

16. *Audientia litterarum contradictarum*, DDC 1.1387–1399; see Sayers, *Papal Judges Delegate* 55–56; Peter Herde, *Audientia litterarum contradictarum: Untersuchungen über die päpstlichen Justizbriefe und die päpstliche Delegationsgerichtsbarkeit vom 13. bis zum Beginn des 16. Jahrhunderts* (2 vols. Bibliothek des Deutschen Historischen Instituts in Rom 31–32; Tübingen 1970).

17. Brundage, *Medieval Origins* 135–137, 376–389. Sayers, *Papal Judges Delegate* 148–150; Katherine Christensen, '"Rescriptum auctoritatis uestre": A Judge Delegate's Report to Pope Alexander III', *The Two Laws: Studies in Medieval Legal History Dedicated to Stephan Kuttner*, ed. Laurent Mayali and Stephanie A. J. Tibbetts (Studies in Medieval and Early Modern Canon Law 1; Washington, D.C. 1990) 40–54; Harry Dondorp, 'Review of Papal Rescripts in the Canonists' Teaching', ZRG Kan. Abt. 76 (1990) 172–253, and Dondorp, 'Review of Papal Rescripts in the Canonists, Part II', ZRG Kan. Abt. 77 (1991) 32–110 at 51–60.

18. Alexander III to Bishop Arnulf of Lisieux, March 5, 1177, 1 Comp. 1.21.14 (X 1.29.9; JL 14219).

19. Pope Alexander III to Bishop John of Chartres, 1 Comp. 1.21.16 (X 1.29.11, JL 13835), and Pope Alexander III to the same bishop of Chartres, 1 Comp. 1.21.2 (X 1.29.1, JL 13770) (wrongly addressed to Exeter in 1 Comp., to London in X, and to Bath or Exeter in JL); Pope Celestine III to Master Columban, 2 Comp. 1.13.1 (X 1.30.2, JL 17667); Pope Innocent III to Archbishop Robert of Rouen, Sept. 1, 1210, 4 Comp. 1.2.1 (X 1.3.24, Potth. 4072). On these decretal collections, see Kenneth Pennington, 'Decretal Collections 1190–1234', *The History of Canon Law in the Classical Period, 1140–1234: From Gratian to the Decretals of Pope Gregory IX* (History of Medieval Canon Law; Washington, D.C. 2008) 293–317.

judges to sub-delegate all or part of the process to a member of his own staff or to any other competent person: 'he can lawfully delegate the beginning, the middle, and the end of the case committed to him, not only jointly but separately'.[20]

The growth and standardization of the system of delegated jurisdiction can be traced through the decretal collections. The local judges conducted their cases in accordance with generally applied rules of procedure, which were progressively refined through the twelfth and early thirteenth centuries. Roman law had provided little explicit guidance on the exercise of delegated jurisdiction, so that many problems of practice and authority arose in the conduct of cases that necessitated authoritative definition. As questions of procedure or substance arose in specific cases, judges requested advice and clarification from the papal curia. One well-known and highly important response from Pope Alexander III to Bishop Richard of Winchester in July 1177 illustrates not only the practice of consultation but also the high standard of professional expertise involved in the process. The papal rescript survives intact in many early English decretal collections, where it is provided with a descriptive heading and marginal rubrics calling attention to the various questions defined in the letter. The summary given below is taken from the unpublished collection of decretals that belonged to the Augustinian house of Bridlington.[21] Under the general title 'Quot iudicibus et in quibus delegatus possit delegare' ('To how many judges and in what circumstances may a [judge] delegate sub-delegate') the decretal is divided into eight segments, of which the first six deal with judges delegate and the judicial process:[22]

(a) 'Delegatus condelegato causam delegare potest etiam si hoc in litteris non apponatur, sed non appellatione remota': a delegate can sub-delegate to

20. 'Licite possit et principium, et finem, et medium causae sibi commissae, non solum coniunctim, sed etiam divisum delegare'. Innocent III to Archbishop Hubert Walter of Canterbury, March 27, 1204, 3 Comp. 1.18.6 (X 1.29.27, Potth. 2163); see Alexander III to Bishop [Gilbert] of London, 1 Comp. 1.21.4 (X 1.29.3, JL 13990); Alexander III to Archbishop Richard of Canterbury, 1 Comp. 1.21.7 (X 1.29.6, JL 13796); and Alexander III to Bishop Richard of Winchester, July 21, 1177, 2 Comp. 1.12.1 (X 1.29.18, JL 14156). For a full discussion of the procedure in judge-delegate courts, see Sayers, *Papal Judges Delegate* 42–99; see also Helmholz, 'Canonists and Standards of Impartiality'; Stanley Chodorow, 'Dishonest Litigation in the Church Courts', *Law, Church and Society: Essays in Honor of Stephan Kuttner*, ed. Kenneth Pennington and Robert Somerville (The Middle Ages; Philadelphia 1977) 187–206.

21. See Charles Duggan, 'Decretal Collections from Gratian's *Decretum* to the *Compilationes antiquae*: The Making of the New Case Law', Hartmann and Pennington *History* 246–292 at 261–262.

22. Oxford, Bodleian Library 357, fol. 85v (Bridl. 23). For the component parts, cf. JL 14156 (parts a, b, d–f, h), 14152 (part c), 14154 (part g), discussed in Charles Duggan, 'Papal Judges Delegate and the Making of the "New Law" in the Twelfth Century', *Cultures of Power: Lordship, Status, and Process in Twelfth-Century Europe*, ed. Thomas Bisson (Philadelphia 1995) 172–199 at 178–180, reprinted in Charles Duggan, *Decretals and the Creation of 'New Law' in the Twelfth Century: Judges, Judgements, Equity and Law* (Aldershot 1998) no. I.

one or more others, to hear and resolve the matter at issue or to hear statements and take evidence, while reserving judgment to himself. Everything is subject to his will and satisfaction, though he cannot delegate a case *appellatione postposita,* even if it was commissioned to him *appellatione remota*—without leave of appeal. And if a case is commissioned to two judges, one of them can commit judgment to his colleague or to another, even if the commission does not state that one can proceed without the other.

(b) 'Si quis crimen obicit testi, qui contra eum producitur': if anyone imputes a crime against a witness brought against him, of such a nature that he could prevent him bearing witness in a civil case, his objection shall be heard; and if it can be proved in civil process, the witness cannot be admitted to give testimony against him, but neither should he be punished because of it.

(c) 'Inhibita appellatione, deferendum est appellationi facte ex incidenti quaestione, sine qua principalis causa non poterit terminari': the question is, should a case be left undecided when appeal has been made on an incidental question, even though the principal matter was commissioned without leave of appeal? If the question arising is such that the principal issue cannot be decided without it, the hearing of the whole case should be intermitted in deference to the appeal, until the superior judge, to whom appeal was made, decides otherwise about the whole affair—'aliter de tota causa disponat'.

(d) 'Si diverse littere impetrantur diversis iudicibus, priores preiudicant': if a litigant secures letters of commission from the apostolic see, and his adversary has the same matter commissioned to other judges, the former should proceed to hearing and settlement, unless the later letters mention the earlier commission. But if the earlier commission is mentioned in the later, the case is thereby removed from the earlier judges, since the later were not obtained by fraud—'non sint tacita veritate impetrate'. Moreover, if a case is commissioned in the presence and with the assent of the parties, of whom one has the case later committed to another, concealing the earlier commission and not informing his adversary, the party guilty of such deceit and fraud should be condemned to pay the expenses thereby incurred by his opponent.

(e) 'Nullus cogitur ad ferendum testimonium': the Roman Church has not been accustomed (*minime consuevit*) to compel anyone to testify.

(f) 'Delegatus potest sententiam executioni mandare, si ordinarius noluerit': if the diocesan bishop neglects to mandate execution of the sentence imposed by the judge delegate, the latter, by virtue of his delegation by the Roman pontiff, has full power to order its execution.

A more succinct summary of the powers of a judge delegate can scarcely be imagined. Not surprisingly, this letter, in whole or in parts, was transmitted through the whole tradition of canonical collections until four of its chapters, including parts a and d, were received into the *Gregorian De-cretales* of 1234.[23]

More than fifteen years later, Dean John of Rouen submitted a series of comparable questions on judge-delegate procedure to Celestine III. The reply, *Prudentiam tuam* (June 17, 1193), was widely circulated in decretal collections. Its treatment in the Sigüenza Collection is typical of the way in which judicial principles and procedures were distinguished and defined by professional canonists. The letter is set out in seven paragraphs, of which six are provided with rubrics highlighting their juridical significance: 'Counter appeals', 'The interpretation of rescripts', 'The competence of courts' (twice), 'The office and power of a judge delegate', 'Concerning a charge of excommunication'. The whole letter, except part d, was transmitted to the *Gregorian Decretales,* where it is distributed in three sections through Books One and Two.[24]

The delegate's jurisdiction was not confined to the region or kingdom in which he operated. A case arising from an unpaid debt incurred in Bologna by a delegate to the Third Lateran Council (March 1179) provides a striking illustration both of the international character of the new law and of the long reach of a judge delegate. Following the complaint of Master Stephen of Blois, that he had given sureties for debts incurred in Bologna by Master G. de Insula and Master Peter of Blois (then chancellor of Archbishop Richard of Canterbury),[25] which had not been repaid, Pope Lucius III issued two sets of letters (November–December 1181), respectively to Bishop John of Norwich and Archbishop Richard of Canterbury.[26] The pope mandated each recipient

23. From the Worcester Collection (Wig. 6.2) through the Appendix and 'Bamberg' collections to the *Decretales*: see H.-E. Lohmann, 'Die Collectio Wigorniensis (Collectio Londinensis Regia): Ein Beitrag zur Quellengeschichte des kanonischen Rechts im 12. Jahrhundert', ZRG Kan. Abt. 32 (1933) 123–124, 180–181. Parts a, d, g, and h reached X: 1.29.6, 1.3.3, 3.38.8, 1.28.3.

24. Part a: 2 Comp. 2.3.1 (X 2.4.2), parts b–d: 2 Comp. 2.19.16 (X 2.28.41 *om.* part d, but inserted in Friedberg's edition); parts e–f: 2 Comp. 1.12.3 (X 1.29.21). See Duggan, 'Decretal Collections' 277–278.

25. R. W. Southern, 'Peter of Blois: A Twelfth-Century Humanist?' *Medieval Humanism* (New York 1970) 105–132; see Christopher R. Cheney, *English Bishops' Chanceries, 1100–1250* (Publications of the Faculty of Arts of the University of Manchester 3; Manchester 1950) 33–35; and Cheney, *From Becket to Langton: English Church Government 1170–1213* (Manchester 1956) 52–53, 61–69.

26. To John of Norwich: *Decretales ineditae,* ed. Chodorow and Duggan 113–114 no. 66; for the corresponding letter to Richard of Canterbury: 1 Comp. 3.18.5 (X 3.22.3, JL 14963). For Lucius III's decretals relating to surety and loan, see Peter Landau, 'Bürgschaft und Darlehen im Dekretalenrecht des 12. Jahrhunderts: Zugleich zur Biographie des Peter von Blois und des Stephan von Tournai', *Festschrift für Dieter Medicus zum 70. Geburtstag,* ed. Volker Beuthien et al. (Köln-Berlin-Bonn-München 1999) 297–316. Professor Landau's suggested identification of the plaintiff Master S. in the Canterbury decretal with Stephen of Tournai is not persuasive. When the letter was issued in November/December 1181, Stephen was abbot of St. Geneviève in Paris, and it is extremely unlikely that he would have been called 'Magister Stephanus' in a legal document issued by the papal chancery, especially one impetrated in person ('Constitutus in presentia nostra') and addressed to a third party. Nowhere in his recorded letters was he called 'magister', and he identified himself as 'Stephanus de S. Genovefa' or 'Frater Stephanus' in his two letters to Lucius III (PL

to compel the debtor under his jurisdiction to release Master Stephen from the bond, if the charges were confirmed; and if the debtor denied the debt or interest, he should be compelled to take the oath of calumny (against trickery, deception, or false or malicious action),[27] notwithstanding custom which is contrary to law—'consuetudine que legi contraria est non obstante, iuramentum calumnie subire cogatur'. Even more significantly, since it would be difficult for Stephen to bring his witnesses to England, the respective commissioners (Norwich and Canterbury) were ordered to instruct Bolognese judges to act in their place (*vice tua*), examine the witnesses, and send back their sealed depositions, with comments on the veracity both of the witnesses and their evidence. If the accused disdained to appear or stand to judgment, they should be deprived of their ecclesiastical benefices, and their incomes assigned to the payment of the debts until the creditors were satisfied. In this remarkable case, the guarantor of debts incurred in Italy sought relief through an appeal to Lucius III, and the pope ordered two English prelates to collaborate with colleagues in Bologna, who were given the task of establishing the veracity of the plaintiff's allegations.

Ordines iudiciorum

The *ordines iudiciorum* contain important evidence about the evolution of jurisprudential thought on the role of judges delegate.[28] Concern with due process and proper form is also characteristic of the early decretal collections, which were made for the guidance of judges.[29] The seventh book of the highly influential Worcester Collection, for example, compiled from the decretals received by active English judges in the late 1160s to 1181, contains eighty-one chapters under the title 'Ad informandum iudices in diversis casibus quandoque emergentibus' (For the instruction of judges in diverse cases whenever they arise).[30]

But these collections of current law were made within a rapidly evolving context of contemporary jurisprudence, in which rules of procedure derived

211 nos 82 and 86). Nor is there any evidence to suggest that the plaintiff in the Norwich letter (Master Stephen of Blois) was the well-known Master Peter of Blois, the defaulting debtor in the Canterbury letter. On suretyship in the broader European context, see Kenneth Pennington, 'The Ius commune, Suretyship, and Magna carta', RIDC 11 (2000) 255–274.

27. Later defined by Tancred, *Ordo judiciarus* 201–202: 'Juramentum calumniae est, cum quis jurat se bona fide et non calumniandi animo agere vel respondere'. For its introduction into canon law, see Anne J. Duggan, '"Justinian's laws, not the Lord's": Eugenius III and the Learned Laws', *Eugenius III, the Cistercian Pope*, ed. Andrew Jotischky and Iben Fonnesberg-Schmidt (in press).

28. Litewski, *Zivilprozeß* 41, 84–97, and passim.

29. See Pennington, 'Jurisprudence of Procedure'.

30. A similar interest in process is evident in the treatment of decretals in the *Collectio Seguntina*; see Duggan, 'Decretal Collections' 290–291.

from Roman law were adduced to provide the foundation of canonical process. From the early twelfth century, there existed a close symbiosis between canonical process and the civil law. The first known treatise on judicial procedure was composed by the Bolognese civilian Bulgarus (1125–1141) for Cardinal Aimeric, chancellor of the Roman Church (1123–41);[31] the first handbook compiled in England (ca. 1140–1160), the (Pseudo)-*Ulpianus de edendo,* was devised in the circle of the Lombard Master Vacarius, who introduced the teaching of Roman law to England in the 1140s.[32] Its twenty-two titles defining the judicial process from the formulation of claim by a plaintiff (Title 1, *De edendo*) to judgments, arbitrations, judges, and appeals (Titles 19–22, *De sententiis, De arbitriis, De iudicibus, De appellationibus*) were derived from the *Codex Justinianus.*[33] Although constructed as an academic model, it circulated in England, the Anglo-Norman world, Lotharingia, and northern Italy and was absorbed into the teaching and practice of canon law. Its influence can be found in the *Olim* (after 1177), which cites papal decretals,[34] in the *Iudicandi formam,* compiled in Westphalia (mid-1170s), which cites the *Decretum,* the *Codex,* and the *Digest;*[35] in *Quia iudiciorum quedam sunt preparatoria* (the so-called *Ordo Bambergensis*), compiled in England or Ireland (after 1182), which attempted an integration of civil and decretal law;[36] and in the very influential *Editio sine scriptis* by Richard de Mores (Ricardus Anglicus, ca. 1190), which more successfully made the desired synthesis between Roman process and the new law of papal decretals.[37] It should be noted, however, that the terms 'Ordo iudicia-

31. Bulgarus, 'Excepta legum', ed. Wahrmund, *Quellen* 4.1, p.1; on the dating and contents of Bulgarus's letter, see Pennington, 'Ordines' chapter above.

32. Peter Stein, 'Vacarius and the Civil Law', *The Character and Influence of the Roman Civil Law: Historical Essays* (London 1988) 167–185; and his essays, 'Vacarius and the Civil Law in England' and 'The Liber pauperum', *The Teaching of Roman Law in England around 1200,* ed. Francis de Zulueta and Peter Stein (Selden Society, Supplementary Series 8; London 1990) xxii–vii, xxviii–xxxvii. Also Jason Taliadoros, *Law and Theology in Twelfth-Century England: The Works of Master Vacarius (1115/20–c.1200)* (Disputatio 10; Turnhout 2006).

33. (Pseudo)-*Ulpianus de edendo,* ed. Gustav Haenel, *Incerti auctoris ordo iudiciorum* (Leipzig 1838); cf. see London, BL Royal 10 B. iv, fols. 1r–9v; Fowler-Magerl, *Ordo* 65–73, and her 'Ordines' 30, 60–62, 94, 102–103, 105. The *tituli* are cited from Ann Arbor, University of Michigan Library 52, fol. 53r–58rb, listed in Fowler-Magerl, *Ordo* 65–68.

34. *Olim,* ed. J. Tamassia and J. B. Palmieri, *Biblioteca iuridica medii aevi. Scripta anecdota antiquissimorum glossatorum* (3 vols. Bologna 1913–1914, 1892, 1901) 2 (1892) 229a–248a (where wrongly attributed to Johannes Bassianus). See Fowler-Magerl, *Ordo* 73–80, and her 'Ordines' 61. For the view that the author was 'un canoniste anglais ou écossais relevant de l'école parisienne', probably Rodo[r]icus Modicipassus, see André Gouron, 'Qui a écrit l'ordo "Olim edebatur?"' *Initium* 8 (2003) 65–84 at 79–84, reprinted with the same pagination in *Pionniers du droit occidental au Moyen Âge* (Aldershot 2006) no. XIII. See Peter Landau, 'Rodoicus Modicipassus—Verfasser der Summa Lipsiensis', ZRG Abt. 92 (2006) 340–354.

35. Fowler-Magerl, *Ordo* 91–92, 273–89, and her 'Ordines' 62.

36. Johann F. von Schulte, ed., 'Der Ordo iudiciarius des Codex Bambergensis P I 11', *Sitzungsberichte Wien* 70 (1872) 289–326; see Fowler-Magerl, *Ordo* 105–106, and her 'Ordines' 62.

37. *Die summa de ordine iudiciario des Ricardus Anglicus,* ed. Wahrmund, *Quellen;* see Fowler-Magerl, 'Ordines' 11, 32, 62, 81, 94–5, 105, 118, and her *Ordo* 114–119. Richard de Mores, successively

rius' or 'Libellus de ordine iudiciorum' did not appear before the 1190s, and the first work consistently called 'Ordo iudiciarius' in the manuscripts was the *Editio sine scriptis* (by Ricardus Anglicus) just cited. Linda Fowler-Magerl suggests that it was the attachment of that title to Richard's work that popularized the term and led to its retrospective association with earlier works that had circulated without that title.[38]

By the beginning of the thirteenth century, the fusion between civilian and canonical concepts and process was demonstrated in the work of Tancred of Bologna, whose *Ordo iudiciarius* marked the culmination of a century of systematic writing on procedural questions. Writing in the wake of the Fourth Lateran Council, which had devoted fourteen canons to procedural matters, Tancred set out to provide a full guide to the proper handling of ecclesiastical cases. He divided his work into four books, dealing respectively with the persons involved (the judge, the parties, and their advisers), the preparation of the case, the *litis contestatio*,[39] and finally, the sentences, appeals, and the *restitutio in integrum*.[40]

From about the same time as Tancred's *Ordo iudiciarius* comes the short summary of process contained in the early thirteenth-century formulary *A. B. C. judices*. Concerned principally with the processes of delegated jurisdiction, it provides a useful aide memoire for judges delegate in the form of the standard letters issued at the various stages of delegated litigation.[41] It is set out in sixteen 'forms', and traces the passage of a delegated case from the first citation of the litigants to a series of possible outcomes:

(1) Form of the first citation on receipt of the papal mandate: the judges A. B. C. to the rector T. of a certain church, setting a time and place for the rector to appear before them.[42]

(2) Form of the second citation, the first peremptory summons: the judges to the defendant, following his failure to appear or send a suitable

---

canon of Merton and prior of the Augustinian house of Dunstable (1202–1242), was an active judge delegate in his own right, with no fewer than 48 cases recorded: see Sayers, *Papal Judges Delegate* 114 and Appendix A (iii).

38. Fowler-Magerl, *Ordines* 105.

39. On the terminology of procedure see Donahue, 'Procedure' 83–94, 104–111; and Litewski, *Zivilprozeß* 70–71, 121–123, 284–309, and passim (litis contestatio), and 525–537 and passim (in integrum restitutio).

40. L. Chevalier, DDC 7.1146–1165.

41. For the extant manuscripts, now in London (British Library and Lambeth Palace), Cambridge (Gonville and Caius College), Baltimore, the Vatican, Montecassino, and Oxford (Bodley), see F. Donald Logan, 'An Early Thirteenth-Century Formulary', *Collectanea Stephan Kuttner IV*, SG 14 (Bologna 1967) 75–87 at 77–79; and Sayers, *Papal Judges Delegate* 45–49. The British Library copy is in a volume including the early English primitive decretal collection *Regalis*: see Duggan, *Twelfth-century Decretal Collections* 82 n. 1.

42. Litewski, *Zivilprozeß* 253–262 and passim.

responsalis to the first citation, issuing a second citation, which constitutes the first peremptory summons.[43]

(3) Form of excuse: the clerk N. to the judges A. B. C., explaining that he could not appear when summoned, since he was judge in another case, for which he had set the date before receiving the citation.[44]

(4) Form of the third citation, the second peremptory summons: the judges to the defendant, warning him that they will proceed with the case, if he fails to appear.

(5) Form of the third peremptory summons, for a person of rank: the judges to the defendant: in consideration of the defendant's status, the judges can issue a third peremptory summons.

(6) Form of the letter of commission of the judge: the judge A. to his fellow judges B. and C.: since he is prevented by other commitments from being present in the case between N. and H., he commissions one of his clerks to act in his place, except for the formal presentation of the case and definitive judgment.

(7) Form of a judge's letter of excuse for absence: the judge C. to his fellow judges A. and B.: he notifies his colleagues that he cannot be present to hear the case committed jointly to them. They are to proceed with their commission, and he is informing the parties.[45]

(8) Form of a letter by which the defendant appoints a proctor: the clerk N. to the judges A. B. C.: since he cannot be present, he commissions a proctor E. (the bearer of his letter) with full powers to act for him, and he is informing the other party.[46]

(9) Form of a letter to the judge ordinary ordering execution of an interlocutory sentence: the judges delegate to the judge ordinary: on N's failure to appear in response to several letters and a peremptory summons, the judges issue an interlocutory judgment against him (after taking counsel), and give possession of the church to his adversary H. to protect the integrity of the property (*causa rei servanda*), pending final judgment, and by the authority of the pope committed to them, they mandate the bishop of the diocese not to defer execution of their sentence.[47]

(10) Request to the judges delegate on behalf of a litigant: to the judges B. and C.: an unidentified source requests the judges to listen earnestly to the plea of H., the bearer of the letter.

(11) Form of a letter recording a settlement made by the litigants: general notification by the judges A. B. C. in the case between the clerks N.

43. Ibid. 272, 282.
45. Ibid. 275–285, 295–298.
47. Ibid. 456–457, 478–483.

44. Ibid. 396–399 and passim.
46. Ibid. 164–174.

and H.: the parsonage to remain with H., but N. to have the vicarage, in return for an annual payment.

(12) Form of a letter of execution of a definitive sentence: the judges delegate to the judge ordinary: having fully considered all the evidence presented by the plaintiff N., they adjudge the church to him, and order the judge ordinary to execute the judgment without delay.

(13) Charter containing the judgment: *De re iudicata*. Formal instrument containing the final sentence.[48]

(14) Form of reference to the pope of a doubtful matter: the judges A. B. C. to the pope (Innocent III), reporting their actions, carried out by his authority. After examining the witnesses of both sides, their claims and objections, and consulting with legal experts, they decided to refer the matter to the pope, sending copies of the commission and the evidence and arguments of both sides, to secure an equitable judgment from him; and they set a date for both parties to appear in his presence.

(15) Form of a letter mandating the judge ordinary to execute the sentence, including the financial penalty imposed on the loser.

(16) Form of a letter of revocation sent by judges delegate to earlier judges: Masters C. and D. to Bishop A. and Abbot B.: on receipt of Pope Innocent's commission, they request Bishop A. and Abbot B. to withdraw from the hearing and execution of the case between N. and H., which has been transferred to themselves by papal mandate.[49]

This dry little pamphlet has small literary merit, but it illustrates what William Longchamp called 'the solemnity of the law'[50] in delegated jurisdiction and the role of the judge delegate in the establishment of formal canonical process. 'The judges delegate were not simply passive agents of papal authority. Their judgments helped to shape the law in their own regions; their questions to the curia elicited definitions on difficult or contentious points of law or procedure; and the collections of decretals compiled in the households of notable English judges delegate provided the sources from which the new decretal law of the entire Latin Church derived'.[51] The office and functions of the papal judge delegate were created by the interplay of current practice in the courts, academic debate in the schools of law, and papal and conciliar

---

48. Ibid. 475–478, 482, 492, 506, 534.

49. Logan, 'Early Thirteenth-Century Formulary' 77 n.4.

50. William de Longchamp, *Practica legum et decretorum* (c. 1183–89), ed. E. Caillemer, 'Le droit civil dans les provinces Anglo-Normandes au xiie siècle', *Mémoires de l'Académie nationale des Sciences, Arts et Belles-Lettres de Caen* (1883) 157–226, c. 6 at p. 205: 'In all legal transactions, the order and solemnity of the law are to be observed'. Litewski, *Zivilprozeß* 52–53, 217–18, 311–312, 330–331, and passim.

51. Duggan, 'Papal Judges Delegate' 178.

definitions. As Thomas Bisson has observed: 'A dynamic and inexorable logic impelled clerks newly schooled in Gratian, the decretals, and canonist cases to prescribe their procedures, to expect written instructions, and to seek to synthesise their expertise in judicial process, appeals and (in the words of *Wigorniensis*) the "instruction of judges in diverse cases".'[52]

Papal judges delegate became less important in the later Middle Ages. They were, however, crucial players in the development and evolution of ecclesiastical courts in the twelfth and thirteenth centuries.

52. Thomas N. Bisson, 'Introduction' *Culture, Power and Personality in Medieval France* (London 1991) 4.

PART 2

The Structure and Practice of the Courts in Several Lands

8

The Ecclesiastical Courts: Introduction

Charles Donahue Jr.

Historians of medieval canon law in the twentieth century paid less attention to case material (with the exception of papal decretals) than they
did to legislative and doctrinal material, less attention to archival material than to manuscript material. The reasons for this relative neglect of
case and archival material are complicated and need not concern us here.
So much needs to be done in so many areas that one can hardly criticize
scholars for focusing on one thing that ought to be done rather than another thing that ought to be done. What needs asserting is that the history
of medieval canon law as a legal system is not going to be written until we
have a better idea than we do now of how law and practice fitted together,
how the various doctrines of the academic law shaped and were shaped
by the societies within which they were applied, and what role canon law,
as opposed to other bodies of law, played in the lives of different people
across the Latin West during the Middle Ages and beyond.[1]

Some progress has been made in these areas in the various studies of
the interrelationship of canon law and politics, and some attention is now
being paid to the 'consilia' of later medieval canonists, another important

1. See Charles Donahue Jr., *Why the History of Canon Law Is Not Written* (Selden Society Lectures; London 1984).

source of the history of the relationship between the academic law and practical reality. Until quite recently, however, one source of that history, the records of the medieval ecclesiastical courts, had hardly been touched.

Recently, a growing body of research has been published on the workings of the medieval ecclesiastical courts of the Latin Church both in England and on the Continent. A listing of those published before 1992 appears in the margin.[2] More recent work is surveyed in Donahue and McDougall, 'France'.[3] One work is so important that it must be mentioned in the text: R. H. Helmholz, *The Canon Law and Ecclesiastical Jurisdiction from 597 to the 1640s* is a comprehensive account of the church courts in England and the law applied in them between the dates mentioned.[4]

Our picture of the workings of the ecclesiastical courts Europe-wide is still woefully incomplete, but enough has emerged that we can begin to write their history. For reasons that will become apparent below, our starting point will be around the year 1200. The chapters that follow this introduction will trace the history of the ecclesiastical courts in France, very broadly conceived, England, Spain, and most of the Latin-rite parts of Eastern Europe.[5] This introduction will attempt to give a common frame of reference for what follows.

2. The following lists book-length studies and editions published between 1967 and 1992, followed by a selective list of older studies. Adams and Donahue, *Select Canterbury Cases*; Ingeborg Buchholz-Johanek, *Geistliche Richter und geistliches Gericht im spätmittelalterlichen Bistum Eichstätt* (Eichstätter Studien n. F. 23; Regensburg 1988); Gero Dolezalek, *Das Imbreviaturbuch des erzbischöflichen Gerichtsnotars Hubaldus aus Pisa, Mai bis August 1230* (Forschungen zur neueren Privatrechtsgeschichte 13; Köln 1969); Donahue, *Records 1, 2*; Othmar Hageneder, *Die geistliche Gerichtsbarkeit in Ober- und Niederösterreich: Von den Anfängen bis zum Beginn des 15. Jahrhunderts* (Forschungen zur Geschichte Oberösterreichs 10; Graz 1967); Richard H. Helmholz, *Marriage Litigation in Medieval England* (Cambridge 1974); Lefebvre-Teillard, *Officialités*; Simon Ollivant, *The Court of the Official in Pre-Reformation Scotland* (Stair Society 34; Edinburgh 1982); *John Lydford's Book*, ed. Dorothy M. Owen (Historical Manuscripts Commission JP 22; London 1974); Hans Paarhammer, *Rechtsprechung und Verwaltung des Salzburger Offizialates (1300–1569)* (Dissertationen der Universität Salzburg 8; Wien 1977); Jane E. Sayers, *Papal Judges Delegate in the Province of Canterbury, 1198–1254* (Oxford Historical Monographs; London 1971); *Liber sentenciarum van de officialiteit van Brussel (1448–1459)*, ed. Cyriel Vleeschouwers and Monique van Melkebeek, 2 vols. (Verzameling van de Oude Rechtspraak in België 7.1–2; Brussel 1982–1983); Richard M. Wunderli, *London Church Courts and Society on the Eve of the Reformation* (Speculum Anniversary Monographs 7; Cambridge, Mass. 1981). Older studies include: Fournier, *Officialités*; Nikolaus Hilling, *Die Offiziale der Bischöfe von Halberstadt im Mittelalter* (Kirchenrechtliche Abhandlungen 72; Stuttgart 1911; reprinted Amsterdam 1965); Georg May, *Die geistliche Gerichtsbarkeit des Erzbischoffs von Mainz im Thüringen: Das Generalgericht zu Erfurt* (Erfurter Theologische Studien 2; Leipzig 1956); Léon Pommeray, *L'officialité archidiaconale de Paris aux XVe–XVIe siècles: Sa composition et sa compétence criminelle* (thèse, droit, université de Paris; Paris 1933); Otto Riedner, *Das Speirer Offizialatsgericht im 13. Jahrhundert* (Inaug.-Diss. Universität Erlangen; Speyer 1907); Heinrich Straub, *Die geistliche Gerichtsbarkeit des Domdekans im alten Bistum Bamberg von den Anfängen bis zum Ende des 16. Jahrhunderts: Eine rechtsgeschichtliche Untersuchung* (Münchener Theologische Studien, Kanonistische Abteilung 9; Munich 1957); Brian L. Woodcock, *Medieval Ecclesiastical Courts in the Diocese of Canterbury* (London 1952).

3. 338–339.

4. The Oxford History of the Laws of England 1; Oxford 2004.

5. Donahue and McDougall, 'France' 300–343; Helmholz, 'England' 344–391; García, 'Spain'

We may begin with the fact that by the year 1500, there were organized ecclesiastical courts in all, or virtually all, the dioceses in Western Christendom. These courts were usually called 'officialities', a term derived from the technical name of the judge (officialis) who presided over them.[6] While the officialities varied considerably among themselves in organization, subject-matter and personal jurisdiction, and procedure, they had certain elements in common that seem to reflect the transnational character both of the common canon law and of the church as an institution. We rarely find a sentence of an ecclesiastical court that violates a basic rule of law found in the academic writers; we rarely find a court that does not seem to be applying one or another form of Romano-canonical procedure; and the patterns of geographical jurisdiction almost always reflect the familiar ideal type of the hierarchical church: pope, archbishop (metropolitan), bishop, archdeacon (frequently but not always), with room for occasional courts of rural or urban deans (archpriests), below the level of the archdeacon, and for 'peculiars' (jurisdictions exempt from one or more elements in the hierarchy).

At the same time there were some remarkable divergences. The subject-matter and personal jurisdiction of the church courts varied markedly from time to time and place to place. Sometimes these divergences seem to reflect open or tacit understandings reached between the ecclesiastical and the secular authorities; sometimes they may reflect differences in the underlying societies. An example of the former might be the differing treatment of criminous clerks in England and in France in the later Middle Ages.[7] An example of the latter might be the large number of cases concerning informal, 'de presenti' marriages in England and the relative absence of such cases from the French records.[8]

The problem is complicated by the fact that jurisdiction in law and jurisdiction in fact frequently differed; knowledge of a court's legal jurisdiction does not always tell the researcher what he or she will find there. For example, by the fourteenth century the English church courts' jurisdiction over cases concerning lay debts (other than those pertaining to marriage or testaments) was not recognized by the secular courts and was hardly defended as a matter of law even by churchmen; yet the English

---

392–425; Erdő, 'Eastern Central Europe' 426–462. García, 'Spain', seeks to discover what was happening in the ecclesiastical courts in the Iberian Peninsula on the basis of synodal legislation about them. Since it was written, some work has been done on the court records themselves. See Donahue, *Records* 1 VIII, IX; Donahue and McDougall, 'France'.

6. In England, if the jurisdiction was that of a bishop, they tended to be called 'consistory courts'. This term is also found in Germany, for example, Regensburg.

7. See 317

8. See 318.

church courts in fact heard thousands of such cases.[9] On the other hand, the French church courts' jurisdiction to hear 'de presenti' marriage cases seems never to have been disputed, but in fact they heard relatively few such cases.[10]

Not only does jurisdiction in fact differ widely from time to time and place to place, but there are also wide differences in the procedures employed. A great variety of procedures were encompassed under the broad heading 'Romano-canonical procedure'.[11] Some courts seem to have heard practically no civil cases; some courts practically no criminal.[12] Some courts regularly employed recognizable variants of 'long form' procedure; others made use of summary procedures. And there was a bewildering variety of the latter, ranging from the occasional consolidation of terms in a procedure that otherwise follows the long-form 'ordo' quite strictly to the one- or two-session hearings typical of criminal cases in the English archdeacons' courts and the northern French diocesan courts.[13]

Given the state of our knowledge of what was actually happening in the wide variety of English and Continental church courts in the Middle Ages, it would be rash to attempt any definitive explanation of these similarities and differences in jurisdiction and procedure. We can, however, begin to sketch the outlines of how these differences developed and to give a preliminary account of the records that survive from various courts in various places both in England and on the Continent.

The Origins of the Officialities

We have said that by 1500 there were organized ecclesiastical courts in virtually every diocese in the Latin West; the same cannot be said of the year 1200. Indeed, recent research would suggest that with the possible exception of the papal court, there were no organized ecclesiastical courts in the West in the year 1200.[14] That is not to say that there were no ecclesiastical proceedings. Bishops had been hearing cases since the late Ro-

9. See Richard H. Helmholz, 'Assumpsit and *fidei laesio*', *Law Quarterly Review* 91 (1975) 406–432.

10. See 272.

11. See Donahue, 'Procedure' 118–124.

12. Compare, for example, Charles Donahue, 'The Canon Law on the Formation of Marriage and Social Practice in the Later Middle Ages', *Journal of Family History* 8 (1983) 154 n. 40 (no surviving records of civil cases from the diocesan officiality of Châlons-en-Champagne), with Charles Donahue, 'Roman Canon Law in the Medieval English Church: Stubbs vs. Maitland Re-Examined after 75 Years in the Light of Some Records from the Church Courts', *Michigan Law Review* 72 (1974) 703–704 (virtually no records of criminal cases from the consistory court of York).

13. See Adams and Donahue, *Select Canterbury Cases* p. 57–59, 68–71; Lefebvre-Teillard, *Officialités* 71–83.

14. See Helmholz, 'England' 350–351; cf. Brundage, *Medieval Origins* 421–424.

man Empire; disputes were resolved and ecclesiastical discipline enforced in local councils and synods, and from the middle of the twelfth century, papal judges delegate heard cases in many, if not most, dioceses. By the year 1200, too, many bishops and some lesser ecclesiastical dignitaries had members of their curiae who were denominated 'officiales'. These various elements combined to produce the organized ecclesiastical courts presided over by an official that began to emerge in the middle of the thirteenth century.[15]

Episcopalis audiencia

Soon after the recognition of the church by the Roman emperor in the fourth century, we hear of bishops performing a judicial function. The Roman emperors recognized this function as legitimate, and, at least in some instances, enforced the bishops' judgments with secular sanctions. We are, however, ill-informed as to how the episcopal courts worked. We know that Christians were encouraged not to bring their disputes before secular courts and that the bishops had some, as yet quite ill-defined, role in the maintenance of church discipline. Our information, which comes largely from secular sources, suggests that episcopal jurisdiction over private disputes was, at least in some sense, dependent on the consent of the parties, and some of our sources suggest that the bishops played a role more as mediators, conciliators, or arbitrators than strictly as adjudicators of such disputes.[16]

The collapse of Roman secular power in the West probably enhanced the dispute-resolution function of the bishops. At the same time, as the sole remaining representatives of Roman order, the bishops became involved in peacekeeping functions, which were at once related to, and somewhat distinct from, their nebulous jurisdiction over matters of ecclesiastical discipline. By the time of the Carolingian reforms, it is possible to speak of two separate but related episcopal functions that we would

---

15. What follows, in so far as it describes the situation prior to 1100, is at once both well known and highly problematical. The ecclesiastical sources may be pursued in Lotte Kéry, *Canonical Collections of the Early Middle Ages (ca. 400–1140): A Bibliographical Guide to the Manuscripts and Literature* (History of Medieval Canon Law; Washington, D.C. 1999).

16. Adriaan J. B. Sirks, 'The episcopalis audientia in Late Antiquity', *Droit et Cultures* 65 (2013) 79–88; Francisco José Cuena Boy, *La 'episcopalis audientia'* (Serie Derecho 3; Valladolid 1985); Maria Rosa Cimma, *L'Episcopalis audientia nelle costituzioni imperiali da Costantino a Giustiniano* (Torino 1989); Pier Giovanni Caron, 'La competenza dell'episcopalis audientia nella legislazione degli imperatori romani cristiani', *Il diritto romano-canonico quale diritto proprio delle comunità cristiane dell'oriente mediterraneo: IX colloquio internazionale romanistico-canonistico* (Città del Vaticano 1994) 267–276; Noel Emmanuel Lenski, 'Evidence for the *Audientia episcopalis* in the New Letters of Augustine', *Law, Society, and Authority in Late Antiquity*, ed. Ralph W. Mathisen (New York 2001) 83–97.

roughly describe as judicial: First, the bishops retained from Roman times a dispute-resolution function. Second, the bishops had the responsibility to enforce ecclesiastical discipline in their dioceses, a responsibility that many of the early councils describe in terms of a duty to visit their dioceses.[17]

Charlemagne incorporated the bishops in his program of reform. The traditional dispute-resolution and disciplinary functions of bishops were enhanced by their association with the secular power of the emperor. At the same time, the bishops became great secular lords, and like all secular lords of their time, they were expected to resolve disputes and enforce discipline. While certain types of matters were thought peculiarly appropriate for ecclesiastical jurisdiction (marriage, for example),[18] there was in fact an increasing blurring of the distinction between matters to be dealt with by secular officers and matters to be dealt with by ecclesiastical officers.

Councils and Synods

Bishops were not the only ecclesiastical judges of the late antiquity. Councils, both general and local, also performed adjudicatory functions, particularly in matters concerning lay and clerical discipline. The canons of the councils from late antiquity and from the early Middle Ages also suggest that a wide variety of matters of church discipline came before these councils, although we cannot always tell whether they were heard in the form of individual cases or in the form of reports and questions from the clergy. The distinction between legislation and adjudication is both Roman and modern; it is not, however, nearly so sharp in medieval law, particularly in the law of the early Middle Ages. Hence, what looks to us like conciliar legislation may, in some instances, be a generalization of a judgment that a given council had reached in a particular case.[19]

The development of ecclesiastical jurisdiction after the death of Charlemagne reflects both the blurring of the distinction between secular and ecclesiastical adjudication and the blurring of the distinction between legislation and adjudication. Bishops, making use of delegated power from

17. See generally, Noël Coulet, *Les visites pastorales* (Typologie des sources du Moyen Age occidental 23; Turnhout 1977, with a *mise à jour* 1985).

18. See Pierre Daudet, *Études sur l'histoire de la juridiction matrimoniale: Les origines carolingiennes de la compétence exclusive de l'Église (France et Germanie)* (Paris 1933).

19. See Wilfried Hartmann, *Kirche und Kirchenrecht um 900: Die Bedeutung der spätkarolingischen Zeit für Tradition und Innovation im kirchlichen Recht* (MGH Schriften 58; Hannover 2008); Rudolf Pokorny, 'Die Textgattung Capitula episcoporum', *Capitula episcoporum* (MGH Capitula episcoporum 4; Hannover 2005) 3–64; Philippe Godding, *La Jurisprudence* (Typologie des sources du Moyen Age occidental 6; Turnholt 1973).

the emperor, began themselves to delegate adjudicatory power to members of their curiae and to local ecclesiastical officers. Canons of cathedrals, archdeacons, and archpriests (deans) began to exercise ecclesiastical authority in regularly held meetings, known as synods (itself a Latinization of the Greek word meaning 'council'). Regino of Prüm's *De synodalibus causis* gives us an account, probably somewhat idealized, of the operations of these synods at the beginning of the tenth century.[20] Much of Burchard of Worms's great collection of canons, dating from the first quarter of the eleventh century, seems to have been written with ecclesiastical synods in mind, but of this we can be less certain.[21]

The ecclesiastical synod of the Carolingian and Ottonian periods might have developed into the organized ecclesiastical courts that we see in the later Middle Ages, and in some areas there may have been a transition from the synod to the officiality without any sharp break. The evidence now available would suggest, however, that in most areas the officiality represents a new beginning.[22] In some jurisdictions the functions of the synod became incorporated in the officiality; in most the synod remained, transmuted into an institution that was more legislative in character. This remark is particularly true of episcopal synods. The evidence would suggest that below the level of the bishop the transition was not nearly so sharp. Archdeacons began to employ officials at approximately the same time as did the bishops. These officials became the judges of the archdeacons' courts at approximately the same time that officials took over the episcopal courts, or just a bit later. But perhaps because the archidiaconal court met more frequently than did the bishop's synod, the transition from the synod-like archidiaconal chapter to the professionalized archidiaconal chapter was more gradual. Episcopal visitation was also revived, and became in some areas a bridge between the officiality and the synod.

The reason that a sharp break was necessary in most areas is related at once to the decline of episcopal authority in the tenth century, to the growth of abuses that the Gregorian reformers of the eleventh century sought to eradicate, and to the development of Romano-canonical procedure in the twelfth century. With the collapse of the Carolingian order in

---

20. *Reginonis abbatis Prumiensis libri duo de synodalibus causis et disciplinis ecclesiasticis*, ed. [Hermann] F. G. A. Wasserschleben (Leipzig 1840, reprinted Graz 1965); most recently *Das Sendhandbuch des Regino von Prüm (Regionis Prumiensis Libri duo De synodalibus causis et disciplinis ecclesiasticis)*, ed. and trans. Wilfried Hartmann (Ausgewählte Quellen zur deutschen Geschichte des Mittelalters 42; Darmstadt 2004).

21. PL 140.537–1058.

22. See Colin Morris, 'From Synod to Consistory: The Bishop's Courts in England, 1150–1250', JEH 22 (1971) 115–123; Helmholz, 'England' 346–350.

the tenth century, jurisdiction exercised by bishops, like jurisdiction exercised by secular counts, fell increasingly into the hands of local notables, at least some of whom were not particularly notable. Ecclesiastical jurisdiction was frequently exercised by laymen. Where it was exercised by ecclesiastics, it was frequently indistinguishable from secular jurisdiction. Looking back on this period, the reformers claimed that it was one of total collapse of ecclesiastical discipline.

The reformers of the eleventh century sought to revive the ecclesiastical jurisdiction of the past, but sharply to separate it from secular jurisdiction. Episcopal visitation was revived; in many areas bishops regained control of the synods. It was also made clear that the bishop's jurisdiction in no way partook of secular jurisdiction. This latter point is most strikingly illustrated by the ordinance of William the Conqueror separating episcopal jurisdiction from that of the hundred courts in England.[23] A necessary concomitant of the enhancement of episcopal authority was that the ecclesiastical jurisdiction that had fallen into the hands of lesser ecclesiastics or even laymen had to be either recaptured or bypassed. The development of Romano-canonical procedure in the twelfth century provided the opportunity for it to be bypassed.

The first development that led to the establishment of the officialities was the extraordinary increase in appeals to the papacy and concomitant papal delegations in the mid-twelfth century. The cases brought to the papacy provided an opportunity for the pope not only to clarify and expand the substantive law of the church but also to create—the word does not seem too strong—a new form of procedure for the delegates to use. This procedure was described in increasingly sophisticated 'ordines', and by the beginning of the thirteenth century it was possible to outline a procedure, radically different from that of the old synods, that could be followed in every type of case.[24]

Imitating the papal court, local bishops came to employ the same procedure in cases brought before them without reference to or from the papacy.[25] A striking illustration of this phenomenon is given in the surviving documents from the curia of Hubert Walter, archbishop of Canterbury (1193–1205), discussed above in my essay on procedure. The documentation from Walter's court makes clear that Walter and those surrounding

---

23. See Colin Morris, 'William I and the Church Courts', EHR 82 (1967) 449–463.

24. See Donahue, 'Procedure' above.

25. Winfried Trusen, 'Die gelehrte Gerichtsbarkeit der Kirche' in Coing, *Handbuch* 1 472, suggests that the papacy required the bishops to follow the new procedure, citing a letter of Pope Celestine II to the bishop of Paris, 2 Comp. 2.2.5 (= X 2.2.9).

him were acquainted with the 'ordo' and that they were using it. The documentation also makes clear, however, that Walter's was still not an organized officiality, as that term will come to be understood in the later years of the thirteenth century.

The reason that we cannot speak of an organized officiality in Hubert Walter's time is that we have no evidence of a regularly sitting court staffed by professionals.[26] Like the pope, Walter relied on ad hoc delegations to get cases heard. Each case called for the creation, in some sense, of a new court. There were a number of men trained in canon law in Walter's curia, and they seem to have served frequently as judges and examiners in cases brought before him. Each case, however, depended on a separate delegation.

We also know that Walter and his successor Stephen Langton on several occasions designated a member of their curia as their 'officialis'. These delegations, however, seem to have been delegations of full episcopal power, not simply judicial power, and these delegations, too, seem to have been ad hoc, frequently made when the archbishop was about to be absent from the province. Walter's and Langton's 'officialis', then, was more like what a later age would call a vicar general.[27]

In the case of Canterbury, the development of the 'officialis' of the late twelfth and early thirteenth century into the judge of a regularly sitting ecclesiastical court does not come until the middle of the thirteenth century, and it is connected with the separation of the archbishop's metropolitical court (the Court of Arches) from his diocesan court for the diocese of Canterbury. The first run of records of a court that can clearly be described as those of the officiality of Canterbury (the metropolitical court) dates from the vacancy of the see following the death of Boniface of Savoy in 1270.[28]

The origin of the officiality of Canterbury is one of the few that we can date with some precision, but the pattern of survival of records on the Continent suggests a similar time period for the development of officialities there. As in England, we get references to bishops' officials from the end of the twelfth century onwards. We should be careful, however,

---

26. Trusen, 'Gerichtsbarkeit der Kirche' 469, 473, associates the creation of the officialities with 'Romana ecclesia' (= VI 2.15.3, Innocent IV, 1246), which makes clear that appeal does not lie from the official to the bishop who appointed him. This date fits well with what we are to suggest in the next paragraphs. We are reluctant, however, to make the definition of an officiality depend on this characteristic alone.

27. Adams and Donahue, *Select Canterbury Cases* 7–8.

28. Individual records that strongly suggest that the development took place in the 1250s survive at Hereford. Donahue, *Records* 2 II/01a/3/3. For the 1270 vacancy, see Adams and Donhaue, *Select Canterbury Cases* 37–72, 49–337.

not to assume that this means that the official is the principal judicial officer of the bishop conducting a regularly sitting court. The first surviving records of a regularly sitting episcopal court in France come from the diocese of Mende and date from the 1270s.[29] The development in Italy may have been a bit earlier. There are surviving records from Pisa in the 1230s that suggest that the archbishop's court had been organized by that time.[30] Here, however, as was usual in Italy throughout the Middle Ages, no distinction was made between the official and the bishop's vicar general, and the judge of the court was called 'vicar' not 'official'. The same pattern prevailed in the medieval kingdom of Hungary, while the medieval kingdom of Poland had an official more on the French model.[31]

Concomitant with the rise of the officialities came a decline of the institution of papal judges delegate. This is not to say, of course, that delegations did not occur throughout the Middle Ages, but the quantity of them seems to have become considerably less in the fourteenth century than it was in the thirteenth. In the fourteenth century, too, bishops who received delegations tended to redelegate the cases to their officials. By the end of the thirteenth century, the world of learned amateurs that we see in the late twelfth and early thirteenth centuries has become a world of professionals. In many, if not most, dioceses, the officiality has been established.

The Records of the Officialities

Before we can begin to outline the similarities and differences among the various officialities, we must outline the principal sources of our information. The records of the officialities can be misleading. What looks at first glance like differences among the courts may only be differences among the types of records kept or the types of records that have survived. A register may record only criminal cases, but that does not mean that the court heard no civil cases. There may have been a civil register, now lost, or it may have been the practice to keep records of the civil cases in files of documents (libels, depositions, etc.) with the 'acta' written on the back, as was done in some periods for the consistory court at York.[32]

Nonetheless and despite these difficulties, the records of the courts themselves are our best evidence of what the courts were actually doing. While statutory material, formularies, styles of court, manuals of proce-

---

29. See Donahue and McDougall, 'France' 306.
30. See Dolezalek, *Imbreviaturbuch* 43–71, describes procedure in the Pisan ecclesiastical court.
31. Erdő, 'Eastern Central Europe' 433–439.
32. See Donahue, 'Stubbs vs. Maitland' 657 and nn. 56, 58.

dure, and references in other types of documents must be combed to give us clues as to the activity of the courts that have left no archives of their own, this type of material has often been shown to be misleading when it can be checked against the actual practice documents. Similarly, it is the records that the court itself kept, rather than the occasional survivals that we find in the archives preserved by parties to litigation, that give us our most unbiased sample of a court's jurisdiction and practice.

An international committee known as The Church Courts Records Working Group undertook a survey of the surviving records of the ecclesiastical courts of the Latin Church in the British Isles and on the Continent prior to 1563. Separate volumes of its reports for the Continent and for England were published in 1989 and 1994.[33]

The reports vary in their completeness. Austria (which was expanded to include the whole of the medieval province of Salzburg), France, Hungary (which was expanded to include the whole of the medieval provinces of Esztergom and Kalocsa) and Switzerland are complete, or virtually complete. The Belgian report lacks Liège, but is complete or virtually complete for Tournai, the one Belgian see that has left substantial surviving records. The report for the Netherlands is complete for the records of the bishop of Utrecht and three of the five subordinate medieval chapters in that city.

There were, however, disappointments: The Group's soundings in Germany, Italy, and Spain suggest that there are important archival remains of the medieval church courts in those countries, but in all three cases the Group reported on one, or just a few, archives.[34] Not only are the Group's reports incomplete for the central core of Europe, but they are simply lacking for its outer orbit. The Group was unable to obtain a correspondent in any of the Slavic-speaking countries, and the report on the ecclesiastical provinces of Esztergom and Kalocsa suggests, and in some cases confirms, that there are survivals there.[35] The Group had no correspondent in any

33. Donahue, *Records 1, 2.*

34. Donahue, *Records* 1 IV, VI, IX. In the case of both Italy and Germany, the political and ecclesiastical history of the country has, in some but not all instances, separated the archives from their original custodians without placing them under central control, as they have been in France. In Italy, the problem of partial secularization of the records is compounded by the great notarial tradition of that country. (This problem also exists in the south of France and may exist in Spain.) See 398–399. Since the Working Group published its findings, a major effort has been made to search for marriage cases in Italy, and many have been found. See Donahue and McDougall, 'France' 322–336. We also now have two impressive editions of German records and a few studies. Donahue and McDougall, 'France' 329.

35. Erdő, 'Eastern Central Europe,' covers the medieval kingdom of Poland in addition to the ecclesiastical provinces of Esztergom and Kalocsa.

of the Scandinavian countries, and its plans for reports for Scotland and Ireland went awry.[36]

Granted the incompleteness of the Group's efforts, it is obviously premature to attempt to draw any firm conclusions. The Group has, however, considerably expanded the knowledge of archival materials beyond the local areas in which they lie and hence has enlarged the opportunities for comparative research. Further, there do seem to be some patterns emerging from the reports themselves that may be useful in establishing plans for further research.

As mentioned above and leaving aside what has already been found in the Italian notarial archives (much less what remains to be found there), the earliest court book found on the Continent of Europe is the court book of Mende from the 1270s,[37] and it is highly experimental in nature. The earliest court book in England is from the early fourteenth century, but, continuous records of sessions before the provincial court of Canterbury survive from the 1270s.[38] Prior to the 1270s, we do find in some places individual court documents from litigated cases and, of course, numerous references to cases and to officials. In most places, however, continuous or even broken runs of court documents, much less of court books, do not begin until the late fourteenth or the fifteenth century.

One can, of course, argue that continuous runs of records did exist, at least from the thirteenth century, but that they were destroyed. Each archive has its story of why no early church court records exist, a story usually relating their destruction to some calamitous national or local event. There is no doubt that much has been destroyed. The fact, however, that substantial runs of records do survive, at least in some places, from the fifteenth and sixteenth centuries suggests that more recent events have not been totally destructive. The failure of any such runs of records to survive from earlier periods casts some doubt on the hypothesis that the destruction that has indubitably occurred is completely responsible for the almost total absence of runs of records from the thirteenth and early fourteenth centuries.

The pattern of surviving records, in turn, supports the suggestion

---

36. Although Ollivant, *The Court of the Official*, suggests that most of what survives in Scotland has been described in that book.

37. See Donahue, *Records 1* III/23/3/1.

38. See Donahue, *Records 2* IV/4/20/2 (describing the Rochester consistory court act book of 1347–1348, printed in *Registrum Hamonis Hethe*, ed. Charles Johnson [Canterbury and York Society 48–49; Oxford 1948] 2.911–1043); II/1a/4a (describing the 'Court of Canterbury Rolls' 1270–1273). Adams and Donahue, *Select Canterbury Cases* 17–18 (describing the same rolls); 49–95 (printing three of the rolls).

made above about the development of local church courts as institutions. Of course, church courts, in the sense of ad hoc or part-time bodies or officers employing canon law to resolve disputes or punish offenses against church discipline, existed in many places from late antiquity. But the development of a professionalized, separate institution—the officiality as it is classically understood—is a phenomenon of the later Middle Ages.

A second point that emerges from the Group's reports is more mundane but perhaps no less important: There is more variety in modern archival practice and terminology than there is in the underlying records. The Group established a typology of church court records in their preliminary report,[39] which has held up remarkably well: (1) There are individual documents used in litigation (cause papers, 'procédures', 'Urkunden' [the last term frequently but not invariably applied]). These documents are almost always in the forms that a familiarity with the handbooks of Romano-canonical procedure would lead one to expect: libels, exceptions, positions, articles, depositions, sentences, appeals, etc. (2) Proceedings in open court were normally redacted as acta. (3) The combination of the individual documents together with the 'acta' gives us a 'processus' ('procès', 'Protokolle' [the German word is used both for the 'processus' and for books of 'processus']). (4) Various combinations of acta and/or cause papers can be recorded in books (act books, 'registres', 'Protokolle'). The arrangement of these combinations can be more-or-less chronological, or case-by-case, the former having the disadvantage of making the record of any one case difficult to reconstruct, the latter creating considerable problems of composition and running the risk of being incomplete. (5) A few books consisting only of sentences or only of depositions have been found.[40] (6) Finally, some courts kept various types of 'housekeeping' books. The Group found various types of account books, ranging from full annual accounts, listing all the receipts and expenses of the officiality, to accounts of receipts of a particular kind, such as fees for gracious acts (documents in non-contentious matters approved by or registered with the court) or fines. There are also books recording the names of those fined and/or excommunicated, and books containing lists of proctors or recording proxies. Account books or rolls of various kinds seem to be particularly common in northern France and in the Low Countries, and that fact may give us a clue as to the nature of the officiality as an institution in those areas.

---

39. Charles Donahue Jr., 'Church Court Records on the Continent and in England', *Englische und kontinentale Rechtsgeschichte: Ein Forschungsprojekt*, ed. Helmut Coing and Knut W. Nörr (Comparative Studies in Continental and Anglo-American Legal History 1; Berlin 1985) 63–71.

40. For example, Donahue, *Records* 1 III/43/3 (sentences); III/07/3/2 (registers of depositions).

There are, in addition to the records themselves, a rather large number of formularies drawn from them, various collections of statutes for the courts, and occasionally a style of the court. The pattern of survival of this type of material is almost haphazard, and the Group indubitably missed a good deal of it because their focus was on archives rather than on manuscript libraries, where this type of material is frequently kept.

The Organization of the Officialities

Terminology varied greatly.[41] Different officers were called different things in different areas. There was far less variation in function. As in the case of the records, if we look at function rather than what the officer was called, either then or now, the common elements become more apparent, as do a few very real differences.

Officials

Almost everywhere, the chief judge of the ecclesiastical court is called 'officialis'. The only exceptions are some lower level courts, where there may have been doubt that the jurisdiction-holder had the authority to create an official, and Italy and the kingdom of Hungary, where the office of official was combined with that of the bishop's vicar general. Episcopal officials were the bishop's alter ego in matters delegated to them. In striking contrast to other kinds of delegates, appeal did not lie from the official to the bishop. When the official has acted, the bishop is deemed to have acted, and so appeal must be to the next higher level in the hierarchy.[42]

The characteristic of the official as the bishop's alter ego led to three institutional developments, which can best be seen in the context of the example of the officiality of the province (and diocese) of York. Since York was a metropolitical court, any appeal from a final decision of that court would have to have been taken to Rome. In order to provide an opportunity for review of decisions within the court without forcing the parties to undertake the arduous journey to the papal curia, the court developed an internal appellate system. It did this by ensuring that decisions by the official himself were reserved for the second or even the third instance. Thus, an ordinary case at first instance would be tried before the commissary general of the official. Appeal from the commissary general's decision would be to the audience of the official. Frequently, the official would not

<hr>

41. On the organization of the officialities, see generally Trusen, 'Gerichtsbarkeit der Kirche' 473–479; Litewski, *Zivilprozeß* 133–136.

42. See VI 2.15.3 (Innocent IV, 1246), discussed at 225 and n. 26.

hear the case himself even then, but would delegate the hearing of the appeal to a special commissary, from whom, in turn, appeal could be taken to the official. (The fact that the official could lawfully do this despite the principle 'delegatus non potest delegare' indicates how strongly the notion that the official was more than a mere delegate was felt.)[43]

The York arrangement was more complicated than most, but it was characteristic of the larger officialities generally that the official would not be the only judge of the court. In England, the judges to whom the official delegated his powers were usually called commissaries, the term 'special commissary' normally being reserved for ad hoc delegation, and 'commissary general' for a permanent sitting judge, who presided more frequently than did the official. In Canterbury, there were two general commissaries, one of whom was the regular judge of the appellate court for the province (the Court of Arches) and was frequently also dean of the exempt deanery of Arches, the other of whom presided over the diocesan court at Canterbury.[44] In the diocese of Hereford (a largely rural diocese), the official presided over the court at Hereford, while the commissary general 'rode circuit', holding a court for correctional matters and minor civil cases, which met in the deanery parishes of the diocese.[45]

In France, the term 'commissary' was not in regular use, but many of the officials appointed vicegerents, who acted in the absence of the official.[46] Unlike the English,[47] the French bishops sometimes divided their dioceses into more than one officiality. Thus the principal official of the archbishop of Rouen sat at Rouen, while the ecclesiastical court at Pontoise was presided over by a vicar of the archbishop who was not a delegate of the principal official.[48] Similar arrangements prevailed in the diocese of Elne, where there was one official at Elne and another at Perpignan, and in the diocese of Cambrai, where there was one official at Cambrai and another at Brussels.[49]

---

43. Trusen suggests that he is a 'mandatarius' rather than a 'delegatus': 'Gerichtsbarkeit der Kirche' 474.

44. Donahue, *Records 2* II.

45. Ibid., IV/9.

46. See further Donahue and McDougall, 'France' 315.

47. In England much the same effect could be achieved by the appointment of commissaries for particular regions. In Lincoln diocese in the fourteenth and fifteenth centuries, there were six such commissaries, one for each archdeaconry. In London diocese, there were two, one for London and the other for Middlesex. See Colin Morris, 'The Commissary of the Bishop in the Diocese of Lincoln', JEH 10 (1959) 50–65. In Chichester diocese there were commissary courts of the bishop in the archdeaconries of Chichester and of Lewes. See Donahue, *Records 2* IV/3.

48. Donahue, *Records 1* III/50.

49. Ibid. III/38, II/00, III/43. For the sentence books of the two Cambrai officialities, see Donahue and McDougall, 'France' 315 and n. 34.

A second consequence of the fact that the official was the alter ego of the bishop who appointed him was that if the bishop wanted to hear a case personally, he could not do so in the official's court. At least in England (Continental examples may exist, but are not known), most, if not all, of the bishops had a separate audience court, at which the bishop notionally presided.[50] In the fourteenth century, these courts became regularly sitting courts, presided over by an officer frequently called the auditor of causes. The division of jurisdiction in fact between the officiality and the audience court (in law their jurisdictions seem to have been the same) needs to be further explored. In the present state of research, it would seem that the audience court, as a practical matter, confined its jurisdiction to serious criminal or quasi-criminal matters, including heresy, and to 'causes célèbres'. This fact, coupled with the fact that in most English dioceses minor correctional matters were handled by the archdeacons meant that many English diocesan officialities heard relatively few correctional cases. While no audience courts have yet been found on the Continent, we do find in the later Middle Ages a court of the bishop's vicar general with a similar jurisdiction to that of the English audience courts.[51]

A third consequence of the fact that the official was the bishop's alter ego was that when judicial business became so great that the official could not in fact serve as the bishop's alter ego in the bishop's absence, another mechanism had to be found to allow the see to be administered. We have already seen how the office of the official in the early thirteenth century became divided by the end of the century between the official, 'stricto sensu', and the vicar general, who handled non-judicial business in the bishop's absence. This development occurred both in England and in France at approximately the same time. We may speculate that this development had some effect on the development of a notion of ecclesiastical separation of powers. Of course, judicial and administrative jurisdiction fully resided in the bishop, but if he had an official who was his alter ego for judicial business and a vicar general, who was in fact if not in law his alter ego for administrative business, at least in his absence, it became necessary to think about the divisions between the two types of functions. In this regard, it is interesting and perhaps significant, that the English officialities became in the process more strictly judicial than did the French. In France, the official continued to deal with a number of non-contentious matters, perhaps the most important of which concerned benefices.[52]

<hr>

50. See, for example, Donahue, *Records 2* II/02, IV/12, IV/14, IV/20.

51. Trusen, 'Gerichtsbarkeit der Kirche' 475, 482.

52. See Helmholz, 'England' 354–383; Donahue, 'Process' (example); Donahue and McDougall, 'France' 315–316, 317, 330.

Because of, or perhaps despite, the fact that the official was the bishop's alter ego, officials never developed a separate jurisdiction in their own right, in the way that archdeacons had in previous centuries. The official could be dismissed by the bishop at any time and without showing cause. Of course, many officials continued in office throughout the time that their appointing bishop served. Frequently, the official 'sede plena' would be appointed as official 'sede vacante'. On the basis of what is now known about the fasti of officials, however, it would seem that it was normal for bishops to appoint their own officials upon their taking up the spiritualities of their office. The official was too important a part of episcopal administration to allow the office to become the personal prerogative of one man.

Other Officers of the Officiality

We have already spoken of subordinate judges, the commissary general of the English church courts, and the vicegerent of the French. The courts of Canterbury and York also employed an examiner general, who was charged with examining the witnesses in civil cases. In addition, the official or commissary general could appoint a special commissary for this purpose, a practice that was particularly common when the witnesses resided far from the court. No examiners general so called have yet been found on the Continent, but the officiality of Speyer employed an auditor who had a similar function, and ad hoc delegations of examinations of witnesses probably were common.[53]

The requirement of canon 38 of Lateran IV, *Quoniam contra falsam*, that judicial acts of all sorts be reduced to writing meant that each court had to be equipped with a staff of clerks. Under the provisions of the canon a single notary could perform the function of two clerks, and by the fourteenth century the use of notaries was widespread in the ecclesiastical courts, even in northern Europe, where the notarial tradition was not so strong as it was in the south.[54]

Organization of the clerical staff of the officialities varied widely. Considerably more research is needed before we can be sure what the reasons for these differences are, but from what is now known we may speculate that the differences reflect both differences in the notarial tradition in the areas where the courts sat and also differences in the functions that the courts were called upon to perform.

53. See Trusen, 'Gerichtsbarkeit der Kirche' 476.
54. Kantorowicz, *Gandinus* 1.59–60, discusses the role of notaries in Italian secular courts. See also Brundage, *Medieval Origins* 371–406, and his chapter on the practice of canon law, 407–465.

In southern Europe the ecclesiastical courts would appoint one or more local notaries who would serve as notaries for the court. While these notaries may have served these courts full-time during their period of appointment, they usually did not abandon their professional connections. Hence the notarial registers that they kept while in service to the court would frequently be kept with other registers of their notarial practice and would be combined with those of their predecessors and passed on to their successors.[55] By contrast, in northern Europe the lack of continuity in the notarial profession meant that the court itself would normally keep its own archive. This characteristic gives the impression, which may reflect a reality, of a larger court bureaucracy in the north than in the south.

In England, the clerical staff frequently if not always followed the division of functions of the court between judge and examiner. One group of clerks or notaries would keep the acts of the court. In the fourteenth century these acts came to be recorded in act books. Another group of clerks or notaries would keep track of the depositions. Occasionally, these depositions, too, came to be recorded in separate books.[56]

In northern France, the episcopal officialities seemed to have done larger amounts both of non-contentious business and of criminal business than they did in England. This tripartite division of functions led to a tripartite division of the clerical staff of many of the northern French officialities. The 'sigillifer', seal-bearer, of the court was in charge of the non-contentious business. The 'registrator' of the court kept track of the criminal business. As the name implies, he normally did so in registers, and these have survived in some quantity for the later Middle Ages. The 'receptor actorum', on the other hand, seems to have been largely in charge of the civil business. Although civil registers are not unknown in France, there are far fewer of them than there are criminal registers.[57] Officers with the same titles are also found in German officialities, and in a few of the larger ones the functions of the 'registrator' were further subdivided between an 'audientiarius' who had charge of criminal sentences

---

55. This fact has made church court records in these areas harder to find. Gero Dolezalek was, we believe, the first to point this out in print, and his discovery enabled him to find and publish what remains the earliest published court book of any local ecclesiastical court: Dolezalek, *Imbreviaturbuch*; see Gero Dolezalek, 'Une nouvelle source pour l'étude de la pratique judiciaire au XIII siècle: les livres d'imbreviatures des notaires de cour', *Confluence des droits savants et des pratiques juridiques: Actes du Colloque de Montpellier* (Milano 1979) 225–241. Fortunately, inventories are beginning to be made of the contents of the great southern European notarial *études*, and church court records are appearing in the process. See, for example, Donahue, *Records 1* III/7/2; VI/1/2.

56. See Donahue, *Records 2* II/4/6, IV/16/3/2. The London deposition books are currently being edited online by Shannon McSheffrey: http://consistory.cohds.ca/.

57. See Donahue and McDougall, 'France' 308–312.

and the 'registrator' proper who took charge of the register of citations.[58]

We are less well informed about the lesser officers of the courts than we are about the judges and clerks. At various times, various courts employed criers, guards, summoners, and other sorts of minor functionaries.

Advocates and Proctors

Canon law, like medieval and modern English law, drew a sharp distinction between those lawyers who spoke for a party in court and those who stood in his stead when he could not be present (and frequently even when he was present).[59] This distinction was observed in almost all of the officialities, at least the higher level ones. The advocate corresponded to the modern English barrister. He made arguments for his client in court. The proctor corresponded to the English solicitor. He filed documents in his client's name, he might present a pleading for him orally, but he normally did not speak for him in court when it came to the final disputation.

Advocates are shadowy figures in medieval ecclesiastical court documents. Their arguments were made orally and were not normally recorded. Proctors, on the other hand, are in evidence wherever the actual documents used in litigation have survived, and they are frequently mentioned in the act books when they appear on behalf of a party.[60]

As a general matter, the advocates seem to have been better educated than the proctors. Advocates frequently had university training in canon and civil law, and in some cases they were required to have a university degree before they could be admitted to practice. The advocates who practiced in a given court frequently formed a college; their number was frequently limited, and because they were of the same class and educational level as the judges themselves, they frequently were called upon to aid in performing the court's functions when they were not representing a party in the case.

Sentences in ecclesiastical courts are normally rendered 'cum consilio iurisperitorum nobis assidencium', and enough survives to suggest that at least in some cases ecclesiastical judges sought the advice of the advocates of the court before rendering sentences. In a busy ecclesiastical legal center, like York, we find the advocates serving as special commissaries of the official, as officials of the various archdeacons in the diocese, and as auditors of causes for the dean and chapter's peculiar jurisdiction. On the Continent, legal experts who advised the official were called 'assessors',

---

58. Trusen, 'Gerichtsbarkeit der Kirche' 476; see Kantorowicz, *Gandinus* 1.56–63.
59. See Brundage, *Medieval Origins* 344–370.
60. Ibid., 407–408.

but here, too, the function was frequently performed by advocates of the court.

The proctors, however, even when they regularly practiced before a court, had a different level of education, and the education was of a different type. Proctors frequently began their careers as clerks of the court. They learned on the job. They then became notaries; after this they began to serve as proctors in individual cases. If an advocate could aspire to become an official or a commissary general, the highest office to which a proctor could aspire was registrar (chief clerk) of the court.

Less is known about the proctors and advocates in the courts on the Continent, but enough is known to suggest that the same general career patterns prevailed there. One development on the Continent, however, is markedly different from that in England. In the late thirteenth century in northern France, but not in England, we begin to find an officer called 'procurator curie' or 'promotor'.[61] His function was to conduct criminal cases in the name of the official. He thus became a kind of ecclesiastical prosecutor, and as such was even more an officer of the court than were the proctors and advocates who practiced before the court representing private clients.

Inquisitions into Heresy

Cases of heresy were sometimes heard before the regular officialities. As is well known, however, in some areas and in some periods, special inquisitors were appointed to deal with matters of heresy. The literature on this topic is large and polemical.[62] We confine ourselves here to one point: The development of the Roman Inquisition and the Spanish Inquisition in the sixteenth century has led too many historians to assume that the direct antecedents of these institutions are to be found in the Middle Ages. They are not. This is not to say, of course, that prosecution of heresy was new in the sixteenth century, nor that inquisitorial procedure was new. What was new was the establishment of a separate ongoing institution that devoted itself to the prosecution of heresy in a given area and had institutional continuity over a period of generations. Medieval inquisitions were ad hoc. The pope or a bishop would appoint an inquisitor, a special commissary of the appointing officer, who had the power to conduct inquisitions into heresy in a given region, or for a given period.

61. See Donahue and McDougall, 'France' 316.
62. See ibid., 318–319.

Jurisdiction of the Officialities: Geographical

In principle, the jurisdiction of an officiality was territorial. In contested cases, it would depend on the parish of residence of the defendant. The familiar ideal type of the hierarchical church would see some form of jurisdiction inhering in the parish priest, broader jurisdiction in the dean (archpriest), yet broader jurisdiction in the archdeacon, with the broadest first-instance jurisdiction in the bishop. Appeal would then lie from the court of the bishop to that of the metropolitan (archbishop) and from there to the pope. Medieval practice never completely conformed to this type, although its basic structure can be seen everywhere. At the lowest level, jurisdiction in the external forum (as opposed to jurisdiction in the confessional) was rarely, if ever, exercised at the parish level, and only occasionally at the level of the rural or urban dean.[63] The archidiaconal level is normally the lowest level of the ecclesiastical hierarchy at which we find a regularly sitting court.

Archidiaconal jurisdiction varied widely from time to time and place to place. Episcopal efforts, supported by the papacy, at the end of the twelfth and beginning of the thirteenth century to limit archdeacons to relatively minor correctional matters and to exclude marriage cases from their competence met with varying degrees of success. In a large diocese, like that of York, archdeacons continued to hear marriage cases well into the fourteenth century and perhaps beyond. In the diocese of Hereford, however, even minor correctional jurisdiction seems to have been taken over by the commissary general of the bishop's official by the beginning of the fifteenth century. The archdeacon of Paris was hearing a wide range of both civil and criminal cases at the end of the fifteenth century, but this jurisdiction seems to have declined markedly in the sixteenth century.[64] In most places where the archidiaconal court was active, appeal lay from the archidiaconal court to the court of the bishop's official, but not in all places. In Canterbury, for example, the bishop's diocesan official and the archdeacon divided criminal jurisdiction in the diocese on a geographical basis, and appeal lay from both courts directly to the metropolitical court, the Court of Arches. While every area has its own story,[65] it seems as a general matter that the jurisdiction of the archdeacons declined as the Middle Ages wore on.

63. See the discussion with references in Donahue, *Records 2* IV/00/31.

64. Pommeray, *L'Officialité archidiaconale*.

65. The situation in the medieval kingdom of Hungary was particularly complicated. See Erdő, 'Eastern Central Europe' 440–443.

The ideal type of hierarchical jurisdiction also admitted a number of exceptions in the form of exempt jurisdictions. Exempt jurisdictions are almost everywhere a product of a time in which episcopal power was weak and the officialities were not well established. Exemptions came in great variety and were frequently bitterly contested over long periods of time. They were generally held by religious corporations—monastic houses, chapters of cathedrals, and collegiate churches being the normal holders—but they were sometimes held by individual religious officers like bishops, who might be exempt from their metropolitan and subject to jurisdiction only of the Holy See (for example, Burgos), or archdeacons or deans, who might be exempt from regular episcopal jurisdiction or more broadly exempt. In Eastern Europe, this latter type of exemption was so common that it might almost be said to be the norm. Again as a general matter, exemptions seem to have had the greatest effect in the area of minor correctional jurisdiction. This type of case was unlikely to be appealed, so the court that had jurisdiction at first instance was likely to be the only court that would take cognizance of the case. Though there are some notable exceptions, as the Middle Ages wore on, exempt jurisdictions tended to be confined to cognizance of this type of case.

Exemptions were not the only exceptions to the ideal type of hierarchical jurisdiction. Members of the hierarchy frequently exercised jurisdiction out of their order in the hierarchy. This was most notable in the case of the pope, who as universal ordinary could hear any case he chose to hear at any time. Higher ecclesiastics, too, sometimes heard cases without reference to the inferior tribunal that might be expected to hear the case at first instance. This was frequently done by virtue of the legatine powers that the higher ecclesiastic might have. Finally, some of the primates (who were frequently themselves legates) exercised what was at once a kind of supra-metropolitan and a quasi-papal first-instance jurisdiction. This jurisdiction was particularly notable in the case of the archbishop of Lyon and the archbishop of Esztergom. In the case of the latter, it seems to have compensated for the unusually large number of exempt jurisdictions that existed in the provinces of Esztergom and Kalocsa.[66]

Personal and Subject-Matter Jurisdiction

Medieval canon law made wide claims about the subject-matter jurisdiction of the courts Christian. It claimed jurisdiction 'ratione personae'

---

66. For Lyon, see Donahue and McDougall, 'France' 314; for Esztergom and Kalocsa, see Erdő, 'Eastern Central Europe' 440–443.

over all cases in which a clerk, at least a clerk who wore a tonsure, was the defendant. A similar jurisdiction was claimed over cases involving scholars (most of whom were clerks or on their way to becoming clerks), crusaders and 'miserabiles personae' (the poor, widows, and orphans). Canon law claimed jurisdiction 'ratione materiae' over spiritual cases, that is, cases concerning the faith, the administration of the sacraments, vows, ecclesiastical censures, elections to ecclesiastical office, and all matters concerning ecclesiastical benefices. It also claimed jurisdiction 'ratione materiae' over questions that concerned the cure of souls, and questions accessory to such questions, such as those that concerned ecclesiastical revenues, tithes, oblations and obventions, and rights of patronage.[67]

If we ask what types of cases the ecclesiastical courts in fact heard, the list given in the preceding paragraph is at once too broad and too narrow. In some instances the jurisdiction of the ecclesiastical courts was limited because the secular authorities objected to it, and the ecclesiastical courts expressly or tacitly conceded the matter. In other instances it was limited because the ecclesiastical courts lost jurisdiction in a kind of free competition with other types of courts. Similarly, the ecclesiastical courts frequently acquired jurisdiction beyond what they seem to have claimed because the secular courts did unwilling or unable to handle a given type of case as satisfactorily as did the ecclesiastical courts. The secular courts would in their turn tacitly or expressly concede their jurisdiction to the ecclesiastical jurisdiction. Finally, throughout the Middle Ages there seem to have been a number of areas where neither the ecclesiastical nor the secular courts had exclusive jurisdiction, but jurisdiction over a given case might be taken by one or another court depending on the choice of the parties and the interest of the court in the matter.

The situation is obviously complex, and the details are best left to the individual chapters. We confine ourselves here to the major types of jurisdiction and the major areas of controversy:

Ratione Personae

Jurisdiction over crusaders and 'miserabiles personae' never seems to have been a major source of controversy. But those records of the ecclesiastical courts that have been studied do not reveal that this jurisdiction was extensive, and those settlements between the ecclesiastical and secular authorities that have survived rarely mention it.[68] The claim of jurisdiction over 'miserabiles personae' may be the source of ecclesiastical juris-

---

67. Fournier, *Officialités* 64–127.
68. It is mentioned in the Hungarian legislation: Erdő, 'Eastern Central Europe' 443–448.

diction to appoint tutors and curators for orphans, a jurisdiction that we
see extensively exercised in some places in France and occasionally in England.[69]

Jurisdiction over clerks, however, was hotly controverted in a number
of countries. Jurisdiction over criminous clerks was the principal issue
in the Becket controversy of the 1160s in England, and it was again one
of the principal issues at the Assembly of Vincennes in France in 1329. In
both cases the result was a compromise, and in both cases the result was
a shared jurisdiction between the ecclesiastical and the secular authorities.
In France, the ultimate punishment of those clerks convicted of serious
crimes rested with the secular authorities; in England, it remained with
the church, at least for the first offense.[70]

Ecclesiastical Property

The church claimed a broad jurisdiction over cases involving ecclesiastical property. Any case that involved property dedicated to pious uses or
the appointment to an ecclesiastical office or revenues owed to the church
was, in principle, a spiritual case and one that should be exclusively in the
ecclesiastical domain. In a world, however, where a very large amount of
productive property was in the hands of one or another ecclesiastical institution, where the appointment to an ecclesiastical office involved substantial secular consequences, and where the revenues owed the church
affected both the value of the ecclesiastical office and the taxing power
of the secular government, secular authority did not concede the broad
jurisdiction claimed.

In England, the secular courts claimed initial jurisdiction to determine
whether land claimed by an ecclesiastic had been dedicated to pious uses
or was in fact secular property of the ecclesiastic (the assize *utrum*). The
secular courts also claimed jurisdiction over all cases involving the right
to appoint to church benefices (advowsons), and over all cases involving
church revenues that exceeded one-fourth of the value of the benefice

69. Fournier, *Officialités* 80–81; J.-Ph. Lévy, 'L'officialité de Paris et les questions familiales à la
fin du XIVe siècle', *Études d'histoire de droit canonique dédiées à Gabriel Le Bras* (Paris 1965) 2.1265–
1294 at 1265–1266, 1284–1294; Helmholz, *Ecclesiastical Jurisdiction* 430 with references. The count of
the cases involving tutors and curators for orphans in Lévy, 'L'officialité de Paris' is made more
precise (77) in C. Donahue, *Law, Marriage, and Society in the Later Middle Ages: Arguments about
Marriage in Five Courts* (New York 2007) T&C no. 535

70. Compare Leona C. Gabel, *Benefit of Clergy in the Later Middle Ages* (Smith College Studies in History 14; Northampton 1929); Christopher R. Cheney, 'The Punishment of Felonious
Clerks', EHR 51 (1936) 215; Helmholz, 'England' 351–356, with Robert Génestal, *Le privilegium
fori en France* (2 vols. Bibliothèqe de l'École des Hautes Études, Sciences religieuses 35, 39; Paris
1921–1924); and François Olivier-Martin, *L'assemblée de Vincennes de 1329 et ses conséquences* (Paris
1909).

(tithes, pensions). After considerable controversy, the church seems to have conceded the claim of secular jurisdiction over advowsons in turn for the right of the bishop to determine the suitability of the candidate proposed for the ecclesiastical office. The church also retained jurisdiction over cases involving the possession of benefices. Jurisdiction of cases involving church revenues remained controversial.

As the practice developed in the later Middle Ages, further mutual accommodations emerged: Cases concerning the ownership or possession of land were heard in the secular courts. What had initially been a jurisdiction to determine what type of land was involved became a jurisdiction in the secular courts to determine the ultimate question of the ecclesiastic's right to the land (the assize 'utrum' became the 'parson's writ of right'). Ecclesiastical jurisdiction over questions concerning the possession of benefices seems to have resulted, at least in some instances, in a jurisdiction that determined the right to the patronage. Further, cases concerning ecclesiastical revenues were heard by the church courts without regard to the one-fourth rule.[71]

In France, where the royal courts never claimed exclusive jurisdiction over the right to appoint to an ecclesiastical benefice, the ultimate results by the end of the Middle Ages seem to have been less favorable to the ecclesiastical jurisdiction. While questions concerning the benefice itself and its holder were still occasionally heard in the ecclesiastical courts, most cases concerning ecclesiastical property and revenues had become the exclusive concern of the secular courts.[72]

Marriage

The church claimed exclusive competence to determine whether or not a couple was validly married and whether or not they could be separated. Ancillary to this jurisdiction was a claim to jurisdiction over cases of legitimacy and cases concerning marital property.

Throughout our period and throughout the West, the church courts had exclusive jurisdiction over whether or not a couple was validly married in the eyes of the church and whether or not they could be separated. The exclusive competence of the church courts in the area of the secular effects of marriage was considerably more controversial.

In England, after a period of much controversy in the thirteenth century, the secular courts came, as a general matter, to judge for themselves questions of legitimacy. This is because the English secular courts refused

71. See Helmholz, 'England' 356–361.
72. See Donahue and McDougall, 'France' 320, 323–324.

to accept the principle of legitimation by subsequent matrimony, and the ecclesiastical courts refused to adjudicate the question of whether a child had been born before or after the solemnization of his parents' marriage. Similarly, in the case of dower (a form of marital property), the secular courts insisted that the endowment should have been made when the couple were married at the church door, thus permitting a secular jury to determine the question of marriage 'vel non', normally without reference to the ecclesiastical courts.[73]

Neither dower nor legitimation by subsequent matrimony was as much of a concern in France as it was in England; hence at the beginning of our period the exclusive competence of the ecclesiastical courts in France over matters concerning marriage was fuller than it was in England. By the end of our period, however, the secular courts seem to have captured much of the jurisdiction over cases that involved the secular effects of marriage, and they rarely, if ever, referred marriage questions to the ecclesiastical courts. We also get some hints at the end of our period that the French secular courts were refusing to recognize marriages that had been entered into without parental consent, a principle that was to become a principle of French secular law with the adoption of the Ordonnance of Blois (1569).[74]

By the end of the Middle Ages, marriage litigation was also markedly different in France from what it was in England. Marriage litigation in France was largely a criminal matter. In England, although there were criminal marriage cases, there were also a large number of civil cases to balance the criminal ones. In France, too, by the end of the Middle Ages, and probably considerably before, marriage cases dealt either with the contract of marriage ('matrimonium per verba de futuro') or with separations. In England, on the other hand, the modal marriage case was a case for the enforcement of an informal 'de presenti' marriage. The relations with the secular jurisdiction in the two countries do not account for these differences; the explanations for them must be sought in differing ecclesiastical institutions and social practices.[75]

Testaments

The classical canon law did not make broad claims for ecclesiastical jurisdiction over testaments.[76] The claim to jurisdiction over property dedi-

---

73. See, with qualifications, Helmholz, 'England' 369, 389–390.
74. See Donahue and McDougall, 'France' 323, 328–330.
75. Donahue, *Law, Marriage* chapter 12.
76. See Trusen, 'Gerichtsbarkeit der Kirche' 486, for references (X 3.26.10–11) suggesting a jurisdiction where the testament was redacted in 'canonical form'.

cated to pious uses did involve a claim to jurisdiction over that portion of a testament that made charitable legacies, but that claim cannot fully account for what happened in some areas. In some areas—England is notable but not the only example—the ecclesiastical courts acquired exclusive jurisdiction over the probate of testaments, the supervision of administration of testaments, and disputes involving them. Ecclesiastical courts also had jurisdiction over the distribution of the chattels of those who died intestate. The origins of this jurisdiction are mysterious but are probably connected with the notion that the making of a testament was a pious act in which the testator had an opportunity to prepare his soul for the next world by doing right with what was his in this world. That the jurisdiction continued in England until the end of the Middle Ages and beyond is probably due to the following facts: First, testamentary gifts of most land were not possible until well into the fourteenth century, and not officially possible until 1540; and second, until close to the end of the Middle Ages the procedures of the secular courts were not well suited to dealing with testamentary administration.[77]

The fact that there are relatively few testamentary matters to be seen in the northern French ecclesiastical courts would suggest that the testamentary jurisdiction of the English ecclesiastical courts was the product of reasons peculiar to that country. Doubt is cast on that hypothesis, however, by the fact that preliminary analysis of the records of the French ecclesiastical courts suggests that some of these courts also heard a number of testamentary cases. Further, the settlement between the ecclesiastical and secular courts in Hungary in the fifteenth century also concedes testamentary matters to the ecclesiastical courts. As in so many areas in this chapter, this topic needs further comparative exploration.[78]

Contracts

The canon law made no general claim to hear cases concerning the contracts of laymen, and, so far as we are aware, no local church did either. In the jurisdictional disputes of the twelfth century some claim was made by the church courts to hear cases that involved contracts made under oath, on the ground that breach of faith was a sin peculiarly within the competence of the church. It seems clear that in the period before the organization of the officialities some church courts did hear such cases, but the cases largely disappeared from the church court dockets at the

77. Helmholz, 'England' 369–373.
78. Donahue and McDougall, 'France' 311, 318, 320, 321, 325; Erdő, 'Eastern Central Europe' 448.

time of the jurisdictional settlements in the late thirteenth and fourteenth centuries.

Beginning in the middle of the fourteenth century and extending into the first decades of the sixteenth century, the English church courts once again obtained jurisdiction over cases involving breach of an ordinary contract that had been consummated with an oath. The jurisdiction was hardly defended as a matter of law by churchmen and was never conceded by the secular courts, but the church courts in fact heard thousands of such cases. The reason that the church courts did this is probably connected with the inability of the secular courts to deal satisfactorily with cases involving oral promises. The reasons for the decline of the jurisdiction are mysterious, but lie largely beyond our period.[79]

The English contract jurisdiction is so far the most extensively documented if we are speaking of contentious matters. The French officialities did, however, serve as registries for contracts (as did some of those in England), and in some periods the French ecclesiastical courts also proceeded against clerks, and in some cases, against laymen for nonpayment of debt. It is not always clear whether those cases involving laymen were dependent on contracts that had previously been registered in the officiality. Breach of faith jurisdiction was also recorded in the Hungarian settlements of the fifteenth century.[80]

Miscellaneous Personal Actions

The canon law did not claim jurisdiction over personal actions where laymen were the defendants, except, perhaps, in instances where there was 'default of justice' in the secular courts. Where the defendant was a cleric, canon law claimed exclusive jurisdiction. The reality was considerably messier. In no area where the jurisdiction of secular and ecclesiastical courts has been studied comparatively did the church courts succeed in maintaining exclusive jurisdiction of all personal actions involving the clergy, and in almost every area they heard, at least in some periods, certain kinds of personal actions involving lay defendants.

The most common type of jurisdiction over personal actions concerned assault on the clergy. This offense involved automatic excommunication, an excommunication that could, in theory, be lifted only by the pope. A careful study of the English records shows that while the ecclesiastical courts in that country heard such cases, they rarely insisted that

79. See further Helmholz, 'England' 377–380.
80. See Donahue and McDougall, 'France' 320–322, 324, 326; Erdő, 'Eastern Central Europe' 448.

the defendant undertake the journey to Rome.[81] A substantial number of French records of such cases also survive, and it may be possible to determine what the practice was in such cases in those courts.

The English ecclesiastical courts are also notable for the wide jurisdiction that they had throughout the Middle Ages over cases of defamation. The origins of this jurisdiction are in a canon of a provincial council (Oxford, 1222), and such cases remained an important element of the church courts' jurisdiction over laymen throughout the Middle Ages. The English ecclesiastical law of defamation has no obvious parallels in the canon law of the universal church. It differs from common canon law and continental canonical practice in that the latter refer to the Roman law concept of 'iniuria', which includes both physical and verbal assault.[82]

Despite these differences, Continental parallels do exist. In some periods the French ecclesiastical courts entertained cases involving physical assault, and in a few cases, verbal assault. They never seem, however, to have developed the sophisticated body of law on the topic that the English courts were forced to develop because they defined their jurisdictional reach differently from the Continental law.[83]

Criminal Cases

Criminal cases were at once the mainstay of many ecclesiastical courts, and the topic about which we can say the least. The reason is that except for heresy cases tried by the inquisition or 'causes célèbres', like the trial of Joan of Arc, the records that these cases have left are terse in the extreme. By the end of the Middle Ages in most areas of the Latin West, there was an ecclesiastical court, largely, if not exclusively, concerned with correctional matters. In France in the smaller dioceses the bishop's officiality did the job. In England and in the larger French dioceses, the task seems to have been undertaken by archidiaconal and exempt jurisdictions.

On the broadest level the claim of the church courts to hear such cases was based on the notion that the courts were charged with the correction of sin (jurisdiction 'ratione peccati').[84] The claim proves too much because virtually every secular crime is also a sin; yet the church courts rarely claimed jurisdiction to deal with secular crimes. What will be defined as

---

81. See Helmholz, 'England' 352.

82. See *Select Cases on Defamation to 1600*, ed. Richard H. Helmholz (Publications of the Selden Society 101; London 1985) xiv–xvi. See generally Helmholz, 'England' 370–372.

83. See Donahue and McDougall, 'France' 320–321, 325, 326.

84. See Trusen, 'Gerichtsbarkeit der Kirche' 486, citing a decretal of Innocent III (X 2.1.13) that suggests a broad jurisdiction on this account.

an 'ecclesiastical crime', then, depends on what sins the secular authorities are not concerned with. That, in turn, produces an odd assortment of crimes, most of which concern either an individual's relations with God or the church, or which concern sex: Heresy, sacrilege, witchcraft, perjury, and Sabbath-breaking are notable in the first category; fornication, adultery, infanticide, and sodomy are notable in the other. The one offense that does not fit well into either category and that was enforced in some ecclesiastical courts in some periods was usury.[85]

The claim to jurisdiction 'ratione peccati' also proves too much because not every sin, even one that the secular authorities did not regard as a crime, was punished in the ecclesiastical courts. The church does not judge about things hidden, and many medieval sinners had to answer only to their confessors and not to the courts. Nonetheless, many offenses that today we would regard as private were thought of as public matters in the Middle Ages. Unpublished heresy is the most notable example; sexual offenses are certainly the most common on the records. We are dealing, then, with a society that brought certain sins before ecclesiastical courts. What they brought before the courts differed from time to time and place to place. The criminal records of the English ecclesiastical courts seem remarkably concerned with the illicit sexual relations of the laity; those of the Spanish ecclesiastical courts (at least those whose records have been examined so far) seem hardly concerned with them at all.[86] Given the intractable nature of the source material, it is not surprising that more comparative work has not been done, but the opportunity exists for the researcher with patience and a good command of statistical techniques to tease out some interesting conclusions about the varying relationships between the church, society, and morality, particularly in the later Middle Ages. We only regret that we cannot report the results here, because the work has not been done.

Procedure of the Officialities

We have suggested above that the officialities were founded, at least in part, in response to the development of Romano-canonical procedure.[87]

85. For example, Dolezalek, *Imbreviaturbuch* 89–95, 109–111, 119–122, 127–128.

86. The only study specifically of the criminal records in Spain that I know of suggests that the only illicit sexual relations that the court pursued were those of the clergy: Yolanda Serrano Seoane, 'El sistema penal del tribunal eclesiastico de la diocesis de Barcelona en la Baja Edad Media: Estudio', *Clio y Crimen* 3 (2006) 334–428; 430–508, at section 4.1.4.

87. A fuller, but eminently readable, account of the procedure of the officialities is found in Fournier, *Officialités* 128–287. Fournier's account is well supported with citations to the common law, but it lacks firm grounding in practice documents. The account of Adams and Donahue,

It is not surprising, therefore, that the earliest records of the officialities reveal a quite careful adherence to the procedure found in the 'ordines iudiciarii'. By the end of our period, although the elements of the long-form 'ordo' were never completely lost, most courts had introduced various 'summary' elements into their procedure. This characteristic is most notable in criminal cases and is therefore most notable in those courts, such as those of northern France, where the criminal mode had come to dominate in contentious proceedings. As in the case of substantive jurisdiction, the variations in procedures are numerous and complex, and the details are best left to the individual chapters. At the risk of oversimplifying, we confine ourselves here to outlining two ideal types of procedure, which we will call 'long-form' and 'summary'. Few, if any, courts adhered to the ideal types precisely as we shall outline them here. Rather, the ideal types represent poles on a spectrum. Depending on the court's practice and also on the requirements of the case, a court could and would pick and choose elements from each to arrive at some sort of blend.

Long-form Procedure

Long-form procedure assumed that there were two parties to the case. It thus fitted better with civil cases and private prosecution of criminal cases. It was characterized by distinct stages, and although the passage from one stage to another did not strictly preclude return to a prior stage, the expectation was that the stages would proceed in orderly fashion until judgment was reached. Each stage of the procedure was evidenced by writing, the claims and defenses of the parties being incorporated in documents normally prepared by their proctors, the actions of the court being recorded in its 'acta', and the proofs presented being written down (if they were not already in writing). All of these written elements combined formed a 'processus', which would then serve as evidence of what the court had decided and as a record in the event of an appeal.

The basic stages of long-form procedure have been well described in a number of places, and we can do it quite briefly here:[88]

Citation.   We are poorly informed about how cases were begun. The writers on procedure suggest that the plaintiff (actor) made an oral complaint or presented a written libel to the court asking that the judge cite

---

Canterbury Cases p. *37–72*, is specific to the practice of the Court of Canterbury in the 1270s. Probably the best general account is Helmholz, *Ecclesiastical Jurisdiction* chapter 5 and 604–626, which covers a wide range of English sources; Lefebvre-Teillard does the same for France in her period: *Officialités* 44–86.

88. See the references in n. 87.

the defendant (reus).[89] The 'acta' do not normally record this stage of the proceeding; so we do not know whether there was any sifting of complaints *ex parte* by the judge. It seems unlikely that the libel was usually presented at this time, since the 'acta' normally first mention the presentation of the libel to the court after the defendant had appeared.[90]

The judge drew up a mandate of citation, usually addressed to the rural dean or to the archdeacon of the place where the defendant resided, bidding him to summon the defendant to appear on a day assigned, in a certain place and before a certain judge, to hear the charges brought against him.[91] To prove that he had heeded the mandate, the dean or archdeacon certified the court of his action. This certificate of citation is normally the first document from the case that we have in the files of cause papers, and it is also normally the first stage of the proceedings recorded in the 'acta'.

Contumacy.   At the first session of the court the parties either appeared, in person or by proctor, or they failed to appear.[92] If neither party appeared, normally nothing was recorded, and the case disappeared from view. If the plaintiff failed to appear and the defendant did appear, the case was usually dismissed. If the defendant failed to appear, and the plaintiff did, the plaintiff would petition that the defendant be declared contumacious. A first absence from the court might be overlooked, and the parties summoned to the next session, but continued absence meant that the absentee would be declared contumacious. The usual penalty for contumacy was suspension, which probably prevented the offender from receiving communion and perhaps from attending services in church ('ab ingressu ecclesie suspensus'). For continued contumacy the judge decreed the absent party excommunicate.

Libel.   Once the parties appeared in court, either in person or by proctor (and the letters of proxy, if any, read), the plaintiff presented his libel.[93] The civil libel (libellus conventionalis) contained the names of the parties and of the judge, a brief statement of the charges against the defendant,

---

89. For example, Tancred, *Ordo* 2.2.3, p. 131.

90. See Guilelmus Durantis, *Speculum iudiciale* 2.1.[4]de competentis iudicis aditione 3.1, 2 vols. (Basel 1574; reprinted Aalen 1975) 1.400; see generally Litewski, *Zivilprozeß* chapter 6.

91. Summoners, apparently as delegates of the archdeacon or dean, are already mentioned in England in the middle of the thirteenth century. See Adams and Donahue, *Canterbury Cases* p. 38 and n. 8. Later they seem to have been attached to the staff of the court.

92. On contumacy, see Tancred, *Ordo* 2.3.4.1, p. 135–139; Litewski, *Zivilprozeß* chapter 7.

93. The procedural writers lavished much attention on *libelli*. For example, William of Drogheda devotes over 200 sections to the topic; William of Drogheda, *Summa aurea*, in Wahrmund, *Quellen* 2.2.196–292; see generally Nörr, 'Literatur' 392–393; Litewski, *Zivilprozeß*, index s.v. Klageschrift, *libellus*.

and a request for redress. It was possible at this stage for the defendant to put forward a counterclaim (libellus reconventionalis).

Exceptions.   As soon as the parties appeared in court and the proxies and libel had been read, exceptions could be put forward.[94] Exceptions were either peremptory or dilatory in effect. Peremptory exceptions were those that, if admitted and proved, entitled the defendant to a judgment on the merits, much like a substantive defense in modern law. They might be proposed at any time before the conclusion of the case but were seldom put forward until after issue had been joined (litis contestatio). At least in English practice, exceptions were normally proposed as part of the exceptions to the witnesses and what they said (exceptiones in testes et in dicta eorum). Dilatory exceptions were divided into declinatory exceptions—those questioning the jurisdiction of the court (declinatoria fori)[95] or the right of the opposing party to sue—and other dilatory exceptions— such as those which claimed that the libel was imprecise or that the plaintiff had violated a pact not to sue for a period of time. As a general matter, such exceptions had to be made before the 'litis contestatio', either because the law required it or because the judge, as he normally did, set a term for proposing all dilatory exceptions.

Litis contestatio.   Joining of issue to the libel (litis contestatio) marked the close of the preliminary stage of the suit and the beginning of the judgment (iudicium).[96] The plaintiff renewed his claim or accusation; the defendant then formally took issue with it. Normally he denied all the statements in the libel. Occasionally, he might raise a substantive defense at this point. Immediately after issue was joined, both parties appeared in person or by proctor to take oaths of calumny and/or of speaking the truth.[97]

Proof.   The basic principle of proof in Romano-canonical procedure, as in modern procedure, was that the party asserting a fact had to prove it (onus probandi incumbit ei qui dicit).[98] This meant that the burden of proving his case in chief rested on the plaintiff. The law of proof was highly technical and complex. As a general matter, however, a burden of proof could be discharged by the admission of the opposing party, the sworn statement

---

94. On exceptions, see Tancred, *Ordo* 2.5, pp. 139–146; Litewski, *Zivilprozeß*, index s.v. Einreden, *exceptio*.

95. Recusal of a judge (recusatio) on the ground of bias or interest had the effect of a declinatory exception. Tancred, *Ordo* 2.6, pp. 146–150.

96. On 'litis contestatio', see Tancred, *Ordo* 3.1, pp. 196–201; Litewski, *Zivilprozeß*, index s.v. *litis contestatio*.

97. Tancred, *Ordo* 3.2, pp. 201–207.

98. For more detail on proof, and references, see Donahue, 'Procedure' 83–96; Litewski, *Zivilprozeß* chapter 9A.

of two unexceptionable witnesses, or an authentic document. The first of these methods was the most commonly employed in practice.

After the oaths were taken, the plaintiff was assigned three terms (exceptionally four) by the judge to make positions and to produce witnesses. The defendant could then except to the witnesses and what they said. If the exceptions were admitted, he too would obtain probatory terms, notionally three or four, although there was less rigidity about the number in practice. The plaintiff could submit a replication to the defendant's exceptions and obtain similar probatory terms. This was as far as the procedure normally went, although there was no ban on the defendant's submitting a rejoinder (duplicatio), the plaintiff a surrejoinder (triplicatio), and so on until all participants were exhausted.

Positions.   In some cases the plaintiff's proctor drew up a document in which every statement in the 'libellus' became the subject of a separate clause and to which the defendant was to reply.[99] These documents were called 'positions' because each clause began with the words 'pono' or 'ponit quod'. The defendant then answered each clause, and his answer was written on the document. Usually the answers were brief: 'credit, non credit, dubitat, credit contrarium', etc.

Articles, interrogatories, and depositions.   At each term for the production of witnesses the party having the burden of proof could produce one or a number of witnesses.[100] These would be sworn in the presence of the adverse party if he chose to be present, and their examination would be committed, usually, to someone other than the judge.

Witnesses were examined in accordance with a set of articles drawn up, on the basis of the libel or exception to be proven, by the party having the burden of proof. The opposing party could submit a set of interrogatories: questions to be put to the witnesses by way of cross-examination.

On the basis of the articles and interrogatories, the witnesses were examined separately and in secret. Their replies were written down (usually in Latin during our period) and sealed by the examiners. After the proponent of a given claim or defense had exhausted his probatory terms or had renounced further production of witnesses, the depositions of the witnesses were published, that is, read in open court, and copies provided to the parties. The common law forbade introduction of further testimony on either side after the publication, if the testimony was on the same ar-

---

99. Tancred's account of this stage of the procedure, *Ordo* 3.3, pp. 307–309, does not quite reflect later practice, but it is close; cf. Litewski, *Zivilprozeß* 356–361.

100. On articles, interrogatories, and depositions, see Donahue, 'Procedure' 83–96.

ticles as that of the witnesses whose testimony had been published or on articles directly contrary. The rule was designed to prevent subornation of perjured testimony, but it was frequently evaded in practice. The device by which it was evaded was to except to the witnesses on the ground that they had perjured themselves. Proof of the perjury would then proceed just like proof of an article directly to the contrary of the one on which testimony had already been published.[101]

Exceptions to witnesses.   Exceptions against the persons of witnesses, on the ground that for one reason or another they were barred from testifying in a church court, could be raised when the witnesses were produced.[102] It was possible, however, and common, to reserve the right to raise such exceptions until after publication of the testimony. Almost invariably in our records exceptions both to the witnesses and their statements are raised after the publication of the plaintiff's testimony. These exceptions usually form the core of the defense.

Documentary proof.   In addition to the testimony of witnesses, the parties might bring in documents to support their claim, and these might be admitted as evidence at any time before the formal conclusion of the case had been declared.[103] Oral testimony was preferred to written evidence, however. Even where documentary evidence of an event was available, the practice was to introduce live witnesses, who might, in turn, refer to the documentary evidence.

Conclusion.   At least in some courts, the judge often set a term within which the parties had to produce all further evidence, a 'terminus ad proponendum omnia in facto consistencia'. This term is not described in the standard contemporary procedural writers. It seems to have combined the term for exceptions to witnesses, that for producing documentary evidence, and probably that for allegations and disputations by the advocates.[104] Following this term the judge would declare a conclusion in the case and set a term for hearing the sentence.

Sentences and review at first instance.   Sentences were of two kinds: interlocutory sentences, which were temporary in nature, such as decisions to accept or quash exceptions, and definitive sentences, which completed the proceedings.[105] In both, the judge reviewed the procedural facts

---

101. See Donahue, 'Procedure' 110.

102. For considerable detail on these exceptions, and references, see Donahue, 'Procedure' 83–94.

103. On documentary proof, see Tancred, *Ordo* 3.13, pp. 248–257.

104. On allegations, see Tancred, *Ordo* 3.15, pp. 261–268; Litewski, *Zivilprozeß* chapter 9B.

105. On sentences and review at first instance, see Tancred, *Ordo* 4.1–4.4, pp. 268–290; Litewski, *Zivilprozeß* chapter 10.

of the case; then he pronounced judgment on the issue before him. Sentences are disappointing documents for the legal historian because they usually say little or nothing about why the judge found as he did.

There are also relatively few definitive sentences; most cases never seem to have made it to the definitive sentence stage. One reason for this is that the church encouraged litigants to make settlements and compositions out of court and to drop proceedings before they reached the final decision.

The proceduralists tell us a considerable amount about the execution of judgments,[106] but we are comparatively ill-informed about how it actually worked in practice. A judgment in favor of the defendant, would, of course, normally require no execution. A judgment in favor of the plaintiff would, probably at the plaintiff's request, be forwarded to the dean or archdeacon where the defendant resided and be published by him. If the defendant refused to obey it, excommunication could be ordered by the court, and in many areas the secular arm could be invoked to aid in the execution.

A definitive sentence could be challenged on appeal. It was also possible to petition the issuing court to reverse its judgment by means of a process variously called a 'quaestio' or 'petitio' or 'querela falsi'. As the name implies, the ground of the petition was that the sentence had been based on false evidence. The 'restitutio in integrum' was another means by which a sentence might be revoked by the issuing court. It was granted by the judge at the prayer of one who was injured by a decision rendered as the result of fraud or some negligence, such as that of a proctor, for which the petitioner was not responsible.[107]

Appeals.   Romano-canonical procedure was notorious for the freedom with which it allowed appeals.[108] Appeal could be taken from a definitive sentence, from some harm (gravamen) that had been done to the appellant either judicially or administratively, or even from some harm that was threatened to the appellant (provocatio). Appeals could be made either in open court before the judge 'a quo' or, in special circumstances, elsewhere, in the presence of witnesses. Immediately after his appeal, the appellant was required to apply to the judge 'a quo' for 'apostoli', letters certifying the appeal.[109] Whether 'apostoli' were issued or not, once an appeal was made, the law required that pending appeal, the appellant be

---

106. For example, Tancred, *Ordo* 4.4, pp. 285–290; Litewski, *Zivilprozeß*, chapter 12.
107. See Tancred, *Ordo* 4.3.3, pp. 282–285; ibid., 4.6, pp. 305–314.
108. On appeals, see Tancred, *Ordo* 4.5, pp. 291–305; Litewski, *Zivilprozeß* chapter. 11.
109. See Litewski, *Zivilprozeß* 513–516 and Duggan 230–231.

kept in the state he was in at the time the appeal was made. Until the higher court confirmed or quashed any sentence of the lower court, execution of that sentence was suspended, and anything done after the appeal to the detriment of the appellant by the inferior judge or an opponent would be annulled.

After taking his appeal, the appellant normally sought an inhibition and citation mandate from the appellate court. These mandates normally gave the grounds of the appeal and set a date for the first appearance in the appellate court. Often a sentence of a lower court resulted in the excommunication of the appellant. Many appeals, therefore, required a provisional absolution (absolutio ad cautelam) granted by the appellate court for the duration of the case on appeal.

Once the parties were before the appellate court, the appellant produced his libel. Rather than reciting the facts of the case once again, it was common for the libel simply to state the grounds of the appeal. The petition for relief followed. The appellant then had to prove his appeal and the factual grounds for it, unless the appellee confessed the validity of the appeal. Sentence for the appeal, whether the appeal had been confessed or proven, took the form of an interlocutory decree pronouncing in favor of the jurisdiction of the appellate court and sending to the judge 'a quo' for the' processus' to be reviewed by the appellate court.

If the case had not proceeded to a definitive sentence in the lower court or if an error in the proceedings of the lower had vitiated all or part of the proceedings below, further pleadings might be made and depositions taken in the appellate court on the substantive issues in the principal case. The procedure in such cases resembled procedure at first instance.

Tuitorial appeals.[110] In England it was possible to obtain some of the advantages of an appeal to the Apostolic See while, at the same time, obtaining the advantage of protection from the metropolitical court in the process. This procedure, known as 'tuitorial appeal', is particularly interesting because it seems frequently to have led to an 'agreement to proceed with the principal' in the metropolitical court: that is, once the appellant had proven his appeal and the grounds for it, the appellant and the appellee agreed to proceed with the case in the metropolitical court as if it had been a direct appeal to that court. Procedure in tuitorial appeals was in England one of the sources for the development of summary process.

---

110. See Adams and Donahue, *Canterbury Cases* 64–72.

Summary Procedure

Long-form Romano-canonical procedure is best adapted to civil cases where the parties can afford to take their time.[111] It calls for the judge to play a relatively passive role. It is particularly well suited to cases in which a settlement or compromise is possible, because by the time the case has reached the sentence stage the parties have a clear idea of the nature of the record on which the judge is going to base his conclusion.

Long-form procedure is, however, complicated. If the parties are not themselves legally trained or cannot afford lawyers, it is likely to bog down, and the multiple possibilities for appeal that it affords means that it favors the wealthy and the persistent.[112] It is also not a particularly appropriate procedure where the judge is expected to take a more active role. Where speedy decisions are desirable, where the parties are unsophisticated, where the enforcement of criminal law is at stake, where a costly process gives undue advantage to one side or the other, long-form procedure is less than ideal. These disadvantages of long-form procedure are apparent to us today and were equally apparent in the Middle Ages.

There was another disadvantage of long-form procedure that may be less apparent to us today, but which, though not normally mentioned except in the criminal context, probably also played a role in the various efforts that were made to reform the procedure: Long-form procedure gave the defendant a large advantage. In civil cases, long-form procedure advantaged the defendant because delay almost always advantages defendants; in criminal cases, it advantaged the defendant because the standard of proof was high. Reform came in the form of a more summary process, which varied markedly from jurisdiction to jurisdiction and from case to case, and which combined a number of different elements from different sources.

---

111. The generalities offered in this section are supported with references in Pennington, 'Introduction' 24–29; Donahue, 'Procedure' 116–117 (development of summary procedure); Helmholz, 'England' 380–383 ('ex officio' procedure in England); Donahue and McDougall, 'France' 332–335 ('ex officio' procedure in France); also see Adams and Donahue, *Canterbury Cases* p. 57–59.

112. This characteristic of long-form procedure can be exaggerated. Many studies of courts using this procedure have remarked that they could be quite efficient, and the success, at least in some periods and in some areas, of the ecclesiastical courts in attracting business that was not within their exclusive jurisdiction suggests that they did a better job than did other contemporary courts. In this regard, we probably should discount lay complaints about the delays in the ecclesiastical courts. Litigants throughout history have complained of delays; lawyers know better. For a recent study published in two different versions, see Richard H. Helmholz, 'Undue Delay in the English Ecclesiastical Courts (circa 1350–1600)', *The Law's Delay: Essays on Undue Delay in Civil Litigation*, ed. Cornelis [Remco] H. van Rhee (Ius commune Europaeum 47; Antwerp 2004) 131–139; Helmholz, 'Due and Undue Delay in the English Ecclesiastical Courts (ca. 1300–1600)', *Within a Reasonable Time: The History of Due and Undue Delay in Civil Litigation*, ed. C. H. van Rhee (Comparative Studies in Continental and Anglo-American Legal History 28; Berlin 2010) 73–92.

Some of these elements represented revivals or survivals of institutions that had existed before the invention of long-form procedure. Methods of proof that antedated the Romano-canonical forms of witness proof remained in effect in many areas, particularly in the lower criminal courts. The most widespread of these methods of proof was canonical purgation, in which the defendant swore to his innocence and then had to produce a certain number of oath-helpers to support his oath. Another was the use of groups of local people in a sworn inquest. While this latter method of proof seems never to have been expressly used by the officialities, we find at times witnesses being used in ways much more like a jury than like canonical witnesses. We also find this institution at the accusation stage of criminal cases where the Carolingian synodal witness seems to have become by the fourteenth century the presenting body of churchwardens. All of these methods of procedure have the advantage of giving an essentially inscrutable answer to the question posed at the stage of the proceeding at which they are used and are, therefore, more expeditious.

Again in the criminal area, we find various methods being employed to increase the efficiency of the prosecution. The authorization of inquisitorial procedure under Innocent III had effects that went far beyond the institutions that go under the name of inquisitions (which were confined to particular areas and were largely concerned with the prosecution of heresy). Judges with criminal jurisdiction could and did proceed on the basis of information reported to them ('fama publica referente') to question the party or parties accused in open court. This questioning frequently produced a confession of guilt or a confession of criminal conduct. While the parties to such charges were normally entitled to a written article outlining the charges against them, in lower level courts they rarely asked for such articles and there is little evidence that they ever got them.

We now have the elements of the one- or two-session case record that is so typical of the lower-level criminal courts in England and of the northern French officialities in the later Middle Ages. On the basis of the presentment of churchwardens in England or of the promotor in France, an individual or a couple would be cited before the court and charged with, let us say, fornication. The judge would interrogate the defendant(s). The procedure was technically one 'ex officio mero' in England and 'ex officio promoto' in France, but at this level of court the distinction was without a difference. The crime would frequently be confessed and a penance, normally a fairly light one, would be imposed. If the charge were denied, the case would proceed to proof. In England, proof was almost invariably by means of compurgation. In France, witnesses might be introduced by the promotor, although frequently the decisory oath was used. The whole case would be over in one or two sessions.

The speed and cheapness of the procedure meant that many cases that previously had been the subject of normal instance procedure could be brought as criminal cases. Almost any civil marriage case could be turned into a criminal marriage offense, and if the aggrieved party could get quicker results and more cheaply at that (because the promotor was paid by the defendant and not by the offended party), the incentive to go the criminal route was considerable. Only separation cases seem, as a general matter, to have escaped the criminalizing trend in France in the later Middle Ages. Marriage cases were not the only ones subject to this tendency to criminalization. We find, for example, a number of defamation cases being tried in the same manner before the London commissary's court at the end of the fifteenth century.[113]

Movement in the direction of summariness is not only characteristic of criminal cases. As the proceduralists made clearer the amount of discretion that the judge had in dealing with the stages of the case, many judges experimented with reducing the number of stages. We have already mentioned one, the 'terminus ad proponendum omnia', which, it would seem, represented a combination of what were notionally separate terms to except to witnesses, to produce documentary evidence, and for allegations and disputations. A more radical reduction in terms is found in the practice in English tuitorial appeals, where all the possible defenses, substantive and procedural, had to be combined in one pleading known as a 'factum contrarium seu exclusorium'.[114] By the fifteenth century parties in the consistory court of York were using the 'factum contrarium' in first-instance marriage cases.[115] Already in the fourteenth century, the same court seems to have authorized proctors to combine positions and articles in the same document.

At the beginning of the thirteenth century the records of church court proceedings suggest that cases employing Romano-canonical procedure were largely cases involving the wealthy. By the end of the fifteenth century a substantial percentage of the population was involved in the ecclesiastical legal system, but the long-form procedure would seem to have been used in only a very few cases, and these were cases, not surprisingly, that involved the wealthy and the persistent. It is hard to know whether the simplified procedure that most people got was a fairer procedure than

113. Wunderli, *London Church Courts* 68–72.
114. Adams and Donahue, *Canterbury Cases* p. 69 n. 7.
115. For example, Peron c. Newby (1414–1415), York, Borthwick Institute, CP. F. 68.

what they got at the beginning of our period because we have no basis of comparison. What we can say is that long-form Romano-canonical procedure, although it was a substantial intellectual achievement and one that was to have considerable influence in shaping modern law, was not something that the church could afford to use when it began processing large numbers of cases in the later Middle Ages.

Conciliar and Synodal Legislation

Before attempting a conclusion, let us return briefly to a topic that we left at the beginning of the thirteenth century in order to pursue the development of the officialities as an institution: local councils and synods. These continued in many places throughout the Middle Ages, and in some places beyond that period. They generated, among other things, a large body of conciliar canons and synodal statutes, some of which have been given modern editions.[116] Local ecclesiastical statutes deserve more space than we can give them here; the focus here is on what these statutes can tell us about the work of the ecclesiastical courts. In particular, we ask whether, in the absence of actual court records or of an adequate exploration of those that exist, we can make any kind of meaningful statement about what the ecclesiastical courts were doing in a given time and place on the basis of conciliar or synodal legislation.

Those who work with medieval church-court records have long since abandoned the older notion that the answer to that question is 'of course'. If the question that we are asking is how did the law and the society in which it was embedded interact, the best evidence for that interaction is the records of the courts themselves. If we accept even mild versions of the predictive theory of law with which we began the chapter 'Procedure', then the best basis for making that prediction is the behavior of the courts. Despite these facts, I would like to offer two examples here, examples where we have both the local legislation and court records, both of which suggest, in different ways, that the local legislation alone does offer some evidence of what may have been happening in the courts.[117]

There is a remarkable register of proceedings in the consistory court

116. For example, *Councils and Synods II: A.D. 1205–1313*, ed. Frederick Maurice Powicke and Christopher R. Cheney (2 vols. Oxford 1964); *Les statuts synodaux français du xiiie siècle*, ed. Odette Pontal and Joseph Avril (5 vols. Paris 1983–2001); *Synodicon hispanum*, ed. Antonio García y García et al. (8 vols. Madrid 1981–2007); *Concilia Poloniae: Źródła i studia krytyczne*, ed. Jakub Sawicki (10 vols. Warsaw 1945–1963).

117. These examples are drawn from Charles Donahue, 'Thoughts on Diocesan Statutes: England and France, 1200–1500', *Canon Law, Religion, and Politics: Liber Amicorum Robert Somerville*, ed. Uta-Renate Blumenthal, Anders Winroth, and Peter Landau (Washington, D.C. 2012) 253–271.

of the bishop of Ely, dating from the years 1374 to 1382, known in the literature as the *Ely Act Book*.[118] The synodal statutes of Ely diocese have a somewhat checkered history, and no one seems to have undertaken an organized revision of them as was done in some other English dioceses. Christopher Cheney detects three recensions in the four known manuscripts.[119] While Cheney's evidence for placing the final recension before 1276 is not overwhelming, there is no reason to doubt that the final version that we have of these statutes was in existence before the end of the thirteenth century. It survives in two manuscripts, one of which is known as the *Vetus liber archidiaconi Eliensis*, where the copy of the statutes is in an early fourteenth-century hand, and in a similar collection of material for the use of the official of Ely, where the basic copy of the statutes is in a fourteenth-century hand that has not been dated more precisely.[120] That this version of the statutes was known to the court of the *Ely Act Book* seems virtually certain.

There can also be little doubt that the diocesan synod was an institution that was alive and well in the diocese of Ely in the fourteenth century.[121] There are numerous references to it in the *Ely Act Book*. The manuscript of the official that contains the statutes also contains rubrics for holding the synod. The statutes were known; they may even have been read at synod, but is there any evidence that they were being applied in the official's or the archdeacon's court?

The answer to this question would seem to be 'no'. Court registers do not, as a rule, contain many references to the formal law. The *Ely Act Book* contains more than most. There are, for example, specific references to the constitutions of Clement V on summary procedure, the provincial constitution that formed the basis of actions for defamation, and the provincial constitution of John Stratford on clandestine marriage (1342) (of which more shortly).[122] But nowhere in the *Ely Act Book* is there a reference to the diocesan statutes.

The argument rests on more than the absence of citation. The Ely diocesan statutes contain a provision on clandestine marriage[123] that would

---

118. Cambridge University Library, Ely Diocesan Registry MS. D2/1. See Donahue, *Law, Marriage* 218, with references. An edition of this volume by Marcia Stentz and Charles Donahue is in press: *The Register of the Official of the Bishop of Ely: 21 March 1374–28 February 1382* (2 vols. Ames Foundation; Cambridge, Mass. forthcoming 2016). The page proofs may be viewed online: http://amesfoundation.law.harvard.edu/ ElyAB_AFinal.pdf.

119. *Councils and Synods II* 1.515–516.

120. *Councils and Synods II* 1.515.

121. See Dorothy M. Owen, 'Synods in the Diocese of Ely in the Later Middle Ages and the Sixteenth Century', *Studies in Church History* 3 (1966) 217–222.

122. See *Register of Ely* Citations to Canon Law, 2.1011–1014.

123. As is well known, the definition of 'clandestine marriage' was quite problematical, rang-

have been noticeable in the Act Book if it were being applied, even if was not cited. In common with Bishop Grosseteste's statutes for Lincoln and many others, the Ely statutes contain a general provision on clandestine marriage: 'Clandestine marriages should be very strictly forbidden in churches, whatever sort of clandestine marriage.'[124] Similar provisions may be found in statutes of virtually all the English dioceses.[125] The authority for them is, of course, the well-known canon *Cum inhibitio* of Lateran IV,[126] although English legislation on the topic may be found even before the council. After the portion of the statutes derived from Grosseteste's statutes, the Ely legislator added two more provisions on clandestine marriage. The first repeats the provision of Lateran IV that clergy who participate in clandestine marriages shall be suspended from office for three years.[127] The second applies to the laity:[128]

Parish priests shall also forbid their parishioners frequently and publicly under pain of excommunication, and the parishioners present shall explain this to their dependents ('familiis'), that they ought not presume to contract marriages or espousals without the presence of priests and the solemnity of banns. Otherwise, the principal persons should know that before they are admitted to instruct about their right, they are to undergo a public whipping, and others who gave consent or authorization are to suffer the same penalty.

The injunction to parish priests that they tell their flock frequently about the prohibition of clandestine marriage is quite common, as is the threat of excommunication if they do not do so. (I have, however, never seen the threat applied.) The threatened penalty, however, for those who marry or contract 'sponsalia' not in the presence of a priest and without publication of banns is unusual; it may be unique. The offenders are to undergo a public whipping 'before they are admitted to instruct about their right'. This is a somewhat difficult phrase, but its meaning seems

---

ing all the way from a marriage in which no one except the couple was present to one that was quite public but lacked one or more of the usual solemnities, such as promulgation of banns or the blessing of the parish priest.

124. Ely (1239 X 1256) c. 25, in *Councils and Synods II* 1:520: 'Clandestina quoque matrimonia districtius in ecclesiis solempniter inhibeantur, quolibet genere clandestini matrimonii'.

125. See Michael Sheehan, 'Marriage and Family in English Conciliar and Synodal Legislation', *Essays in Honour of Anton Charles Pegis*, ed. J. Reginald O'Donnell (Toronto 1974) 205–214; reprinted in Michael Sheehan, *Marriage, Family, and Law in Medieval Europe: Collected Studies*, ed. James K. Farge (Toronto 1996) 77–86.

126. Lateran IV (1215) c. 51 (= X 4.3.3).

127. Ely (1239 X 1256) c. 32, in *Councils and Synods II* 1.521.

128. Ely (1239 X 1256) c. 33, in *Councils and Synods II* 1.521–522: 'Inhibeant eciam presbiteri parochiales frequenter et puplice parochianis suis sub pena excommunicacionis, et parochiani presentes suis famulis hoc exponant, ut sine presbiterorum presencia et bannorum edicione matrimonia sive sponsalia contrahere non presumant. Alioquin sciant se principales persone, priusquam ad docendum de iure suo admittantur, publice fustigacioni subdendos, et alios qui consensum vel auctoritatem prestiterunt eadem pena feriendos'.

reasonably clear. Participants in a clandestine marriage are to be whipped before they will be allowed to show that they have married clandestinely and are therefore entitled to be regarded as married.

As is well known, the canon 51, *Cum inhibitio copule coniugalis,* of Lateran IV prescribed that marriages were not to take place until the banns had been proclaimed. It did not, however, change the basic rule that marriages made by the consent of the parties without solemnity or ceremony, without the presence of a priest or the publication of banns, were, nonetheless, valid marriages. Penalties were laid down for clergy who participated in clandestine marriages, but what was to be done with the laity who formed such marriages was left to the local churches to decide. As we will see, the French church, as a general matter, provided that participants in clandestine marriages would be automatically excommunicated. No English legislation went that far. But the Ely legislator did prescribe a public whipping for such people as a condition of their marriage being recognized.

This statute was not being enforced by the official of Ely in the years 1374 to 1382. There are 93 cases in the register, some begun as instance cases, some begun as office cases, in which a marriage is sought to be enforced. In virtually all of these cases one or more of the marriages at stake were clandestine, in the sense that they were entered into without the promulgation of banns. In none of them is there any indication that the parties alleging the marriage were whipped before they were allowed to allege the marriage. Indeed, there is no indication that any of the parties to a clandestine marriage were punished for the clandestine marriage alone.[129]

The only parties to a clandestine marriage who were punished were those who were determined to have violated John Stratford's constitution *Humana concupiscentia* of 1342.[130] A fair reading of that statute suggests that it concerns those who knowing of an impediment (or having a reasonable suspicion of one) nonetheless have their marriages solemnized are automatically excommunicated. That is not the way in which the Ely court read the statute, and the register gives us the court's argument for its rather strange interpretation:[131]

129. Donahue, *Law, Marriage* 230–231, 279–280.

130. *Concilia Magnae Britanniae et Hiberniae,* ed. David Wilkins, 4 vols. (London 1737) 2:707.

131. *Register of Ely* 647–648: 'Cum in generali concilio proinde sit statutum ut cum matrimonia sint contrahenda in ecclesiis per presbyteros publice propona[n]tur competenti termino prefinito ut infra illum qui voluerit et valuerit legitimum impedimentum opponat. Et ipsi presbyteri nichilominus investigent utrum aliquod impedimentum obsistat. Cum autem apparuerit probabilis coniectura contra copulam contrahendam, contractus interdicatur expresse donec quid fieri debeat super eo manifestis constiterit documentis. Quodque omnes et singuli matrimonia inter

The general council has accordingly established that when marriages are to be contracted, they shall be announced by the priests in [their] churches, with an adequate term fixed beforehand within which whoever wishes and is able to may adduce a lawful impediment in opposition to the marriage. The priests themselves shall also investigate whether any impediment stands in the way [of the proposed marriage]. When there appears a credible reason against the proposed union, the contract shall be expressly forbidden until there has been established by clear documents what should be done about it. Any and every person who contracts marriage with another, has it solemnized, or is present at the solemnization of such a marriage who knows of a lawful impediment or has a reasonable ('verisimilem') suspicion thereof shall, and does, incur a sentence of major excommunication in accordance with the provincial constitution.

The problem with this explanation is that the first three sentences quote the canon *Cum inhibitio* of Lateran IV, while the last describes, more loosely, Stratford's constitution. The two constitutions are clearly related. What is not clear is that Stratford and his council intended that the sanction of automatic excommunication apply to those who married during the pendency of the investigation or even in violation of the inhibition described in *Cum inhibitio.* That is, however, the way in which the Ely court interpreted it. Parties were cited and punished for violations of *Humana concupiscentia* if they married during the pendency of a case before the court, even if it later turned out that the marriage was valid, but they were not cited or punished for violations of *Humana concupiscentia* if they entered into an invalid marriage, so long as a case about it was not pending. In at least some of these cases we strongly suspect that the parties were aware of the invalidity or, at least, had a reasonable suspicion of it.[132]

The evidence of the *Ely Act Book* thus suggests that by the last quarter of the fourteenth century the Ely diocesan statutes were no longer being applied in the episcopal consistory court.[133] Provincial constitutions were being applied, but the interpretation of them was, to say the least, free. If all we had were the statutes and not the Act Book, we would get many things wrong about what was happening in the Ely consistory court in the last quarter of the fourteenth century. We would not, however, get it totally wrong. Clandestine marriage was clearly a matter of concern.

---

se contrahentes et ea solempnizari facientes impedimenta legitima scientes aut suspicionem habentes verisimilem eorundem, huiusque matrimoniorum solempnizacioni interessentes maioris excommunicacionis sentencia a constitucione provinciali in proximo articulo superius recitata [a reference to the citation of *Humana concupiscentia* in the previous entry] fuerint et sint ipso facto dampnaliter involuti'.

132. Details in Donahue, *Law, Marriage* 281–285.

133. Stentz and Donahue speculate that there may be a reference to an otherwise unknown diocesan statute about abjuration 'sub pena nubendi'; *Register of Ely* 1014. The reference is, however, vague, and the provision in question is not found in the statute book to which we have been referring.

On the basis of the statutes we might suspect that the courts were hearing cases involving clandestine marriage, and that suspicion would not be mistaken. If we noticed that the Ely diocesan provision about whipping was unusual, if not unique, in English legislation on the topic of clandestine marriage, we might suspect that it was not being fully enforced more than 75 years after it was promulgated, or not enforced at all. That suspicion would also be correct. If we noticed that the most recent provision on the topic of clandestine marriage (about a generation before the date of the Act Book) was a provincial constitution that dealt with those who had their marriages solemnized despite knowledge or suspicion of their invalidity, we might suspect that there would be some enforcement of this provision. That, too, turns out to be correct, though it would be hard to predict just how it was being enforced.

On another topic, if we noticed that there was a provincial statute that authorized the ecclesiastical courts to hear defamation cases and we were aware that the central royal courts in England in this period did not hear such cases, we might suspect that the consistory court of Ely would be one of those places to which a man or woman who had been the victim of defamation might turn to obtain redress. That suspicion, too, would be correct; after marriage cases, cases of defamation are the most common type of case in the *Ely Act Book*.[134]

The situation in France was substantially different from that in England. Diocesan synodal statutes in France in the later Middle Ages continued to be made, and they continued to be organized in a pattern specific to such statutes. In England organized diocesan statutes seem to have died out at the end of the thirteenth century. That the English were still taking local ecclesiastical legislation seriously in the later Middle Ages is indicated by the massive commentary on the provincial constitutions of Canterbury by William Lyndwood.[135] Lyndwood, however, focused on statutes at the provincial level (including, as has been shown, raising some diocesan statutes to the level of provincial in order to include them),[136] and Lyndwood organized his discussion according to the titles of the books of papal decretals (iudex, iudicium, clerus, conubia, crimen), rather than using a form of organization specific to local ecclesiastical legislation.

Not only were the French continuing to issue diocesan synodal stat-

---

134. *Register of Ely* table 6, p. cxxxvi.

135. William Lyndwood, *Provinciale seu Constitutiones Angliae* (Oxford: H. Hall, 1679; reprinted Franborough 1968).

136. See Christopher R. Cheney, 'William Lyndwood's Provinciale', *The Jurist* 21 (1961) 405–434 and Brian Ferme, *Canon Law in late Medieval England: A Study of William Lyndwood's Provinciale with particular Reference to Testamentary Law* (Studia et Textus Historiae Iuris Canonici 8; Roma 1996).

utes, they were also enforcing them, in some cases quite strictly. We turn here to the diocese of Cambrai, where we have, as we do in the case of Ely, substantial survivals of records of the ecclesiastical courts, in this case sentence books from the officiality at Cambrai and from the co-equal officiality at Brussels from the mid-fifteenth century.[137]

French statutes on the topic of clandestine marriage were strict.[138] Such marriages subjected the parties to automatic excommunication. There are two Cambrai diocesan statutes on the topic, one that focuses on clandestine marriage generally and one that focuses on the formation of marriage by words of the future tense followed by sexual intercourse between the parties. Both statutes were being enforced in the Cambrai sentences of the fifteenth century. There are considerably more that fall under the second provision than under the first.[139]

What is different about the Cambrai statutes from the general run of French synodal statutes is that they also insist that the 'sponsalia de futuro' be public. They do not excommunicate those who contract 'sponsalia de futuro' privately (though they do excommunicate those who, having contracted them, then form a marriage by subsequent intercourse). The control over 'sponsalia de futuro' is exercised in a different way. In the thirteenth century, private 'sponsalia de futuro' are prohibited; indeed they are said to be invalid. Also, the parish priest may not proclaim the banns or solemnize the marriage of those who have so contracted without license from the bishop.[140] This may not be a direct violation of Alexander III's decretal *Quod nobis ex tua parte*, but it is certainly in a different spirit.[141]

Emendation of these canons followed in the compilation of synodal statutes made in 1287 X 1288 and again in the early years of the fourteenth century. The early fourteenth-century version reads:[142]

137. Details, including specific references to the cases, may be found in Donahue, *Law, Marriage* chapters 8–9. Cambrai was, of course, not in France in the Middle Ages, and most of its extensive diocese is now in Belgium, and much of that in an area of Belgium that does not now, and never has, spoken French. The diocese was, however, in the province of Reims and can be regarded for our purposes as 'French'.

138. Donahue, *Law, Marriage* 33.

139. See Cambrai (early 14th century) cc. [81], [82], in *Les statuts synodaux français du xiiie siècle. IV: Les statuts synodaux de l'ancienne province de Reims (Cambrai, Arras, Noyon, Soissons et Tournai)*, ed. Joseph Avril, (Collection de documents inédits sur l'histoire de France, sér. in 8°, 23; Paris 1988) 160; and in *Les actes de la province ecclésiastique de Reims*, ed. Thomas Gousset (4 vols. Reims 1842–1844) 2.452. The material for the later Middle Ages and early modern period in the latter is drawn from the best printed texts that were available at the time. Some of the attributions are probably wrong, and the texts printed could almost certainly be improved by careful work with the manuscripts, but for our purposes they will suffice.

140. Cambrai (1238–1240) cc. [89]–[90], in *Statuts synodaux français IV* 45.

141. X 4.3.2.

142. *Statuts synodaux français IV* 160: [80] Inhibeant presbyteri parrochiales subditis suis ne sponsalia contrahant seu dent fidem de matrimonio inter eos pariter contrahendo nisi coram

[80] Parish priests shall prohibit their subjects ('subditis') from contracting 'sponsalia' or giving faith of contracting marriage to each other, except, at a minimum, before the priest of one of those who wishes to contract, and this should be in a public place, a church, for example, or a cemetery or a chapel and before many other trustworthy people. And if they otherwise contract 'sponsalia', unless they repeat them within eight days before one of the above priests, the priest should not proceed to the proclamation of the banns or the solemnization of them without our special license [i.e., of the bishop] or that of our official. And anyone who presumes to do this (knowingly) shall know himself suspended by this very fact.

This provision is, in many ways, an improvement from the point of view of statutory drafting. The sanction for not contracting publicly is changed from invalidity of the 'sponsalia' (something that was probably not within the power of the bishop or the synod to do) to the requirement that a special license be obtained from the bishop or his official (on which occasion, presumably, a penance could be imposed) in order to proceed with the proclamation of the banns and the solemnization. Perhaps more important, and by way of concession to the fact that medieval people, like modern, normally first found out whether someone was willing to marry them in a private setting, clandestine 'sponsalia de futuro' were not forbidden. Rather, the couple were enjoined to publicize them within a week after they were made. This period of a week remained a feature of the Cambrai legislation throughout the Middle Ages and was being enforced in the mid-fifteenth-century sentences that we see in our registers.

The Cambrai courts also regularly fined couples for failure to solemnize their marriages after sponsalia had been entered into, and the fines mention a period 'fixed by law'. That the failure to solemnize 'sponsalia' (unless they were remitted before the bishop or his official) would be an offense is clearly implied in the legislation, but no fixed period for solemnization is laid down. I have been unable to find such legislation, though I have no doubt that it existed. Because I have been unable to find the legislation, I do not know what the period was; it is never given in the sentences.[143] It could have been as short as a month from the time of entering into or publication of the 'sponsalia' because that would have given ample time for the three successive proclamations of the banns on Sundays or

---

presbytero alterius saltem contrahere volentium, et hoc in loco publico: ecclesia videlicet cymeterio vel capella et coram pluribus fidedignis, et si aliter contraxerint sponsalia, nisi infra octo dies ea reiterent coram altero de presbyteris antedictis, non procedant presbyter ulterius ad bannorum publicationem, vel matrimonii sollempnisationem, sine nostra vel officialis nostri licentia speciali, et qui hoc (scienter) ['scienter' in *Actes de Reims* 452, but not in *Statuts synodaux français IV* 160] facere presumpserit ipso facto se noverit esse suspensum'.

143. It may have been forty days because that is the period mentioned in a number of the sentences where a couple is ordered to solemnize their marriage.

feast days called for in *Cum inhibitio*. Clearly, this legislation was designed to turn marriage promises into solemnized marriages quickly.

Cambrai was not the only northern French diocese to have such provisions. Similar provisions can be found in statutes of Tournai from the beginning of the fourteenth century, and in statutes of Liège of 1288.[144] The fifteenth-century cases from Châlons-en-Champagne reported in Beatrice Gottlieb's 'Getting Married in Pre-Reformation Europe' suggest that similar provisions were in effect there.[145] There is a Soissons provision on the same topic, though it is classified as a 'consilium' and not a 'preceptum'.[146] Around 1454, if we can rely on Gousset's edition, however, the bishop of Amiens adopted a collection of synodal statutes that said nothing about the celebration of 'sponsalia de futuro', excommunicated those who contracted 'per verba de presenti' clandestinely, but then repeated the injunction of *Quod nobis ex tua parte* that those who wish to publicize such marriages be received by the church and blessed.[147]

There is another Cambrai statute of relevance to our cases, appearing first in this form in the Cambrai collection of 1287 X 1288 and carried over into that of the early fourteenth century:[148]

[83] Item, we excommunicate all those who propose false impediments against marriages, or who knowingly conceal the truth, out of affection, [superior] order or favor, or for any other reason, and will that priests frequently denounce them as excommunicate for this reason. Even if no one offers opposition at the proclamation of the banns, but the priest has a probable or true suspicion (versimilem aut veram coniecturam) against the marriage, he should not proceed to solemnize the marriage without consulting with us or our official of Cambrai about this. If he does to the contrary, he will be held to the penalty for [being present at a] clandestine marriage.

144. *Statuts synodaux français IV*, 331–333 (Tournai); ibid., 45–47 nn. 148, 150, 152, 154, 158, 160 (references to Liège).

145. PhD diss., Columbia University, 1974.

146. Soissons (1403) c. 50, in *Actes de Reims* 2:631 (= Soissons [end of the 13th century] c. 53, in *Statuts synodaux français IV* 297): 'Prohibeant sacerdotes frequenter laicis sub excommunicatione, ne dent fidem sibi de contrahendo, nisi sacerdote praesente, et pluribus aliis, et si fecerint eo absente, non faciat edicta seu banna.' By contrast, clandestine marriages seem to be punished with automatic excommunication. Soissons (1403) c. 55, in *Actes de Reims* 2.632 (= c. 58 in *Statuts synodaux français IV*, 298); cf. *Actes de Reims* c. 48, 2.631 (= c. 51 in *Statuts synodaux français IV* 297).

147. X 4.3.2; Statutes of Jean Avantage (c. 1454) c. 5.10, in *Actes de Reims* 2.712. I strongly doubt that this provision was new in 1454. *Quod nobis ex tua parte* was directed to the bishop of Beauvais, right next door, as it were, to Amiens.

148. *Statuts synodaux français IV* 161: '[83] Item excommunicamus omnes qui contra matrimonia falsa impedimenta proposuerint, vel vera celaverint scienter, amore, precepto vel favore, vel alia quacumque de causa, et volumus eos excommunicatos propter hoc frequenter a presbyteris nuntiari. Quod si nemo bannorum proclamationi se opposuerit, et loci presbyter verisimilem aut veram contra matrimonium habeat coniecturam, nobis aut officio nostro Cameracensi inconsultis super hoc, ad solempnisationem matrimonii non procedat, et si contra hoc fecerit, pena pro clandestinis nuptiis imposita teneatur'.

The general thrust of this statute is clearly designed to encourage the raising of objections, but it could be used to penalize those who raise objections that turn out not to be provable, particularly since the *'scienter'* requirement does not have to be taken as applying to 'those who propose false impediments'. This statute may be the authority for a penalty that we find quite often in the cases, imposed for 'frivolous opposition' to a marriage.

A relevant addition to the basic statutes of Cambrai is recorded in the fourteenth century. In 1313, a synod imposed *ipso facto* excommunication on those who separated themselves without judgment of the church.[149] This statute was also being applied in our fifteenth-century cases.

Once more, the question is how much of the practice of the courts of Cambrai could we have surmised if all that we had was the statutes themselves and not the evidence of their enforcement? The fact that the basic Cambrai statute was emended both, it would seem, to bring it more into compliance with the common law of the church and in response to what may have been practical difficulties with its enforcement suggests an ongoing interaction between the lawmakers and the court. The emphasis in the statutes on 'sponsalia de futuro' certainly suggests that there was some kind of ongoing effort to regulate them. We might suspect that the locus of that effort was the episcopal courts. That suspicion would be correct. We might wonder if a set of statutes that seem to have reached their final form early in the fourteenth century was still being enforced in the middle of the fifteenth, but the presence of similar statutes in nearby dioceses with manuscript witnesses dating from the fifteenth century might allow us to conclude, correctly, that they probably were. We probably, however, would not be able to guess that a statute that seems designed to encourage raising objections to marriages was, in fact, being used to punish those who raised them and then could not prove them. Overall, the detail in the statutes and the presence of similar statutes elsewhere in the region gives us more confidence than we had for Ely that some enforcement activity was probably taking place.

In the chapters that follow, both that on Spain and that on Eastern Central Europe make considerable use of local legislation to infer what was happening in the courts. What we have done here suggests that such evidence must be used with caution, but it is evidence. In all cases, however, it needs to be qualified. The presence of a local statute on a given topic 'suggests' that the local ecclesiastical courts 'may have' or 'probably' did something in response to it.

---

149. In *Actes de Reims* 2:502.

The Achievement of the Officialities

Granted the state of our knowledge and of what remains to be done, any assessment of the achievement of officialities must be highly preliminary. From the vantage point from which we are writing, however, some relatively clear conclusions seem to be emerging as well as numerous areas that call for more research:

1. Despite the undeniable achievements of the papacy and of the academic canonists in shaping the canonical legal system, the local courts were the vehicles by which that system was carried to a majority of the population. Had the officialities not been founded in the middle of the thirteenth century, canon law would have remained, at best, of practical concern only to the higher-level clergy and a few rich lay people with marriage problems. Had it so remained, the academic development might not have continued. As it was, canon law in the later Middle Ages affected the lives of a very large percentage of the population. While the majority of those saw it only in the somewhat primitive form of the low-level criminal courts, a substantial group, certainly a much more substantial group than would have been possible had there been only the papal court and papal delegates, used the canonical system as a device for dispute resolution.

2. In many areas the local ecclesiastical courts seem to have filled a real social need. Nothing required fourteenth- and fifteenth-century Englishmen to bring cases of contract to the ecclesiastical courts. Indeed, they ran the risk of royal prohibition if they did so. Yet over a century and a half they brought such cases to the church courts in the thousands, and the result, if recent research has it right, was a permanent effect on English contract law.

3. Competition, if it does not always engender efficiency, almost always engenders thought. The fact that the local ecclesiastical tribunals existed side-by-side with secular ones prompted men who were concerned with the law to think about the best way to do things. The English chancellors who adopted and adapted a form of Romano-canonical procedure in the fifteenth century for use in what was to become one of the most important courts in the English legal system did not have to learn about this procedure by reading books. There were examples of it in every English diocese. By the end of the fifteenth century, Romano-canonical procedure was the norm for almost all the higher level secular courts on the Continent, and there can be little doubt that one of the most important means of the transmission of this procedure from books to practical reality was the example of the local ecclesiastical courts.

4. At the same time, the local ecclesiastical courts were not institutions totally imposed from above. What they did was not completely contained in books or in the pronouncements of popes. They reflected the societies in which they were found, and this fact proved to be at once the source of their strength and ultimately, later, the source of their downfall. We have suggested that there is little that we find in the records of the local ecclesiastical courts that is contrary to the common canon law. At the same time much that happened in the local ecclesiastical courts is simply not to be found in the common canon law, or at least not be found there in a very developed form. Canon law gives a wide play to custom, and many courts clearly took advantage of this fact when they dealt with such areas as tithes, ecclesiastical revenues, testaments, and contracts. Canon law also tells us what the law is in many kinds of cases, but does not require that the case be brought. French society in the later Middle Ages found the canon law of marriage contracts and of separation to be useful; English society found the law concerning 'de presenti' marriages useful. Neither society found useful what the other society found useful. A lawyer who had practiced before the consistory court of York in the fifteenth century would have had to go through extensive retraining in order to operate effectively in the officiality of Troyes in the same period.

5. To balance against these considerable achievements, we must note that the ecclesiastical courts, like all bureaucracies, had a tendency to indulge in their processes for their own sake. In many dioceses, they operated largely out of the direct control of the bishop. They were highly professional, but also highly bureaucratic. Bureaucracies must be supported, and while there is little evidence to support the more extreme charges of the reformers about the size and scope of the fees that they charged and the fines that they imposed, there is an increasing sense from the records, particularly from the criminal courts, that the broader functions of courts tended to be submerged in the pursuit of revenue. This characteristic was already noted by Chaucer at the end of the fourteenth century, and it is perhaps significant that he notes it not of a bishop's official but of an archdeacon. The two least attractive characters in the *Canterbury Tales* are the pardoner and the summoner, a minor official of an archidiaconal court.

6. While the local ecclesiastical courts proved adaptive to the societies in which they found themselves, they ultimately failed, paradoxically, because they were adaptive but not adaptive enough. The story of the failure of the ecclesiastical courts lies beyond our period, but at the end of our period we can begin to see things that will ultimately prove destructive. At the end of the fifteenth century, considerably before Reformation

was formally in the wind, the ecclesiastical courts in London experienced a loss of jurisdiction at the hands of a lay society that wanted stricter sanctions imposed on those appearing before the ecclesiastical courts, particularly for sexual offenses.[150] In the same period, and perhaps in response to the same kind of pressure, we see a great increase in criminal jurisdiction of the ecclesiastical courts in northern France.[151]

In a world in which there was considerable consensus about the desirability of at least outward religious uniformity, the local ecclesiastical courts could play a somewhat paternalistic role. The sanctions need not be too severe; they could be enforced as much by community pressure as by the judges themselves. When that consensus broke down, as it did in sixteenth-century Europe, the old methods no longer worked. The ecclesiastical courts became agents of religious repression and came close to collapsing of their own weight, as in England, or lost much of their jurisdiction to an increasingly autarchic regime, as in France.[152]

We close, then, with a quotation from a great Biblical scholar who had considerable doubts about the move of the church to law. I am not sure that I agree with him, but his point of view is well worth considering as we seek to assess the achievement of medieval officialities:[153]

As long as law is confined to the business of the Church, and as long as the Church has business to manage, there appears no convincing reason at the moment why legal processes should not be employed. But observe that I speak of the business of the Church. Law, it seems, should not touch the Christian life of the Church; here it is an intrusion of a secular factor. The church is empowered to exercise leadership in the Christian life, but this is not a leadership of the law. It is leadership of another type.... Only when something other than the true mission of the Church is the objective are we likely to turn to means which are quite suitable to these objectives; and I mean the use of power. Power is profane and adapted to profane purposes; but why should the Church have profane purposes? Order can be achieved by other means than law; and... we can ask whether the failures of the Church may not be connected with our failures to achieve a truly ecclesiastical order.

150. See Wunderli, *London Church Courts* 101–102; see generally ibid., chapter 4.

151. See Donahue and McDougall, 'France'.

152. Nothing is ever as simple as one's generalizations would like to make it. The ecclesiastical courts in England experienced a remarkable revival in the reign of Elizabeth I, only to decline again in the period of the religious wars of the seventeenth century, and one should be uncomfortable making general statements about the ecclesiastical courts in France after 1539 when so little has been done with their records. For the first point, see Richard H. Helmholz, *Ecclesiastical Jurisdiction* 4; for a remarkable beginning on a contradiction of the second point, see Kevin Saule, 'L'officialité de Beauvais et l'enfermement des curés délinquants au xviiᵉ siècle: Entre rigueur et indulgence', *Les officialités dans l'Europe médiévale et moderne: des tribunaux pour une société chrétienne, Actes du colloque international de Troyes, 27–29 mai 2010*, ed. Véronique Beaulande-Barraud et Martine Charageat (Turnhout 2014) 205–24.

153. John L. McKenzie, SJ, 'Law in the New Testament', *The Jurist* 26 (1966) 180.

9

France and Adjoining Areas

Charles Donahue Jr. and Sara McDougall

This chapter discusses the late medieval ecclesiastical courts in continental western Europe from the North Sea to the Pyrenees, from the Atlantic to the modern borders of Germany and Italy. It thus includes the modern Netherlands, Belgium, and Switzerland, in addition to modern France.[1] While there were considerable variations in the structure and practice of the ecclesiastical courts within this large area, the variations do not correspond to the modern political or linguistic boundaries, and they all can be discussed within a broader framework that was not unique to this area but was typical of it.

Discussion of the ecclesiastical courts in this region must begin with the pioneering work of Paul Fournier: *Les officialités au moyen Âge: Étude sur l'organisation, la compétence et la procédure des tribunaux ecclésiastiques ordinaires en France de 1180 à 1328.*[2] Published in 1880 on the basis of a thesis at

1. The boundaries of the medieval kingdom of France were not so wide as those of modern France. Therefore, the Western part of the medieval empire is included in this chapter. Medieval ecclesiastical jurisdiction in this region did not correspond to modern political boundaries, and sometimes ignored contemporary political boundaries. These facts, coupled with the fact that the editors of this volume did not assign a chapter on ecclesiastical courts to any of the smaller western European countries, suggested that 'France' in this chapter should be very broadly defined.

2. (Paris 1880; reprinted Aalen 1984); see Donahue, 'Ecclesiastical Courts' 276–277.

the École des chartes, Fournier's is a remarkable work that remains to this day readable and in many ways unsurpassed. We should note, however, the chronological, subject-matter, and geographical limitations indicated in his subtitle. Fournier was largely concerned with the 'long' thirteenth century. He begins with what he conceived to be the origins of organized officialities in France (with an emphasis on the north), and he ends on the eve of the assembly of Vincennes. He did not know what we know today about the surviving records of the French officialities from the period with which he was concerned, and he quite legitimately ignored the substantial surviving records from later periods.

For each of his three topics—organization, competence, and procedure—Fournier painstakingly pieced together charter evidence. While there is certainly more that can be said about this evidence, Fournier's work is likely to remain fundamental. On the other hand, where Fournier lacked charter evidence—and this is particularly true of the section on procedure—he filled in his story with evidence from canonistic writing, notably Tancred and Durantis. While we are not yet ready to replace Fournier's work on the procedure of the thirteenth-century French officialities, recent work with surviving records unknown to Fournier gives an impression of considerably greater diversity of legal practice than a reading of Fournier's pages would lead one to expect.[3]

A second difficulty with Fournier's work is his starting point. All too often, one gets the impression from his work that wherever we find a charter that mentions the 'official' of a bishop or an archdeacon, we are to assume that there was an organized officiality, as that term was understood in the fourteenth and later centuries. The fact is, however, that the term 'official' in the late twelfth and early thirteenth centuries did not mean what it later came to mean. The official of the late twelfth and early thirteenth centuries is the ancestor both of the later official and of the later vicar general. The process by which the organized officiality of the later Middle Ages emerged was gradual, with all the characteristics of the later officialities not firmly in place, at least in most areas, until the mid- to late thirteenth century.[4]

Finally, Fournier's book has self-imposed limitations of subject matter. He is concerned with 'ordinary tribunals'—courts in a quite narrow sense—and only those courts that exercised 'ordinary' jurisdiction. This means that he did not consider at any length methods by which disputes

3. For an example, see the records at Le Puy, discussed 326–328 below; on the general topic of procedure, see 'The Procedure of the French Officialities' 331–336.
4. See 'The Origins of the French Officialities' 303–308.

were resolved and ecclesiastical discipline administered—arbitrations, synods, visitations, for example—nor did he consider at any length 'extraordinary' tribunals, notably papal judges delegate and inquisitions into heresy.[5]

Anne Lefebvre-Teillard's *Les officialités à la veille du concile de Trente* was published as a Paris thesis in law in 1973.[6] The 'veille' of the title is the period from 1490 to 1540. Like Fournier's, her findings have stood the test of time. Unlike Fournier, Lefebvre makes extensive use of the records of the officialities themselves. Her chapters on organization, procedure, and competence make it quite clear that considerable variation existed in her period in all three areas, under an umbrella of an ideal type quite like that described by Fournier. Also unlike Fournier, she devotes three chapters to substantive matters, marriage and divorce, obligations, and family patrimony, showing again considerable variation under the uniform umbrella provided by the canon law taught in the universities. Like Fournier, Lefebvre focuses on contentious cases heard by ordinary organized tribunals and thus does not consider at any length other methods by which the law might have been enforced or disputes resolved.

Ideally, this chapter should contain a general history of ecclesiastical courts in our area from their origins into the sixteenth century, focusing on those periods and those subjects that are not covered in Fournier and Lefebvre. The state of research, however, means that we can only offer an inconsistent and incomplete picture. What we will do is suggest where Fournier's conclusions are still valid and where they need revision, what has been done to fill the chronological gap between Fournier and Lefebvre, and what needs to be added before the picture can be regarded as in any sense complete. Throughout, we will rely on the work of a growing group of international researchers whose recent contributions have greatly enriched our understanding of the French officialities by studying the priorities and jurisdictional reaches of the different courts in their exercise of justice, the interaction between the people who came before these courts and their officers, and also the place of these courts in their societies. In addition to highlighting the work that has been done, we will

5. For an investigation into the world of papal judges delegate in this region, see Emily W. Wood, 'The Execution of Papal Justice in Northern France, 1145–1198' (PhD diss., Harvard University 2009). While this study is a good start, more could certainly be done. For further discussion on inquisitions into heresy, see 318–319.

6. (Bibliothèque d'histoire du droit et droit romain 19; Paris 1973.) In the period intervening between Fournier and Lefebvre, there was a relatively brief but suggestive survey by Jean Gaudemet, 'La juridiction écclésiastique', *Histoire des institutions françaises au moyen age. 3: Institutions écclésiastiques*, ed. Fernand Lot and Robert Fawtier, (Paris 1962) 257–279. See also Jean Gaudemet, *Le gouvernment de l'Église à l'époque classique* (Histoire du droit et des institutions de l'Église en occident 7.2; Paris 1979) 166–171.

point to several fruitful avenues yet to be explored as we work to fill out the picture first sketched by Fournier.

The Origins of the French Officialities

An appendix to Fournier's *Officialités* gives a diocese-by-diocese account of the first time that the word 'officialis' appears in a charter.[7] The dates vary; they tend to be later in the south than in the north. The earliest references date from the end of the pontificate of Alexander III (1151–1179): Reims (1178), Amiens (1178, 'minister' rather than 'officialis'), Beauvais (before 1180, 'ministerialis'), Noyon (1183), Chartres (before 1187), Rouen (before 1183). By 1223 there are additional references from the following dioceses: Arras (1206), Cambrai (1180 X 1191), Châlons-en-Champagne (1203), Laon (1209), Senlis (1207), Soissons (1203), Térouanne (1203), Tournai (1216),[8] Sens (1200), Meaux (1204), Orléans (1216), Paris (1204), Troyes (1200), Avranches (1199 X 1210), Bayeux (1164 X 1205), Coutances (1202), Évreux (1208), Lisieux (1218), Séez (1217), Tours (1215), Angers (1224), Le Mans (1191), Nantes (1223), Bourges (1209), Cahors (1220), Limoges (1201), Verdun (1203). In short, we can document the existence of an episcopal officer called 'official' in most of the dioceses of northern France by the death of Innocent III (1215), and the pattern is sufficiently widespread that one might assume that there were others for whom we do not have documentation.

None of the work done since Fournier casts any doubt on this basic conclusion. What this work does cast doubt on is a proposition that Fournier never quite stated, but which he probably believed and which the structure of his book implies: that the 'officials' in French dioceses from 1178 to 1215 did the same things that 'officials' of French dioceses did a hundred years later. Here is where Fournier's evidence should be reviewed (much of it is still unpublished). What Fournier tells us about the unpublished documents and examination of those that have been pub-

---

7. Fournier, *Officialités* 309–313.

8. The document probably dates from December of 1215; *Documenten uit de praktijk van de gedingbeslissende rechtspraak van de Officialiteit van Doornik: Oorsprong en vroege ontwikkeling (1192–1300)*, ed. Monique Vleeschouwers van Melkebeek (Iuris scripta historica, uitgeven door het Wetenschappelijk Comité voor Rechtsgeschiedenis van de Koninklijke Academie voor Wetenschappen, Letteren en Schone Kunsten van België 1; Brussel 1985) No. 1, p. 7. For the argument that the official himself dates from 1203, see Monique Vleeschouwers van Melkebeek, *De officialiteit van Doornik: Oorsprong en vroege ontwikkeling (1192–1300)* (Verhandelingen van de Koninklijke Academie voor Wetenschappen, Letteren en Schone Kunsten van België, Klasse der Letteren, 47.117; Brussel 1987) 40–56. Vleeschouwers's work shows what can be done to expand on Fournier's base; it also shows, however, that radical changes in Fournier's conclusions about the dating of an officer called 'official' are not likely to emerge from such efforts.

lished suggest the following qualifications to Fournier's never-stated conclusion about the origin of the French officialities:

(1) The French 'official' of the period from 1178 to 1215 was not only a judicial officer. This is not to say that he did not sometimes act as a judge. Bishops also acted as judges, and so did their officials. It is striking, however, how few early references to 'officials' can be firmly connected with contentious matters. The process by which officials came to be connected exclusively with both contentious and non-contentious legal matters was gradual, and that point had certainly not been reached by 1215.

(2) The connection between the official and the use of Romano-canonical procedure was loose in this period. There are certainly some French documents from this period that reflect an awareness of the norms of Romano-canonical procedure. Sometimes such documents also mention officials, and in these instances we may assume that the official had some legal training. There is, however, nothing from this period that suggests that an official must have legal training.

(3) When the official comes to be thought of not only as an officer but also as an institution—that is, when we can speak not only of 'officials' but also of 'officialities'—is vague. This development, too, had almost certainly not happened by 1215. The word 'officiality' hardly existed at that time. The development of the institution can probably be traced in the development of its seal. By 1250, many officials had separate seals of their offices. The primitive form of the legend of these seals is 'sigillum curie domini episcopi X' (where 'X' is the name of the diocese).[9] This tells us that the 'court' of the bishop was being considered as separate, in some sense, from the bishop himself, but it does not tell us what the functions of that court were. By way of analogy, we should remember that it is not until well into the thirteenth century that we get any indication that the 'curia' of the king of France was divided into specialized groups for legal, financial, and administrative or political matters, and it would be dangerous to assume that this development occurred much earlier on the ecclesiastical side.[10]

Granted the scrappy nature of the evidence, it will probably not be possible to identify the precise moment at which there came to be organized officialities in more than a few dioceses. Nonetheless, the evidence now

---

9. Fournier, *Officialités* 303–305. Tournai's legend is even vaguer: 'Sigillum sedis Tournacensis'; Vleeschouwers, *Officialiteit* 93–100.

10. See Jacques Ellul, *Histoire des institutions. 3: Le Moyen Age* (7th ed. Paris 1976) 266–271; see generally *Histoire des institutions. 2: Institutions royales,* ed. Fernand Lot and Robert Fawtier (Paris 1958).

available points to the gradual development of organized officialities over the course of the thirteenth century. By the end of the century, many, if not most French dioceses, had officers known as 'officials' who presided over institutions that performed three separate but related functions: (1) hearing disputes that were within the cognizance of the bishop in his capacity as ordinary rather than in his capacity as secular lord, (2) enforcing ecclesiastical discipline by means of bringing criminal proceedings against delinquents, and (3) putting a seal that served as the bishop's seal on a large group of transactions, all of which had some specifically legal content. The official was aided in the performance of his functions by various subordinate officers and a clerical staff. The institution kept a separate body of records. It employed some form of Romano-canonical procedure in dealing with contentious matters, and it met to hear such matters on a regular basis. The official and the higher officers within the officiality had some form of legal training, normally university training in law leading to at least a bachelor's degree. It is highly unlikely that many, if any, French dioceses had an institution with all of these characteristics much before 1250.

While it is not possible to rehearse all the evidence that supports this last proposition, we can give some indications of the nature of the argument: There is no direct evidence of an institution with these characteristics within our geographical area prior to the late 1260s. The first description that we have of such an officiality is in a document styled *Privilegia curie remensis archiepiscopi*, which dates from 1269 and has long been in print.[11] It reports the establishment of standards of conduct for officers, advocates, proctors, and notaries of the court by a constitution of the officials of Reims (there were two of them) dated in 1267.[12] It also reports customs of the court that give us most of the characteristics that we have identified above as those of an 'organized officiality'. The court itself, the document reports, was established in the late twelfth century. We may, however, treat this statement with some skepticism since the subsequent history of the court given in the document makes clear that there was little institutional continuity between the officials of the late twelfth century (who certainly existed) and those who constituted the organized offciality in the 1250s or 1260s.[13]

---

11. This document appears in *Archives législatives de la ville de Reims*, ed. Pierre Varin (Collection de documents inédits sur l'histoire de France; Paris 1840) 1.6–33.

12. Ibid. 12–16. For an account of some of the background, see Gaudemet, 'Juridiction ecclésiastique' 276–278.

13. For a somewhat different point of view and much more information, see Odile Grand-

Actual court records date from just a bit after this time.[14] There is considerable record material in a curious work known as the *Liber practicus de consuetudine remensi*, a combination of a formulary and style of the archiepiscopal court at Reims, with substantial academic commentary.[15] The earliest dates of the court records in the formulary are in the 1280s. The earliest known court book that survives in France in something like its original form is a register of cases (in process form) from the diocese of Mende. It contains cases dated between 1268 and 1272.[16] Just a bit later is a court book from Le Puy that will be discussed below.[17]

It is, of course, possible to infer the existence of institutions for which we have no direct evidence. The burden, however, is on those who would argue for the earlier existence of organized officialities: They have to explain why an institution that has left a considerable deposit of records dating from the late thirteenth century to the end of the Middle Ages and beyond left no records at all from the earlier Middle Ages.

There is also indirect evidence for the proposition that organized officialities in France date from the middle of the thirteenth century. We have already noted above that the earliest 'officials' played a role quite similar to that of the later vicar general. They performed a wide range of episcopal functions and were particularly noticeable in the absence of the bishop. Édouard Fournier has carefully traced the rise of the vicar general.[18] It was really not possible for the official to develop his specialized functions and institution until there was someone who could play the broader and less well-defined role of the vicar general. In most dioceses, vicars general did not appear until the mid- to late thirteenth century.

One of the clearest indications that we are dealing with an institution rather than an event is the maintenance of a body of records that belong to the institution. In the absence of the records themselves a good indication that such records were being kept is evidence that there was an

---

motte, 'Les officialités de Reims', *Bulletin d'information de l'Institut de recherche et d'histoire des textes* 4 (1955) 77–106. The full story will not be told until the material concerning the history of the chapter of Reims is integrated into the history of the officiality; for example, Ludwig Falkenstein, 'Zur Stellung des Reimser Metropolitankapitels in Stadt, Diözese und Kirchenprovinz während des 12. und 13. Jahrhunderts', *Proceedings Berkeley 1980* 551–562.

14. By 'court records', we mean records that we have some reason to believe were maintained by the court itself. Records of judicial activity, normally in charter form, are much earlier.

15. *Archives législatives*, ed. Varin, 1.35–344.

16. Donahue, *Records 1* III/23/3/1. Jan K. Bulman, *The Court Book of Mende and the Secular Lordship of the Bishop* (Toronto 2008), makes a start on this book, but much more could be done with it.

17. Donahue, *Records 1* III/24/4; see 326–328.

18. Édouard Fournier, *L'origine du vicaire général et des autres membres de la curie diocésaine* (2nd ed. Paris 1940).

officer whose task it was to keep the records. Court notaries in northern France have been studied in some dioceses, and continuous bodies of notaries can be traced back to the middle of the thirteenth century and not much before. In the dioceses of Reims, Laon, and Soissons, a continuous body of notaries can be traced from 1239; the equivalent date in Tournai is 1245; in Liège, 1252.[19]

Further indirect evidence is impressionistic, but tends in the same direction. In England, one gets the impression that the proportion of significant cases being heard by papal judges delegate declined over the course of the thirteenth century. This is not to say, of course, that the institution of papal judges delegate did not exist at the end of the century. But it was no longer true, as it had been at the beginning of the century, that every significant canonic dispute was heard by papal judges delegate. One reason for this might be that by the end of the century there were local officialities in which litigants had sufficient confidence that they no longer took all their significant disputes to the court of Rome. Lacking a detailed study of papal judges delegate in this period for France, we can only say that we would not be surprised to discover the same situation in France.[20]

A final note of caution: Monique Vleeschouwers van Melkebeek appears to be arguing that the Tournai officiality originated earlier in the thirteenth century than what we have suggested above was the norm.[21] She has also published the charters on which she is relying.[22] Her charters show what it is possible to do with persistence, even when all that one has is charter evidence. They also show that the official of Tournai was frequently involved in judicial matters in the 1210s and 1220s. They show an extensive, perhaps precocious, use of Romano-canonical procedure. Whether they show that Tournai had an organized officiality, as we have defined that term above, is a matter of more doubt. In any event, not much turns on it. It is possible that Stephen of Tournai's see produced an officiality a generation in advance of all the other northern European ones. (Compare the somewhat precocious development of an officiality at Durantis's see at Mende, though the book antedates Durantis's becoming the bishop there.)[23] The important point is that the evidence that we now

<hr>

19. Vleeschouwers, *Officialiteit* 100–101.

20. For England, see Jane Sayers, *Papal Judges Delegate in the Province of Canterbury, 1198–1254: A Study in Ecclesiastical Jurisdiction and Administration* (Oxford 1971). The move of the papal court to Avignon and the creation of the Rota may well have changed this situation, at least so far as benefice litigation was concerned. See Guillaume Mollat, *Les papes d'Avignon* (10th ed. Paris 1965) 482–494; Mollat, 'Contribution à l'histoire de l'administration judiciaire de l'Église romaine au XIVᵉ siècle', RHE 32 (1936) 876–928.

21. Vleeschouwers, *Officialiteit*.   22. Vleeschouwers, *Documenten*.

23. See 306.

have suggests that few, if any, other sees in this area followed suit until about a generation after Tournai.

The Records of the French Officialities

In the French archival world the received wisdom is that the French Revolution was largely responsible for the loss of the records of the French officialities. While the Revolution is certainly to blame for some of the loss, its effects can be exaggerated. The fact that relatively little survives from before 1450 in places that have quite impressive holdings after that date suggests that the Hundred Years' War was probably more destructive than was the Revolution. Then too, random fires, the religious wars of the seventeenth century (particularly in the east), and two wars in the twentieth century have all taken their toll.

The notion that the Revolution destroyed most of the records of 'ancien régime' officialities has had ill effects. Relatively little archival research has been done on the French officialities since Fournier's pioneering work, though some has been done quite recently.[24] It turns out that quite an extensive body of records survives. Of 129 medieval dioceses, the seats of which lay within the boundaries of modern France, 53 have left records from one or more of their officialities. Altogether 73 French officialities are represented in the reports of the Church Courts Records Working Group.[25] Not only do these records exist, but the French archival tradition has seen to it that they are, by and large, well-housed, well-preserved, and accessible to the user.

The situation in Belgium is similar.[26] A major deposit of records at Tournai was destroyed in the Second World War, but some material from this see remains, as does some material from Cambrai and Liège. Representative documents also exist from the various officialities in the diocese of Utrecht, and a large amount of widely scattered material exists in Switzerland.[27]

The list given below shows all the sees or provinces within our geographical area that are known to have left records of one or more officiality.[28] The name of the province in square brackets means that the provincial court has left no known surviving records or that it lies outside of our geographical area, but one or more of the subordinate sees lie within our area and have left surviving records:

---

24. See 338–343.   25. Donahue, *Records 1* 59.

26. Ibid. 51–53.   27. Ibid. VII, X.

28. Based on what is found in Donahue, *Records 1* II, III, VII, X. The order of the list follows *Die päpstlichen Kanzleiordnungen von 1200 bis 1500*, ed. Michael Tangl (Innsbruck 1894; reprinted Aalen 1959) 1–32.

Lyon (Lugdunensis)
Autun (Eduensis)
Langres (Lingonensis)

Sens (Senonensis)
Paris (Parisiensis)
Chartres (Carnotensis)
Orléans (Aurelainensis)
Troyes (Trecensis)

[Reims (Remensis)]
Châlons-en-Champagne
   (Cathalaunensis)
Cambrai (Cameracensis)
Tournai (Tornacensis)
Amiens (Ambianensis)
Senlis (Silvanectensis)
Beauvais (Belvacensis)

Rouen (Rothomagensis)
Bayeux (Baiocensis)
Sées (Sagiensis)

[Tours (Turonensis)]
Le Mans (Cenomanensis)
Nantes (Nanetensis)
Saint-Brieuc (Briocensis)
Tréguier (Trecorensis)

Bourges (Bituricensis)
Clermont (Claromontensis)
Saint-Flour (Sancti Flori)
Rodez (Ruthenensis)
Limoges (Lemovicensis)
Mende (Mimatensis)
Le Puy (Aniciensis sive Podiensis)

Bordeaux (Burdegalensis)
Poitiers (Pictaviensis)
Maillezais (Malleacensis)
Angoulême (Englolismensis)
Périgeux (Petragoricensis)

[Narbonne (Narbonensis)]

Nîmes (Nemausensis)
Elne (Elnensis)

Toulouse (Tholosanus)
Pamiers (Appamiarum)

Aix-en-Provence (Aqensis)
Apt (Aptensis)
Fréjus (Foroiuliensis)
Sisteron (Sistericensis)

Arles (Arlelatensis)
Marseille (Massiliensis)
Avignon (Avinionensis)
Orange (Aurasicensis)
Vaison (Vasionensis)
Cavaillon (Cavalicensis)
Carpentras (Carpentoracensis)

[Vienne (Viennensis)]
Die (Diensis)
Grenoble (Gracionopolitanum)
Genève (Gebbensis)

[Tarentaise (Tarentasiensis)]
Sion (Sedunensis)

[Besançon (Bisuntinus)]
Basel (Basiliensis)
Lausanne (Lausanensis)

[Embrun (Ebredunensis)]
Digne (Dignensis)

[Köln (Coloniensis)]
Liège (Leodiensis)
Utrecht (Traiectensis)

[Mainz (Maguntina)]
Konstanz (Constantiensis)
Chur (Curiensis)

[Trier (Treverensis)]
Toul (Tullensis)

Virtually all of these records are unpublished. Some of them have come to light only as the result of the work of the Church Court Records Working Group. Obviously, much work needs to be done with this large body of unpublished material. In the meantime, there are five major published collections of church court records from our area and time period:

(1) The register of the officiality of Cerisy, an exempt monastic jurisdiction encompassing twenty-five Norman parishes, is one of the earliest of the French church court records and certainly the earliest to be edited.[29] The register contains material dating from 1314 to 1485, but not every year is covered. There is a large gap between 1346 and 1369 and another between 1414 and 1451. The purpose of the record seems to have varied over its long course of compilation. Initially, it records both proceedings conducted by the official at the monastery and those conducted by him during his regular visitations of the parishes within the jurisdiction. The former records contain a number of civil marriage cases; the latter are almost exclusively criminal. As time goes on, visitation and criminal material predominates, although it is not clear whether this reflects a change in jurisdiction or simply a change in record-keeping practices. Sexual offenses predominate throughout, although a wide variety of ecclesiastical offenses (defamation, witchcraft, striking a cleric) may be found.

(2) In marked contrast to the wide chronological reach of the Cerisy court book, the published civil register of the diocesan officiality of the bishop of Paris covers only the years 1384 to 1387.[30] Almost all the cases are civil cases, but there are hundreds of them. A wide range of subject matters is covered. The cases concerning marriage and the family have received some attention in the literature.[31]

(3) Approximately contemporaneously with the publication of the Paris register, two Dutch scholars published a seven-volume collection of material relating to the history of ecclesiastical jurisdiction in the diocese

29. 'Le registre de l'officialité de Cerisy', ed. Gustave Dupont [and Léopold Delisle], *Mémoires de la société des antiquaires de Normandie*, 3ᵉ série 10, no. 30 (1880) 271–662. Paul Le Cacheux, 'Un fragment de registre de l'officialité de Cerisy', *Bulletin de la Société des antiquaires de Normandie* 43 (1935) 291–315, edits records from 1474 to 1480 and 1485 that Dupont and Delisle missed. Digital editions: http://archive.org/stream/mmoiresoinormgoog#page/n285/mode/2up; http://gallica.bnf.fr/ark:/12148/bpt6k57321593. The manuscript was destroyed in 1944.

30. *Registre des causes civiles de l'officialité de Paris, 1384–1387*, ed. Joseph Petit and Paul Marichal (Collection des documents inédits sur l'histoire de France; Paris 1919), http://hdl.handle.net/2027/pst.000057437200.

31. See Jean-Philippe Lévy, 'L'officialité de Paris et les questions familiales à la fin du XIVᵉ siècle', *Études d'histoire de droit canonique dédiées à Gabriel Le Bras* (2 vols. Paris 1965) 2:1265–1294; Charles Donahue, *Law, Marriage, and Society in the Later Middle Ages: Arguments about Marriage in Five Courts* (New York 2007) chapter 7.

of Utrecht in the Middle Ages.[32] The 'jurisdiction' of the title is broadly defined. Hence, two of the volumes concern the geographical division of the diocese and contain various accounting records that show how the parishes and archdeaconries were organized; two volumes concern the division of subject-matter jurisdiction between the secular and ecclesiastical courts and contain collections of material on the topic that were compiled in the sixteenth century on the basis of earlier material; one volume contains synodal statutes and documents concerning visitations; one volume contains ordinances regulating the officials and formularies, and the final volume contains a miscellany of material concerning West Friesland.

(4) From the opposite end of our area geographically is a two-volume collection of material relating to the officialities of Aix and Marseille.[33] The material published is all to be found in various formularies. It concerns principally, though not exclusively, forms of mandates issued by the officials, as opposed to documents used by the parties in litigation.

(5) Most recently, the massive sentence book of the official of the bishop of Cambrai at Brussels that dates from 1448 to 1459 and a collection of sentence registers from the official of the same bishop at Cambrai, covering, with some gaps, the years 1438 to 1453 have been published.[34] The two collections contain almost 3,000 sentences, some interlocutory, but most definitive. Both civil and criminal sentences are represented. Marriage matters constitute the great bulk of the cases, though other subjects (testaments, church property, clerical discipline) are also found. Quite different in content, but almost as interesting, are the account books of the officiality of Tournai, which have also been published recently.[35]

All these books are well done, and it is no criticism of them to say that neither individually nor as a whole do they fully represent what survives. Both the Dutch and southern French collections suffer from the fact that, so far as the courts themselves are concerned, they give us statutes and/or formularies rather than actual cases. Statutes represent an ideal at a particular time. They tell us what the statute-giver hoped would happen, not

---

32. *Bronnen voor de geschiedenis der kerkelijke rechtspraak in het bisdom Utrecht in de middeleeuwen*, ed. Jan G. C. Joosting and Samuel Muller (7 vols. 's-Gravenhage 1906–1924).

33. *Recueil de lettres des officialités de Marseille et d'Aix*, ed. Roger Aubenas (2 vols. Paris 1937–1938).

34. *Liber sentenciarum van de officialiteit van Brussel (1448–1459)*, ed. Cyriel Vleeschouwers and Monique van Melkebeek (2 vols. Verzameling van de Oude Rechtspraak in België, 7.1–2; Brussel 1982–1983); *Registres de Sentences de l'Officialité de Cambrai (1438–1453)*, ed. Cyriel Vleeschouwers and Monique van Melkebeek (2 vols. Recueil de l'ancienne jurisprudence de la Belgique, 7e sér.; Bruxelles 1998).

35. *Compotus sigilliferi curie Tornacensis; Rekeningen van de officialiteit van Doornik: 1429–1481*, ed. Monique Vleeschouwers van Melkebeek (3 vols. Bruxelles 1995).

what necessarily did happen. Further, most statutes deal with relatively minor matters concerning the organization of the officiality; they rarely deal with substantive points about its business. By contrast, formularies frequently give us a piece of a record in an actual case. Unless the formulary is unusually full, however, it is rarely possible to tell the whole story of a given case from the formulae, nor, normally, is it possible to tell whether the formula was a usual or an unusual one, because formularies were used to record both.

Similar problems with representativeness are presented by the three major editions of actual court records. As we have seen, Cerisy was a small exempt jurisdiction and may have been atypical in many ways. There are also questions of whether the record actually records the same thing over its long course of composition. By contrast, the Paris, Cambrai, and Brussels registers cover relatively narrow time frames. They give us a snapshot of a certain kind of activity at a particular point. In the case of Paris, we can see the progress of civil litigation, but not much of criminal. In the case of Cambrai and Brussels, we see those cases (both civil and criminal) that produced sentences, but we see only the sentences. Much that might explain those sentences is simply not there. The legal, as opposed to the financial and social, content of the Tournai account book is even smaller.

While the bulk of the surviving records is such that one cannot hope that they all will be published, clearly more should be published. In particular, since so much of the material that survives from this region for the later Middle Ages is criminal, one would hope that someone would undertake a critical edition of one of the great runs of criminal registers that survive from the archdeacon's court of Paris and from the episcopal officialities of Troyes and Châlons-en-Champagne.[36] As it is, one must work with the printed material, aware of its deficiencies, with microfilm or photographs (which are not always obtainable), and in the fleeting moments that one gets to spend with the records themselves. Incentive for editions and for further research has recently been provided by the archives of the département de l'Aube, which houses the records of the officiality of Troyes. They have made digitized versions of the entirety of the fifteenth-century registers available on their website.[37] We hope other archives might soon follow this most promising example.

36. Donahue, *Records 1* III/59, III/63, III/43. The earliest Troyes register has been edited: Jean Bréban, 'Registre de l'officialité épiscopale de Troyes, 1389–1396 (Archives de l'Aube G 4170)' (thèse, droit, dact., université de Paris 1954), but it is atypical, dealing as it does largely with non-contentious and some civil matters.

37. http://www.archives-aube.fr/s/9/registres-de-l-officialite-de-troyes/resultats/?

The Organization of the French Officialities

The Officials

There was always some resistance to expanding the number of officials. It would seem that the power of the official was too great and too
closely related to that of the person whom he represented to permit its
easy multiplication. The model of the hierarchical church seems to have
envisioned one official for each bishop, and, perhaps, to have tolerated an
official for the archdeacon if the archdeacon's jurisdiction was tightly controlled.[38]

The reality was considerably messier. Some of the variations from the
model can be traced to jurisdictional complexities that existed at the time
of the origins of the officiality; some seem to have been the product of
increasing business, and some the product of political changes. We list below a number of officialities that are known to have varied from the norm
of only one official per diocese. We list only those officialities that have
left surviving court records. The number of oddities that are recorded
elsewhere far exceeds this number, but the surviving court records are the
best test of the reality, and they certainly give us enough illustrations for
our purposes here.

The large diocese of Utrecht was divided into eleven archdeaconries.
Nine of these archdeaconries were possessed corporately by collegiate
churches. The canons, without participation by the bishop, elected one
of their number as provost, who exercised ordinary power as archdeacon.
Five of these collegiate churches were in Utrecht; four others were scattered about the country. In addition the 'chorepiscopus', a canon of the
cathedral not in episcopal orders, exercised archidiaconal powers over a
small group of parishes, and there was an archdeacon, called 'provost',
of West-Friesland, who was also a canon of the cathedral. Appeal from
sentences of the officials of these archdeaconries lay to the official of the
bishop. Utrecht records also mention 'provisores', who were appointed by
the bishop to exercise jurisdiction, in some cases 'quasi-ordinaria' and in
some cases 'delegata', in certain areas. Appeal from the 'provisiores' also
lay to the official principal in Utrecht.[39]

In modern Belgium, the dean of Brugge in the diocese of Tournai had
an ecclesiastical court, which was taken over as a subordinate court of the

---

38. For this model of the officiality with citations to the common canon law, see Fournier,
Officialités 12–24, 133–142; Winfried Trusen, 'Die gelehrte Gerichtsbarkeit der Kirche', Coing,
Handbuch 1.473–475.

39. Donahue, *Records 1* 163–164.

bishop sometime in the late thirteenth or early fourteenth century. It operated throughout the Middle Ages. There are also occasional references to separate officialities in Oudenaarde and Lille.[40] The bishop of Cambrai, as we have seen, maintained a separate officiality in Brussels.[41]

In the north of modern France there were a number of important monastic jurisdictions that were exempt from episcopal control, at least as a matter of first instance. In addition to Cerisy, already mentioned, records have survived from the officialities of the abbeys of Fécamp and Montivilliers (all in the province of Rouen) and of Corbie (Reims).[42] The ecclesiastical court structure in the diocese of Paris was complicated. Records have survived from the officialities of the bishop, the cathedral chapter, the archdeacon of Brie, the archdeacon of Paris, and the exempt jurisdiction of Saint-Germain, which, like some of the abbeys mentioned above, also had secular jurisdiction over its territory.[43] Records survive of the jurisdiction, it would seem, of both the great archdeacon of Chartres and of the cathedral chapter.[44] The archbishop of Rouen maintained a separate vicar at Pontoise, who has left a number of surviving records.[45]

In central France the most complicated jurisdictional situation was that of Lyon. Records survive from the archbishop's primatial court, from his metropolitical and diocesan court (which were sometimes combined and sometimes separated and are frequently mentioned in the records of the archbishop's council), from a separate criminal diocesan court, known as the 'cour d'excès', from a combined court that the archbishop maintained with the cathedral chapter, from the court of the chapter of Saint-Jean, and from that of the chapter of Saint-Just.[46] The cathedral chapter of Limoges maintained a separate court, as did the cathedral chapter of Sens and that of Bourges.[47] The chapter of Saint-Julien-du-Sault in the diocese of Sens and the chapter court of Saint-Pierre in the diocese of Nantes have also left a few surviving records.[48]

---

40. Ibid. 51–53.   41. See 311.

42. Donahue, *Records 1* III/47, 48, 49, 40. These exemptions go back a long way. See Jean-François Lemarignier, *Étude sur les privilèges d'exemption et la juridiction ecclésiastique des abbayes normandes depuis les origines jusqu'à 1140* (thèse, droit, université de Paris 1937).

43. Donahue, *Records 1* III/56, 57, 58, 59, 60.

44. Ibid., III/54; see Lucien Merlet, 'Registre des officialités de Chartres', BEC 17 (1856) 574–594; Carole Avignon, *L'Église et les infractions au lien matrimonial: mariages clandestins et clandestinité. Théories, pratiques et discours. France du nord-ouest (XIIe–milieu XVI siècle)* (thèse, université de Paris-Est 2008) 333, especially n. 984. The caution expressed in Donahue, *Records 1*, about Merlet's descriptions of the jurisdictions remains, but at least two different courts seem to be involved.

45. Donahue, *Records 1* III/50. See Marie-Charlotte Demeunynck, *Le vicariat de Pontoise ou l'officialité foraine de Rouen à Pontoise (1255–1789)* (thèse, École des chartes, Paris 1933); see [Paris], École Nationale des Chartes, *Positions des thèses* (Paris 1933) 15–20.

46. Donahue, *Records 1* III/29, 30, 33, 34, 35, 36, 37.

47. Ibid. III/22, 51.   48. Ibid. III/62, 69.

Exempt or separate jurisdictions were fewer in the south, perhaps because of the larger number of dioceses. The bishop of Elne, however, maintained a separate officiality at Perpignan, and the bishop of Saint-Flour at Arpajon.[49]

In the mountainous East, evidence of numerous small jurisdictions abounds. The bishop of Grenoble maintained officialities both at Grenoble and at Chambéry.[50] Swiss archives contain various documents indicating jurisdictional activity by the archdeacon of Basel, the chapter of Lausanne, various archdeacons and deans in the diocese of Lausanne, the archpriest of Vintschgau and the dean of Engadin (diocese of Chur), and the deans of Sitten and Valeria (diocese of Sion).[51]

Subordinate Officers

Within the officiality itself, there were numerous subordinate officers. We hear occasionally of officials appointing 'vice-gerentes' or 'locumtenentes', who were their deputies for all matters. The number of known examples is small, however, and until further study proves otherwise, we may doubt whether such officers were regular members of the court, as opposed to someone appointed ad hoc as the circumstances required.[52] The larger officialities, however, did make use of various subordinate officers to perform pieces of the official's task. Thus, by the end of our period the Paris diocesan officiality had two 'auditores': one, apparently, for civil cases, the other for criminal. The Paris court also seems to have made use of commissaries for the purpose of taking depositions.[53]

By the end of the thirteenth century, the clerical staff of the officialities, at least the larger ones in the north, was divided into three parts, each under the head of a different subordinate of the official, and each charged with a different type of business.[54] The 'sigillifer', seal-bearer, of the court was in charge of the non-contentious business. In marked con-

---

49. Ibid. III/38, 27.   50. Ibid. III/73.

51. Ibid. X/3, 5, 6, 7, 8, 12.

52. Fournier, *Officialités* 25; Lefebvre, *Officialités* 35 and n. 59. Since we are disagreeing here (mildly) with both Fournier and Lefebvre, let us make our disagreement more precise. We are not denying that many, perhaps most, officials appointed substitutes when they had to be away from their seats or even when it was inconvenient for them to sit in court on a given day. What we are questioning is whether many, if any, French officialities had a permanent officer like the English commissary general. The fact that letters to officials are regularly addressed 'to the official of X or his vicegerent (or *locumtenens* in the south)' does not tell us anything about the permanence of the officer in question.

53. Fournier, *Curie diocésaine* 188–195; Lefebvre, *Officialités* 36–37.

54. Lefebvre, *Officialités* 33–34; Fournier, *Officialités* 26–27. The evidence here is largely from Reims, but Trusen, 'Gelehrte Gerichtsbarkeit' 476–477, offers enough other examples that we can have some confidence that we are not dealing with a phenomenon unique to Reims.

trast to England, and perhaps other areas, the officialities in our area were notable for the amount of non-contentious business that they did, though the surviving court records from later periods feature far more evidence of contentious business. In the thirteenth century (and probably for some time thereafter, though the evidence for subsequent centuries is spotty), a great deal of relatively routine legal business, notably business involving benefices and routine dispensations, passed under the seal of the officiality.[55] The 'registrator' of the court kept track of the criminal business. As the name implies, he normally did so in registers, and these have survived in some quantity for the later Middle Ages.[56] The 'receptor actorum', on the other hand, seems to have been largely in charge of the civil business. Although civil registers are not unknown in France, there are far fewer of them than there are criminal registers.[57]

In the second half of the thirteenth century in northern France, by a process that is still not well traced, the 'registrator' came to be called the 'procurator curie' or the 'promotor'.[58] The function of the promotor was to conduct criminal cases in the name of the office of the bishop. He thus became a kind of ecclesiastical prosecutor, and as such was even more an officer of the court than were the proctors and advocates who practiced before the court representing private clients. The purview and number of these promotors, at least in the fifteenth-century diocese of Troyes, proved the subject of considerable complaint on the part of municipal and royal officials, a topic to which we will return when we deal with the jurisdiction of the French officialities.[59]

The legal functions of a prosecutor and the clerical functions that the former 'registrator' performed were not the same, and there is some ev-

---

55. Lefebvre, *Officialités* 33–34; Fournier, *Officialités* 26–27. See generally Louis Carolus-Barré, 'L'organisation de la juridiction gracieuse à Paris dans le dernier tiers du XIIIe siècle: L'officialité et le Châtelet', *Le Moyen Age* 69 (1963) 417–435.

56. Fournier, *Officialités* 28–29; Lefebvre, *Officialités* 34. For criminal registers, see 312.

57. Fournier, *Officialités* 27–28. For examples of civil registers, see Donahue, *Records 1* III/7/3 (Marseille), III/10/3 (Carpentras), III/59/3/2 (Paris archdeacon). Since Donahue, *Records 1* was compiled, the Carpentras records have been examined more closely. Of 24 fifteenth-century registers noted in the handlist at the archive, only two are listed as criminal registers, and one which is not listed as either civil or criminal (B 3324) is, in fact, a criminal register. Fifteen registers are listed as civil, and three that are not listed as either civil or criminal turn out to be civil (B 3322A, B 3324bis, and 3325). Many of these registers are in bad condition, having suffered water damage in a previous repository. They remain, however, a remarkable set of records that, with patience, can be made to yield up their secrets. For recent scholarship, see Elizabeth Hardman, *Justice, Jurisdiction and Choice: The Church Courts of Carpentras in the Fifteenth Century* (Ph.D. diss., Fordham University, New York 2010).

58. P. Fournier's account (*Officialités* 27–28) has now been replaced by É. Fournier, *Curie diocésaine* 196–229; see Lefebvre, *Officialités* 34. What is still unclear is whether the development that É. Fournier painstakingly traces for Reims occurred in other dioceses, and when.

59. See 325.

idence that the mixture was not a complete success. By the end of the fourteenth century we see a new officer—called in French 'greffier', and in Latin, frequently simply 'notarius curie' or 'scriba'—who was in charge of keeping track of the criminal records.[60] Further evidence that the functions of a prosecutor and the functions of a clerk did not mix well is found in the fact that in a number of officialities in the later Middle Ages we find an officer, called the 'receptor emendarum', whose function, as the name implies, was to collect the fines imposed by the court. This office was sometimes combined with that of the 'sigillifer' or with that of the promotor.[61]

The question is, what happened to the receptor actorum? Lefebvre reports that he is not to be found in any of the records she examined from the later Middle Ages.[62] She speculates that his function was taken over by the 'sigillifer'. This speculation may be correct, but there is little in the surviving civil registers that would confirm it. All of the civil registers that have been examined carefully were composed by notaries, men who describe themselves as 'notarius curie', or, occasionally, as at Brussels and Paris, 'scriba'.[63] In some areas, particularly in the south, this function may have been performed by notaries who had another practice, and who served on an ad hoc, or even case-by-case basis. In most areas, however, the notary who served as the court's notary enrolled all the cases, or at least all the cases of a particular type, for a period of several years. In the south, too, we sometimes find the court's records for a given period kept in the notarial étude to which the court's notary belonged, while in the north, if they survive at all, these records survive as part of the court's own archive.[64]

As we noted above, there are relatively few civil registers that survive from the officialities.[65] We will note below that as the Middle Ages progressed there was a tendency for civil procedure to become accommodated to criminal procedure, on the one hand, and 'gracious' procedure on the other.[66] The ambivalence in many officialities over who was responsible for records of civil cases goes hand in hand with an ambivalence about civil procedure generally. Much, of course, depends on what one assumes about what is missing. It seems hard, however, to believe that

60. Lefebvre, *Officialités* 34.
61. Ibid. 36.
62. Ibid. 34 at n. 37.
63. *Liber sentenciarum* 1.62; Petit, *Registre* 190.
64. See e.g. Donahue, *Records 1* III/7/2.
65. See 316.
66. See 'The Procedure of the French Officialites' 331–336.

dioceses such as Troyes and Châlons-en-Champagne, which have left us such a remarkable series of records of criminal cases, would not have left us at least something on the civil side, if the civil jurisdiction had been anything like as extensive as the criminal jurisdiction.[67]

In the diocese of Nîmes and in the exempt officiality of Montivilliers we find an officer called 'magister testamentorum', who was concerned, as the name implies, with jurisdiction over testamentary matters.[68] In Montivilliers he also dealt with the intestates' estates. Further research will probably turn up other officers performing similar functions, because, as we shall see, some officialities in our area had extensive testamentary jurisdiction.

Inquisitions into Heresy

As was already suggested in Donahue 'The Ecclesiastical Courts: Introduction', medieval inquisitions into heresy were ad hoc.[69] Nonetheless, during the thirteenth century and the first half of the fourteenth, there were a sufficient number of inquisitors into heresy in the south of France that such inquisitors almost became a regular feature of ecclesiastical jurisdiction in this area during this period. Records have survived from inquisitions at, among other places, Toulouse, Albi, Carcasonne, and Pamiers.[70] Appointments of inquisitors, whether by a bishop or the pope, were made so frequently that one might say that inquisitors were beginning to be a permanent institution. A permanent institution did not develop, however, for the wave of Catharism and Waldensianism that prompted the sustained inquisitions of the thirteenth and fourteenth centuries subsided, and ecclesiastical attention shifted elsewhere.[71]

Renewed interest in prosecuting both the Waldensians, who would later join the Protestant Reformation, and also the various forms of alleged witchcraft and heresy referred to as 'Waldensian', began again in the fifteenth century, most notably with prosecutions in the Dauphiné and Arras, with scattered pockets of prosecution throughout much of France.

<hr>

67. See Donahue, *Records 1* III/63.

68. Lefebvre, *Officialités* 35–36; Fournier, *Officialités* 31.

69. Donahue, 'Ecclesiastial Courts' 266.

70. See *Le registre d'inquisition de Jacques Fournier (Évêque de Pamiers, 1318–1325)*, ed. Jean Duvernoy (3 vols. Paris 1978); *Processus Bernardi Delitiosi: The Trial of Fr. Bernard Délicieux, 3 September–8 December 1319*, ed. Alan Friedlander (Transactions of the American Philosophical Society 86.1; Philadelphia 1996); Mark G. Pegg, *The Corruption of Angels: The Great Inquisition of 1245–1246* (Princeton 2001); *Livre des sentences de l'inquisiteur Bernard Gui: 1308–1323*, ed. Annette Pales-Gobilliard (2 vols. Paris 2002); see also http://jean.duvernoy.free.fr/sources/sinquisit.htm.

71. For two good accounts, with references, see Walter Wakefield, *Heresy, Crusade and Inquisition in Southern France, 1100–1250* (London 1974); Élie Griffe, *Le Languedoc cathare et l'Inquisition (1229–1329)* (Paris 1980).

These isolated prosecutions of alleged witches as 'vaudois' were followed by a massive effort to repress 'actual' Waldensians in 1487, called for by the pope and the parlement of Grenoble acting with inquisitors.[72] In the earlier fifteenth-century examples, secular courts in some cases took the lead, while in other cases, as in Arras, officialities conducted the proceedings with or without the inquisitor delegated to that diocese. Apart from these isolated and rather spectacular prosecutions, in at least some parts of northern France, such as the diocese of Troyes, the officiality tried a handful of cases in tandem with the local inquisitor, who judged these cases with the official.[73] All of this took place alongside the best-known trials that made use of inquisitors in our period: that of Joan of Arc and of her rehabilitation.[74] In both cases a bishop appointed special commissaries to hear a particular case. Once the case was concluded, the body disbanded. Apart from the prosecutions in southern France in the thirteenth and fourteenth centuries,[75] there is little evidence for an organized inquisition in our period, and it is quite clear that there was never anything in France on the scale, or with the permanence, of the Spanish Inquisition established in the late fifteenth century, or its parallels and successors in Italy and the Spanish territories.

The Jurisdiction of the French Officialities

The Division between Secular and Ecclesiastical Jurisdiction

Recent work with the records of the French officialities allows us considerably to expand what is generally known about their geographical jurisdiction. While a complete picture may never emerge, granted how much has been lost, our knowledge, particularly of the activities of special jurisdictions, has expanded considerably.[76] Our understanding of the

72. Pierette Paravy, *De la chrétienté romaine à la Réforme en Dauphiné. Évêques, fidèles et déviantes (vers 1340–vers 1530)* (2 vols. Collection de l'École française de Rome 183; Paris 1993). For the 'vaudois' of Arras, see Henry Charles Lea, *A History of the Inquisition of the Middle Ages* (3 vols. New York 1888; reprinted Cambridge 2010) 3.519–533. For prosecutions of superstition, sorcery, and usury in Rouen that did not make use of delegated inquisitors, see Vincent Tabbagh, 'Rouen 1438: De l'extension du champ de la répression judiciare en situation de crise', *De la déviance à la délinquance, XVe–XIXe siècle*, ed. Benoît Garnot (Dijon 1999) 13–39.

73. Troyes, Archives départementales de l'Aube, G4171, fol. 16r (blasphemy), G4171, fol. 46r (resistance to efforts on the part of the bishop to suppress local 'pagan' practices); G4171, fol. 143 (heresy).

74. For a modern recounting of the story with references to the primary material, see Charles Wood, *Joan of Arc and Richard III* (Oxford 1988) 125–151.

75. See sources and literature cited in nn. 70–71; cf. Émmanuel Le Roy Ladurie, *Montaillou, village occitan de 1294 à 1324* (Paris 1975) (to be treated with caution as history but great fun to read).

76. For example, Fabrice Delivré, 'Les Officialités primatiales en France (v. 1420–1520): Réforme et Pratique Juridictionnelle', *Les officialités dans l'Europe médiévale et moderne: des tribunaux pour une société chrétienne: Actes du colloque international de Troyes, 27–29 mai 2010*, ed. Véronique Beaulande-Barraud and Martine Charageat (Tournout 2014) 75–90.

jurisdictional settlements between the church and the secular power is, however, more limited, but we do have a growing body of research upon which to draw.[77]

The beginning years of the sixteenth century saw a considerable tension between ecclesiastical and secular jurisdiction, a tension that frequently became the subject of proceedings before the parlement of Paris. The cases are nicely summarized by Lefebvre, and from them she concludes that the advocates of the king, with considerable help from the parlement, were trying to establish and enforce four principles: (1) A bishop, because he has no territory, has no jurisdiction to impose any physical penalties. He can only impose spiritual sanctions. The principle was most controverted in the case of arrests. The king's advocates also attempted to apply it to the imposition of pecuniary sanctions. (2) The ecclesiastical courts had no jurisdiction in the purely personal cases of laymen. The king's advocates certainly sought to apply this principle to cases of defamation and assault, which some church courts heard quite frequently. They may have intended to apply this principle to the large number of contract cases that some church courts heard under the rubric of excommunication for debt. (3) The king's advocates wished to exclude the church courts from taking jurisdiction of cases in which both the church courts and the secular courts had traditionally been competent. Cases involving testaments were notable in this group. (4) The king's advocates wished to exclude the ecclesiastical courts entirely from cases involving questions of possession, an exclusion that would have had the effect of depriving the church courts of much of their jurisdiction in matters of benefices and tithes.[78]

Of these four efforts, the second and fourth met with some success during this period. The first article of the 'ordonnance' of Villers-Cotterêts of 1539 reads: 'Let it be known that we have forbidden and now forbid our subjects from citing lay people before judges of the church in purely personal actions, on penalty of loss of the case and an arbitrary

---

77. Fournier, *Officialités*; François Olivier-Martin, *L'assemblée de Vincennes de 1329 et ses conséquences* (Paris 1909); Robert Génestal, *Le privilegium fori en France* (2 vols. Bibliothèqe de l'École des Hautes Études, Sciences religieuses 35, 39; Paris 1921–1924); Robert Génestal, *Les origines de l'appel comme d'abus* (Bibliothèqe de l'École des Hautes Études, Sciences religieuses 63; Paris 1951); Jean-Pierre Royer, *L'Église et royaume de France au XIVe siècle d'après le 'Songe du Vergier' et la jurisprudence du Parlement* (Bibliothèque d'histoire du droit et du droit romain 15; Paris 1969); Lefebvre, *Officialités*; Jean-Louis Gazzaniga, 'Les États généraux de Tours de 1484 et les affaires de l'Église', RHD 62 (1984) 31–45; Jacques Krynen, 'Le roi "Très Chrétien" et le rétablissement de la Pragmatique Sanction: Pour une explication idéologique du gallicanisme parlementaire et de la politique religieuse de Louis XI', *Églises et pouvoir politique : Actes des journées internationales d'histoire du droit d'Angers, 30 mai–1er juin 1985* (Angers 1987) 135–149; Delivré, 'Les Officialités primatiales'.

78. Lefebvre, *Officialités* 127–134.

fine.'[79] The statute does not seem to have been applied to contractual matters, but may have contributed to the considerable decline in the number of cases that has been noted in some of the registers in this period.[80] Lefebvre concludes:[81]

Despite the assaults suffered at the end of the fifteenth century, the competence of the officialities at the dawn of the sixteenth century was still very important: engagements, marriage, separation of spouses, heresy, and sacrilege were within their exclusive competence. Either directly, by means of obligations entered into under oath, or indirectly, by means of excommunication for debt, they had cognizance of contracts. In competition with the royal justices, they were judges of testaments and tithes; they punished incest, adultery, illicit sexual relations, and separated lepers from the world of the faithful. Finally, the reputation that they enjoyed among litigants meant that litigants, despite the futile efforts of the royal agents, continued to submit to them many personal quarrels of all sorts.

But their position was threatened. The stubbornness of their adversaries, which caused internal repercussions within the church, was eventually going to triumph. Already when the Council finally began its work in the little village of Trent, the officialities no longer had the right of cognizance of personal causes of lay people; in many cases their right to punish lay people was contested, and in those situations where they still could do so, they were only permitted to impose a spiritual sanction.

The competence over testaments and tithes was withering; the privilege of the forum was narrowing; even marriage cases, the last bastion, were suffering restrictions. At the same time that the king was thinking about legislating directly about these matters if he did not obtain satisfaction at the Council, his agents wanted to obtain cognizance of separation of spouses.

Testing these propositions would take us far beyond our period. Unquestionably the church courts in France lost a considerable amount of jurisdiction in the early modern period, though the substantial survivals of records from the sixteenth, seventeenth, and even the eighteenth centuries would suggest that this topic, too, needs further exploration. From our point of view, however, the point is that the same paragraphs could have been written about the situation after the assembly of Vincennes in 1329.[82] Indeed, similar paragraphs have been written, without the control over the record material that allowed Lefebvre to assess so positively the situation at the beginning of the sixteenth century. Recent research, moreover, might suggest that some decline in jurisdiction as the result of pressure from the secular authorities—a decline that Lefebvre hints was

79. Ibid. 127.

80. Ibid. 128. Lefebvre's statistics, however, show a decline in criminal jurisdiction with an unexplained increase in civil jurisdiction.

81. Ibid. 143 (CD translation).

82. Olivier-Martin, *Assemblée de Vincennes*, remains fundamental.

beginning in 1500—had already happened in some courts over the course of the second half of the fifteenth century, but definitely not as early as 1329.[83]

From the time of the formation of the officialities in the thirteenth century until their ultimate decline in the eighteenth century, there were constant tensions between the ecclesiastical courts and the secular courts. From the point of view of the secular jurisdiction, the ecclesiastical courts were supposed to confine themselves to purely spiritual matters. Their broad claims of jurisdiction by reason of the person were never fully conceded, nor were their claims of jurisdiction by reason of the subject matter when the matter concerned what F. W. Maitland called 'that debatable land which is neither very spiritual nor very temporal'.[84] If a tithe is an offering to the church, commanded by the law of God and of his church, it is also a tax on property, one that may be of critical importance in the livelihood of both the tithe-giver and the tithe-receiver (who may not even be a clergyman). If a testament is an expression of a man's settling of his final accounts before he stands before the throne of judgment, it is also an intergenerational disposition of property. If a criminous clerk is under the jurisdiction of the church because of his orders, he has also offended, perhaps grievously offended, the secular order. Men of good will have difficulty finding principled resolutions of such questions of competence, and not all those who engaged in the debate were of good will.

It is not surprising, therefore, that the matter was controversial, nor, indeed, that no firm resolution could be reached. The arguments and their tentative resolutions from the thirteenth to the sixteenth centuries remained pretty much the same. In the fourteenth century, we have ample evidence that documents French kings, lords, and municipal authorities taking aim at selected officialities, seeking in particular to limit their jurisdictional powers over the laity. Municipal authorities in Amiens, for example, regularly appealed their jurisdictional disputes with the officiality of Amiens to the parlement of Paris.[85] Other municipalities and royal officials similarly appealed all manner of jurisdictional disputes with ecclesiastical authorities to the parlement. Such efforts continued throughout the fifteenth century; they focused on the prosecution of the laity in

---

83. See 324–325.

84. Frederic William Maitland, *Roman Canon Law in the Church of England: Six Essays* (London 1898; reprinted New York 1968) 56.

85. *Documents inédits concernant la ville et le siège du bailliage d'Amiens: extraits des registres du Parlement de Paris et du Trésor des chartes*, ed. Édouard Maugis (3 vols. Amiens 1908–1921) 2.31–33 (referring to decisions of 1336 and 1388, and printing a complaint of 1406, all concerning competence in cases of adultery).

church courts, particularly for moral delicts.[86] Monique Vleeschouwers has studied similar efforts on the part of communal and seigniorial powers to limit ecclesiastical jurisdiction in Burgundian lands, motivated at least in part, as she points out, by an interest in laying hold of the revenues that came with such judicial competence.[87]

In our area, as in virtually every other area of western Europe, jurisdiction over marriage cases was conceded to the church courts, while there might be some debate around the edges where the secular effects of marriage were concerned. Adultery cases, technically within the purview of church courts in this region, sometimes saw secular prosecution, and jurisdictional battles between secular and church authorities over the power to prosecute adultery were a relatively frequent feature of the fifteenth century. Legal separations, if granted by church courts in northern France, appear to have had their financial implications worked out in secular courts. In southern France, however, secular courts both granted separations and handled the financial implications.[88] In our area as in virtually every other area of western Europe, spiritual crimes were cognizable in the ecclesiastical courts, and there would be jurisdictional overlap only when the crime became a matter of political concern, as in the case of heresy at some times in our period, or in the case of witchcraft, beginning at the end of our period. In some places in our area, in marked contrast to many other areas of Western Europe, the church courts had extensive jurisdiction over contract. This jurisdiction was a matter of fact; it does not seem to have been strongly defended even by churchmen. In some places in our area, in contrast with some other areas in Western Europe, the church courts had considerable jurisdiction over testaments. In our area, in contrast with others, criminous clerks were turned over to the secular arm after conviction. In our area, in contrast with others, possessory actions concerning tithes and benefices were shared with the

86. For example, for Troyes, see Théophile Boutiot, 'Recherches sur la juridiction du roi sur celle de l'evêque dans le Bailliage de Troyes et sur les coutumes de ce bailliage', *Mémoires de la Société académique d'agriculture, des sciences, arts et belles-lettres de l'Aube 36* (1872) 6–74; see also Troyes, Archives départementales de l'Aube, G137.

87. Monique Vleeschouwers van Melkebeek, 'Conflits de jurisdiction au niveau diocesain dans les Pays bourguignons de par deça', *Les juristes dans la ville: Urbanisme, société, économie, politique, mentalités,* ed. Jean-Marie Cauchies (Publication du Centre Européen d'Études Bourguignonnes 40; Neuchâtel 2000) 33–47.

88. Susan McDonough, 'She Said, He Said, and They Said: Claims of Abuse and a Community's Response in Late Medieval Marseille', *Journal of Women's History 19* (2007) 35–58; for comparison to Italy see Diego Quaglioni, '"Divortium a diversitate mentium": La separazione personale dei coniugi nelle dottrine di diritto comune (appunti su una discussione)', *Coniugi nemici: La separazione in Italia dal XII al XVIII secolo,* ed. Silvana Seidel Menchi and Diego Quaglioni (I processi matrimoniali degli archivi ecclesiastici italiani 1; Atti del primo, secondo e quarto seminario; Annali dell'Istituto storico italo-germanico in Trento, Quaderni 53; Bologna 2000) 95–118.

secular courts. At some periods, such actions would seem to have been more within the cognizance of the ecclesiastical courts than within the cognizance of the secular courts.[89]

The resulting pattern of settlement was unstable. Wide variations seem to have existed across our geographical area, variations that are probably not the product simply of loss of records.[90] In the fifteenth century, the sentence books of the officiality of Cambrai (outside of the jurisdiction of France entirely) and the records of the officiality of Carpentras (a complicated jurisdictional situation involving both the pope and the dauphin) both reveal a considerably wider jurisdiction than what we would expect in an ecclesiastical court.[91] If the court in Carpentras seems to have dealt with far fewer marriage cases than did those in the north, it was quite active in other respects. To give one example, as a recent dissertation has demonstrated, the court served as an important venue for debt litigation.[92]

There is no evidence that the officiality of Troyes exercised jurisdiction over contractual matters in the later part of the fifteenth century. Such a jurisdiction is well evidenced in the same court in the late fourteenth century. This difference may the product of loss of records. There are no records of civil cases at Troyes for the fifteenth century. As we have already suggested, however, it seems hard to believe that had the civil jurisdiction of the officiality of Troyes been anything like as extensive as its criminal jurisdiction it would not have left us some evidence of it to go along with records of the criminal jurisdiction that do survive. If there was in fact a marked decline in contractual jurisdiction of the court from the end of the fourteenth to the later part of the fifteenth, that decline could be explained by the fact that at the end of the fourteenth century, the monarchy was preoccupied by war. When the monarchy became stronger after the war, the church courts, at least in the north, may have lost ground.[93]

At present, we know of a handful of local disputes in Northern France

89. In addition to the literature cited in n. 77, this paragraph is based on a survey of the subject-matter jurisdiction revealed in Donahue, *Records 1* II, III, VII, X.

90. It should be recalled that the jurisdictional pattern was simply 'outlined' at the assembly by Pierre Cuignières and other advocates on behalf of the king. Their theories were not embodied in the subsequent royal order. See Olivier-Martin, *Assemblée de Vincennes*.

91. See Donahue, *Records 1* III/43, 10. A sample of six months of Carpentras cases from 1436 (B3322), for example, reveals a large number of debt cases (particularly debts on ordinary sales), including cases involving voluntary and involuntary bankruptcy (cessio bonorum, missio in possessionem), cases concerning tithes and benefices, cases involving inheritance, even one case of physical damage to a house. Most, though not all of these cases, involve members of the clergy on one side or the other. See the next sentence and accompanying note.

92. Hardman, 'Justice, Jurisdiction and Choice'.

93. For contractual jurisdiction at Troyes in the late fourteenth century, see Bréban, 'Registre de Troyes' (n. 36). For the absence of any civil registers in the fifteenth century, see 318.

that went to the parlement, all over the 'excesses' of the church courts in their handling of the laity.[94] To return the example of Troyes, in the first half of the fifteenth century, the officiality in Troyes acted on its claimed competence over adultery, murder involving clergy, violence, insults, and even promises under oath to keep the peace (assecurationes), in order to prosecute and punish hundreds of laypeople in the diocese. Relations with local secular authorities, meanwhile, worsened; we hear of reciprocal imprisonments and excommunications or banishments of the opposing party's court officers. After protracted litigation before the parlement of Paris, in 1461, the parlement ordered the officiality of Troyes to reduce the number of promotors it employed and to refrain from the 'ex officio' prosecution of the laity for offences the parlement considered as falling under secular jurisdiction—a lengthy list that included adultery, blasphemy, and homicide.[95] Preliminary investigations into this question show a noted absence of adultery and homicide prosecutions after 1465, in marked contrast to the earlier records.[96]

Once more, it may be significant that the restriction of the jurisdiction at Troyes came after, indeed just after, the end of the war. The hypothesis that the end of the war led to the monarchy being more able to engage in incursions into the jurisdiction of the officialities may explain more than the situation at Troyes; it may explain why the issues about jurisdiction raised in the early sixteenth century are so similar to those raised at the assembly of Vincennes.

There are also variations in jurisdiction that seem to be related to geography, but in different ways. For example, testamentary jurisdiction seems to be most in evidence in Normandy and in the south.[97] To explain the former we might look to the equally strong testamentary jurisdiction of the English church courts; to explain the latter we might argue that testaments were generally more important in the south than in the north.

94. For a transcription of a mid-century (before April 1452) complaint from the archbishop of Reims about secular incursions into what he claimed as ecclesiastical jurisdiction, see Nöel Valois, *Histoire de la Pragmatique sanction de Bourges sous Charles VII* (Archives de l'histoire religieuse de la France; Paris 1906) 206–220. For jurisdictional conflicts in Amiens, see 322. For Amiens and Troyes, see Sara McDougall, 'The Transformation of Adultery in France at the End of the Middle Ages', LHR (2014) 491–524. See also Claude Gauvard, 'Honneur de Femme et Femme d'Honneur en France à la fin du Moyen Âge', *Francia* 28 (2001) 159–191; Cyril Pons, 'Les affaires d'adultère en France du Nord du XIIIe au début du XVIe siècle', *Matrimonio y sexualidad. Normas, praticas y transgresiones en la Edad Media y principios de la Epoca Moderna*, ed. Martine Charageat (Mélanges de la Casa de Velázquez 33; Madrid 2003) 113–124.

95. G137 (n. 86); Boutiot, 'Recherches sur la juridiction'.

96. See McDougall, 'Transformation of Adultery'; Gauvard, 'Honneur de Femme'; Pons, 'Affaires d'adultère'.

97. Fournier, *Officialités* 31; *Les testaments de l'officialité de Besançon (1265–1500)*, ed. Ulysse Robert (2 vols. Collection de documents inédits sur l'histoire de France; Paris 1902–1907); Lefebvre, *Officialités* 35–36; Donahue, *Records* 1 III passim, especially III/7/4.

The point is this: Until the surviving records are carefully examined for the types of cases that they reveal across time and across regions, it is probably dangerous to generalize on the basis of what is known of the claims that church and crown made when they faced each other in debate. The assembly of Vincennes and the ordonnance of Villers-Cottêrets were important, but we cannot assume that what happened always complied with their terms, even in the areas where they were in effect.

The Range of Subject-Matter Jurisdiction in Fact

To get some sense of this last point, let us examine one register of an episcopal officiality, that of the bishop of Le Puy for the years 1270 to 1274.[98] This record is, in many ways, highly atypical, and it considerably antedates the assembly of Vincennes. What it shows, however, is how far the subject-matter jurisdiction of an episcopal officiality could vary from the norm and still be recognizably that of an episcopal officiality.[99] (It should also be noted that further study of this book is clearly called for.)

The subject-matter jurisdiction represented in our Le Puy register is very broad and is almost entirely concerned with matters that could be treated in a secular court. We find a number of actions for 'iniuria', both physical and verbal, though the latter seem to predominate. The offending words are frequently given in the vernacular (Occitan). There are also a number of contract actions, mostly for the collection of debts, some of which had been previously registered with the court. There are several actions for dowry, several requests for the appointment of tutors for orphaned children, and an order to pay 'alimenta' to a woman who was found to have been the wife of a man (it not being clear whether he was deceased or whether this was a separation case). Cases concerning property are less common, but they exist: One man seeks the return of several

---

98. Le Puy, Archives départementales de la Haute-Loire, G260. Another book, G261, contains similar material, mostly, if not all, dated in 1283, when the see was vacant and the officers of the court were appointed by the king. See Donahue, *Records 1* III/24/4. The significance of this record was not, however, known when *Records 1* was written.

99. The only use of this book in print that we know of is in Étienne Delcambre, 'Le paréage du Puy', BEC 92 (1931) 121–169, 285–344, especially 137–149. A description follows: The book is arranged by cases rather than by dates, and the clerk normally began a new page for each case. There may be more than 100 cases in a register of 137 folios. The record contains the 'acta' in the case and occasionally the depositions. There are some sentences. A few original documents are folded into the quires. From a procedural point of view the book is notable for its use of Romano-canonical procedure throughout. Instance procedure is far more common than 'ex officio' procedure, although there are a couple of examples of what seems to be the latter. Some cases seem to have been pleaded orally, some in writing. The 'acta' are notable in that they frequently give the substantive arguments of the lawyers. There is an extensive use of positions throughout the book, and these are normally answered both by the adverse party's proctor and by the adverse party him- or herself.

mules, which the defendant claims were given him as a pledge; another seeks an order against his neighbor who is preventing him from constructing a stone and plaster wall.[100] A number of cases concern the administration of decedents' estates.

The chief judge of the court throughout the book is Master Armand de Fayno. He is variously described as the judge of the court of Le Puy (iudex curie Aniciensis) or bailiff of the court of Le Puy (baiulus) or official of the court of Le Puy (officialis). In 1273, another man, Guillaume de Rochabero, is the bailiff, but Armand is still the judge. An occasional mention of appeal from a judgment of the court speaks of appeal to the king, not to the archbishop of Bourges or to the pope.

The first question that such a document raises is, can this be called an ecclesiastical court at all? None of the cases that the court dealt with in this period had to be in an ecclesiastical court. Although there are cases that concern marriage, there appear to be no marriage-enforcement actions and no separation cases. There also appear to be no cases that deal with ecclesiastical property, such as tithes or benefices.

In the thirteenth century, the bishop of Le Puy was not only the bishop of the territory around Le Puy; he was also the secular lord of much of the same territory. He held his lands nominally of the king of France, and as French royal power extended into Languedoc, this nominal relationship became more of a reality. In 1307 the bishop agreed to a 'paréage' with the king, whereby the secular jurisdiction in the area would be presided over by two judges, one appointed by the bishop, the other by the king.[101] But our document dates from more than a generation before this happened.

There is some evidence in the record that the bishop's bailiff had his own court.[102] We may suspect that this court concerned itself with criminal matters, though we cannot tell whether it dealt with both secular and ecclesiastical crimes. The absence of marriage cases in the surviving record is puzzling, but then again the relative absence of marriage cases is characteristic of the south.[103] It is possible that tithe and benefice matters were dealt with in another court, but it is also conceivable that they were dealt with administratively rather than judicially. In short, the officiality of

---

100. G260 (n. 98), fol. 14v, 47r.

101. Delcambre, 'Le paréage', tells the story well.

102. For example, G260, fol. 20r, where Marc Bellonis, clerk of the church of Le Puy, complains that Bartholomée Maleti, citizen of Le Puy, defamed him before the bailiff.

103. See Charles Donahue, 'The Canon Law on the Formation of Marriage and Social Practice in the Later Middle Ages', *Journal of Family History* (1983) 152. Of approximately 100 cases in the Carpentras court book from the second half of 1436 (n. 91), only one deals with marriage, and this is a divorce case, on the ground of bigamy.

Le Puy in the late thirteenth century probably dealt largely with a run of personal actions quite indistinguishable from those which one would find in a secular court at the same time.

That, of course, raises the question whether the official was aware of the sharp distinction between spiritual and secular matters that had been characteristic of canonic writing since the time of the Gregorian reform. It is hard to imagine that he was not. The sophistication of the procedure suggests that the personnel of the court were well acquainted with at least one aspect of the common law of the church; they were probably acquainted with others as well. Some division between secular and ecclesiastical matters was probably made for purposes of appeals, for it is inconceivable that the court could have denied a party the right to appeal to the pope in an appropriate case. The references, however, to appeals are few.

One Area of Subject-Matter Jurisdiction—Marriage

One area of subject-matter jurisdiction that was exercised by virtually all ecclesiastical courts in our area was jurisdiction over marriage. There are a number of studies in print.[104] They focus on the fourteenth, fifteenth, and early sixteenth centuries, and on cases concerning marriage in northern France and the Low Countries. While some of these studies have provoked controversy, it is important to emphasize the considerable agreement among them.

In the first place, in marked contrast to England, and, it would appear,

104. For our region, see Lévy, 'Questions familiales' (n. 31) (study of marriage and family cases in the printed register of the episcopal officiality of Paris); Lefebvre, *Officialités* 147–221 (focuses on the period from 1490–1540, and for the marriage material relies particularly on the records of the Paris archdeacon's court); Beatrice Gottlieb, *Getting Married in Pre-Reformation Europe: The Doctrine of Clandestine Marriage and Court Cases in Fifteenth-Century Champagne* (PhD diss., Columbia University 1974) (based on the late-fifteenth-century records of Troyes and Châlons-en-Champagne); Gottlieb, 'The Meaning of Clandestine Marriage', *Family and Sexuality in French History*, ed. Robert Wheaton and Tamara Hareven (Philadelphia 1980) 49–83 (summary of the argument of the dissertation, with some additional material); Anne Lefebvre-Teillard, 'Règle et realité dans le droit matrimonial à la fin du moyen-age', RDC 30 (1980) 41–54 (based on Lefebvre, *Officialités*, with additions); Donahue, 'Social Practice' (based on an attempt to survey the whole); Monique Vleeschouwers-van Melkebeek, 'Aspects du lien matrimonial dans le *Liber sentenciarum de Bruxelles*', TRG 53 (1985) 43–97 (based on the records of the Cambrai officiality [n. 34]); Charlotte Christensen-Nugues, 'Mariage consenti, mariage contraint: L'abjuration sub pena nubendi à l'officialité de Cerisy, 1314–1346', *Médiévales* 40 (2001) 101–111; Donahue, *Law, Marriage*, chapters 7 and 8; Emmanuël Falzone, '"Ad secunda vota rite convolare posse": Le remariage des personnes veuves à la fin du moyen âge dans les registres de sentences de l'officialité de Cambrai (1438–1453)', RHE 102 (2007) 815–836; Sara McDougall, *Bigamy and Christian Identity in Late Medieval Champagne* (Philadelphia 2012); Avignon, 'L'Église et les infractions'; Ruth M. Karras, *Unmarriages: Women, Men, and Sexual Unions in Medieval Europe* (Philadelphia 2012) esp. chapter 4 (once more, the Paris archdeacon's court).

Germany, the number of cases dealing with an informal exchange of 'de presenti' consent to marry is small.[105] Cases in which a marriage is sought to be enforced almost always concern espousals of the future tense. Second, and again in marked contrast to England, and perhaps Germany, the number of cases that deal with separation is relatively high.[106] These cases not only concern the separation from bed and board that is well known from the common canon law but also separation of goods. The standard for granting the latter was less strict than that for granting the former. Indeed, in some areas separations, particularly, but probably not only, of goods, may have been de facto a matter of consent of the parties, whatever may have been the standard de jure.[107] Third, and once more in marked contrast with England, there is considerable evidence of attempts to enforce rules against 'clandestinity'. In some areas—Châlons-en-Champagne and Troyes are notable—couples were regularly fined for having exchanged even 'de futuro' promises of marriage privately, and throughout our area, criminal penalties for non-solemn marriages seem to have been the norm.[108] Finally, and perhaps most controversially, there is a tendency, as the fifteenth century goes on, for ordinary marriage enforcement cases to be heard on the criminal side of the court.[109] Separation cases, however, seem to have remained largely a civil matter.

105. For our region, see literature cited in n. 104 and Donahue, 'Social Practice' 149–155 (challenged in Andrew J. Finch, 'Parental Authority and the Problem of Clandestine Marriage in the Later Middle Ages', LHR 8 [1990] 189–204; answered in Charles Donahue, 'Clandestine Marriage in the Later Middle Ages: A Reply to Finch', LHR 10 [1992] 315–322); for England, see Sheehan, 'The Formation and Stability of Marriage in England in the Fourteenth Century: Evidence of an Ely Register', *Mediaeval Studies* 53 (1971) 228–263; Richard Helmholz, *Marriage Litigation in Medieval England* (Cambridge 1974); Donahue, *Law, Marriage* chapters 2–6; for Germany, see Rudolf Weigand, 'Zur mittelalterlichen kirchlichen Ehegerichtsbarkeit: Rechtsvergleichende Untersuchung', ZRG (KA) 98 (67) (1981) 213–247; reprinted in Weigand, *Liebe und Ehe im Mittelalter* (Biblioteca eruditorum 7; Goldbach 1993) 307*–341*; Klaus Lindner, *Courtship and the Courts: Marriage and Law in Southern Germany, 1350–1550* (PhD diss., Harvard Divinity School 1988); see also the literature about Germany cited in n. 110.

106. See Charles Donahue Jr., 'English and French Marriage Cases in the Later Middle Ages: Might the Differences Be Explained by Differences in the Property Systems?' *Family, Property and Succession*, ed. Lloyd Bonfield (Comparative Studies in Continental and Anglo-American Legal History 10; Berlin 1992) 339–366, reprinted in *Miscellanea Domenico Maffei Dicata: Historia-Ius-Studium*, ed. Antonio García y García and Peter Weimar (4 vols. Goldbach 1995) 4.283–310.

107. Compare Vleeschouwers, 'Aspects' 67–74, with Lefebvre, *Officialités* 191–192, 201–204, and Levebvre, 'Règle et réalité' 51–54. Perhaps the debate can be resolved on the basis of the distinction between the ground of the sentence (usually, if not always, something more than consent) and the means by which the ground was proved (sometimes, perhaps quite frequently, the confession of both parties). See Donahue, *Law, Marriage* chapter 10.

108. Donahue, 'Social Practice' 153–154, with references; Gottlieb, 'Meaning' 58–65.

109. Donahue, 'Social Practice' 154 and n. 40 (again, challenged by Finch, 'Parental Authority', and answered by Donahue, 'Reply to Finch'). For examples of more marriage cases heard 'on the criminal side,' see McDougall, *Bigamy*, Avignon, 'L'Église et les infractions', and the edition of Monique Vleeschouwers van Melkebeek cited in n. 35.

Except for the somewhat loose standards that we occasionally find for separations, nothing in these records would be surprising to someone who was acquainted with the common canon law on the topic of marriage. Canon law did not require the ecclesiastical courts to hear 'de presenti' marriage cases, if such cases did not arise, and the canonists certainly did not approve of clandestine marriages or even clandestine exchanges of promises to marry. Nonetheless, the nature and scope of marriage jurisdiction in late medieval France is different from that of its close neighbor England, and different again (we can be less certain about this) from its neighbor Germany.[110] Exactly what combination of different institutions and different social attitudes produced such different results is a topic that merits further exploration.[111]

The same may be said of other areas of the subject-matter jurisdiction of the officialities. The records reveal the importance of gracious jurisdiction, but exactly how gracious jurisdiction worked in different areas needs more study, as does consensual jurisdiction, particularly in the area of contracts, and what seems to be the steady increase in criminal business toward the end of the Middle Ages. Ecclesiastical disputes-resolution mechanisms other than that of the officialities have hardly been studied at all. The records contain a number of references to arbitration, but the circumstances under which it was used have not been the subject of a detailed study.[112] As already noted, we lack for France a study of papal judges delegate comparable to that which Jane Sayers has done in England.[113] (And neither country has a study of papal judges delegate in what we assume was their period of decline in the fourteenth and fifteenth centuries.) We now possess a splendid bibliography of material on visitations in France in our period.[114] But this material has not been studied from the point of view of how visitation jurisdiction was combined with that of the officialities.[115]

110. Weigand, *Liebe und Ehe* 245*–387*; Christian Schwab, *Das Augsburger Offizialatsregister (1348–1352): Ein Dokument geistlicher Diözesangerichtsbarkeit: Edition und Untersuchung* (Forschungen zur kirchlichen Rechtsgeschichte und zum Kirchenrecht 25; Köln 2001); Christina Deutsch, *Ehegerichtsbarkeit im Bistum Regensburg (1480–1538)* (Forschungen zur kirchlichen Rechtsgeschichte und zum Kirchenrecht 29; Köln 2005); Kirsi Salonen, 'Marriage Disputes in the Consistorial Court of Freising in the Late Middle Ages', *Regional Variations in Matrimonial Law and Custom in Europe, 1150–1600*, ed. Mia Korpiola (Medieval Law and Its Practice 12; Leiden 2011) 189–209.

111. For a start, see Weigand, 'Ehegerichtsbarkeit'; Anne Lefebvre-Teillard, 'Une nouvelle venue dans l'histoire du droit canonique: La jurisprudence', *Proceedings Berkeley 1980* 647–675; Donahue, *Law, Marriage* chapter 12.

112. For examples, see *Liber sentenciarum* nos. 484, 606, 1030, 1143. There are also a number of references in the Le Puy register (n. 98). See Alfred R. Julien, 'Evolutio historica compromissi in arbitros in iure canonico', *Apollinaris* 10 (1937) 187–232, 544–569.

113. Sayers, *Papal Judges Delegate* (n. 20). Wood, 'Execution of Papal Justice' (n. 5), is a start.

114. CNRS, *Répertoire des visites pastorales de la France. 1: Anciens diocèses* (4 vols. Paris 1977–).

115. See generally Noël Coulet, *Les visites pastorales* (Typologie des sources du moyen age oc-

The Procedure of the French Officialities

Both Fournier and Lefebvre give accounts of procedure before the officialities.[116] The pattern of procedure, both civil and criminal, that emerges from their accounts is remarkably like that given in Donahue's chapter 'Ecclesiastical Courts'.[117] It is thus recognizably the pattern of Romano-canonical procedure. We have already suggested that Fournier's account is deficient in that he relies on the work of the proceduralists when he has no contemporary records to support his account. Where he does have contemporary records, however, the fit is close. Relatively little that he found in his charters cannot be fitted into the overall pattern described by Tancred and Durantis. Lefebvre's account is supported much more fully with contemporary records. While there have been some changes since the thirteenth century, the overall impression that she leaves is one of close correspondence to the patterns of procedure suggested in the proceduralists.

More recent work with the records does not upset these conclusions. There is, indeed, relatively little that the records indicate about the procedure of the French officialities that cannot be supported from the works of the writers on procedure, particularly if we remember that the proceduralists are usually careful to note that much that they say can be modified by local custom and that the judge has considerable discretion to tailor the procedure to the needs of the case. At the same time, reading the records of any given officiality gives the impression that there is much about the procedure that was followed in different courts that would be hard to predict from reading the proceduralists. In particular, if one had the impression from the proceduralists that there were sharp distinctions between long-form and summary, civil and criminal, and contentious and non-contentious procedure, one might be surprised to discover that the records present not dichotomies but continua between and among these various categories.

Considerable support for this proposition will be found in the examination of one folio from the register of officiality of Paris that we find in Donahue's chapter 'Procedure'.[118] The cases there described all occurred on

---

cidental 23; (Turnhout 1977). For specific studies, see, for example, Marie-Thérèse Lorcin, 'Des commandes pour les orfèvres: La visite pastorale du diocèse de Lyon en 1469', *Cahiers d'histoire* 24 (1979) 21–48; Pierre-Clément Timbal and Bernadette Auzary, 'Visites décanales faites dans l'archidiaconé de Paris en 1468–1470', *Revue d'histoire de l'Église de France* 62 (1976) 349–360.

116. Fournier, *Officialités* 128–290; Lefebvre, *Officialités* 44–86.

117. Donahue, 'Ecclesiastical Courts' 276–287.

118. Donahue, 'Procedure' 119–124.

Monday, January 2, 1385. It turns out that it is possible to generalize from what occurred on that day to the entire register, which covers approximately three years. While it would be dangerous to draw firm conclusions from one register covering a bit more than three years to what this court was doing over the long course of its existence, much less to what procedure was like in the officialities of the whole of France in this period, the register certainly suggests a blending of long-form and more summary procedures and a mixture of contentious and non-contentious matters.

The relative absence of criminal cases in the Paris register is probably a peculiarity of this court or of its record-keeping.[119] The criminal jurisdiction of the archdeacon of Paris is well documented in the late fifteenth and early sixteenth centuries, and it is possible that the bulk of the criminal cases were handled in that court in the fourteenth century as well.[120] In the fifteenth century, the French officialities, at least those in the north, turned much more to criminal procedure, seemingly almost to the exclusion of civil procedures. And it is to that topic that we now turn.

Much of what survives from the French officialities in the later Middle Ages concerns criminal cases, and while the criminal prosecutions of adultery, bigamy, blasphemy, and clandestine marriage have all been the subject of recent study, much needs to be done with the procedure in these cases.[121] Both Pommeray's study of the archidiaconal officiality of Paris and Gottlieb's of marriage cases in Champagne give us material from which a start can be made, but neither of these studies is concerned with procedure as such.[122] A careful study of criminal procedure in the French officialities in the later Middle Ages is clearly called for. We offer here two records in order to suggest what the issues are:

Colin Tanneur and Perette, daughter of Jehannot Doulsot of Villers-en-Argonne,[123] were cited for clandestinity [on January 4, 1494].

Perette, daughter of Jehannot Doulsot, confessed under oath that on St. Andrew's day last past Colin Tanneur, son of Jehan Tanneur, came by night to her

---

119. There are, however, some criminal cases. See Charles Donahue, '*Ex officio* Cases in the Officiality of Paris, 1384–1387', *Mélanges en l'honneur d'Anne Lefebvre-Teillard*, ed. Bernard d'Alteroche, et al. (Paris 2009) 393–412.

120. See Léon Pommeray, *L'officialité archdiaconale de Paris aux XVe–XVIe siècles* (Paris 1933). One document indicates that this jurisdiction was equally active in the middle of the fourteenth century. See Donahue, *Records* 1 III/59/3/2 (AN, Z[10] 25).

121. Christelle Walravens, 'Insultes, blasphèmes ou hérésie? Un procès à l'officialité épiscopale de Troyes en 1445', BEC 154 (1996) 485–507; Avignon, 'L'Église et les infractions'; Sara McDougall, *Bigamy*; McDougall, 'The Opposite of the Double Standard: Gender, Marriage, and Adultery Prosecution in Late Medieval France', *Journal of the History of Sexuality* 23 (2014) 206–225.

122. Pommeray, *L'officialité archidiaconale de Paris*; Gottlieb, 'Getting Married'.

123. The guess in Donahue, 'Social Practice' 148 n. 17, that this is the Villers in question is supported by the reading 'nemus'.

father's house. Colin asked her about contracting marriage with her, and after many words had between them the said Colin Tanneur promised by the faith of his body that he would take her to wife and that he would never have another except her. And Perette likewise promised all these things to him. The promises having thus been made, at that time the said Colin gave her a silver ring[124] in the name of marriage, and when he had handed it over, the speaker gave the same Colin another ring of polished pewter[125] in the name of marriage, which the same Colin accepted. Asked who was present when these promises were made between them, she said that no one was, but he further said to her that nevertheless he would hold to the right that he had promised her.

Colin Tanneur confessed under oath that on the feast of St. Andrew the Apostle he went to the house of the father of the said Perette and there promised the same Perette that he would take her to wife, and she promised [the same] to him in like manner. Asked who was present, he said no one was.

The official sentenced each of them to one pound of wax and [to pay] the costs of the letters of the promotor, and they were enjoined to proceed within a week to solemnize the said marriage.[126]

The substantive significance of this case is discussed above.[127] Procedurally it is significant in that it is one of dozens like it. The parties are cited before the court. They tell their stories under oath. The judge sentences them to a fine (frequently the fine is quite small). If a marriage is involved, the judge also makes a ruling about the marriage—in this case, that the parties are to proceed to solemnization. We know that the case is a criminal case because the promotor gets his expenses paid and because of the fine. It is striking, however, how little difference there is between this case and the similar cases about promises to marry that were tried civilly before the Paris episcopal officiality a century earlier.

Why was this case prosecuted criminally? The easy answer is because there was a rule in the diocese of Châlons-en-Champagne against secret exchanges of promises to marry. But how did the promotor find out about this particular clandestine exchange? Since no one was there when the promises were exchanged, someone must have talked. One may suspect that Colin, having made his promise, balked at fulfilling it, or, considering how quickly he admitted it when he appeared before the official, perhaps the parents of either or both parties objected to the marriage. The point, however, is that the presence of the promotor allowed either

124. Possibly 'pin'. Gottlieb translates 'ring', following DuCange, s.v. *virga*.

125. Gottlieb translates 'amber,' the classical meaning of 'electrum', but if the reading 'contriti' is right, 'pewter' seems more likely.

126. The transcription of the case translated here may be found in Donahue, *Law, Marriage*, T&C 1292 (available online at http://www.cambridge.org/download_file/202931). The case is discussed in Gottlieb, *Getting Married* 201–202; Gottlieb, 'Meaning' 55; Donahue, 'Social Policy' 148–149.

127. See 329.

Colin or Perette, or both, to turn what would have been a relatively costly civil proceeding into a relatively cheap criminal one.

We can see the parties using the prosecutor to achieve their own ends even more clearly in the following case:[128]

Today [March 28, 1489][129] there appeared before the official the promotor and Jeanne Maire, plaintiffs, that is, the promotor in an office case and Jeanne in a case of defloration and matrimony, on the one side, and Tassin Joville, defendant, on the other. The said Jeanne, plaintiff, said that her relatives ['parentes'] had agreed on the sum of 3 gold écus to be handed over to her. She was content with that. So far as the promises of marriage are concerned she asserted that he promised her by words of the future tense two years ago in the month of March, and before and after he had known her carnally many times and about this she defers to his oath. He [Tassin] questioned under oath acknowledged that he had promised to take her as wife if she behaved herself and if she did not abandon him for another man, and afterwards he knew her carnally. But he says that she afterwards abandoned him for a certain clerk, the master of the same plaintiff, to wit, Master Geoffroi Gueroult. Questioned by the official if she abandoned him in the time intervening between the promise and the carnal knowledge, he says that she abandoned him for the same clerk. The plaintiff was examined about the same matter, and she replied under oath that the said clerk knew her carnally within the last half year and not before, and that the promises with the defendant were made two years ago and the carnal knowledge likewise. The official assigned to the parties a day and a week hence for saying and proposing whatever they would and especially to the defendant for saying and proposing whatever he would say against his own said confession and against the aforesaid. And the said defendant made amends for the aforesaid deflowering, and the amends were taxed at 2 gold écus, and it was modified on account of poverty and in favor of matrimony to 1 gold écu. Next the said Jeanne had received 2 gold écus, and Jean de Guitelles, the brother-in-law of the said Tassin, went surety to the same Jeanne for the other écu and promised to pay before the day was out, and when this was done, she said that she was satisfied about the said 3 écus, and he was delivered from prison.

Nominally, this is a criminal case. It is brought by the promotor in the name of the office of the official, and the defendant has been arrested and put in prison. In fact, however, the case is brought by Jeanne making use of the promotor to provide her with legal support. The record reflects the mixed nature of the proceeding by saying that the promotor sues on behalf of the office, while Jeanne sues on behalf of herself. Many of the late northern French records are not so clear. Perhaps the mixed nature of

128. Paris, Archives Nationales, Z^{10} 19, fol. 96, edited in Pommeray, *L'officialité archdiaconale de Paris* No. 81, 547–548.

129. Pommeray, *L'officialité archdiaconale de Paris*, No. 81, 547–548, reports the date here as 1488. Elsewhere, he reports it as Saturday, March 28, 1489, and Saturday, March 28, 1499; ibid. 334, 377. The last is impossible, granted the bracketing dates of the register, and the only year of the ones in question in which March 28 fell on a Saturday was 1489.

this case was made more apparent because Jeanne was so clearly suing for monetary compensation. Other cases where the result is not the award of money damages proceed as if they were brought entirely by the promotor. But the fact is that however the case is styled the procedure is similar. The judge takes an active role in questioning the parties. Normally witnesses are not introduced. The entire proceeding is based on what the parties say, and frequently they agree as to what has happened.

Both parties in this case agree that there was a promise of marriage conditioned on the good behavior of Jeanne. The legal issue was an old one, and the answer was clear enough. If Jeanne and Jean had had intercourse after the promise and before the condition was broken, they were married. Jeanne's subsequent infidelity did not make her any less Jean's wife.[130] But the fact is that the court fines Jean for having deflowered Jeanne, and Jean pays Jeanne 3 écus. Jean has not admitted that the intercourse came before the infidelity. It is open to Jeanne to pursue him civilly as her husband, and the court reduces Jean's fine on account of Jean's poverty and 'favore matrimonii'. A day is even set for the case to proceed, but apparently it does not.[131] We may speculate that despite the involvement of the promotor, Jean will not be compelled to marry Jeanne if Jeanne is satisfied with her compensation. Whether they will marry others will depend on their consciences, their confessors, and, perhaps, on the results of subsequent proceedings.[132]

The point, however, about this case is not what it tells us about the substantive law of espousals followed by intercourse in the Paris archidiaconal court. The point about this case, at least for this section, is what it tells us about procedure. What it tells us is that criminal procedure has come to dominate over civil procedure by the end of the fifteenth century in the Paris archdeacon's court. The same may be said of the court of the official of Châlons-en-Champagne and of that of Troyes, both of which have left extensive records from the same period.[133] There are some cases brought civilly in the officiality of Cambrai, both in the city itself and at Brussels, but here, too, criminal procedure dominates.[134] By this period it also dominates in the court of the official of Cerisy and in many of the other officialities of northwestern France studied by Carole Avignon.[135]

---

130. Ibid. 334.

131. None of Pommeray's references to the case (ibid. 334, 377, 547–548) mentions further proceedings.

132. We should not get the impression that promotors never pursued the unwilling and forced them to marry. They did. Here, however, for reasons that are only partially discernible from the record, the promotor seems to have backed off.

133. See 318.

134. See 311.

135. See 310; Avignon, 'L'Église et les infractions'.

The same is not true in the south of France. There extensive records survive that suggest that normal civil procedure in relatively long form was still the rule in the officiality of Marseilles.[136] Similar records exist for the officiality of Carpentras. At Carpentras too there is a separate set of registers that shows us that purely 'ex officio' procedure was also in operation.[137] Civil registers are not totally lacking for northern France. The provincial court at Sens has left us one register from the late fifteenth century that shows us that in that court, long-form procedure was alive and well.[138]

The records are sufficiently spotty that firm conclusions are dangerous. It does seem to be the case, however, that as the Middle Ages came to a close, the officialities in our region were increasingly making use of criminal forms and criminal procedures. The trend was more notable in the north than in the south, more notable in courts that had a large number of cases dealing with quite ordinary people. The southerners—perhaps because of their Roman-law tradition—and the rich continued to use forms of procedure that followed the long-form 'ordo' more closely. The northerners and those of modest means had gone over to a much more truncated procedure in which the promotor played a key role.

The Achievement of the French Officialities

Granted how much needs to be done before a comprehensive history of the ecclesiastical courts in this region can properly be written, it would be foolish to attempt any definitive assessment of their accomplishments. What we now know would suggest that the officialities in northern France and the southern Low Countries had by the end of the Middle Ages succeeded in bringing their brand of justice to a wide variety of people. They did this by shortening the procedure and by making extensive use of the promotor and of procedures adapted from the criminal 'ordo'. The evidence from the south of France would suggest that this development had not progressed as rapidly or as far by 1500. The evidence from the outer fringe of our area (Utrecht in the north and modern Switzerland in the east) has been insufficiently explored to allow us even to guess what was happening there. (The work that has been done with the Utrecht records suggests a pattern more like the southern French one.)[139]

Courts in areas that were subject to the jurisdiction of the French king experienced competition for jurisdiction from a powerful competitor. The

---

136. Donahue, *Records 1* III/7.
138. Donahue, *Records 1* III/53/3/2.

137. See n. 57.
139. See Donahue, *Records 1* VII.

records would suggest, however, that despite the assembly of Vincennes, despite the strong bias to secular jurisdiction of the parlement of Paris, and despite the development of the 'appeal comme d'abus', ecclesiastical courts within the kingdom of France remained powerful and effective institutions into the sixteenth century and that their jurisdiction was not, as a whole, narrower than that in other kingdoms, such as England, where secular government was also strong.[140] Whether this situation changed in the sixteenth century and how it changed are questions beyond our temporal scope.

The ultimate, and at this point unanswerable, question is whether justice was served. In their effort to reach a wider population, the ecclesiastical courts of northern France developed an extensive bureaucracy, and bureaucrats have to be supported. The records of the northern French officialities focus quite heavily on the revenue-raising functions of the courts, and while such activities are evidenced elsewhere, the comparatively larger quantity of such material from northern France may be telling us something about the importance of revenue-raising in that part of the world. Without getting deeply into the debate in the literature over the extent of the use of the sanction of excommunication in the northern part of our region, we can say that there was clearly a heavy reliance on that sanction, not only for substantive violations of the church's laws but also for procedural violations.[141] Finally, any legal system that depends on processing a large number of cases in which the parties appear, by and large, without counsel, are questioned by the judge, and are urged to confess, runs the risk of violating what from a modern standpoint are tenets of fundamental fairness. Judged by the standards of their time, the ecclesiastical courts in our region were probably as fair, if not fairer, than the secular courts, just as they were as efficient, if not more efficient. But thoughtful men viewing the system around the turn of the sixteenth century might have been led to wonder whether it was appropriate for the church to be in the judicial business at all, or to be in it in quite the way that it was. Those questions were raised quite trenchantly in the sixteenth century, but the consequences of that change in attitude lie well beyond our chronological scope.

---

140. For the 'appel comme d'abus', see Génestal, *Appel comme d'abus* (n. 77).

141. See Elisabeth Vodola, *Excommunication in the Middle Ages* (Berkeley 1986) 140–145, and literature cited in n. 63; Véronique Beaulande[-Barraud], *Le Malheur d'être exclu? Ex communication, réconciliation, et société a la fin du moyen âge* (Paris 2006).

Recent Research on the Late-Medieval Church Court Records of Western Europe

The previous parts of this chapter are based on a draft that was written in 1992. While we have made considerable effort to update the chapter in the light of recent research, it is quite possible that the chapter would not have been organized the way it is or have treated the topics that it did had it begun with the research of the last twenty years. We offer here, therefore, a brief survey of that research with some suggestions as to where we might go from here.[142]

Lingering for a moment on the question of the achievements of these officialities, recent research has emphasized the primary interest of these courts in two main areas: the regulation of marriage and the prosecution of clerical concubinage.[143] There is general agreement that these courts took vigorous and proactive measures to protect the sacrament of marriage from abuse, investigating and prosecuting any violations they detected, including the clandestine unions described above and bigamous marriages. The courts also summoned and sanctioned hundreds of clergy and their alleged mistresses, generally ordering them to pay fines and to quit each other's company. Clerical concubinage may, however, have been a lesser concern for these courts; the fines were generally quite small, though they were demanded with regularity. Success in both areas is quite difficult to measure. Both clerical concubinage and illegal marriage practices seem to have persisted well into the sixteenth century. It is hard to know whether the officials and their promotors were pleased with the results of their ongoing efforts.

Turning to a broader examination of our current understanding of northern French officialities, we see that recent research has made diverse use of the surviving records of the fifteenth-century French officialities, offering a rich account of the activity of a handful of church courts, including Paris, Brie, Rouen, Chartres, Troyes, Châlons-en-Champagne, Troyes, Brussels, Cambrai, Tournai, and (in the only example of recent work on a southern French officiality) Carpentras.[144] This work has been greatly influenced by previous and ongoing research in the English church

---

142. What follows is entirely the work of McDougall, though Donahue completely agrees with it.

143. Vleeschouwers van Melkebeek, 'Aspects'; Vincent Tabbagh, 'Recherches sur l'adultère et sa répression par les officialités de France septentrionale a la fin du moyen âge', *La petite délin-quance du Moyen Age à l'époque contemporaine*, ed. Benoît Garnot (Dijon 1998) 393–402; Donahue, *Law, Marriage*; Avignon, 'L'Église et les infractions'; McDougall, *Bigamy*; Karras, *Unmarriages*.

144. For Northwestern France, see Avignon, 'L'Église et les infractions.' For the Champagne region: Walravens, 'Insultes'; Beaulande, *Malheur d'être exclu*; McDougall, *Bigamy*. For Belgium and Northeastern France, see Vleeschouwers van Melkebeek, 'Aspects'; Vleeschouwers van Melkebeek, 'Self-Divorce in Fifteenth-Century Flanders: The Consistory Court Accounts of the Diocese of Tournai', TRG 68 (2000) 83–98; Vleeschouwers van Melkebeek, 'Incestuous Marriag-

court records.[145] The last several years have also seen a wealth of research on Italian officialities.[146] There has also been work on the German dioceses of Regensburg, Augsburg, and Freising,[147] and on Iberian,[148] Swiss,[149] Swedish,[150] and Hungarian[151] officialities.

es: Formal Rules and Social Practice in the Southern Burgundian Netherlands', *Love, Marriage, and Family Ties in the Later Middle Ages*, ed. Isabel David et al. (International Medieval Research 11; Turnhout 2003) 77–95; Vleeschouwers van Melkebeek, 'Marital Breakdown before the Consistory Courts of Brussels, Cambrai and Tournai: Judicial Separation *a mensa et thoro*', TRG 72 (2004) 81–89; Falzone, 'Ad secunda vota.' For Carpentras, see Hardman, 'Justice, Jurisdiction and Choice'.

145. Helmholz, *Marriage Litigation*; Michael M. Sheehan, *Marriage, Family, and Law in Medieval Europe: Collected Studies*, ed. James K. Farge (Toronto 1996); Frederik Pedersen, *Marriage Disputes in Medieval England* (London 2000); Shannon McSheffrey, *Marriage, Sex, and Civic Culture in Late-Medieval London* (Philadelphia 2006); Sara M. Butler, *The Language of Abuse: Marital Violence in Later Medieval England* (Leiden 2007); Donahue, *Law, Marriage*; Sara M. Butler, *Divorce in Medieval England: From One to Two Persons in Law* (Routledge Research in Medieval Studies 4; New York 2013).

146. In particular a series of collected studies edited by Silvana Seidel Menchi and Diego Quaglioni: *Coniugi nemici*; *Matrimoni in Dubbio: Unioni controverse e nozze clandestine in Italia dal XIV al XVIII* (I processi matrimoniali degli archivi ecclesiastici italiani 2; Annali dell'Istituto storico italo-germanico in Trento, Quaderni 57; Bologna 2001); *Trasgressioni: seduzione, concubinato, adulterio, bigamia (XIV–XVIII secolo)* (I processi matrimoniali degli archivi ecclesiastici italiani 3; Annali dell'Istituto storico italo-germanico in Trento, Quaderni 64; Bologna 2004); *I tribunali del matrimonio (secoli XV–XVIII)* (I processi matrimoniali degli archivi ecclesiastici italiani 4; Annali dell'Istituto storico italo-germanico in Trento, Quaderni 68; Bologna 2006). Other studies include Christine Meek, 'Women, the Church and the Law: Matrimonial Litigation in Lucca under Bishop Nicolao Guinigi (1394–1435)', *Chattel, Servant or Citizen: Women's Status in Church, State and Society*, ed. Mary O'Dowd and Sabine Wichert, (Institute of Irish Studies, Queen's University, Belfast, Historical Studies 19; Belfast 1995) 82–90; Cecilia Cristellon, 'L'ufficio del giudice: Mediazione, inquisizione, confessione nei processi matrimoniali veneziani (1420–1532)', *Rivista Storica Italiana* 115 (2003) 851–898; Cristellon, 'Marriage and Consent in Pre-Tridentine Venice: Between Law Conception and Ecclesiastical Conception, 1420–1545', *Sixteenth Century Journal* 39 (2008) 390–418; Cristellon, *La carità e l'eros: Il matrimonio, la Chiesa, i suoi giudici nella Venezia del Rinascimento, 1420–1545* (Annali dell'Istituto storico italo-germanico in Trento 58; Bologna 2010); Corinne Wieben, *A Kind of Marriage: Marriage in Dispute in Medieval Lucca (1341–1361)* (PhD diss., University of California at Santa Barbara 2010).

147. Rudolf Weigand, 'Die Rechtsprechung des Regensburger Gerichts in Ehesachen unter besonderer Berücksichtigung der bedingten Eheschließung nach Gerichtsbüchern aus dem Ende des 15. Jahrhunderts', AKKR 137 (1968) 403–463, reprinted in Weigand, *Liebe und Ehe* 245*–305*; Deutsch, *Ehegerichtsbarkeit*; Schwab, *Augsburger Offizialatsregister*; Salonen, 'Marriage Disputes.'

148. For example, the works of Martine Charageat: 'Pour une étude de la conflictualité matrimoniale (xive–xvie siècles): Les archives de l'officialité césearaugustaine', *Les officialités dans l'Europe médiévale et moderne* 245–258; 'Témoins et témoignages en Aragon aux xve–xvie siècles', *La preuve en justice de l'antiquité à nos jours*, ed. Bruno Lemesle (Rennes 2003) 149–169; 'Copula carnal: La preuve de mariage dans les procès à Saragosse au xve siècle', *Mélanges de la Casa de Velazquez* 33 (2003) 47–63; *La délinquance matrimoniale: Couples en conflit et justice en Aragon (XV–XVI siècle)* (Paris 2011); 'Typologie des procès canoniques matrimoniaux à Saragosse (xve–xvie siècle)', *Sínodos diocesanos y legislación particular: Estudios históricos en honor al Dr. D. Francisco Cantelar Rodriguez* (Bibliotheca Salmanticensis 10; Salamanca 1999) 217–232. See also Yolanda Serrano Seoane, 'El sistema penal del tribunal eclesiastico de la diócesis de Barcelona en la Baja Edad Media', *Clio y Crimen* 3 (2006) 334–428, 430–508; Federico Rafael Aznar Gil, 'Penas y sanciones contra los matrimonios clandestinos en la península Ibérica durante la baja edad media', *Revista de estudios históricos-jurídicos* 25 (2003) 189–214.

149. Marie-Ange Valazza Tricarico, 'L'officialité de Genève et quelques cas de bigamie à la fin du moyen âge: L'empêchement de lien', *Zeitschrift für schweizerische Kirchengeschichte* 89 (1995) 99–118; Valérie Lamon Zuchuat, 'Mariages clandestins dans le diocèse de Sion à la fin du Moyen Age', *Annales valaisannes* (2004) 7–25; Zuchuat, *Trois pommes pour un mariage: L'Église et les unions clandestines dans le diocèse de Sion, 1430–1550* (Cahiers lausannois d'histoire médiévale 46; Lausanne 2008).

150. Mia Korpiola, *Between Betrothal and Bedding: Marriage Formation in Sweden 1200–1600* (Leiden 2009).

151. Peter Erdő, 'Eheprozesse im mittelalterlichen Ungarn', ZRG Kan. Abt. 103 (1986) 250–276.

There have also been efforts to bring these studies together into a broader comparative framework. In 2006 researchers working on marriage litigation in courts throughout medieval Europe met to present and discuss their findings. The results, edited by Mia Korpiola, offer a unique opportunity to survey and compare recent discoveries.[152] In 2010, researchers working on officialities of France, Spain, Italy, and England met to present their findings; the proceedings of that conference have just been published and are summarized in the last chapter.[153]

Narrowing our focus to the subject of this chapter and what we can call—in convenient if anachronistic shorthand—the Franco-Belgian region, recent research in this area has most often focused on marriage litigation or matters related to marriage, such as legal separation, adultery, and bigamy.[154] At the same time, researchers have also examined more diverse topics such as excommunication, debt, punishment, blasphemy, jurisdictional conflicts, and the regulation of midwives.

To offer a few examples, researchers have utilized the surviving records of the officialities in the Île-de-France to analyze both marital and non-marital relationships and also the efforts of church courts to regulate midwives.[155] Records of the Champagne region have been used to study both prosecution and punishment, as well as social practice. Topics have included clandestine marriage, the prosecution and practice of bigamy, adultery and blasphemy prosecutions, the role of excommunication as punishment, as well as the use of fines and the more limited use of public penance and imprisonment. For example, Véronique Beaulande-Barraud examined the social and spiritual effects of excommunication, a tool that the officiality in Châlons used primarily to punish violence against clerics and clandestine marriage.[156] For northwestern France, Carole Avignon has studied the practice and prosecution of clandestine marriage, and Vincent Tabbagh has examined adultery prosecutions, sacramental practices, church and state relations, and similar topics, both within the kingdom of France and in Burgundy.[157]

---

152. Korpiola, *Regional Variations*.

153. Charles Donahue Jr., 'By Way of a Conclusion', *Les officialités dans l'Europe médiévale et modernes* 325–338.

154. Donahue, *Law, Marriage*.

155. Tiffany D. Vann Sprecher and Ruth M. Karras, 'The Midwife and the Church: Ecclesiastical Regulation of Midwives in Brie, 1499–1504', *Bulletin of the History of Medicine* 85 (2011) 171–192; Karras, *Unmarriages*.

156. Beaulande, *Malheur d'être exclu*.

157. Avignon, 'L'Église et les infractions'; Carole Avignon, 'Marché matrimonial clandestin et officines de clandestinité à la fin du Moyen Âge: l'exemple du diocèse de Rouen', *Revue Historique* 655 (July 2010) 515–549; Avignon, 'Les couples clandestins devant la justice d'Église. Réflexions sur la normalisation matrimoniale judiciaire dans la France du Nord-Ouest à la fin du Moyen Âge',

One particular frustration of working with the French portion of the Franco-Belgian records is the difficulty of placing the court prosecutions by a given officiality in their local social or judicial context. Scholars studying the officialities of the Burgundian Low Countries can avail themselves of a wealth of social, economic, and judicial sources for the region. Northern France, outside of Paris, offers a much more limited range of materials. For example, the church court records for fifteenth-century Troyes are rich, but no secular court records survive. The *Grandes Jours* of Troyes, which have not been the subject of scholarly study since the nineteenth century, seem to concern mostly civil matters.[158] We have some of the deliberations of the municipal council of Troyes, but preliminary efforts to study their relationship to the officiality have yielded little information. The records of the parlement of Paris, the court of highest appeal for this area, certainly could have many more appeals involving the Troyes officiality than have been identified thus far, but at present the databases provided by the *Centre d'études d'histoire juridique* (CEHJ), while valuable resources for research on the fourteenth century and for a range of other questions, do not yet include the bulk of the fifteenth-century registers, the period for which we have the greatest number of surviving officiality registers.[159] Nevertheless, there is every reason to hope for the discovery of more material. The French archives, particularly the underutilized municipal archives—now usually housed in the relevant municipality's *Médiathèque*—cry out for further attention.

Drawing on the work that has been done so far, we can attempt some generalizations, but only with caveats. At least at present it seems that, in comparison with church courts in England, Germany, or Italy, the northern French and Belgian courts appear to have had a quite different character from that of other European courts studied so far, most clearly when in the case of marriage litigation. That difference lies in a distinctly aggressive and proactive style of prosecuting. The English courts on the whole appear to have had a far more passive role in the adjudication of marital disputes, with the bulk of the proceedings taking place in instance cases. What we know of German and Italian courts suggests a similar handling of marriage cases. Franco-Belgian courts, meanwhile, at

---

Couples devant les justices: Du Moyen Âge à l'époque contemporaine, ed. Claude Gauvard and Alessandro Stella (Paris 2013) 77–98; Vincent Tabbagh, 'Adultère'; Tabbagh, 'La pratique sacramentelle des fidèles d'après les documents épiscopaux de France du Nord (XIIIe–XVe siècle)', *Revue Mabillon* 12 (2001) 159–204; Tabbagh, 'Le prince face aux communautés ecclésiales: René, Charles, Louis, Philippe et les autres', *René d'Anjou (1409–1480): Pouvoirs et gouvernement*, ed. Jean-Michel Matz and Noël-Yves Tonnerre (Paris 2011) 355–372.

158. Théophile Boutiot, *Recherches sur les Grandes Jours de Troyes* (Troyes 1852).

159. http://www.ihd.cnrs.fr/spip.php?article255.

least in the fifteenth century, acted quite often 'ex officio', at the instigation of the court, and acted with seeming urgency to regulate marriage practice. These northern French courts also spent a great deal of time punishing the sexual offences alleged against members of the clergy and laity, though clergy usually predominated among the offenders fined for their illicit sexual activity. Some courts, such as the officiality in Troyes, also punished hundreds of acts of violence, defamation, and blasphemy throughout the century.

There are, however, some good reasons to hesitate in making this comparative claim. With the exception of Lucca, criminal records in Italy and Spain are spotty.[160] For example, only a handful of fifteenth-century criminal prosecutions have survived in Barcelona, and the criminal records of Saragossa have not yet been made available.[161] Until they have been studied, we cannot know whether and how marital offences were criminally prosecuted. For Augsburg, at least, we know that the bishop did not have criminal jurisdiction, and if other German bishops lacked criminal jurisdiction, we can assume that the German officialities handled marital offences less aggressively. Even some English courts may have had a more prosecutorial character than prior research has sometimes indicated.[162]

Looking ahead, there are many ways in which the records of the officialities of northern France could be put to further use. The records of Troyes, for example, offer rich materials on the Hundred Years War and its aftermath, including the prosecution of clerics who committed homicide or fought as brigands. The regulation of violence unconnected with the war, including sexual violence, and the policing of insults are also found in these records. The testimony of witnesses is harder to find, but it does exist, and has not been much used in recent studies. The minor clergy, their involvement in their communities, including both their sexual practices and their involvement in gambling, or relations between laity and clergy more broadly could be explored in these records. For southern France,

---

160. Wieben, 'Kind of Marriage' 5; Guy Geltner, 'I registe criminali dell'Archivio archvescovile di Lucca: Prospettive di ricerca per la storia sociale del medioevo', *Il patrimonio documentario della Chiesa di Lucca: Prospettive di ricerca: atti del Convegno internazionale di studi*, ed. Sergio Pagano and Pierantonio Piatti (Firenze 2010); Geltner, 'Patrolling Normative Borders after the Black Death: The Bishop of Lucca's Criminal Court', *Center and Periphery: Studies on Power in the Medieval World in Honor of William Chester Jordan*, ed. Katherine L. Jansen, Guy Geltner, and Anne E. Lester (Leiden 2013) 169–180. For Venice, criminal records from the fifteenth century have not survived; see Cristellon, 'L'ufficio del giudice'.

161. Charageat, 'Typologie' 217; Serrano Seoane, 'Sistema penal'.

162. Lawrence R. Poos, 'The Heavy-Handed Marriage Counsellor: Regulating Marriage in Some Later-Medieval English Local Ecclesiastical-Court Jurisdictions', *AJLH* 39 (1995) 291–309; Richard Wunderli, *London Church Courts and Society on the Eve of the Reformation* (Cambridge, Mass. 1981); Donahue, *Law, Marriage* 278–296.

the rich, if geographically isolated, records of Mende and Le Puy, both because of their age and the peculiar nature of the jurisdiction, have been neglected for too long. The fascinating, multicultural records of Perpignan, though more a part of the Catalan tradition than anything comfortably recognizable as French, offer materials of considerable interest. As already mentioned, institutional studies, comparative studies, and further examinations of jurisdictional questions could all be enlightened by these records.

There is much more to be done.

IO

Local Ecclesiastical Courts In England

R. H. Helmholz

This chapter describes the main features of the canon law as they were put into practice within the courts of the medieval English church. It is based primarily upon evidence found in the surviving records of these courts, but it also attempts to relate practice to the formal canon law that is described in other contributions to this volume. Where possible, the chapter also places ecclesiastical jurisdiction within its contemporary context, in particular that of the English legal system as a whole. Although many points remain on which our knowledge is incomplete, enough research has now been done on the records of the spiritual courts in England so that a reliable picture of the overall jurisdiction exercised by these courts can be drawn. The chapter attempts to provide that picture, pointing out the lacunae in our knowledge as well as dealing more fully with those areas where that knowledge is fuller.

The focus in these pages lies almost exclusively on the external forum, that is, on the jurisdiction exercised by the public courts of the church. These were the consistory courts of archdeacons and bishops and also the appellate tribunals of archiepiscopal and papal courts. This chapter deals only incidentally with the internal forum, even though it is evident (and worth emphasizing to a greater extent than sometimes occurs) that the law of the church was put to use and was also of crucial importance within the penitential forum.[1] The reasons for this omission are, first, the space limitations of the overall project and, second, the absence of records of the 'law in action' by which practice within the internal forum could meaningfully be described. Nonetheless, it is crucial that the *existence* of this forum be recognized and considered. Indeed, some aspects of external court practice cannot be understood without reference to the regulation of the lives of men and women that occurred through confession and penance.

One additional limitation of this contribution lies in the absence of a separate, detailed treatment of the procedure used in England's spiritual courts. The subject is dealt with under individual subject matter headings where possible and appropriate. The limitations of space must again justify this sort of treatment. In most areas of practice, the English courts seem to have applied a slightly simplified form of the Romano-canonical procedure found in contemporary manuals, the result being a system not greatly different from that applied elsewhere in Europe.[2] To some extent, however, it must remain an open question how far one can make the otherwise quite reasonable assumption that canonical procedure did not vary markedly from one country to another.

The Sources

In the total number of jurists who contributed to the development and elaboration of the canon law and the Ius commune, England stands far down the list.[3] Perhaps it is the least among the European kingdoms. This seems to be the situation, at least if one excludes the twelfth century, when England was for a time a center for the collection of papal decretals and the study of canon law.[4] Only the names of John of Atho (d. 1350) and William Lyndwood (d. 1446) are at all well known from the later medi-

---

1. See Winfried Trusen, 'Forum internum und gelehrtes Recht im Spätmittelalter', ZRG Kan. Abt. 57 (1971) 131–157; and Joseph Goering, 'The Internal Forum and the Literature of Penance and Confession', *History*, ed. Hartmann and Pennington 379–428; and Atria A. Larson, *Master of Penance: Gratian and the Development of Penitential Thought and Law in the Twelfth Century* (Studies in Medieval and Early Modern Canon Law 11; Washington, D.C. 2014).

2. See Knut W. Nörr, *Romanisch-kanonisches Prozessrecht: Erkenntnisverfahren erster Instanz in civilibus* (Enzyklopädie der Rechts- und Staatswissenschaft, Abteilung Rechtswissenschaft; Berlin-Heidelberg-New York 2012).

3. Leonard Boyle, 'The "Summa Summarum" and Some Other English Works of Canon Law," *Proceedings Boston 1963* (MIC Subsidia 2; 1965) 415.

4. See Charles Duggan, *Twelfth-century Decretal Collections and Their Importance in English History* (University of London Historical Studies 12; London 1963); and his chapter 'Decretal Collections from Gratian's *Decretum* to the *Compilationes antiquae*: The Making of the New Case Law', *History*, ed. Hartmann and Pennington 246–292; Stephan Kuttner and E. Rathbone, 'Anglo-Norman Canonists of the Twelfth Century: An Introductory Study', *Traditio* 7 (1951) 279–358.

eval period, and they were primarily commentators on the constitutions enacted by English provincial and diocesan councils, not on the general Western canon law.[5] Their principal accomplishment was to bring local, English law within the framework of the Ius commune. As such, their works are of great importance in understanding the history of ecclesiastical jurisdiction in England, but they were of much lesser importance in the wider history of the medieval canon law.

Despite its scarcity of accomplished canonists, to its credit or good fortune, England stands very high in the extent of preservation of official records from its spiritual courts. Perhaps it is the leader among European nations.[6] Precedent books and other informal notebooks of ecclesiastical lawyers exist in some quantity.[7] The archives of the consistory courts are also very rich, both in the form of act books—formal day-by-day records of the procedure taken in the courts—and in the form of cause papers—the documents used to introduce pleadings, to record evidence, and to promulgate sentences in litigation.[8] Bishops' registers and other incidental sources also fill gaps in the evidence.[9] Of course, one could wish for more, and there is certainly much research left to do in what remains. The records of cases appealed to the papal court, for example, have been left so far almost entirely unexplored.[10] We do not yet know much about what they contain. And much the greatest part of the material from the local, consistory courts has remained in manuscript. However, for the years from the mid-thirteenth century, the surviving manuscript evidence has now been explored fully enough to allow for us to discern the basic shape of spiritual jurisdiction as it was exercised in England's local ecclesiastical courts.

---

5. Their works are accessible in *Provinciale (seu Constitutiones Angliae) cui adjiciuntur Constitutiones Legatinae d. Othonis et d. Othobonis* (Oxford 1679, reprinted 1968). See also John H. Baker, *Monuments of Endlesse Labours: English Canonists and Their Work 1300–1900* (London 1998).

6. See *The Records of the Medieval Ecclesiastical Courts, Part I: The Continent*, ed. Charles Donahue Jr. (Berlin 1989) 26; and Donahue, *Part II: England* (Berlin 1994).

7. See 'The Canonists' Formularies', in Dorothy M. Owen, *The Medieval Canon Law: Teaching, Literature and Transmission* (Cambridge 1990) 30–42.

8. See John S. Purvis, *An Introduction to Ecclesiastical Records* (London 1953) 64–95; Anne Tarver, *Church Court Records: An Introduction for Family and Local Historians* (Chichester 1995).

9. See David M. Smith, *Guide to Bishops' Registers of England and Wales: A Survey from the Middle Ages to the Abolition of Episcopacy in 1646* (London 1981).

10. A happy if partial exception is Ludwig Schmugge, *Marriage on Trial: Late Medieval German Couples at the Papal Court*, trans. Atria A. Larson (Studies in Medieval and Early Modern Canon Law 10; Washington, D.C. 2008).

Early Development of Ecclesiastical Jurisdiction

Organization of the Spiritual Courts

No historian has examined thoroughly the stages by which ecclesiastical jurisdiction assumed the durable form reached by the end of the thirteenth century. However, the story of the creation of a system of ecclesiastical justice in England undoubtedly begins earlier than the establishment of regular, organized tribunals. A separate sphere of spiritual jurisdiction began to emerge in the second half of the eleventh century. It grew from the twin springs of the energetic kingship of William I and the Gregorian reform movement. The latter is sufficiently treated elsewhere in this volume. The former was effected by a royal ordinance forbidding the hearing of ecclesiastical pleas within the hundred courts or any similar forum presided over by secular men, and also guaranteeing that decisions of spiritual matters should be made 'according to the episcopal laws'.[11] The precise purpose of this ordinance and the extent of its immediate implementation remain subjects of uncertainty,[12] but at least two matters are tolerably clear. First, the ordinance stated a rule of separation of spiritual from secular affairs upon which almost all men agreed in principle, however much they might disagree about details and areas of overlap. The acceptance of this principle was an essential precondition for carving out a separate sphere for the enforcement of the canon law. Second, the ordinance itself did not create a system of ecclesiastical courts. It served to separate spiritual from secular pleas, no doubt, but it did not establish a functioning system of courts. In many ways, the reforming decree may even have left the organization of courts in England as it had long existed. Most spiritual pleas were dealt with in synods or through other traditional means.

Even during the second half of the twelfth century, when records of ecclesiastical litigation become more abundant, only the most halting steps towards the creation of an organized system of courts were taken. No regularly compiled records of spiritual courts exist, and indeed there were no regularly constituted diocesan tribunals, such as later ages would

11. 'Ordinance of William I on Church Courts' (1072 x 1085 as printed in *Councils and Synods with Other Documents relating to the English Church: I A.D. 871–1204*, ed. Dorothy Whitelock, Martin Brett, and C. N. L. Brooke (Oxford 1981) 623–624.

12. See Colin Morris, 'William I and the Church Courts', EHR 82 (1967) 449–463; Frank Barlow, *The English Church 1066–1154* (London 1979) 150–154. See generally 'Introduction' in Adams and Donahue, *Canterbury Cases* 6–12; Colin Morris, 'From Synod to Consistory: The Bishops' Courts in England 1150–1250', JEH 22 (1971) 115–123; David M. Smith, 'St Hugh's Administration of the Diocese of Lincoln', *Saint Hugh of Lincoln*, ed. Henry Mayr-Harting (Oxford 1987) 19–47.

know as consistory courts. Ecclesiastical disputes were decided in dioc-esan gatherings[13] or in the local chapters of archdeacons and rural deans.[14] These meetings combined administrative, judicial, and purely spiritual functions, and they provided no guarantee that experts in the canon law would be present. Litigation was also commonly dealt with by the bishop (or archdeacon) personally—acting by virtue of his office[15]—or by an offi-cer specially appointed by the bishop to hear and determine a specific con-troversy.[16] All of these gatherings were traditional ways of dealing with ecclesiastical disputes. They were in harmony with William's ordinance, and not then wholly out of keeping with the law of the church. None amounted to the organization of what we would consider proper, profes-sional courts.

The one sign of movement towards the creation of regular courts that is found in the surviving evidence is the increasing numbers of men de-scribed as episcopal *officiales*. Later on, the term *officialis* was the title com-monly given to the presiding officer of a consistory court, and some have thought that the occurrence of the word itself signaled the existence of a system of diocesan courts. We now know that the term did not. During the years around the turn of the thirteenth century, the *officialis* was more like an agent or vicar general, acting when necessary in the place of the bishop or archdeacon. When absence, illness, or inconvenience rendered the prelate's presence difficult, this official acted instead.[17] Such action of course included acting in a judicial capacity. But the early *officialis* was not necessarily the judge he later became. He carried out administrative du-ties as often as he heard spiritual causes, he was not necessarily trained as a lawyer, and he did not sit in a regular consistory court.[18]

13. See the examples in *English Episcopal Acta II: Canterbury 1162–1190*, ed. Christopher R. Cheney and B. E. A. Jones (London 1986) No. 47a (1174 x 1181); *Chronicle of Battle Abbey*, ed. Eleanor Searle (Oxford 1980) 126–127; *Cartulary of Oseney Abbey*, ed. H. E. Salter (Oxford Historical Society 90; Oxford 1929) No. 745.

14. Examples: *Luffield Priory Charters Part I*, ed. G. R. Elvey (Northants. Record Society 22; Aylesbury 1968) No. 67A (1178 x 1192); *Cartulary of Cirencester Abbey, Gloucestershire*, ed. C. D. Ross (Oxford 1964) No. 611 (1207); *Reading Abbey Cartularies I*, ed. B. R. Kemp (Camden Society 4th ser. 31; London 1986) No. 345 (1173 x 1174).

15. Examples: *English Episcopal Acta II*, No. 41 (1162 x 1164); *Magna Vita sancti Hugonis II*, ed. H. Farmer and D. Douie (London 1962) 29–30; *Annales Prioratus de Dunstaplia* (RS 36:3; London 1864–1869) 65 (1221).

16. Examples: *Cartulary of Cirencester Abbey*, Nos. 417, 448 (1148 x 1167); *The Letters of Arnulf of Lisieux*, ed. Frank Barlow (Camden Society 3rd Ser. 61; London 1939) No. 67 (ca. 1170); *Autobiogra-phy of Giraldus Cambrensis*, trans. and ed. Harold E. Butler (London 1937) 56.

17. Examples: *Letters of Arnulf*, No. 57 (1170); Benedict of Peterborough, *Gesta regis Henrici secundi*, ed. William Stubbs (RS 49:2; London 1867) 77 (1189); *Reading Abbey Cartularies I*, No. 155 (1191).

18. David M. Smith, 'The "Officialis" of the Bishop in Twelfth and Thirteenth Century Eng-land: Problems of Terminology', *Medieval Ecclesiastical Studies in Honour of Dorothy M. Owen*, ed.

The absence of a formalized court system did not mean that there was an absence of litigation. Indeed, one of the features of the late twelfth century is the large increase in the number of disputes subjected to formal decision by judges applying the canon law. This explosion is evident from sources of several kinds. Not only did contemporary documents more often describe legal procedure that is unmistakably canonical,[19] but complaints about the excessive 'legalization' of the church began to be heard with increasing frequency.[20] Quasi-judicial actions by archdeacons poking into the private lives of English men and women furnished a particular source of discontent.[21] Secular sources from this period also began to describe the *curia Christianitatis* as a regular feature of English legal life.[22] Indeed it was during this period that jurisdictional objections against the activities of the 'courts Christian' on the part of the temporal courts took the legal form they retained during the medieval period and beyond: the royal writ of prohibition.[23] Evidently, spiritual courts were thought to exist—indeed, did exist—before they were organized into the more formal system of consistory courts familiar from the later Middle Ages.

The most fully studied, and probably the most important, institutions of ecclesiastical justice during the period between 1150 and 1250 were the tribunals composed of papal judges delegate.[24] Recourse to the papacy, either by way of appeal or original complaint, became relatively frequent during the second half of the twelfth century, particularly after the collapse of King Henry II's plan to restrict appeals to Rome.[25] Actual trial of these disputes was normally entrusted to local dignitaries, who were instructed to hear and decide the cause according to the law set out in the papal re-

M. J. Franklin and C. Harper-Bill (Woodbridge 1995) 201–220, and the remarks in Donahue, 'Ecclesiastical Courts' 254–256, and Donahue and McDougall, 'France' 303–308.

19. See e.g. the documents in Adams and Donahue, *Canterbury Cases* 1–3 (1194 x 1204); and also Baltimore, Md., Walters Art Gallery W.15, fol. 79v–81v (ca. 1200).

20. E.g. Peter of Blois, *Epistolae* (PL 207) Ep. 19, 25, 26; *The Letters of John of Salisbury: The Early Letters*, ed. W. J. Millor and Harold E. Butler (London 1955) 4 (complaining about 'vigorous use of legal subtleties' in order to frustrate justice); Roger of Wendover, *Flores Historiarum*, ed. H. G. Hewlett (RS 84:1; London 1886) 259–260 (account of meeting a *iurisperitus* in Hell).

21. Case of the burgesses of Scarborough, in William fitz Stephen, 'Vita sancti Thomae', in *Materials for the History of Thomas Becket*, ed. J. C. Robertson (RS 67:3; London 1877) 44 (Henry II's complaint that by such activities archdeacons and rural deans were yearly extorting more money than he himself received).

22. *Treatise on the laws and customs of the realm of England commonly called Glanvill*, IV, 13 and XII, 22, ed. G. D. G. Hall (London 1965) 52–53, 146–147.

23. Ibid.; see also Christopher R. Cheney, *From Becket to Langton* (Manchester 1956) 110.

24. See Jane E. Sayers, *Papal Judges Delegate in the Province of Canterbury 1189–1254* (Oxford 1971); and the chapter by Charles Duggan, 'Judges Delegate,' above.

25. 'Constitutions of Clarendon' (1164) c. 8, *Stubbs' Select Charters*, ed. H. W. C. Davis (9th ed. London 1913) 165; there is also a useful commentary in H. G. Richardson and G. O. Sayles, *The Governance of Mediaeval England from the Conquest to Magna Carta* (Edinburgh 1963) 295–302.

script. Delegated justice was a vital link between England and the papacy, and it was a mechanism by which the new canon law penetrated into ordinary English practice. Contemporary activities by such papal judges delegate have left many tracks on the historical record from this period.

These tracks become less obvious in the historical record after the second half of the thirteenth century, and the likely reason for the change is that it was during this period that the consistory courts took organized shape. Whether from the press of litigation, the inconvenience of requiring recourse to the Roman court, or the better organization of ecclesiastical justice spurred by the publication of the Gregorian Decretals in 1234, the surviving evidence from after the middle of the century shows a court system in operation. A formal sign of the change was the increasing coupling of the term *officialis* with a diocese or location rather than with the bishop who had appointed him.[26] As yet, the steps by which the change occurred have been studied in detail only for the diocese of Canterbury. The study demonstrated that, at least by 1270 and perhaps a decade or two before, a court had emerged 'as a distinct institution with its own body of records and its own personnel'.[27] Some uncertainty about the date and pace of change remains, but the other evidence so far surveyed equally suggests that the organization of regular consistory courts was accomplished during the second half of the century.[28]

It would, of course, be inaccurate to equate the organization of a court system with the penetration of the canon law in England. It would be closer to the mark to say that for more than a century the canon law was regarded as the source of a distinct jurisdiction in England but that convening of a court to deal with a specific piece of litigation was regarded as a special (and usually unfortunate) event. Such a court would apply the canon law, but the court would not be a permanent institution. This was the way, for example, in which papal jurisdiction was exercised. A separate panel of papal judges delegate was convened for each case. No regular papal court was ever established in England, and none was ever proposed. Local ecclesiastical courts prior to the middle years of the thirteenth century must have been regarded in a similar light.

Application of the canon law was, of course, expected within the courts that were convoked. In the century between 1150 and 1250, knowledge and use of the canon law made great forward strides in England, as it

---

26. Thus *officialis Sarisburiensis* in lieu of *officialis episcopi Sarisburiensis*. See e.g. *The Great Chartulary of Glastonbury*, ed. A. Watkin (Somerset Record Society 59; Frome 1947) No. 89 (1276).

27. Adams and Donahue, *Canterbury Cases 25*.

28. See generally Colin Morris, 'From Synod to Consistory: The Bishops' Courts in England, 1150–1250', JEH 22 (1971) 115–123.

did elsewhere on the continent. The two English universities, Oxford and Cambridge, began providing training in both canon and civil law.[29] Faculties in the two laws existed throughout the medieval period. Notaries, familiar on the continent, were trained in England, though perhaps more by apprenticeship than by formal schooling. Their skills were employed principally in recording the documents necessary for the exercise of ecclesiastical jurisdiction, and the registrars (together with many of the proctors) in the consistory courts held the status of papal (or occasionally imperial) notary public.[30] Ecclesiastical lawyers (advocates and proctors) were also a regular feature of legal life in the consistory and other diocesan courts, though apparently not every court was staffed by trained advocates. Towards the end of the Middle Ages, the ecclesiastical lawyers practicing in London joined together to form a separate educational and dining institution. It came to be known as Doctors' Commons.[31] This institution became the focus of canonical and admiralty jurisdiction in England, both in study and practice. Its strength must help to explain the resistance to wholesale changes in the law inherited from the Middle Ages during the period when ecclesiastical jurisdiction first came under sustained attack at the end of the fifteenth century.

Structure and Personnel of the Courts, 1300–1500

Several of the individual consistory courts in England have been investigated in detail, although more thoroughly for the sixteenth century than for the medieval period.[32] These studies have demonstrated some variety in the ways these courts operated, just as there was variation in the jurisdictional divisions between the courts of bishops, archdeacons, and other dignitaries. However, consistent patterns of operation do seem to have existed across the land, and as long as the historian remembers the fact that exceptions existed, those patterns can be usefully surveyed. Most consistory courts met about every three weeks, except during their late summer recess, and usually they met in the cathedral church of the diocese. Not infrequently, however, consistories were also held at intervals elsewhere within the diocese in another large church.[33] Most such consistories occu-

29. Paul A. Brand, *Origins of the English Legal Profession* (Oxford 1992) 143–157.

30. See Christopher R. Cheney, *Notaries Public in England in the Thirteenth and Fourteenth Centuries* (Oxford 1972); Nicholas Bennett, 'Pastors and Masters', *The Foundations of Medieval English Ecclesiastical History: Studies presented to David Smith*, ed. P. Hoskin et al. (Woodbridge 2005) 40–62.

31. George D. Squibb, *Doctors' Commons: A History of the College of Advocates and Doctors of Law* (Oxford 1977).

32. See generally R. L. Storey, *Diocesan Administration in Fifteenth-Century England* (2nd ed., York 1972).

33. See, for instance, the description by B. Dunning, 'The Wells Consistory Court in the Fif-

pied more than one day, two or three days being normal and sufficient to transact both instance and ex officio litigation.

The judge of the diocesan court was called the 'official principal'. He was appointed by the bishop. Often, however, the official sat by deputy instead, sometimes called the 'commissary general', and the act books show that litigants were not sure to meet the same judge at every session. After the judge, the registrar was probably the most important court official. At least, he was the most permanent, and it was to this humble figure, invariably a notary public, acting in accord with a papal decretal,[34] that we owe the compilation of the court records that have been so largely preserved into modern times and that have allowed the history of the spiritual courts to be described in detail.

Most consistory courts were also served by four to six proctors, usually limited in number, so that one would have to die or retire before another could take his place. Some of the proctors were university graduates, but most seem not to have been. Only the judges and the advocates, where the latter were employed, were invariably university trained in either the civil or canon law. Almost everywhere there were summoners or apparitors, whose responsibility included the citation of parties to appear in the spiritual tribunals. However, the offices of *sigillator* and *procurator fiscalis*, which are found in many courts on the continent,[35] do not seem to have been used in England.

The citations and sentences of the spiritual courts were enforced by orders of suspension from entry into the parish church in the first instance, and then by major excommunication. Interdicts and minor excommunication, although theoretically available under the canon law, seem rarely to have been used in English practice.[36] As will be noted below, persons who remained obdurately excommunicate for more than forty days could be imprisoned upon application by the litigants or courts to the royal chancery. Studies so far undertaken suggest that this draconian penalty was in regular but not particularly frequent use in the consistory courts. It is clear that initiative for the process came more from the litigants themselves than from the court officers. The act books commonly record such initiatives, and the judges commonly provided a specific term for the par-

---

teenth Century', *Proceedings of the Somersetshire Archaeological and Natural Historical Society* 106 (1962) 46–61.

34. X 2.19.11 (*Quoniam contra falsam*), from Fourth Lateran Council (1215), c. 38.

35. E.g. Hans Foerster, 'Die Organisation des erzbischöflichen Offizialatsgerichts zu Köln bis auf Hermann von Wied', ZRG Kan. Abt. 11 (1921) 254–350 at 304, 337.

36. The former was, however, well known from the famous interdict placed on the kingdom during the reign of King John (1199–1216); see Peter D. Clarke, *The Interdict in the Thirteenth Century: A Question of Collective Guilt* (Oxford 2007).

ty against whom royal sanctions were to be invoked to appear and show cause why application to the chancery should not proceed.

Probably more important to note than this special process, at least from the legal point of view, was the considerable variety of sanctions available in the English spiritual tribunals.[37] Whereas the only remedy available in personal actions within the common law courts quickly came to be money damages, the ecclesiastical courts were open to more tailored remedies. Monetary awards, as in tithe causes; orders for specific performance, as in suits to enforce contracts; public apologies and public penance, as in defamation disputes; and injunctions, as in cases of jactitation of marriage, were all available in the ecclesiastical forum. Public penance has attracted the most notice from historians, probably because of its 'picturesque' character, but it was only one of several remedies used as a matter of course.

Appeals lay from the consistory courts of the province of Canterbury to the archiepiscopal court, called the Court of Arches, which met in the church of St. Mary-le-Bow, London. In the smaller northern province of York, appeals proceeded to the provincial court that met in York minster. From there appeals could go to the papal court.[38] England also knew a procedure called the 'tuitorial appeal', under which a litigant appealed directly both to the Roman court and 'for protection' also to the archbishop of Canterbury.[39] Called a *suggestio,* the document that contained such appeals commonly alleged the likelihood—indeed, the virtual certainty—of immediate harm to the appellant, either from his opponent or from unlawful action by the lower court. It was to avoid this immediate harm that the protection of the archiepiscopal see was invoked. Ordinarily, this protection was to last a year and a day, although the period could be extended.

In practice, tuition meant more than an order for retention of the status quo; it entailed process about the litigation itself, before the archbishop's court or before the archbishop himself. In theory only the immediate danger alleged by the appellant was being investigated. The result, however, of the widespread use of tuitorial appeals was to enlarge archiepiscopal jurisdiction at the expense of that of the suffragan bishops, since the

37. See R. E. Rodes Jr., *Ecclesiastical Administration in Medieval England: The Anglo-Saxons to the Reformation* (Notre Dame, Ind. 1977) 89–99.

38. For the continuing practice, see, e.g. R. N. Swanson, 'A Canon Lawyer's Compilation from Fifteenth-Century Yorkshire', JEH 63 (2012) 260–272.

39. See 'Modus procedendi in tuitoriis negociis', *The Medieval Court of Arches,* ed. F. Donald Logan (Canterbury and York Society 95; London 2005) 85–90; I. J. Churchill, *Canterbury Administration* (London 1933) 1.460–467; and Donahue, 'Ecclesiastical Courts' 283.

tuitorial appeal permitted objection and obstruction before the issuance of a definitive sentence by the lower court. This expansion was resented by the suffragans, as was the archbishop's prerogative in testamentary matters. The procedure was also open to objection under the canon law. It might have been challenged as an interference with the ordinary course of appeals to the papacy.[40] The papacy, considered as the 'universal ordinary', had the right to hear immediate appeals from all corners of Christendom under the canon law. Here it was being admitted in theory but sidestepped in practice. Whatever may explain its popularity, the tuitorial appeal came to be firmly established in English practice. No exception to its legality has so far been discovered among the surviving acta of the ecclesiastical courts, and if there were such an exception, the historical record shows that it was not successful.

The Scope Of Spiritual Jurisdiction In England

Jurisdiction *ratione personae*

Separation of the clerical order from subjection to lay power had been one of the cardinal tenets of the Gregorian reforms. It was natural, therefore, that the medieval canon law should have held that, except for special situations, clerics should be subject only to spiritual jurisdiction. The first chapter of the title *De foro competenti* in the Gregorian Decretals stated the rule that clerics were to be convened before their bishop; the second that a secular judge who presumed to 'distrain or condemn' a cleric without papal permission was himself to be excommunicated.[41] The rule applied both in civil and criminal matters. A considerable jurisprudence, normally treated under the heading of the *privilegium fori,* grew up around this jurisdiction based upon clerical status.[42] Its most immediate practical consequence was that a considerable part of the activity of most ecclesiastical tribunals would be devoted to a wide range of subjects that touched individual clerics but that would not otherwise have been heard there.[43]

This did not happen in England. Except for clergy accused of serious crimes, the jurisdiction of the ecclesiastical courts was restricted to a jurisdiction based upon subject matter. Even the action for assaulting a cleric,

---

40. See 'Introduction', in Adams and Donahue, *Canterbury Cases* 64–68.

41. See X 2.2.1–2; the principal exception in the canon law was for feudal questions between clerics and laymen; it was admitted that the feudal lord ordinarily had jurisdiction in such circumstances. See X 2.2.6.

42. Fournier, *Officialités* 64–82.

43. See the discussion by Winfried Trusen, 'Die gelehrte Gerichtsbarkeit der Kirche', *Handbuch* I, ed. Coing 483–485.

which did form a regular part of English ecclesiastical jurisdiction,[44] was treated as creating a separate subject-matter category; matrimonial or testamentary matters were treated in the same way. Actions to punish assaults on clerics were not regarded as arising under the wider *privilegium fori*. This great source of business and contention, so vital for most of the spiritual courts on the continent,[45] never took hold in England.

Moreover—and what seems even more striking from the canonical point of view—the bishops themselves enforced the common law's restrictive rules on this subject. They did so by regularly executing the royal courts' citations summoning clerics in civil cases to appear in the temporal forum. Sheriffs executed writs of summons against lay defendants; the bishops carried out the identical function when the defendant was in holy orders,[46] in effect making themselves party to violation of this principle of the canon law. In fact, the bishops actually helped to enforce temporal sentences against clerics. Where a common law court had rendered a judgment that a cleric owed money damages as a consequence of litigation, the bishop of the diocese in which the cleric was beneficed served the writ of execution, including levying execution against the cleric's property, if necessary, to collect the judgment debt.

Exclusion of ecclesiastical jurisdiction *ratione personae* in England was challenged in a cause heard in the papal court in the 1370s. The result there was a clear victory for what one might call the 'high church position'. The *consuetudo anglicana,* which accorded to the king jurisdiction 'in clericos solutos in actionibus civilibus', was held to be invalid by the Roman Rota. It was treated as an *abusus* rather than a valid custom. Arguments based upon long-time observance within the English courts, on apparent acquiescence in the situation by the English clergy, and even on the custom's long continued toleration by the papacy, were all rejected by the Rota in favor of the view that under the law the king 'has no jurisdiction over clerics and can have none'.[47] The *privilegium fori,* based upon a principle that was thought essential to the church's law, was not a rule that individual actors, no matter how numerous, could abrogate by renunciation or by repeated actions to the contrary.

<hr>

44. R. H. Helmholz, '"Si quis suadente" (C.17 q.4 c.29): Theory and Practice', *Proceedings Cambridge 1984* 425–438.

45. E.g. G. May, *Die geistliche Gerichtsbarkeit des Erzbishofs von Mainz in Thüringen des späten Mittelalters* (Leipzig 1956) 138–144.

46. To my knowledge, no historian has investigated this interesting aspect of the relations between church and state. It can be best approached through examination of the section of bishops' registers containing royal writs, on which see Smith, *Guide.*

47. Decisio 840, Decisiones antiquae, *Dominorum de Rota decisiones novae, antiquae et antiquiores* (Turin 1579) 360.

It must therefore stand as a tribute to either the strength of the English kings, the pusillanimity of the English clergy, or the ingrained habit of allowing custom to determine jurisdiction,[48] that this decision had no apparent impact on the shape of the canon law's jurisdiction in English practice. We know little more about the Rota's decision than its existence; none of the background or even its substance has been unearthed.[49] Nor do we know whether or not its implementation afterwards was seriously sought by the English bishops. What we do know is that nothing changed outwardly as the result of it. Clerics continued to be summoned before the courts of the common law in civil matters. The bishops continued to execute the royal writs summoning clerics to appear in civil actions before the king's justices, and they continued to help secure payment of money judgments against clerics subject to their jurisdiction.

In criminal matters, however, the situation was quite different. Archbishop Thomas Becket had taken his stand against King Henry II on this jurisdictional issue.[50] The prestige that Becket's martyrdom (1170) brought in its wake ensured the triumph of his position, and this meant that in English practice all clerics accused of serious crimes came to be punished only in the spiritual forum. The system chosen, as it was worked out over the course of the thirteenth century, required the cleric accused of a felony to appear first before a secular court and to 'plead his clergy' if he sought to assert his clerical privilege.[51] Bishops also appointed officers to attend these proceedings, to assert the claim on behalf of the church, and to take charge of the person of the cleric who asserted it. If the cleric could prove his status—normally by reading a passage from the Latin Psalter—he was dismissed to his bishop in the company of this officer. In time, the secular courts came also to make a preliminary inquest as to the cleric's guilt or innocence, but this did not affect the status of the cleric found guilty by the inquest. He was released to the bishop nonetheless.

48. This was a rule of the canon law itself. See e.g. the *Glossa ordinaria ad* X 2.13.13 s.v. *in tua.* It was, of course, always to be tested by the reasonableness of the custom, as it was in this case.

49. For what is known about it, together with speculation about the circumstances of the dispute's coming before the Rota, see Walter Ullmann, 'A Decision of the Rota Romana on the Benefit of Clergy in England', *Collectanea Stephan Kuttner* (SG 13; Bologna 1967) 455–489.

50. Secondary literature on this subject is very large; see generally Frank Barlow, *Thomas Becket* (Berkeley-Los Angeles 1986). On the legal issues of this famous dispute, see Richard Fraher, 'The Becket Dispute and Two Decretist Traditions', JMH 4 (1978) 347–368.

51. The standard work on the subject is L. C. Gabel, *Benefit of Clergy in the Later Middle Ages* (Smith College Studies in History 14; Northampton, Mass. 1929); augmented and updated by John G. Bellamy, *Criminal Law and Society in Late Medieval and Tudor England* (London 1984) 115–164; and A. K. McHardy, 'Church Courts and Criminous Clerks in the Later Middle Ages', *Medieval Ecclesiastical Studies in Honour of Dorothy M. Owen*, ed. M. J. Franklin and C. Harper-Bill (Woodbridge 1995) 165–183. A more summary recent treatment is found in R. N. Swanson, *Church and Society in Late Medieval England* (Oxford and New York 1989) 149–153.

No systematic records of canonical trials of clerics in the spiritual forum have been preserved, if indeed they ever existed. The guilt or innocence of accused clerics was not determined at regular sittings of the consistory courts, but instead by a tribunal convoked in response to a special order of the bishop. Episcopal registers thus contain the only extant entries relating to the matter. The procedure found in them included incarceration of the cleric in the bishop's prison pending trial, a preliminary inquest to determine the existence of *fama publica* against him, and a public proclamation calling for any party who wished to prove the cleric's guilt to appear and undertake that task.[52] Finally canonical purgation was used to determine guilt or innocence where (as was normal) no accuser appeared. Assuming a finding of guilt, the penalty was degradation from holy orders and, in flagrant cases of 'incorrigible' clerics, an indefinite prison sentence.[53] Assuming successful purgation, however, the accused was 'restored to his pristine reputation', and 'perpetual silence' was imposed upon his accusers.

The judgment of English historians about the procedure used in such cases has been uniformly unfavorable. F. W. Maitland regarded it as 'little better than a farce'.[54] The author of the standard work on the subject called it 'an empty form favorable to the accused'.[55] These opinions have rested upon the very high percentage of clerics who, being accused of crimes, successfully 'purged' themselves of the charge. Very, very few of the entries in the episcopal registers record a conviction. Almost all record the reverse. Lately, it has been suggested that the apparent dominance of successful purgations may reflect the nature of the registers rather than the nature of the proceedings. The registers should be regarded only as 'notifications of successful purgation' rather than full records.[56] Thus the unfavorable judgments may rest on a skewed sample. As yet, however, no final consensus on the question has emerged.

For the historian of the canon law, of greater interest is the question of the relation of this procedure to the canonical texts. It was more favorable to the clerical order than the system found in the *Corpus iuris canonici*. The canon law held that under some circumstances a degraded cleric should

<hr>

52. On the role of *fama* in the ordo iudiciarius see Antonia Fiori, 'La valutazione processuale della personalità dell'accusato: Dall'infamia alla "capacità a delinquere del colpevole",' *Einfluss der Kanonistik* 4.157–172; and Pennington, 'Introduction' 10.

53. William Lyndwood, *Provinciale* 322 s.v. *perpetuo carceri*. For what is known about bishops' prisons, see Ralph B. Pugh, *Imprisonment in Medieval England* (Cambridge 1968) 134–138.

54. Frederick Pollock and Frederic W. Maitland, *History of English Law* (2 vols. 2nd ed. Cambridge 1898) 2.443.

55. Gabel, *Benefit* 113.

56. See Swanson, *Church and Society* 153.

be handed over to the secular power for punishment.[57] In England, both trial and punishment of all clerics were reserved exclusively to the church, although some crimes became exempt from the privilege by virtue of statutes enacted by Parliament during the later Middle Ages. Thus, one might fairly conclude that English practice deviated from the canon law both on the criminal and on the civil side. In the former it adopted Gregorian assumptions in an extreme form; in the latter it refused to adopt Gregorian assumptions at all.

Litigation involving Benefices and Ecclesiastical Patronage

Loss of most of the records of the Court of Arches[58] and the failure of any historian, so far at least, to explore records of English litigation at the papal court make it hazardous to generalize about the subject of causes relating to ecclesiastical benefices as part of the canon law as enforced in England. We do know that the decision about the right of patronage was a subject of jurisdictional dispute. Both church and state made claims over the subject, and these claims appear to have been mutually exclusive. The king's courts claimed the right to try all matters relating to the rights of patrons of benefices.[59] The canon law claimed the same right for the church.[60] Moreover, if we were to regard only the complaints of official representatives of each side, it would appear that in each case the other side was not only the aggressor but also an overly successful aggressor. On the one hand, a royal justice complained in the sixteenth century that the bishops had acted in so 'presumptuous' a fashion as almost to 'make question of all the patronages of the realm'.[61] On the other hand, however, contemporary ecclesiastical lawyers complained equally loudly that the temporal courts had prevented the courts of the church from taking 'notice of a canonical "ius patronatus" or anie allegation thereof'.[62] We must, therefore, temporarily put aside such self-serving complaints and examine what information is actually to be found in the medieval records of the courts.

---

57. See C.11 q.1 c.18 and *Glossa ordinaria* ad idem.

58. Probably in the Great Fire of London of 1666. See M. D. Slatter, 'The Records of the Court of Arches', JEH 4 (1953) 139–153.

59. W. R. Jones, 'Relations of the Two Jurisdictions: Conflict and Cooperation in England during the Thirteenth and Fourteenth Centuries', *Studies in Medieval and Renaissance History* 7, ed. W. M. Bowsky (Lincoln, Nebraska1970) 102–132; *Select Ecclesiastical Cases from the King's Courts 1272–1307*, ed. David Millon (Selden Society 126; London 2009) ci–cviii.

60. X 2.1.3 (*Quanto divina*) decretal of Alexander III addressed to King Henry II. See generally Peter Landau, *Ius Patronatus: Studien zur Entwicklung des Patronats im Dekretalenrecht und der Kanonistik* (Cologne 1975); Paul Thomas, *Droit de propriété des laïques sur les églises et le patronage laïque au moyen age* (Bibliothéque de l'École des Haute Études, Sciences Religieuses 19; Paris 1906).

61. See Case of *Quare impedit* (1587) in Gouldsborough's Reports 52 (75 *English Reports* 989).

62. London Metropolitan ArchivesMS. 11448, fol. 127v (16th century) per Dr. Steward.

At first sight, the evidence suggests the victory of the position of the royal courts from at least the start of the thirteenth century, and relative quiescence thereafter. The records of the royal courts contain many disputes over advowsons, most of them brought by means of a royal writ called *Quare impedit*.[63] The records of the courts of the church do not. Most act books contain almost no litigation dealing with beneficial matters, and even in the archiepiscopal court at York, where one might expect some such cases from the northern province, the number of causes involving such questions is tiny. Moreover, none of the causes that are found in the ecclesiastical archives were clashes between patrons over the right to the *ius patronatus*. English custom conceded to the church the right to decide questions such as whether a person presented to a benefice was sufficiently literate or whether he had committed simony in return for the presentment. Disputes over such matters do figure in the surviving records, and of course they involved no violation of jurisdictional principles of either canon or English common law. From what one can tell in the absence of actual reports of the cases, they were decided according to the law of the church. Their existence in the records makes the absence of disputes about the ius patronatus particularly telling.

A more complete look suggests greater caution in assuming that the church conceded full jurisdiction to the courts of the king. First, throughout the period, the church operated a parallel system of inquiry into the patronage of vacant churches. Before a candidate for a benefice could be admitted and inducted, bishops caused to be convoked a special, local inquest to determine the suitability of the candidate and the status of the benefice. These were called inquests *de iure patronatus*.[64] Made up of twelve men—sometimes six incumbents of nearby churches and six laymen, sometimes simply twelve clerics—these inquests met under the presidency of an archdeacon, rural dean, or other person appointed by the bishop. They normally were held on site; that is, in the relevant parish church. Several articles were put at these inquests and, as their title suggests, one of these was: Who is the lawful patron? If it was determined that the patronage was *not* held by the person presenting the cleric, it appears that the process would not go forward. Thus the church maintained its own check on questions involving the ius patronatus, and in the judgment of the principal student of the subject, the conflict between tempo-

63. Joshua C. Tate, 'The Origins of *Quare Impedit*', *Journal of Legal History* 25 (2004) 203–219.

64. The fundamental article is J. W. Gray, 'The *Ius Praesentandi* in England from the Constitutions of Clarendon to Bracton', *EHR* 67 (1952) 481–509. More recent and helpful also is Joshua C. Tate, 'The Third Lateran Council and the *Ius Patronatus* in England', *Proceedings Esztergom 2008*, 589–600.

ral and ecclesiastical jurisdictions 'was not, in fact, finally settled' during this period.[65] Because these inquests were convoked ad hoc, they have left little evidence in the regular records of the courts, and this may explain the appearance of the church's acquiescence in the claims of the crown.

Second, even in the absence of detailed exploration of the Vatican archives, it is apparent that litigation about English benefices took place in Rome throughout the Middle Ages.[66] Extant papal letters refer to beneficial questions,[67] and since the papal court was not subject to intimidation or to direct threat by royal writs of prohibition, it is certainly more likely that questions of patronage were raised directly in that forum. Moreover, the growing system of papal provision of benefices had direct potential for conflict with the English common law courts' jurisdiction over advowsons. Although it appears that, as a matter of prudence, the popes did not normally intrude intentionally upon the rights of lay patrons, nonetheless it is equally clear that clashes did sometimes occur. So much depended upon the initiative of candidates for the benefices that it would have been quite unrealistic to expect candidates not to take advantage of the possibilities of papal provision. It seems that they did. Indeed, the records of the archiepiscopal court at York contain disputes that grew directly out of such conflicts.[68]

Third, examination of the detailed questions raised in litigation has shown the impossibility of rigorous separation between legal questions involving patronage and those involving other aspects of claims involving benefices. The English common law's claim to exclusive jurisdiction depended on the ability to maintain that dividing line. Although this was a theoretically defensible position, and although it did take care of many problems, in fact it also left room for disputes about on which side of the dividing line a particular question fell.[69] Self-interest of the contestants magnified the possibility. For example, suppose a vicar's title was contested for allegedly being the product of simony, but the vicar disputed the

65. Gray, 'Ius Praesentandi' 508. Gray's conclusion extended only to the end of the thirteenth century, but the system of inquests clearly continued into the sixteenth century, if not later. See, for example, British Library, London, Add. 41503 (late 15th-century English formulary) fol. 45–46: 'Commissio ad inquirendum de iure patronatus'.

66. See Jane E. Sayers, 'Proctors Representing British Interests at the Papal Court, 1198–1415', *Proceedings Strasbourg 1968*, 143–163.

67. See *Calendar of entries in the papal registers relating to Great Britain and Ireland (1362–1404)* 4, No. 325 (1390) (benefice of Bognor Regis, diocese of Winchester).

68. E.g. Burthan c. Wymark and Kexby, Archives of the Archbishop of York, Borthwick Institute of Historical Research, York, C.P.E.133 (1386); a dispute over possession of the parish church of Sproatley, involving claims to the benefice 'virtute gracie auctoritate apostolica,' but involving in name only the contending clerics, not the patrons.

69. See Gray, 'Ius Praesentandi' 497, noting 'the difficulty of distinguishing between the question of patronage and that of incumbency'.

allegation. Suppose further that patronage of the benefice was in dispute and that each patron had presented a candidate to replace the vicar in possession. Because decision of any case brought by the writ of *Quare impedit*—the normal form in which patronage cases were raised in the royal courts—depended in part on the factual questions of which person had last presented and whether the benefice was currently vacant, decision in the spiritual courts on the question of simony could easily have a decisive impact on litigation in the royal courts.[70] Issues of 'plenarty' mattered in each forum, and each was affected by decisions in the other. Therefore, it would seem that collisions were inevitable and frequent, even though we can see only parts of each in the surviving records.

The force of these arguments is difficult to deny. Nonetheless, it is equally evident that the English system of double jurisdiction must have been tolerable, because it was in fact tolerated. Indeed, the system appears overall to have been stable and durable. It lasted without great change well into the sixteenth century. There must therefore have been mitigating mechanisms, practical means by which the system dealt effectively with jurisdictional conflicts. The most conspicuous such mechanism appearing in the records is the availability of compromise,[71] often achieved through fastening annual pensions upon a benefice in dispute. These pensions amounted to fixed charges upon the revenues accruing from the benefice, payable to someone other than the incumbent.[72] Thus could the revenue arising from the benefice be shared by the party whose claims to the benefice and its patronage were formally rejected. Subsequent payment of these charges could be enforced in either the royal or the ecclesiastical forum, and the surviving records demonstrate the frequency with which this mechanism was used in practice.[73]

The royal courts contributed to making the situation tolerable by permitting the plea of plenarty to block the bringing of many suits over ecclesiastical benefices. No one has yet systematically investigated the subject, and conclusions about it must be tentative. Yet, it does seem that in some

---

70. See John Mallory, *Quare Impedit* (London 1737) 77, 142–144.

71. It is particularly important in this respect to emphasize that in personal actions, judgments in the royal courts were for money damages only. Injunctive relief was not directly available. In the ecclesiastical forum the opposite was the case. Thus there was no overt duplication of remedies, leaving greater room for compromise where there was direct overlap in subject-matter jurisdiction.

72. Canonical learning on the subject is contained in Hieronymus Gigantis († 1560), *Tractatus de pensionibus ecclesiasticis* (Venice 1542). See also R. H. Helmholz, 'The Canon Law of Annual Pensions', *Recto ordine procedit magister: Liber amicorum E.C. Coppens*, ed. L. Berkvens et al. (Brussels 2012) 161–173.

73. E.g. *Rotuli Ricardi Gravesend, diocesis Lincolniensis*, ed. F. N. Davis (Lincoln Record Society 20; Lincoln 1925) 139–140. See generally Millon, *Select Ecclesiastical Cases* lxxxviii–ci.

situations the common law permitted defendants in suits of *Quare impedit* to plead that the benefice was not vacant, after the admission and induction of an incumbent. The practical effect of such a plea, where successful, was to choke off the claims of outstanding rights to the patronage.[74] This is so because it would have prevented the claimant from raising the question of patronage at all; no actual dispute about whether it could be exercised would exist after the vacancy had effectively been filled. Pleas of plenarty thus operated as a practical bar to continuation of such disputes, even while they allowed the common law courts to maintain their theoretical monopoly on litigation over advowsons. The reason for allowing the plea's expansive scope, as a later common lawyer noted, was in order to prevent 'the disturbance and hindrance of Divine Service'.[75]

It is, of course, also important to remember that in most cases the English church acquiesced in the established custom that accorded jurisdiction to the royal courts.[76] Patronage disputes were routinely handled in the common law courts. Their outcomes were respected, and even introduced as evidence, in the ecclesiastical forum.[77] The jury-like procedure used in inquests *De iure patronatus* was unlikely to produce different results than those emanating from the royal courts, and indeed these inquests were always meant more to protect the ecclesiastical ordinary from inducting the wrong person to a benefice (and from consequent litigation) than they were to assert the independence of spiritual jurisdiction.[78] It was the exceptional case that caused friction. In this, of course, jurisdiction over beneficial matters was no different than several other areas of subject-matter jurisdiction that lay in dispute between the courts of church and state.

Tithes, Oblations, and Taxation

Surprisingly little scholarly work has been undertaken on the subject of the financial system of the English church as it was enforced in the ecclesiastical courts. There have, however, been useful investigations of the nature and variety of tithes and oblations owed to parish churches.[79] Like

74. See Mallory, *Quare Impedit* 139, noting that where the plea of plenarty was made after six months from the date of a parson's induction, it barred all private parties in a suit brought with this writ. The origins of the utility of this plea may be statutory; see 25 Edw. III, st. 6, cc. 7, 8 (1351).

75. Mallory, *Quare Impedit* 139.

76. See Lyndwood, *Provinciale* 316 s.v. *jure patronatus*: 'Sed consuetudo dat cognitionem foro temporali, et hoc fateri videtur haec constitutio in hoc loco'.

77. E.g. notice of the result of litigation in the royal courts was included in a fifteenth-century ecclesiastical formulary: British Library, London, Add. 41503, fol. 45–46.

78. See Mallory, *Quare impedit* 167.

79. A valuable study, although covering only the years just prior to the Reformation, is R. Houlbrooke, *Church Courts and the People during the English Reformation 1520–1570* (Oxford 1979) 117–150. See generally Swanson, *Church and Society* 209–217, and references given therein.

the subject of benefices, most of what attention has been devoted to the legal aspects of the subject has been concentrated on the areas of overlap and of potential conflict with the royal courts.[80] Scholarly energy has also been expended on exploring the difficult question of the extent of evasion of tithes, and on the even more inscrutable inquiry into whether or not the laity paid their tithes willingly.[81] However, on the basis of published works and a preliminary survey of the court records, a few general, if necessarily tentative, conclusions emerge about the role of the ecclesiastical tribunals.

First, tithe litigation played a proportionately smaller role in court practice than several other types of causes, although some of the more complicated tithe disputes did drag on longer than most other kinds of litigation. Woodcock's survey of the commissary court at Canterbury during the medieval period found that the number of tithe causes introduced in the court there fluctuated between thirty-nine (1397) and four (1517).[82] That general pattern, allowing for variation from one year to another without ever becoming terribly large in total volume, seems to have held true in most dioceses. In the consistory court of Lichfield, for example, only thirteen of the 259 causes introduced between 1465 and 1467 related to tithes.[83] Litigation dealing with breach of faith and with various probate matters outnumbered causes relating to tithes and customary offerings in almost all late medieval English act books. It was only after the Reformation, when monastic tithes fell into the hands of the laity, that litigation relating to tithes came to play a more dominant role in court practice.

Second, at least the outlines of the litigation heard in the English ecclesiastical courts followed the lines laid out by the canon law texts. Although lay infeudation of tithes was not entirely unknown in England, in fact there was very little of it, at least compared to the contemporary situation in France and Spain. Moreover, in the several areas where the English secular law proscribed the collection of tithes, it seems that the ecclesiastical courts nonetheless entertained suits for enforcement unless actually prevented from doing so by the introduction of a writ of prohibition. Thus, suits for recovery of tithes for minerals,[84] agistment,[85] new

80. See Norma Adams, 'The Judicial Conflict over Tithes', EHR 52 (1937) 1–22.

81. The best review of the literature on the subject is Giles Constable, 'Resistance to Tithes in the Middle Ages', JEH 13 (1962) 172–185.

82. See Brian L. Woodcock, *Medieval Ecclesiastical Courts in the Diocese of Canterbury* (Oxford 1952) 86.

83. Taken from act book B/C/1/1, Joint Record Office, Lichfield.

84. See A. G. Little, 'Personal Tithes', EHR 60 (1945) 70.

85. For example, *Prior and Convent of Hospital of St. John of Jerusalem c. Carter et al.* (York 1402–1403), Borthwick Institute of Historical Research, York, C.P.F.7: a 'causa decime agistamenti sive pasture'.

mills,[86] and great wood[87] can all be found in medieval act books, despite their seeming contravention of the common law's rules. This is not to say that all tithes were paid, much less that they were paid willingly. Evidence from the medieval act books themselves shows that some tithes were not paid and indeed had not been paid from time immemorial. However, whenever customary exemptions from the tithe obligation were actually challenged in the church's judicial forum, they seem regularly to have been disallowed.[88] The courts attempted to enforce the canon law's rule that tithing customs must be reasonable and that a prescriptive right to pay no tithe at all was always invalid. What one cannot say, on the basis of the surviving evidence, is whether such tithes were in the end actually collected.

Third, custom played a prominent part in English tithe litigation. Reliance on custom is only to be expected. As a source of the obligation itself, as a determining factor in the allocation of particular tithes among the clergy, and as a justification for alternatives to full payment of tithes in kind, custom held an important place in the canon law itself. It could also be the source of legitimate obligation. Thus it should be no surprise to see custom being pleaded and sometimes tested in canonical litigation. And that is what one does find. It was common for plaintiffs seeking to recover tithes withheld to allege that they had been owed these tithes 'de consuetudine laudabili prescripta' from a time beyond which the memory of man did not run.[89] Many suits involved determination of the precise customary manner of paying tithes, as for instance whether a tithe payer was obliged to separate the tenth and himself deliver it to the tithe barn.[90] It was somewhat less common, though also not infrequent, to find custom being alleged as a reason for nonpayment of full tithes in kind.[91] Without doubt, these are the most interesting of the surviving cases from a strictly

---

86. For example, *Merryng, vicar of Wednesbury c. Whitchurche, vicar of St. Mary* (Canterbury 1415), Canterbury Cathedral Library, Deposition book X.10.1, fols. 58–61.

87. For example, *Ex officio c. Whitherot* (Lincoln 1517), Lincolnshire Archives, Lincoln, Act book Cj/2, f. 37.

88. *Vicar of Carisbrooke c. Fleitt et al.* (Winchester 1517), Hampshire Record Office, Winchester, Act book 1, f. 114v, brought to record arrearages of tithe wool for seven years. The defendants, 'dixerunt quod de consuetudine non solverunt decimas [de] lockes', but the official 'pronunciavit dictam consuetudinem fore illegitimam et omnino nullam ac irrationabilem'.

89. For example, *Mag. John Gilby, rector of Kneesall c. Bakster* (York 1405–1407), Borthwick Institute of Historical Research, York, C.P.F.14: 'Item ponit quod de consuetudine laudabili prescripta ac a x xx xxx xl l lx annis ac citra et ultra et per ipsa tempora necnon a tempore et per tempus cuius initii memoria hominum non existit observata....'

90. *Prior and Chapter of Durham c. Thomholme* (York 1452), Borthwick Institute of Historical Research, York, C.P.F.188.

91. For example, *Cowprey, rector of Birdham c. Hybardy* (Chichester 1507), East Sussex Record Office, Chichester, Act book Ep. I/10/1, f. 25v: a suit brought for tithes of a water mill. The defendant's answer was that 'non solet solvi temporibus preteritis'. The matter was put to arbitration.

legal standpoint. Unfortunately, the absence of records of actual legal arguments in the medieval archives of the English church prevents us from speaking with authority on the treatment that was actually accorded to such claims. It must be enough to note their ubiquity.

Fourth, a surprisingly large percentage of the tithe suits found in the instance act books of the ecclesiastical courts concerned not the purposeful withholding of tithes by laymen who allegedly owed them, but instead the question of which cleric held the right to tithes that were not themselves in dispute. To some extent the impression may be slightly exaggerated if one looks only at instance act books and cause papers, the most common surviving muniment, since enforcement of this obligation occurred also on the ex officio side or in the penitential forum. Nevertheless, it remains striking how often disputes centered around the division of tithes rather than their nonpayment.[92] Indeed, many suits that began against apparently defaulting parishioners actually turn out to have been about deciding the question of entitlement among competing clerics. One discovers this in the records in those cases in which another ecclesiastic appeared as an intervening party in order to defend his rights.[93]

Widespread monastic appropriation of parish churches had inevitably led to widespread division of tithes in England. The normal division was for the greater tithes to be held by the monastery or rector, the lesser tithes by the vicar. But the apparent simplicity of this system may easily conceal the complexity of the issues actually raised in litigation. Some of the longest and most complicated of the causes to be found in medieval act books involved the question of whether tithes were due to one institution rather than to another. Frequent questions involved the extent of parish boundaries, the proper treatment of tithes of new crops or products, the status of past agreements or prescriptive rights, the coverage and validity of papal grants of privilege, and the complexities caused by the movement of goods and chattels from one parish to another during the tithe year.

Finally, one must take note of the many cases heard by the ecclesiastical courts about other kinds of financial obligations that were based upon custom alone. The *causa subtractionis iurium ecclesiasticorum* was a very fre-

92. Normally indicated in the records by being styled a *causa spoliationis decimarum* or simply a *causa decimarum*, whereas most suits brought to collect tithes where none had been paid were called a *causa subtractionis decimarum*.

93. E.g. *Atte Well, rector of Hastingleigh c. Scot* (Canterbury 1374), Canterbury Cathedral Library, Act book Y.l.l, fol. 61v, which was begun to collect tithes from a parishioner, but became such an action when the prior and Convent of Horton intervened to protect their rights to the same tithes.

quent entry in medieval act books. Although it could cover questions as concrete as interference within a churchyard, a great many of such cases involved purely customary oblations owed by parishioners. The mortuary payment, owed to an incumbent as a matter of custom upon the death of one of his flock, and Peter's Pence, originally a voluntary payment made to the papacy, are the best known of these oblations. There were many others. Their proliferation and uncertain legal status made for disputes and suits to secure their enforcement. Payment of 'church rates' levied by the parishioners for the church's use was another monetary obligation enforced in the spiritual tribunals in England.[94] Likewise, suits were brought to collect special taxes levied in Convocation upon English benefices.[95] Suits begun by proctors in the ecclesiastical courts to collect fees from clients were another regular aspect of spiritual litigation.[96] To a modern observer, it is striking how frequently these tribunals were concerned with collecting money. A contrast between the spiritual ends of the canon law and the protection of the Church's concrete and substantial interests is apparent, sometimes in a disquieting way, in many of the activities of England's spiritual courts.

Marriage and Divorce

During the Middle Ages, cases involving marriage and divorce occupied a significant part of the litigation heard by the English ecclesiastical courts.[97] The majority of such cases at all times involved disputes over the formation of marriage rather than its annulment. The normal question upon which the outcome of disputes depended was whether or not the parties had entered into a contract of marriage by *verba de praesenti*, not (as is true today) whether they were entitled to an annulment because of

94. For example, *Rector of Mutford et al. c. Grangia* (Canterbury 1305), Lambeth Palace Library, London, Act book MS. 244, fol. 66: a suit brought for impeding collection of 'partes Christi que vocantur Cristesdoles.'

95. For example, *Ex officio c. Botselde* (Lichfield 1534), Joint Record Office, Lichfield, Act book B/C/10/1, fol. 34.

96. Normally styled *cause salarii*.

97. The following summary of the law relating to marriage and divorce is largely based on the author's *Marriage Litigation in Medieval England* (Cambridge 1975), together with Christopher Brooke, *The Medieval Idea of Marriage* (Oxford 1989); George Duby, *Two Models of Medieval Marriage*, trans. E. Forster (Baltimore 1978); James A. Brundage, *Law, Sex, and Christian Society in Medieval Europe* (Chicago 1987); D. Giesen, *Grundlagen und Entwicklung des englischen Eherechts in der Neuzeit* (Bielefeld 1973); Michael M. Sheehan, 'The Formation and Stability of Marriage in England from the Eleventh to the Fourteenth Century', *Mediaeval Studies* 33 (1971) 228–263; Frederik Pedersen, *Marriage Disputes in Medieval England* (London and Rio Grande 2000); and Charles Donahue Jr., *Law, Marriage, and Society in the Later Middle Ages* (Cambridge 2007). See also the marriage cases discussed by Donahue, 'Ecclesiastical Courts' 271–272, 287–292; and his chapter 'Procedure' 104–111.

the existence of a diriment impediment.[98] The words subject to interpretation and dispute in these litigated cases had almost always been spoken privately, before a few witnesses or even no witnesses at all, and one party was refusing to complete the marriage and to have it duly solemnized. A suit was therefore necessary to enforce the contract of marriage, according to the church's law that treated clandestine marriages as valid, even if illicit. In these cases, and with the few minor exceptions such as practice always produces, the English ecclesiastical tribunals seem to have followed the formal canon law of marriage. Both questions of interpreting the language used by the parties and those raised by the Ius commune's requirements of proof were decided according to the canonical texts.

Over the course of the later Middle Ages, both the relative and the absolute importance of matrimonial litigation in the English courts declined. For example, in 1373–1374, thirty-five matrimonial causes were heard yearly by the commissary court at Canterbury, easily making this the largest single type of litigation. In the fifteenth century, however, the average never exceeded twenty and was often less than ten.[99] The number was dwarfed by litigation to enforce simple contracts entered into by pledge of faith.[100] This decline in the amount of matrimonial litigation may have reflected an increasing acceptance by the laity of the church's rules against clandestine marriages. They raised special difficulties of proof and were sometimes regarded by the parties involved as mere agreements to marry at some point in the future. Thus these cases gave rise to dispute more often than marriages preceded by banns and duly celebrated. With greater general adherence to the rules against clandestine marriages naturally followed the decline in numbers of cases that is found in the act books.

The successful suit to enforce a marriage contract ended with a decision holding that the parties had spoken words sufficient to constitute a valid marriage and an order requiring them to solemnize the union in their parish church. The unsuccessful suit ended with a judicial statement that the parties were free to marry elsewhere and also with a dismissal to their consciences, at least where the suit had failed for want of proof. In English practice, most matrimonial litigation seems to have been instigated by one of the parties involved; that is, brought on the instance side of ecclesiastical jurisdiction. These cases were not entirely absent from the ex officio side, however, and indeed questions involving marriage

---

98. This has been shown to be a consistent European pattern; see, for example, Kirsi Salonen, 'Marriage Disputes in the Consistorial Court of Freising in the Late Middle Ages', *Regional Variations in Matrimonial Law and Custom in Europe, 1150–1600,* ed. M. Korpiola (Leiden 2011) 189–209.

99. Brian L. Woodcock, *Medieval Ecclesiastical Courts* 85.

100. Ibid. 84.

arose incidentally in a variety of disciplinary causes. For instance, ex officio prosecutions against persons accused of open fornication could involve a question of matrimonial law if either party asserted that the other had made a promise to marry. The remaining act books similarly contain ex officio prosecutions begun against parties for 'reclaiming' during the reading of banns of marriage, for living with a person suspected not to be one's spouse, for impeding a valid marriage, and even for having more than one living spouse. Incidentally but inevitably, all such proceedings required the courts to implement the canon law of marriage.

Divorce *a vinculo* occupied a smaller place in matrimonial litigation in medieval England than did suits brought to enforce marriage contracts. The relative paucity of such suits shows that it is incorrect to assume that grounds could have been found to annul virtually any marriage and that the laity habitually took advantage of such grounds to escape from unions found unprofitable or irksome.[101] Though fewer in number than might have been expected, the cases that were brought seem to have been decided along principles laid down by the formal law. Thus divorces were granted based upon the existence of prohibited degrees of affinity and consanguinity, the exertion of sufficient force to sway the will of a normal man or woman, the fact of continuing sexual impotence, or the lack of sufficient canonical age on the part of one or both of the parties. Some of the more minor grounds for annulment—disparity of cult, the impediment of crime, and mistake of person—are not found in the remaining records. However, the most likely explanation lies in their rarity in the lives of contemporary men and women rather than in a serious disjunction between theory and practice in the canon law of marriage.[102]

The English ecclesiastical tribunals also dealt with several areas of law related to the marriage bond but not touching it directly.[103] Judicial separation, called divorce *a mensa et thoro*, was easily the most conspicuous of these. All those found in the English records were brought either for physical cruelty on the part of the husband or for adultery on the part of the husband or wife.[104] Heresy, called 'spiritual fornication' by the canon-

101. An older statement of this view is T. A. Lacey, *Marriage in Church and State* (London 1912). Charles Donahue has breathed some new life into it in 'A Legal Historian Looks at the Case Method', *Northern Kentucky Law Review* 19 (1991) 21–31.

102. On the widespread knowledge among the laity of the canon law on these points, see Pedersen, *Marriage Disputes* 59–84; Sam Worby, *Law and Kinship in Thirteenth-Century England* (Royal Historical Society Studies in History, new series; Woodbridge-Rochester 2010) 68–91.

103. See Sara M. Butler, *The Language of Abuse: Marital Violence in Later Medieval England* (Leiden 2007) 68–81.

104. See Sara M. Butler, *Divorce in Medieval England: From One to Two Persons in Law* (New York 2013).

ists to accommodate it within existing legal norms, does not appear in the records. In fact, the number of ordinary judicial separations seems to have been limited in practice. A requirement of demonstrable, substantial physical harm; a judicial willingness to find condonation or forgiveness by the aggrieved spouse; and the enforcement of canonical rules of proof held down the number of successful claims. Other minor areas of competence, similarly limited in numbers in English practice, included restitution of conjugal rights, suits brought by one spouse against the other for deserting the conjugal home, and suits brought by mothers to require fathers to contribute to the support of their illegitimate children.

Cases involving trial of questions of legitimacy of birth, long a *cause célèbre* in canonical theory,[105] were only occasionally brought within England's consistory courts.[106] Perhaps, however, the apparent scarcity results from peculiarities of record preservation. Such disputes were often referred to the spiritual forum by the English common law courts, but they were usually dealt with by special commissions created ad hoc by the bishop and have left little trace on the ordinary court records. Also largely missing from the medieval act books, but for reasons substantial rather than formal, are causes involving property rights dependent upon marriage. Litigation involving gifts between husband and wife or gifts made in consideration of marriage, which claim a separate title in the Gregorian Decretals, were normally dealt with in England by the temporal courts. According to the English common law, only when the validity of the marriage itself was at issue was reference to be made to the spiritual forum. Insofar as the surviving ecclesiastical court records give an accurate impression of the realities, the common law rule here was also the fact.

Last Wills and Testaments

One of the special characteristics of the courts of the English church was its testamentary jurisdiction. Developing gradually and indeed almost imperceptibly over the course of the twelfth and thirteenth centuries, the 'general custom' of the realm came to grant to the church the right to determine the validity of the last wills and testaments of laymen.[107] The church also held the authority to supervise the administration of decedents' estates, whether decedents had died testate or intestate. Although not without parallel on the continent, this was a broader jurisdiction than

---

105. For example, X 4.17.7 (*Causam quae*); for England, see Frederic W. Maitland, *Roman Canon Law in the Church of England* (London 1898) 53–56.

106. See my 'Bastardy Litigation in Medieval England', *Canon Law and the Law of England* (London 1987) 188.

107. Lyndwood, *Provinciale* 170 s.v. *insinuationem*. See Donahue, 'Ecclesiastical Courts' 273–274.

existed in many parts of Europe,[108] since it was by no means restricted to charitable bequests.[109] Certainly, it was broader than the regime referred to in the canonical texts.[110]

English probate jurisdiction was nevertheless limited in several ways. In some areas of the country, for example, special custom allocated probate matters to local secular courts.[111] Probably the most significant limitation stemmed from the common law rule that, in the absence of valid local custom, land could not be left by will.[112] Although in practice inroads were made in this rule during the Middle Ages,[113] by and large it was observed, restricting ecclesiastical jurisdiction extended to interests in chattels or personal property. Even so restricted, however, probate remained a vital source of revenue and power for the spiritual courts. It was one that English ecclesiastical lawyers everywhere fought to defend against both the claims of the courts of other dioceses and those of the royal courts.

Perhaps the most notable feature of the English testament was the lack of formality required to establish the testament's formal validity.[114] Although English probate practice was determined at most points directly by the Roman and canon laws, a more relaxed view was taken on the question of the formalities requisite to sustain the validity of a testament. For instance, no fixed number of witnesses was required—neither the number found in the Roman law nor that endorsed in the Decretals.[115] The courts sought to discern and to enforce the last wishes of a decedent without regard for form. It was commonly stated in court papers that a

108. Compare, for example, Anne Lefebvre-Teillard, *Les officialités a la veille du Concile de Trente* (Paris 1973) 251–263.

109. Lyndwood sought to bring practice into harmony with the law by asserting that 'quaelibet voluntas testatoris rationabilis dici potest pia'; see Lyndwood, *Provinciale* 169 s.v. *residuis*. See Brian E. Ferme, *Canon Law in Late Medieval England: A Study of William Lyndwood's Provinciale with Particular Reference to Testamentary Law* (Rome 1996).

110. E.g. X 3.26.3 (*Nos quidem*).

111. See e.g. *Estate of Tyly* (Hereford 1470), Herefordshire Record Office, Act book O/9, p. 55: the widow appeared before the commissary court and 'allegat se non teneri ad probationem testamenti ex consuetudine patrie'. She was assigned a day to prove the custom.

112. See A. W. B. Simpson, *History of the Land Law* (2nd ed. Oxford 1986) 62, 139.

113. The most fundamental being the 'use', on which see 'The Early Enforcement of Uses', *Canon Law and the Law of England*, 341–53; and S. DeVine, 'The Franciscan Friars, the Feoffment to Uses, and Canonical Theories of Property Enjoyment before 1535', *Journal of Legal History* 10 (1989) 1–22.

114. The fundamental work on the development and nature of the English testament is Michael M. Sheehan, *The Will in Medieval England: From the Conversion of the Anglo-Saxons to the End of the Thirteenth Century* (Studies and Texts 6; Toronto 1963). Also valuable, although principally devoted to a later period, is Lloyd Bonfield, *Devising, Dying and Dispute: Probate Litigation in Early Modern England* (Farnham 2012).

115. See R. H. Helmholz, *Roman Canon Law in Reformation England* (Cambridge Studies in English Legal History; Cambridge 1990) 13–14.

decedent had made a 'testamentum continens ultimam suam voluntatem'.[116] These words seem carefully chosen. The testament was regarded as enforceable because it contained what the decedent had willed up to the moment of his death. When one English civilian later came to defend the compatibility of English practice with the Ius commune, he suggested that in England all testaments might be regarded as military testaments.[117] His words seem justified by the results. Although many matters involving testaments were litigated in England, few of them seem to have involved direct challenges to their validity on grounds of lack of formality or testamentary incapacity. Disputes over the collection of assets, the payment of legacies, and other details of probate administration were much more frequent.

A valid testament might be made orally, in writing, or by some combination of the two. Nuncupative testaments were of course harder to prove than written testaments, but both were equally valid. Indeed, this equality was carried to the point of allowing oral revocations of written testaments. Most of the testaments noted in the surviving records were made very close to the testator's death, often on the deathbed itself, and then reduced to writing by one of the witnesses to it. There may, however, have been a slight tendency towards greater planning and consequently greater use of writing over the course of the later medieval period. In theory, testamentary validity depended upon an executor being named, the English equivalent to the civilian rule requiring the nomination of the *haeres*.[118] In practice, however, even this requirement was relaxed. The courts would appoint an administrator *cum testamento annexo* where the decedent had declared his last wishes regarding disposition of his property without also naming an executor.[119] The administrator would be required to see that these last wishes were carried out.

The law of testamentary capacity as enforced in the English spiritual courts generally followed the outlines of the Ius commune. That is, any person not expressly prohibited from leaving a property by will was permitted to do so.[120] Boys under the age of 14, girls below the age of 12, idiots, and unpardoned traitors are examples of those prohibited. In two

116. Taken from *Lumley and Parkynson c. Oldewoode* (York 1528), Borthwick Institute of Historical Research, York, CP.G.139.

117. *Owen c. Brett* (Court of Arches 1605), Worcester Record Office, Collectanea B, 794.093 BA 2470, f. 159: 'Haec obtinent de iure civili, sed in Anglia nos testamur iure militari quo iure testamenta sunt libera a solemnitatibus iuris civilis et relinquuntur in sola observatione iuris gentium'.

118. Lyndwood, *Provinciale* 172 s.v. *intestatis*.

119. See William S. Holdsworth, *History of English Law* (17 vols. 5th ed. London 1942) 3.536–541.

120. See Accursius, *Glossa ordinaria*, ad Inst. 2.12, echoed in Henry Swinburne, *Brief Treatise of Testaments and Last Wills* (1st ed. London 1590) Part 2 § 1.

situations, however, the general custom of the realm prohibited testation: villeins and married women. There is evidence to show that the spiritual courts would prove testaments by women if offered the chance, but by the fifteenth century at the latest such testaments rarely came before the courts. It is not clear whether this occurred because of actual interference from the common law judges or because of societal assumptions that neither class of persons could own property.[121]

By the end of the Middle Ages, freedom of testation for free adult male testators had been achieved in most parts of England. Early on, the Roman law of *legitim,* which required that a third of a decedent's estate be left to his children and also to his wife, seems to have prevailed in the spiritual forum.[122] Except for the northern province of York and a few pockets within the province of Canterbury,[123] this restriction disappeared.[124] The payment of a testator's debts, funeral expenses, and ecclesiastical dues continued to take precedence, restricting freedom of testation. However, the child's right not to be disinherited had been reduced to the more tenuous status of a local custom. Again, the reasons for this development are obscure. Certainly it occurred in tandem with the greater prevalence and the growing acceptance of devising real property through the 'use', but this does not seem a wholly satisfactory explanation.[125]

The actual proving of testaments was one of the most profitable, although unfortunately one of the least fully studied, areas of canonical practice in medieval England. In principle, probate took place before the bishop of the diocese in which the decedent was domiciled. Prescriptive custom and compositions in the wake of jurisdictional disputes created many exceptions to this rule, however. The most important was for *bona notabilia.* Where a person died possessing goods worth more than £5 in more than one diocese, his testament was to be proved before the court of the archbishop, creating in the southern province the so-called Prerogative Court of Canterbury, England's most important probate court. Its records exist in profusion for the medieval period, and it is among them that the testaments of most important Englishmen are today to be found.

The executor named in a testament had the primary responsibility for

---

121. I have tried to lay out the evidence on the former and to do some theorizing about it in 'Married Women's Wills in Later Medieval England', *Wife and Widow in Medieval England,* ed. Susan S. Walker (Ann Arbor, Mich. 1993) 165–182. See also Michael M. Sheehan, 'The Influence of Canon Law on the Property Rights of Married Women in England', *Mediaeval Studies* 25 (1963) 109–124.

122. See my *Canon Law and the Law of England* 247–262.

123. These 'pockets' included the City of London, however.

124. See the arguments on the point in Swinburne, *Brief Treatise* Part 3 § 16.

125. See generally J. M. W. Bean, *The Decline of English Feudalism 1215–1540* (Manchester 1968).

presenting the testament to the competent judge for proof. However, other persons interested in the estate, including legatees and if necessary the decedent's creditors, had a secondary right if the executor defaulted. There were two basic forms that proving the will could take: proof 'in common form' or proof 'in solemn form of law'.[126] The former amounted to proving by the oath of the executor and one or two other witnesses that the document offered was the decedent's true last will. Procedure was informal and, at least within broad limits, it lay in the discretion of the judge exactly what proof to require. Solemn form required full proof by witnesses and was appropriate where a protest against validity had either been made or was expected. Solemn form furnished greater security against subsequent challenge; common form probate was subject to upset by any subsequent challenge within thirty years. This challenge then required that one later make solemn form proof. According to modern commentators, however, common form proof was much the more frequent in practice.[127]

Grant of letters of administration occurred after requiring the administrator to take an oath faithfully to administer the estate and to make a final accounting of that administration before the judge who had proved the testament. Administrators were required to submit for whatever scrutiny the ecclesiastical judges cared to give them written inventories of the assets collected and of the debts paid. Many have survived.[128] Apart from these formal requirements, practice left it to private parties to object to failures to carry out the decedent's last will. The surviving act books in fact contain objections of many sorts. Legacies had not been fulfilled. Debts had not been paid. Children had not been cared for. Goods had been appropriated without right by relatives or strangers. The inventory was incomplete. A codicil was being overlooked or suppressed. As noted above, many more such suits are found in the medieval act books than contests over the validity of the testaments themselves.

The Law of Defamation

Despite the slender authorization found in the *Corpus iuris canonici*, the English church exercised jurisdiction over all forms of defamation throughout the Middle Ages, on both its instance and its ex officio sides. Indeed, defamation became one of the principal headings of spiritual ju-

---

126. See e.g. the description in John Godolphin, *The Orphan's Legacy, or a Testamentary Abridgment* (1st ed. 1674) part 1, chapter 20.

127. Houlbrooke, *Church Courts* 93.

128. See, for example, *Wills and Inventories Illustrative of the History, Manners, Language, Statistics, etc. of the Northern Counties of England*, ed. J. Raine (Surtees Society 2; London 1835).

risdiction in England. No distinction was drawn between clerics and lay-men. Either might sue or be sued in the spiritual forum for slanderous ut-terances. A few local secular courts also offered a remedy in the thirteenth century.[129] However, with the apparent exception of the city of London,[130] this jurisdiction disappeared over the course of the fourteenth century. At no point did the medieval royal courts provide a direct alternative to the ecclesiastical remedy. Only during the sixteenth century did the common law extend its reach to cover common defamatory utterances. Thus slan-der was treated as a *tout spirituell offence* in England throughout the Middle Ages.[131]

The basis for the earliest law of defamation in England was not the Roman law of *iniuria,* which was, at least to a limited extent, canonized in the Gregorian Decretals.[132] The basis was instead a provincial constitution promulgated by the Council of Oxford in 1222.[133] The constitution visited excommunication *latae sentenciae* upon any person who 'before good and substantial persons, for the sake of hatred, profit or favor, or for whatever other reason, did maliciously impute a crime to any person not previously of ill fame, by reason of which purgation at the least is awarded against him or he is harmed in some other manner'.

Among the obvious and noteworthy features of this constitution was its restriction to imputations of a crime. This necessarily excluded much abusive language that would have been actionable under the Roman law of iniuria. Also noteworthy is its express requirement of malice. Requiring that a speaker's malicious intent be proved allowed the courts to exclude much justifiable, but otherwise actionable, language from the constitu-tion's coverage. Finally, the close link between defamation and canonical purgation, found at the constitution's end, provided both the practical mechanism for initiating prosecutions under it and a connection with the learning found in the canonical texts.

Early practice in England may have followed this constitution's word-ing literally, by requiring the imputation of an actual crime.[134] If so, the requirement was soon relaxed. Probably it would have been all but impos-sible to enforce exactly, unless it had been limited to cases of actual mali-

<hr>

129. See R. H. Helmholz, *Select Cases on Defamation to 1600* (Selden Society 101; London 1985) lii–lxv.

130. F. Rexroth, *Deviance and Power in Late Medieval London* (Cambridge 2007) 191–217.

131. Year Book 12 Henry VII, Trinity term 1497 (London 1679 ed.) f. 24b.

132. See X 5.36.9 (*Si culpa tua*) and *Glossa ordinaria* ad idem.

133. See Powicke and Cheney, *Councils* 1.107. This constitution was commonly referred to in canonical practice, from its incipit, as *Auctoritate dei patris.*

134. See the cases collected and printed in Adams and Donahue, *Canterbury Cases,* and re-marks in its 'Introduction' 94–96.

cious prosecution, and the ecclesiastical lawyers would not readily have accepted such a limitation of their jurisdiction. By the fourteenth century, what might be called 'general imputations' of criminal conduct—as by calling someone a thief without specifying what actual theft he had committed—are commonly found in the surviving act books.[135] Imputations of mere personal 'defects'—such as illegitimacy, or professional incompetence, or simple verbal abuse stopping short of general allegations of criminality—would, however, still have been excluded from the jurisdiction of the spiritual courts.

Nevertheless, the development signaled an expansion in the concept of actionable verbal wrongs, and during the fifteenth century even this line was breached. English law moved towards applying the law of iniuria by making a remedy available where merely 'contumelious, vituperative or slanderous words' had been spoken maliciously.[136] The term used most frequently in the surviving records to describe the nature of the expanded remedy was *convicium*.[137] The motives that lay behind this jurisdictional enlargement were never stated by the lawyers who encouraged it. Perhaps no more complicated explanation for this development is required than the natural desire for an expanded remedy on the part of persons slandered, coupled with the compatibility of the change with the canon and Roman laws. No English common law rule stood in the way of the change. The royal courts treated the matter as falling within ecclesiastical competence, and they offered no alternate remedy until well into the sixteenth century.

In one respect, however, it is possible to suggest that the expansion of ecclesiastical jurisdiction to encompass mere insults did build upon developments in the English temporal law. This change took place during the same period in which the royal courts were restricting the ability of the spiritual tribunals to hear defamation causes involving the imputation of a secular crime. To call someone a 'thief' would not have been actionable under the new common law rule, whereas to call someone a 'whore' would be, because in England the substantive crimes involved lay on different sides of the jurisdictional boundary between the courts of church and state. This restriction, at first without any move by the common law to hear slander cases themselves, was a development of the last third of

135. See, for example, the cases collected in *Before the Bawdy Court*, ed. P. Hair (London 1972) noted at 252–253.

136. The full form of this pleading can be seen in Helmholz, *Select Cases* No. 8.

137. One early case was actually recorded as a *causa iniuriarum sive convicii*, following Roman law terminology: *Adane c. Ricard* (Canterbury 1462), Canterbury Cathedral Library, Act book Y.1.7, fol. 139v.

the fifteenth century, and it is conceivable that the ecclesiastical courts were 'making up' for this loss by expanding their own definition of actionable defamation to include *convicium*.

Throughout the medieval period, defamation included both a criminal and a civil side in the English spiritual forum. A *causa diffamationis* could be brought by the party defamed, but it also might come by way of an ex officio proceeding. In most respects, little hinged upon the form. The remedy was the same in either case. However, the criminal side of the church's jurisdiction did have the effect of allowing the courts to proceed even when no specific individual had complained. Thus, where the person defamed was dead, the courts could nonetheless proceed against the slanderer.[138] Moreover, many prosecutions were undertaken against 'common defamers' and 'scolds' in similar circumstances.[139] In these ex officio prosecutions there was a concern for restoring the public harmony, which had been disturbed by malicious speech, as well as a desire to restore the reputation of the person slandered.

On both the criminal and civil sides of defamation, the remedy under English practice was recantation and public penance. These were treated as a prerequisite for absolution from the constitution's mandatory sentence of excommunication. No monetary damages were awarded. This restriction may have followed from a restriction adopted by the common law. The royal courts held that the church should act only *ad correctionem peccati* in defamation cases, and that principle was thought to rule out monetary awards. In a formal sense, and probably in reality as well, the English courts obeyed this rule. Any payment of compensation to the victim of a defamatory utterance was made as part of private settlement. It was not made part of a specific order. The order that was commonly made against defendants at the end of successful defamation suits—to abstain from all further defamation of the plaintiff—emphasized the same point. The jurisdiction was designed to restore public peace and the injured person's reputation. Use of public recantation to effect this goal was authorized by a text found in the *Decretum*,[140] and therefore it may have been one of those situations where following the common law rule also meant following a respectable canon law precedent as well. It might, in fact, have seemed quite sensible to the ecclesiastical lawyers themselves.

138. E.g. *Ex officio c. Harris* (London 1491), London Metropolitan Archives, Act book MS. 9064/4A, f. 5v: a prosecution for defaming the *corpus et anima* of John Philip, a deceased priest.

139. E.g. *Ex officio c. Forest*, noted in W. Hale, *A Series of Precedents and Proceedings in Criminal Causes* (London 1847) 68. See also Sandy Bardsley, *Venomous Tongues: Speech and Gender in Late Medieval England* (Philadelphia 2006).

140. See C.5 q.1 c.3; D.46 c.5.

One might easily conclude, in light of the foregoing, that defamation in England was a local and peculiar custom, with little reference being made in practice to either Roman or canon law. However, that impression would not be accurate, because many of the questions that arose in practice were habitually answered from the ample resources of the Ius commune. The best medieval example of this habit comes from the pages of William Lyndwood's *Provinciale*. For example, in dealing with the important question of the how the requirement of malice was to be interpreted—when it could be presumed, in what circumstances it could be overcome, and what results followed from its existence—Lyndwood drew answers from the Roman law's Code and Digest; from Gratian's *Decretum* and the Gregorian Decretals; and from commentaries by Hostiensis, Johannes Andreae, and Henricus Bohic.[141] The Ius commune thus was relevant even to this special aspect of canonical practice in England. Indeed, jurisdiction over defamation in England provides a concrete situation in which the canon law filled a gap in secular remedy. Broadly speaking, it even might have been regarded by some reasonable men as an example of canonical jurisdiction, acting *ex defectu justitiae*; that is, in default of an appropriate remedy in the more natural, temporal forum.

Breach of Faith

From the moment of the first appearance of a distinct ecclesiastical jurisdiction in England, the spiritual tribunals were entertaining suits brought for the violation of an oath. In the records such causes were styled as *fidei laesio*, or sometimes simply as perjury. Despite the name, most often these matters were not what a modern reader would regard as perjury; that is, deliberately making a false statement while under oath. Although such instances existed, most *causae perjurii* found in the records turn out to have been brought by private parties to secure the specific enforcement of a sworn promise to perform a contractual obligation. King Henry II's Constitutions of Clarendon (1164) contained a provision forbidding invocation of this kind of spiritual jurisdiction to sue for the collection of debts,[142] a sign both that the breach of faith then existed as a part of ecclesiastical competence and that it was being used in exactly this way. That is, it was being used to enforce secular obligations that could also have been enforced, under a slightly different rationale, in the royal courts themselves.

---

141. See *Provinciale*, 346, s.v. *malitiose*.

142. Found in c. 15 in *Stubbs' Select Charters* (Oxford 1921) 167: 'Placita de debitis quae fide interposita debentur, vel absque interpositione fidei, sint in justitia regis'.

The canon law that grounded this aspect of ecclesiastical jurisdiction was not simple custom. Johannes Tuetonicus's *Glossa ordinaria* to the *Decretum* stated a contemporary understanding when he noted that an oath 'added materially' to a simple promise.[143] Texts from the Decretals also enunciated the principle that 'care should be taken that those things which were promised should be brought to fruition'.[144] A decretal of Boniface VIII included in the *Liber Sextus* held specifically that a layman might legitimately be brought before a spiritual tribunal, even in the case of a purely pecuniary transaction, when an oath had been part of that transaction.[145] The fifteenth-century English canonist William Lyndwood thus built upon legitimate canonical tradition when he spoke in defense of the church's extensive jurisdiction over breach of faith. Because 'perjury directly concerns irreverence towards God,' he wrote, it therefore follows that 'an ecclesiastical judge rightly takes cognizance of oaths' in the wholesale form found in the English act books.[146]

What happened in the English courts indeed did require defending. Jurisdiction over oaths turned out to have put the English spiritual tribunals in the business of petty debt collection. The canon law did not insist on any substantial formalities to constitute an oath. Almost any addition to a simple promise would do: 'by my faith' was held to be sufficient. Thus, when anyone entered into a contract, it became possible to secure an ecclesiastical remedy in case of breach simply by adding three words to a promise to pay a debt. This happened on a surprisingly large scale.[147] Agreements to deliver goods, convey land, construct houses, or accept arbiters' awards all became actionable in the church courts because the promisor had agreed, under some form of oath, that he would be bound to perform. Most such cases involved simple debts for services rendered or goods delivered, and by the fifteenth century they had come to dominate litigation within the English spiritual courts. Hundreds of such cases each year were being heard in the commissary court at Canterbury.[148] Where the sworn promise was proved,[149] the ecclesiastical courts would order promisors to perform the obligation thereby incurred, also backing the order with the threat of

---

143. See *Glossa ordinaria* to C.22 q.5 c.17 (*Iuramenti*), s.v. *distantiam*: 'tamen plus operatur sacramentum quam simplex promissio'.

144. X 1.35.3 (*Qualiter in Sardinia*).   145. Sext 2.2.3 (*Cum C. laicus*).

146. *Provinciale* 315 s.v. *periurio*.

147. See 'Assumpsit and Fidei Laesio', *Canon Law and the Law of England* 266–268.

148. See Woodcock, *Medieval Ecclesiastical Courts* 84, 89–92.

149. The requirement of some sort of oath, although seemingly minimal to modern eyes, seems to have been kept up in court practice. See, for example, *Taylour c. Todyone* (Rochester 1439), Kent County Archives (Maidstone) DRb Pa 1, fol. 112, in which the defense offered was that the defendant 'nunquam prestitit sibi fidem'.

excommunication.[150] English practice was thus very like the contemporary practice that was so much resented and controverted in Germany.[151]

A partial reason for this flood of litigation, as opposed to its canonical justification, must be found in the weaknesses in the contemporary secular law of contracts in England. Indeed, strictly speaking, there was no such law. Analogous to the situation in classical Roman law, in England all that existed was a series of discrete common law remedies, each covering a slightly different form of obligation and each requiring a different writ or form of action. The writ of debt was the chief among these, and its limitations as a means of enforcing contractual obligations were several.[152] This writ, for example, could only be brought to recover money and only for a fixed price that had been agreed on before or at the time the contract was made. It could not be used for executory contracts, those in which there had not been performance on one side. Moreover, where the contract had been oral, it could be met in the royal courts by the defendant's wager of law, an unsatisfactory method of proof to plaintiffs. The common law of contracts, in other words, provided a fragmented regime to potential litigants. It was one that sophisticated merchants could live with, but its limitations required advanced planning. The English ecclesiastical courts ameliorated some of its imperfections. By making the promise itself the source of liability, as the canon law itself encouraged, the spiritual courts provided a legal resource for ordinary parties—and indeed for commercial life more generally—that the secular courts did not. This was another instance where, in a broad sense, the canon law moved *ex defectu justiciae* into what would otherwise have been regarded as an area appropriate for temporal jurisdiction.

The English church's jurisdiction over breach of faith came under effective attack in the last three decades of the fifteenth century. This attack formed part of a more general offensive against what the common lawyers regarded as the 'excesses' of the spiritual courts. However, the church's jurisdiction over cases involving breach of faith litigation was by far the most immediate and prominent victim of the attack.[153] By issu-

150. For example, *Rodyng c. Baker* (Hereford 1493), Herefordshire Records Office (Hereford) I/1, p. 95: 'Unde monitus est quod perimpleat promissum suum citra vigiliam Michaelis proximo futuram una cum expensis x d. sub pena excommunicationis'.

151. See Justus Hashagen, 'Zur Charakteristik der geistlichen Gerichtsbarkeit vornehmlich im späteren Mittelalter', ZRG Kan. Abt. 6 (1916) 205–292, especially 213–216.

152. See John H. Baker, *Introduction to English Legal History* (4th ed. London 2002) 326–327, 342; David Millon, 'Ecclesiastical Jurisdiction in Medieval England', *University of Illinois Law Review* (1984) 621–638 at 636–638.

153. See R. L. Storey, 'Clergy and Common Law in the Reign of Henry IV', *Medieval Legal Records Edited in Memory of C. A. F. Meekings* (London 1978) 347–351.

ing writs of prohibition and expanding the procedural reach of the fourteenth century statute of *Praemunire,* the royal courts effectively restricted the ability of litigants to invoke spiritual jurisdiction to enforce promises to fulfill secular obligations. The result was a dramatic loss in litigation for the courts of the church. By the end of the first decades of the sixteenth century, only promises to pay distinctly spiritual obligations and disciplinary cases for perjury that had occurred within the ecclesiastical courts themselves remained as parts of spiritual jurisdiction. By the 1520s, jurisdiction over breach of faith had become a shell of what had been only a few decades before.

Ex Officio Proceedings

The canon law treated a surprisingly limited number of public criminal offenses as inherently spiritual in nature and therefore subject to exclusive ecclesiastical jurisdiction. For example, adultery, though concededly a violation of the sacrament of marriage, was regarded as being 'of mixed forum' by the *communis opinio* of the jurists.[154] It seemed vital to the canonists only that the definition of the offense be left to canonical principles. This approach left the actual exercise of jurisdiction over adultery, and many other such offenses, to local custom. In some parts of Europe, adultery among the laity was dealt with exclusively by temporal courts. However, in England this is not what happened. There, criminal prosecution of sexual offenses of all kinds came within the ambit of ecclesiastical jurisdiction. With very few exceptions it remained an exclusive jurisdiction. This jurisdictional division was confirmed by the enactment *Circumspecte agatis* (1286), made by King Edward I in favor of the rights of the church.[155] The numerical importance and continuance of this jurisdiction has led English historians to associate ecclesiastical courts and the canon law itself with repression of sexual peccadilloes as though this had been the church's primary aim.

However one-sided or even unfair such a characterization of the canon law may be, in earlier centuries it is true that the English customary jurisdiction was a considerable one. Jurisdiction over sexual offenses was exercised ex officio, in the name and at the instance of the court. Often, records of these cases were kept in separate registers or act books, and

154. See Julius Clarus, *Practica criminalis* (Venice 1595) Quaest. 37, No. 3. With English practice, compare the evidence in Daniela Lombardi, 'Il reato di stupro tra foro ecclesiastico e foro secolare,' *Transgressioni: Seduzione, concubinato, adulterio, bigamia (XIV–XVIII secolo),* ed. S. Seidel Menchi and D. Quaglioni (Bologna 2004) 351–382.

155. Its text is contained in *Councils and Synods II: A.D. 1205–1313* 974–975.

many of these books positively bulge with prosecutions dealing with the sins of the flesh. In terms of numbers, prosecutions for fornication and other sexual offenses constituted the greater part of ex officio matters pretty much throughout the medieval period.[156]

They did not stop with such offences, however. Among the offenses of the laity dealt with on the ex officio side of the spiritual courts in England were blasphemy, fornication, assault on clerics, contempt of ecclesiastical jurisdiction, infanticide, misbehavior in or absence from church services, pandering, usury, sodomy, trading or working on Sundays and holy days, and witchcraft. Some matters, notably perjury or defamation, were handled both on the instance and office sides. It is a miscellaneous list, but it was a relatively stable one during the Middle Ages. Only in the sixteenth century was the scope of the Church's subject-matter jurisdiction curtailed on the criminal side, and even then the restrictions were relatively minor.

In some respects, jurisdiction over criminal matters was quite a bit more dispersed than over instance causes. Many dignitaries, such as deans or prebendaries of cathedral churches, held courts that exercised jurisdiction over criminal matters. They rarely judged instance cases.[157] Even rural deans in many parts of the land held chapters periodically to deal with ex officio matters.[158] On the other hand, in some respects criminal jurisdiction was at the same time less dispersed, being effectively reserved to the bishops acting in person, in a court of audience, or by a court of special commission. Heresy cases, for example, seem to have been dealt with in this way. There were such prosecutions, many of them initiated in response to the movement of thought begun by John Wycliff. However, in England these heresy cases were not dealt with by a separate institution of inquisitorial courts. There was no organized Inquisition.[159] Likewise, most cases of clerical misbehavior, including clerics accused of felonies claimed from the royal courts, were dealt with by courts specially convoked by the appropriate bishop.

Under the canon law, private parties were given the opportunity to

---

156. See Richard M. Wunderli, *London Church Courts and Society on the Eve of the Reformation* (Speculum Anniversary Monographs 7; Cambridge, Mass. 1981) 81: 'Venereal offenses dominate court records'.

157. See, for example, Sandra Brown, *The Medieval Courts of the York Minster Peculiar* (York 1984) 8–9; Lawrence R. Poos, *Lower Ecclesiastical Jurisdiction in Late-Medieval England* (British Academy, Records of Social and Economic History, n.s. 32; Oxford 2001) xi–lxiv.

158. See, for example, Jean Scammel, 'The Rural Chapter in England from the Eleventh to the Fourteenth Century', EHR 86 (1971) 1–21.

159. Swanson, *Church and Society* 338–347.

prove the criminal matter against any person accused of a crime, and—in form, at least—this opportunity was afforded in practice. Proclamations to that effect were routinely made in the parish church of the person accused. However, it is true that the court records produce very few instances in which a private party actually stepped forward in response to such a proclamation. The normal procedure in ex officio cases required persons accused of offenses to undergo canonical purgation in the absence of response, assuming, of course, that they denied their guilt. Canonical purgation required defendants to swear a formal oath that they were innocent and to find a number of compurgators able to swear that they believed the oath to be true. The canon law left the number of compurgators to judicial discretion. It also provided that, although the defendant brought compurgators with him in the first instance, the judges might act to disqualify unsuitable candidates. Both of these efforts to limit potential abuse in the system seem to have been observed in English usage. At least, no fixed pattern in numbers has been discerned, and compurgators brought by defendants were sometimes disqualified by order of the judge. Perhaps there were many abuses in the system. It has been often criticized by historians. It lasted, however, for a very long time.

The sanctions against convicted lay offenders at the disposal of the spiritual courts in England were normally confined to requiring the performance of public penance, except where the guilty party himself wished to commute the penance by making a charitable payment. It is difficult to be sure how often and at whose initiative such commutation actually occurred, but studies so far undertaken certainly show that it was not infrequent in practice.[160] It should also be stressed that virtually all persons accused of criminal offenses were required to pay court costs and that these expenses were not negligible in amount. Even most of those who successfully underwent canonical compurgation did not leave without being ordered to pay these costs, the theory apparently being that it was fair to impose this burden upon any person who had been the source of public fame against himself.

The most serious form of public penance required appearance in penitential garb in one's parish church, usually on Sunday, and it was often coupled with a public admission of guilt and recantation or renunciation of the conduct. There were varieties of severity in the ways such public penance could be performed, in line with the canonical rule that penalties

---

160. See Wunderli, *London Church Courts and Society* 51–52; my impression is that the figures given there are higher than they would have been in most provincial courts.

rested in the sound discretion of the judge. At times, the courts simply required a private apology to the party injured, issued a public monition against the party convicted, or dismissed him *sub spe melioris vitae*. Excommunication was, of course, regularly used in English practice, but it was not, strictly speaking, a penal sanction in the canon law. Rather, it was reserved for cases of deliberate contumacy; its primary object was to bring the contumacious party into willing obedience to the law, not to impose a punishment upon him. Whether this was purely a theory or an accurate description remains a puzzling question. Certainly excommunication could have worldly consequences.

Ecclesiastical Courts and English Temporal Law

Intervention against Canonical Jurisdiction

From time to time in this chapter mention has been made of conflicts between the royal and the ecclesiastical courts. In such places it has taken note of the king's writ of prohibition as the principal means by which the temporal courts attempted to limit and control the scope of ecclesiastical jurisdiction. Almost from the earliest days of the emergence of a separate spiritual jurisdiction in England, the king and his officers presumed to police the uncertain boundaries between pleas that belonged to the church and those that belonged to the crown. This policing was accomplished not by general ordinance but by ordering the parties and judges in specific cases before the ecclesiastical courts to cease from that litigation when the underlying plea properly belonged to the cognizance of the temporal courts. It goes without saying that the royal courts' view of what matter belonged to what court did not necessarily coincide with the canonical position. The purpose of the writ of prohibition was to put the secular view into effect.

Most litigation in the common law courts originated by writ, and this litigation directed against the church was no exception. Writs of prohibition were available from the king's chancery, and by the thirteenth century, it was settled that some were available *de cursu*.[161] That means that areas of law where the spiritual courts commonly encroached on royal court jurisdiction were recognized by the chancery, and in them persons who had been sued in an ecclesiastical court had a "ready made" writ to prevent the encroachment. Only the details of the particular case had to

---

161. The fundamental works are G. B. Flahiff, 'The Writ of Prohibition to Court Christian in the Thirteenth Century', *Mediaeval Studies* 6 (1944) 261–313, and 7 (1945) 229–290; and Millon's 'Introduction', *Select Ecclesiastical Cases* xix–lxxxvii.

be varied from writ to writ. Thus, there were writs *de cursu* for attempts to exercise ecclesiastical jurisdiction over land held by feudal tenure, rights of advowson, trespass, and lay debts and chattels. A party aggrieved had merely to apply to the chancery and pay the requisite fees, and the prohibition would be made available. Served on the litigants on the other side and on the officers of the ecclesiastical court, it subjected them to monetary penalties and eventually to more serious sanctions if they continued litigation in the spiritual forum. A procedure was made available to appeal the justice of these writs, called a writ of 'consultation' in then current usage,[162] but that procedure too required submitting the case to the jurisdiction of the royal court in order to undo the effects of the prohibition.

Writs of prohibition could also be framed for special circumstances; they were then called writs *de precepto* in English usage. These writs were intended for cases where an ecclesiastical court had violated a principle of jurisdictional law in a way not covered by a *de cursu* writ, and their availability allowed the royal courts to adapt—and also to expand—the reach of this common law method of control. The form of these writs did not have the fixed phrasing of the *de cursu* writs, and they were apparently prepared by a separate group of clerks in the royal chancery.[163] Potentially, they left determination of the scope of ecclesiastical jurisdiction subject to the desires of chancery clerks and the judges of the English common law. Moreover, in various parts of England, local courts apparently took action against litigants who had violated the bounds of local jurisdictional rules by suing in an ecclesiastical court.[164] These prosecutions, roughly equivalent to prohibitions, await investigation, but their existence is beyond doubt.

Despite their potential, prohibitions did not become the means for large-scale encroachments on spiritual jurisdiction, at least not until the very end of the medieval period. Why did this seemingly inevitable development not occur? Why did more defendants secure them? Uncertainties remain, but there were several reasons that prohibitions did not become the means for large-scale and continuous attacks on the church's medieval jurisdiction. First, prohibitions required individual litigants to seek them out. They were never issued automatically. They also cost money. Since

---

162. 'Statute of Consultation' (1289–1290), *Statutes of the Realm* (London 1810) 1.108.

163. See A. E. Stamp, 'The Court and Chancery of Henry III', *Historical Essays in Honour of James Tait*, ed. J. Edwards, V. Galbraith, and E. F. Jacob (Manchester 1933) 306–308.

164. E.g. Portur v. Maydenstan (Borough of Great Yarmouth 1288), Norfolk Record Office Norwich C 4/9, s.d. Monday after feast of St. James, the allegation tracking the wording used in the royal writs: viz., 'traxit in placitum in curia Christianitatis de catallis que non sunt de testamento vel matrimonio coram decano de Gerven…'.

this was so, prohibitions necessarily subjected litigants to the uncertainties and costs of securing and serving the writ. Introducing a writ of prohibition in an ecclesiastical court also could subject litigants to the possibility of 'counteraction.' Although the spiritual courts obeyed writs of prohibition when they received one, they sometimes went on to subject the person who had procured the prohibition to a sentence of excommunication for interfering with the legitimate exercise of their spiritual jurisdiction.[165] Such severely practical considerations discouraged wider use of the writ.

Moreover, several statutes and otherwise authoritative pronouncements from the common law side recognized the scope of existing ecclesiastical jurisdiction. These statutes and pronouncements restricted the freedom of all actors to expand common law jurisdiction at the expense of the church's jurisdiction. The so-called statute 'Circumspecte agatis' (1286) ordered the king's judges to 'act circumspectly' in challenging the church's jurisdiction,[166] and indeed it appears that the royal judges did not ordinarily seek to confine the church's courts to the narrowest of jurisdictional confines. Third, the outcome in prohibition cases was not predictably in favor of the party procuring the writ. Under accepted common law procedure, whether or not a party incurred liability for failure to obey the writ depended in the earliest period on wager of law (compurgation) by that party himself. Later on, the decision was by the verdict of a lay jury and, finally, by determination within the chancery based largely on the libel introduced in the ecclesiastical forum.[167] Since the issue being tried in attachments on prohibitions was never simply whether the writ had been issued but whether the underlying case in the ecclesiastical court was outside proper ecclesiastical jurisdiction, leaving the decision to these uncertain methods of proof meant that many litigants in the spiritual courts might well have been discouraged from seeking the writ in the first place. Examination of the ecclesiastical court records has shown the relative infrequency with which prohibitions were introduced in practice. These three factors may help explain the reason.

An attack on the church's jurisdiction did in fact occur, starting in the 1480s. However, the principal means used was not the established writ of prohibition, but instead a fourteenth-century statute originally aimed at

---

165. See R. H. Helmholz, 'Writs of Prohibition and Ecclesiastical Sanctions in the English Courts Christian', *Canon Law and the Law of England* 77–99; Millon, 'Ecclesiastical Jurisdiction' 636–668.

166. The text is given in *Councils and Synods* 974–975. See also E. B. Graves, 'Circumspecte agatis', EHR 43 (1928) 1–20; 'Articuli cleri' (1315–16), *Statutes of the Realm* (London 1810) I.171.

167. See R. H. Helmholz, 'The Writ of Prohibition to Court Christian before 1500', *Canon Law and the Law of England* 59–76.

restricting the powers exercised by the papacy, the statute of *Praemunire*.[168] This statute was given an expansive reading: it was held to apply to proceedings in consistory courts within England as well as those at the papal court. Such a reading permitted litigants to overcome some of the procedural limitations of writs of prohibition. Beginning slowly, the statute of *Praemunire* had an end result that was dramatic: elimination of a significant part of the church's medieval jurisdiction and establishment of a more effective means by which the consistory courts could be brought under supervision of the common law judges. Indeed, over the course of the sixteenth century, the procedure for issuance of writs of prohibition was itself improved in the service of establishing the practical supremacy of the English common law.

Cooperation between Spiritual and Temporal Courts

Real and persistent as jurisdictional conflicts between the two systems in England were, it would be mistaken to characterize relations between them simply in terms of antagonism and mutual recrimination. There were areas of active cooperation, areas in which the two court systems habitually aided one another. Three examples can be discussed here: imprisonment by the temporal courts of obdurate excommunicates, enforcement by the spiritual courts of common law judgments against clerics, and mutual decision of contested litigation that involved both questions of land title and legitimacy of birth.

The first of these three provides one instance where the common law courts embraced the principles of the canon law. The canon law held that, where spiritual sanctions failed, the judge had the right to 'invoke the secular arm' in an effort to effect the reformation of the person subject to ecclesiastical jurisdiction.[169] England accepted this part of the canon law. It became a customary rule of the common law that if any person remained excommunicate for forty days or more, the bishop could apply to the royal chancery for a writ *de excommunicato capiendo* by which the sheriff would be ordered to imprison the person until he made satisfaction to the church.[170] Although technically a matter of royal discretion, so firmly entrenched in the English legal system did this procedure become that it

---

168. There was more than one such statute: 27 Edw. III, st. 1, c. 1 (1354); 38 Edw. III, st. 1, c. 5 (1364); 4 Hen. IV, c. 23 (1403).

169. For canonical authority and commentary, see X 2.1.10; *Glossa Ordinaria*, ad X 1.31.1; and Lyndwood, *Provinciale* 349–352.

170. The fundamental study is F. Donald Logan, *Excommunication and the Secular Arm in Medieval England* (Studies and Texts 15; Toronto 1968). See also Elisabeth Vodola, *Excommunication in the Middle Ages* (Berkeley-Los Angeles 1986) 180–190.

survived the Reformation and indeed lasted into the nineteenth century.[171] Both in threat and in deed, the temporal sword was wielded in support of the spiritual.

The king's chancery, as the canon law itself, insisted upon checks against abuse of the procedure. Appeals—at least most appeals—within the system of ecclesiastical courts suspended the process. If the person imprisoned offered suitable guarantees of obedience, he would be released despite a bishop's refusal to accept the guarantees. The persons who could initiate the process were also limited. At least nominally it had to be the bishop himself who requested issuance of the royal writ against the excommunicate. Thus requests by consistory court judges were subject to episcopal oversight. And, where abuse was flagrant, the chancery might even refuse the writ as an initial matter. Nonetheless, it was always true that the writ was *de cursu,* issued in common form and without separate investigation of the underlying facts. It was used in practice to blunt the force of royal writs of prohibition, as well as to deal with true instances of contempt for spiritual sanctions.

The request for 'caption' was not made automatically in ecclesiastical court practice. In instance litigation, and despite the formal language used, the process was usually initiated by the party aggrieved, not by the judge. Moreover, the excommunicated person customarily was cited to a special term in the spiritual court to show cause (if he could) why he should not be subject to 'caption'. These hearings took place. Contemporary act books produce many examples,[172] and this largely explains the lengthy delays from time of excommunication to that of 'signification' to the chancery—often much longer than the prescribed forty-day period. Excommunicates thus always had a chance to explain why they should not be treated as contumacious, and very likely also to come to terms with the party on the other side, if compromise remained possible.

In making 'signification' of excommunicates available, the common law was indirectly enforcing the sentences of the spiritual courts. The op-

---

171. The most likely explanation for the disappearance of the writs from the chancery files by the end of the sixteenth century (see Logan, *Excommunication* 156–157) is a technical one: the writ was made returnable before the Court of King's Bench by statute: 5 Eliz. c. 23 (1563). It would thus not have been kept in the chancery files. See also *Guide to the Contents of the Public Record Office, Volume 1 (Legal Records, Etc.)* (London 1963) 115.

172. E.g. *Rayny c. Rayny* (Lichfield 1466), Lichfield Joint Record Office, Act book B/C/1/1, fol. 79r, 86r, 93v. The defendant in a suit for restitution of conjugal rights was first cited to appear December 3 to show cause why he should not be suspended *ab ingressu ecclesie;* then to appear January 14 to show cause why he should not be excommunicated; then February 20 to show cause why he should not be 'signified' to the chancery for caption. He appeared only in response to the final citation.

posite situation also obtained: the spiritual courts enforced the judgments of temporal courts. As noted above, the *privilegium fori* went largely unobserved in medieval English practice. Clerics sued and were sued in common law courts, despite the canonical prohibitions. However, the royal courts did not push this temporal jurisdiction to its logical conclusion, in that they left to the church the execution of judgments against clerics who held no lay freehold. The church regularly undertook what can only be called 'collection work' in response to directions from the royal courts. The system seems to have worked in the following way.[173] After a final judgment in a common law court had been entered against a cleric who had been a party to a civil suit and after the sheriff had found that the cleric held no lay fee, a judicial writ called *levari facias* was issued to the cleric's bishop.[174] The writ ordered him to levy upon the man's ecclesiastical possessions in order to collect the judgment. In response, the bishop directed either the *officialis* of his consistory court or some other episcopal officer to carry out the writ, normally by sequestering and selling chattels that belonged to the cleric by virtue of his ecclesiastical benefice. The proceeds of this action were turned over to the royal court in due course. This process was an entirely normal part of English legal life, and it was used to deal with a wide variety of substantive claims; debt and trespass seem to have been the most frequent.

Execution of the judgments of the common law courts amounted to adding express episcopal sanction to English violation of the canonical *privilegium fori*. On the other hand, it appears that English ecclesiastical officials did—at least informally—exercise independent judgment in executing these royal writs. They did not, for example, seize property that was essential to the Church's pastoral function. The cleric involved must be left with enough to sustain himself, to pay the parish's servants, and to carry out necessary spiritual ministrations.[175] Neither chalices nor glebe lands were sold; grain was. And even grain was sold only to the extent that it did not prejudice the essential interests of the church. When one examines actual practice, it is clear that episcopal returns to writs of *levari*

---

173. What research on the subject has been done appears in Churchill, *Canterbury Administratio* I.520–21, and the 'Introduction', *Royal Writs Addressed to John Buckingham, Bishop of Lincoln, 1363–1398*, ed. A. K. McHardy (Lincoln Record Society 86; Bury St. Edmunds 1997) xii–xxvi. For examples of the writ see A. Fitzherbert, *New Natura Brevium* (London 1704) 265–267.

174. The writ to bishops was actually put in the plural form out of respect for the recipients (i.e., *levari faciatis*), but in common parlance the writ itself was referred to in the same singular form in which it went to sheriffs.

175. See e.g. *Registers of Roger Martival, Bishop of Salisbury 1315–1330, Volume III: Royal Writs*, ed. S. Reynolds (Canterbury and York Society; London 1965) nos. 21 (1315), 30 (1316), 67 (1316), 448 (1324), and 784 (1328).

facias served to excuse the cleric (and the bishop) from full execution of the writ, as often they did fully to satisfy the judgment. Violation of the letter of the canon law thus seems actually to have carried with it practical advantages to the church. Conscientious bishops might well have found the system preferable to allowing collection of judgment debts to fall directly into the hands of English sheriffs, even if the result would have been difficult to defend under strict canonical principles.

The intersection between jurisdictions over freehold land and over marriage and divorce provides a third and slightly different example of cooperation between temporal and spiritual tribunals in medieval England. The common law courts claimed the right to try title to land; the ecclesiastical courts claimed competence in all questions involving marriage and illegitimacy. In most situations, these claims remained distinct, but where they did not, the stage was set for confrontation. Where title to land was disputed by one claimant on the grounds that the other was of illegitimate birth and incapable of inheriting under English law, who would decide the question? And what force would the decision reached in one forum have in the other?

In England the pattern for deciding such cases was set as early as the reign of Henry II (1154–1189). Its principal outlines followed the procedure endorsed in canonical texts.[176] Where title to land was at issue, upon a plea of illegitimacy in the royal courts, proceedings were suspended. A writ was sent to the bishop, requiring him to try the limited issue of the claimant's legitimate birth and then to return a certificate containing the answer to the royal judges. Judgment would be given by the common law judges on the basis of the bishop's certificate. Conversely, the spiritual courts would make no claim to deal with the question of title to the land involved. They restricted the scope of their inquiry to the question of legitimacy of birth.

In the course of things, conflicts almost inevitably developed in making this system work. The most celebrated such conflict involved children born to a man and woman who married only after the child's birth. The canon law treated such children as fully legitimate. The common law, following a baronial decision of 1236, treated them as illegitimate. There was unhappiness and disagreement about the resulting situation. The bishops refused to certify such children as bastards. The common law judges then refused to allow bishops to decide the question at all. Instead the judges determined to submit the question of legitimacy to lay juries. Much has

---

176. The writ is found in *Glanvill* VII 14, p. 87. The principal canonical texts were X 4.17.5 (*Lator praesentium*) and X 4.17.7 (*Causam quae*).

been written about the conflict.[177] In fact, so much has been written about it that the ordinary case has all but disappeared from view. And surely the ordinary case matters at least as much as the exceptional. Despite awkwardness and loss of time, in most cases the two court systems worked together in harmony in deciding such cases. The bishops received and answered the writs requiring them to determine legitimacy.[178] The common law judges respected the outcome as determined in the episcopal certificates, in effect deferring to the jurisdiction of the spiritual forum. Such voluntary, customary deference characterized relations between common law and canon law as often as did the more famous conflicts. In many different circumstances crown and church depended on each other.[179]

Conclusion

Up until the present generation, the English church's courts described in this essay have not provoked the admiration of many of the historians who have discussed them. About these courts and the canon law applied in them, the greatest of English legal historians, F.W. Maitland, had little good to say, and quite a bit that was not.[180] More often than not, the church's courts have been treated quite summarily by historians. Indeed, their importance has sometimes been dismissed almost out of hand. They have been treated as declining and unpopular institutions.[181]

Today, echoes of this view persist. However, at least in the growing body of work devoted expressly to the ecclesiastical tribunals—work in which this writer has admittedly taken part—things stand rather differently. The pendulum may even have swung too far in the opposite direction. In their vigorous exploitation of jurisdictional rights, in their resonance with contemporary values, in their persistence well into modern times,

---

177. See Maitland, 'Church, State, and Decretals', *Roman Canon Law* 52–56; N. Adams, '*Nullius filius*: A Study of the Exception of Bastardy in the Law Courts of Medieval England', *University of Toronto Law Journal* 6 (1946) 361–384; R. H. Helmholz, 'Bastardy Litigation in Medieval England', *Canon Law and the Law of England* 187–210; W. R. Jones, 'Relations of the Two Jurisdictions: Conflict and Cooperation in England during the Thirteenth and Fourteenth Centuries', *Studies in Medieval and Renaissance History* 7 (1970) 139–141; John L. Barton, 'Nullity of Marriage and Illegitimacy in the England of the Middle Ages', *Legal History Studies 1972*, ed. D. Jenkins (Cardiff 1975) 28–49; 'Introduction' to Adams and Donahue, *Canterbury Cases* 84–86.

178. See, for example, *Register of Robert Hallum, Bishop of Salisbury 1407–17*, ed. J. M. Horn (Canterbury and York Society; n.p. 1982) nos. 1065–1066 (1408).

179. See the many examples in *Petitions to the Crown from English Religious Houses, c. 1272–c. 1485*, ed. G. Dodd and A. K. McHardy (Canterbury and York Society; n.p. 2010).

180. For example, *History of English Law* 2.389: 'the incalculable harm done by a marriage law which was a maze of flighty fancies and misapplied logic'.

181. For example, T. F. T. Plucknett, *A Concise History of the Common Law* (5th ed. Boston 1956) 742: 'Such a jurisdiction was never popular in the middle ages' (speaking of the church's testamentary jurisdiction).

and in their ability to influence the English common law itself, the ecclesiastical courts today command more respect among historians than they did fifty years and more ago.[182] The courts are recognized as having played a lasting and important role in the history of law and society.[183] They are also regarded as furnishing an important point of contact with the legal world of the European continent and with the history of the canon law that is the subject of this volume. The English ecclesiastical courts now seem to deserve some legitimate place both in works about the development of English common law and in those devoted to the history of the wider canon law.

182. See generally the useful treatment of Javier Martínez-Torrón, *Derecho angloamericano y derecho canónico* (Madrid 1991).

183. See, for instance, the work of Martin Ingram, *Church Courts, Sex and Marriage in England, 1570–1640* (Cambridge 1987); R. B. Outhwaite, *The Rise and Fall of the English Ecclesiastical Courts, 1500–1860* (Cambridge Studies in English Legal History; Cambridge 2006); R. H. Helmholz, *The Canon Law and Ecclesiastical Jurisdiction from 597 to the 1640s* (Oxford History of the Laws of England 1; Oxford 2004).

II

Ecclesiastical Procedure in Medieval Spain

Antonio García y García†

Introductory Note by Charles Donahue Jr.

A first draft of this essay was written almost twenty years ago, but Father García's health prevented him from bringing it completely up-to-date. Since then, two developments have taken place that are not reflected here. (1) The Church Court Records Working Group has published a very preliminary survey of the surviving medieval church court records in Spain.[1] This survey suggested that though difficult to access, such records did exist; in what quantity it was hard to determine. The publication also suggested, somewhat surprisingly, that cases of marriage and sexual offenses, except perhaps those of the clergy, were not a major concern of the medieval ecclesiastical courts in Spain, as they were in so many other places. This is not what we would expect from the surviving synodal legislation. (2) A small body of literature has been published dealing with marriage and sexual offenses in the church courts, principally in what was in the Middle Ages the kingdom of Aragon.[2] This literature seems largely

---

1. Richard Helmholz, chapter 9, Donahue, *Records 1*.

2. E.g. the works of Martine Charageat: 'Pour une étude de la conflictualité matrimoniale (xive–xvie siècles): Les archives de l'officialité césearaugustaine', *Officialités*, ed. Beaulande and Charageat 245–258; 'Témoins et témoignages en Aragon aux xve–xvie siècles', *La preuve en justice de l'antiquité à nos jours*, ed. Bruno Lemesle (Rennes 2003) 149–169; 'Copula carnal: La preuve de

to be based on the records of Barcelona and Zaragoza that the Church Court Records Group had already identified.[3]

Faced with this seeming paradox, the obvious solution is to call for further research. It is quite possible that the impression gained by the Church Court Records Working Group on the basis of short visits to the archives was simply wrong. It is also possible that a comprehensive study of the surviving material would reveal that although it does contain material dealing with marriage and sexual offenses, such cases form a relatively small proportion of the surviving material and probably of what once existed. Considering the success that a team of researchers has had in Italy in identifying hitherto unknown repositories of records of the church courts, it seems likely that a similar effort in Spain would uncover a great deal more than is now known, because this material in Spain, as in Italy, has remained largely in the hands of the Church.[4]

In the meantime, it makes sense to publish the results of Father García's research. It is based largely on the synodal legislation of Spain, of which he was a master. (He was the general editor of the Synodicon Hispanum.) As noted in my 'Ecclesiastical Courts', the study of synodal legislation independent of the court records can be misleading, but where it is possible to compare the two, the former frequently provides a guide to what is in the latter.[5] The reader who is interested in what the ecclesiastical courts in Spain actually did should remember our suggestion that synodal legislation provides only probabilistic evidence of court practices. How probable depends on judgments that will vary depending on the legislation and its context and on the willingness of the reader to take risks. We leave those judgments to the reader.

---

mariage dans les procès à Saragosse au xve siècle', *Mélanges de la Casa de Velazquez* 33 (2003) 47–63; *Mariage, couple et justice en Aragon à la fin du Moyen Age* (thèse, Sorbonne; Paris 2001); 'Typologie des procès canoniques matrimoniaux à Saragosse (xve–xvie siècle)', *Sinodos diocesanos y legislacion particular: Estudios históricos en honor al Dr. D. Francisco Cantelar Rodriguez* (Bibliotheca Salmanticensis 10; Salamanca 1999) 217–232. See also Yolanda Serrano Seoane, 'El sistema penal del tribunal eclesiastico de la diocesis de Barcelona en la Baja Edad Media', *Clio y Crimen* 3 (2006) 334–428, 430–508; Federico Rafael Aznar Gil, 'Penas y sanciones contra los matrimonios clandestinos en la península Ibérica durante la baja edad media', *Revista de estudios históricos-jurídicos* 25 (2003) 189–214.

   3. Donahue, *Records 1* 181–188.

   4. See Donahue and McDougall, 'France' 339, references in n. 146.

   5. See Donahue, 'Ecclesiastical Courts' 287–296.

The Problem of Sources

There has not yet been a study of the administration of ecclesiastical justice over the course of the Middle Ages in the Iberian peninsula that examines the many aspects of medieval canonical procedure in Spain. Such a study would include the origin and evolution of ecclesiastical tribunals, the types of tribunals, the division of jurisdiction between ecclesiastical and secular courts, the procedure used in the administration of justice in the various church councils and diocesan synods, the range and ratios of different kinds of cases, whether and how the norms of the 'ordo iudiciorum' were observed in conciliar judgments, and the local variations on canonical procedure in Spain.

One of the reasons for the absence of such a pre-existing study and a serious hindrance to a complete treatment of the subject here arises from the fact that the series of procedural records of the medieval courts—that is, the 'acta causae' or 'acta processus'—do not survive in their original manuscript form in Spain. England and Italy, in contrast, and other countries as well, still possess rich archives of court documents.[6] It is most unusual to find manuscripts of ecclesiastical court cases dating from the Middle Ages in Spanish archives. This fact explains the absence of modern literature on the subject: there are not enough sources or records from the courts for legal historians to produce comprehensive studies.

Another difficulty lies in the fact that the catalogues and inventories in Spanish archives[7] liberally use and misuse the word 'proceso' and its equivalents to refer to fragments in the archives that are usually nothing like the records of court cases or even parts of those records. They are, instead, documents that mention some aspect of a court case that took place or might have taken place. At other times they refer to lawsuits that did not result in a formal judicial process that might have resolved the conflict. These disputes were resolved by compromises or settlements, or arbitration, or by extrajudicial administrative decisions. In some cases, there are summaries of the original records, but these summaries are not sufficient to understand how the case was handled.

For the study of ecclesiastical justice in this period, we need the com-

---

6. See the two examples from the Bolognese archives discussed in Pennington, 'Introduction' above.

7. For information concerning catalogues in the ecclesiastical archives in Spain, see *Guía de los archivos y las Bibliotecas de la Iglesia en España*, 1: *Archivos* (2 vols. León 1985), and the up-dated *Guía de los archivos de la Iglesia en España*, ed. José M. Martí Bonet (Barcelona 2001).

plete record of each stage of the process. It does not suffice to have documents that mention a given dispute when, as is often the case, we do not know whether or not that dispute gave rise to an actual process in court. Nor is it enough to have detached fragments that could have formed a part of an actual process or of one that did not take place. For example, in the case of depositions of witnesses or of proxies—to mention some pieces that are often found in the archives—we cannot be sure, without more information, whether they formed part of a judicial procedure or an administrative one. The documentation that we possess throws little light on the modes of proof of the 'ordo iudiciorum' that was followed in a particular legal conflict.

Before entering into the core of the argument of this chapter, perhaps it would be appropriate to try to explain why, although there are some exceptions, the procedural records of the Middle Ages from the Iberian peninsula have not, by and large, survived. While my opinion on the matter cannot be proven at this point—since there are no definite proofs for negative claims—I believe that the explanation lies simply in the fact that it was not customary to commit the procedural records to writing. If I am right, it is not surprising that they have not survived.[8] We may add to this fact a pervasive negligence in the care and conservation of the documents. We might still ask why this negligence was not so great in the case of other sorts of documents that were, in fact, less important than procedural records when it came to guaranteeing protection of the laws. The Fourth Lateran Council of 1215 promulgated canons 35 to 40, establishing canonical procedural norms for the church. The council (canon 38) outlined the obligation to preserve the records that the activities of the courts produced.[9] The Iberian peninsula seems to have been one of the places where the regulations of canon 38 were not observed. This neglect of the canon is, perhaps, not surprising; the council encountered quite a few difficulties in the attempt to put its regulations into practice in the Iberian peninsula and elsewhere.

The Reception of Medieval Roman-Canonical Procedure

Until the middle of the twelfth century, ecclesiastical courts in the Iberian peninsula were governed by Visigothic legal norms, with small modifications in those rules promulgated by the kings of the *Reconquista* (Re-

8. See, however, Donahue, *Records* 1 IX.
9. COD 184–186.

conquest). The information that we have is just as inadequate for a precise description of secular procedure as it is for describing canonical procedure. Many aspects of the secular procedure have yet to be explained, since the sources do not provide enough information. The information for Visigothic canonical procedure is even more fragmentary; for more information on this subject, we refer the reader to the literature that already exists, since our own objective in this chapter is not the Visigothic period, but the medieval Ius commune. Much work has been done on various forms of the judicial procedure[10] and on the practices of Iberian secular courts.[11]

Visigothic legal procedure interests us here only insofar as it was practiced in the Iberian peninsula until the introduction of medieval Roman-canonical procedure. A good illustration of this situation is the Council of Coyanza, probably held in 1055; it recognized as the principal source the canonical collection called the *Hispana* in an augmented version.[12] That the *Hispana* was being used is supported by the fact that the codices were copied into the twelfth century—many examples from the eleventh and twelfth centuries survive.[13]

10. On ecclesiastical procedure during the Visigothic period and the Early Middle Ages, see Eduardo de Hinojosa, 'La jurisdicción eclesiástica entre los visigodos', *Obras* (3 vols. Madrid 1948–1974) 1.1–23 (although the article is from 1881); Celestino Blanco Cordero, *El fuero especial del clero y su desarrollo en España hasta el s. VIII* (Salamanca 1944); José M. Rodríguez Devesa, 'Contribución al estudio de las penas en el derecho canónico de la época visigoda', *Revista de Estudios Penales* (1945) 2–6; José Maldonado and Fernández del Torco, 'Líneas de influencia canónica en la historia del proceso español', AHDE 23 (1953) 467–494; Georg May, 'Die Belegung kirchlicher Vergehen mit Infamie durch den Staat in römischen und westgotischen Reichs', ÖAKR 15 (1964) 177–188. On the subject of arbitration, see Antonio Merchán Álvarez, *El arbitraje: Estudio histórico-jurídico* (Seville 1981) and his 'Arbitraje y el derecho común', *El Derecho Común y Europa del derecho de el Escorial: Jornadas Internacionales de Historia del Derecho de El Escorial, 3–6 de Junio de 1999: Actas* (Madrid 2000) 121–156; Antonio Fernández de Buján Fernández, 'Contribución al estudio histórico-jurídico del arbitraje', *Revista jurídica Universidad Autónoma de Madrid* 8 (2003) 215–240 and his 'Cienca jurídical europea y derecho comunitario: "Ius romanum, Ius commune",' *Studi in onore di Antonio Metro,* ed. Carmela Russo Ruggeri (Pubblicazioni della Facoltà di Giurisprudenza della Università di Messina 243; Milano 2009) 363–402.

11. Concerning secular procedure, see Santos M. Coronas González, 'El derecho de Asturias en la alta Edad Media', *Libro del I Congreso Jurídico de Asturias* (Oviedo 1987) 73–95; Benjamin González Alonso, 'La justicia', *Enciclopedia de Historia de España, 2: Instituciones políticas: Imperio* (Madrid 1988) 343–417; J. López Ortiz, 'El proceso en los reinos cristianos de nuestra reconquista antes de la recepción romano-canónica', AHDE 14 (1942–1943) 184–226; and Isabel Ramos Vázquez, 'El proceso ordinario en el fuero de Andújar', *Buletin del Instituto de Estudios Giennenses* (2008) 221–256; idem, 'El proceso en rebeldía en el derecho castellano', AHDE 75 (2005): 721–754; idem, 'Aspectos procesales en el Fuero latino de Sepúlveda', *Los Fueros de Sepúlveda,* ed. Javier Alvarado Planas (Sine loco 2005) 213–230; Mercedes Galán Lorda, 'Algunos aspectos procesales en el Fuero General de Navarra', *Iacobus* 15–16 (2003) 113–172.

12. See Lotte Kéry, *Canonical Collections of the Early Middle Ages (ca. 400–1140): A Bibliographical Guide to the Manuscripts and Literature* (History of Medieval Canon Law; Washington, D.C. 1999) 61–72. See my article, 'Concilios y sínodos en el ordenamiento jurídico del Reino de León', *El Reino de León en la Alta Edad Media,* 1: *Cortes, concilios, y fueros* (Fuentes y estudios de historia leonesa 48; León 1988) 386–389.

13. Kéry, *Canonical Collections* 62–63 and 68.

The Gregorian reform had little impact on procedure in the Iberian peninsula, although the same could not be said for other aspects of the reform.[14] The Iberian Christian kingdoms—in all cases but Catalonia—pass directly from Visigothic canon law to the medieval Ius commune, which was imposed rapidly from the time of Gratian to that of the first decretists. Roman-canonical procedure entered the Iberian peninsula through the following channels: the Roman tradition, scholars, imported books, books produced in the Peninsula, and the canonical reception of Roman law.[15]

The Roman legal tradition, which survived, though unevenly, in the former territories of the Roman Empire, facilitated the reception of Roman law in countries of written law, such as Italy, most of southern France, the Iberian peninsula, and, to a lesser degree, other geographical areas. Focusing on the Iberian peninsula, we see that the greater or lesser intensity of the Roman legal tradition generally coincides with the areas in which the Visigothic *Forum iudicum* was most widely diffused. Since the twelfth century, this legal collection of Visigothic law had also circulated in a Castilian version and adaptation, along with other versions in Portuguese and Catalán.[16] The *Forum iudicum*, as is well known, represents a notable reception of what is called 'vulgar Roman law'.[17]

The reception of the Ius commune shaped the development of procedural law. As early as the 1180s, the Italian Ugo, or Ugolino de Sesso, seems to have been teaching at the University of Palencia.[18] (It was the oldest of the Spanish universities, but it closed in the thirteenth century.) Following

14. See my book *Iglesia, Sociedad y Derecho* (2 vols. Bibliotheca Salmanticensis 74–89; Salamanca 1985–1987) 2.369–389.

15. Antonio Pérez Martín, 'La producción de códices jurídicos en España: Ius commune y iura propria', *Juristische Buchproduktion im Mittelalter*, ed. Vincenzo Colli (Studien zur europäischen Rechtsgeschichte 155; Frankfurt am Main 2002) 567–598; and his 'La difusión de la obra de Rolandino en España', *Rolandino e l'ars notaria da Bologna all'Europa: Atti del Convegno Internazionale di Studi Storici sulla Figura e l'Opera di Rolandino*, ed. Giorgio Tamba (Per una storia del notariato nella città europea 5; Milan 2002) 759–789. More generally see Aquilino José Iglesia Ferreirós, '¿Hay juristas en el Medioevo Peninsular?' *Initium* 16 (2011) 3–25 and idem, 'Qué és un jurista en el selge XIII?' Jaume I I el seu temps 800 anys després: Econtres acadèmics de Castelló, Alacant I Valencia, Actes, ed. Rafael Narbona Vizcaíno (Valencia 2012) 279–304.

16. *Fuero Juzgo en latin y castellano* (La Real Academia Española; Madrid 1815); Veronica Orazi, *El dialecto leonés antiguo (Edición, estudio lingüistico y glosario del 'Fuero Juzgo' según el ms. escurialense Z.III.21)* (Madrid 1997); Mónica Castillo Lluch, 'Las lenguas del Fuero juzgo: Avatares históricos e historiográficos de las versiones romances de la Ley visigótoca, I', *e-Spania* 13 (2012), http://e-spania.revues.org/20994.

17. *Liber iudiciorum in Leges Visigothorum*, ed. Karl Zeumer (MGH LL 1; Hannover-Leipzig 1902) 33–456. See Marie Regina Madden, *Political Theory and Law in Medieval Spain* (New York 1930) chapter 2; Lisi Oliver, *The Body Legal in Barbarian Law* (Toronto Anglo-Saxon Series 9; Toronto 2011) 176–177, 190–191, and passim.

18. Paola Maffei, 'Ugolino da Sesso', DGI 2.1994; Fowler-Magerl, *Ordo* 200, 223–224, 243; the three tracts are edited by Gonzalo Martínez Díez, 'Tres lecciones del siglo XII del Estudio General de Palenzia', AHDE 61 (1991) 391–449; Aquilino José Iglesia Ferreirós, 'Rex superiorem non recognoscens: Hugolino de Sesso y el Studium de Palencia', *Initium* 3 (1998) 1–205.

the pure Bolognese tradition, Ugolino wrote three treatises on procedural law, which we will discuss below. In these treatises he referred to Palencia and Castile.[19]

Another master appears in the Castilian royal court, also active in the middle of the thirteenth century, also Italian, called Jacobo Giunta, usually known in the Spanish tradition as Jacobo el de las Leyes, who also wrote three procedural treatises. It has been suggested that this Jacobo may also have been the author of the third *Partida* of the *Siete Partidas* of Alfonso the Wise, the Partida that focused on procedural law.[20] The works of Jacobo Giunta are also distinctive because they were written in Castilian. This use of Castilian shows both the expressive force of this Romance language, which had become an appropriate vehicle for learned thought by the middle of the thirteenth century, and that the sophisticated language of Roman-canonical medieval procedure could be made intelligible in Castilian for legal practitioners.

Aside from these treatises on procedural law written by Bolognese jurists, we should mention other authors who were used extensively in the Iberian peninsula during this period. There is evidence in two manuscripts at the University of Salamanca. The texts date from the first half of the thirteenth century. One includes the first edition of Tancred of Bologna's *Ordo iudiciorum*, while the other manuscript contains an abbreviated recension by Bartolomaeus Brixiensis.[21] The second of these codices, the one that contains the abbreviated version of Tancred's *Ordo*, was used by a member of the monastic community of the Galician monastery of Sobrado de los Monjes, in the extreme northwest of Galicia.[22] He acted as

19. Domenico Maffei, 'Fra Cremona, Montpellier e Palencia nel secolo XII: Ricerche su Ugolino da Sesso', REDC 47 (1990) 34–51 which also appeared in RIDC 1 (1990) 9–30; Gonzalo Martínez Díez edited Ugolino's three procedural treatises in *Actas del II Congreso de Historia de Palencia*, ed. Maria Valentina Calleja González (6 vols. Palencia 1990) 4.155–191.

20. Jacobo el de las Leyes, *Oeuvres 1: Summa de los nueve tiempos de los pleitos: Edition et étude d'une variation sur un thème*, ed. J. Roudil (Paris 1986); Fowler-Magerl, *Ordo* 144; Fowler-Magerl, 'Ordines' 92–93. See the introductions to *Las Siete Partidas*, trans. Samuel Parsons Scott and ed. Robert I. Burns (5 vols. The Middle Ages; Philadelphia 2001); and Rafael R. Gilbert Sánchez de la Vega, 'Jacobo el de las leyes en el studio juridico hispánico', *Glossae* 5–6 (1993) 255–278.

21. On the recensions of Tancred's *Ordo* and Bartolomaeus Brixiensis's adaption, see Fowler-Magerl, *Ordo* 129–130; on Tancred's *Ordo*, see Pennington, 'Ordines' 144–148. See also Antonio Pérez Martín, 'El ordo iudiciarius "Ad summariam notitiam" y sus derivados: Contribución al estudio de la literatura procesal castellana', *Historia Instituciones Documentos* 8 (1981) 195–266 and 9 (1982) 327–423; and his 'La producción de códices jurídicos en España: Ius commune y iura propria', *Juristische Buchproduktion im Mittelalter*, ed. Vincenzo Colli, (Studien zur europäischen Rechtsgeschichte 155; Frankfurt am Main 2002) 567–595.

22. Salamanca, Biblioteca de la Universidad Civil 2681, fol. 1ra–126rb (*Ordo iudiciarius* of Tancred). The codex dates to the middle of the thirteenth century. The text we are citing was copied in Spain somewhat later. A complete text of Tancred's *Ordo* was in the library of the Monastery of Alcobaça that is now in Lisbon, Biblioteca Nacional Alcobaça CCCIV/202.

a lawyer for his abbot in the royal curia on all contentious matters relating to the monastery. This fact is established by the hitherto-unnoticed proxy that the abbot sent to King Alfonso X the Wise that is copied into the manuscript.[23] A similar case occurs with Civil 2681 in the same library, which contains the abridgement of Tancred's original work, a codex that until now has also been unknown to researchers, and that belonged to a practicing lawyer who worked in the court of the bishop of Barcelona.[24]

There are many medieval 'ordines iudiciarii' that survive as manuscripts in Spanish libraries. But in the case of these two codices from Salamanca we also have evidence that they were used by legal practitioners, with their first names, family names, and an indication of the courts before which they practiced. Many other manuals of procedural law, written by authors outside of the school of Bologna, also appear in medieval Spanish libraries. We will refer to these other manuals at greater length below when we describe the 'ordo iudiciorum' of medieval procedure.

The Origin and Evolution of Ecclesiastical Tribunals

The Visigothic councils—and particularly the canons of the councils held at Toledo—were frequently formed as tribunals to judge the most delicate questions affecting both the church and kingdom. Among other well-known cases, these councils were held in order to deal with violent successions to the royal throne, a pattern that was so often repeated in the Visigothic kingdom that Gregory of Tours called it the 'Visigothic disease'. Thus, canon 75 of the Fourth Council of Toledo (633) ruled on the deposition of King Suintila and his replacement by Sisenand.[25] Canons 3 through 4 and 7 of the Fifth Council of Toledo (636) also dealt with this thorny problem. At the Sixth Council of Toledo (642), canons 16 through 18 treated the same issue. The Seventh Council of Toledo (642) dealt with the overthrow of Tulga and the accession of Chindasuinth. And the Eighth Council of Toledo (653), for its part, favored a general amnesty for those who conspired against King Chindasuinth. The Twelfth Council of Toledo (681) was convened to deal with the deposition of King Wamba by Erwig.[26]

23. Salamanca, Biblioteca de la Universidad Civil 2689, fol. 126r.

24. Salamanca, Biblioteca de la Universidad Civil 2689, fol. 3ra–31ra (the *Ordo iudiciarius* of Tancred in Bartolomaeus's recension). This is from the same period as the one above. The text alluded to the curia of Barcelona. Also La Seu d'Urgell Bibl. capit. 2086, fol. 94r–105v, 173ra–174rb.

25. Renan Frighetto, 'Aspectos da teorica política isidoriana: O cânone 75 do IV Concilio de Toledo e a Constituiçao Monárquica do reino visigodo de Toledo', *Revista de ciências históricas* 12 (1997) 73–82.

26. See the chapter titled 'El juramento de fidelidad in los concilios visigóticos', in my *Iglesia,*

The Sixteenth Council of Toledo (693) summoned King Egica to render judgment on Sisbert, Archbishop of Toledo, for having failed to make an oath of loyalty to his sovereign. The council, in which many bishops participated, condemned the archbishop of Toledo, who was a sort of patriarch in the Visigothic church. They inflicted on him the penalties of excommunication, degradation, loss of all his property, and exile. These examples show clearly the judicial role that these mixed clerical and lay councils frequently played.

The symbiotic relationship between royal and ecclesiastical power can be seen in the canons of the Council of Coyanza (1055), mentioned earlier. The difference in this case is that the church was, at that time, was stronger than the monarchy—the reverse of what was the case in the Visigothic era. It also was operating at a different historical moment, that of the kings of the Reconquista. At the Council of Coyanza regulations were established that reflected the church's preoccupation with the way that the secular authorities were governing. In Visigothic Spain the bishops who gathered in the councils had legislated on matters relating to the government of the kingdom with the secular authorities—legislation which, in principle, also had civil application. In the case of the Council of Coyanza, the bishops' decrees took canonical and secular legislation of the Visigothic period as a point of reference, although they introduced the more limited norms that the most recent Castilian kings of the Reconquista had promulgated.[27]

Such was the situation in the Peninsula at the advent of medieval Ius commune, which had an early reception in Spain. The Spanish courts received the Ius commune in all its aspects, including the new norms of the 'ordo iudiciarius'. Besides the two procedural treatises written by Ugolino de Sesso and Jacobo Giunta (de las Leyes) , discussed in the previous section, other works that were written outside the Peninsula circulated in the Peninsula. Included in this group is a treatise originally written in Latin—the *Libellus fugitivus* of Nepos de Montealbano—and later translated into Castilian.[28] Eventually, other procedural writings were composed by Castilian jurists who were trained in the Roman-canonical procedure of the

---

Sociedad y Derecho 2.281–308. Francisco Javier Guzmán Armario, 'La politica exterior de los visigodos en Hispania: Un ensayo sobre la debilidad del reino de Toledo', *Estudios sobre patrimonio, cultura y sciencia medievales* 15 (2013) 215–234 at 229–232.

27. José María Magaz, 'La reforma del clero secular en el Concilio de Coyanza', *La reforma gregoriana en España: Seminario de historia de la iglesia*, ed. J. M. Magaz and Nicolás Álvarez de las Asturias (Madrid 2011) 17–54; and Gonzalo Martínez Díez, 'Alta edad media: La reforma religiosa y el concilio de Coyanza', *La Iglesia en la historia de Espana*, ed. José Antonio Escudero (Madrid 2014) 185–198.

28. Giovanna Murano, 'Ricerche sul "Libellus fugitivus",' *Aevum* 79 (2005) 417–460.

Ius commune. They used the procedural treatises written by the Bolognese jurists, and we will describe them at the end of this chapter.

The diocesan synods also provide us with evidence when medieval Roman-canonical procedure was used at the local level. When they allude to litigious matters, papal documents sent to the Peninsula presuppose that the Roman-canonical procedural model was in force.[29]

The large number of Iberian students who were trained by the law faculty in Bologna and at other Italian universities, and in Spain and abroad, also exercised an important influence. Leaving aside Bologna and other universities in Italy and southern France, the following universities were founded in the Peninsula between the twelfth and the fifteenth centuries: Palencia (ca. 1180), Salamanca (1218–1219), Tudela (1259), Coímbra-Lisbon (1288–1289), Lérida (1300), Valladolid (1346), Huesca (1354), Calatayud (1415), Barcelona (1454), Saragossa (1474), Gerona (1483), Palma de Mallorca (1483), and Sigüenza (1489).[30] Many jurists trained by these law faculties later taught at universities or at cathedral or municipal schools. But what is most interesting from the point of view of this chapter is that the majority of them practiced law in ecclesiastical courts or in chancelleries of secular authorities, quite a few of which were specifically involved in the administration of justice. As a result, they contributed significantly to the introduction, strengthening, and monopolistic power of the norms of the Ius commune in the courts.[31]

The development of the Iberian ecclesiastical tribunals from the twelfth to the fifteenth centuries was shaped by the double reality of new norms that emerged from the procedural law itself and from the early or later reception and implementation of those norms in the tribunals. Changes and innovations in the Ius commune were introduced by papal decretals and

29. Demetrio Mansilla Reoyo, *La documentación pontificia hasta Inocencio III, 965–1216* (Monumenta Hispaniae Vaticana, Sección Registros 1; Rome 1955); Mansilla, *La documentación pontificia de Honorio III, 1216–27* (Monumenta Hispaniae Vaticana, Sección Registros 2; Rome 1965); Augusto Quintana Prieto, *La documentación pontificia de Inocencio IV, 1243–54* (Monumenta Hispaniae Vaticana, Sección Registros 7; Rome 1987); Ildefonso Rodríguez de Lama, *La documentación pontificia de Alejandro IV, 1254–1261* (Monumenta Hispaniae Vaticana, Sección Registros 5; Rome 1976).

30. For the early Spanish universities see María Jesús Fuente Pérez, *La primera Universidad hispana: El Estudio General de Palencia* (Palencia 2012); Fuente Pérez, *La Universidad de Salamanca en el siglo XIII: Constituit scholas fieri salamanticae* (Salamanca 2011); José Goñi Gaztambide, 'Alejandro IV a la Universidad proyectada por Teobaldo III en Tudela (1259)', *Príncipe Viana* 69 (2008) 835–839; Mariano Peset Reig, 'Orígenes de la Universidad de Coimbra', *Península: Revista de estudos ibéricos* (2003) 71–86; Peset Reig, 'Universidades medievales: Los orígenes de Lisboa/Coimbra', *Historia de la Universidad de Salamanca* (3 vols. Acta Salmanticensia: Historia de la Universidad 61; Salamanca 2004–2006) 3.1065–1086. Juan Pemán Gavín, 'Sobre la elección del rector en la universidad medieval: El caso del Estudio General de Lérida', *Derecho y arhumentación histórica*, ed. Teresa Peralta Escuer (Lleida 1999) 125–149.

31. See my chapter, 'El *Studium Bononiense* y la Península Ibérica', *Iglesia, Sociedad y Derecho* 1.45–76.

councils, such as the Fourth Lateran Council of 1215, canons 35 through 40, which established many rules on court procedure.[32] In the fourteenth century Pope Clement V's decretal *Saepe* established the norms for summary procedure—'simpliciter et de plano et sine strepitu iudicii'—that Spanish courts adopted.[33]

We must bear in mind that the implementation of procedural norms was by no means automatic. For example, the implementation of the canons of the Fourth Lateran Council was quite uneven in the various parts of Christian Europe. In the Iberian peninsula during the thirteenth century, their observance was quite weak in Castile and stronger in the kingdoms of the Crown of Aragon.[34] By contrast, after the legatine Council of Valladolid in 1322, they were implemented more strongly in Castile.[35] For this reason, one might presume that, although the thirteenth-century ecclesiastical tribunals used the 'ordo iudiciarius', they were not established in accordance with all of its requirements nor did they function entirely according to its rules.

Types of Tribunals

The legislation in Spanish synods distinguished between cases that must necessarily go to the bishop's tribunal or to the tribunals of his vicars-general, and those that could be judged by lesser vicars and archpriests or archdeacons. In the *Synodicon* of Portugal (Guarda 1500), the cases that had to go to the bishop's tribunal were personal actions where 300 reales or more were at stake, disputes between churches concerning property in land, those concerning the ownership of the tithes (including quantities less than 300 reales), matrimonial and criminal cases, and those concerning benefices. Local (pedáneos) vicars, auditors (ouvidores), and archpriests were, however, given the power to receive all kinds of complaints and to send those who were presumed guilty to the bishop or his vicar-general. They could judge cases of verbal wrongs (injúrias verbais)

---

32. These canons were later incorporated into the law of the church in the Decretals of Pope Gregory IX: X 2.28.59–60, X 1.3.28, X 2.19.1, X 2.13.18, and X 1.43.8. See Pennington, 'Introduction' 17–23.

33. Clem. 5.11.2. See above, Pennington, 'Introduction' 26–29.

34. Peter Linehan, *The Spanish Church and the Papacy in the Thirteenth Century* (Studies in Medieval Life and Thought 4; Cambridge 1971), and the Spanish translation (Salamanca 1975); García y García, 'El Concilio IV Lateranense y la Península Ibérica', *Iglesia, Sociedad, y Derecho* 2.187–208; García y García, 'Primeros reflejos del Concilio IV Laternanense en Castilla', *Iglesia, Sociedad, y Derecho* 2.209–235.

35. Adeline Rucquoi, 'El Cardenal legado Guillaume Peyre de Godin', REDC 47 (1990) 493–516; García y García, 'Las constituciones del Concilio legatino de Valladolid (1322)', *Ecclesia Militans. Studien zur Konzilien und Reformationsgeschichte Remigius Bäumer zum 70. Geburtstag gewidmet* (Paderborn 1988) 1.111–127; Manfred Gerwing, 'Wilhelm Petrus von Godino OP', LMA 9.183.

that did not amount to 300 reales, if these cases were not appealed to the tribunal of the bishop or the vicar-general. They could also enforce the constitutions of the bishop but not dispense from them. They could hear 'feitos de residuos', even if they exceeded 300 reales, so long as appeal was taken, either ex officio or by a party to the vicar general.[36]

The vicar of Portalegre was also authorized to judge all types of civil cases, concerning any problem, and to try criminal cases brought civilly—but not cases concerning marriage or benefices—with the possibility of appeal to the bishop or his vicar general. The extent of the vicar's jurisdiction was established for the benefit of the parties involved, so that they did not have to travel the long road to Guarda, and the vicar had long experience with these types of cases.[37]

According to the Synod of the Administração de Valença do Minho of 1482, appeals did not go to Braga but to a vicar who lived in Porto, outside of the territory of this Administração.[38]

Norms similar to those we have just described for Portugal were promulgated in the synods of León and Oviedo. The Leonese bishop Juan del Campo passed an extra-synodal constitution in 1355, which was made ratified by the Leonese synods of 1406 and 1426. The legislation decreed that archpriests could not hear matrimonial cases, nor deal with cases involving wills or other suits where the amount at stake exceeds six maravedis.[39]

Canon 5, of the Synod of Alfonso de Cusanca (1426) modified Juan del Campo's constitution, raising the maximum sum from six maravedis to sixty in cases that could be judged by tribunals inferior to those of the bishop and the vicar-general.[40] This change is probably due to the monetary inflation in Castile.

Canons 18, 20, 46, and 49 of the Synod of Oviedo, celebrated by Bishop Gutierre Gómez of Toledo in 1377, established that matrimonial cases are reserved to the bishop or his vicar-general, just as major cases (causae maiores) are reserved for the Roman curia. The synod requires expertise in the law from all those concerned in such cases, and prohibits archdeacons from trying them, under penalty of 500 maravedis. Confirming previous constitutions, it insists that neither archdeacons nor their vicars can

---

36. Synod of Pedro Vaz Gavião, c. 69, *Synodicon Hispanum,* ed. Antonio García y García (11 vols. to date; Madrid 1981) 2.261 (hereafter referred to as SH). The precise meaning of *feitos dos residuos* is unclear, and the provisions concerning appeal of such judgments are more complicated than the summary given here.

37. Ibid.; Margarida Garcez Ventura, 'Noticia sobre a rota de Santiago no sul de Portugal: Os contributos da toponimia em Portalegre e Elvas', *Jacobus* 15–16 (2003) 173–186.

38. Synod of Justo Baldino, c.1 (SH 2.449).

39. Constitution of Juan del Campo (SH 3.293).

40. Synod of Alfonso de Cusanca, c.5 (SH 3.311).

hear cases outside of their territories, nor hear criminal cases of the clergy or cases relating to benefices.[41] The Oviedo Synod of 1381 decrees that archpriests cannot hear cases or pronounce sentences of excommunication.[42] The canon refers to the constitutions of its predecessors and to those of Cardinal Gil Torres.[43] Included under the title 'archpriests' were those who are called in law 'arcedianos' (archdeacons). The same regulation is contained in the Oviedo Synod of 1382, where it says, among other things, that archdeacons are very inappropriately called 'archpriests'.[44] This suggests that the misuse of the title was extensive in the diocese of Oviedo, and doubtless also in the other dioceses whose synods objected to this usage.

Other synods of León and Oviedo speak of the judicial vicars of archdeacons. In 1267, the Synod of León[45] ordered that archdeacons could not keep judicial vicars in their archdeaconries to hear cases except in the city of León. The same rule was repeated in more detail in a Synod of 1406.[46] The substance of the canon was reiterated for the dean of the chapter and the archdeacons in the Synod of Oviedo of 1378.[47] It admonished ecclesiastical judges (the dean, archdeacons, and others) that they were not allowed to make judgments outside of their territory, under penalty of suspension for six months.[48]

The Synod of Léon in 1303 ordered that a settlement that two parties had been able to reach before going to court must be respected.[49] The Synod of Oviedo of 1377 observes that an agreement, composition, or release is not valid in marriage cases.[50]

In the synods of Salamanca, too, we encounter various rules that refer to tribunals or competent jurisdiction. For example, the *Libro sinodal* of 1410—both its Latin and its Castilian versions—emphasized that marriage cases belong to the bishop's court or that of his vicar. It also pointed out that just as private penance belonged to the confessor, public or judicial penance belonged to the bishop or his vicar.[51]

In the Synod of Salamanca of 1497, notaries and clerks were prohibited

<hr>

41. SH 3.406, 412–413.

42. Constitutions of Gutierre Gómez de Toledo, c.9 (SH 3.436–437).

43. Gil Torres, *Statuta pro Capitulo Salamantino a. 1245 et pro Capitulo Abulensi a. 1250, Iglesia castellano-leonesa y curia romana en los tiempos del rey San Fernando*, ed. D. Mansilla, (Madrid 1945) 328–329. The statutes for Salamanca are reedited by A. Riesco Terrero in *Ius Canonicum* 17 (1977) 244–250.

44. Synod of Gutierre Gómez de Toledo, c.7 (SH 3.443–444).

45. Synod of Martín Fernández, c.22 (SH 3.240).

46. Synod of García Rodríguez de Carreño, c.5 (SH 3.300–301).

47. Synod of Gutierre Gómez de Toledo, c.20, n. 47 (SH 3.413).

48. Synod of Gutierre Gómez de Toledo, c.20, n. 48 (SH 3.413).

49. Synod of Gonzalo Osorio, c.8 (SH 3.263–264).

50. Synod of Gutierre Gómez de Toledo, c.18 (SH 3.406).

51. Gonzalo de Alba, *Liber Synodalis*, c.73 (SH 4.164–165, 284–285).

from giving documents certifying that couples who claim they were not married were indeed not married, if they had not received a decision from a legitimate judge deciding the question.[52]

The Synod of Salamanca in 1451 referred to the bishop as a temporal lord.[53] It decreed, in effect, that the cases from the towns in the diocese should be judged by local judges (judices pedanos) whom the bishop had placed there by virtue of his temporal lordship, and that such cases were to be heard in the episcopal audience in Salamanca only on appeal. The Synod of Salamanca of 1497 ordered that no sentence of a judge who claimed to have papal authority be executed if it is not first shown to the bishop or his provisor.[54] Canon 52 of the same synod ordered that no notary issue a document of separation or divorce unless the case had first been tried by a competent judge.[55]

Proof that the ecclesiastical jurisdiction over the clergy was violated by the secular authorities can be found in the fact that the synods of Salamanca repeatedly call attention to the problem and insist that the ecclesiastical jurisdiction be respected.[56] It seems clear that the lower courts established by the bishop as a temporal lord were different from the lower ecclesiastical courts of the archdeacons, lesser vicars, etc. These canons do not insist that cases under the jurisdiction of the bishop as temporal lord be judged by the same judges as those who hear ecclesiastical cases. The synods also ordered that neither clerics who have received their first tonsure nor married clerics could benefit from ecclesiastical jurisdiction if they do not wear the ecclesiastical garb.[57]

The Synod of Mondoñedo of 1447 stated that it had been the custom of the dean, the precentor, the archdeacons, and the master of the schools to try matrimonial cases and to render sentence in them; this custom was condemned. The synod also recorded the fact that earlier bishops had placed ecclesiastical judges in the town of Ribadeo, an office that the ab-

52. Synod of Diego de Deza, c.52 (SH 4.419).

53. Synod of Gonzalo de Vivero, c.30 (SH 4.346–347), José Luis Martín Martín, 'Un prelado medieval y su corte: Gonzalo de Vivero (Salamanca, 1447–1480)', *El historiador y la sociedad: Homenaje José María Mínguez*, ed. Pablo de la Cruz Díaz Martínez et al. (Salamanca 2013) 147–162.

54. Synod of Diego de Deza, c.30 (SH 4.388–389), Helen Nader, 'Deza, Diego de', *The Christopher Columbus Encyclopedia*, ed. Silvia A. Bedini (New York 1992) 222–223.

55. Ibid. c.52 (SH 4.319).

56. Synod of Diego de Anaya y Maldonado, c.5 (SH 4.30–31, where the constitutions of King Juan I and Enrique III were mentioned); Luis Enrique Rodríguez San Pedro Bezares, 'Don Diego de Anaya y Maldonado, fundador del Colegio de San Bartolomé de Salamanca: 1357–1437', *Derecho, historia y universidades: Estudios dedicados a Mariano Peset* (2 vols. Valencia 2007) 2.557–565;Synod of Gonzalo de Alba, c.2–3 (SH 4.52–55); Synod of Gonzalo de Vivero c.28 (SH 4.337–343, which alluded explicitly to the abuses committed in these matters); Synod of Diego de Deza, c.32 and 38 (SH 4.390–391 and 395–396).

57. Synod of Gonzalo de Alba, c.2–3 (SH 4.52–55);Synod of Diego de Deza, c.32 (SH 5.390–391).

bot and prior of the town generally had held; this practice was also prohibited. This prohibition extended not only to the hearing of the entire
case, but any part of it.[58]

The Synod of Tuy in the year 1482 established that the clergy and peas-
ants on church land had a special court, and it imposed penalties on judges who tried to exercise jurisdiction over them and on clergy who obeyed
a summons from a secular judge.[59]

A Synod of Coímbra recorded that the prior of the regular canons in
Coímbra did not have jurisdiction to try ecclesiastical cases. Tolerance of
'such a great usurpation' would prejudice the church of Coímbra in the
future.[60]

The Synod of Lisbon of 1307 forbade a declaration of nullity of marriage without the intervention of the church.[61]

Up to the present time no one has found the complete record of a
procedure of any episcopal or lower ecclesiastical tribunal, and thus I am
unable to illustrate the procedure in any specific way. I can do so only
indirectly through the synodal regulations, which generally deal with the
correction of abuses.[62]

Some of the judicial activities of papal judges have been found that
shed light on procedural norms. One case that took place between 1239
and 1251 and aimed to clarify whether the monastery of Castañeda was
autonomous or subject to the bishop of Astorga provides good evidence.[63]
A similar case, which I have also been able to study, took place in 1253
between the monastery of Silos (Burgos) and a parish in the vicinity.[64] I
have also been able to examine the surviving part of a court case in 1334
between the archbishop of Santiago de Compostela, in the role of papal
judge conservator of the Dominicans and Franciscans, and the parish
priests of Vivero (Lugo).[65] None of the three examples survive in their entirety, but, to judge from the parts we have, they were carried out entirely
according to the procedural norms that was then in force.

---

58. Synod of Pedro Arias de Baamonde (SH 1.32–34).

59. Synod of Diego de Muros, c.27, 41, 44 (SH 1.364, 372, 373–374).

60. Synod of Estavão Anes Brochardo, c.2 (SH 2.195).

61. Synod of João Martins de Solhaes, c.15 (SH 2.310).

62. See Charles Donahue's introduction to this chapter.

63. See my article, 'El proceso canónico en la documentación medieval leonesa', *El Reino de
León en la Alta Edad Media 2: Ordenamiento jurídico del reino* (León 1992) 565–655; see also Jorge Díaz
Ibáñez, 'La potestas jurisdiccional del obispo y cabildo catedralicio burgalés durante el siglo XV',
Medievalismo 22 (2012) 75–97.

64. García y García, 'La justicia eclesiástica en la España Medieval: Un pleito legatino de Silos
(1253)', *Società, istituzioni, spiritualità: Studi in onore di Cinzio Violante* (2 vols. Centro italiano di
Studi sull'Alto Medioevo, Collectanea, 1; Spoleto 1994) 1.395–407.

65. García y García, 'Un proceso conservador entre juez conservador pontificio, Santiago de
Compostela, 1334', BMCL 19 (1989) 55–59.

The Division of Jurisdiction between Secular and Ecclesiastical Tribunals

We will examine this problem first from the point of view of synodal norms, and then compare the doctrine found in the *Siete Partidas*.[66] Many diocesan synods declared with great force that the secular authorities did not have jurisdiction over the clergy, who could be judged only by the ecclesiastical courts of the church. A Synod of Túy even extended this judicial authority to farmers working in church lands.[67] The same clerical privilege was enjoyed by clergy of first tonsure and married clergy, so long as they wore clerical garb. Consequently it was considered an offense against ecclesiastical liberties or immunities when those who had a right to have their cases judged by the church were summoned before a secular tribunal.

One may add some other synodal references to the relations between the secular and ecclesiastical authorities. For instance, there is a whole series of texts in the *Synodicon* of Portugal against those who obstructed the exercise of ecclesiastical jurisdiction. In some of these texts the punishments are directed both against the secular authority that interfered in ecclesiastical cases and against those who resorted to secular courts or who volunteered to answer before them.[68] The Synod of Porto of 1496 referred to the abusive practice of the clergy in minor orders who had committed offenses and, in order to escape secular justice, had pretended to have a benefice in some church.[69]

Following the norms of canon 18 of the Fourth Lateran Council, the Synod of Braga of 1281 prohibited any cleric from pronouncing sentences of blood or holding the office of seneschal for any lay lord.[70] According to the Synod of Braga in 1505[71] (which reproduced the text of the 1496 Synod of Porto)[72] and the Synod of Guarda in 1500,[73] those who made complaints

---

66. *Las Siete Partidas*, trans. Scott vol. 1.

67. Synod of Diego de Muros, c.41, 44 (SH 1.372–374); Synod of Diego de Avellaneda, 2.1.5 (SH 1.434), 3.3.1 (SH 1.451), 3.21.2 (SH 1.503–504); Mondoñedo, Synod of Pedro Pacheco (1534), c.31 (SH 1.62); Orense, *Contituciones antiguas*, c.38 (SH 1.121–122).

68. Synod of Martinho Pires de Oliveira, c.1 (SH 2.33); Braga, Synod of Diogo de Sousa, c.44 (SH 2.176); Évora, Synod of Martinho Afonso, c.3 (SH 2.206); Évora, Synod of Martinho III, ca. pr. (SH 2.212); Valença do Minho, Synod of Frei Baldino, c.2 (SH 2.449).

69. Synod of Diogo de Sousa, c.57 (SH 2.400); See Amadeu Torres, 'Diogo de Sousa, metropolita de Braga, na Europa do Renascimento', *Revista portuguesa de humanidades* 10 (2006) 493–503.

70. Synod of Aires Vasques, c.2 (SH 2.298). See Fourth Lateran Council c.18 (= X 3.50.9) (being the seneschal of a temporal authority was not specifically prohibited in c.18, but its prohibition is very much in the spirit of the canon); José Sánchez Herrero, 'El sínodo de Braga de 1281 en el contexto conciliar y sinodal portugués, castellano y ecuménico', *IX centenário da dedicaçao da Sé de Braga: Congresso internacional: Actas* (3 vols. Braga 1990) 2.317–357.

71. Synod of Diogo de Sousa, c.33 (SH 2.164–165).

72. Ibid. c.35 (SH 2.380–381).

73. Synod of Pedro Vaz Gavião, c.71 (SH 2.263).

against the clergy in an ecclesiastical court had to give security that they would abide by its rulings and had to renounce the jurisdiction of secular courts. According to the 1500 Synod of Guarda, the *priostes* or collectors of the incomes and profits of the churches had to renounce secular authority and abide by the ecclesiastical jurisdiction of the bishop.[74] The Synod of Lisbon of 1248 excommunicated those who had recourse from an ecclesiastical tribunal to a secular one.[75]

As is well-known, the violation of the right of asylum was connected to a process that was designed to control those who had recourse to the right.[76] There are some norms concerning this in the Synod of Lisbon of 1307, which discussed abuses committed in churches by those who fled secular justice and were sheltered there.[77] But the Synod of Valença do Minho of 1444 promulgated a sentence of excommunication against secular authorities who violently abduct people who were sheltered in the churches under the law of asylum.[78]

To summarize the synodal legislation, we might say that the church had to confront an invasion into ecclesiastical jurisdiction by the secular courts—which was at times almost systematic. But these disputes did not mean that one side was totally right and the other totally wrong. Many sources of the period evidence this fact, for example, the Portuguese concordats and the *Summa de libertate ecclesiastica* of Egas, the bishop of Viseu.[79] The same idea is found in documents from Castile, where the work of Egas also circulated. (Indeed, the five codices that are known today have all been found in Castile.)[80] In Aragon things were no different. It suffices to mention the dispute between the bishop of Valencia and the secular authority—in this case represented by the *Justicia valenciano*—concerning the jurisdiction over clergy who bore arms.[81]

74. Ibid. c.36 (SH 2.244).

75. Synod of Aires Vasques, c.2 (SH 2.298).

76. See Karl Shoemaker, *Sanctuary and Crime in the Middle Ages, 400–1500* (New York 2011); and William Chester Jordan, 'A Fresh Look at Medieval Sanctuary', *Law and the Illicit in Medieval Europe*, ed. Ruth Mazo Karras et al. (Philadelphia 2008) 1–16.

77. Synod of João Martins de Soalhaes, c.14 (SH 2.310).

78. Synod of João Afonso Ferraz I, c.15 (SH 2.432–433).

79. See E. de Melo Peixoto, 'Derecho concordatario medieval portugués', REDC 35 (1979) 305–338; García y García, *Estudios sobre la canonística portuguesa medieval* (Madrid 1976) 257–281, which includes a critical edition and study of this *Summa* at 257–281. Hermínia Vasconcelos Vilar, 'In Defence of Episcopal Power: The Case of Bishop Egas of Viseu', *Carreiras eclesiásticas no Ocidente Cristão: Séc. XII–XIV* (Estudos de história religiosa 5; Lisbon 2007) 221–244. See also the article cited in the following note.

80. See my article, 'El aporte de la canonística a la teoría política medieval: Del caso portugués al castellano', *Génesis medieval del estado moderno: Castilla y Navarra (1250–1370)*, ed. Adeline Rucquoi (Valladolid 1987) 49–66.

81. See my article, 'Relaciones entre la Iglesia y el Estado en Valencia a principios del s. XV',

The fourth *Partida* emphatically affirms that procedures for marriage cases had to be tried 'before the judges of the Holy Church'.[82] There was nothing odd about this; ecclesiastical jurisdiction had been generally respected in such cases throughout Christendom since the twelfth century, and in some areas since the tenth. This idea occurred even more explicitly in other secular legal works during the reign of Alfonso X of Castile, like the *Espéculo* and the *Fuero Real*.[83] In this context, it becomes clear that the authority of the church over marriage cases referred not only to the dissolution of the bond but also to all cases concerning matrimonial matters. In the fourth *Partida* the grounds given for this exclusive jurisdiction of the church were the divine institution of marriage by Christ and its spiritual character and nature.

What is not so clear in the *Partidas* was jurisdiction over the secular issues connected to matrimonial cases, such as the restitution of goods or earnest of marriage (*arras matrimoniales*), and the return of the dowry. In some cases it seems that the *Partidas* authorized the ecclesiastical judge to intervene, based on the notion that an accessory issue follows the principal. But in other cases—as, for example, in cases of adultery—the *Partidas* seemed to allow the intervention of both the civil and the ecclesiastical courts. If the wronged party was seeking a separation on this ground, he or she had to appear in an ecclesiastical court. If, however the wronged party was seeking the punishment of the adulterous party, the fourth *Partida* dictated that secular criminal justice should hear the complaint.[84] It is not clear that the justice of the church was excluded in this case, even where only punishment and not separation was being sought. A decretal of 1206 by Innocent III seems to have anticipated the *Partidas* and allowed intervention by a secular judge.[85] At least that is how the canonists understood the decretal in their commentaries. In cases that could carry the sentence of death, the church preferred, for obvious reasons, to have the secular judge intervene.[86]

Escritos del Vedat 9 (1979) 235–246, reprinted in *Primer Congreso de Historia del Pais Valenciano: Celebrado en Valencia del 14 al 18 abril de 1971, 2: Prehistoria, Edades Antiqua y Media* (Valencia 1981) 773–781.

82. *Las Siete Partidas*, 4 Partida 9 pr, trans. Scott 917.

83. *Espéculo* 4.14.4, *Fuero Real* 3.2.7; Joseph F. O'Callaghan, 'On the Promulgation of the Espéculo and the Fuero Real', *Alfonso X, the Cortes and Government in Medieval Spain* (Selected Studies 604; Aldershot 1998) III (translated from Spanish essay of 1985).

84. *Las Siete Partidas*, 4 Partida 9.2, trans. Scott 917–918.

85. 3 Comp. 1.22.2 (X 1.38.5): 'Si vir accuset uxorem de crimine adulterii coram iudice saeculari ad penam legitimam infligendam . . . seque ad penam talionis adstringere'.

86. On the subject of marriage in the *Partidas*, see especially Esteban Martínez Marcos, *Las causas matrimoniales en las Partidas de Alfonso el Sabio* (Consejo superior de investigaciones cientificas, Instituto San Raimuno de Peñafort; Salamanca 1966) 55–69.

The Role of the Local Councils and Diocesan Synods

This section describes the occasions when local councils and diocesan synods met as tribunals to adjudicate legal rights and wrongs. It is clear that in these cases we are not dealing with truly judicial processes, but rather with arbitrations or conciliar or synodal decisions that did not follow procedural norms.[87] It is obvious that even in this latter instance, these cases were not handled as they could, or should, have been through judicial channels.

The oldest known references for the period of the Reconquista come from the time of the Gregorian reform and from legatine councils that were summoned, directed, and presided over by papal legates. This fact limits our knowledge of the role of bishops as makers of conciliar decisions, but the evidence of judicial activity in legatine councils is considerable.

The earliest conciliar decision that we know of is that of the Council of Husillos (Palencia 1080), presided over by the papal legate Ricardo Milhaud. The text of the council's decisions does not survive, but a diploma from the period recorded that this council resolved a dispute between the archbishops of Toledo and Osma on the one hand, and the archbishop of Burgos on the other, concerning the borders of the diocese of Burgo de Osma.[88] The new boundaries of Burgo de Osma were explained in great detail in this document.

The Council of Palencia in 1101 was presided over by the same papal legate. It decreed that the sporadic disputes over the boundaries of the suffragan dioceses of Braga should be laid before the tribunal of the pope or that of his legates in the kingdom of León.

In the bull *Officii nostri nos* Pope Pascal II awarded the dioceses of León and Oviedo to the province of Toledo on May 4, 1099. A short time later, at the councils of Palencia (1101) and Carrión (1103), the bishops in question objected to Pascal's decision.[89] They alleged that the pope's decision was based on a mistaken historical assumption—that the dioceses in question had belonged to Toledo during the Visigothic era—which was not in fact the case. Pascal II accepted their argument in a later decretal, *Actorum synodalium*.[90]

At Palencia (1101) the bishops also demanded payment of a third part of the tithes from monasteries, which the monks had paid to them in ear-

---

87. See my article 'Concilios y sínodos' 353–494; and my 'Legislación de los concilios y sínodos del reino leonés', *El Reino de León en la Alta Edad Media, 2: Ordenamiento jurídico del Reino* (Colección Fuentes y Estudios de Historia Leonesa; León 1992) 7–114.

88. Odilo Engels, 'Husillos, Konzil von (1088)', LMA 5.232.

89. Fidel Fita y Colomé, 'Bulas inéditas de Urbano II: Illustraciones al concilio nacional de Palencia (5–8 diciembre 1100)', *Boletín de la Real Academia de la Historia* 24 (1894) 547–553.

90. PL 163.60–62 (Mansi 20.982–984).

lier times—or so the bishops argued—and had not paid illegally, falsely claiming that they were exempt or that they were freed of the obligation by long disuse. If we are to believe the evidence of a note in a codex from the monastery of San Millán de la Cogolla, Cardinal Ricardo Milhaud, the papal legate at the council, rejected the bishops' claim and noted that they should not try to collect what their predecessors had renounced.[91]

The Council of Carrión of 1103 was presided over by the archbishop of Toledo, Bernard of Cluny. It served as a platform for his reaction to the status of Braga as a metropolitan see, which the council had reaffirmed. Bernardo obtained a reaffirmation of the primacy of Toledo, but the primacy of his see was long disputed.[92]

Another long and tedious case between Archbishop Diego Gelmírez of Compostela and the bishop of Mondoñedo over the possession of some archdeaconries was discussed in the papal curia, in the Council of Carrión of 1103, and in the Council of León of 1107. A final resolution was reached in 1122.[93]

Another matter that was heard in a conciliar forum was the removal of the see of Mondoñedo from its old location, a few kilometers from the coast, to a much more secure place 30 kilometers further inland in the current province of Lugo. This translation was agreed upon at the Council of Palencia in 1113.

Although the judicial function of the councils was a very ancient institution, Archbishop Diego Gelmírez of Compostela chose an informal meeting of bishops, gathered in Segovia in the year 1118 to consecrate the new archbishop of Braga.[94] He also wanted the council to consider a lawsuit that he was bringing against the archbishop of Braga over the possession of a lordship of the archdiocese of Compostela that was within the territory of Braga. The bishops gathered in Segovia (those of Toledo, Salamanca, Osma, and Porto) decided to delegate the final decision of this matter to the bishops of Lugo and Orense, who would meet for the purpose in the city of Tuy.

The legatine Council of Valladolid of 1123, summoned and presided

---

91. María Isabel Falcón Pérez, 'San Millán de la Cogolla', LMA 7.1185–1186.

92. See Mansi 20.1185–1186; see 'La primacia de las Españas de la iglesia de Toledo: Origen, descripción y oposición durante la Edad Media', *Nuevas aportaciones de jóvenes medievalistas*, ed. Jesús Brufal Sucarrat (Lleida 2014) 11–28.

93. See Georg Gresser, *Die Synoden und Konzilien in der Zeit des Reformpapsttums in Deutschland und Italien von Leo IX. bis Calist II. 1049–1123* (Konziliengeschichte, Reihe A: Darstellungen; Paderborn-München-Wien-Zürich 2006) 345–346.

94. Bernard F. Reilly, 'Gelmirez, Diego, Archbishop of Compostela (c. 1070–1140)', *Key Figures in Medieval Europe*, ed. Richard K. Emerson and Sandra Clayton-Emerson (New York 2006) 245–246; see also the essays in *Compostela and Europe: The Story of Diego Gelmirez*, ed. Manuel Castiñeiras (Milan 2010).

over by Cardinal Deusdedit, was involved in the judgment of a case that the British historian Richard Fletcher has called 'the Zamora imbroglio'.[95] This council dealt with the question of whether the diocese of Zamora belonged to the province of Toledo, Braga, or Compostela. The diocese had been re-established in 1121; its first bishop of the new foundation was a disciple of Bernard of Cluny, archbishop of Toledo. Alon, bishop of Astorga, raised the question of jurisdiction at the Council of Valladolid in 1123, where the legate Deusdedit agreed with the archbishop of Toledo that it was subject to Toledo. Pope Calixtus II reserved to himself the power to resolve this complicated dispute but died on December 13, 1124, without having resolved it. Afterwards Zamora appeared as a suffragan of Compostela, but the question was not finally settled until two centuries later, when it was definitively made suffragan of Compostela, a decision that lasted until the Concordat of 1851.

The very fact that jurisdictional issues like this one, and in general all cases relating to the sporadic disputes over the boundaries of dioceses, passed through papal legates, legatine councils, the pope and his curia, shows quite clearly how complicated these problems were. They were the result of the Islamic conquest and the Christian re-conquest of the Iberian peninsula. These jurisdictional disputes did not plague the other kingdoms of medieval Christendom.

The episcopal assembly in León in 1135 (which does not rank as a council proper) was gathered to attend the coronation of King Alfonso VII. It produced an agreement between the bishops of Saragossa and Sigüenza about territories disputed between the two dioceses. The legatine Council of Burgos in 1136 resolved controversies over the boundaries of the dioceses of Burgos, Osma, Sigüenza, and Tarazona. It also focused on similar problems that the Aragonese bishops had in Catalan territory. These examples make clear that these kinds of decisions were ordinarily made by legatine councils, but the León example shows that they were also made by gatherings of bishops that do not properly qualify as councils. Boundaries of dioceses were not the only issue with which bishops dealt. A non-conciliar meeting of bishops, which took place in Lisbon in 1191, dealt with conflicts over the boundaries of parishes.

We turn now to another theme of the Gregorian reform: the deposition of abbots and bishops who did not embrace the reform, and their substitution by those who did. This often happened in councils. Under the old law of the church, the deposition of bishops was the responsibility of

95. Richard A. Fletcher, *The Episcopate in the Kingdom of León in the Twelfth Century* (Oxford 1978) 195.

their metropolitans, with or without their suffragans, as the case might be. The pope could hear such cases only by way of appeal. With the Gregorian reform, such depositions were reserved to the pope, as the *Dictatus papae,* among other sources, clearly proclaimed: 'That he alone [the pope] can depose or reinstate bishops' (n. 3); 'That, in a council, his legate, even if a lower grade, is above all bishops, and can pass sentence of deposition against them' (n. 4); 'That the Pope can depose the absent' (n. 5); 'That he has authority to transfer to the bishops when necessity requires' (n. 13).[96] Iberian examples show quite clearly that these Gregorian principles existed not only in theory but in practice.[97]

In the Council of Burgos (1081), the abbot of the monastery of Sahagún was deposed because he was not sufficiently 'Gregorian', and Bernard of Cluny was put in his place. Later Bernard moved to the archiepiscopal see of Toledo (1086–1124). He presided as papal legate over a number of councils.[98]

Prelates were also deposed for more ordinary reasons. The Council of Husillos (Palencia, 1088) decided to replace the Bishop Santiago Diego Paláez with the abbot Pedro de Cardeña. In this case the reason for this deposition was that the bishop had been a prisoner of the king for several years. The pope later restored him to his office.

The Council of Palencia of October 25, 1113, which the archbishop of Toledo, Bernard of Cluny, presided over as papal legate, decided, among other things, to install Pedro, the queen's chaplain, to the episcopal see of Lugo. He was named and consecrated in the name of the council, because the metropolitan of Braga, who normally had jurisdiction, had been suspended. Thus the papal legate at the Council of Palencia performed a task that would normally have been the responsibility of the metropolitan.

The Council of Sahagún of 1121, which was convened under the papal legate Cardinal Boso in order to examine whether or not the bishop of Burgos had been elected canonically, imposed (canon 3) the penalty of suspension on bishops and abbots who did not attend the council. Hence, the council concluded, 'the bishop of Avila is suspended'.[99]

---

96. *Das Register Gregors VII* (2 vols. MGH Epp. sel. 2; Munich 1990, reprint of Berlin 1920) 2.1, 202–208.

97. On the *Dictatus papae* see Agostino Paravicini Bagliani, 'Dictatus papae', ed. André Vauchez et al., *Encyclopedia of the Middle Ages* (2 vols. Chicago 2000) 1.434; and Horst Fuhrmann, 'Papst Gregor VII. und das Kirchrecht: Zum Problem des Dictatus papae', *Miscellanea Domenico Maffei Dicata: Historia - Ius - Studium,* ed. Antonio García y García and Peter Weimar (4 vols. Goldbach 1995) 1.1–27.

98. Juan F. Rivera Recio, *El arzobispo de Toledo, Don Bernardo de Cluny (1086–1124)* (Publicaciones del Instituto español de Historia eclesiastica, Monografias 8; Rome 1962).

99. García y García, 'Concilios y sínodos' 482.

At the Council of Carrión in 1139, presided over by Cardinal Humbert, the bishops of León and Salamanca were deposed, along with the abbot of Samos. The conciliar documents give no explanation of the reasons for these depositions. Their positions were filled by other men who were disciples of the Archbishop Diego Gelmírez of Compostela. The Council of León (1133) provided Archdeacon Berenguer, who was also attached to Diego Gelmírez, as bishop to the see of Salamanca.[100]

The legatine Council of Oviedo of 1143 provided a bishop to the see of Oviedo. According to documents connected with this council, it also settled various unresolved conflicts among a number of churches, all of them related to questions of property or conflicting jurisdictions.

At the legatine Council of Valladolid in 1155, the papal legate Jacinto Bobo suspended the archbishop of Braga for not having attended the council and for not having properly excused himself for his absence. The Valladolid Council of 1155 also dealt with a dispute that was pending between the monasteries of Carracedo and Cluny.

A letter from Innocent III reprimanded Guillermo, the bishop of Zamora, for not having attended the Council of Salamanca in 1175. It is only because of this papal letter that we know that this council took place. The bishop argued that he had not been able to attend because he was in the service of the king, but the papal legate Jacinto Bobo did not consider this a valid excuse. Guillermo had the unexpected and unwanted honor of appearing in this unflattering position through successive decretal collections; the letter was ultimately included in the Decretals of Gregory IX.

As has already been suggested, diocesan boundaries and deposition of bishops were not the only legal matters that councils considered.[101] We can consider the following examples: Three conciliar assemblies, which were not true councils, had proceedings for the canonization of saints, a matter which had been the province of the bishops since ancient times, but which at the end of the twelfth century, Pope Innocent III reserved for the pope.[102] Assemblies that took place in Coímbra (1163) and in León (1173) dealt with two separate cases. In the first of these assemblies the archbishop of Braga, along with the bishops of Coímbra, Porto, Lamego, and Viseu and the canons regular of Santa Cruz de Coímbra, met in the monastery of Santa Cruz, and canonized its first prior, who was called Teotónico. This canonization was later confirmed by Innocent III. The second assembly was a gathering

---

100. Mariel Pérez, 'Diego Gelmírez, obispo de Santiago Compostela (1100–1139)', *Arqueología, Historia y Viajes sobre el Mundo Medieval* 46 (2013) 86–95; on Diego see n. 94 above.

101. This section discusses 1 Comp. 2.20.29 (X 2.28.19).

102. On canonization trials in general see Thomas Wetzstein, *Heilige vor Gericht: Das Kanonisationverfahren im europäischen Spätmittelalter* (Forschungen zur Kirchlichen Rechtsgeschichte und zum Kirchenrecht 28; Köln-Weimar-Wien 2004).

of various bishops, abbots, and notables of the kingdom of León, along with the king, presided over by Cardinal Jacinto Bobo, who came together for the purposes of transferring relics of, and then canonizing, the martyrs Claudio, Lupercio, and Víctor. A gathering similar to these two assemblies—only much better documented—resulted in the canonization of San Roseado de Celanova or de Dumio; it was carried out by the same Cardinal Bobo. As canonization was developing into a privilege that was reserved to the bishop of Rome, the papal legate Jacinto Bobo, once he became Pope Celestine III, issued a second document in which he confirmed as pope the canonization that he himself had approved as a cardinal bishop.[103]

A matrimonial problem that very much occupied and preoccupied the bishops was the marriage within the prohibited degrees contracted between Alfonso IX and Doña Teresa, who were related by blood in the second collateral degree.[104] This problem divided the episcopate of the kingdom. The contracting parties and the bishops who had supported the royal marriage incurred serious penalties. All this took place at the Council of Salamanca in 1191 to 1192, presided over by the papal legate Raniero. The papal curia was also preoccupied with the marriage. As a final matter, let us note that the procedure of the Romano-canonical medieval common law was not used in any of the cases I have just described.

The Legal Profession

Martín Pérez's *Libro de las confesiones,* written about the year 1316 in the kingdom of León,[105] explains at greater length and depth than any other source what we might call the ethical obligations of the legal profession. In the second part of his work there are various chapters devoted to these questions, and the different professionals to the law courts march through its pages. The treatise indicated the ordinary abuses that were often committed, or could be committed, by each professional. It gives confessors suggestions and guidance about how to handle those who repent.[106]

The diocesan synods also contain numerous rules concerning judges,

---

103. See my *Estudios sobre la canonística portuguesa medieval* (Madrid 1976) 157–172. There is an earlier and more imperfect edition in French, in RDC17 (1968) 3–15; also Damian J. Smith, 'The Iberian Legations of Cardinal Hyacinth Bobone', *Pope Celestine III, 1191–1198: Diplomat and Pastor,* ed. John Doran and Damian J. Smith (Aldershot 2008) 81–112.

104. Inés Calderón Medina, 'Las arras de doña Teresa: El tratado entre Alfonso IX de León y Sancho I de Portugal de 1194', *Castilla y el mundo feudal: Homenaje al professor Julio Valdeón,* ed. Maria Isabel del Val Valdivieso et al. (3 vols. Valladolid 2009) 2.443–456.

105. Martín Pérez, *Libro de las confesiones: Una radiografía de la sociedad medieval española,* ed. Antonio García y García and Francisco Cantelar Rodríguez (Biblioteca de Autores Cristianos; Madrid 2002); cf. Hélène Thieulin-Pardo, *Confesionario: Compendio del Libro de las confesiones de Martín Pérez (Sources 2; Paris 2012).*

106. See Brundage, 'Practice' above for a broad consideration of the role of jurists in society.

arbiters, lawyers, notaries, clerks, bailiffs, experts, and witnesses. We will take a brief look at some synods in the western part of the Peninsula as examples of these regulations.

There is a paragraph in the *Liber synodalis* of Salamanca of 1410, later used in the dioceses of Segovia (1440) and Cuenca (1446), which listed the questions that confessors were to ask secular judges or bailiffs: Had they done justice to all who asked for it? Had they violated the property rights of the church? Had they made or applied ordinances that infringed on the immunities of the church? If the penitents were lawyers, they should be asked whether they had maliciously defended an unjust cause, received pay from both the litigating parties, revealed the secrets of one party to the other causing the former to lose his case, or failed to help poor people to make a case.[107] The Synod of Tuy of 1497 decreed that notaries were required to keep protocols and registers.[108]

In the Synod of Braga in 1505 clergy were prohibited from serving as advocates or proctors in secular cases, a rule that the same bishop had established earlier at the Synod of Porto in 1496.[109] All of these texts make an exception for clergy who plead in their own defense, the defense of their families, or the defense of the poor.

A matter that received special attention at the synods is the fixing of legal fees. Among other sources, the Synod of Braga, of about 1286, contains a quite detailed list of fees for lawyers and clerks in cases brought to court by a church or monastery. The canon stipulates that no lawyer should receive more than 20 pounds for a case. If the institution was not wealthy, the advocate could charge 15 pounds; if it was poor, 10. Notarial documents were priced according to length and according to whether they were parchment or paper.[110]

The Synod of León of 1303 fixed the fees for different stages of a case:

---

107. Bernardo de Alba, *Liber synodalis* (1410), c.48 (SH 4.110–112 for the Latin text, and 225–227 for the Castilian). On the subject of synodal books, see Bernardo Alonso Rodríguez, Francisco Cantelar Rodríguez, and Antonio García y García, 'Para la historia de un concepto: Liber synodalis', *Studia in Honorem Eminentissimi Cardinalis Alphonsi M. Stickler* (Studia et textus historiae iuris canonici 7; Rome 1992) 1–11.

108. Constitutions of Pedro Beltrán, c.3 (SH 1.388–389).

109. Synod of Diogo de Sousa, c.12 (SH 2.148), taken from c.14 of theSynod of the same bishop held in Porto in 1496 (SH 2.363–364); Synod of Mateus, c.12 (SH 2.300), Synod of João Afonso Ferraz I, c.10 (SH 2.430). On clergy's practice of law see James A. Brundage, *The Medieval Origins of the Legal Profession: Canonists, Civilians, and Courts* (Chicago-London 2008) 174–179, 194–198, 208–209, 469–471.

110. Synod of Frei Telo, c.2–3 (SH 2.30–31): 'Item statuimus quod in audientia Bracarensi nemo advocatorum accipiat ultra xx. libras in causa alicuius ecclesie sive monasterii, et in causis mediocrum ecclesiarum sive monasteriorum advocati libras xv. sint contempti, in minoribus vero decem'. (Unfortunately the text has lacunae, due to the deterioration of the manuscript. 'Contempti' is odd in this context, and may not be correct; perhaps 'advocati qui accipiunt plus quam libras xv.' is to be understood.)

for a summons 4 solidi, for an interlocutory sentence nothing, for a letter of warning to a contumacious litigant 4 solidi, and for the final judgment 2 solidi.[111] The Synod of Salamanca of 1410 dealt with the same subject, describing in detail the procedure that judges should follow in pronouncing a sentence of excommunication, indicating the fee that can be charged for each of the judicial acts (citation, warning, finding of contempt, etc.) in such cases.[112]

The 1451 Synod of Salamanca regulated the way in which clerks redact the processes of cases. It ordered that the cases be arranged in the form of a book, and it fixed the fee for the copy of each document that they have to give at the request of a party. The fee fluctuates between 2 and 4 maravedi for each of the different acts.[113]

The Synod of Salamanca in 1497 contained an extensive list of fees that fixed the compensation of the notaries of the chancery of the bishopric of Salamanca for entering various judicial acts. It is the most extensive and detailed list of fees that we have in the first five volumes of the *Synodicon hispanum*. There were also instructions about how the acts of a process should be entered.[114]

To emphasize again: none of these councils followed the norms of the 'ordo iudiciorum' of Romano-canonical medieval Ius commune. Instead, we find, at most, a simple conciliar deliberation, not a judicial one. Lists of court fees and other matters of an administrative nature do not always appear in the synods. Where they do appear, however, the lists of fees give us some sense of what was being done in the courts, and the references in them to the stages in the procedure correspond with what we would expect to find on the basis of the norms of the 'ordines'.

The 'Ordo iudiciorum'

We will look, first, at the manuals or 'ordines iudiciorum' that circulated throughout the Peninsula.[115] Then we shall examine the rules found

---

111. Synod of Gonzalo Osorio, c.20 (SH 3.268).

112. Synod of Bernardo de Alba, c.12 (SH 4.63–66).

113. Synod of Gonzalo de Vivero, c. 30 (SH 4.346–347). The maravedi is a medieval coin; it began as a gold coin but became the generic name for many coins. E. Flentes Gauzo, 'Ordenamiento de moneda y maravedi de oro en la Cortes Leonesas de 1202', *Gaceta numismatica* 136 (1999) 19–31.

114. Synod of Diego de Deza, c. 53 (SH 4.419–426). This list of fees is edited in the same volume as the cited synod, although it is not technically part of the synod proper.

115. Fowler-Magerl, *Ordo* and 'Ordines'; also Antonio Pérez Martín, 'El ordo iudiciarius "Ad Summariam notitiam" y sus derivandos: Contribución al studio de la literature procesal castellana', *Historia Instituciones Documentos* 9 (1982) 327–423; and Peter Johanek, 'Ordo iudiciarius', *Die deutsche Literatur des Mittelalters: Verfasserlexikon* 11 (2004) 1083–1090; See Pennington, 'Ordines' above.

in the medieval Spanish synods about the organization of legal processes. The extant documentation is not sufficient to let us know how the procedures in episcopal tribunals in the Iberian peninsula in the early Middle Ages were organized. As suggested above, it is probably safe to assume that justice was administered in accordance with the norms contained in the canonical collection *Hispana* and in the rudimentary legislation of the nascent Christian kingdoms of the Reconquista.[116]

In the later Middle Ages, the story goes hand-in-hand with that of the 'ordines iudiciarii' or 'ordines iudiciorum'. The rules of procedural law were scattered throughout Justinian's codification. Starting in the twelfth century, jurists systematized and commented on the procedural texts in these collections. This gave rise to the procedural manuals known as the 'ordines iudiciarii' or 'ordines iudiciorum'. Sometimes, the jurists wrote tracts that dealt with one part or stage of the procedure.[117]

Gratian's *Decretum* was completed in the middle of the twelfth century. It represents the beginning of canonical jurisprudence.[118] The *Decretum* laid down norms of procedure, but Gratian did not thoroughly discuss all aspects of procedure, although he did devote causae 2 through 6 to the subject. This partial canonical vacuum was filled in on the basis of the 'ordines iudiciarii' written by the civilians and canonists. The decretals and conciliar canons promulgated by Popes Alexander III and Innocent III, which provided key elements in the procedure were crucial for the evolution of procedure norms. These canons were included in the second book of the collections of decretals which became the 'sedes materiae' for discussing procedure.

From the beginning of the thirteenth century, however, the distinction between the civilian 'ordines iudiciarii' and those of the canonists became less and less relevant. Both integrate the Roman and canonical procedural systems within the unitary conception of the Romano-canonical medieval Ius commune. Indeed, as we will soon see, a single 'ordo iudiciorum' dealt with all types of cases. In practice each tribunal made use of the part that was most relevant to its concerns.

Which 'ordines iudiciarii' circulated on the Iberian peninsula and to what extent? We can answer this question, at least partially, from two per-

---

116. Text at n. 12. See Lotte Kéry, *Canonical Collections of the Early Middle Ages (ca. 400–1140): A Bibliographical Guide to the Manuscripts and Literature* (History of Medieval Canon Law; Washington, D.C. 1999) 61–72; and most recently Eric Knibbs, 'The Interpolated Hispana and the Origins of Pseudo-Isidore', ZRG Kan. Abt. 130 (2013) 1–71.

117. See Pennington, 'Ordines' above.

118. Peter Landau, 'Gratian and the Decretum Gratiani', Hartmann and Pennington *History* 22–54; most recently Kenneth Pennington, 'The Biography of Gratian, the Father of Canon Law', *Villanova Law Review* 59 (2014) 679–706, augmented in Italian RIDC 25 (2014) 25–60.

spectives: In the first place, we see the dissemination of 'ordines iudicia-rii' composed abroad by non-Iberian authors. In fact, their manuscripts are still held in the libraries of the Peninsula, well-known works of the medieval procedural literature ranging chronologically from the twelfth to the fifteenth centuries. We find such authors as Pillius de Medecina, Placentinus, Tancredus, Roffredus de Benevento, Bonaguida de Arezzo, Rolandinus Passageri, Bartolus de Saxoferrato, and many others.[119] Aside from surviving manuscripts in Spain, there are inventories of manuscripts that are now lost contain many procedural works.[120]

Second, we have numerous works composed in Spain by foreign authors and by authors native to the Iberian kingdoms. But before listing these works, it is important to point out the existence of general legal collections in Castile with important procedural jurisprudence, such as the *Siete Partidas* and the *Fuero Real* of King Alfonso X the Wise, the *Ordenamiento de Alcalá* and the *Ordenamiento de Montalvo*. These works were glossed by various Castilian authors, including the anonymous authors of glosses on the *Ordenamiento de Alcalá,* the glosses of Arias de Balboa on the *Fuero Real,* the glosses of Alfonso Díaz de Montalvo on the *Ordenamiento* that and on the *Fuero Real.* The glosses on the *Partidas* very important and culminate in the middle of the sixteenth century with the ordinary gloss of Gregorio López.[121] Although these are collections of Castilian law, it is important to bear in mind that the reception of the jurisprudence of the Ius commune took place through these collections.

Among the authors of treatises who wrote in Castile that dealt exclusively with procedure, the following deserve special mention:

(1) Ugo or Ugolino de Sesso, *Tractatus de appelatione, Tractatus de recusatione iudicum,* and *Tractatus de testibus,* preserved in Archivo de la Corona

119. For information about these jurists, see Pennington, 'Ordines' above.

120. See the catalogues of Iberian libraries with medieval backgrounds in Paul O. Kristeller, *Latin Manuscript Books before 1600. A List of the Printed Catalogues and Unpublished Inventories of Extant Collections,* revised by Sigrid Krämer (4th ed. MGH Hilfsmittel 13; Munich 1993), as well as the catalogues of medieval manuscripts in Spanish libraries or publications later arising from them: Antonio García y García, 'Los manuscritos jurídicos medievales de la Hispanic Society of América', REDC 18 (1963) 501–560; García y García, 'Manuscritos jurídicos de la Catedral de Sigüenza', *Xenia Medii Aevi historiam, illustrantia oblata Thomae Kaeppeli O.P.* (Storia e Letteratura, Raccolta di Studi e Testi 141; Rome 1978) 27–50; García y García, *Iter hispanicum* (Codices operum Bartoli a Saxoferrato recensiti 2; Florence 1973); A. García y García and R. Gonzálvez Ruiz, *Catálogo de los manuscritos jurídicos medievales de la Catedral de Toledo* (Rome-Madrid 1970); A. García y García, F. Cantelar Rodríguez, M. Nieto Cumplido, *Catálogo de los manuscritos e incunables de la Catedral de Córdoba* (Bibliotheca Salmanticensis 6; Salamanca 1976); *Catálogo de los manuscritos jurídicos de la Biblioteca Capitular de La Seu d'Urgell,* ed. Antonio García y García et al. revised and augmented by Martin Bertram and Paola Maffei, with the collaboration of Benigne Marquès Sala and Marta Pavón Ramírez (La Seu d'Urgell 2009) with a rich and detailed bibliography.

121. *Las Siete Partidas del sabio rey don Alonso el nono* [sic] (3 vols. Salamanca 1555), with the marginal glosses of Gregorio López.

de Aragón San Cugat 55 fol. 138ra–145ra. For more information about the author and his work, we refer the reader to studies by Domenico Maffei and G. Martínez Díez.[122] The author of these treatises taught and wrote at the University of Palencia around 1190, and also seems to have taught at Montpellier. He has nothing to do with his namesake Ugolino Presbeteri but seems to have been born into a Ghibelline family from Sesso, whose castle is found near Reggio Emilia. He was later bishop of Vercelli in 1214 and died in 1235.[123]

(2) Ordo iudiciarius 'Ad summariam notitiam'. Its oldest recension was written after 1234 (the date of Gregory IX's *Liber Extra*), to which various additions were later made. It was attributed to Petrus Hispanus, but we do not know which one of the various men who went by this name was the author of this work. Ten manuscripts of this work are known, four of which are in Spanish libraries (Córdoba, Escorial, and Seo de Urgel).[124] There are derivatives of this widely disseminated work, in other 'ordines iudiciarii' known by their incipits: *Quoniam plerique* by Martino de Fano, *Ut nos minores* by Arnulfo de París, and *Hec sunt*, attributed, almost certainly mistakenly, to Bartolus de Saxoferrato. More complicated is the relationship of three procedural works written in the Iberian peninsula with *Ad summariam notitiam* and with each other: the *Summa de los nove tienpos de los pleytos* by Jacobo Junta (Jacobo de las Leyes),[125] *Los nueve tiempos de los pleitos* of Arias de Balboa,[126] and the *De como se parten los pleytos* of Doctor Infante.[127] Pérez Martín has demonstrated the relationship of *Ad summariam notitiam* to Fernando Martínez de Zamora, *Summa aurea de ordine iudiciario* (of which more below), and in the fourth book of Juan de Berberio (Jean Barbier), *Viatorum utriusque iuris*.[128]

(3) Rodrigo de Palencia's *Tractatus de positionibus* survives in Córdoba, Biblioteca del Cabildo 150, fol. 6vb–8vb, which must have been written before 1254, the date of the author's death.[129]

---

122. Domenico Maffei, 'Fra Cremona, Montpellier, e Palencia nel secolo XII: Ricerche su Ugolino da Sesso', REDC 47 (1990) 35–51; this essay also appeared in RIDC 1 (1990) 9–30. Also Paola Maffei, 'Ugolino da Sesso', DGI 2.1994.

123. Paola Maffei, 'Ugolino da Sesso', in DGI 2.1994.

124. Fowler-Magerl, *Ordo* 142–44. Edition by Pérez Martín, 'El ordo iudiciarius "Ad Summariam notitiam"' 330–342.

125. All these works are listed by Fowler-Magerl, *Ordo* 142–144.

126. Antonio Pérez Martín, 'El arte de la "disputatio" en Vicente Arias de Balboa (ca. 1368–1414)', *Die Kunst der Disputation: Probleme der Rechtsauslegung und Rechtsanwendung im 13. und 14. Jahrhundert*, ed. Manlio Bellomo (Schriften des Historischen Kollegs, Kolloquien 38; Munich 1997) 229–248 and Pérez Martín's other essays cited in his notes.

127. These three works are edited in parallel in Pérez Martín, 'El ordo iudiciarius' 343–353.

128. Jean Barbier, *Viatorum utriusque iuris* (Lyon 1488), which is extremely rare, but most of which is now available online, http://www.archive.org/details/OEXV4SUP34_P1. There are also a number of sixteenth-century printings.

129. See my article, 'Magister Rodericus Palentinus', *Homenaje a Fray Justo Pérez de Urbel,*

(4) *Margarita de los pleitos,* a work written in Castilian, a language that became a suitable vehicle for the expression of learned thought from the middle of the thirteenth century. The editor of this text attributes it to the jurist Fernando Martínez de Zamora but does not provide conclusive evidence to that effect.[130] The vernacular was used in many diverse works of humanistic learning—especially legal writings from the time of Alfonso the Wise.

(5) Fernando Martínez de Zamora, *Summa aurea de ordine iudiciario,* which appears to have been written somewhat before May 31, 1252, the date that Alfonso X began his reign, since the work is dedicated to this monarch when he was still a prince. In the manuscript in which this work survives, it appears with Castilian municipal statutes.[131]

(6a) Jacobo Junta (Giunta) (Jacobo de las Leyes), a distinguished jurist,[132] wrote *Flores de las leyes* or *Flores del derecho,* also dedicated to Prince Alfonso (the future king Alfonso the Wise). To judge by the large number of manuscripts in which it survives, it circulated widely. It was also translated into Portuguese and Catalan. Fragments of this work are found as appendices to municipal statutes. At least ten codices of the Castilian text are known.

(6b) Jacobo also wrote *Doctrinal de los juicios,* a handbook of procedure, dedicated to his son Bonajunta. This treatise appears to anticipate the Third *Partida,* to which Jacobo is usually thought to have contributed. Only two manuscripts are known. We do not know the date of its composition.[133]

(6c) Jacobo also wrote *Summa de los nove tienpos de los pleytos.* We do not know the date of its composition. As discussed above (no. 2), it is a summary of *Ad summariam notitiam.*

(7) Bachiller Fernando, *Formulario Procesal* (my title), which appears to have been written in 1445. The formularies are written in Castilian, while the citations are in Latin. It appears to be more of a work in progress than a finished document. It survives in Toledo, Biblioteca del Cabildo 41–8 fol. 9r–79v. The author sometimes called himself a bachelor of civil law and at other times a bachelor of canon law, at the University of Salamanca. The

O.S.B. (2 vols. Silos 1977) 2.111–115, reprinted and updated in *El derecho común en España: Los juristas y sus obras* (Murcia 1991) 79–82.

130. Joaquín Cerdá, 'La *Margarita de los pleitos* de Fernando Martínez de Zamora: Texto procesal del s.XIII', AHDE 20 (1950) 634–738; see Joseph F. O'Callaghan's introductory essay, 'Alfonso X and the Partidas', *Las Siete Partidas,* ed. Burns, 1.xxx–xl.

131. Pérez Martín, 'El ordo iudiciarius'.

132. Robert A. MacDonald, 'Jacobo de las Leyes', *Medieval Iberia: An Encyclopedia* (New York 2003) 433; Antonio Pérez Martín, 'Jacobo de las Leyes: Datos biográficos', *Glossae* 5–6 (1993) 279–332.

133. 'Doctrinal de los juyzios de Jacobo de las Leyes: Edicion critica', ed. Victor Ruiz (PhD diss., New York University 1991).

place names that appear in the forms are all taken from Salamanca and in other cities in Castile and León.[134]

(8) Juan (Doctor) Infante's *Forma libellandi* is a formulary, sometimes accompanied by legal notes, which includes at the end a treatise titled *De commo se parten los pleytos en diez tienpos* (How court cases are divided into ten stages), discussed above (no. 2).[135] It enjoyed a wide circulation; there are more than twenty printed editions before 1561.[136] It seems to have been written between 1474 and 1484, since it refers to the reigns of both Pope Sixtus IV (1471–1484) and Ferdinand the Catholic (1474–1516). Most likely, the author studied at the University of Salamanca; he is mentioned as a bachelor of law there in 1467, and in 1480 as a doctor and prebendary.[137]

In the *Summa* of Fernando Martínez de Zamora there were two forms given for the definitive sentence in matrimonial cases at ecclesiastical courts.[138] The work described how a complaint should be put before a bishop in a case of clerical concubinage.[139] The same section described the procedure for carrying out an inquisition, based entirely on canonical sources.[140] In another passage there were three lists of cases reserved for particular authorities:[141] eight for the pope, twenty-three for bishops, and eighteen for archbishops. Another part of the text reproduced a document known as the *Formulario de Sahagún*, which includes thirty legal forms, largely dealing with matrimonial cases.[142] This formulary from the monastery at Sahagún is particularly interesting because the monastery is in the territory of León; the rest of the *Summa de ordine iudiciario* is a work imported from beyond the Pyrenees. It would seem that the abbot of Sahagún used the formulary in the administration of justice for people other than monks. In this *Summa,* there are about twice as many references to canon law as to civil law.

In the diocesan synods there were many individual rules directed at those who were conducting court cases. Thus the Synod of Salamanca of

134. García y García and Gonzálvez Ruiz, *Catálogo* 159–160 n. 85.

135. Antonio Sánchez Aranda, 'Algunas aportaciones sobre la forma "libellandi" en el "ordo iudiciorum privatorum" castellano', *La aplicación del derecho a lo largo de la historia: Actas II Jornadas de Historia del Derecho de la Universidad de Jaén*, ed. Juan Sáinz Guerra et al. (Jaén 1997) 273–290. *Forma libellandi: Compuesta por el muy famoso doctor infante* (Seville 1500, 1512, Burgos 1500).

136. A. Palau y Dulcet, *Manual del librero hispanoamericano* (Barcelona 1954) 7.52–53.

137. F. Marcos Rodríguez, *Extractos de libros de claustros de la Universidad de Salamanca* (Salamanca 1964) 106 and 309, nn. 301 and 1319.

138. Fernando Martínez de Zamora, *Summa*, Title 10, nn. 34–43 (Pérez Martín, 'El ordo iudiciarius' 382–383).

139. Ibid. Title 12, nn. 31–39 (Pérez Martín, 'El ordo iudiciarius' 397–398).

140. Ibid. Title 12, nn. 40–81 (Pérez Martín, 'El ordo iudiciarius' 398–402).

141. Ibid. Title 14, nn. 1–51 (Pérez Martín, 'El ordo iudiciarius' 403–405).

142. Ibid. Title 15, nn. 1–119 (Pérez Martín, 'El ordo iudiciarius' 405–417).

1410 has a quite full 'ordo iudiciarius' on how to pronounce sentences of excommunication. It points out that 'this has not been observed for a very long while in our bishopric'.[143] This section was supplemented in another part of the same synod.[144]

There are also many rules in the various synods concerning the interrogation of witnesses. Perjury is subjected to punishment in Santiago (1289), León (1303), in the ancient Constitutions of Orense (from the end of the fifteenth century), in Salamanca (1451), which refers to the constitutions of the legatine Council of Valladolid in 1322, and again in Salamanca (1497), which imposes a fine of a silver mark on perjurers.[145] The Synod of Compostela (1328) decrees that cloistered nuns may not be cited to appear or appear in person at a trial.[146] The Synod of Tuy (1482) decrees that clerics who are beneficed in a church in the diocese cannot testify against the bishop, the chapter, or another cleric who was beneficed in the same church as they are.[147]

The Synod of Compostela (1436) decrees that judges should decrease the rents (çensos) and fees of patronage (padroados) paid by beneficed clerics proportionally according to the income of the benefice.[148]

The Porto Synod of 1496 modified the days on which episcopal audiences were open. Tuesdays, Thursdays, and Saturdays had been stipulated since antiquity. The synod introduced the modification that if any of these days is a holiday, the audience was to open the preceding day, out of regard for the people who come from far away in order to attend a trial.[149]

The 1500 Synod of Guarda decreed that no one—under pain of excommunication 'ipso facto incurrenda'—may come to trial accompanied by powerful secular or ecclesiastical persons.[150] According to this synod, complaints should not be brought against rectors of churches during Lent.[151] Again according to this synod, trials may not be held in churches or cemeteries.[152]

---

143. Synod of Gonzalo de Alba, c.12 (SH 4.63–66).

144. Synod of Gonzalo de Alba, c. 14 (SH 4.67).

145. Synod of Rodrigo González de León, c.37 (SH 1.280); León, Synod of Martín Fernández, c.21 (SH 3.260); Constituciones antiguas de Orense, c.49 (SH 1.124); Salamancan Synod of Gonzalo de Vivero, c.13 (SH 4.322–323); Salamancan Synod of Diego de Deza, c.39 (SH 4.396–397); legatine Council of Valladolid of 1322, c.5 (Juan Tejada y Ramiro, Colección de canones y de todos los concilios de la iglesia españa (5 vols. Madrid 1849–1855) 3.482).

146. Synod of Berengario de Landora, c.1 (SH 1.308).

147. Synod of Diego de Muros, c.6 (SH 1.351).

148. Synod of Lope de Mendoza, c.1 (SH 1.328).

149. Synod of Diogo de Sousa, c.58 (SH 2.400–401).

150. Synod of Pedro Vaz Gavião, c.75 (SH 2.264–265).

151. Synod of Pedro Vaz Gavião, c.42 (SH 2.247).

152. Synod of Pedro Vaz Gavião, c.73 (SH 2.263–264).

Safe-conducts given to ecclesiastical persons in connection with cases of homicide or wounding, are regulated by a constitution in the Synod of Braga of 1505.[153]

The Synod of León of 1426 promulgated various rules concerning notifications and summonses, anticipating the case of a summons that no one dared to serve personally. Summons should be proclaimed or announced in a place as close as possible to the location of the person being sought.[154] No blank letters of summons or other judicial matters should be given out, according to the Leonese Synod of 1485–1500.[155]

The 1410 Synod of Salamanca contained detailed instructions concerning the way that judicial summons should be prepared.[156] The Synod of Salamanca in 1451 decreed that the acts of court be recorded in the form of a book so that no one could remove them, as had happened earlier.[157] The Salamancan *Liber synodalis* of 1410 decreed that confessors must refer to the bishop in the case of those couples who wish to marry but who are probably prevented from doing so by some impediment.[158] This norm was repeated in a decree of the Synod of Salamanca of 1497.[159]

By Way of a Conclusion

After reviewing the conciliar legislation, it is possible to draw some conclusions about types of cases that the ecclesiastical courts in the Iberian peninsula were hearing. Other chapters in this book suggest that an important part of ecclesiastical jurisdiction in the western Middle Ages was matrimonial cases, including impediments to marriage, adultery, and the dissolution of the bond. What we have seen in the evidence of the councils and synods does not suggest that such was the case in the Peninsula, although our base of evidence here may be misleading. The focus of the councils and synods seems to be matters of property, particularly ecclesiastical benefices. There also seem to be cases concerning wills, rents, and other disputes over worldly goods.

Another important topic of the cases was conflict over jurisdictional rights and diocesan boundaries of ecclesiastical institutions. These would be handled in councils or in informal gatherings of bishops that do not

153. Synod of Diogo de Sousa, c.57 (SH 2.189–190).
154. Synod of Alfonso de Cusanca, c. 1 (SH 3.308).
155. Synod of Alonso de Valdivielso, the text of which does not survive (SH 3.315).
156. Synod of Gonzalo de Alba, c.12 (SH 4.63–66).
157. Synod of Gonzalo de Vivero, c.30 (SH 4.346–347).
158. Gonzalo de Alba, Liber synodalis de 1410, c.73 (SH 4.165–167 [Latin] 283–286 [Castilian]).
159. Synod of Diego de Deza, c.52 (SH 4.419).

qualify, strictly speaking, as councils. Intra-diocesan jurisdictional disputes would have gone to the episcopal tribunals.

Metropolitan judicial authority seems to have been rarely exercised in the Iberian Peninsula. There are reasons for this anomaly: for instance, the fact that the archbishop of Braga had a number of his suffragans in Galicia, where the bishops were more dependent on the archbishop of Santiago than on Braga. Conversely, Santiago had suffragans in Portugal, where the same phenomenon took place in reverse. And as we have seen, there were other dioceses, like Astorga, where no one knew for certain who the metropolitan was; Toledo, Santiago, and Braga all claimed it. Other dioceses like León and Oviedo were exempt, and outside of any metropolitan jurisdiction.

Conflicts with the secular authorities are prominent, not only those disputes between the civil and ecclesiastical jurisdictions but also those cases concerning the conflicting interests that both powers had in the entire adjudicatory process. This chapter represents a basic gathering of sources and bibliography, as well as a preliminary analysis of the subject. A detailed history of procedure in Spain has yet to be written.

12

Ecclesiastical Procedure in Eastern Central Europe

Péter Cardinal Erdő

The present volume is primarily concerned with presenting Latin canon law, yet it is well known that Latin ecclesiastical legal culture did not totally predominate in Eastern Europe; the West had frontiers where Latin culture ceased. This chapter deals with the eastern portion of Central Europe, where territories of Latin culture were located east of German and Italian territories (the Empire).[1] In the High Middle Ages and the later Middle Ages, two states dominated this region, Hungary (with the Kingdom of Croatia) and Poland (the Polish-Lithuanian state). The frontiers and areas of influence of these states changed many times during this period. This turbulent history impinged on the existence of many ecclesiastical courts, particularly because the eastern frontiers of these states were largely identical with the eastern frontier of Latin culture. Efforts at political and cultural expansion by both of these territories were often intertwined with the expansion of Latin ecclesiastical organization.

1. The present chapter expands upon some previous publications of the author: 'A középkori officiálisi bíráskodás írott emlékei Lengyelországban és Magyarországon', *Magyar Könyvszemle* 110 (1994) 117–129; 'Tribunali ecclesiastici medievali in Polonia e in Ungheria', *Studi Medievali* 36 (1995) 323–343; 'Mittelalterliche Offizialate in Ungarn und in Polen', BMCL 23 (1999) 16–34.

For that reason, due to later changes in the borders of states, what follows applies to places currently in Ukraine, Romania, and other countries. The main emphasis, however, will be on the ecclesiastical courts in what is today Croatia, Hungary, Slovakia, Poland, and Transylvania (western Romania). Medieval ecclesiastical relations were defined by the hierarchical organization.[2] The primary focus of this essay will be on the ecclesiastical provinces of Esztergom, Kalocsa, Gniezno, and Lviv (Lwów).[3] Dalmatia, on the other hand, which was largely subject to the Venetian republic yet belonged in part to Hungary, causing frequent conflicts between these two powers, still belonged to the Italian sphere in terms of hierarchy and culture.[4] Bohemia, where 'the penetration of learned law (i.e., Ius com-

2. For the history of diocesan organization in Poland, see Władysław Abraham, *Organizacia Kościoła w Polsce do XII w.* (2nd ed. Lwów 1893); Abraham, *Gniezno i Magdeburg* (Kraków 1921); Abraham, *Powstanie organizacji Kościoła łacińkiego na Rusi* 1 (Lwów 1904); Abraham, 'Założenie biskupstwa łaciskiego w Kamieńcu Podolskim', offprint of *Księga pamiątkowa ku uszczeniu 250-tej rocznicy założenia Uniwersytetu Lwowskiego przez króla Jana Kazimierza r. 1661* (Kraków 1911); Karl Völker, *Kirchengeschichte Polens (Grundriss der slavischen Philologie und Kulturgeschichte*, ed. Reinhold Trautmann and Max Vasmer 7; Leipzig 1930); Zygmunt Wojciechowski, *L'État polonais au moyen âge: Histoire des institutions* (Paris 1949) 149–157; Bolesław Kumor, 'Granice metropolii i diecezji polskich (966–1939): Metropoliarum ac dioecesium Polonarum confinia', *Archiwa, Biblioteki i Muzea Kościelne* 18 (1969) 289–352, 19 (1969) 271–351, 20 (1970) 309–404, 22 (1971) 319–402, 23 (1971) 361–397, 24 (1972) 361. On the diocesan organization of Lithuania, see Tadeusz Krahel, 'Die anfängliche Organisation der Kirche in Litauen', *La cristianizzazione della Lituania: Atti del Colloquio Internazionele di Storia Ecclesiastica, in occasione del VI Centenario della Lituania cristiana, 1387–1987. Roma, 24–26 Giugno 1987*, ed. Paulius Rabikauskas (Pontificio Comitato di Scienze Storiche, Atti e Documenti 2; Città del Vaticano 1989) 159–174. On the diocesan organization of Hungary, see György Györffy, *István király és műve* (2nd ed. Budapest 1983) 177–190, 316–328, 554 (bibliography); Györffy, 'Zu den Anfängen der ungarischen Kirchenorganisation auf Grund neuer quellenkritischer Ergebnisse', *AHP* 7 (1969) 79–113; Horst Fuhrmann, 'Provincia constat duodecim Episcopatibus: Zum Patriarchatsplan Erzbischofs Adalbert von Hamburg-Bremen', *Collectanea Stephan Kuttner* (SG 11; Bologna 1967) 389–404, 396–398; Tivadar Ortvay, *Geographia ecclesiastica Hungariae ineunte seculo XIV* (2 vols. Budapest 1891); Péter Gyetvai, *Egyházi szervezés főleg az egykori déli magyar területeken és a bácskai Tisza mentén* (Dissertationes Hungaricae ex historia Ecclesiastica 7; Munich 1987), with a dubious position on matters under dispute; Erik Fügedy, 'Esztergomi Érsekség', *Korai magyar történeti lexikon (9–14. század)*, ed. Gyula Kristó, Pál Engel, and Ferenc Makk (Budapest 1994) 202; Gyula Kristó, 'Szent István püspökségei', also in *Korai magyar történeti lexikon; Írások Szent Istvánról és koráról* (Szeged 2000) 121–135; László Koszta, 'A váci püspökség alapítása', *Századok* 135 (2001) 363–375; Péter Erdő, 'A főváros területének egyházmegyei hovatartozása az évszázadok során', *A katolikus Budapest: Általános történeti szempontok. Plébániák*, ed. Margit Beke (2 vols. Budapest 2013) 1.17–37. On Croatia see, for example, Ante Gulin, *Hrvatski srednjovjekovni kaptoli* (Zagreb 2001); and n. 4 below.

3. Cf. *Die päpstlichen Kanzleiordnungen von 1200 bis 1500*, ed. Michael Tangl (Innsbruck 1894, reprinted Aalen 1959) 1–32 (Provinciale); Conrad Eubel, *Hierarchia catholica medii aevi sive summorum Pontificum, S.R.E. Cardinalium, Ecclesiarum Antistitum series ab anno 1198 usque ad annum 1431 perducta* (2nd ed. Münster 1913) vol. 1.

4. On the history of the diocesan organization of Dalmatia, see Alfred Felbinger, 'Die Primatialprivilegien für Italien von Gregor VII. bis Innozenz III. (Pisa, Grado und Salerno)', *ZRG Kan. Abt.* 37 (1951) 95–163, especially 134–152; Ivan Kukuljević Sakcinski, *Codex diplomaticus regni Croatiae, Dalmatiae et Slavoniae* (2 vols. Zagreb 1874–1875) 2.52, 55, 56–58, 99; Atanazije Matanić, *De origine tituli 'Dalmatiae ac totius Croatiae primas'* (Pontificium Athenaeum Antonianum Fac. Theol. Theses ad lauream 89; Rome-Subiaco 1952); Vinko Foretić, 'La chiesa di Ragusa (Dubrovnik) in rapporto alla Chiesa di Spalato (Split)', *Vita religiosa morale e sociale ed i concilii di Split (Spalato) del*

mune)' proceeded 'roughly in the same temporal rhythm and along the same paths as in Germany',[5] despite similarities to its eastern neighbors,[6] the prestige of the University of Prague, and its influence on the procedure of Hungarian ecclesiastical courts,[7] belonged to the empire.[8]

For Hungary, as is the case to some degree with Croatia and Slovakia, it seems proper to end the medieval period with 1526, the beginning of Turkish rule in Hungary. Archival sources as well as printed editions are organized on that principle, and historiography in general has adopted that year as the end of the period.

---

secc. X–XI: Atti del symposium internazionale di storia ecclesiastica, Split, 26–30 settembre 1978 (Medioevo e umanesimo 49; Padua 1982) 405–415; Lothar Waldmüller, *Die Synoden in Dalmatien, Kroatien und Ungarn: Von der Völkerwanderung bis zum Ende der Arpaden (1311)* (Konziliengeschichte, Reihe A; Paderborn-Munich-Vienna-Zürich 1987) 150–153.

5. Norbert Horn, 'Die legistische Literatur der Kommentatoren und der Ausbreitung des gelehrten Rechts', Coing, *Handbuch* 1.261–364 at 310. More generally David Kalhous, *The Anatomy of a Duchy: Political and Ecclesiastical Structures of Early Přemyslid Bohemia* (East Central and Eastern Europe in the Middle Ages, 450–1450, 19; Leiden-Boston 2012).

6. For example, in 1266 an 'officialis' is mentioned in Prague, and the first 'officialis' is mentioned in a document in Olomouc (Olmütz) in 1267; see Winfried Trusen, 'Die gelehrte Gerichtsbarkeit der Kirche', Coing, *Handbuch* 1.467–504, 470; Elemér Balogh, *Középkori bajor egyházi bíráskodás* (Bibliotheca Instituti Postgradualis Iuris Canonici Universitatis Catholicae de Petro Pázmány nominatae 3.2; Budapest 2000) 38–41, 113–114. On the 'officialis' in Western Europe see Donahue, 'Ecclesiastical Courts' passim above, and most recently the essays in Beaulande and Charageat, *Officialités.*

7. Cf. Péter Erdő, *Geschichte der Wissenschaft vom kanonischen Recht: Eine Einführung* (Kirchenrechtliche Bibliothek 4; Berlin 2006) 113 n. 69;. Kinga Körmendy, *Studentes extra regnum: Esztergomi kanonokok egyetemjárása és könyvhasználata 1183–1543* (Bibliotheca Instituti Postgradualis Iuris Canonici Universitatis Catholicae de Petro Pázmány nominatae 3.9; Budapest 2007) 101–129.

8. On ecclesiastical jurisdiction in the Czech territory, see the classical publication of the acts of the ecclesiastical court of justice of Prague: *Acta iudiciaria consistorii Pragensis (Soudní akta konsistoře pražské)*, ed. Ferdinand Tadra (7 vols. Prague 1893–1900); see Emil Ott, *Beiträge zur Receptionsgeschichte des römisch-kanonischen Processes in den böhmischen Ländern* (Leipzig 1879); Ott, 'Das Eindringen des kanonischen Rechts, seiner Lehre und Praxis in Böhmen und Mähren während des Mittelalters', ZRG Kan. Abt. 3 (1913) 54–56; Zdeňka Hledíková, 'De l'histoire de la jurisdiction ecclésiastique de temps avanthussite: Actes juridiciaires de l'archévêché de Prague', *Zápisky katedry Československých dějin a archivního studia* 5 (1961) 43–46; Hledíková, 'Z diplomatické praxe pražského oficialátu ve druhé plovíné 14. století', *Sbornik archivnich prací* 22 (1972) 135–162; Václav Vaněček, 'La penetrazione del diritto romano e canonico nel territorio dell'odierna Cecoslovacchia a partire dalla seconda metà del IX secolo sino alla prima metà del secolo XIV', *Atti del convegno internazionale di studi Accursiani, Bologna 21–26 ottobre 1963* (3 vols. Milan 1968) 3.1275–1291; Miroslav Boháček, 'Das römische Recht in der Praxis der Kirchengerichte der böhmischen Länder im 13. Jahrhundert', *Collectanea Stephan Kuttner* (SG 11; Bologna, 1967) 275–304; Boháček, *Einflüsse des römischen Rechts in Böhmen und Mähren* (IRMAe 5.11; Mediolani 1975); Jaroslav Polc, *Česká církev v dějinách* (Prague 1999) 50–51; Zdeňka Hledíková, Jan Janák, and Jan Dobeš, *Dějiny správy v Českých zemích od počátků po současnost* (Prague 2005); Petr Elbel, 'Oficialat v olomoucké diecézi ve středověku (od počatků v 50. letech 13. století do 50. let 15. století)', *Sacri canones servandi sunt: Ius canonicum et status ecclesiae saeculis XIII–XV,* ed. Pavel Krafl (Opera Instituti historici Pragae C.19; Prague 2008) 324–342; Jan Adámek, 'Korektor kléru arcidiecéze pražské jako trestní soudce', *Sacri canones* 343–351; Jiří Kejř, 'K rozšíření kanonistických rukopisů v českých zemích', *Sacri canones* 363–370 at 364; Dominik Budský, 'Matrimonial Cases Reflected in the *Processus iudiciarius secundum stilum Pragensem*', *Law and Marriage in Medieval and Early Modern Times: Proceedings of the Eighth Carlsberg Academy Conference on Medieval Legal History 2011,* ed. Per Andersen, Kirsi Salonen, Møller Sigh Helle, and Helle Vogt (Copenhagen 2012) 77–82; Budský, '*Processus iudiciarius secundum stilum Pragensem* and Its Author', ZRG Kan. Abt. 98 (2012) 324–340.

Sources and the State of Research

Available documents on the activities of ecclesiastical courts vary dramatically between the Polish and the Hungarian regions. While protocol books and archives of ecclesiastical courts in the fifteenth century survive for Poland in many places, hardly a single protocol book from the period before 1526 survives for Hungary.[9] The earliest ecclesiastical court archives which are preserved in what is now Poland are to be found in Gniezno (Gnesen), Kraków (Krakau) and Poznań (Posen).[10] There are also collections of consistorial acts to be found in the diocesan archives of Lubaczow, Lublin, Olsztyn, Przemysl, Włocławek and Wrocław (Breslau).[11] Similar documents survive and have been published in Lviv, (Lwów, Lemberg). Hence it is possible to do extensive work on Poland using printed editions of documents in ecclesiastical court protocol or consistory books.[12] In addition, one can also use individual documents that survive outside juridical archives. In Hungary, in contrast, due to the destruction of ecclesiastical juridical archives during the period of Turkish domination (1526–1686), one is compelled to use individual documents, which are mostly to be found today in the State Archive in Budapest.[13] It is rare for

9. Protocol books were of course kept in Hungary too (see Bónis, 'Entwicklung' 221), but they have been lost. A late and incomplete exception is found in the Primatial Archive of Esztergom: Esztergomi Prímási Levéltár, Acta Consist. (sine numero), 133 pp., bound (half-leather). *Protocollum Annorum 1525, 1532, 1564* (register of trials from the years of 1525 and 1532, pp. 2–78; register of trials from the year 1564, pp. 79–130). See Péter Erdő, 'Das älteste Protokollbuch des Vikariatsgerichts von Esztergom (Ungarn)', De Iure Canonico Medii Aevi: *Festschrift für Rudolf Weigand* (SG 27; Bologna 1996) 71–84 (= Erdő, *Kirchenrecht im mittelalterlichen Ungarn: Gesammelte Studien* [Aus Religion und Recht 3; Berlin 2005] 105–113); Erdő, 'Ungarn (Kirchenprovinzen von Esztergom und Kalocsa)', Donahue, *Records* 1 123–158, 127. Another categorically rather strange 'Protocol Book' compiled before the spread of Roman canonical procedure was the *Registrum Varadinense*, which does not primarily deal with ecclesiastical jurisdiction. See below.

10. There is now a complete catalogue of the Kraków records up to the middle of the sixteenth century. Elżbieta Knapek, ed., *Akta oficjalatu i wikariatu generalnego krakowskiego do połowy XVI wieku* (Polska Akademia Umiejętności, Rozprawy Wydziału Historyczno-Filozoficznego, Ogólnegozbioru, 110; Kraków 2010).

11. See Tadeusz Pawluk, *Prawo Kanoniczne wedlug Kodeksu Jana Pawla II* (Olsztyn 1985) 1.165; Stanisław Librowski, 'Archiva kościoła katolickiego w Polsce', *Encyklopedia katolicka* (Lublin 1973–) 1.877–886, 880–884.

12. The most important editions are the following: Bolesław Ulanowski, *Acta capitulorum nec non iudiciorum ecclesiasticorum selecta, 2: Acta iudiciorum ecclesiasticorum dioecesium Gnesnensis et Posnaniensis (1403–1530), 3.1: Acta iudiciorum ecclesiasticorum dioecesium Plocensis, Wladislaviensis et Gnesnensis (1422–1533)* (Monumenta medii aevi historica res gestas Poloniae illustrantia 16, 18; Kraków 1902–1908); Wilhelm Rolny, *Acta officii consistorialis Leopoliensis antiquissima* (Leopoli 1927–1930) 1.1482–1485. 2.1490–1498. Cf. Izabela Skierska, 'Źródła do badania praktyk religijnych w średniowiecznej Polsce: Akta kapituł I sądów kościelnych', *Archiwa, Biblioteki i Muzea Kościelne* 87 (2007) 173–195.

13. For a list of known Hungarian court documents, see Erdő, 'Ungarn'. For a short description of a great number of different documents regarding the activity of Hungarian church courts, the most essential publication is György Bónis, *Szentszéki regeszták. Iratok az egyházi bíráskodás történetéhez a középkori Magyarországon*, ed. Elemér Balogh (Jogtörténeti Tár 1.1; Budapest 1997).

the bulk of documents from a court to be found in a particular archive so as to form a coherent collection. The documents survive, but they are scattered in various archives and printed editions. A considerable number of medieval documents are to be found in the ecclesiastical archives of northwest Hungary. However, it is only with the Prímási Levéltár in Esztergom that a collection of ecclesiastical court records can be found in a diocesan archive containing documents from the period before 1563.[14]

Research on the history of ecclesiastical jurisdiction has been pursued in Poland with greater interest and intensity than has been the case in the region that belonged to Hungary in the Middle Ages. Beyond the fact that the sources in Poland are more plentiful, one reason for this difference is that the medieval history of ecclesiastical institutions documents organic links between the Polish church and the regions of Silesia and Pomerania. Further, literary discussions between German and Polish scholars on the history of ecclesiastical hierarchy and jurisdiction have been frequent. There were even clandestine German translations of relevant Polish scholarly publications before the Second World War.[15] There was the rare occasion of a literary debate between Polish and Hungarian authors on the origins of the Latin ecclesiastical organization in Galizia. The Hungarians tended to emphasize the role of Louis the Great (king of Hungary, 1342–1382, king of Poland, 1370–1382), who had concerned himself extensively with establishing a Latin church structure in Galizia.[16]

Institutional History: Prehistory

Autonomous ecclesiastical jurisdiction matured from the time of Christianization of these lands until the second half of the thirteenth century.

Hungary

Some researchers have detected the signs of a distinct ecclesiastical jurisdiction as early as the laws of the first Hungarian king, St. Stephen

14. There are three collections of court records to be found in this archive: (1) the 'Archivum Ecclesiasticum Vetus' (AEV), with documents before 1778, is significant for documents through 1526, for trials in the second instance (particularly before the Primate-Archbishop) between 1526 and 1563; (2) the 'Acta Consistorialia' (Acta Consist.) are fundamental for court records after 1526; (3) the 'Archivum Saeculare' contains many documents from the period before 1526 (the subdivisions of this collection are marked by letters of the Latin alphabet, e.g. 'F-2-24'). See Erdő, 'Ungarn' 124, 126; György Bónis, *Útmutató az esztergomi Prímási Levéltárhoz* (Levéltárileltárak 24; Budapest 1964) 235–236; Gyula Prokop, 'Az Esztergomi Prímási Levéltár', *Magyarország Levéltárai*, ed. Péter Balázs (Budapest 1983) 272–280.

15. See Karol Koranyi and Jadwiga Koranyiowa, *Bibliografia historyczno-prawa za lata 1937–1947: Bibliographia historico-iuridica annorum 1937–1947* (2 vols. Roczniki Towarzystwa Naukowego w Toruniu, Rocznik 55 za rok 1950 Zeszyt 1–2; Toruń 1953–1959).

16. Antal Pór, 'Nagy Lajos király, a halicsi érseksèg alapítója', *Katholikus Szemle* 14 (1900) 109–122.

(1000–1038).[17] Others doubt this early distinction because of the combination in the laws of St. Stephen of spiritual and secular penalties, which are seen as supplementing one another, so that in the case of serious offenses against ecclesiastical commandments, ecclesiastical penalties rose to the point where the acts were punished by secular penalties. In crimes such as murder, killing a spouse, or perjury, however, ecclesiastical and secular penalties remained parallel and distinct.[18] These scholars argue that the king stood at the apex of all jurisdiction, and that the entire system relied upon royal power in the last instance.[19] Still, there are texts that appear to demonstrate the opposite. In the laws of Stephen,[20] as well as in the mirror of princes attributed to him,[21] some passages proclaim the 'privilegium fori'. The authorship of this mirror of princes is in dispute, however,[22] and some authors infer that the law passages are interpolations from the latter half of the eleventh century, more specifically from the period of King Andrew I (1046–1060).[23] Even if that is the case, it is at least proof that there was a serious effort to establish the 'privilegium fori' as early as the middle years of the eleventh century. According to the oldest of the three codes of St. Ladislaus (Ladislaus I, 1077–1095), which 'probably was composed in the time of his predecessor',[24] the royal judge could summon anyone 'exceptis presbyteris et clericis necnon comitibus'.[25] In the so-called *Sancti Ladislai regis decretorum liber secundus*[26] (about 1077), there are still traces of double trials for clerics.[27] The compilation made in the time

17. *Decretorum Sancti Stephani liber* 1.13–14, ed. Levente Závodszky, *A Szent István, Szent László és Kálmán korabeli törvények és zsinati határozatok forrásai* (Budapest 1904; reprinted Pápa 2002) 145–146; cf. György Bónis, *Középkori jogunk elemei: Római jog, kánonjog, szokásjog* (Budapest 1972) 20–21; Elemér Balogh, 'Die Einführung der kirchlichen Gerichtsbarkeit in Bayern: Eine komparative Studie über Kontakte und Parallelen der geistlichen Gerichte von Bayern und Ungarn im Mittelalter', *De processibus matrimonialibus* 17–18 (2010–2011) 81–110 at 86–88.

18. Cf. Waldmüller, *Synoden* 111.

19. Ibid.

20. *Decretorum Sancti Stephani liber* 1.2; 1.4; 1. 5 (3), ed. Závodszky 143–144.

21. *De institutione morum ad Emericum ducem*, ed. Závodszky, *Szent István, Szent László és Kálmán* 131–140; Albin F. Gombos, *Catalogus fontium historiae hungaricae aevo ducum et regum ex stirpis Arpad descendentium ab anno DCCC usque ad annum MCCCI* (4 vols. Budapest 1937–1943) no. 4686.

22. Tamás Bogyay, *Stephanus Rex: Versuch einer Biographie* (Vienna-Munich 1975) 44; cf. also, despite its age, Stephan Ladislaus Endlicher, *Die Gesetze des hl. Stephans: Ein Beitrag zur ungarischen Rechtsgeschichte* (Vienna 1849) 16.

23. Cf. Jakub Sawicki, 'Zur Textkritik und Entstehungsgeschichte der Gesetze König Stephans des Heiligen', *Ungarische Jahrbücher* 9 (1929) 395–425 at 424; György Bónis, 'Die Entwicklung der geistlichen Gerichtsbarkeit in Ungarn vor 1526', ZRG Kan. Abt. 49 (1963) 174–235 at 181–183.

24. Bónis, 'Entwicklung' 184.

25. *Decretorum Ladislai liber* 3.25, ed. Závodszky, *Szent István, Szent László és Kálmán* 179.

26. *Decretorum Ladislai liber* 2, ed. Závodszky 166–171.

27. According to the *Decretorum Ladislai liber* 2.13, the penalty for a cleric who has committed a theft of high value is that he should be 'ab episcopo suo degradetur, et iudicio vulgari dampnetur' (Závodszky, 170). Cf. Robert Génestal, *Le privilegium fori en France du Décret de Gratien à la fin du XIVe siècle* (2 vols. Bibliothèque de l'École des Hautes Études 35, Sciences religeuses; Paris 1921–1924) 2.xxx and n. 1.

of King Coloman (1096–1115), whose laws are known as *Colomanni regis decretorum liber primus*,[28] thoroughly regulated clerical jurisdiction.[29] It established that no secular judge could summon a cleric,[30] and that in disputes between a cleric and a layperson, the judge of the accused was competent.[31] The 'episcopi' and 'archipresbyteri' are named here as ecclesiastical judges. In the resolutions of the purely ecclesiastical synod of Esztergom held under the leadership of Archbishop Laurentius (1105–1116), the *Synodus Strigoniensis prior*,[32] it was commanded that trials concerning clergy and ecclesiastical properties should be 'canonice finiantur' (can. 1),[33] that clerics should only be deposed 'ordine canonico' (can. 23),[34] and that no cleric 'in causis ecclesiasticis' could leave the episcopal court and turn to the king or to a secular judge (canon 25).[35] Canon 66 of the same synod even mandated, 'Ut omnes archidiaconi breviarum canonum habeant'.[36] The research of Alexander Szentirmai established that these 'archidiaconi' correspond to the archipresbyteri of Ius commune. According to him, the Hungarian archidiaconus was the parish priest of a castle, with limited powers as a judge.[37] Along with Bónis, all that can be said is, 'In this virtually "non-literate time", it is virtually impossible to say how the jurisdiction of the ecclesiastical princes and the archpriests functioned.... Any trial was oral, probably ending with a ruling by the high ecclesiastic'.[38] The earliest known Hungarian church court charter is from the year 1134.[39]

Ecclesiatical jurisdiction was already quite extensive in the first half of the thirteenth century but still rather traditional and primitive. Our prima-

---

28. *Decretorum Colomanni liber* I, ed. Závodszky, *Szent István, Szent László és Kálmán* 181–194.

29. Cf. Bónis, 'Entwicklung' 185–186.

30. *Decretorum Colomanni liber* 1.14, ed. Závodszky 185: 'Nullus presumat secularis iudex sigillum clerico dare'.

31. Ibid. 1.6, ed. Závodszky 184; better in Bónis, 'Entwicklung' 185 n. 26: 'Si vero clericus causam habet cum laico, per iudicis sigillum laicus cogatur; si vero laicus habet causam cum clerico, per sigillum episcopi vel archipresbyteri clericus cogatur ab eisque cum iudice suo examinentur'.

32. *Synodus Strigoniensis prior*, ed. Závodszky, *Szent István, Szent László és Kálmán* 197–206. On the date of this synod (1100 or 1104/5), see Monika Jánosi, 'Az első ún. esztergomi zsinati határozatok keletkezési problémái,' *Acta Universitatis Szegediensis: Sectio Historica* 83 (1986) 23–30; Gábor Thoroczkay, 'Megjegyzések a Hartvik-féle Szent István-legenda datálásának kérdéséhez', *Írások az Árpád-korról: Történeti és historiográfiai tanulmányok* (TDI Könyvek 9; Budapest 2009) 67–87 at 73–74; Thoroczkay, 'Még egyszer a Hartvik-féle Szent István-legenda datálásáról', *Magyar Könyvszemle* 121 (2005) 213–218; Szabolcs Anzelm Szuromi, 'Les sources et l'effet des deux premiers Synodes d'Esztergom (1100–1112)', RIDC 21 (2010) 93–104 at 93–94.

33. Ed. Závodszky 198.

34. Ibid. 200.

35. Ibid. 200.

36. Ibid. 205.

37. Alexander Szentirmai, 'Der Ursprung des Archidiakonats in Ungarn', ÖAKR 7 (1956) 231–244 at 240.

38. Bónis, 'Entwicklung' 187.

39. *Codex diplomaticus regni Croatiae, Dalmatiae et Slavoniae*, ed. Tadija Smičiklas (14 vols. Zagreb 1904–1916) 2.42, a court certificate issued by Felicianus, archbishop of Esztergom.

ry source of knowledge about this is the *Registrum Varadinense*.[40] Bishops, followed by their archdeacons and vice-archdeacons, occasionally also abbots[41] and provosts,[42] even the vicar of the archdeacon,[43] practiced their judicial competence both in civil complaints by clerics as well as in criminal matters such as theft, robbery, murder, poisoning and 'maleficia'.[44] A similar procedure was used before both ecclesiastical and secular courts. Following formal complaint and response, the judge would send the accused, but often the plaintiff as well,[45] to a chapter meeting to undergo the ordeal of glowing iron[46] or render a special oath, such as on the grave of St. Ladislaus in Oradea (Grosswardein, Nagyvárad).[47] Although bishops often decided cases as judges delegated by the king,[48] there are also examples of common jurisdiction by ecclesiastical and secular judges[49] in trials where there is no indication of any royal delegation to an ecclesiastical and a secular judge.[50] Conflicts between archdeacons and bishops were not typical. It was quite exceptional when an archdeacon asserted his competence over against the bishop of the newly erected see of Sirmium in 1232.[51] Even before 1241 (when the Mongols attacked), scholarly canonical procedure and written trials were rather widespread, particularly as a result of numerous appeals to the Holy See. These cases were usually delegated to three-member courts organized for the occasion in response to papal orders. These courts then proceeded according to the canons. Pa-

40. *Registrum Varadinense examinum ferri candentis ordine chronologico digestum*, ed. János Karácsonyi and Samu Borovszky (Budapest 1903); see Imre Zajtay, 'Le registre de Varad: Un document judiciaire du XIIIᵉ siècle', RHD 32 (1954) 527–562; Bónis, 'Entwicklung' 193; Vince Bunyitay, *A Váradi püspökség története alapításától a jelenkorig* (Nagyvárad 1883, reprinted 2000) 1.69–80.

41. E.g. ibid. nos. 43, 183, 211, pp. 170, 220, 230.

42. E.g. ibid. no. 379, p. 302.

43. See *Codex diplomaticus Arpadianus continuatus*, ed. Gusztáv Wenzel (12 vols. Pest 1860–Budapest 1874) 3.33, document from 1262.

44. See Bónis, 'Entwicklung' 193.

45. See *Registrum Varadinense* no. 163, p. 212.

46. Examples of the use of this ordeal in trials before ecclesiastical judges are in the *Registrum Varadinense* nos. 23, 169, 183, 381, pp. 163, 215, 220, 304. Cf. C.2 q.5 c.15, *Nobilis homo*, that permitted the ordeal; it is a palea that is in none of the early Vulgate Gratian manuscripts. It was found in fifteen pre-Gratian canonical collections, including Regino 2.303 and Burchard 16.19; Balogh, 'Einführung' 96.

47. See, for example, *Registrum Varadinense* no. 340, p. 282.

48. For example, in 1225, *Registrum Varadinense* no. 341: 'Rex delegavit causam eorum Thomae, Agriensi episcopo, et Salomoni bano dicidendam'; and no. 342: 'coram Desiderio episcopo a rege Andrea delegato' (p. 283).

49. See n. 41.

50. E.g. *Registrum Varadinense* no. 166 (1217, bishop and *comes*), 195 (1219, *curialis comes* and abbot), 307 (1221, 'iudice eorum Madian et iudice archidiacono Petro') pp. 213–214, 224–225, 268. Cf. Bónis, 'Entwicklung' 193–194.

51. *Vetera monumenta historica Hungariam sacram illustrantia*, ed. Augustinus Theiner (2 vols. Rome 1859–1860) 1.1, 103.

pal legates (particularly between 1228 and 1234) settled many legal disputes themselves, helping to spread knowledge of canonical procedure.[52]

Poland

Until the beginning of the thirteenth century, the Polish church was rather strictly subordinated to secular authority.[53] Although lay investiture was very quickly eliminated by the initiative of the papacy, and the canonical election of bishops was established, the church was only able to enforce the privilegium fori at a late date.[54] Hence ecclesiastical jurisdiction had little potential for development.[55] As in Hungary the use of ordeals was found in Polish courts before the middle of the thirteenth century.[56] In this matter, one can infer a certain analogy with Hungarian conditions. The first traces of economic as well as juridical immunity are to be found in Poland in the twelfth century.[57] Archdeacons were functioning from the end of that century.[58] In the time of Archbishop Henryk Kietlicz of Gniezno (1199–1219), synods, particularly that of 1215 in Wolborz,[59] were used to establish the immunity of ecclesiastical jurisdiction.

52. See Bónis, 'Entwicklung' 194–195.

53. Special thanks should go to P. Hieronim Fokcinski, SJ, rector of the Pontificio Istituto di Studi Ecclesiastici in Rome, to his colleagues, and to Mons. Leonard Flisikowski for their significant assistance in finding and studying the Polish sources and literature.

54. See Stanisław Kutrzeba, *Historia ustroju Polski w zarysie* 1 (Kraków 1931) 49–50; Adam Vetulani, 'Die Einführung der Offizialate in Polen: Ein Beitrag zur Verbreitungsgeschichte des bischöflichen Offizialats im Mittelalter', *Collectanea Theologica* 15 (1934) 277–322 at 284–285; Wojciechowski, *L'État polonais* 160–161.

55. On Polish jurisdiction before the introduction of immunities in the thirteenth century, see Zygmunt Wojciechowski, *Sadownictwo prawa polskiego w dobie przedimmunitetowej* (Lwów 1930), reviewed by Zygmunt Marian Jedlicki in RHD (1932) 339–343; Zdzisław Kaczmarczyk, *Immunitet sądowy i jurisdykcja poimmunitetowa w dobrach Kościoła w Polsce do końca XIV w.* (Poznań 1936), reviewed by Heinrich Felix Schmid in ZRG Kan. Abt. 28 (1939) 643–660; Tadeusz Silnicki, *Organizacja archidiakonatu w Polsce* (Lwów 1927), reviewed by Heinrich Felix Schmid in ZRG Kan. Abt. 17 (1928) 686–691.

56. See Emil Meyer, 'Ordalien im Posener Lande', *Deutsche wissenschaftliche Zeitschrift für Polen* 33 (1937) 71–76; Władysław Semkowicz, 'Jeszcze o przysiędze no słońce w Polsce', *Studia Historyzne ku czci Stanislawa Kutrzeby* (Krakow, 1938) 1.429–444; Heinrich Felix Schmid, *Die rechtlichen Grundlagen der Pfarrorganisation auf westslawischen Boden und ihre Entwicklung während des Mittelalters* (Weimar 1938) 977.

57. Wojciechowski, *L'État polonais* 162.

58. Cf. Bolesław Kumor, 'Archidiakonat', *Encyklopedia katolicka* (Lublin 1973–) 1.869–873; Pawluk, *Prawo Kanoniczne* 165; Silnicki, *Organizacja*; Bernhard Panzram, 'Die Gerichtsbarkeit der schlesischen Archidiakone im Mittelalter: Ein Beitrag zur Frage der Sendgerischtsbarkeit', *Zeitschrift des Vereins für Geschichte Schlesiens* 72 (1938) 161–184; Józef Nowacki, *Dzieje archidiecezji poznańskiej*, 2: *Archidiecezja poznańska w granicach historycznych i jej ustrój* (Poznań 1964) 288.

59. Józef Umiński, *Henryk Arcybiskup Gnieźnieński zwany Kietliczem, 1199–1219* (Lublin 1926) 109; Adam Vetulani, *Statuty synodalne Henryka Kietlicza* (Kraków 1938) 37; Ignacy Subera, 'Powstanie i rozwój właściwości sądow kościelnych w Polsce', *Prawo kanoniczne* 11 (1968) 57–80 at 58.

The Origin and Development of the Officialate

Poland

Even though an independent ecclesiastical jurisdiction was established in Poland later than was the case in Hungary, the order was opposite in the case of the introduction of the officialate. In Poland the office of the episcopal 'officialis' spread very early and rapidly. The 'officialis' is first mentioned in the statutes of the papal legate James (then archdeacon of Liège, later Pope Urban IV), which he issued at the provincial synod of 1248 of the Polish church in Wrocław (Breslau). The original text of these statutes does not survive; it was reissued in 1262 and 1263 by Pope Urban IV for the ecclesiastical provinces of Riga, Gniezno, and Salzburg, as well as for the region of Bohemia and Moravia, in response to the request of the legate at that time.[60] Canon 10 of this later redaction stated:

About the nomination of the 'officialis' in each cathedral... we order that all of you shall appoint your own 'officialis' in your own cities next to the cathedral and leave him in place. He shall be a well-educated man, careful and righteous, who shall be entrusted by the bishop to substitute him fully in hearing the cases and in practice of the ecclesiastical censure. And you all, in those matters that belong to him, shall be aware, that the major questions—if necessary—shall be referred to you. And every 'officialis' must have the sigil of their lord for warrants and sealing other acts carried out before him. . . . And he shall minister justice for the wise and the unwise, reserving the right of the archdeacons, who practice ecclesiastical censure in their archdeaconate; one can make an appeal from them to the aforementioned 'officialis', from the 'officialis' to the archbishop himself or to his official in reasonable causes. Every 'officialis' must return his office on the feast of St. John into the hands of the bishop.[61]

This regulation was not introduced in all Polish dioceses. Kraków was an exception, since the bishop had named an 'officialis' before Cardinal Guy

---

60. Vetulani, 'Einführung' 285.

61. 'De constituendo officiali in qualibet ecclesia cathedrali: . . . mandamus: ut quilibet vestrum officialem suum in civitate sua iuxta ecclesiam cathedralem constituat, et relinquat, virum utique literatum, providum et discretum, cui vices suas committat plenarie in causis audiendis, et censura ecclesiastica exercenda. Vos autem in his quae ad eum pertinent specialiter intendatis, ut maiora, si opus fuerit, ad vos referantur. Et habeat quilibet officialis sigillum curiae domini sui, pro citationibus et aliis actis coram ipso habitis sigillandis. . . . Et ipse se exhibeat sapientibus et insapientibus, iustitiae debitorem; salvo iure archidiaconorum, qui consueverunt in suis archidiaconatibus censuram ecclesiasticam exercere; a quibus tamen potuerit ad dictum officialem, et ab ipso officiali ad ipsum archiepiscopum vel officialem eius, ex causis rationalibus appellari. Quilibet autem officialis officium suum, in festo S. Johannis, teneatur in manus episcopi singulis annis resignare'; *Antiquissimae constitutiones synodales provinciae Gnesnensis*, ed. Romuald Hube (Petersburg 1856) 27–28. In the realm of Bohemia throughout the Middle Ages, archdeacons did not have independent jurisdictions; see Polc, *Česká církev* 50–51; Hledíková, Janák, and Dobeš, *Dějiny správy* 175, 178; Izabela Skierska, 'Sądownictwo oficjałów okręgowych (foralnych) w późnośredniowiecznej Polsce', *Sacri canones* 352–360 at 352.

reissued Legate James's rules at the provincial synod of Wrocław in 1267.[62] This reissue was particularly vigorous. Legate Guy required the establishment of an 'officialis' in every diocese of the ecclesiastical province of Gniezno and all its suffragans on threat of suspension.[63] The severity of regulation arose from the specific Polish situation, since there was a close link between the introduction of the 'officialis' court and the struggle for the privilegium fori.[64] After 1267 the 'officialis' quickly became a permanent element in the organization of ecclesiastical courts in Poland.[65] The struggle between the bishops and the archdeacons played no role in the introduction of the 'officialis' in Poland. The two papal legates, James and Guy, were Frenchmen who established French practices. According to Vetulani, imitation of French institutions is palpable in the following: 'in establishing the competence of the 'officialis', the bishop reserves the right to keep the 'causae maiores'; the regulation concerning the keeping of routine records; the possession and style of seal; finally … the specification of grounds for appeal'. The practice of naming the 'officialis' annually as well as renewing the oath of office annually were also taken from prevailing practice in parts of France.[66]

There was one difference from French practice in that every bishop in Poland only had at first one 'officialis, iuxta ecclesiam cathedralem'. The regional 'officiales', whose competence was restricted to a particular part of the diocese, became typical only later. They were called *officiales foranei* in Poland only from the start of the sixteenth century.[67] The net of regional officialates was constructed toward the end of the fourteenth century, though they were to be found significantly earlier in a few dioceses.[68] The principal 'officialis' and the regional 'officiales' were often named from the ranks of the archdeacons.[69] As a rule, the borders of regional officialates corresponded to those of archdeacons' districts.[70] On the basis of ref-

---

62. See Vetulani, 'Einführung' 297, 301–305.

63. See ibid. 295

64. Ibid. 297–299.

65. Ibid. 306.

66. Ibid. 293–295.

67. See ibid. 321 n. 200.

68. See ibid. 321. On the institution of 'officiales foranei' in Poland, see also Piotr Hemperek, 'Oficjalaty okręgowe w Polsce', *Roczniki Teologiczno-Kanoniczne* 18, no. 3 (1971) 51–73 (listing the regional officialates); Skierska, 'Sądownictwo' 352–360. For the maps and the boundaries of Polish officialates and archdeaconates, see *Historia kościoła w Polsce* 2², ed. Bolesław Kumor and Zdzisław Obertyński (Poznań-Warszawa 1979); *Atlas historyczny Polski: Województwo łęczyckie w drugiej polowie XVI wieku*, 2: *Komentarz*, ed. Henryk Rutkowski (Warszawa 1998) 34–35; Skierska, 'Sądownictwo' 353.

69. For example, in Pultusk, magister Thomas de Zanach, 'archidiaconus et officialis Poltoviensis' (Ulanowski, *Acta capitulorum*, 3¹ nos. 1, 16, 48, 58, 101 [1448–1469]); *magister*, later *decretorum doctor* Mathias de Sluzewyecz, 'archidiaconus et officialis Poltoviensis' (ibid. 3¹ nos. 101, 102, 126 [1473–78/82?]); cf. Vetulani, 'Einführung' 308–309.

70. So, for example, in Łowicz (1522), see Ulanowski, *Acta capitulorum* 2.viii and 431–433; Vetulani, 'Einführung' 321; Skierska, 'Sądownictwo' 355.

erences in the documents, two varieties of Polish regional 'officiales' can be distinguished, a majority bearing only the title 'officialis' together with the name of the place where their court had its seat, distinguished from the central personage, who was called 'officialis generalis'.[71] Some district or regional 'officiales', however, such as the officialis of Pomerania or of Warsaw, held the title 'officialis generalis' due to the political importance of their district. In 1450 the 'officialis' of Pomerania styled himself as 'spiritualibus et temporalibus vicarius, officialis per terram Pomeraniae generalis',[72] and from 1452 the 'officialis' of Warsaw used the title 'archidiaconus Varschoviensis vicariusque... in spiritualibus et officialis in ducatibus Mazoviae generalis'.[73] The title 'officialis generalis', according to Vetulani, probably developed by analogy with 'vicarius generalis'. The chief officialis and a few others who held the office of vicar general called themselves 'officialis generalis'.[74]

From the second half of the fifteenth century, the principal 'officialis' was simultaneously vicar general (vicarius in spiritualibus).[75] It occasionally happened elsewhere in Europe that the offices of 'officialis' and vicar general were held by the same person,[76] but this combination was the rule in Poland, and it affected the structure of the diocesan archives.[77]

The competence of the officialate was defined by the legatine synods of 1267 and 1279, when secular recognition of the 'privilegium fori' was mandated. Clerics could not be called before secular courts for either civil or criminal cases. Later this privilege was recognized in the case of counterclaims as well.[78] It should be noted that the synod of the legate Philip of Fermo, which took place in the Hungarian capital of Buda in 1279

71. Adam Vetulani, 'Prawne stanowisko oficjałow biskupich w Polsce w XV stuleciu', *Studia historyczne ku czci Stanisława Kutrzeby* (Kraków1938) 1.471–491 at 491.

72. Jan Fijałek, 'O archidiakonach pomorskich i urzednikach biskupich w archidiakonacie pomorskim diecezji włocławskiej w XI–XIV wieku', *Roczniki Towarzystwa Naukowego w Toruniu* 6 (1899) 125–172 at 170–172.

73. Bolesław Ulanowski, ed., 'Acta ecclesiae collegiatae Varsoviensis', *Archiwum Komisji Prawniczej* 6 (Kraków 1897), p. 21 no. 66

74. Vetulani, 'Prawne' 482.

75. Pawluk, *Prawo Kanoniczne* 165; Nowacki, *Dzieje archidiecezji poznańskiej* 202.

76. Trusen, 'Die gelehrte Gerichtsbarkeit' 475, 482; Balogh, *Középkori bajor* 58.

77. See Pawluk, *Prawo Kanoniczne* 165.

78. Subera, 'Powstanie' 61–65, 80. See Jan Fijałek and Adam Vetulani, *Statuty synodalne wieluńsko-kaliskie Mikołaja Trąby z r. 1420* (Polska Akademia Umiejetnosci: Studi i materialy do historii ustawodawstwa synodalnego w Polsce 4; Kraków 1951) 36–37: Lib. II, 'De foro competenti': 'Irrefragibili constitucione sanccimus, ut nullus clericus clericum... ad iudices trahant seculares.... Si vero laicus fuerit, sive citans actor sit sive reus reconveniens, excommunicationis sentenciam ipso facto incurrat.... Ecclesiasticis iudicibus districcius inhibemus, ne laicos ad instanciam quorumcumque clericorum vel laicorum pro causis secularibus seu mere civilibus ad suum consistorium citari faciant aut de cognicione causarum huiusmodi se aliquatenus intromittant, nisi forte miserabilium personarum vel in defectu iudicis secularis'.

and issued decrees for both Poland and Hungary,[79] also concerned itself with the privilegium fori (§ 27, 60–64). Due to the resistance of princes and knights, ecclesiastical courts were not allowed to rule over real property (legacies, etc.). In the fourteenth century, Casimir the Great reserved to himself cases touching royal or state interest. In negotiations with the bishops, Casimir secured jurisdictional competence for secular courts over cases involving tithes. Later there were conflicts between the nobility and the clergy over the jurisdiction of ecclesiastical judges over cases concerning the ownership of land, wills, tithes, and other services. In such cases kings often intervened in ecclesiastical trials.[80] From the thirteenth century on, but particularly after 1433,[81] ecclesiastical courts were assured that the secular arm (bracchium saeculare) would carry out their sentences.[82] Kings often forbade or interrupted ecclesiastical trials in cases tied with the interests of the state or of the king through orders (litterae inhibitoriae).[83] Although ecclesiastical judges usually obeyed the royal will, differences of opinion over the limits of competence of ecclesiastical courts were frequent, and hence there were royal incursions until the middle of the sixteenth century. In 1542 an ecclesiastical synod and an assembly of estates accepted the same list of cases belonging to ecclesiastical courts. Royal interventions ceased only in 1565, following the suspension of the secular execution of ecclesiastical sentences.[84]

Concerning the competence of regional 'officiales', it should be noted that they could receive a general mandate for all marital matters[85] from the bishop.[86] In the jurisdiction of the regional 'officialis' of Lublin (un-

79. Hube, ed., *Antiquissimae constitutiones* 72–164 (using the Petersburg manuscript).

80. Walenty Wójcik, 'Interwencje monarsze u sędziów kościelnych w Polsce XV–XVI wieku', *Czasopismo Prawno-Historyczne* 19² (1967) 89–105 at 95–99, 104.

81. 'Edict of Władysław Jagiello', *Volumina legum* (8 vols. 2nd ed. Petersburg 1859–1860) 1.88; cf. Subera, 'Powstanie' 69; Wojciechowski, *L'État Polonais* 161.

82. Cf. Walenty Wójcik, 'Pomoc świecka dla sądownictwa kościelnego w Polsce średniowiecznej', *Prawo Kanoniczne* 3, nos. 3–4 (1960) 33–61.

83. Wójcik, 'Interwencje' 98; Subera, 'Powstanie' 70–71.

84. Wójcik, 'Interwencje' 104–105; Wójcik, 'Procedura w załatwianiu spraw małżeńsich w oficjalacie okręgowyn w Sandomierzu', *Roczniki Teologiczno-Kanoniczne* 9, no. 1 (1962) 99–127 at 124 (after 1565 executors attempted to use 'admonitio', 'poenitentia publica', monetary fines, prison, and often even excommunication).

85. This general mandate was not a delegation of a plenitude of power; rather it can be seen as a sign of the 'potestas ordinaria'. Innocent IV, in his bull of 1246, *Romana ecclesia*, attributed 'to the permanent episcopal judge the position of one with a mandate, hence a *iudex ordinarius*'; see Trusen, 'Die gelehrte Gerichtsbarkeit' 473. In Polish documents there are frequently express mentions of an 'auctoritas ordinaria' of the regional 'officialis' (Ulanowski, *Acta capitulorum* 2, no. 923). Perhaps that is why the use of the term 'officialis foraneus' was avoided in Poland until the sixteenth century, since the term was used in the West for a delegate of the bishop (Vetulani, 'Prawne' 485–486; cf. Trusen, 'Die gelehrte Gerichtsbarkeit' 481).

86. On the limits of competence of the various ecclesiastical courts in matrimonial cases, see the synodal decrees of Kraków (Jan Fijałek, *Najstarsze statuty synodalne krakowskie biskupa*

der the bishop of Kraków), the overwhelming majority of trials between 1452 and 1498 consisted of marital cases.[87] The situation was similar in many other courts (e.g., Sandomierz). At the beginning of the modern era, questions of marital property were less important than cases of annulment and separation.[88] The 'officialis generalis' had the same court as the bishop (idem auditorium). The same applied to the regional officialis, and there was no appeal from them to the 'officialis generalis' of the same bishop.[89] There were, however, restrictions on the monetary value of a case (ratione valoris). In some trials there could be an objection on the grounds that a regional 'officialis' had no competence in cases which exceeded a certain amount (such as twelve marks).[90]

Regional 'officiales' were nominated by the bishop himself and not by the official general, who otherwise at times might have appointed commissioned judges.[91] In times of vacancy at the bishop's see (sede vacante), the vicar of the chapter might have affirmed the regional 'officiales' but was entitled to appoint others with the task as well.[92] Besides the judges (officiales), 'instigatores' (ecclesiastical prosecutors) also played an important role in such courts.[93] After the Council of Trent it was common for the judge in marital decisions to seek the advice of other persons.[94]

Notaries also played an important role in Polish ecclesiastical jurisdictions. There is a significant corpus of surviving work permits granted to notaries from the fifteenth century.[95]

Nankera [Kraków 1915] 51); of Wielun and Kalisz (1420; Fijałek and Vetulani, *Statuty synodalne wieluńsko-kaliskie* 86, on secular and ecclesiastical competence in general, 36–37, on the 'officialis', 29–30); of Wrocław (1410; Mortimer de Montbach, *Statuta synodalia dioecesana sanctae Ecclesiae Wratislaviensis* [Wratislaviae 1855] 18–20, 34–36, 63–66); and of Chelm (fifteenth century; Jakub Sawicki, *Najdawniejsze statuty synodalne diecezij chełmskjej z XV w.* [Lublin 1948] 170–173). Cf. Skierska, 'Sądownictwo' 357 (regional 'officialis' as 'commissarius specialiter deputatus' of the bishop).

87. Piotr Hemperek, 'Sprawy małżeńskie w oficjalacie okręgowym w Lublinie w XV w.', *Roczniki Teologiczno-Kanoniczne* 17 (1970) 27–44.

88. Wójcik, 'Procedura' 99–102, 126.

89. Vetulani, 'Prawne' 485; cf. Skierska, 'Sądownictwo' 358 (appeal from the regional 'officialis' to the archbishop of Gniezno as metropolitan).

90. For such records see Ulanowski, *Acta capitulorum* 2, nos. 1891, 1894–1896 (for 1458), 1907 (for 1460), 1917 (for 1462); See Vetulani, 'Prawne' 484; Skierska, 'Sądownictwo' 357 (30, 40, or 50 marks in the sixteenth century).

91. Skierska, 'Sądownictwo' 356.

92. Ibid. 356–357.

93. Cf. Walenty Wójcik, 'Instygator w oficjalacie okręgowym w Sandomierzu', *Prawo Kanoniczne* 2 (1959) 331–383, 359; Vetulani, 'Prawne' 484; Nowacki, *Dzieje archidiecezji poznańskiej* 226. Skierska, 'Sądownictwo' 359; Pennington, 'Introduction' 10; Brundage, 'Practice' 56–59; and Donahue, 'Procedure' 83; and passim above.

94. See Wójcik, 'Procedura' 120, 127.

95. Antoni Gąsiorowski, *Notariusze publiczni w Wielkopolsce schyłku wieków średnich: Katalog admisji w Gnieźnie i w Poznaniu 1420–1500* (Poznań 1993). On 'notarii', see Antoni Gąsiorowski, 'Admisje notariuszy publicznych w Wielkopolsce schyłku wieków średnich', *Społeczeństwo Polski średniowiecznej*, ed. Stefan Kazimierz Kuczyński (Warszawa 1992) 5.274.

In case of ecclesiastical litigations, the place of the official proceedings was often the lodging of the 'officialis'. For example, in Warsaw 1412 ('in domo habitacionis honorabilis viri domini Alberti canonici et officialis Warszoviensis').[96] The oldest known document issued by a Polish 'officialis' dates from 1286.[97]

Concerning the education of participants, particularly the judges of Polish ecclesiastical courts, one must acknowledge that they were well-trained canonists. They were often called 'magister' or 'doctor decretorum'.[98] The 'officiales', even regional 'officiales',[99] applied the principles of Roman-canonical procedure with the necessary technical knowledge.[100] The majority of regional 'officiales'—at least in certain parts of Poland—were only learned in law (iuris periti) without academic degrees.[101] Regional officials working in the diocese of Gniezno usually did not become bishops nor did they acquire leading positions in the civil government. Besides their position as an official, they had a prebendal stipend in a collegiate church or the post of vicarage or some other less rewarding benefice.[102]

The situation in Lithuanian territories was peculiar. Christianity was established there relatively late. There was also a difference between territories under the influence of the Teutonic Knights and other parts of the country. In Vilnius[103] up until the end of the fifteenth century, regional organization following the 'old model' was typical and consisted of the officialate and the general vicariate having jurisdiction all over the diocese plus an archidiaconate for the capital.[104] In the diocese of Medininkai there was no archidiaconate until 1527.[105]

Hungary

At the outset I should repeat that the term 'officialis' is used in Hungary for a secular estate administrator[106] and it is rarely applied to an ecclesiasti-

96. *Liber formularum ad ius canonicum spectantium, ex actis Jacobi de Kurdwanów, episcopi Plocensis, maxima parte depromptarum*, ed. Bolesław Ulanowski, *Archiwum Komisji Prawniczej* 1 (1895) 1–36 at 36.

97. Vetulani, 'Einführung' 306.

98. See Vetulani, 'Einführung' 310–311. According to the author, the stipulations concerning juristic education of archdeacons in the synodal statutes issued for Poland and Hungary by the legate Philip of Fermo (1279) were instigated by conditions in Hungary.

99. See Hemperek, 'Sprawy.'   100. See Vetulani, 'Einführung' 311.

101. Skierska, 'Sądownictwo' 359.   102. Ibid.

103. Jerzy Ochmański, *Biskupstwo Wileńskie w średniowieczu: Ustrój i uposażenie* (Poznań 1972) 17, 19, 32–44, 55–60.

104. Krahel, 'Die anfängliche Organisation' 170.

105. Ibid.

106. On the division of Hungarian dioceses into 'officiolati' and the role of the 'officiales', which included military duties, see József Holub, *Egy dunántúli egyházi nagybirtok élete a középkor végén* (Pannónia 62; Pécs 1943) 17; Erik Fügedi, 'Az esztergomi érsekség gazdálkodása a XV.század végén'; Fügedi, *Koldulό barátok, polgárok, nemesek, Tanulmányok a magyar középkorról* (Budapest 1981) 114–237, esp. 124–125, 174–179.

cal judge, save as a formula in papal documents.[107] Yet this usage indicated that the Holy See saw Hungarian ecclesiastical courts (usually headed by a vicar general) and courts of the 'officialis' found elsewhere in Europe to be one and the same institution. This identification was also established in the canonical literature.[108] It is to be seen at once that the court of the vicar general in Hungary is extensively identical with courts of the principal 'officialis' or 'officialis generalis' (particularly in Poland in the fifteenth century).

The spread of Romano-canonical procedure was complete in Hungary for all practical purposes by 1279 (Concilium Bundense [Buda], anno 1279, canons 24, 39, 56).[109] The courts of the vicar general (functionally equivalent to the officialate), however, only became characteristic as the typical ecclesiastical court in the first half of the fourteenth century. An important impulse to this development, and probably also for the development of the terminology of ecclesiastical jurisdiction, was the period of service of the legate Gentilis (1308–1311). Gentilis issued a series of legal regulations, once again for both Hungary and Poland, and constructed a broad jurisdiction. His collaborators (auditors, papal notaries as recordkeepers or representatives of the parties, cursors, advocates) were mostly academically trained Italian canonists.[110] This could be one of the reasons why Hungarian vicarial courts had a terminology resembling that in Italy.[111] Also, the later vicars general of Hungarian bishops were often themselves Italian.[112] From the 1380s until the beginning of the sixteenth century, for

107. E.g. Theiner, *Vetera monumenta historica Hungariam* 2.36 (1358); *Monumenta Vaticana historiam Hungariae illustrantia* (6 vols. Series I; Budapest 1885–1891) 1.3, 37, 63 (1389–1390); cf. Bónis, 'Entwicklung' 203. Usually, the Roman Curia used different terms for the diocesan judges in Hungary and in Poland; see Augustinus Barbosa, *Ius Ecclesiasticum Universum* (2 vols. Lugduni 1645) Lib. I cap. XV § 12, p. 1.205b: 'Romanae autem Curiae stylus observat, ut in expeditionibus seu delegationibus ad Italiam, Hungariam, Dalmatiam, Epyrum et Cretam et partes Orientales, Siciliam et Corsicam concernentibus Cancellaria verbo vicario utatur; sed ultra montes Alpinas, ut in Hispania, Gallia, Germania, Polonia, Anglia et in ultramarinis, ut in Africa, officiales nuncupantur'; see Trusen, 'Die gelehrte Gerichtsbarkeit' 481–482; Balogh, *Középkori bajor* 57–58.

108. For example, Fredericus Petruccius Senensis, *Consilia sive Responsa, Quaestiones et Placita* (Venice 1570) 127 no. 4; see Trusen, 'Die gelehrte Gerichtsbarkeit' 481; and Litewski, *Zivilprozeß* 1.133–135, 461–462. For a detailed discussion of 'officialis' and 'vicarius' in the early modern period, see Augustino Barbaro, *Tractatus varii: De axiomatibus iuris* (Lyon 1651) 268–269.

109. Carolus Péterffy, ed., *Sacra Concilia Ecclesiae Romano-Catholicae in Regno Hungariae Celebrata* (2 vols. vol. 1: Posonii 1741, 2nd ed.: Vienna 1742; vol. 2: Posonii 1742), 2nd ed. 1.111, 114, 120–221.

110. *Monumenta Vaticana historiam Hungariae illustrantia* 1², 43, 100, 101–112, 126–150, 154–177, 188–267, 356–362; see Bónis, 'Entwicklung' 198, 202.

111. See Trusen, 'Die gelehrte Gerichtsbarkeit' 481–482; Trusen, 'Gericht, Gerichtsbarkeit, III. Kanonisches Recht', LMA 4.1325–1326.

112. See György Bónis, 'Olasz vikáriusok Magyarországon a reneszánsz korban és a Beneéthy-formuláskönyv', *Levéltári közlemények* 44–45 (1974) 89–101 at 97–98; Bónis, 'Vicari italiani in Ungheria durante il Rinascimento', *Rapporti veneto-ungheresi all'epoca del Rinascimento*, ed. Tibor Klaniczay (Studia humanitatis 2; Budapest 1975) 181–193. Italian jurists and canonists also worked at Hungarian church courts in the early sixteenth century; see László Solymosi, 'Az 1515. évi veszprémi zsinat és a vallásos élet', *Tudomány és művészet Veszprémben a 13–15. században*, ed. Zsu-

example, there were nine Italian vicars general in Esztergom, and the situation was similar in other dioceses as well. Secular legislation sought to exclude Italian jurists and other foreigners from the vicariate (Art. 32, 1495; Art. 35, 1500). Vicars, including those who were born Hungarians, were well-educated canonists, almost exclusively 'doctores decretorum'.[113] All of them, however, had to go abroad to study, since no university was able to survive for any period of time in medieval Hungary.[114]

The relationship between archdeacons and vicars general in Hungary was not a disputed one. In fact it even happened that the vicar could be archdeacon at the same time.[115] Some members of the chapters bore archdeaconal titles as well as having appropriate benefices, while they were also ambassadors of the king.[116] The old archidiaconates continued to ex-

---

zsanna Fodor (Veszprémi Múzeumi Konferenciák 6; Veszprém 1996) 57–77, 62–64 (Italian vicars in Veszprém; Dalmatians, especially the role of the Statileo/Statilič family from Trogir); Kinga Körmendy, 'A jogtudó magyar értelmiség és a Curia Romana a 16. század elején', *Tanulmányok a magyarországi egyházjog középkori történetéről: Kéziratos kódexek, zsinatok, középkori műfajok*, ed. Péter Erdő (Bibliotheca Instituti Postgradualis Iuris Canonici Universitatis Catholicae de Petro Pázmány nominatae III/3; Budapest 2002) 211–223 at 222 (some Italian canonists were invited from the *Curia Romana*); Körmendy, *Studentes* 107–108.

113. See Bónis, 'Entwicklung' 220–21; Körmendy, *Studentes* 101–114, 114–116 (vicars and church court associates of Esztergom who finished their studies in Vienna), 116–121 (those having studied in Padua), 121–126 (those having studied in Bologna). For an exception, see Péter Erdő, 'Sull'uso dell'opera del Panormitano nei centri diocesani dell'Ungheria tardomedievale', *Niccolò Tedeschi (Abbas Panormitanus) e i suoi Commentaria in Decretales*, ed. Orazio Condorelli (I libri di Erice 25; Roma 2000) 89–102.

114. See Erdő, *Geschichte der Wissenschaft* 86–87 n. 10. Just as other East-European students, the vast majority of pupils from Transylvania studied canon law at western universities. Theology and civil law were studied by a far smaller number of them; see Sándor Tonk, *Erdélyiek egyetemjárása a középkorban* (Bucharest 1979) 99–100. In Hungary during the last decades of the thirteenth century, canonists who finished their studies at Italian universities took almost at once the leading positions in the chancellery of the king's court and in chancelleries of the high aristocracy and also episcopates and other more important benefices; see György Bónis, *A jogtudó értelmiség a Mohács előtti Magyarországon* (Budapest 1971) 23–25; Jacques Verger, 'Les étudiants slaves et hongrois dans les universités occidentales (XIIIᵉ–XVᵉ siècles)', *L'Église et le peuple chrétien dans les pays de l'Europe du Centre-Est et du Nord (XIVe–XVe siècles): Actes du colloque par l'École française de Rome* (Collection de l'École française de Rome 128; Roma 1990) 83–106; Petar Runje, 'Hrvatski studenti u Padovi 1470.–1480', *Mogućnosti* 42 (1995) 117–123; Stanko Andrić, 'Studenti iz slavonsko-srijemskog međurječja na zapadnim sveučilištima u srednjem vijeku (1250.–1550.)', *Croatia Christiana Periodica* 37 (1996) 117–151; Nella Lonza, 'Blasius of Moravče, a Fifteenth-century Canon of Zagreb and His Legal Manuscripts', *Sacri canones* 444–455 at 445 ('in the fifteenth century students from the northern part of Croatia were known to attend the universities in Vienna, Cracow, Prague and Paris [if rarely], and those in Italy [more usually]. If they wanted to study law, Italy was certainly the best choice'); Körmendy, *Studentes* 172–222, 230–231 (fifteenth-century Canons of Esztergom with university degrees in canon law or civil law).

115. Theiner, *Vetera monumenta historica Hungariam* 1.673 (1344). Approximately half of the general vicars of Esztergom had some sort of archidiaconal benefices as well during the late Middle Ages or ascended in the hierarchy from benefices of this kind. The financial value of these benefices played a significant role in this respect; see Körmendy, *Studentes* 102, 185–186 (no. 68), 189 (no. 87), 190 (no. 90), 204 (no. 134).

116. For example: Thomas of Piestány, archdeacon of Hont and Nitra between 1413 and 1430, was ambassador of King Sigismund; see Körmendy, *Studentes* 184–185, no. 68.

ercise their juridical functions in the first half of the fourteenth century without disturbance. Toward the middle of that century some archdeacons endorsed their court documents as 'vicevicarius' or 'delegatus'.[117] In the meantime (in 1344), King Louis the Great forbad archdeacons to judge disputes with a value of more than a mark. Still, in 1515 the diocesan synod of Veszprém suspended the right of archdeacons to deal with disputes except as the result of episcopal mandate, but the same synod permitted them to deal with debts up to four marks.[118]

It frequently happened that some ecclesiastical dignitaries (archdeacons, canons, abbots, priors) performed juridical functions far from their home areas as delegates or vicevicarii. There were examples in cases of the absence of the vicar general that his appointee endowed with general jurisdiction ran the affairs. The vicar general of the archbishop of Esztergom Ippolito D'Este was Donato Aretino de Marmellis, canon of Ferrara. In his absence—as 'in dicto vicariatus officio iudex generaliter surrogatus'—Nicolaus de Athya, the archdeacon of the cathedral, held the jurisdiction.[119] Legal commentators in general did not think that vicar generals had the right to appoint a vicar general for their own posts. For this reason they used different terms for their permanent deputies.[120] According to the doctrine, under normal circumstances, the vicar had to have a separate assignment from the bishop to commission a permanent deputy.[121] Particular cases could be delegated by the vicar to others.[122]

In some periods it was also quite common for these same persons (as well as many bishops and foreign prelates) to perform juridical activities on the basis of a papal delegation. It happened that Hungarian canonists who possessed different prebendal benefices acted as judges on the basis of papal delegation, for example, Dominicus Galli de Waradino, a 'doctor decretorum' who studied in Padua between 1400 and 1402 ('olim rector dominorum Ultramonantorum') and was counselor to King Sigismund at the Council of Constance (1415–1416).[123]

117. See Bónis, 'Entwicklung' 204.

118. Péterffy, ed., *Sacra Concilia Ecclesiae* I.234; *Constitutiones synodales ecclesiae Vesprimiensis anni MDXV—A veszprémi egyház 1515. évi zsinati határozatai*, ed. László Solymosi (Budapest 1997) 79; cf. Alexander Szentirmai, 'Das Recht der Erzdechanten (Archidiakone) in Ungarn während des Mittelalters', ZRG Kan. Abt. 43 (1957) 132–201 at 186–187.

119. See Bónis, *Szentszéki regeszták* no. 3679.

120. See Iacobus Sbrozzi, *Tractatus de vicario episcopi, officio eius, et potestate constituenda, exercenda, et finienda* (Venetiis 1592) Lib. II, q. 66, § 1–2, fol. 81ra: 'an vicarius Generalis episcopi possit constituere alium vicarium generalem? Respondeo, regulariter non posse'.

121. See ibid. Lib. II, q. 66, § 15, fol. 81vb.

122. Ibid. §§ 21–22, fol. 82rb.

123. See Körmendy, *Studentes* 185. On the special role of the circle of canonists having studied at Padua at the Council of Constance, see Dieter Girgensohn, 'Studenti e tradizione delle opere di Francesco Zabarella nell'Europa Centrale', *Studenti, università, città nella storia padovana: Atti del*

Monastic leaders of higher rank (superiores maiores) and also monastic chapters carried out jurisdictional functions over members of the monastic order and at times over others as well. In these cases the secular jurisdiction of the landlord (manorial court) was connected to or mixed with the functions of ecclesiastical jurisdictional practice.[124]

The vicarial court (officialate court) did not spread uniformly throughout the entire country as the normative institution of jurisdiction, according to the documents that survive. In the first half of the fourteenth century, court records, for example in Esztergom and Győr, were still composed predominantly—but not exclusively—in the name of the bishop (or archbishop, respectively),[125] while in Eger the vicar general was already identified as the issuing authority. In the first decades of the fourteenth century the episcopal judge was often also described as the 'viceiudex et cancellarius', the 'iudex et cancellarius', the 'yconomus', or the 'vicesgerens'.[126] In the fifteenth century the judge was the 'vicarius in spiritualibus', often called the 'vicarius in spiritualibus et causarum auditor generalis' in diplomas.[127] This twofold title is an indication that administration and jurisprudence could be clearly distinguished in Hungary as well. In modern times the vicar general was also called the 'officialis'. Still, in Hungary this title did not apply to the vicar general's office as judge, but to his administrative activities. It is in this sense that Paul Khlósz writes on the archbishops of Esztergom:

They sometimes established a single person in their own place in the diocese of Esztergom to whom they committed both voluntary and necessary jurisdiction, and he was called the 'vicarius in spiritualibus' as well as 'causarum auditor generalis'. Sometimes, however, two distinct persons received the spiritual care and the governance of this diocese, so that one was called the 'officialis seu vicarius

---

convegno Padova 6–8 febbraio 1998, ed. Francesco Piovan and Luciana Sitran Rea (Contributi alla storia dell'Università di Padova 34; Trieste 2001) 127–176; Ansgar Frenken, 'Die Rolle der Kanonisten auf dem Konstanzer Konzil: Personen, Aktivitäten, Prozesse', Sacri canones 398–417 at 401–403 (Polish canonists who had studied at Padua and were at the Council of Constance).

124. See Bónis, Szentszéki regeszták no. 3647.

125. See for example Bónis, Szentszéki regeszták nos. 653 and 693 (for 1313 and 1318, Esztergom, archbishop), 729 (for 1322, Esztergom, vicar), 797 (for 1328, Esztergom, 'in spiritualibus vicarius generalis... cuius cognitioni universe cause nostro examini producte subiacent').

126. See Bónis, 'Entwicklung' 203; Bónis, Szentszéki regeszták nos. 545 (for 1300, Eger, viceiudex), 667 (for 1313–1321, Eger, 'vicecomes'), 687 (for 1317, Eger, 'iudex et cancellarius').

127. See Alexander Szentirmai, 'Die ungarische Diözesankurie im Spätmittelalter', ZRG Kan. Abt. 48 (1962) 164–221 at 206. In contrast to German customs, in Salzburg it was usually the vicar general who took the post of official as well; in most cases these two functions were entrusted to the dean of the cathedral, who bore the title 'decanus et iudex' and later 'vicarius in spiritualibus generalis [ecclesie] et officialis curie Salczburgensis'; see Hans Paarhammer, Rechtsprechung und Verwaltung des Salzburger Officialates. 1300–1569 (Dissertationen der Universität Salzburg 8; Wien 1977) 7, 28; Balogh, Középkori bajor 113–114.

in spiritualibus generalis', and the other, to whom the trying of disputes in court was granted, was called the 'causarum auditor generalis'.[128]

There were no regional 'officiales' in Hungary, but in the archdiocese of Esztergom (and in the exempt territories subject to this archbishop and primate), as well as in the dioceses of Alba Julia (Karlsburg, Gyulafehérvár) and Zagreb (Agram, Zágráb) there were other permanent courts, which corresponded to some degree to the regional 'officialis'; they were erected for autonomous populations or as a result of special historical circumstances. No diocese was completely subdivided into regional vicariates. In the archdiocese of Esztergom the prior of Bratislava (Pressburg, Pozsony) held a special position, since he was 'officialis' and vicar general 'tam in foro contensioso, quam conscientiae' of the archbishop of Esztergom since 1469. He was competent for the priorate or archidiaconate of Bratislava, respectively. The prior named his own vicar, who led the court.[129] The competence of the vicar general of Bratislava is strikingly similar to the situation of the 'officialis generalis' of Warsaw, though with the distinction that the 'officialis' of Warsaw was not always the prior of the collegiate church there, although this vicariate was more or less tied with that collegiate church. Another vicar general of the archbishop of Esztergom was the prior of the collegiate chapter of Spišska Kapitula (Zips, Szepeshely). He was 'tamquam vicarius in ipsa Ecclesia scepusiensi in spiritualibus' of the archbishop of Esztergom.[130] The prior named his vicar himself, who led the court of Spišska Kapitula.[131] The 'canonica visitatio' of 1629 established, 'utraque iurisdictione, tam fori iudicialis, seu contentiosa, quam voluntaria praepositos praedictos usos fuisse'.[132] The geographical boundaries of the prior's jurisdiction[133] confirm that this was essentially a structure to guarantee the autonomy of the Saxons in Spiš (Zips).[134] At times of vacancy of the post of prior, the chapter itself chose the vicar for the judge's function.[135] These vicars asked the advice of canons and other wise (lay)men when deciding

128. Paulus Khlósz, *Praxis seu forma processualis fori spiritualis, in Mariano-Apostolico Hungariae Regno usu recepta* (2nd ed. Tyrnaviae 1794) 18–19. The separation of the posts of vicar general and diocesan judge cannot be documented until the end of the Middle Ages in Hungary.

129. See Erdő, 'Ungarn' 138.

130. See the letter of Archbishop Nikolaus Oláh of June 1, 1560; Carolus Wagner, *Analecta Scepusii sacri et prophani* (4 vols. Vienna-Posonii-Cassoviae 1773–1778) 1.380–382.

131. See Wagner, *Analecta* 1.374–375; see Bónis, *Szentszéki regeszták* no. 2431 (for 1436).

132. See Wagner, *Analecta* 2.283

133. See ibid. 2.283–284; Ortvay, *Geographia* 1.53–57.

134. On the history of the priorate, see Márton Pirhala, *A szepesi prépostság vázlatos története kezdetétől a püspökség felállításáig* (Lőcse 1899).

135. See Bónis, *Szentszéki regeszták* nos. 2431 (for 1436, vicar of provost in office), 2122 (for 1419, 'canonicus vicariusque loci eiusdem electus per capitulum in spiritualibus generalis'), and 2396 (for 1434).

on judgments;[136] which also happened at other ecclesiastical jurisdictions in Hungary, but the peculiar circumstance concerning civil affairs was that here the Zipser Willkür was of legal force.[137] The Saxons in Transylvania, far from Esztergom, also had their own ecclesiastical courts. Their region was exempt and subject to the archbishop alone. 'As early as 1295 the diaconate of Braşov (Kronstadt, Brassó) stood directly under the archbishop of Esztergom, who issued orders to all the pastors of Sibiu (Hermannstadt, Nagyszeben) and Braşov in spiritual matters'.[138] Georg Daniel Teutsch remarked on the two ecclesiastical courts of the Transylvanian Saxons, 'In ecclesiastical life each individual community constituted a chapter, certainly already at the time of original immigration. In this chapter the pastors freely elected a deacon as their head, who headed the ecclesiastical administration in many matters as the bishop did elsewhere, and independently of the bishop'.[139]

The rise of the sole independent 'regional vicariate' of the diocese of Alba Julia might be due to geographical position. In the fourteenth and fifteenth centuries, the 'vicarius de extra Mezes' of that Transylvanian bishop decided the legal disputes of the portion of the diocese lying in the great plain. According to the rules, this office was overseen by the pastor of Satu Mare (Szatmár, Szatmárnémeti) or of Tăşnad (Tasnád).[140] The diocese of Zagreb also had a priorate (Čazma, Csázma), which was combined with a vicariate court. The prior of Čazma resided in Zagreb as a member

---

136. Ibid. nos. 2122 and 2396.

137. See Béla Szabó, 'A szepesi jog forrásai', *Jogtörténeti tanulmányok* (Pécs 2005) 8.443–463.

138. See Georg Daniel Teutsch, *Geschichte der Siebenbürger Sachsen,* ed. and rev. Friedrich Teutsch (4 vols. 4th ed. Hermannstadt 1899–1926) 1.87. The archbishop of Esztergom had already permitted in 1264 the deacon of Sibiu to start legal proceedings as court of first instance in the territory of the deanary; see Bónis, *Szentszéki regeszták* no. 379; the deacon of Sibiu later used the title 'decanus Cibiniensis locique dicti in spiritualibus causarum auditor generalis'; ibid. no. 4323; see nos. 4325, 4343, 4350, 4363–4365, 4367. Similar rights were given by the archbishop of Esztergom to the deacon of Braşov. These rights were renewed at times by the archbishop; see ibid. nos. 2136–2167 (for 1420, the vicar of the chapter of Esztergom gives the power of chastisement and absolution for a year to the deacon of Sibiu and Braşov), 4355 (for 1525: 'Nos… damus et concedimus tibi auctoritatem omnes et singulas causas civiles et criminales, ad forum nostrum ecclesiasticum in et sub dicto decanatu Brassoviensi spectantes audiendi, cognoscendi et fine debito terminandi, sententiasque per te in eisdem latas exequendi… et gerendi, que alias decanis Brassoviensibus concedi a sede et ecclesia nostra Strigoniensi consueta fuerunt'). The Saxons of Transylvania had their own professionals who had been qualified at foreign universities; see for example Maja Philippi, 'Kronstädter und Burzenländer Studenten an der Wiener Universität 1382–1525', *Beiträge zur Geschichte von Kronstadt in Siebenbürgen,* ed. Paul Philippi (Siebenbürgisches Archiv 17; Köln-Wien 1984) 179–224. The experience of the independent jurisdiction of the two deanaries had its effect still in 1870 during the reorganization of ecclesiastical jurisdiction of the local Lutheran Church; see Paul Philippi, *Land des Segens? Fragen an die Geschichte Siebenbürgens und seiner Sachsen* (Siebenbürgisches Archiv 3.39; Köln 2008) 297 n. 7.

139. Teutsch, *Geschichte* 42.

140. Bónis, 'Entwicklung' 204; cf. János Karácsonyi, 'Az erdélyi püspökség Erdélyen kívül eső föesperestségei', *Batthyáneum* 1 (1911) 38–46.

of the chapter there. The judge of the consistory was the 'locumtenens' of the prior.[141] The Benedictine abbey of Pannonhalma (Abbatia S. Martini) lay outside the diocese of Esztergom and was independent of the jurisdiction of the archbishop of Esztergom. It had its own territory (area of jurisdiction) and, like the bishops, its own consistory.[142] Written relics of its medieval functioning relate chiefly to monastic jurisdition.[143] This was not a regional officialate. Even in the archdiocese of Kalocsa, where there were two vicariates general (Kalocsa and Bács), these were not regional officialates; rather, for specific historical reasons, there coexisted two seats of the archbishop with two cathedral chapters, which together elected the archbishop. Both vicars could try cases of the second instance from suffragan bishops.[144]

In times of vacancy of the episcopal see the provisional governor or administrator appointed a vicar to try and decide law cases. For example, in 1409 the diocese of Pécs was temporarily led by the bishop of Zagreb (as 'gubernator'). He mandated that the chapter should choose a vicar for judge's function and appointed the chosen person accordingly.[145] In 1442 in Esztergom, an administrator was leading the archdiocese. His vicar was Matheus de Vicedominis (Matteo Vicedominisi da Piacenza), a 'Doctor decretorum'[146] who had been the vicar general earlier there.[147]

The medieval sources do not answer the question whether there was a separate jurisdiction for Eastern Rite Catholics in Hungary. However, Pope Leo X gave allowance, even prescribed on May 16, 1521, that in those dioceses where Greeks (Greek Rite Catholics) lived besides Latins, but where there was only a Latin bishop, the Latin bishop had the authority to nominate a Greek vicar freely or after election to decide the cases that involved Greeks. He had also obligated the metropolitans to appoint a Greek judge for the appeals in such cases.[148] A written document from

---

141. See Erdő, 'Ungarn' 158.

142. See *A pannonhalmi Szent Benedek Rend története*, ed. László Erdélyi and Pongrác Sörös (12 vols. Budapest 1902–1916) 4.168–175.

143. See Bónis, *Szentszéki regeszták* no. 3988, also 3925, 4198–4199.

144. See Menyhért Érdújhelyi, *A kalocsai érsekség a renaissance-korban* (Zenta 1899) 166–194; Tamás Bogyay, 'Kalocsa', LThK 5.1264; Erdő, 'Ungarn' 151–152; Bónis, *Szentszéki regeszták* nos. 3698 (for 1495, 'A predecessoribus nostris episcopis olim fuisse distinctas parochias pertinentiarum, que ad vicariatum Bachiensem, que item ad vicariatum Colocensem pertinere debeant. Eam igitur distinctionem nos nequaquam volumus pervertere'), 4148 (appeal from the vicar of the bishop of Transylvania to the vicar of Bács), 4353 (for 1525, appeal from the locumtenens of the provost of Časma to the vicar of the archbishop of Kalocsa in Bács).

145. Bónis, *Szentszéki regeszták* no. 1883.

146. Ibid. no. 2188.

147. Ibid. no. 1675 (for 1399) and passim; see Körmendy, *Studentes* 182 no. 58.

148. Bónis, *Szentszéki regeszták* no. 4290: 'episcopus circa negotia et causas dictorum Grecorum, vicarium Grecum ipsis Grecis gratum, vel per ipsos Grecos eligendum... deputare,

1525 survived, however: it was about a case being heard by the vicar general of Esztergom (Latin) where the respondents were Greeks.[149]

The jurisdictional competence of ecclesiastical courts in Hungary was unitary.[150] In the fourteenth century this competence was only regulated by custom. In the course of the fifteenth century a series of secular laws enumerated the competences of ecclesiastical courts. Ecclesiastical courts were granted jurisdiction over (1) matters related to the sacraments; (2) questions of belief and heresy; (3) testaments; (4) marital cases and related issues, particularly claims for dowry, paraphernal property, and daughter's quarter, as well as 'donationes propter nuptias'; (5) conflicts concerning tithes on property and persons, with their related isses; (6) usury; (7) matters concerning widows and the poor, excepting property questions; (8) violation of oaths and perjury (in other words, complaints concerning contracts confirmed by oath); (9) any case which resulted in the use of the ecclesiastical sanction 'hominis vel canonum' (including deeds 'of violence, the shedding of blood and the injury or plundering of clerics and women').[151] According to Article 14 of the royal law of 15 April 1405, the 'specialis presentia' of the king was to rule on conflicts of jurisdiction between ecclesiastical and secular judges.[152]

At the beginning of the fifteenth century, secular authority tried to siphon off most of the cases from the ecclesiastical jurisdictions. Antipope John XXIII had remitted many cases to lay courts that belonged to ecclesiastical jurisdictions previously. However, the Council of Constance in its decision of July 1, 1415, addressed to the archbishop of Esztergom and to the bishops of Hungary, recalled the antipope's decision.[153] At the beginning of the fifteenth century, royal mandates of transfer were sent to ecclesiastical judges, usually on the grounds that the trial concerned real

---

quodque in causis appellationis ad metropolitanum… dictus metropolitanus similiter in dictis causis iudicem Grecum deputare teneatur'; ed. János Török, *Magyarország prímása. Közjogi és történeti vázlat* (2 vols. Pest 1859) 2.94.

149. See Erdő, "Das älteste Protokollbuch," 79 (= Erdő, *Kirchenrecht* 110): 'Domine Agathe contra Grecos'.

150. For a general view, see Szentirmai, 'Diözesankurie' 200–206.

151. Bónis, 'Entwicklung' 224–225.

152. Ibid. Bónis, 'Az egyházi és világi jog határai a középkorban', *Eszmetörténeti tanulmányok a magyar középtkorról*, ed. György Székely (Memoria Saeculorum Hungariae 4; Budapest 1984) 235–241.

153. Bónis, *Szentszéki regeszták* no. 2027: 'in eodem Regno Hungarie… dotium et rerum paraphrenalium, quarte puellaris, testamentorum, iniuriarum sexus feminei ac quedam alie cause miserabilium personarum dumtaxat pertinere consueverint et pertinerent ad cognitionem iudicum ecclesiasticorum, saltem de consuetudine similiter legitime prescripta, tamen dictus Balthasar tunc papa voluit et concessit, quod omnes ille cause non per ecclesiasticos, ut prius fieri consuevit, sed de cetero per laicos iudices deberent terminari et decidi'. Josephus Nicolaus Kovachich, *Monumenta veteris legislationis Hungaricae, quae nunc primum detecta* (Claudiopoli 1815) 2.14.

or even movable property. Often the grounds or pretext for a mandate of transfer was that the ecclesiastical judge was 'suspectus'. In other cases the royal command was motivated by the privileges of royal free or mining towns. The towns attempted to limit the jurisdiction of consistories in cases involving testaments and even resorted to violence to do so. In these towns only pious bequests remained reserved to the ecclesiastical court. As a rule, clerics conceded to these royal commands, but often they set such mandates aside (through the middle of the fifteenth century), or obeyed them only with a reservation ('de foro meo esse credo, salvis constitutionibus ecclesiae', etc.).[154] Toward the end of the fifteenth century the custom spread of commencing all legal disputes of the urban population before the civil magistracy. Only once the case was declared to be ecclesiastic in that court was one allowed to turn to the consistory. King Matthias Corvinus sanctioned this custom through an act of his own.[155]

On the basis of the surviving documents, it can be inferred that cases concerning matrimony (suits concerning recognition as marital partners, establishment of the legitimacy of a marriage, cases concerning betrothal, nullification of marriage and separation) were relatively rare (3 to 5 percent of all court cases). In contrast, property cases arising from marriage (claims for dowry, paraphernalia and daughter's quarter, or donationes propter nuptias) made up the majority of all cases. This percentage applies to the entire country.[156] There was also frequent litigation before ecclesiastical judges concerning tithes, benefices, ecclesiastical property, and testaments.[157] So it happened that marital cases in the strict sense were relatively less frequent in Hungary than in Poland. The cause could have been the more limited competence of Polish ecclesiastical courts, for example, in matters of inheritance. Still, as mentioned above, Hungarian consistory courts had also lost a great deal of their jurisdictional authority in the course of the fifteenth century.

It was a peculiarity of the ecclesiastical court in Esztergom that the archbishop, as primate of Hungary, was entitled to try any ecclesiasti-

---

154. Bónis, 'Entwicklung' 227–229. Concerning the jurisdiction of church courts at the beginning of the sixteenth century, see, for example, *Constitutiones synodales ecclesiae Vesprimiensis anni MDXV*, ed. Solymosi, 94: 'statuitur et etiam de iure est statutum, ne quis de testamentis, dotaliciis, quartis puellaribus et rebus paraphrenalibus et aliis causis ecclesiasticis vel nisi talis casus comprehendatur in Bulla Coena Domini, cognoscere vel iudicare praesumat sine speciali licentia sui episcopi vel eius vicarii'.

155. See, for example, Martinus Georgius Kovachich, *Formulae sollennes styli in cancellaria, curiaque regum, foris minoribus ac locis credibilibus, authenticisque Regni Hungariae olim usitati* (Pesthini 1799) 212 (for 1481).

156. See Péter Erdő, 'Eheprozesse im mittelalterlichen Ungarn', ZRG Kan. Abt. 72 (1986) 250–276. Archdeacons also dealt extensively with such cases; see Szentirmai, 'Erzdechanten' 188.

157. See Erdő, 'Ungarn' 131–135.

cal case in the country as a court of first instance, and to receive appeals against the decisions of any ecclesiastical judge in the country. Although this privilege was documented in the later Middle Ages (1451, 1513),[158] there is no separate series of documents for the primatial court before 1563.[159] However, there are many examples that the archbishop of Esztergom delegated a judge for particular cases who could take over the case even in situations when the litigation was conducted by the vicar himself.[160] However, this happened in other dioceses as well.[161]

Hungarian vicarial courts applied the standard norms of canonical procedure. There were, however, some peculiarities: advocates assisted in the composition of the sentence, despite the fact that this was forbidden by secular law (Art. 35, 1500). The fiscal attorney (officii instigator, procurator fiscalis, procurator officii ecclesiae) appears as early as the fifteenth century, but he is only found routinely at the beginning of the sixteenth century. He also had the responsibility to act as plaintiff against those who injured the privileges or property of the church. This institution could give rise to abuse: the vicar could hardly be impartial in cases concerning his own church.[162] As early as the start of the fifteenth century, the vicar called upon secular nobles to consult on the rights of women. Such matters were decided together with assessors, including experts on the local customary law.[163] Later this tradition vanished, since cases with a secular ramifications were increasingly drawn to secular courts. Mixed courts survived longest in local vicariates (Spišska Kapitula, Tăşnad) as well as in the lowest courts (archdeacons, vice-archdeacons).[164] It was a further peculiarity that the vicars

158. Pope Leo X gave extended jurisdictional privileges to cardinal Tamás Bakócz, archbishop of Esztergom, primate of Hungary and 'legatus a latere' (July 18, 1513): 'ecclesiales ac spirituales ac prophanas causas quaslibet ad forum ecclesiasticum quomodolibet pertinentes, tam in prima instantia, quam prime et aliarum appellationum quarumlibet, a quibuscumque iudicibus ordinariis legatis et delegatis, etiam per nos et sedem apostolicam deputatis… per te vel per alium seu alios audiendi, cognoscendi et fine debito terminandi… concedimus facultatem'; Theiner, *Vetera monumenta historica Hungariam* 2.595.

159. See Alexander Szentirmai, 'The Primate of Hungary', *The Jurist* 20 (1961) 27–46, 36–37; Péter Erdő, 'Il potere giudiziario del Primate d'Ungheria', *Apollinaris* 53 (1980) 272–292, 54 (1981) 213–231; Erdő, 'Das Primatialgericht von Esztergom-Budapest', *De processibus matrimonialibus* 6 (1999) 39–53; cf. Bónis, *Szentszéki regeszták* no. 4141 (Leo X, May 6, 1513); 4143 (Leo X, July 18, 1513); Theiner, ed., *Vetera monumenta historica Hungariam* 2.597.

160. For example Bónis, *Szentszéki regeszták* no. 2787 (for 1454).

161. Bónis, 'Entwicklung' 222 n. 188.

162. See ibid.

163. Thus, for example, *Codex diplomaticus domus senioris comitum Zichy*, ed. Imre Nagy, Iván Nagy, Dezső Véghely, Ernő Kammerer, and Pál Lukcsics (12 vols. Budapest 1871–1931) 12.94 (for 1414); Bónis, *Szentszéki regeszták* no. 1972. The vicar of Oradea in 1414 transcribed a decision of the palatine from 1399 ('una cum nostris coassessoribus utriusque status, ecclesie videlicet et secularis, de lege et consuetudine regni expertis deliberantes'); ibid., no. 1970 (for 1414, the vicar of Eger decided together with 'honest noblemen').

164. See Bónis, 'Entwicklung' 222–223.

used some forms of Hungarian law, for instance, in estimating monetary fines, punishing false prosecution, and (even at the start of the fifteenth century) in overseeing oaths of purgation with numerous oath-helpers.[165] In the general law of the church, 'divorce' was not possible, not even in time of war, neither due to enslavement subsequent to marriage nor in the case of captivity. It is a symptom of the spread of an abuse when Leo X imposed strict sanctions against these very practices in his constitution *Sacrosanctae universalis ecclesiae* of August 9, 1515,[166] specifying that these types of divorce were common in Czech lands, Poland, and Hungary.[167]

Notaries took part in ecclesiastical litigations in Hungary as well, and particular documents in proof were made by imperial notaries.[168] The right of appointing notaries belonged to the pope or to the emperor of the Holy Roman Empire, but 'this right was usually wielded by the ecclesiastical leaders of the countries'.[169] The scriveners of the chapters often had the notary functions as well.[170] The decrees of the vicar were countersigned by papal or imperial notaries. Since the fifteenth century we can also find permanent papal or imperial notaries[171] working in ecclesiastical courts of the vicar.[172] Often, the notaries were people having studied at foreign universities who, after working for a while beside the vicar, became members of the chapter, or even vicars themselves. The prestige of the position of the notary is shown by the fact that some of them worked as notaries having prebendal benefices.[173] Notaries in ecclesiastical courts could work as attorneys (procuratores) too.[174]

Hungarian judicial 'libelli' of vicars—as it is proved by a number of documents enduring through the centuries—were stamped by the special seal of the vicar's office, occasionally though only by the vicar's private seal.[175]

165. Ibid.

166. Ed. Theiner, *Vetera monumenta historica Hungariam* 2.629.

167. Cf. Erdő, 'Eheprozesse' 268–269.

168. See Bónis, *Szentszéki regeszták*, nos. 1858 (for 1408), 3653–3654, 3661, 3662 (a priest of the diocese of Eger, vicecomes of the Lateran Palace, was a papal and imperial notary), 4149 (for 1514). Pontifical notaries: ibid. nos. 3930, 4192, 4202; Bónis, 'A sasadi tizedper közjegyzői a XV. század derekán', *Levéltári közlemények* 42 (1971) 102–113.

169. *Monumenta Ecclesiae Strigoniensis*, ed. Crescens Lajos Dedek et al. (Esztergom 1874–1999) 3.532–533; Körmendy, 'A jogtudó' 214–215.

170. Körmendy, *Studentes* 112.

171. See Zoltán Kovách, *Az esztergomi Főszékesegyházi Könyvtár története a 11. századtól 1821-ig* (Budapest 2006) 13.

172. Bónis, 'Entwicklung' 221 n. 195 (for 1438, Esztergom 'Consistorii Strigoniensis causarum scriba et notarius').

173. Körmendy, *Studentes* 112.

174. Ibid.

175. Bónis, *Szentszéki regeszták* no. 1755 (for 1401, Eger 'propter carentiam sigilli nostri vicariatus sigillo Johannis lectoris et canonici dicte ecclesie Agriensis vices nostras gerentis fecimus consignari'); 4311 (for 1513, 'VICARIATUS STRIGONIENSIS'). For medieval Hungarian seals of

The place in which ecclesiastical cases were heard was usually the dwelling of the vicar or of the head of the court[176] or a place belonging to the cathedral (porticus ecclesie Strigoniensis).[177]

Written Sources of Court Activities

The activities of ecclesiastical courts are preserved by various types of documents. The most important of these are the 'ordines iudiciarii' used by the courts themselves; the protocol books kept on trials;[178] the formularies; the individual acts or charters, which are particularly important for Hungary because of the lack of protocol books; and some chapter statutes or synodical statutes, which might also contain prescriptions on the activities of the officialates. These last varieties, however, already belong more to literary genres that are not primarily oriented to courts.

Court Ordinances

The ecclesiastical courts of these countries made use primarily of foreign 'ordines iudiciarii'. However, in Poland, particularly in the sixteenth century and after, works of this sort by native authors were also circulated. In Poland the following works were printed:[179]

Johannes Urbach, *Processus iudiciarius eximij Doctoris iuris canonici Johannes de Urbach,* Impressum Cracouie per Florianum Vnglerium [circa 1516], 4°, 56 leaves.

Grzegorz Szamotulski, *Processus Juris Breuior Joannis Andr. per Gregorium Shamotulanu[m] Juris pontificii doctore[m] pro tyrunculis resolutus cum practica exemplari in Regno Poloniae circa Strepitum fori spiritualis observari solita* [no place, no date], 83 leaves.[180]

Grzegorz Szamotulski, *Processus Juris breuior Joa[n]nis Andr. [...] denuo*

---

vicars' office see Bernát Lajos Kumorovitz, *A magyar pecséthasználat története a középkorban* (2nd ed. Budapest 1993) pictures 24, 25, 31, 34; cf. Bónis, 'Entwicklung' 221 n. 186.

176. See for example Bónis, *Szentszéki regeszták* nos. 1799 (for 1403, in the room of cardinal Valentinus, administrator of the diocese of Pécs); 3989 (for 1505–1506, Esztergom, the lodging of the vicar); 4017 (for 1507, Veszprém, in the house of Caspar de Nagoch *substitutus vicarius*); see Erdő, 'Das älteste Protokollbuch' 79 (= Erdő, *Kirchenrecht* 109), for January 2, 1525: 'dominus demetrius episcopus iudex in domo solito residens sedet pro tribunali'.

177. See Bónis, *Szentszéki regeszták* nos. 3989, 4015, 4292 and Deimling's chapter above passim.

178. See Pennington, 'Jurisprudence of Procedure' above.

179. Concerning a formulary preserved in manuscript, see, for example, Adam Vetulani, 'Gnieźnieński rękopis formularza Martina de Ebulo', *Prawo Kanoniczne* 4 (1961) 211–222. For a general discussion of the 'ordines iudiciarii', see Fowler-Magerl, 'Ordines'. For other records of church courts in Poland (for example, *acta consistorialia*) see Skierska, 'Źródła' 173–195.

180. See *Polska bibliografia prawa kanonicznego od wynalezienia druku do 1940 R.,* vol. 1: *Od wynaleziena druku do 1799. R.* (Lublin 1960) 213 no. 1795.

iterum reuisus et auctus, Impressum Cracouiae per Florianu Vnglerium Anno 1531, 95 leaves.

Grzegorz Szamotulski, *Processus Juris Brevior Joannis Andr.* [...] *tertio iterum reuisus et auctus,* Cracouiae ex Officina Vngleriana Anno Dni M.D.XXXVII. 124 leaves.[181]

For the distribution of manuscript literature of procedural law in Poland, one must refer to the extensive manuscript catalogs of Polish libraries. It is worth mentioning that there are a number of copies in Polish libraries of the manuscript *Processus iudiciarius secundum stilum Pragensem* by Nicholas Puchník. These were in use and copied for local use mainly during the Middle Ages in the same region.[182] The prevalence of the more extensive work beginning with 'Circa processum iudiciarium in causis delegatis', which is also related to Prague—the so-called Prague 'ordo iudiciarius'—was also significant, especially in Silesia. Title labels and colophons in certain manuscripts prove its use in Wrocław[183] and elsewhere in Poland, too.[184] Nicolaus de Schweidnitz is generally considered its author.[185]

In Hungary use was made of adapted foreign 'ordines iudiciarii'. Canonical works of other genres were also copied for use in Hungary.[186] For

181. This work also appeared in Venice in 1573 (*Polska bibliografia* 1.213 no. 1798). The first edition mentioned above is from 1524; see Schulte, *Geschichte* 3.768.

182. See Kraków, Biblioteka Jagiellońska 326, fol. 119r–126v; Wrocław, Ossolineum 1628/1 fol. 86r–95v; Wrocław, Biblioteka Uniwersytecka U.II.O.1, fol. 215r–243v; Gdańsk, Biblioteka Polskiej Akademii Nauk Mar.F.30, fol. 292v–296v; Gdańsk, Biblioteka Polskiej Akademii Nauk Mar.F.294, fol. 266v–273r; see Dominik Budský, 'Processus iudiciarius secundum stilum Pragensem Mikuláše Puchníka (Rozbor dochovanych rukopisů)', *Studie o rukopisech* 39 (2009 [2010]) 255–277, 258–259, 262–263, 268–270 and Budský, 'Nicholas Puchnik, a Portrait of a Medieval Canonist', BMCL 30 (2013) 123–140.

183. Gyula Gábor, 'Adatok a középkori magyar könyvírás történetéhez', *Magyar Könyvszemle* 20 (1912) 302–315 at 313; Leipzig, BU 922, fol. 100–145v; Leipzig, BU 933, fol. 2–62, fol. 2: title lines: 'Incipit processus iudiciarius novus per Johannem Schusseler Wratislaviensem prage pronunciatus', which is a false attribution; see Rudolf Helssig, *Die lateinischen und deutschen Handschriften der Universitätsbibliothek Leipzig 3. Die juristischen Handschriften* (Leipzig 1905, reprinted Wiesbaden 1996) 59; Leipzig, BU 938, fol. 60–111, on fol. 60: title line 'Processus iudiciarius consistorii wrat(islaviensis)'. In the same codex, copied by the same hand, there is a collection of formulae as well, fol. 1–59v, fol. 1: title line 'Summa sive formularius curie episcopalis quo utuntur Officiales pragenses Wratzlavienses Olomucenses et ceteri iuxta ritum et consuetudinem notariorum in spiritualibus'; see Helssig, *Die lateinischen und deutschen Handschriften* 66.

184. For example in Plock: 'Liber formularum... ' *Jacobi de Kurdwanów,* ed. Ulanowski 1–362; Płock, Biblioteka Kapituly H.19, fol. 201–215 (the ordo iudiciarius 'Circa processum iudiciarium in causis delegatis').

185. Augsburg, SB 2° Cod 312, fol. 198ra–216vb, fol. 216vb; see Wolf Gehrt, *Handschriftenkataloge der Staats- und Stadtbibliothek Augsburg 4. Die Handschriften 2° Cod 251–400e* (Wiesbaden 1989) 108; Karl Heiz Keller, *Kataloge der Universitätsbibliothek Eichstätt. Die mittelalterlichen Handschriften* (Wiesbaden 2004) 3.87 (Eichstätt BU Cod. st 490, fol. 8va–38vb, referring to Leipzig BU 922, fol. 100–145v and Leipzig BU 933); see Fowler-Magerl, 'Ordines' 71.

186. See for example: Gyula Gábor, 'Adatok a középkori magyar könyvírás történetéhez', *Magyar Könyvszemle* 18 (1910) 6–9, 'Johannes Occam, Directorium iuris,' Wien, ÖNB 2146; Kinga Körmendy, 'A középkori egyetemi oktatásával és a 15. századi esztergomi vikáriusok

example a number of works of canon law were copied or obtained for the Collegium Christi of Esztergom.[187] Thomas of Piestány, who became a 'Doctor decretorum' in Prague in 1402, copied the Prague 'ordo iudiciarius' in Esztergom and slightly reworked it, replacing the sigla P with S (hence in the place of Prague he put Strigonium-Esztergom).[188] Thomas of Piestány, King Sigismund's ambassador to King Ferdinand of Aragon in 1415 was vicarius generalis of Esztergom in 1423 and 1424.[189] In the same way, about 1420 the *Summa de processu iudicii* attributed to Johannes Andreae[190] was adapted to the usage of the diocese of Eger.[191] Interesting fragments of the *Speculum iudiciale* of Guilielmus Durantis also survive in Hungary,[192] just as fragments survive from another ordo iudiciarius possibly used in Hungary.[193] The version of Nicholas Puchník's *Processus Iudiciarius* of Prague that was used in Wrocław was copied by the Transylvanian Jacob Haas 'de Enydino Maiori' (Aiud, Nagyenyed) together with other works of canon law at Aiud.[194]

---

olvasmányaival, működésével kapcsolatos kéziratos források az esztergomi egyház 1543 előtti könyvállományában', *Tanulmányok a magyarországi* 157–188 at 178–179. Péter Erdő, 'Középkori kánonjogi kódextöredékek Esztergomban. Adalékok egy nyomtatott katalógushoz', *Tanulmányok a magyarországi* 69–74.

187. See Körmendy, 'A kánonjog' 179–183.

188. Gábor, 'Adatok' (1912) 308–313; Bónis, *Középkori* 27, 51 n. 48; Körmendy, *Studentes* 70; see also Göttingen, BU Luneb. 48, fol. 86–126; *Bibliotheca Hungarica. Kódexek és nyomtatott könyvek Magyarországon 1526 előtt*, ed. Csaba Csapodi and Klára Csapodiné Gárdonyi (3 vols. Magyar Tudományos Akadémia Könyvtárának Közleményei. Új sorozat 23, 31, 33; Budapest 1988, 1993, 1994) 3 no. 374 (data about lost works). The incipit of the work is 'Circa processum iudiciarium in causis delegatis', and its explicit reads, 'que Omnia habentur in spe. de app. qualiter autem' (Gábor, 'Adatok' [1912] 310). This refers to the work attributed to Nicolaus de Schweidnitz and not to Nicholas Puchník's *Processus iudiciarius*. See Theodor Muther, *Die Geschichte des römisch-canonischen Prozesses in Deutschland während des vierzehnten und zu Beginn des fünfzehnten Jahrhunderts* (Rostock 1872) 52–75.

189. See Körmendy, *Studentes* 70, 184–85, no. 68. On documents related to his activity as judge in the function of vicar general, see Bónis, *Szentszéki regeszták* nos. 2220, 2221, 2226, 2227.

190. See Schulte, *Geschichte* 2.225 (the work also survives in several manuscripts in Prague).

191. See Bónis, *Közepkori* 27; Gábor, 'Adatok' (1912) 314.

192. Budapest, Eötvös Loránd Tudományegyetem Könyvtára, U.Fr.1.m.102; see *Fragmenta latina condicum in Bibliotheca Universitatis Budapestinensis*, ed. László Mezei et al. (Fragmenta codicum in bibliothecis Hungariae 1¹; Budapest 1983) 114–115.

193. Budapest, Eötvös Loránd Tudományegyetem Könyvtára, U.Fr.1.m.103; see *Fragmenta*, 1¹.115; Péter Erdő, 'Codici manoscritti di diritto canonico e loro frammenti in Ungheria', *Apollinaris* 61 (1988) 341–354 at 349.

194. München, BU 8° Cod. 152, fol. 121v–163v, fol. 163v, cf. fol. 116r and 197r; Natalia Daniel, *Die lateinischen mittelalterlichen Handschriften der Universitätsbibliothek München: Die Handschriften aus der Oktavreihe* (Wiesbaden 1989) 128–129; see Budský, 'Processus Mikuláše Puchníka' 265. On the *Processus iudiciarius secundum stilum Pragensem*, see Miroslav Boháček, 'Processus iudiciarius secundum stilum Pragensem', *Akademiku Václavu Vojtíškovi k 75. narozeninám pracovníci Archivu ČSAV, Práce z Archivu ČSAV* (Prague 1958) 5–35; Budský, 'Processus iudiciarius' and Budský, 'Nicholas Puchnik'.

Formularies

The literary genre of the formulary book and the 'artes notariae' must be distinguished from one another.[195] Yet the titles of the various works as well as their inner structure hardly permit us to make an absolute division of these two categories.

We will consider several 'artes notariae', for example:

(1) The *Ars notaria* connected with the name of Johannes Uzsai. This work may be called the oldest significant formulary in Hungary.[196] It was written between 1346 and 1350. In it, besides secular formulas, there are formulas connected with ecclesiastical jurisdiction in the diocese of Eger (Erlau).[197]

(2) The Formulary of Bartholomew of Tapolcza. This ecclesiastical formula collection was composed at the University of Vienna in 1385. It contains the records of two marital trials related to Székesfehérvár (Stuhl-weissenburg).[198] Since the work has a very heterogeneous composition, no definitive conclusions can be drawn, either concerning the frequency of trial types presented as examples or concerning ecclesiastical jurisdiction in the country.[199]

The following formularies belong to a genre distinct from the work of Bartholomew of Topolcza. They are private collections of juridical procedure, composed within a court for its internal use. They are thus outstanding witnesses to the operation of courts. The oldest known formulary composed and used in Hungary is the work of Vagnolus de Mevania,[200] who composed his collection during the legation of Gentilis in Hungary, when Vagnolus was serving as a notary of the legate. However, this book contains no information about specifically Hungarian conditions.[201] A book of formulae written and printed abroad (*Formularium advocatorum et procuratorum Romanae curiae et Regii parlamenti* [Basel 1493]) and used in Hungary was the incunabulum in which a file of litigation was copied right after the colophon. This litigation was carried out in front of Tommaso Amadeo da

---

195. Guido van Dievoet, *Les coutumiers, les styles, les formulaires et les 'artes notariae'* (Typologie des sources du moyen âge occidental 48; Turnhout 1986) 75–77.

196. See G. Bónis, 'Uzsai János Ars Notariája', *Filológiai Közlöny* 6 (1961) 229–260.

197. Kovachich, ed., *Formulae* 1–154. The two known manuscripts (Vienna, ÖNB 3452; ÖNB 4276, fol. 104–139) witness to a structure differing from the cited edition; see Bónis, *Középkori* 30.

198. László Fejérpataky, ed., 'Tapolczai Bertalan oklevélformulái a XIV. szazadból' *Magyar Könyvszemle* 11 (1886) 44–66.

199. See Erdő, 'Eheprozesse' 252.

200. BAV lat. 4013.

201. See Bónis, *Középkori* 29.

Ferrara, vicarius generalis of Esztergom.[202] The following formularies, in contrast, are bound up with Hungarian ecclesiastical courts:

(1) The Formulary of Vitus Huendler (vicar of Pécs). The collection derives from the fifteenth century. The author had been *suffraganus in pontificalibus* in Pécs, Oradea (Grosswardein, Nagyvárad), Alba Julia, and Zagreb between 1448 and 1465. The work has only been partly published. [203]

(2) The Formulary of Johannes Magyi. The collection primarily reflects the practice of the ecclesiastical court of Eger in the period of Bishop Johannes Beckensloer. His documents on ecclesiastical jurisdiction derive from the years from 1468 to 1476.[204] The work contains about 500 formulas which are taken partly from the royal chancellery (nos. 1–58, from 1476), partly from the chapter of Buda (nos. 109–227, 300–359, from 1476–1480), from episcopal collections (nos. 256–299, 362–364, from 1468–1476), or are tied with municipal law, ecclesiastical courts or the activities of notaries (nos. 59–108; 228–255; 360–361, 365–458, from 1477–1493).[205] This formulary is a demonstration of the organic involvement of secular law (primarily Hungarian customary law) with canonical and municipal law.

(3) The Formulary of Matthew Beneéthy. This work documents the activities of the archiepiscopal vicar at Esztergom from 1500 to 1512.[206] It is unpublished.[207] Not considering the fragments, it contains 521 formulas, mostly from the period of service of the Esztergom vicar Tommaso Amadeo da Ferrara. Some texts in the collection derive from his successor, Demetrius of Nyás. Both vicars general were doctors of canon law.[208]

(4) The Formulary of Doctor Michael (vicar of Pécs). The work was composed at the start of the sixteenth century. It is unpublished. The sole manuscript is to be found in the Chapter Archive of Esztergom.[209]

202. Magyar Tudományos Akadémia Könyvtára, Kézirattár, Inc. 362; see Csapodi, Csapodiné 1–2, no. 738.

203. Josephus Koller, ed., *Historia Episcopatus Quinqueecclesiarum* (7 vols. Posonii-Pesthini 1782–1812) 4.246–359. The manuscript is Klosterneuburg, ML 941; see János Csontosi, 'Könyvárbúvárlatok Ausztriában', *Magyar Könyvszemle* 15 (1890) 38–39; Bónis, *Középkori* 43.

204. Kovachich, ed., *Formulae* 155–458; see György Bónis, 'Magyi János formuláskönyve és a gyakorlati jogtanítás', *Jubileumi Tanumányok*, I: *A pécsi egyetem történetéből*, ed. Andor Csizmadia (Pécs 1967) 232–233.

205. See Bónis, *Középkori* 153–155.

206. Ibid. 44–45; Bónis, 'Olasz'; Bónis, 'Un formulaire de l'officialité primatiale hongroise de 1512', *Recueil de Mémoires de la Société d'Histoire du Droit Écrit* 7 (1970) (= Mélanges Pierre Tisset) 31–40; Erdő, 'Eheprozesse' 252.

207. Manuscript: Alba Julia (Romania), Bibliotheca Batthyanyana, I.152; see Róbert Szentiványi, *Catalogus concinnus Librorum MSS Bibliothecae Batthyanyanae* (4th ed. Szeged 1958) no. 152. A number of its parts were published or reviewed by Bónis, *Szentszéki regeszták*: nos. 3817–3913, 3961, 3976, 3989, 3992, 3995, 4002, 4020, 4032–4033, 4036, 4044, 4048–4049, 4057, 4062, 4065–67, 4073, 4082–4094, 4099, 4105–4120, 4151, 4181, 4184.

208. See Bónis, *Középkori* 44; Körmendy, *Studentes* 107–108.

209. Esztergom, Főkáptalani Levéltár, Ladula 50, liber primus, pp. 1–70 and 112–85; it contains

(5) The Formulary of Demetrius of Nyás (vicar of Esztergom). This work can be seen as the second, expanded edition of the Formulary of Matthew Beneéthy. To Beneéthy's work it adds many documents (about 70) from 1511 to 1521. The collection is the most important ecclesiastical formulary of medieval Hungary. It is unpublished.[210]

There are texts related to the functioning of ecclesiastical courts in Hungarian civil formularies, for example in the so-called Werbőczy book of formulae, which is kept in the Cathedral Library of Esztergom.[211]

Of the formularies used in Poland, we shall mention a few which have appeared in modern printed editions:

(1) *Formulae ad ius canonicum spectantes, ex actis Petri Wysz, episcopi Cracoviensis (1392–1412) maxima parte depromptae.*[212]

(2) *Liber formularum ad ius canonicum spectantium, ex actis Jacobi de Kurdwanów, episcopi Plocensis, maxima parte depromptarum*[213] (end of the fourteenth and beginning of the fifteenth centuries).

(3) *Liber formularum ad ius polonicum necnon canonicum spectantium in codice Regiomontano asservatarum.*[214]

(4) Formulas connected to canon law can be found in the *Codex epistolaris saeculi decimi quinti. Ex antiquis libris formularum, Corpore Naruszeviciano autographis archivisque plurimis collectus.*[215]

---

court formulas of the officialate of Pécs (some of them dated, e.g. 1512, 1515, 1516). Concerning this formulary (with some published formulas), see Szentirmai, 'Diözesankurie' 209, 210–211, 215, 217; see Erdő, 'Ungarn' 149. A number of its parts were published or reviewed by Bónis, *Szentszéki regeszták*: nos. 4133, 4135, 4147, 4165, 4168–4169, 4183, 4186, 4188, 4193.

210. Manuscript, Esztergom, Főszékesegyházi Könyvtár II.507 ('Formularium secundum modum et stilum ecclesiae Strigoniensis'); see Bónis, *Középkori* 45. A number of its parts were published or reviewed by Bónis, *Szentszéki regeszták*: nos. 3976, 4015, 4020, 4033, 4036, 4048, 4062, 4065–4066, 4073, 4089–4092, 4104, 4106–4107, 4111–4121, 4146, 4151–4153, 4155, 4159, 4177, 4179, 4181–4182, 4184, 4201, 4225, 4230, 4248–4249, 4251, 4254, 4256, 4258–4261, 4263–4265, 4269–4270, 4275, 4280, 4283, 4288, 4292–4294, 4296–4297.

211. Esztergom, Főszékesegyházi Könyvtár II, 521; see Kovách 52, no. 16; Ferenc Eckhart, 'Formuláskönyv Werbőczy István hivatali működése köréből', in *Emlékkönyv dr. viski Illés József ny. r. egyetemi tanár tanári működésének negyvenedik évfordulójára*, ed. Ferenc Eckhart and Alajos Degré (Budapest 1942) 151–160. For church-related parts, see Bónis, *Szentszéki regeszták* nos. 4156–4157.

212. Ed. Bolesław Ulanowski, *Archiwum Komisji Historycznej* 5 (1889) 265–358.

213. Ed. Bolesław Ulanowski, *Archiwum Komisji Prawniczej* 1 (1895) 1–36 (separately printed Kraków 1893); reviewed by Władysław Abraham, *Kwartalnik Historyczny* 7 (1893) 340–341; see Walenty Wójcik, 'Uprawnienia oficjałów okręgowych w Sandomierzu w sprawach małżeńskich', *Roczniki Teologiczno-Kanoniczne* 8, no. 4 (1961) 77–100 at 84.

214. Ed. Bolesław Ulanowski, *Archiwum Komisji Prawniczej* 1 (1895) 169–256.

215. August Sokołowski and Józef Szujski, eds., *Codex epistolaris saeculi decimi quinti: Ex antiquis libris formularum, Corpore Naruszeviciano autographis plurimis collectus* (Monumenta medii aevi historica 2; Kraków 1876).

There was also a close connection in respect of usage of formularies among Silesia, Bohemia, and some parts of Germany.[216] Works written or used in this region infuenced ecclesiastical judicial practice in other regions of Poland and even in Hungary.[217] The history of the formulary collection of Ferdinand Palacios, bishop of Lugo, legate in Hungary from 1419 to 1423, permits one to discern a particular tie between the jurisdiction of papal legates and court practice in Hungary and Poland. The formulas probably deal with the judicial activities of the legate in Hungary, but the collection ended up in Kraków.[218]

Protocol Books and Documents

As mentioned above, hardly any medieval protocol books used by ecclesiastical courts have survived in Hungary.[219] In Poland, in contrast, there are printed editions of the documents of ecclesiastical courts produced on the basis of protocol books.

Following are examples for the ecclesiastical province of Gneizno:

(1) Gniezno, officialate general of the archbishop (*consistorium generale*);[220]

(2) Archdiocese of Gneizno, Wielun, regional officialate;[221]

(3) Archdiocese of Gniezno, Łowicz (the archbishop long resided in Łowicz);[222]

(4) Archdiocese of Gniezno, Kalisz;[223]

216. See above n. 183.

217. See above nn. 188 and 183.

218. *Monumenta Romana Episcopatus Vesprimiensis* (4 vols. Budapest 1896–1908) 3.lxi; Bónis, *Középkori* 43.

219. For an exception, see above n. 9.

220. Ed. Ulanowski, *Acta capitulorum* 2.1–388, no. 1–811 (for 1404–1531). See Antoni Gąsiorowski and Izabela Skierska, 'średniowieczni oficjalowie gnieźnieńscy', *Roczniki historyczne* 61 (1995) 37–86 (73–83: list of 'officiales' and general vicars of Gniezno from the thirteenth century to 1513); Gąsiorowski and Skierska, 'Oficjalaty okręgowe w późnośredniowiecznej archidiecezji gnieźnieńskiej', *Czasopismo Prawno Historyczne* 47 (1995) 91–126 at 118–124. In 1503 there were eight regional officialates in the archdiocese of Gniezno: Kamień (see Antoni Gąsiorowski and Izabela Skierska, 'Początki oficjalatu kamieńskiego archidiecezji gnieźnieńskiej [wieki XIV–XV]', *Kwartalnik Historyczny* 103 [1996] 3–21), Kalisz (see Izabela Skierska, 'Oficjalat kaliski w XV wieku', *Rocznik Kaliski* 25 [1994–1995] 95–132), Uniejów, Łęczycą, Łowicz, Wieluń, Łęgonic, and Kurzelow; see Skierska, 'Sądownictwo' 354.

221. Ed. Ulanowski, *Acta capitulorum* 2.389–430, no. 812–890 (for 1459–1500); 933–944, no. 1979–1999 (for 1500–1512); 3¹.333–356, no. 794–858 (for 1513–1531); see Walenty Patykiewicz, 'Późniejsze oficjaty gnieźnieńskie', *Roczniki Teologiczno-Kanoniczne* 5 (1958) 117–122. In 1510 Archbishop Jan Łaski appointed Stanisław Kłomnicki to regional 'officialis' of both Wielun and Kalisz; see Skierska, 'Sądownictwo' 357.

222. Ed. Ulanowski, *Acta capitulorum* 2.431–456, nos. 891–932 (for 1469–1481).

223. Ed. Ulanowski, *Acta capitulorum* 2.457–872, nos. 933–1848 (for 1403–1535); see Skierska, 'Oficjalat kaliski' 117–125 (list of 'officiales' of Kalisz from 1430 to 1502).

(5) Poznań, officialate general of the bishop;[224] from the end of the fourteenth century the 'officialis' is also vicar general, and from the middle of the fifteenth century, this is the rule until the end of the eighteenth century; after the division of the two offices, the judge of the bishop is often known as auditor generalis;[225]

(6) Diocese of Poznań, Kalisz Pomorski[226] (fourteenth to sixteenth century), regional officialate;

(7) Diocese of Poznań, officialate of Czersk/Warszawa (from 1405 in Warsaw);[227]

(8) Diocese of Poznań, Swiebodzin (first known 'officialis' in 1444), regional officialate;[228]

(9) Diocese of Poznań, Pszczew (1415–1505), regional officialate;[229]

(10) Plock, officialate general of the bishop[230] ('curia episcopalis', by turns in Plock and Pultusk);

(11) Włocławek, officialate general of the bishop;[231]

(12) Włocławek, Gdańsk (Danzig), officialate 'terre Pomeranensis';[232]

(13) Kraków, officialate general of the bishop;[233]

(14) Diocese of Kraków, Lublin, regional officialate;[234]

(15) Diocese of Kraków, Sandomierz, regional officialate.[235]

For the ecclesiastical province of Lviv (Lwów), the consistorial acts of the archiepiscopal official general from 1482 to 1498 are particularly im-

---

224. Ed. Ulanowski, *Acta capitulorum* 2.457–872, nos. 933–1848 (for 1403–1535); see Izabela Skierska, 'Konsystorz poznański w XV wieku', *Ostrów Tumski—kolebka Poznania. Materiały z sesji naukowej Poznań, 4 listopada 2003 roku*, ed. Leszek Wilczyński (Poznań 2004) 79–135.

225. Nowacki, *Dzieje archidiecezji poznańskiej* 202–236 (with a description of the archival materials on this court).

226. See ibid. 239–243.

227. Ed. Ulanowski, *Acta capitulorum* 2.873–898, no. 1849–1889 (for 1448–1492); see Nowacki, *Dzieje archidiecezji poznańskiej* 236–239 (since 1416–1417, the Warsaw 'officialis' has been vicar general, hence 'officialis generalis'); Władysław Padacz, 'Rys historyczny sądownictwa kościelnego na terenie Archidiecezji Warszawskiej', *Wiadomosści Archidiecezjalne Warszawskie* 55 (1965) 233–237.

228. See Nowacki, *Dzieje archidiecezji poznańskiej* 243–244 (referring to the records).

229. For documents of this officialate, see Nowacki, *Dzieje archidiecezji poznańskiej* 245.

230. Ed. Ulanowski, *Acta capitulorum* 3¹.1–216, nos. 1–453 (for 1448–1530).

231. Ibid. 217–332, nos. 454–793 (for 1422–1533).

232. Ibid. 365–80, nos. 878–916 for (1467–1500).

233. On the documents of this court see, for example, Bolesław Ulanowski, 'Praktyka w sprawach małżeńskich w sądach duchownych w wieku XV', *Archiwum Komisji Historycznej* 5 (1889) 87–193. See also Knapek, ed., *Akta* (this work also contains an introduction outlining the history of the court in considerable detail [in Polish with English summary]).

234. For the documents of this court, see Knapek, *Akta*. See Piotr Hemperek, *Oficjalat okręgowy w Lublinie XV–XVIII w.* (Lublin 1974).

235. Cf. Piotr Bober, 'Najstarsze księgi oficjalatu sandomierskiego', *Polonia Sacra: Kwartalnik teologiczny* 4 (1951) 155–159 (with references to protocol books 'ab anno Dni 1398'). Walenty Wójcik, 'Uprawnienia oficjałów okręgowych w Sandomierzu w sprawach małżeńskich', *Roczniki Teologiczno-Kanoniczne* 8 (1961) 77–100.

portant.[236] The old sources for the other Polish officialates have also been edited in part. Texts and specialized studies usually are concentrated on the sixteenth century.[237] Inquisition records are also known for Poland.[238]

For the vicarial courts (officialates) of Hungary there is a thorough, if not exhaustive, list of individual documents, including printed ones. The following vicarial courts stand on this list:

Ecclesiastical province of Esztergom:

(1) Esztergom, court of the archiepiscopal vicar general[239] (or of the archbishop himself);

(2) Archdiocese of Esztergom, Bratislava, court of the provost;[240]

(3) Archdiocese of Esztergom, Spišska Kapitula, court of the provost;[241]

(4) Esztergom (exempt region in Transylvania), court of the deacon of Braşov;[242]

(5) Esztergom (exempt region in Transylvania), court of the deacon of Sibiu;[243]

(6) Eger, vicar general of the bishop;[244]

236. Rolny, ed., *Acta officii*.

237. For example, Walenty Wójcik, 'Officjalat okręgowy w Tarnowie w latach 1535–1575', *Prawo Kanoniczne* 2 (1959) 3853–90; Wójcik, 'Organizacja okręgowego oficjalatu radomskiego w latach 1531–1540', *Roczniki Teologiczno-Kanoniczne* 5 (1958) 305–308; Wójcik, 'Organizacjia i działalnosc oficjalatu okregowego w Kielcach w latach 1551–1635', *Roczniki Teologiczno-Kanoniczne* 10 (1963) 29–37; Ewa Wółkiewicz, 'Organizacja konsystorza wrocławskiego w średniowieczu', *Kultura prawna w Europie środkowej*, ed. Antoni Barciak (Katowice 2006) 240–261, 244–245, cited by Skierska, 'Sądownictwo' 359–60 (the bishops of Wrocław did not nominate regional officials, but only a general 'officialis' who functioned in Wrocław; however, from 1384 bishops mandated *commissarii* calling them *auditor causarum* for the territory of every single archdeaconate).

238. Bolesław Ulanowski, 'Examen testium super vita et moribus Beguinarum, per inquisitionem hereticae pravitatis in Sweydnitz anno 1332 factum', *Archiwum Komisyi Historiycznej* 5 (1889) 233–255.

239. Erdő, 'Ungarn' 126–136. About the functioning of this court a number of parts of documents were published or reviewed by Bónis: *Szentszéki regeszták* nos. 293 (for 1244), 298 (for 1244), 313 (for 1248), 458, 461–464, 469–471, 476, 480–481, 497, 500–503, 505–510 (for 1297)—in these cases the archbishop was personally issuing the documents; 729 (for 1322)—from this time on, usually the vicar general is named as the issuer of the bill; 797 (for 1328), 1864–1865, 2188, 2936, 2942, 3528 (for 1486, in case of sede vacante the vicar of the chapter's vicar), 3989, 4335, and passim. See Norbert C. Tóth, Bálint Lakatos, and Gábor Mikó, *A pozsonyi prépost és a káptalan viszálya (1421–1425): A szentszéki bíráskodás Magyarországon—a pozsonyi káptalan szervezete és működése a XV. század elején* (Subsidia ad historiam medii aevi Hungariae inquirendum 3; Budapest 2014) 23–39.

240. Erdő, 'Ungarn' 137–138; Bónis, *Szentszéki regeszták* nos. 460 (for 1284, the provost of Bratislava personally decided), 555, 2138, 2181; see ibid. nos. 1822, 3600–3601, etc. See Tóth, Lakatos, and Mikó, *A pozsonyi prépost* 41–162, 391–429.

241. Erdő, 'Ungarn' 140–141; Bónis, *Szentszéki regeszták* nos. 1500, 1625, 1814, 1824, 1836, 1960, 2009, 2122, 2169, 2205, 4045, etc. On May 6, 1513 Pope Leo X cancelled the 1459 edict of Pope Pius II regarding the privileges of the provost of Spiš. Leo's letter was necessary, because the provost had exceeded the extent of his jurisdiction; Bónis, *Szentszéki regeszták* no. 4140.

242. Erdő, 'Ungarn' 136–137; Bónis, *Szentszéki regeszták* nos. 2137, 4355, etc. see 4339.

243. Erdő, 'Ungarn' 139; Bónis, *Szentszéki regeszták* nos. 379, 1562, 2136, 4323, 4325, 4329, 4343, 4348, 4350, 4363–65, 4367, 4374, etc. See 4339.

244. Erdő, 'Ungarn' 141–146. Bónis, *Szentszéki regeszták* nos. 309 (for 1246–1275, the viceiudex of

(7) Győr, vicar general of the bishop; [245]

(8) Nitra, vicar general of the bishop; [246]

(9) Pannonhalma, court of the territorial abbot;[247]

(10) Pécs, vicar general of the bishop;[248]

(11) Vác, vicar general of the bishop;[249]

(12) Veszprém, vicar general of the bishop;[250]

Ecclesiastical province of Kalocsa:

(1) Kalocsa, vicar general of the archbishop (two vicariates of equal rank in Kalocsa and Bács);[251]

(2) Alba Julia, vicar general of the bishop; [252]

(3) Diocese of Alba Julia, court of the vicar *extra Mezes*;[253]

(4) Csanád, vicar general of the bishop;[254]

(5) Oradea, vicar general of the bishop; [255]

(6) Zagreb, vicar general of the bishop;[256]

---

the bishop), 317 (for 1248–1265, the bishop), 545 (for 1300, viceiudex), 551–552 (for the beginning of the fourteenth century archdeacons), 554, 687 (for 1317, 'viceiudex et cancellarius'), 756 (for 1325, vicar), 1775, 1778, 1831, 1834, 1885, 1889, 1905, 3415 (for ca. 1480, 'nullitas matrimonii'), 3920, 4134, 4345, 4371, 4373, and passim.

245. Erdő, 'Ungarn' 146–148; Bónis, *Szentszéki regeszták* nos. 320 (for 1249, the bishop), 721 (for 1322, the bishop), 759 (for 1325, vicar), 2146, 2192, 2939, 3657, 3922 (for 1501, 'in officio vicariatus iudex surrogatus'), 4366, 4368, etc.

246. Erdő, 'Ungarn' 148; Bónis, *Szentszéki regeszták* nos. 1879, 2053, 2147.

247. Erdő, 'Ungarn' 138–139. Bónis, *Szentszéki regeszták* nos. 3988 (monastic case), 3925 (*capitulum generale*), 3926 (the convention of Pannonhalma objected to the decision of the abbot), etc.

248. Erdő, 'Ungarn' 148–149; Bónis, *Szentszéki regeszták* nos. 318 (provost with the authority of the bishop in marital cases), 519 (for 1297, the bishop), 656 (for 1313, 'vices gerens in spiritualibus generalis'), 660 (for 1313, the archdeacon of the cathedral as surrogate for the bishop), 663 (for 1314, oeconomus and vicar), 700 (for 1319, oeconomus), 1878, 1883, 1890, 4171, 4174, etc.

249. Erdő, 'Ungarn' 149–150; Bónis, *Szentszéki regeszták* nos. 1860, 1862, 1875, 3204, 4145, etc.

250. Erdő, 'Ungarn' 150–151; Bónis, *Szentszéki regeszták* nos. 325 (for 1251, the bishop), 352 (for 1258, the bishop), 394 (for 1266, diocesan oeconomus), 1776 (for 1412, vicarius), 1790a (for 1403), 4007, 4334, 4346–47, 4360, etc.

251. Erdő, 'Ungarn' 151–152; Bónis, *Szentszéki regeszták* nos. 3698, 4148, 4353 (Bács), etc.

252. Erdő, 'Ungarn' 152–153; Bónis, *Szentszéki regeszták* nos. 615 (for 1308–1322, vicarius), 703, 732, 1794, 1843, 1849–1850, 3934, 4012, 4071, 4148 (for 1514, an appeal to the vicar of Bács), 4291, 4299, 4309, 4364, etc.

253. Erdő, 'Ungarn' 153–155; Bónis, *Szentszéki regeszták* nos. 670 (for 1315), 679 (the parish priest of Satu Mare is the vicar), 715–716 (the vicar named after his territory: *de ultra Mezes*), 1818 (the seat of the vicar is Tăşnad), 1861, 1869, 2159–2161, 2163, 2166, 2168, 4215, 4217–4218, 4252, 4266, etc.

254. Erdő, 'Ungarn' 155–156; Bónis, *Szentszéki regeszták* nos. 1561, 1795–1796, 1808, 1873, 1901, 2013, 2184, 2368, 2370–2373, 2375, 2377, 3918, etc. See ibid. no. 1573 (for 1391, on Pope Boniface IX's commission to the bishop of Csanád to carry out punitive litigation, accusatory procedure: 'postquam accusare ceperit et se inscripseri'). *Monumenta Vaticana historiam Hungariae illustrantia* (6 vols. Series I; Budapest 1885–1891) I¹.173.

255. Erdő, 'Ungarn' 156–157; Bónis, *Szentszéki regeszták* nos. 1337, 2008, 2495, 4300.

256. Erdő, 'Ungarn' 157–158; Bónis, *Szentszéki regeszták* nos. 1883–1884, 1886, 2154 (for 1420, chapter's vicar), 4372, etc. In 1478 the diocese of Zagreb had fourteen archdeaconates, but only one regional officialate; see Nada Klaić, *Povijest Hrvata u razvijenom srednjem vijeku* (Zagreb 1976) 270; Lonza, 'Blasius of Moravče' 447.

(7) Diocese of Zagreb, court of the provost of Čazma.[257]

There was no separate inquisitorial court functioning on a regular basis in Hungary. However, due to King Sigismund's demand, the pope delegated the Observant Franciscan Jacob of Marchia (Jacobus de Marchia) as inquisitor against Hussitism in 1436. At the same time he was vicar of Bosnia at the order's province there.[258]

Conclusion

Although ecclesiastical jurisdiction commenced functioning somewhat earlier in Hungary than in Poland, Hungarian ecclesiastical courts were not yet completely autonomous in the eleventh and twelfth centuries. In the thirteenth century the institution of the officialate was introduced to Poland by papal legates in its classic French form, while the terminology and form of the same (or practically the same) institution in Hungary was influenced by numerous Italian canonists active there. Here as well the role of the legates was important. In the fifteenth century the competence and structure, as well as the theoretical division and practical composition of the office of vicar general and of episcopal judge (the 'officialis' or 'causarum auditor generalis'), as well as the recordkeeping of the Polish and Hungarian consistories, were quite similar. One difference at this time was that the regional officialate had not spread in its classic form in Hungary.

257. Erdő, 'Ungarn' 158; Bónis, *Szentszéki regeszták* nos. 3642, 3648–3650, 4161 (for 1516, the provost as 'curie legationis causarum... auditor iudex et commissarius specialiter deputatus'), 4192 and 4196 (for 1516, 1517, the provost of Čazma), 4203, 4206–4209, 4213–4214 (the 'locumtenens' of the provost of Čazma), 4241 (locumtenens), etc.

258. Bónis, *Szentszéki regeszták* nos. 2444, 2455; see Daniele Solvi, 'Giovanni da Capestrano inquisitore e la dissidenza francescana', *S. Giovanni da Capestrano: Un bilancio storiografico: Atti del Convegno Storico Internazionale, Capestrano, 15–16 maggio 1998*, ed. Edit Pásztor (Quaderni di provincia oggi 30; L'Aquila 1999) 25–46 at 35–36. Another Observant Franciscan, Michael of Šibenik (Sebenico), had also asked his delegation from Rome to be inquisitor against Hussitism in 1421; Bónis, *Szentszéki regeszták* no. 2176.

Selected Bibliography of Printed and Secondary Sources

Abbondanza, Roberto. 'Bagarotto (Bagarotto dei Corradi)', DBI 5 (1963) 170–174.

Ackermann, Markus R. 'Mittelalterliche Kirchen als Gerichtsorte', ZRG Germ. Abt. 110 (1993) 530–545.

Adams, Norma. 'The Judicial Conflict Over Tithes', EHR 52 (1937) 1–22.

Adams, Norma, and Charles Donahue Jr. *Select Cases from the Ecclesiastical Courts of the Province of Canterbury c. 1200–1301* (Selden Society 95; London, 1981).

Appelt, Heinrich. 'Die Anfänge des päpstlichen Schutzes', MIÖG 62 (1954) 101–111.

Aubenas, Roger. *Contribution a l'histoire des officialités au moyen-age: Recueil de lettres des officialités de Marseille et d'Aix* (2 vols. Paris 1937–1938).

Avignon, Carole. 'Les couples clandestins devant la justice d'Église: Réflexions sur la normalisation matrimoniale judiciaire dans la France du Nord-Ouest à la fin du Moyen Âge', *Couples devant les justices: Du Moyen Âge à l'époque contemporaine*, ed. Claude Gauvard and Alessandro Stella (Paris 2013) 77–98.

———. *L'Église et les infractions au lien matrimonial: mariages clandestins et clandestinité. Théories, pratiques et discours: France du nord-ouest (XIIe–milieu XVI siècle)* (Thèse, Paris– Est 2008).

———. 'Marché matrimonial clandestin et officines de clandestinité à la fin du Moyen Âge: l'exemple du diocèse de Rouen', *Revue Historique* 655 (2010) 515–549.

Avril, Joseph, *Les statuts synodaux français du xiiie siècle. IV: Les statuts synodaux de l'ancienne province de Reims (Cambrai, Arras, Noyon, Soissons et Tournai)* (Collection de documents inédits sur l'histoire de France, sér. in 8°, 23; Paris 1988).

Aznar Gil, Federico Rafael. 'Penas y sanciones contra los matrimonios clandestinos en la península Ibérica durante la baja edad media', *Revista de estudios históricos-jurídicos*, 25 (2003) 189–214.

Baker, John H. *Monuments of Endlesse Labours: English Canonists and Their Work 1300–1900* (London 1998).

Baldwin, John. 'The Intellectual Preparation for the Canon of 1215 against Ordeals', *Speculum* 36 (1961) 613–636.

Balogh, Elemér. 'Die Einführung der kirchlichen Gerichtsbarkeit in Bayern: Eine komparative Studie über Kontakte und Parallelen der geistlichen Gerichte von Bayern und Ungarn im Mittelalter', *De processibus matrimonialibus* 17–18 (2010–2011) 81–110.

Bartlett, Robert. *Trial by Fire and Water: The Medieval Judicial Ordeal* (Oxford 1986).

Bartocci, Andrea. 'Giovanni d'Andrea (Johannes Andreae de Bononia)', DGI (2013) 1.1008–1012.

Barton, John L. *Roman Law in England* (IRMÆ 5.13a; Milan 1971).

Baschet, Jérôme. *Les Justices de l'au-delà: Les représentations de l'enfer en France et en Italie (XIIe–XVe siècle)* (Bibliothèque des Écoles françaises d'Athènes et de Rome 279; Paris 1993).

Baumgärtner, Ingrid. 'Was muß ein Legist vom Kirchenrecht wissen? Roffredus Beneventanus und seine "Libelli de iure canonico",' *Proceedings Cambridge 1984* 223–245.

Beaulande[-Barraud], Véronique. *Le Malheur d'être exclu? Excommunication, réconciliation, et société à la fin du Moyen Âge* (Histoire ancienne et médiévale 84; Paris 2006).

Bellamy, John G. *Criminal Law and Society in Late Medieval and Tudor England* (London 1984).

———. *The Criminal Trial in Later Medieval England: Felony before the Courts from Edward I to the Sixteenth Century* (Toronto-Buffalo 1998).

Bellomo, Manlio. 'Intorno a Roffredo Beneventano: Professore a Roma?', *Scuole, diritto e società nel mezzogiorno medievale d Italia* (2 vols. Studi e ricerche dei 'Quaderni catanesi' 8; Catania 1985) 1.135–181.

Benatti, Corrado. 'Guido da Suzzara', DGI (2013) 1.1093–1094.

Benson, Robert L. 'Plenitudo potestatis: Evolution of a Formula from Gregory IV to Gratian', *Collectanea Stephan Kuttner* (SG 14; Bologna 1968) 195–217.

Berger, Adolf. *Encyclopedic Dictionary of Roman Law* (Transactions of the American Philosophical Society; new ser., 43.2; Philadephia).

Bergmann, Friedrich, ed. *Pillii, Tancredi, Gratiae Libri De iudiciorum ordine* (Göttingen 1842).

Bernhardt, John W. *Itinerant Kingship and Royal Monasteries in Early Medieval Germany, c. 936–1075* (Cambridge Studies in Medieval Life and Thought 4th series 21; Cambridge 1993).

Bertram, Martin. *Kanonisten und ihre Texte (1234 his Mitte 14. Jh.): 18 Aufsätze und 14 Exkurse* (Education and Society in the Middle Ages and Renaissance, 43; Leiden-Boston 2013).

———. 'Goffredo da Trani', DGI (2013) 1.1038–1039.

———. 'I manoscritti delle opere di Rolandino conservati nelle biblioteche italiane e nella Biblioteca Vaticana', *Rolandino e l'ars notaria da Bologna all'Europa: Atti del Convegno Nazionale di Studi Storici sulla figura e l'opera di Rolandino*, ed. Giorgio Tamba (Milan 2002) 683–718.

Bertram, Martin, and Maguerite Duynstee, 'Casus legum sive Suffragia monachorum: Legistische Hilfsmittel für Kanonisten im späteren Mittelalter', TRG 51 (1983) 317–363.

Bettetini, Andrea. 'Tancredi da Bologna', DGI (2013) 2.1930–1931.

Bisson, Thomas N. *The Crisis of the Twelfth Century: Power, Lordship, and the Origins of European Government* (Princeton 2009).

Blaauw, Sible de. *Cultus et décor: Liturgie en architectuur in laatantiek en middeleeuws Rome* (Delft 1987) trans. into Italian *Cultus et décor: Liturgia e architettura nella Roma tardoantica e medievale*, by Maria B. Annis (Studi e Testi 355–356; Vatican City 1994).

Blanco Cordero, Celestino. *El fuero especial del clero y su desarrollo en España hasta el s.VIII* (Salamanca 1944).

Blanshei, Sarah Rubin. *Politics and Justice in Late Medieval Bologna* (Medieval Law and Its Practice; Leiden-Boston 2010).

Blumenthal, Uta-Renate. 'Rom in der Kanonistik', *Rom im hohen Mittelalter: Studien zu den Romvorstellungen und zur Rompolitik vom 10. zum 12. Jahrhundert: Reinhard Elze zur Vollendung seines siebzigsten Lebensjahres gewidmet*, ed. Bernhard Schimmelpfennig and Ludwig Schmugge (Sigmaringen 1992) 1–19 reprinted *Papal Reform and Canon Law in the 11th and 12th centuries* (Collected Studies 618; Aldershot 1998).

————. 'Conciliar Canons and Manuscripts: the Implications of Their Transmission in the Eleventh Century', *Proceedings Munich 1992* 357–379, reprinted *Papal Reform and Canon Law in the 11th and 12th centuries* (Collected Studies 618; Aldershot 1998).

Boháček, Miroslav. 'Zur Geschichte der Stationarii von Bologna', *Symbolae Raphaeli Taubenschlag dedicatae,* ed. Isabella Bieżuńska-Małowist (3 vols. Eos 48.1–3; Vratislaviae–Varsoviae 1957) 2.241–296, reprinted as 'Nuova fonte per la storia degli stazionari bolognesi', SG 9 (1966) 409–460.

————. 'Le opere delle scuole medievali di diritto nei manoscriti della Biblioteca Capitolare di Olomouc', SG 8.305–421.

Bonfield, Lloyd. *Devising, Dying and Dispute: Probate Litigation in Early Modern England* (Farnham 2012).

Bónis, György. *Középkori jogunk elemei: Római jog, kánonjog, szokásjog* (Budapest 1972).

————. *Szentszéki regeszták: Iratok az egyházi bíráskodás történetéhez a középkori Magyarországon,* ed. Elemér Balogh (Jogtörténeti Tár 1.1; Budapest 1997).

————. 'Die Entwicklung der geistlichen Gerichtsbarkeit in Ungarn vor 1526', ZRG Kan. Abt. 49 (1963) 174–235.

Borgolte, Michael. *Die mittelalterliche Kirche* (Enzyklopädie deutscher Geschichte 17; Munich 1992).

————. *Petrusnachfolge und Kaiserimitation: Die Grablegen der Päpste, ihre Genese und Traditionsbildung* (Veröffentlichungen des Max-Planck-Instituts für Geschichte 95; Göttingen 1989).

Boutiot, Théophile. 'Recherches sur la juridiction du roi sur celle de l'evêque dans le Bailliage de Troyes et sur les coutumes de ce bailliage', *Mémoires de la Société académique d'agriculture, des sciences, arts et belles-lettres de l'Aube* 36 (1872) 6–74.

————. *Recherches sur les Grandes Jours de Troyes* (Troyes 1852).

Brand, Paul M. *Origins of the English Legal Profession* (Oxford 1992).

Brandileone, Francesco. *Saggi sulla storia della celebrazione del matrimonio in Italia* (Milan 1906).

Bréban, Jean. *Registre de l'officialité épiscopale de Troyes, 1389–1396* (Archives de l'Aube G 4170; Dissertation, Paris 1954).

Brenk, Beat. *Tradition und Neuerung in der christlichen Kunst des ersten Jahrtausends: Studien zur Geschichte des Weltgerichtsbildes* (Vienna 1966).

Bresslau, Harry. *Handbuch der Urkundenlehre für Deutschland und Italien* (2 vols. 2nd ed. Leipzig 1912–1931) 1.240, trans. into Italian A.M. Voci-Roth *Manuale di diplomatica per la Germania e l'Italia* (Pubblicazioni degli Archivi di Stato, Sussidi 10; Rome 1998).

Brommer, Peter. *Capitula episcoporum: Die bischöflichen Kapitularien des 9. und 10. Jahrhunderts* (Typologie des sources du Moyen Age occidental 43; Turnhot 1985).

Brooke, Christopher N. L. *The Medieval Idea of Marriage* (Oxford 1989).

Browe, Peter. *De Ordaliis: In usum exercitationum et praelectionum academicarum, 2: Ordo et Rubricae: Acta et Facta: Sententiae theologorum et canonistarum* (Textus et documenta, Series theologica; Rome 1933).

Brühl, Carlrichard. *Fodrum, Gistum, Servitium regis: Studien zu den wirtschaftlichen Grundlagen des Königtums* (Kölner Historische Abhandlungen 14.1–2; Cologne–Graz 1968).

————. 'Zur Geschichte der procuratio canonica vornehmlich im 11. und 12. Jahrhundert', *Le istituzioni ecclesiastiche della 'societas christiana' dei secoli XI–XII: Papato, cardinalato ed episcopato: Atti della quinta settimana internazionale di studio, Mendola, 26–31 agosto 1971* (Miscellanea del Centro di Studi Medioevali 7; Milan 1974) 419–431.

Brundage, James A. 'The Calumny Oath and the Ethical Ideals of Canonical Advocates', *Proceedings Munich 1992* 793–805, reprinted *The Profession and Practice of Medieval Canon Law* (Collected Studies,797; Aldershot 2004) no. IV.

————. *Law, Sex, and Christian Society in Medieval Europe* (Chicago–London 1987).

————. 'Legal Ethics: A Medieval Ghost Story', *Law and the Illicit in Medieval Europe*, ed. Ruth Mazo Karras, Joel Kaye, and E. Ann Matter (Philadelphia 2008) 47–56.

————. *The Medieval Origins of the Legal Profession* (Chicago 2008).

————. 'The Monk as Lawyer', *The Jurist* 39 (1979) 423–436.

————. 'Professional Canonists and their Clients: Problems in Legal Ethics', *Proceedings Washington 2004* 857–874.

————. 'Legal Ethics: A Medieval Ghost Story', *Law and the Illicit in Medieval Europe*, ed. Ruth Mazo Karras, Joel Kaye, and E. Ann Matter (Philadelphia 2008) 47–56.

————. 'The Monk as Lawyer', *The Jurist* 39 (1979) 423–436.

Buchholz-Johanek, Ingeborg. *Geistliche Richter und geistliches Gericht im spätmittelalterlichen Bistum Eichstätt* (Eichstätter Studien n.F. 23; Regensburg 1988).

Bukowska Gorgoni, Cristina. 'Foscarari (Foscherari) Egidio', DBI 49 (1997) 277–280.

Bulman, Jan K. *The Court Book of Mende and the Secular Lordship of the Bishop* (Toronto 2008).

Burmeister, Karl Heinz. Das Studium der Rechte im Zeitalter des Humanismus im deutschen Rechtsbereich (Wiesbaden 1974).

Burns, Robert I., ed. *Las Siete Partidas,* trans. Samuel Parsons Scott (5 vols. Philadelphia 2001).

Butler, Sara Margaret. *Divorce in Medieval England: From One to Two Persons in Law* (Routledge Research in Medieval Studies 4; New York 2013).

————. *The Language of Abuse: Marital Violence in Later Medieval England* (Leiden 2007).

Caenegem, Raoul C. van. *The Birth of the English Common Law* (2d ed. Cambridge 1988).

Cahn, Walter. 'Solomonic Elements in Romanesque Art', *The Temple of Solomon: Archaeological Facts and Medieval Tradition in Christian, Islamic and Jewish Art*, ed. J. Gutmann (Missoula 1976) 45–72.

Calabresi, Guido, and A. Douglas Melamed. 'Property Rules and Liability Rules: One View of the Cathedral', *Harvard Law Review* 85 (1972) 1089–1128.

Caprioli, Severino. 'Bonaguida d'Arezzo (de Aretio si dice egli stesso; Aretinus, de Aretinis)', DBI 11 (1969) 512–513.

Caravale, Mario. 'Bencivenne da Siena', DBI 8 (1966) 215–216.

Carbonetti, C. 'Tabellioni e scriniari a Roma tra IX e XI secolo', *Archivio della Società Romana di storia patria* 102 (1979) 77–156.

Carocci, S., ed. *Itineranza pontificia: La mobilità della Curia papale nel Lazio (secoli XII–XIII)* (Nuovi studi storici 61; Rome 2003).

Carolus-Barré, Louis. 'L'organisation de la juridiction gracieuse à Paris dans le dernier tiers du XIIIe siècle: L'officialité et le Châtelet', *Le Moyen Age* 69 (1963) 417–435.

Caron, Pier Giovanni. 'La competenza dell'episcopalis audientia nella legislazione degli imperatori romani cristiani', *Il diritto romano-canonico quale diritto proprio delle comunità cristiane dell'oriente mediterraneo: IX colloquio internazionale romanistico–canonistico* (Città del Vaticano 1994) 267–276.

Charageat, Martine. 'Copula carnal: La preuve de mariage dans les process à Saragosse au XVe siècle', *Mélanges de la Casa de Velazquez* 33 (2003) 47–63.

————. *La délinquance matrimoniale : Couples en conflit et justice en Aragon (XV–XVI siècle)* (Paris 2011).

————. 'Pour une étude de la conflictualité matrimoniale (xive–xvie siècles): Les archives de l'officialité césearaugustaine', Beaulande/Charageat, *Les Officialités* 245–258.

————. 'Témoins et témoignages en Aragon aux XVe–XVIe siècles', *La preuve en justice de l'antiquité à nos jours,* ed. Bruno Lemesle (Rennes 2003) 149–169.

————. 'Typologie des procès canoniques matrimoniaux à Saragosse (XVe–XVIe siècle)',

Sínodos diocesanos y legislación particular: Estudios históricos en honor al Dr. D. Francisco Cantelar Rodriguez (Bibliotheca Salmanticensis 10; Salamanca 1999) 217–232.

Chartularium Universitatis Parisiensis, ed. Heinrich Denifle and Emil Chatelain (4 vols. Paris 1889–1897).

Cheney, Christopher R. *English Bishops' Chanceries, 1100–1250* (Publications of the Faculty of Arts of the University of Manchester 3; Manchester 1950).

———. *From Becket to Langton: English Church Government 1170–1213* (Manchester 1956).

———. *Notaries Public in England in the Thirteenth and Fourteenth Centuries* (Oxford 1972).

———. 'William Lyndwood's Provinciale', *The Jurist* 21 (1961) 405–434.

———. 'The Punishment of Felonious Clerks', EHR 51 (1936) 215–236.

———. 'William Lyndwood's Provinciale', *The Jurist* 21 (1961) 405–434.

Chodorow, Stanley. 'Dishonest Litigation in the Church Courts', *Law, Church and Society: Essays in Honor of Stephan Kuttner,* ed. Kenneth Pennington and Robert Somerville (The Middle Ages; Philadelphia 1977) 187–206.

Christensen, Katherine. '"Rescriptum auctoritatis uestre": A Judge Delegate's Report to Pope Alexander III', *The Two Laws: Studies in Medieval Legal History Dedicated to Stephan Kuttner,* ed. Laurent Mayali and Stephanie A. J. Tibbetts (Studies in Medieval and Early Modern Canon Law 1; Washington DC 1990) 40–54.

Christensen-Nugues, Charlotte. 'Mariage consenti, mariage contraint: L'abjuration sub pena nubendi à l'officialité de Cerisy, 1314–1346', *Médiévales* 40 (2001) 101–112.

Churchill, Irene J. *Canterbury Administration: The Administrative Machinery of the Archbishopric of Canterbury Illustrated from Original Records* (Church Historical Society Publications 15; London 1933).

Cimma, Maria Rosa. *L'Episcopalis audientia nelle costituzioni imperiali da Costantino a Giustiniano* (Torino 1989).

Clarke, Peter D. *The Interdict in the Thirteenth Century: A Question of Collective Guilt* (Oxford 2007).

Classen, Peter. 'Zur Geschichte Papst Anastasius' IV.' QF 48 (1968) 36–63.

Claussen, Peter C. *Chartres–Studien: Zur Vorgeschichte, Funktion und Skulptur der Vorhallen* (Forschungen zur Kunstgeschichte und christlichen Archäologie 9; Wiesbaden 1975).

Cochetti, Maria. 'Repertori e Cataloghi: La biblioteca di Giovanni Calderini', *Studi Medievali 3rd Series* 19 (1978) 951–1032.

Coing, Helmut. *Römisches Recht in Deutschland* (IRMAe 5.6; Milan 1964).

Colli, Vincenzo. *Giuristi medievali e produzione libraria: Manoscritti, autografi* (Stockstadt am Main 2005).

Colliva, Pietro. 'Documenti per la biografia di Accursio', *Atti del Convegno internazionale di studi Accursiani, Bologna 21–26 Ottobre 1963,* ed. G. Rossi (Milan 1968) 2.445–456.

Condorelli, Orazio. 'Un contributo bolognese alla dottrina del processo romano–canonico: Il Tractatus de accusationibus et inquisitionibus di Bonincontro di Giovanni d'Andrea († 1350)', *Einfluss der Kanonistik* 4.65–90.

Constable, Giles. 'Resistance to Tithes in the Middle Ages', JEH 13 (1962) 172–185.

Cornides, Elisabeth. *Rose und Schwert im päpstlichen Zeremoniell: Von den Anfängen bis zum Pontifikat Gregors XIII.* (Wiener Dissertationen aus dem Gebiete der Geschichte 9; Vienna 1967).

Conte, Emanuele. 'Bagarotto (Bagarottus de Coradis)', DGI 1.142–143.

Coronas González, Santos M. 'El derecho de Asturias en la alta Edad Media', *Libro del I Congreso Jurídico de Asturias* (Oviedo 1987) 73–95.

Cortese, Ennio. 'Legisti, canonisti e feudisti: La formazione di un ceto medievale', *Università e società nei secoli XII–XVI: Atti del nono Convegno Internazionale di studio* (Centro Italiano di Studi di Storia d'Arte 9; Pistoia 1982) 195–284.

———. 'Scienza di giudici e scienza di professori tra XII e XIII secolo', *Legge, giudici, giuristi: Atti del convegno tenuto a Cagliari* (Università di Cagliari, Pubblicazioni della Facoltà di Giurisprudenza 26; Milan 1982) 93–148.

———. 'Pillio da Medicina', DGI (2013) 2.1587–1590.

Coulet, Noël. *Les visites pastorales* (Typologie des sources du Moyen Age occidental 23; Turnhot 1977; mise à jour 1985).

Cristellon, Cecilia. *La carità e l'eros: Il matrimonio, la Chiesa, i suoi giudici nella Venezia del Rinascimento, 1420–1545* (Annali dell'Istituto storico italo–germanico in Trento 58; Bologna 2010).

———. 'Marriage and Consent in Pre–Tridentine Venice: Between Law Conception and Ecclesiastical Conception, 1420–1545', *Sixteenth Century Journal* 39 (2008) 390–418.

———. 'L'ufficio del giudice: Mediazione, inquisizione, confessione nei processi matrimoniali veneziani (1420–1532)', *Rivista Storica Italiana* 115 (2003) 851–898.

Cuena Boy, Francisco José. *La 'episcopalis audientia'* (Serie Derecho 3; Valladolid 1985).

Daudet, Pierre. *Études sur l'histoire de la juridiction matrimoniale: Les orgines carolingiennes de la compétence exclusive de l'Église (France et Germanie)* (Paris 1933).

Dean, Trevor. *Crime and Justice in Late Medieval Italy* (Cambridge 2007).

Deér, Jószef. *The Dynastic Porphyry Tombs of the Norman Period in Sicily,* trans. G.A. Gillhoff (Dumbarton Oaks Studies 5; Cambridge, MA 1959).

———. 'Der Anspruch der Herrscher des 12. Jahrhunderts auf die apostolische Legation', AHP 2 (1964) 117–186.

Deimling, Barbara. '*Ad Rufam Ianuam:* Die rechtsgeschichtliche Bedeutung von roten Türen im Mittelalter', ZRG Germ. Abt. 115 (1998) 498–513.

———. 'Das mittelalterliche Kirchenportal in seiner rechtsgeschichtlichen Bedeutung', *Die Kunst der Romanik: Architektur, Skulptur, Malerei,* ed. R. Toman (Köln 1996) 324–327.

Deknatel, F. B. 'The Thirteenth Century Gothic Sculpture of the Cathedrals of Burgos and León', *Art Bulletin* 17 (1935) 243–389.

Del Re, Niccolò. 'Prospero Farinacci giureconsulto romano (1544–1618)', *Archivio della Società Romana di Storia Patria,* 3rd series 28 (1975) 135–220.

Delcambre, Étienne. 'Le paréage du Puy', BEC 92 (1931) 121–69, 285–344.

Delivré, Fabrice. 'Les officialités primatiales en France (v. 1420–1520): Réforme et pratique juridictionnelle', Beaulande/Charageat *Les officialités* 75–89.

Demeunynck, Marie-Charlotte. *Le vicariat de Pontoise ou l'officialité foraine de Rouen à Pontoise (1255–1789)* (Thèse, École des chartes, Paris 1933) (see [Paris], École Nationale des Chartes, *Positions des Thèses* (Paris 1933) 15–20).

Denifle, Heinrich. 'Die Statuten der Juristen-Universität Bologna vom J. 1317–1347, und deren Verhältniss zu jenem Paduas, Perugias, Florenz', *Archiv für Litteratur- und Kirchengeschichte des Mittelalters* 3 (1887) 196–397.

Denny, Don. 'The Last Judgment Tympanon at Autun: Its Sources and Meaning', *Speculum* 57 (1982) 532–547.

Descamps, Olivier. 'Aux origines de la procédure sommaire: Remarques sur la constitution Saepe contingit (Clem., V, 11, 2)', *Einfluss der Kanonistik* 4.45–63.

Destrez, Jean. *La Pecia dans les manuscrits universitaires du XIIIe et du XIVe siècle* (Paris 1935).

Deutsch, Christina. *Ehegerichtsbarkeit im Bistum Regensburg (1480–1538)* (Forschungen zur kirchlichen Rechtsgeschichte und zum Kirchenrecht 29; Köln 2005).

Díaz Ibáñez, Jorge. 'La potestas jurisdiccional del obispo y cabildo catedralicio burgalés durante el siglo XV', *Medievalismo* 22 (2012) 75–97.

Dievoet, Guido van. *Les coutumiers, les styles, les formulaires et les 'artes notariae'* (Typologie des sources du moyen âge occidental 48; Turnhout 1986).

Dolezalek, Gero. *Das Imbreviaturbuch des erzbischöflichen Gerichtsnotars Hubaldus aus Pisa,*

Mai bis August 1230 (Forschungen zur neueren Privatrechtsgeschichte 13; Köln, 1969).

———. 'Une nouvelle source pour l'étude de la pratique judiciaire au XIII siècle: les livres d'imbreviatures des notaires de cour', *Confluence des droits savants et des pratiques juridiques: Actes du Colloque de Montpellier* (Milano 1979) 225–241.

Donahue, Charles, Jr. 'By Way of a Conclusion', Beaulande/Charageat, *Les officialités* 325–338.

———. 'The Canon Law on the Formation of Marriage and Social Practice in the Later Middle Ages', *Journal of Family History* (Summer, 1983) 149–153.

———. 'Church Court Records on the Continent and in England', *Englische und kontinentale Rechtsgeschichte: ein Forschungsproject,* ed. Helmut Coing and Knut W. Nörr (Comparative Studies in Continental and Anglo–American Legal History 1; Berlin 1985) 63–71.

———. 'Clandestine Marriage in the Later Middle Ages: A Reply to Finch', LHR, 10 (1992) 315–322.

———. 'English and French Marriage Cases in the Later Middle Ages: Might the Differences be Explained by Differences in the Property Systems?', *Family, Property and Succession,* ed. Lloyd Bonfield (Comparative Studies in Continental and Anglo–American Legal History 10; Berlin 1992) 339–66, reprinted *Miscellanea Domenico Maffei Dicata: Historia—Ius—Studium,* ed. Antonio García y García and Peter Weimar (Goldbach 1995) 4:283–310.

———. '*Ex officio* Cases in the Officiality of Paris, 1384–1387', *Mélanges en l'honneur d'Anne Lefebvre-Teillard,* ed. Bernard d'Alteroche *et al.* (Paris 2009) 393–412.

———. '"The Hypostasis of Prophecy": Legal Realism and Legal History', *Law and Legal Process: Substantive Law and Procedure in English Legal History,* ed. Matthew M. Dyson and David Ibbetson (Cambridge 2013) 1–16.

———. *Law, Marriage, and Society in the Later Middle Ages: Arguments About Marriage in Five Courts* (New York 2007). (T&C = the numbered 'Texts and Commentary' that accompanied the book, available online http://www.cambridge.org/us/download_file/202931/).

———. 'A Legal Historian Looks at the Case Method', *Northern Kentucky Law Review* 19 (1991) 21–31.

———. 'Malchus's Ear: Reflections on Classical Canon Law as a Religious Legal System', *Lex et Romanitas: Essays for Alan Watson* (Berkeley, Calif. 2000) 91–120.

———. 'Private Law without the State and during Its Formation', *American Journal of Comparative Law,* 56 (2008) 541–566, reprinted *Beyond the State: Rethinking Private Law,* Niles Jansen and Ralf Michaels (Tübingen 2008) 121–143.

———. 'Proof by Witnesses in the Church Courts of Medieval England: An Imperfect Reception of the Learned Law', *On the Laws and Customs of England: Essays in Honor of Samuel E. Thorne,* ed. M. S. Arnold *et al.* (Chapel Hill, N.C. 1981) 127–158.

———. 'Roman Canon Law in the Medieval English Church: Stubbs vs. Maitland Re-Examined after 75 Years in the Light of Some Records from the Church Courts', *Michigan Law Review* 72 (1974) 647–716.

———. *The Records of the Medieval Ecclesiastical Courts: Reports of the Working Group on Church Court Records. 1: The Continent; 2: England* (Comparative Studies in Continental and Anglo–American Legal History, 6, 7; Berlin 1989, 1994).

———. 'Thoughts on Diocesan Statutes: England and France, 1200–1500', *Canon Law, Religion, and Politics: Liber Amicorum Robert Somerville,* ed. Uta–Renate Blumenthal, Anders Winroth, and Peter Landau (Washington, D.C. 2012) 253–271.

———. *Why the History of Canon Law Is Not Written* (Selden Society Lectures; London 1984).

Dondorp, Harry. 'Review of Papal Rescripts in the Canonists' Teaching', ZRG Kan.Abt. 76 (1990) 172–253 and ZRG Kan. Abt. 77 (1991) 32–110.

Drosbach, Gisela, and H.-J. Schmidt, ed. *Zentrum und Netzwerk: Kirchliche Kommunikationen und Raumstrukturen im Mittelalter* (Scrinium Friburgense 22; Berlin–New York 2008).

Duggan, Charles. *Twelfth-century Decretal Collections and Their Importance in English History* (University of London Historical Studies 12; London 1963).

———. 'Decretal Collections from Gratian's *Decretum* to the *Compilationes antiquae*: The Making of the New Case Law', Hartmann-Pennington *History* 246–292.

———. 'Decretals of Alexander III to England', *Miscellanea Rolando Bandinelli, Papa Alessandro III*, ed. F. Liotta (Accademia Senesi degli Intronati; Siena 1986) 85–151.

———. 'Papal Judges Delegate and the Making of the 'New Law' in the Twelfth Century', *Cultures of Power: Lordship, Status, and Process in Twelfth-Century Europe*, ed. Thomas Bisson (Philadelphia 1995) 172–199.

Duggan, Charles, and Stanley Chodorow. *Decretales ineditae saeculi XII, from the Papers of Walther Holtzmann* (MIC, Series B, 4; Vatican City 1982).

Dunning, B. 'The Wells Consistory Court in the Fifteenth Century', *Proceedings of the Somersetshire Archaeological & Natural Historical Society* 106 (1962) 46–61.

Dupont, Gustave [and Léopold Delisle], ed. 'Le registre de l'officialité de Cerisy', *Mémoires de la société des antiquaires de Normandie*, 3ᵉ série 10 (30) (1880) 271–662.

Ellul, Jacques. *Histoire des institutions*, 3: *Le Moyen Âge* (7th ed. Paris 1976).

Elze, Reinhard. 'Das Sacrum "Palatium Lateranense" im 10. und 11. Jahrhundert', *Studi Gregoriani* 4 (1952) 27–54; reprinted *Päpste–Kaiser–Könige und die mittelalterliche Herrschaftssymbolik* (London 1982) no. I.

———. 'Die päpstliche Kapelle', ZRG Kan. Abt. 36 (1950) 145–204; reprinted *Päpste-Kaiser-Könige* no. II.

———. 'Sic transit gloria mundi. Zum Tode des Papstes im Mittelalter', DA 34 (1978) 1–18.

Erdő, Péter. *Geschichte der Wissenschaft vom kanonischen Recht: Eine Einführung* (Kirchenrechtliche Bibliothek 4; Berlin 2006).

———. 'Il potere giudiziario del Primate d'Ungheria', *Apollinaris* 53 (1980) 272–292, 54 (1981) 213–231.

———. 'Codici manoscritti di diritto canonico e loro frammenti in Ungheria', *Apollinaris* 61 (1988) 341–354.

———. 'Eheprozesse im mittelalterlichen Ungarn', ZRG Kan. Abt. 103 (1986) 250–276.

———. 'Tribunali ecclesiastici medievali in Polonia e in Ungheria', *Studi Medievali* 36 (1995) 323–343.

———. 'Mittelalterliche Offizialate in Ungarn und in Polen', BMCL 23 (1999) 16–34.

———. 'Ungarn (Kirchenprovinzen von Esztergom und Kalocsa)', Donahue, *Records 1* 123–158.

———. 'Sull'uso dell'opera del Panormitano nei centri diocesani dell'Ungheria tardomedievale', *Niccolò Tedeschi (Abbas Panormitanus) e i suoi Commentaria in Decretales*, ed. Orazio Condorelli (I libri di Erice 25; Roma 2000) 89–102.

Erler, Adalbert. *Das Straßburger Münster im Rechtsleben des Mittelalters* (Frankfurt, 1954).

Eubel, Konrad. 'Kleinere Mitteilungen', RQ 8 (1894) 494–499.

Evers, H. G. *Tod, Macht und Raum als Bereich der Architektur* (Munich 1939, 2nd rev. ed. Munich 1970).

Falkenstein, Ludwig. 'Zur Stellung des Reimser Metropolitankapitels in Stadt, Diözese und Kirchenprovinz während des 12. und 13. Jahrhunderts', *Proceedings Berkeley 1980* 551–562.

Falzone, Emmanuël. '"Ad secunda vota rite convolare posse:" Le remariage des personnes veuves à la fin du moyen âge dans les registres de sentences de l'officialité de Cambrai (1438–1453)', RHE, 102 (2007) 815–836.

Faußner, Hans Constantin. 'Die Thronerhebung des deutschen Königs im Hochmittelalter und die Entstehung des Kurfürstenkollegiums', ZRG Germ. Abt. 108 (1991) 1–60.

Fehr, Hans. *Das Recht im Bilde* (Erlenbach-Zürich-Munich-Leipzig 1923).

Ferme, Brian E. *Canon Law in Late Medieval England: A Study of William Lyndwood's Provinciale with Particular Reference to Testamentary Law* (Rome 1996).

Fernández de Buján Fernández, Antonio. 'Contribución al estudio histórico-jurídico del arbitraje', *Revista juridica Universidad Autónoma de Madrid* 8 (2003) 215–240.

Ferreri, Tiziana. *Ricerche sul crimen calumniae nella dottrina dei glossatori: Da Irnerio ad Azzone e da Graziano a Uguccione da Pisa* (Archivio per la storia del diritto medioevale e moderno, 15; Noceto 2010).

Ficker, Julius. *Forschungen zur Reichs- und Rechtsgeschichte Italiens* (4 vols. Innsbruck 1868–1874, reprinted Aalen 1961).

Fichtenau, Heinrich. *Lebensordnungen des 10. Jahrhunderts: Studien über Denkart und Existenz im einstigen Karolingerreich* (2 vols. Monographien zur Geschichte des Mittelalters 30; Stuttgart 1984).

———. 'Vom Ansehen des Papsttums im 10. Jahrhundert', *Aus Kirche und Reich: Studien zu Theologie, Politik und Recht im Mittelalter: Festschrift für Friedrich Kempf zu seinem fünfundsiebzigsten Geburtstag und fünfzigjährigen Doktorjubiläum*, ed. Hubert Mordek (Sigmaringen 1983) 117–124.

Figueira, Robert C. 'Papal Reserved Powers and the Limitation of Legatine Authority', *Popes, Teachers and Canon Law in the Middle Ages,* ed. James R. Sweeney and Stanley Chodorow (Ithaca-London 1989) 191–211.

———. 'The Medieval Papal Legate and His Province: Geographical Limits of Jurisdiction', *Apollinaris* 16 (1988) 817–860.

Finch, Andrew J. 'Parental Authority and the Problem of Clandestine Marriage in the Later Middle Ages', LHR 8 (1990) 189–204.

Fiori, Antonia. *Il giuramento di innocenza nel processo canonico medievale: Storia e disciplina della 'purgatio canonica'* (Studien zur europäische Rechtsgeschichte 277; Frankurt am Main 2013).

———. 'La valutazione processuale della personalità dell'accusato: Dall'infamia alla "capacità a delinquere del colpevole",' *Einfluss der Kanonistik* 4.157–172.

———. 'Paucapalea', DGI (2013) 2.1525–1526.

Fischer, Andreas. *Kardinäle im Konklave: Die lange Sedisvakanz der Jahre 1268 bis 1271* (Bibliothek des Deutschen Historischen Instituts in Rom 118; Tübingen 2008).

Fisher, William, Morton J. Horwitz, and Thomas Reed, ed. *American Legal Realism* (New York 1993).

Fleckenstein, Josef. *Die Hofkapelle der deutschen Könige* (MGH Schriften 16; Stuttgart 1959–1966).

Fletcher, Richard A. *The Episcopate in the Kingdom of León in the Twelfth Century* (Oxford 1978).

Flug, Brigitte, Michael Matheus, and Andreas Rehberg, ed. *Kurie und Region: Festschrift für Brigide Schwarz zum 65. Geburtstag* (Geschichtliche Landeskunde 59; Wiesbaden 2005).

Foerster, Hans. 'Die Organisation des erzbishöflichen Offizialatsgerichts zu Köln bis auf Hermann von Wied', ZRG Kan. Abt. 11 (1921) 254–350.

Fournier, Édouard. *L'origine du vicaire général et des autres membres de la curie diocésaine* (2nd ed. Paris 1940).

Fournier, Jacques. *Le registre d'inquisition de Jacques Fournier (Évêque de Pamiers, 1318–1325)*, ed. Jean Duvernoy (3 vols. Paris 1978).

Fraher, Richard M. 'Conviction According to Conscience: The Medieval Jurists' Debate Concerning Judicial Discretion and the Law of Proof', LHR 7 (1989) 23–88.

———. 'IV Lateran's Revolution in Criminal Procedure', *Studia in honorem eminentissimi cardinalis Alphonsi M. Stickler*, ed. R. Castillo Lara (Roma 1992) 97–111.

———. 'Tancred's "Summula de criminibus": A New Text and a Key to the Ordo iudiciarius', BMCL 9 (1979) 29–35.

———. 'The Theoretical Justification for the New Criminal Law of the High Middle Ages: Rei publicae interest ne crimina remaneant impunita', *University of Illinois Law Review* (1984) 557–595.

———. 'Ut nullus describatur reus prius quam convincatur: Presumption of Innocence in Medieval Canon Law', *Proceedings Berkeley 1980* 493–506.

Franceschini, Adriano. *I frammenti epigrafici degli statuti di Ferrara del 1173 venuti in luci nella cattedrale* (Ferrara 1969).

Fransen, Gérard. 'Colligite Fragmenta: La "Summa Elnonensis",' SG 13 (1967) 87–108.

Frauenstädt, Paul. *Blutrache und Todtschlagsühne im deutschen Mittelalter: Studien zur deutschen Kultur– und Rechtsgeschichte* (Leipzig 1881).

Fried, Johannes. *Die Entstehung des Juristenstandes im 12. Jahrhundert: Zur sozialen Stellung und politischen Bedeutung gelehrter Juristen in Bologna und Modena* (Forschungen zur neueren Privatrechtsgeschichte 21; Cologne–Vienna 1974).

———. *Der päpstliche Schutz für Laienfürsten: Die politische Geschichte des päpstlichen Schutzprivilegs für Laien (11.–13. Jahrhundert)* (Abh. Akad. Heidelberg; Heidelberg 1980).

———. 'Die römische Kurie und die Anfänge der Prozeßliteratur', ZRG Kan. Abt. 59 (1973) 151–174.

———. Vermögensbildung der bologneser Juristen im 12. und 13. Jahrhundert', *Università e società nei secoli XII–XVI* (Pistoia 1982) 27–59.

Friedlander, Alan, ed. *Processus Bernardi Delitiosi: The Trial of Fr. Bernard Délicieux, 3 September–8 December 1319* (Transactions of the American Philosophical Society 86.1; Philadelphia 1996).

Frölich, Karl. *Alte Dorfplätze und andere Stätten bäuerlicher Rechtspflege* (Arbeiten zur rechtlichen Volkskunde 2; Tübingen, 1938).

———. *Denkmäler mittelalterlicher Strafrechtspflege in Ost- und Mitteldeutschland* (Arbeiten zur rechtlichen Volkskunde 5; Gießen 1946).

———. *Rechtsdenkmäler des deutschen Dorfs* (Gießener Beiträge zur deutschen Philologie 89; Gießen 1947).

———. *Stätten mittelalterlicher Rechtspflege auf südwestdeutschem Boden, besonders in Hessen und den Nachbargebieten* (Arbeiten zur rechtlichen Volkskunde 1; Tübingen 1938).

———. *Stätten mittelalterlicher Rechtspflege im niederdeutschen Bereich* (Arbeiten zur rechtlichen Volkskunde 4; Gießen 1946).

Fudge, Thomas A. *The Trial of John Hus: Medieval Heresy and Criminal Procedure* (Oxford 2013).

Fuhrmann, Horst. 'Papst Gregor VII. und das Kirchenrecht: Zum Problem des Dictatus Papae', *Studi Gregoriani* 13 (1989) 123–149.

———. 'Ecclesia Romana – Ecclesia Universalis', *Rom im hohen Mittelalter: Studien zu den Romvorstellungen und zur Rompolitik vom 10. bis zum 12. Jahrhundert: Festschrift Elze*, ed. B. Schimmelpfennig and L. Schmugge (Sigmaringen 1992) 41–45.

Gabel, Leona C. *Benefit of Clergy in the Later Middle Ages* (Smith College Studies in History 14; Northampton, Mass. 1929).

Galán Lorda, Mercedes. 'Algunos aspectos procesales en el Fuero General de Navarra', *Iacobus* 15–16 (2003) 113–172.

Ganzer, Klaus. *Die Entwicklung des auswärtigen Kardinalats im hohen Mittelalter. Ein Beitrag zur Geschichte des Kardinalskollegiums vom 11. bis 13. Jahrhundert* (Bibliothek des Deutschen Historischen Instituts in Rom 26; Tübingen 1963).

———. 'Das römische Kardinalskollegium', *Le istituzioni ecclesiastiche della 'societas christiana' dei secoli XI–XII: Papato, cardinalato ed episcopato: Atti della quinta settimana internazionale di studio, Mendola, 26–31 agosto 1971* (Miscellanea del Centro di Studi Medioevali 7; Milan 1974) 153–181.

García y García Antonio. *Iglesia, Sociedad y Derecho* (2 vols. Bibliotheca Salmanticensis 74–89; Salamanca 1985–1987).

———. *Synodicon Hispanum* (5 vols. Madrid 1981–1991).

———. *El derecho común en España: Los juristas y sus obras* (Murcia 1991).

———. 'Concilios y sínodos en el ordenamiento jurídico del Reino de León', *El Reino de León en la Alta Edad Media, 1: Cortes, concilios, y fueros* (León 1988) 353–494.

———. 'El aporte de la canonística a la teoría política medieval: Del caso portugués al castellano', *Génesis medieval del estado moderno: Castilla y Navarra, (1250–1370)* ed. Adeline Rucquoi (Valladolid 1987) 49–66.

———. El proceso canónico en la documentación medieval leonesa', *El Reino de León en la Alta Edad Media II: Ordenamiento jurídico del reino* (León 1992) 565–655.

———. 'La justicia eclesiástica en la España Medieval: Un pleito legatino de Silos (1253)', *Società, istituzioni, spiritualità: Studi in onore di Cinzio Violante* (2 vols. Centro itlaiano di Studi sull'Alto Medioevo, Collectanea 1; Spoleto 1994) 1.395–407.

———. 'Legislación de los concilios y sínodos del reino leonés', *El Reino de León en la Alta Edad Media, 2: Ordenamiento jurídico del Reino* (Colección Fuentes y Estudios de Historia Leonesa; León 1992) 7–114.

———. and Bernardo Alonso Rodríguez, Francisco Cantelar Rodríguez, 'Para la historia de un concepto: Liber synodalis', *Studia in Honorem Eminentissimi Cardinalis Alphonsi M. Stickler* (Studia et textus historiae iuris canonici 7; Rome 1992) 1–11.

Gazzaniga, Jean-Louis. 'Les États généraux de Tours de 1484 et les affaires de l'Église', RHD, 62 (1984) 31–45.

Gaudemet, Jean. *Le gouvernment de l'Église à l'époque classique* (Histoire du droit et des institutions de l'Église en occident 7.2; Paris 1979).

———. 'Durand (Durant, Durante) Guillaume (Guglielmo) detto Lo Speculatore', DBI 42 (1993) 82–87.

———. 'La juridiction écclésiastique', *Histoire des institutions françaises au moyen age. 3: Institutions écclésiastiques*, ed. F. Lot and R. Fawtier (Paris, 1962) 257–279.

———. *Les naissances du droit: Le temps, le pouvoir et la science au service du droit* (Domat droit public; Paris 1997).

Gauvard, Claude. 'Honneur de Femme et Femme d'Honneur en France à la fin du Moyen Âge', *Francia* 28 (2001) 159–191.

Geisthardt, Fritz. *Der Kämmerer Boso* (Historische Studien 293; Berlin 1936).

Geltner, Guy. 'Patrolling Normative Borders after the Black Death: The Bishop of Lucca's Criminal Court', *Center and Periphery: Studies on Power in the Medieval World in Honor of William Chester Jordan*, ed. Katherine L. Jansen, Guy Geltner, and Anne E. Lester (Leiden 2013) 169–180.

———. 'I registre criminali dell'Archivio archvescovile di Lucca: Prospettive di ricerca per la storia sociale del medioevo', *Il patrimonio documentario della Chiesa di Lucca: Prospettive di ricerca: Atti del Convegno internazionale di studi*, ed. Sergio Pagano and Pierantonio Piatti (Firenze 2010).

Genest, Jean-François. 'Le Fonds juridique d'un stationnaire italien a la fin du XIIIe siècle: Materiaux nouveaux pour servir à l'histoire de la pecia', *La production du livre universitaire au moyen age: Exemplar et pecia: Actes du symposium tenu au Collegio San Bonaventura de Grottaferrata en Mai 1983*, ed. Louis J. Battaillon, Bertrand G. Guyot, and Richard H. Rouse (Paris 1988) 133–154.

Génestal, Robert. *Les origines de l'appel comme d'abus* (Bibliothèqe de l'École des Hautes Études, Sciences religieuses 63; Paris 1951).

———. *Le privilegium fori en France* (2 vols. Bibliothèqe de l'École des Hautes Études, Sciences religieuses 35, 39; Paris 1921–1924).

Gennep, Arnold van. *The Rites of Passage*, trans. Monika B. Vizedom and Gabrielle L. Caffee (Chicago, 1960).

Genzmer, Erich. 'Eine anonyme Kleinschrift de testibus aus der Zeit um 1200', *Festschrift Paul Koschaker* (3 vols. Weimar 1939; reprinted Leipzig 1977) 3.376–401.

———. 'Summula de testibus ab Alberico de Porta Ravennate composita', *Studi di storia e diritto in onore di Enrico Besta* (4 vols. Milano 1939) 1.491–510.

Giesey, Ralph E. *The Royal Funeral Ceremony in Renaissance France* (Travaux d'humanisme et Renaissance 37; Geneva 1960).

Gilchrist, John T. *Diversorum patrum sententiae; sive, Collectio in LXXIV titulos digesta* (MIC B:1; Città del Vaticano 1973) trans. Gilchrist *The Collection in Seventy-four Titles: A Canon Law Manual of the Gregorian Reform* (Toronto 1980).

Glass, P. C. 'Papal Patronage in the Early Twelfth Century: Notes on the Iconography of Cosmatesque Pavements', *Journal of the Warburg and Courtauld Institutes* 32 (1969) 386–390.

Godding, Philippe. *La Jurisprudence* (Typologie des sources du Moyen Age occidental 6; Turnhout 1973).

Goering, Joseph. 'The Internal Forum and the Literature of Penance and Confession', Hartmann-Pennington *History* 379–428.

Göller, Emil. *Die päpstliche Pönitentiarie von ihrem Ursprung bis zu ihrer Umgestaltung unter Pius V.* (2 vols. Bibliothek des königlich Preussischen Historischen Instituts in Rom 3–4, 7–8; Rome 1907–1911).

González Alonso, Benjamin. 'La justicia', *Enciclopedia de Historia de España, 2: Instituciones políticas: Imperio* (Madrid 1988) 343–417.

Gottlieb, Beatrice. *Getting Married in Pre-Reformation Europe: The Doctrine of Clandestine Marriage and Court Cases in Fifteenth-Century Champagne* (Ph.D. Columbia University 1974).

———. 'The Meaning of Clandestine Marriage', *Family and Sexuality in French History,* ed. Robert Wheaton and Tamara Hareven (Philadelphia 1980) 49–83.

Gouron, André . 'Sur les formules dites de Stintzing', RSDI 62 (1989) 39–54.

———. 'Le rôle de l'avocat selon la doctrine romaniste du douzieme siècle', *L'Assistance dans la résolution des conflits* (Recueils de la Société Jean Bodin pour L'Histoire Comparative des Institutions 65; Brussels 1998) 7–19, reprinted *Pionniers du droit occidental au Moyen Âge* (Collected Studies 865; Aldershot 2006) no. XV.

———. 'Medieval Courts and Towns: Examples from Southern France', *Fundamina* 30 (1992) 30–46, reprinted *Juristes et droits savants: Bologne et la France médiévale* (Selected Studies 679; Aldershot 2000) no. XIV.

———. 'La potestas statuendi dans le droit coutumier montpelliérain du treizième siècle', *Diritto comune e diritti locali nella storia dell'Europa: Atti del Convegno di Varenna (12–15 June 1979)* (Milan 1980) 95–118.

Gousset, Thomas. *Les actes de la province écclésiastique de Reims* (4 vols. Reims 1842–1844).

Graboïs, André. 'Les séjours des papes en France au XIIe siècle et leur rapports avec le développement de la fiscalité pontificale', *Revue d'histoire de l'église de France* 49 (1963) 5–18; reprinted *Civilisation et société dans l'occident médiéval* (London 1983) no. I.

Gramsch, Robert. 'Kommunikation als Lebensform: Kuriale in Thüringen vom 13. bis zum 16. Jahrhundert', *Kurie und Region: Festschrift für Brigide Schwarz zum 65 Geburtstag* (Geschichtliche Landeskunde 59; Wiesbaden 2005) 417–434.

Grandmottet, Odile. 'Les officialités de Reims', *Bulletin d'information de l'Institut de recherche et d'histoire des textes* 4 (1955) 77–106.

Grebner, Gundula. 'Lay Patronage in Bologna in the First Half of the 12th Century: Regular Canons, Notaries, and the *Decretum*', *Europa und seine Regionen: 2000 Jahre Rechtsgeschichte,* ed. Andreas Bauer and Karl H. L. Welker (Cologne 2007) 107–122.

————. 'Kultureller Wandel und Generationswechsel: Bologneser Notare vom 11. zum 12. Jahrhundert', HZ 36 (2003) 25–41.

Gresser, Georg. *Die Synoden und Konzilien in der Zeit des Reformpapsttums in Deutschland und Italien von Leo IX. bis Calixt II. 1049–1123* (Konziliengeschichte, Reihe A; Paderborn 2006).

————. 'Sanctorum patrum auctoritate – Zum Wandel der Rolle des Papstes im Kirchenrecht auf den päpstlichen Synoden in der Zeit der Gregorianischen Reform', ZRG Kan. Abt. 91 (2005) 59–73.

Griffe, Élie. *Le Languedoc cathare et l'Inquisition (1229–1329)* (Paris 1980).

Grimm, Jacob. *Deutsche Rechtsalterthümer* (2 vols. 4th ed. Leipzig, 1899).

Grassis, Cesare de. *Decisiones Sacrae Rotae* (Roma 1590).

Gray, J. W. 'The *Ius Praesentandi* in England from the Constitutions of Clarendon to Bracton', EHR 67 (1952) 481–509.

Gross, Carl. *Incerti auctoris ordo judiciarius* (Innsbruck, 1870).

Guenée, Bernard. *Tribunaux et gens de justice dans le bailliage de Senlis à la fin du moyen âge (vers 1380–vers 1550)* (Publications de la Faculté des Lettres de l'Université de Strasbourg 144; Strasbourg 1963).

Gui, Bernard (Bernardus Guidonis, bishop of Lodève). *Livre des sentences de l'inquisiteur Bernard Gui: 1308–1323,* ed. Annette Pales-Gobilliard (2 vols. Paris 2002).

Guillemain, Bernard. *La cour pontificale d'Avignon 1309–1376: Étude d'une société* (Bibliothèque des Écoles Françaises d'Athènes et de Rome 201; Paris 1962; reprinted 1966).

Guyon, Gérard D. 'L'avocat dans le procédure des anciennes coutumes médievales bordelaises', RHD 86 (2008) 21–38.

Guyotjeannin, Oliver. 'Juridiction gracieuse ecclésiastique et naissance de l'officialité à Beauvais (1175–1220)', *À propos des actes d'éveques: Hommage à Lucie Fossiet,* ed. Michel Parisse (Nancy 1991) 295–310.

Gy, Pierre-Marie. 'La papauté et le droit liturgique aux XIIe et XIIIe siècles', *The Religious Roles of the Papacy: Ideals and Realities 1150–1330* (Pontifical Institute of Mediaeval Studies, Papers in Mediaeval Studies 8; Toronto 1989) 229–245.

Hack, Achim Thomas. *Das Empfangszeremoniell bei mittelalterlichen Papst-Kaiser-Treffen* (Forschungen zur Kaiser- und Papstgeschichte des Mittelalters 18; Cologne 1999).

Hageneder, Othmar. *Die geistliche Gerichtsbarkeit in Ober- und Niederösterreich: von den Anfängen bis zum Beginn des 15. Jahrhunderts* (Forschungen zur Geschichte Oberösterreichs 10; Graz, 1967).

————. 'Zur Frührezeption des Römisch-kanonischen Prozessverfahrens im Lande ob der Enns', *Festschrift Karl Pivec: Zum 60. Geburtstag gewidmet von Kollegen, Freunden und Schülern,* ed. Anton Haidacher and Hans E. Mayer (Innsbrucker Beiträge zur Kulturwissenschaft 12; Innsbruck 1966) 131–139.

————. 'Weltherrschaft im Mittelalter', MIÖG 93 (1985) 257–278.

Hahnloser, Hans Robert. 'Urkunden zur Bedeutung des Türrings', *Festschrift für Erich*

Meyer zum sechzigsten Geburtstag 29. Oktober 1957: Studien zu Werken in den Sammlungen des Museums für Kunst und Gewerbe Hamburg (Hamburg 1959) 125–146.

Haider, Siegfried. 'Zu den Anfängen der päpstlichen Kapelle', MIÖG 87 (1979) 38–70.

Hallam, Elizabeth M. 'Royal Burial and the Cult of Kingship in France and England 1060–1330', JMH 8 (1982) 359–380.

Hardman, Elizabeth. *Justice, Jurisdiction and Choice: The Church Courts of Carpentras in the Fifteenth Century* (Ph.D. dissertation, Fordham University, New York 2010).

Hartmann, Wilfried. *Kirche und Kirchenrecht um 900: Die Bedeutung der spätkarolingischen Zeit für Tradition und Innovation im kirchlichen Recht* (MGH Schriften, 58.; Hannover 2008).

Hashagen, Justus. 'Zur Charakteristik der geistlichen Gerichtsbarkeit vornehmlich im späteren Mittelalter', ZRG Kan. Abt. 6 (1916) 205–292.

Heckel, R. von. 'Das Aufkommen der ständigen Prokuratoren an der päpstlichen Kurie im 13. Jahrhundert', *Miscellanea Francesco Ehrle: Scritti di storia e paleografia* (Studi e testi 37–42; Vatican City 1924) 2.290–321.

Helmholz, Richard H. *The Canon Law and Ecclesiastical Jurisdiction from 597 to the 1640s* (The Oxford History of the Laws of England, 1; Oxford–New York 2004).

———. *Marriage Litigation in Medieval England* (Cambridge Studies in English Legal History; Cambridge 1974).

———. *Select Cases on Defamation to 1600* (Publications of the Selden Society 101; London, 1985).

———. *The Spirit of Classical Canon Law* (The Spirit of the Laws; Athens–London 1996).

———. *Roman Canon Law in Reformation England* (Cambridge Studies in English Legal History; Cambridge 1990).

———. 'Assumpsit and *fidei laesio*', *Law Quarterly Review* 91 (1975) 406–432.

———. 'Canonists and Standards of Impartiality for Papal Judges Delegate', *Traditio* 25 (1969) 386–404.

———. 'Undue Delay in the English Ecclesiastical Courts (circa 1350–1600)', *The Law's Delay: Essays on Undue Delay in Civil Litigation*, ed. Cornelis [Remco] van Rhee (Ius commune Europaeum 47; Antwerp-Oxford-New York 2004) 131–139.

———. 'Due and Undue Delay in the English Ecclesiastical Courts (ca. 1300–1600)', *Within a Reasonable Time: The History of Due and Undue Delay in Civil Litigation*, ed. Cornelis [Remco] H. van Rhee (Comparative Studies in Continental and Anglo-American Legal History 28; Berlin 2010) 73–92.

———. 'The Canon Law of Annual Pensions', *Recto ordine procedit magister: Liber amicorum E. C. Coppens*, ed. L. Berkvens et al. (Brussels 2012) 161–73.

———. 'Married Women's Wills in Later Medieval England', *Wife and Widow in Medieval England*, ed. Susan S. Walker (Ann Arbor, Michigan 1993) 165–182.

Henssler, Ortwin. *Formen des Asylrechts und ihre Verbreitung bei den Germanen* (Frankfurt 1954).

Herde, Peter. *Audientia litterarum contradictarum: Untersuchungen über die päpstlichen Justizbriefe und die päpstliche Delegationsgerichtsbarkeit vom 13. bis zum Beginn des 16. Jahrhunderts* (2 vols, Bibliothek des Deutschen Historischen Instituts in Rom 31–32; Tübingen 1970).

———. *Beiträge zum päpstlichen Kanzlei- und Urkundenwesen im dreizehnten Jahrhundert* (2d ed. Münchener historische Studien, Abteilung Geschichtlichen Hilfswissenschaften 1; Kallmünz 1967).

———. 'Zur päpstlichen Delegationsgerichtsbarkeit im Mittelalter und in der Frühen Neuzeit', ZRG Kan. Abt. 119 (2002) 20–43.

Herklotz, Ingo. *Gli eredi di Costantino: Il papato, il Laterano e la propaganda visiva nel XII secolo* (La corte dei papi 6; Rome 2000).

Herrmann, Klaus–Jürgen. *Das Tuskulanerpapsttum (1012–1046): Benedikt VIII., Johannes XIX., Benedikt IX.* (Päpste und Papsttum 4; Stuttgart 1973).

Hibbitts, Bernard J. "Coming to our Senses': Communication and Legal Expression in Performance Cultures', *Emory Law Journal* 41 (1992) 874–960.

Hoehne, Hans. 'Pilii Medicinensis Summula de reorum exceptionibus "precibus et instantia",' *Ius commune* 9 (1980) 139–209.

Hilling, Nikolaus. *Die Offiziale der Bischöfe von Halberstadt im Mittelalter* (Kirchenrechtliche Abhandlungen 72; Stuttgart, 1911).

Hirte, Markus. *Papst Innozenz III., das IV. Lateranum und die Strafverfahren gegen Kleriker: Eine registergestützte Untersuchung zur Entwicklung der Verfahrensarten zwischen 1198 und 1216* (Rothenburger Gespräche zur Strafrechtsgeschichte 5; Tübingen 2005).

Hofflich Michael H., and Jasonne M. Grabher, 'The Establishment of Normative Legal Texts: The Beginnings of the *Ius commune*', Hartmann-Pennington *History* 1–21.

Holmes, Oliver Wendell, Jr. 'Natural Law', *Harvard Law Review* 32 (1918) 40–44.

Holtzmann, Walther ed. *Papsturkunden in England, 1: Bibliotheken und Archive in London* (Abhandlungen der Akademie der Wissenschaften in Göttingen, phil.-historische Klasse 25; Berlin 1931).

Horn, Michael. *Studien zur Geschichte Papst Eugens III. 1145–1153* (Europäische Hochschulschriften 3.508; Frankfurt am Main 1992).

Horn, Norbert. 'Bologneser Doctores und Iudices im 12. Jahrhundert und die Rezeption der studierten Berufsjuristen', *Zeitschrift für historische Forschung* 3 (1976) 221–232.

Hugot, Leo. 'Baugeschichtliches zum Grab Karls des Großen', *Aachener Kunstblätter* 52 (1984) 13–28.

Hüls, Rudolf. *Kardinäle, Klerus und Kirchen* (Bibliothek de Deutschen historischen Instituts in Rom 48; Tübingen 1977).

Hyams, Paul. 'Trial by Ordeal: The Key to Proof in Early Common Law', *On the Laws and Customs of England: Essays in Honor of Samuel E. Thorne*, ed. Morris S. Arnold et al. (Chapel Hill 1981) 90–126.

Iglesia Ferreirós, Aquilino José. ' Rex superiorem non recognoscens: Hugolino de Sesso y el Studium de Palencia', *Initium* 3 (1998) 1–205.

Ingram, Martin. *Church Courts, Sex and Marriage in England, 1570–1640* (Cambridge 1987).

Izbicki, Thomas M. 'Problems of Attribution in the Tractatus Universi Iuris (Venice 1584)', *Studi Senesi* 92 (1980) 479–493.

Jerouschek, Günter. '"Ne crimina remaneant impunita": Auf daß Verbrechen nicht ungestraft bleiben: Überlegungen zur Begründung öffentlicher Strafverfolgung im Mittelalter', ZRG Kan. Abt. 89 (2003) 323–337; also published in *Strafrechtsgeschichte an der Grenze des nächsten Jahrtausends*, ed. Barna Mezey (Budapest 2003) 54–84.

Johanek, Peter. 'Ordo iudiciarius', *Die deutsche Literatur des Mittelalters: Verfasserlexikon* 11 (2004) 1083–1090.

Johrendt, Jochen. 'Die Reisen der frühen Reformpäpste—ihre Ursachen und Funktionen', RQ 96 (2001) 57–94.

Johrendt, Jochen, and Harald Müller, ed. *Römisches Zentrum und kirchliche Peripherie: Das universale Papsttum als Bezugspunkt der Kirchen von den Reformpäpsten bis zu Innozenz III.* (Neue Abhandlungen der Akademie der Wissenschaften zu Göttingen, Philologisch-Historische Klasse 2; Berlin 2008).

Jolowicz, Herbert Felix, and Barry Nicholas. *Historical Introduction to the Study of Roman Law* (3d ed. Cambridge 1972).

Joosting, Jan Gualtherus Christiaan. 'Die Summa "Ut nos minores",' ZRG Kan. 17 (1928) 153–227.

Joosting, Jan Gualtherus Christiaan, and Samuel Muller. *Bronnen voor de geschiedenis der kerkelijke rechtspraak in het bisdom Utrecht in de middeleeuwen* (7 vols. 's-Gravenhage 1906–1924).

Jordan, Karl. 'Die Entstehung der römischen Kurie: Ein Versuch', ZRG Kan. Abt. 28 (1939) 97–152, 2nd ed. printed separately Darmstadt 1962).

———. 'Die päpstliche Verwaltung im Zeitalter Gregors VII.', *Studi Gregoriani* 1 (1947) 111–135, reprinted *Ausgewählte Aufsätze zur Geschichte des Mittelalters* (Kieler Historische Studien 29; Stuttgart 1980) 129–153.

———. 'Zur päpstlichen Finanzgeschichte im 11. und 12. Jahrhundert', QF 25 (1933–1934) 61–104; reprinted *Ausgewählte Aufsätze* 85–128.

Jordan, William C. 'A Fresh Look at Medieval Sanctuary', *Law and the Illicit in Medieval Europe,* ed. Ruth Mazo Karras, Joel Kaye, and E. Ann Matter (The Middle Ages; Philadelphia 2008) 17–32.

Julien, Alfred R. 'Evolutio historica compromissi in arbitros in iure canonico', *Apollinaris* 10 (1937) 187–232, 544–569 and as a monograph (Rome 1937).

Kagay, Donald. *The Usatges of Barcelona: The Fundamental Law of Catalonia* (Philadelphia 1994).

Kantorowicz, Ernst H. *The King's Two Bodies: A Study in Mediaeval Political Theology* (Princeton 1957).

Kantorowicz, Herman U. 'Accursio e la sua Biblioteca', RSDI 2 (1929) 35–62 and 193–212.

———. *Rechtshistorische Schriften,* ed. Helmut Coing and Gerhard Immel (Freiburger Rechts– und Staatswissenschaftliche Ablandlungen 30.; Karlsruhe1970).

Karras, Ruth Mazo. *Unmarriages: Women, Men, and Sexual Unions in Medieval Europe* (Middle Ages; Philadelphia 2012).

Kautzsch, Rudolf. *Der Dom zu Worms* (3 vols. Berlin, 1938).

Keller, Hagen. 'Der Gerichtsort in oberitalienischen und toskanischen Städten: Untersuchungen zur Stellung der Stadt im Herrschaftssystem des Regnum Italicum vom 9. bis 11. Jahrhundert', QF 49 (1969) 1–72.

Kelly, John Maurice. *Roman Litigation* (Oxford 1966).

Kéry, Lotte. *Canonical Collections of the Early Middle Ages (ca. 400–1140): A Bibliographical Guide to the Manuscripts and Literature* (History of Medieval Canon Law; Washington, D.C. 1999).

———. 'Inquisitio—denunciatio—exceptio: Möglichkeiten der Verfahrenseinleitung im Dekretalenrecht', ZRG Kan. Abt. 87 (2001) 226–268.

———. *Gottesfurcht und irdische Strafe: Der Beitrag des mittelalterlichen Kirchenrechts zur Entstehung des öffentlichen Strafrechts* (Konflikt, Verbrechen und Sanktion in der Gesellschaft Alteuropas, 10; Köln-Weimar-Wien 2006).

Kevin, Saule. 'L'officialité de Beauvais et l'enfermement des curés délinquants au xviie siècle: Entre rigueur et indulgence', Beaulande/Charageat, *Les officialités* 205–214.

Klapisch-Zuber, Christine. 'Zacharias, or the Ousted Father: Nuptial Rites in Tuscany between Giotto and the Council of Trent', *Women, Family, and Ritual in Renaissance Italy,* trans. Lydia G. Cochrane (Chicago 1985) 178–212.

Klemmer, Klemens. *Von der Linde über den Palast zu einem Haus des Rechts: Katalog zur ständigen Ausstellung im Niedersächsischen Justizministerium* (Regensburg 1991).

Klemmer, Klemens, R. Wassermann, and T. M. Wessel. *Deutsche Gerichtsgebäude: Von der Dorflinde über den Justizpalast zum Haus des Rechts* (Munich 1993).

Knapek, Elżbieta ed. *Akta oficjalatu i wikariatu generalnego krakowskiego do połowy XVI wieku* (Polska Akademia Umiejętności, Rozprawy Wydziału Historyczno-Filozoficznego, Ogólnegozbioru, 110; Kraków 2010)

Knibbs, Eric. 'The Interpolated Hispana and the Origins of Pseudo–Isidore', ZRG Kan. Abt. 130 (2013) 1–71.

Kölzer, Theo. 'Adventus regis', LMA 1 (1977) 170–171.

Körmendy, Kinga. *Studentes extra regnum: Esztergomi kanonokok egyetemjárása és könyvhasználata 1183–1543* (Bibliotheca Instituti Postgradualis Iuris Canonici Universitatis Catholicae de Petro Pázmány nominatae 3.9; Budapest 2007).

———. 'A jogtudó magyar értelmiség és a Curia Romana a 16. század elején', *Tanulmányok a magyarországi egyházjog középkori történetéről. Kéziratos kódexek, zsinatok, középkori műfajok*, ed. Péter Erdő (Bibliotheca Instituti Postgradualis Iuris Canonici Universitatis Catholicae de Petro Pázmány nominatae III/3; Budapest 2002) 211–223.

Korpiola, Mia. *Between Betrothal and Bedding: Marriage Formation in Sweden 1200–1600* (Leiden 2009).

———. *Regional Variations in Matrimonial Law and Custom in Europe, 1150–1600* (Medieval Law and its Practice 12; Leiden 2011).

Kötzschke, Rudolf. 'Das Gericht Werden im späteren Mittelalter Ausübung der Landesgewalt im Stiftsgebiet', *Beiträge zur Geschichte des Stiftes Werden* 10 (1904) 70–126.

Krahel, Tadeusz. 'Die anfängliche Organisation der Kirche in Litauen', *La cristianizzazione della Lituania: Atti del Colloquio Internazionele di Storia Ecclesiastica, in occasione del VI Centenario della Lituania cristiana, 1387–1987. Roma, 24–26 Giugno 1987*, ed. Paulius Rabikauskas (Pontificio Comitato di Scienze Storiche, Atti e Documenti 2; Città del Vaticano 1989) 159–174.

Krynen, Jacques. 'Le roi Très chrétien et le rétablissement de la Pragmatique Sanction. Pour une explication idéologique du gallicanisme parlementaire et de la politique religieuse de Louis XI', *Églises et pouvoir politique. Actes des journées internationales d'histoire du droit d'Angers, 30 mai–1er juin 1985* (Angers 1987) 135–149.

Künßberg, Eberhard von. *Rechtliche Volkskunde* (Grundriß der deutschen Volkskunde in Einzeldarstellungen 3; Halle, 1936).

Kunstmann, Friedrich. 'Über den altesten *Ordo judiciarius*', *Kritische Überschau der deutschen Gesetzgebung und Rechtswissenschaft* 2 (1855) 17–29.

Kuttner, Stephan. 'Analecta iuridica Vaticana (Vat. lat. 2343)', *Collectanea Vaticana in honorem Anselmi M. Card. Albareda a Biblioteca Apostolica edita* (2 vols. Studi e Testi 219–220; Vatican City 1962) 1.415–452.

———. 'Cardinalis: The History of a Canonical Concept', *Traditio* 3 (1945) 160–63; reprinted *The History of Ideas and Doctrines of Canon Law in the Middle Ages* (London 1980) no. IX.

———. 'The Revival of Jurisprudence', *Renaissance and Renewal in the Twelfth Century*, ed. R. L. Benson and Giles Constable (Cambridge, Mass. 1982) 299–323.

———. 'Ricardus Anglicus (Richard de Mores ou de Morins)', DDC 7 (1965) 676–681.

Kuttner, Stephan, and E. Rathbone, 'Anglo-Norman Canonists of the Twelfth Century: an Introductory Study', *Traditio* 7 (1951) 279–358.

Kyer, Clifford Ian. 'The Legation of Cardinal Latinus and William Duranti's "Speculum legatorum",' BMCL 10 (1980) 56–62.

———. 'Legate and Nuntius as Used to Denote Papal Envoys 1245–1378', *Mediaeval Studies* 40 (1978) 473–477.

———. *The Papal Legate and the 'Solemn' Papal Nuncio, 1243–1378: The Changing Pattern of Papal Representation* (Ph.D. dissertation; University of Toronto 1979).

Ladner, Gerhart B. 'The Concept of "Ecclesia" and "Christianitas" and their Relation to the Idea of Papal "Plenitudo Potestatis" from Gregory VII to Boniface VIII', *Sacerdocio e Regno da Gregorio VII a Bonifacio VIII* (Miscellanea Historiae Pontificiae 18; Rome 1954) 1.49–77 reprinted *Images and Ideas in the Middle Ages* (Storia e Letteratura 156; Rome 1983) 2.487–515.

Lamon Zuchuat, Valérie. 'Mariages clandestins dans le diocèse de Sion à la fin du Moyen Age', *Annales valaisannes* (2004) 7–25.

————. *Trois pommes pour un mariage: L'Église et les unions clandestines dans le diocèse de Sion, 1430–1550* (Cahiers lausannois d'histoire médiévale 46; Lausanne 2008).

Landau, Peter. *Europäische Rechtsgeschichte und kanonisches Recht im Mittelalter* (Badenweiler 2013).

————. *Ius Patronatus: Studien zur Entwicklung des Patronats im Dekretalenrecht und der Kanonistik* (Cologne 1975).

————. '*Ne crimina maneant impunita:* Zur Entstehung des öffentlichen Strafanspruchs und der Rechtswissenschaft des 12. Jahrhunderts', *Einfluss der Kanonistik* 2.23–35.

————. 'Die Anfänge der Prozessrechtswissenschaft in der Kanonistik des 12. Jahrhunderts', *Einfluss der Kanonistik* 1.7–23.

————. 'Bürgschaft und Darlehen im Dekretalenrecht des 12. Jahrhunderts: Zugleich zur Biographie des Peter von Blois und des Stephan von Tournai', *Festschrift für Dieter Medicus zum 70. Geburtstag*, ed. Volker Beuthien et al. (Köln-Berlin-Bonn-München 1999) 297–316.

Langbein, John. *Torture and the Law of Proof: Europe and England in the Ancien Régime* (2d ed. Chicago 2006).

Lange, Hermann. *Römisches Recht im Mittelalter, 1: Die Glossatoren* (München 1997).

————. and Maximiliane Kriechbaum. *Römisches Recht im Mittelalter, 2: Die Kommentatoren* (München 2007).

Langton, Stephen. *Acta Stephani Langton Cantuariensis archiepiscopi A.D. 1207–1228*, ed. Kathleen Major (Canterbury and York Society 50; Oxford 1950).

Larson, Atria Ann. *Master of Penance: Gratian and the Development of Penitential Thought and Law in the Twelfth Century* (Studies in Medieval and Early Modern Canon Law 11; Washington, D.C. 2014).

————. 'Early Stages of Gratian's *Decretum* and the Second Lateran Council: A Reconsideration', BMCL 27 (2007) 21–56.

Le Cacheux, Paul. 'Un fragment de registre de l'officialité de Cerisy', *Bulletin de la Société des antiquaires de Normandie* 43 (1935) 291–315.

Le Roy Ladurie, Émmanuel. *Montaillou, village occitan de 1294 à 1324* (Paris 1975).

Lea, Henry Charles. *A History of the Inquisition of the Middle Ages* (3 vols. New York 1888).

Lefebvre, Charles. 'La concession des conservateurs apostoliques au temps d'Innocent IV (1234–1254)', *Ephemerides Juris Canonici* 31 (1975) 116–135.

Lefebvre-Teillard, Anne. 'Une nouvelle venue dans l'histoire du droit canonique: La jurisprudence', *Proceedings Berkeley 1980* 647–675.

————. *Les officialités à la veille du concile de Trente* (Bibliothèque d'histoire du droit et droit romain 19; Paris 1973).

————. 'Règle et realité dans le droit matrimonial à la fin du moyen–age', RDC, 30 (1980) 41–54.

Lehnen, Joachim. *Adventus principis: Untersuchungen zu Sinngehalt und Zeremoniell der Kaiserankunft in den Städten des Imperium Romanum* (Prismata 7; Frankfurt am Main 1997).

Leitmaier, C. *Die Kirche und die Gottesurteile: Eine rechtshistorische Studie* (Wiener rechtsgeschichtliche Arbeiten 2; Vienna, 1953).

Lemarignier, Jean-François. *Étude sur les privilèges d'exemption et la juridiction ecclésiastique des abbayes normandes depuis les origines jusqu'à 1140* (Thèse droit, Paris 1937).

————. 'L'exemption monastique et les origines de la réforme grégorienne', *A Cluny: Congrès scientifique: Fêtes et cérémonies liturgiques en l'honneur des saints abbés Odon et Odilon* (Dijon 1950) 288–340.

Lenski, Noel Emmanuel. 'Evidence for the *Audientia episcopalis* in the New Letters of Augustine', *Law, Society, and Authority in Late Antiquity*, ed. Ralph W. Mathisen (New York 2001) 83–97.

Lévy, Jean-Philippe. *La hierarchie des preuves dans le droit savant du moyen âge* (Annales de l'université de Lyon, 3e sér., droit, fasc. 5; Paris 1935).

———. 'L'officialité de Paris et les questions familiales à la fin du XIVe siècle' *Études d'histoire de droit canonique dédiées à Gabriel Le Bras* (2 vols. Paris 1965) 2.1265–1294.

Linehan, Peter. *The Spanish Church and the Papacy in the Thirteenth Century* (Cambridge Studies in Medieval Life and Thought 4; Cambridge 1971).

———. 'Spanish Litigants and Their Agents at the Thirteenth–century Papal Curia', *Proceedings Salamanca 1976* 487–501.

Lindner, Klaus. *Courtship and the Courts: Marriage and Law in Southern Germany, 1350–1550* (Ph.D. Thesis, Harvard Divinity School, 1988).

Logan, F. Donald. *The Medieval Court of Arches* (Canterbury and York Society 95; Woodbridge, Suffolk 2005).

———. *Excommunication and the Secular Arm in Medieval England* (Studies and Texts 15; Toronto 1968).

———. 'An Early Thirteenth–Century Formulary', *Collectanea Stephan Kuttner* (SG 14; Bologna 1967) 75–87.

Lombardi, Daniela. 'Il reato di stupro tra foro ecclesiastico e foro secolare', *Transgressioni: Seduzione, concubinato, adulterio, bigamia (XIV–XVIII secolo)* ed. Silvana Seidel Menchi and Diego Quaglioni (Bologna 2004) 351–382.

Lonza, Nella. 'La Biblioteca Duecentesca del Canonico Zaratino Iohannes de Scomla', RIDC 3 (1992) 197–219.

———. 'Blasius of Moravče, a Fifteenth–century Canon of Zagreb and His Legal Manuscripts', *Sacri canones* 444–455.

Lorcin, Marie-Thérèse. 'Des commandes pour les orfèvres: La visite pastorale du diocèse de Lyon en 1469', *Cahiers d'histoire* 24 (1979) 21–48.

Lohmann, H.-E. 'Die Collectio Wigorniensis (Collectio Londinensis Regia): Ein Beitrag zur Quellengeschichte des kanonischen Rechts im 12. Jahrhundert', ZRG Kan.Abt. 32 (1933) 123–124, 180–181.

Loschiavo, Luca. 'Bulgaro', DGI (2013) 1.357–359.

Lot, Fernand, and Robert Fawtier. *Histoire des institutions, 2: Institutions royales* (Paris 1958).

Lunt, W. E. *Financial Relations of the Papacy with England to 1327* (Studies in Anglo-Papal Relations during the Middle Ages 1; Cambridge, Mass. 1939).

Lydford, John. *John Lydford's Book,* ed. Dorothy M. Owen (Historical Manuscripts Commission JP 22; London 1974).

Maffei, Domenico. *Giuristi medievali e falsificazioni editoriali del primo cinquecento* (Ius commune, Sonderhefte 10; Frankfurt am Main 1979).

———. 'Fra Cremona, Montpellier e Palencia nel secolo XII: Ricerche su Ugolino da Sesso' RIDC 1 (1990) 9–30.

———. 'Un trattato di Bonaccurso degli Elisei e i più antichi statuti dello Studio di Bologna nel manoscritto 22 della Robbins Collection', BMCL 5 (1975) 73–101.

———. 'Fra Cremona, Montpellier e Palencia nel secolo XII: Ricerche su Ugolino da Sesso', REDC 47 (1990) 34–51, also printed in RIDC 1 (1990) 9–30.

Maffei, Paola. 'Ugolino da Sesso' DGI 2.1994.

Maitland, Frederic William. *Roman Canon Law in the Church of England: Six Essays* (London 1898; reprinted New York 1968).

Maldonado, José, and Fernández del Torco, 'Líneas de influencia canónica en la historia del proceso español', AHDE 23 (1953) 467–494.

Maleczek, Werner. *Papst und Kardinalskolleg von 1191–1216: Die Kardinäle unter Coelestin III. und Innozenz III.* (Publikationen des Historischen Instituts beim Österreichischen Kulturinstitut in Rom 6; Vienna 1984).

————. 'Rombeherrschung und Romerneuerung durch das Papsttum', *Rom im hohen Mittelalter: Studien zu den Romvorstellungen und zur Rompolitik vom 10. zum 12. Jahrhundert: Reinhard Elze zur Vollendung seines siebzigsten Lebensjahres gewidmet,* ed. Bernhard Schimmelpfennig and Ludwig Schmugge (Sigmaringen 1992) 15–27.

————. 'Das Kardinalskolleg unter Innocenz II. und AnakletII', AHP 19 (1981) 27–78.

————. 'Die Kardinale von 1143 bis 1216: Exklusive Papstwähler und erste Agenten der päpstlichen plenitudo potestatis', *Geschichte des Kardinalats im Mittelalter,* ed. Jürgen Dendorfer and Ralf Lützelschwab (Stuttgart 2011) 95–154.

————. 'Boso', LMA 2 (1983) 478–479.

Martines, Lauro. *Lawyers and Statecraft in Renaissance Florence* (Princeton 1968).

Martínez Marcos, Esteban. *Las causas matrimoniales en las Partidas de Alfonso el Sabio* (Consejo superior de investigaciones cientificas, Instituto 'San Raimuno de Peñafort'; Salamanca 1966).

Martínez-Torrón, Javier. *Derecho angloamericano y derecho canónico* (Madrid 1991).

Maugis, Édouard, ed. *Documents inédits concernant la ville et le siège du bailliage d'Amiens: Extraits des registres du Parlement de Paris et du Trésor des chartes* (3 vols. Amiens 1908–1921).

Maussen, Yves. *Veritatis adiutor: La procédure du témoignage dans le droit savant et la pratique française (XIIe–XIVe siècles)* (Università degli studi di Milano, Facoltà di giurisprudenza, Pubbblicazioni dell' Istituto di storia del diritto medievale e moderno 35; Milano 2006)

May, Georg. *Die geistliche Gerichtsbarkeit des Erzbischoffs von Mainz im Thüringen: Das Generalgericht zu Erfurt* (Erfurter Theologische Studien 2; Leipzig 1956).

————. 'Die Belegung kirchlicher Vergehen mit Infamie durch den Staat in römischen und westgotischen Reichs', OAKR 15 (1964) 177–188.

Mazzacane, Aldo. 'Farinacci, Prospero', DBI 45 (1995) 1–5.

————. 'Farinacci, Prospero', DGI (2013) 1.822–825.

Mazzanti, Giuseppe. 'Guido da Suzzara', DBI 61 (2004) 421–426.

McAuley, Finbarr. 'Canon Law and the End of the Ordeal', *Oxford Journal of Legal Studies* 26 (2006) 473–513.

McDonough, Susan Alice. 'She Said, He Said, and They Said: Claims of Abuse and a Community's Response in Late Medieval Marseille', *Journal of Women's History* 19 (2007) 35–58.

McDougall, Sara. *Bigamy and Christian Identity in Late Medieval Champagne* (Middle Ages; Philadelphia 2012).

————. 'The Opposite of the Double Standard: Gender, Marriage, and Adultery Prosecution in Late Medieval France', *Journal of the History of Sexuality* 23 (2014) 206–225.

————. 'The Transformation of Adultery in France at the End of the Middle Ages', LHR 32 (2014) 491–524.

McHardy, A. K. 'Church Courts and Criminous Clerks in the later Middle Ages', *Medieval Ecclesiastical Studies in Honour of Dorothy M. Owen,* ed. M. J. Franklin and C. Harper–Bill (Woodbridge 1995) 165–183.

McKenzie, John, SJ. 'Law in the New Testament', *The Jurist* 26 (1966) 180.

McLean, Alick. *Sacred Space and Public Policy: The Establishment, Decline & Revival of Prato's Piazza della Pieve* (Ph.D. Princeton University, 1993).

————. 'Romanesque Architecture in Italy', *Romanesque: Architecture, Sculpture, Painting,* ed. R. Toman (Cologne 1997) 74–117.

McNair, Mike. 'Vicinage and the Antecedents of the Jury' LHR, 17 (1999) 537–71.

McSheffrey, Shannon. *Consistory Database: Testimony in the Late Medieval London Consistory Court* (http://digitalhistory.concordia.ca/consistory/).

————. *Marriage, Sex, and Civic Culture in Late-medieval London* (Middle Ages; Philadelphia 2006).

Meduna, Brigitte. *Studien zum Formular der päpstlichen Justizbriefe von Alexander III. bis Innocenz III. (1159–1216): Die non obstantibus-Formel* (Sitzungsberichte Vienna 536; Vienna 1989).

Meek, Christine. 'Women, the Church and the Law: Matrimonial Litigation in Lucca under Bishop Nicolao Guinigi (1394–1435)', *Chattel, Servant or Citizen: Women's Status in Church, State and Society,* ed. Mary O'Dowd and Sabine Wichert (Institute of Irish Studies, Queen's University, Belfast, Historical Studies 19; Belfast 1995) 82–90.

Mende, Ursula. *Die Türzieher des Mittelalters* (Denkmäler deutscher Kunst: Bronzegeräte des Mittelalters 2; Berlin, 1981).

Menzinger, Sara. *Giuristi e politica nei comuni di popolo: Siena, Perugia e Bologna, tre governi a confronto* (Ius nostrum, Studi e testi 34.; Roma 2006)

————. 'Foscarari, Egidio (Egidius, Gilius de Foscarariis, Fuscarariis)', DGI (2013) 1.893–894.

Merchán Álvarez, Antonio. *El arbitraje: Estudio histórico–juridico* (Seville 1981).

————. 'Arbitraje y el derecho común', *El Derecho Común y Europa del derecho de El Escorial: Jornadas Internacionales de Historia del Derecho de El Escorial, 3–6 de Junio de 1999: Actas* (Madrid 2000) 121–156.

Merlet, Lucien. 'Registre des officialités de Chartres', BEC, 17 (1856) 574–594.

Merzbacher, Friedrich. 'Der Kiliansdom als Rechtsdenkmal', *Ecclesia Cathedralis: Der Dom zu Würzburg,* ed. R. Schömig (Würzburg 1967) 69–82.

Migliorino, Francesco. *Fama e infama: Problemi della società medievale nel pensiero giuridico nei secoli XII e XIII* (Catania 1985).

Miller, Maureen C. *The Bishop's Palace: Architecture and Authority in Medieval Italy* (Ithaca-London 2000).

————. 'From Episcopal to Communal Palaces: Places and Power in Northern Italy (1000–1250)', *Journal of the Society of Architectural Historians* 54 (1995) 175–185.

Millon, David. 'Ecclesiastical Jurisdiction in Medieval England', *University of Illinois Law Review* (1984) 621–638.

Minnucci, Giovanni. *La capacità processuale della donna nel pensiero canonistico classico, 2: Dalle scuole d'oltralpe a S. Raimondo di Pennaforte* (Quaderni di 'Studi senesi' 79; Milan 1994).

Mnookin, Robert, and Lewis Kornhauser. 'Bargaining in the Shadow of the Law', *Yale Law Journal* 88 (1979) 950–97.

Molin, Jean-Baptiste, and Protais Mutembe. *Le Rituel du mariage en France du XIIe au XVIe siècle* (Théologie historique 26; Paris 1974).

Mollat, Gullaume. 'Contribution à l'histoire de l'administration judiciaire de l'Église romaine au XIVe siècle', RHE 32 (1936) 876–928.

————. *Les papes d'Avignon* (10th ed. Paris 1965).

Morris, Colin. 'The Commissary of the Bishop in the Diocese of Lincoln', JEH 10 (1959) 50–65.

————. 'From Synod to Consistory: The Bishop's Courts in England, 1150–1250', JEH 22 (1971) 115–123.

————. 'William I and the Church Courts', EHR 82 (1967) 449–463.

Müller, Harald. *Päpstliche Delegationsgerichtsbarkeit in der Normandie (12. und frühes 13. Jahrhundert)* (Studien und Dokumente zur Gallia Pontificia 4.1–2; Bonn 1997).

————. 'Gesandte mit beschränkter Handlungsvollmacht: Zu Struktur und Praxis päpstlich delegierter Gerichtsbarkeit', *Aus der Frühzeit europäischer Diplomatie: Zum geistlichen und weltlichen Gesandtschaftswesen vom 12. bis zum 15. Jahrhundert,* ed. Claudia Märtl and Claudia Zey (Zürich 2008) 41–65.

————. 'Entscheidung auf Nachfrage: Die delegierten Richter als Verbindungsglieder zwischen Kurie und Region sowie als Gradmesser päpstlicher Autorität', *Römisches Zentrum und kirchliche Peripherie: Das universale Papsttum als Bezugspunkt der Kirchen von den Reformpäpsten bis zu Innozenz III.* ed. Jochen Johrendt and Harald Müller (Neue Abhandlungen der Akademie der Wissenschaften zu Göttingen, Philologisch–Historische Klasse 2; Berlin 2008) 109–131.

Müller-Mertens, Eckhard. 'Reich und Hauptorte der Salier: Probleme und Fragen', *Die Salier und das Reich, 1: Salier, Adel und Reichsverfassung,* ed. Stefan Weinfurter et al. (Sigmaringen 1991)139–158.

Murano, Giovanna. *Autographa, I.1: Giuristi, giudici e notai (sec. XII–XVI med)* with Giovanna Morelli and Thomas Woelki (Bologna 2012).

————. 'Ricerche sul "Libellus fugitives",' *Aevum* 79 (2005) 417–460. Muther, Theodor. *Die Geschichte des römisch-canonischen Prozesses in Deutschland während des vierzehnten und zu Beginn des fünfzehnten Jahrhunderts* (Rostock 1872).

Napoli, Maria Teresa. 'L'Ordo iudiciarius "Quia utilissimum fore",' ZRG Kan. Abt. 62 (1976) 58–105.

Nörr, Knut Wolfgang. *Romanisch–kanonisches Prozessrecht: Erkenntnisverfahren erster Instanz in civilibus* (Enzyklopädie der Rechts- und Staatswissenschaft, Abteilung Rechtswissenschaft, Berlin-Heidelberg-New York 2012).

————. 'A Propos du Speculum Iudiciale de Guilaume Durand', *Guilaume Durand: Évêque de Mende (vers 1230–1296): Canoniste, legiste et homme politique* ed. P. M. Gy (Actes de la Table Ronde de CNRS. Mende 24–27, Mai 1990; Paris 1992) 63–67.

————. *Iudicium est actus trium personarum: Beiträge zur Geschichte des Zivilprozessrechts in Europa* (Biblioteca eruditorom 4; Goldbach 1993).

————. 'Ordo iudiciorum und ordo iudiciarius', *Collectana Stephan Kuttner* (SG 11; Bologna 1967) 327–344.

————. Päpstliche Dekretalen in den ordines iudiciorum der friihen Legistik', *Ius Commune* 3 (1970) 1–9.

————. 'Päpstliche Dekretalen und römisch–kanonischer Zivilprozess', *Studien zur europäischen Rechtsgeschichte: Helmut Coing zum 28. Februar 1972 von seinen Schülern und Mitarbeitern,* ed. Walter Wilhelm (Frankfurt 1972) 53–65.

————. 'Rechtsgeschichtliche Apostillen zur Clementine *Saepe*', *The Law's Delay: Essays on Undue Delay in Civil Litigation,* ed. C.H. van Rhee (Ius commune Europaeum 47; Antwerp–Groningen 2004) 203–215.

————. *Zur Stellung des Richters im gelehrten Prozeß der Frühzeit: Iudex secundum allegata non secundum conscientiam iudicat* (Münchener Universitätsschriften, Reihe der Juristischen Fakultät, 2; München 1967).

Nottarp, Hermann. *Gottesurteilstudien* (Bamberger Abhandlungen und Forschungen 2; Munich 1956).

Novarese, Daniela. 'Roffredo da Benevento', *Federico II: Enciclopedia Fridericiana* (Rome 2005) 81–105.

Oliver, Lisi, *The Beginnings of English Law* (Toronto 2002).

Olivier-Martin, François. *L'assemblée de Vincennes de 1329 et ses conséquences* (Paris 1909).

Ollendiek, Hans. *Die päpstlichen Legaten im deutschen Reichsgebiet von 1261 bis zum Ende des Interregnums* (Historische Schriften der Universität Freiburg 3; Freiburg, Switzerland 1976).

Ollivant, Simon. *The Court of the Official in Pre–Reformation Scotland* (Stair Society 34; Edinburgh, 1982).

Orlandelli, Gianfranco. '"Studio" e scuola di notariato', *Atti del convegno internazionale di studi accursiani,* ed. Guido Rossi (3 vols. Milan 1968) 1.73–95.

————. 'La scuola di notariato fra VIII e IX Centenario dello Studio bolognese', *Studio bolognese e formazione del notariato, Convegno organizzato dal Consiglio notarile di Bologna col patrocinio della Università degli Studi di Bologna (Bologna, 6 maggio 1989, Palazzo dei Notai)* (Studi storici sul notariato 9; Milan 1992) 23–59.

Outhwaite, R. B. *The Rise and Fall of the English Ecclesiastical Courts, 1500–1860* (Cambridge Studies in English Legal History; Cambridge 2006).

Owen, Dorothy M., 'Synods in the Diocese of Ely in the Latter Middle Ages and the Sixteenth Century', *Studies in Church History* 3 (1966) 217–222.

————. *The Medieval Canon Law: Teaching, Literature and Transmission* (Cambridge 1990, reprint Cambridge 2009).

Paarhammer, Hans. *Rechtsprechung und Verwaltung des Salzburger Offizialates (1300–1569)* (Dissertationen der Universität Salzburg 8; Wien, 1977).

Padoa Schioppa, Antonio. 'Il ruolo della cultura giuridica in alcuni atti giudiziari italiani dei secoli XI e XII', *Nuova rivista storica* 64 (1980) 265–289.

Padovani, Andrea. 'Grazia', DBI 58 (2002) 780–793.

Paolini, Lorenzo. 'La figura dell'arcidiacono nei rapporti fra lo Studio e la città', *Cultura universitaria e pubblici poteri a Bologna dal XII al XV secolo: Atti del II Convegno, Bologna 20–21 maggio 1988*, ed. Ovidio Capitani (Bologna 1990) 31–71.

Paravicini Bagliani, Agostino. *Cardinali di curia e 'familiae' cardinalizie dal 1227 al 1254* (2 vols. Italia Sacra 18–19; Padua 1972).

————. *Il papato nel secolo XIII: Cent'anni di bibliografia (1875–2009)* (Millennio medievale 83, Strumenti e studi 23; Florence 2010).

————. *I testamenti dei cardinali del Duecento* (Miscellanea della Società Romana di Storia Patria 25; Rome 1980).

————. *Il corpo del papa* (Torino 1994, trans. David S. Peterson, *The Pope's Body* Chicago–London 2000).

————. 'Der Papst auf Reisen im Mittelalter', *Feste und Feiern im Mittelalter: Paderborner Symposion des Mediävistenvergandes*, ed. Detlef Altenburg et al. (Sigmaringen 1991) 501–514.

————. 'La mobilità della Curia Romana nel secolo XIII. Riflessi locali', *Società e istituzioni dell'Italia comunale: L'esempio di Perugia (secoli XII–XIV)* (Perugia 1988) 155–278.

————. 'Die Polemik der Bettelorden um den Tod des Kardinals Peter von Collemezzo (1253)', *Aus Kirche und Reich: Studien zu Theologie, Politik und Recht im Mittelalter: Festschrift für Friedrich Kempf zu seinem fünfundsiebzigsten Geburtstag und fünfzigjährigen Doktorjubiläum*, ed. Hubert Mordek (Sigmaringen 1983) 355–362.

————. 'La storiografia pontificia del secolo XIII. Prospettive di ricerca', RHM 18 (1976) 45–54.

Paravy, Pierette. *De la chrétienté romaine à la Réforme en Dauphiné: Évêques, fidèles et déviantes (vers 1340–vers 1530)* (2 vols. Collection de l'École française de Rome 183; Paris 1993).

Pásztor, Edith. 'La curia romana', *Le istituzioni ecclesiastiche della 'societas christiana' dei secoli XI–XII: Papato, cardinalato ed episcopato: Atti della quinta settimana internazionale di studio, Mendola, 26–31 agosto 1971* (Miscellanea del Centro di Studi Medioevali 7; Milan 1974) 490–504.

————. 'Riforma della chiesa nel secolo XI e l'origine del collegio dei cardinali,' *Studi sul Medioevo Christiano, offerti a Raffaello Morghen: Per il 90. anniversario dell'Istituto storico italiano (1883–1973)* (2 vols. Studi Storici 88 and 92; Rome 1974) 2.609–625.

————. 'San Pier Damiani, il cardinalato e la formazione della curia romana', *Studi Gregoriani: Per la storia della 'Libertas ecclesiae'* (Studi Gregoriani 10; Rome 1975) 317–339.

Patze, H. *Fürstliche Residenzen im spätmittelalterlichen Europa*, ed. H. Patze and W. Paravicini (Vorträge und Forschungen 36; Sigmaringen 1991).

Paul, Jürgen. *Die mittelalterlichen Kommunalpaläste in Italien* (Ph.D. Dissertation, Albert-Ludwigs-Universität Freiburg, 1963).

Pavloff, George, *Papal Judges Delegate at the Time of the Corpus Iuris Canonici* (The Catholic University of America, Canon Law Studies 426; Washington, D. C. 1963).

Pedersen, Frederik. *Marriage Disputes in Medieval England* (London 2000).

Pegg, Mark Gregory. *The Corruption of Angels: The Great Inquisition of 1245–1246* (Princeton 2001).

Pennington, Kenneth. *The Prince and the Law, 1200–1600: Sovereignty and Rights in the Western Legal Tradition* (Berkeley–Los Angeles–London 1993).

————. 'The "Big Bang": Roman Law in the Early Twelfth–Century', RIDC 18 (2007) 43–70.

————. 'The Biography of Gratian, the Father of Canon Law', *The Villanova Law Review* 59 (2014) 679–706. Revised and augmented in 'La biografia di Graziano, il Padre del diritto canonico', RIDC 25 (2014) 25–60.

————. 'The *Constitutiones* of King Roger II of Sicily in Vat. lat. 8782', RIDC 21 (2010) 35–54.

————. 'Decretal Collections 1190–1234', Hartmann-Pennington *History* 293–317.

————. 'Due Process, Community, and the Prince in the Evolution of the Ordo iudiciarius', RIDC 9 (1998) 9–47.

————. 'Innocent until Proven Guilty: The Origins of a Legal Maxim', *The Jurist* 63 (2003) 106–124.

————. 'Innocent III and the Ius commune', *Grundlagen des Rechts: Festschrift für Peter Landau zum 65. Geburtstag*, ed. Richard Helmholz, Paul Mikat, Jörg Müller, Michael Stolleis (Rechts- und Staatswissenschaftliche Veröffentlichungen der Görres–Gesellschaft, NF 91; Paderborn 2000) 352–354.

————. 'The Ius commune, Suretyship, and Magna carta', RIDC 11 (2000) 255–274.

————. 'Nicolaus de Tudeschis (Panormitanus)', *Niccolò Tedeschi (Abbas Panormitanus) e i suoi commentaria In decretales*, ed. Orazio Condorelli (Roma 2000) 9–36.

————. 'Law, Criminal Procedure', DMA: *Supplement 1* (New York 2004) 309–320.

————. Roman Law at the Papal Curia in the Early Twelfth Century', *Canon Law, Religion, and Politics: Liber Amicorum Robert Somerville*, ed. Uta-Renate Blumenthal, Anders Winroth, and Peter Landau (Washington, D.C. 2012) 233–252.

————. 'Torture and Fear: Enemies of Justice', RIDC 19 (2008) 203–242.

————. 'A Note to Decameron 6.7: The Wit of Madonna Filippa', *Speculum* 52 (1977) 902–905.

Pérez Martín, Antonio. 'Büchergeschäfte in Bolognese Regesten aus den Jahren 1265 – 1350', *Ius commune* 7 (1978) 7–49.

————. 'El ordo iudiciarius "Ad Summariam notitiam" y sus derivandos: Contribución al estudio de la literatura procesal castellana, 1: Estudio', *Historia Instituciones Documentos 8* (1982) 195–266 and '2: Edición de textos', *Historia Instituciones Documentos 9* (1982) 327–423.

————. 'El arte de la "disputatio" en Vicente Arias de Balboa (ca. 1368–1414)', *Die Kunst der Disputation: Probleme der Rechtsauslegung und Rechtsanwendung im 13. und 14. Jahrhundert*, ed. Manlio Bellomo (Schriften des Historischen Kollegs, Kolloquien 38; Munich 1997) 229–248.

————. Jacobo de las Leyes: Datos biográficos', *Glossae* 5–6 (1993) 279–332.

———— 'La producción de códices jurídicos en España: Ius commune y iura propria', *Juristische Buchproduktion im Mittelalter*, ed. Vincenzo Colli (Studien zur europäischen Rechtsgeschichte 155; Frankfurt am Main 2002) 567–598.

————. 'La difusión de la obra de Rolandino en España', *Rolandino e l'ars notaria da Bo-

logna all'Europa: Atti del Convegno Internazionale di Studi Storici sulla Figura e l'Opera di Rolandino, ed. Giorgio Tamba (Milano 2002) 759–789.

Petit, Joseph, and Paul Marichal, ed. *Registre des causes civiles de l'officialité de Paris, 1384–1387* (Collection des documents inédits sur l'histoire de France; Paris 1919).

Philippe de Beaumanoir. *Coutumes de Beauvaises*, ed. Amédée Salmon (2 vols. Paris 1900, reprinted Paris 1970).

Pini, Antonio Ivan. *Studio, università e città nel medioevo bolognese* (Bolgona 2005).

Planck, Johann Julius von. *Das deutsche Gerichtsverfahren im Mittelalter, nach dem Sachsenspiegel und verwandten Rechtsquellen* (2 vols. Braunschweig 1879).

Planitz, H. 'Die deutsche Stadtgemeinde: Forschungen zur Stadtverfassungsgeschichte', ZRG Germ. Abt. 64 (1944) 1–85.

Pollock, Frederick, and Frederic Maitland. *The History of English Law before the Time of Edward I*, ed. S. F. C. Milsom (2 vols. Cambridge 1968).

Pommeray, Léon. *L'officialité archidiaconale de Paris aux XVe–XVIe siècles: Sa composition et sa compétence criminelle* (Thèse, Paris; Paris 1933).

Pons, C. 'Les affaires d'adultère en France du Nord du XIIIe au début du XVIe siècle,' *Mélanges de la Casa de Velázquez*, 33 (2003) 113–124.

Poos, Lawrence R. 'The Heavy-Handed Marriage Counsellor: Regulating Marriage in Some Later-Medieval English Local Ecclesiastical-Court Jurisdictions', AJLH 39 (1995) 291–309.

Post, Gaines, K. Giocarinis, and Richard Kay. 'The Medieval Heritage of a Humanistic Ideal: "Scientia donum dei est, unde vendi non potest",' *Traditio* 11 (1955) 195–234.

Poumarède, Charles. *Les Usages de Barcelone* (Thèse, Toulouse 1920).

Preuve, La. (4 vols. Receuils de la Société Jean Bodin 16–19; Bruxelles 1963–1965).

Pugh, Ralph B. *Imprisonment in Medieval England* (Cambridge 1968, reprinted Cambridge 1970).

Quaglioni, Diego. '"Divortium a diversitate mentium": La separazione personale dei coniugi nelle dottrine di diritto comune (appunti su una discussione)', *Coniugi nemici: La separazione in Italia dal XII al XVIII secolo*, ed. Silvana Seidel Menchi and D. Quaglioni (I processi matrimoniali degli archivi ecclesiastici italiani, 1: Atti del Primo, Second e Quarto Seminario della Serie 'I Processi Matrimoniali degli Archivi Ecclesiastici Italiani', Annali dell'Istituto storico italo-germanico in Trento, Quaderni 53; Bologna 2000) 95–118.

———. 'Gandino, Alberto', DGI 1.942–944.

Rabikauskas, P. *Die römische Kuriale in der päpstlichen Kanzlei* (Miscellanea Historiae Pontificiae 20; Rome 1958)

———. 'Kanzlei, päpstliche', LMA 5 (1991) 921–22.

Ragusa, Isa. 'Terror Demonum and Terror Inimicorum: The Two Lions of the Throne of Solomon and the Open Door of Paradise', *Zeitschrift für Kunstgeschichte*, 40 (1977) 93–114.

Ramackers, Johannes, ed. *Papsturkunden in Frankreich, 3: Artois* (Abhandlungen der Gesellschaft der Wissenschaften zu Göttingen, 23; Göttingen 1940).

Ramos Vázquez, Isabel. 'El proceso ordinario en el fuero de Andújar', *Buletin del Instituto de Estudios Giennenses* (2008) 221–256.

———. 'El proceso en rebeldía en el derecho castellano', AHDE 75 (2005) 721–754.

———. 'Aspectos procesales en el Fuero latino de Sepúlveda', *Los fueros de Sepúlveda*, ed. Javier Alvarado Planas (Sine loco 2005) 213–230.

Reid, Charles J., Jr. *Power over the Body, Equality in the Family: Rights and Domestic Relations in Medieval Canon Law* (Emory University Studies in Law and Religion; Grand Rapids, Michigan–Cambridge 2004).

Reincke, H., and J. Bolland. *Die Bilderhandschrift des Hamburgischen Stadtrechts von 1497,* annotations by H. Reincke, ed. J. Bolland (Veröffentlichungen aus dem Staatsarchiv der Freien und Hansestadt Hamburg 10: Hamburg, 1968).

Reinle, Adolf. *Zeichensprache der Architektur: Symbol, Darstellung und Brauch in der Baukunst des Mittelalters und der Neuzeit* (Zürich–Munich 1976).

Resnik, Judith, and Dennis E. Curtis. *Representing Justice: Invention, Controversy, and Rights in City-States and Democratic Courtroom* (New Haven 2011).

Riedner, Otto. *Das Speirer Offizialatsgericht im 13. Jahrhundert* (Jur. Diss. Erlangen; Speyer, 1907).

Richards, Jeffrey. *The Popes and the Papacy in the Early Middle Ages* (476–752) (London-Boston-Henley 1979).

Richardson, H. G. 'Studies in Bracton' *Traditio* 6 (1948) 61–104.

Robert, Ulysse, ed. *Les testaments de l'officialité de Besançon (1265–1500)* (2 vols. Collection de documents inédits sur l'histoire de France; Paris 1902–1907).

Roberts, John M. 'Oaths, Autonomic Ordeals, and Power', *American Anthropologist* 67 (1965) 186–212.

Robinson, I. S. *The Papacy 1073–1198: Continuity and Innovation* (Cambridge 1990).

Rodocanachi, Emmanuel. *Les corporations ouvrières à Rome: Depuis la chute de l'empire romain* (2 vols. Paris 1894).

Rodríguez Devesa, José M. 'Contribución al estudio de las penas en el derecho canónico de la época visigoda', *Revista de Estudios Penales* (1945) 2–6.

Rossi, Guido. 'Contributi alla biografia del canonista Giovanni d'Andrea', *Rivista trimestrale di diritto e procedura civile* 11 (1957) 145–152.

Roumy, Franck. 'Le développement du système de l'avocat commis d'office dans la procédure romano-canonique (XIIe–XIVe)', TRG 71 (2003) 359–386.

Rouse, Richard H., and Mary Rouse. 'The Books Trade at the University of Paris, ca. 1250–ca. 1350', *La production du livre universitaire au moyen age: Exemplar et pecia: Actes du symposium tenu au Collegio San Bonaventura de Grottaferrata en Mai 1983,* ed. Louis J. Battaillon, Bertrand G. Guyot, and Richard H. Rouse (Paris 1988) 41–114.

Royer, Jean-Pierre. *L'Église et royaume de France au XIVe siècle d'après le "Songe du Vergier" et la jurisprudence du Parlement* (Bibliothèque d'histoire du droit et du droit romain 15; Paris 1969).

Ruess, Karl. *Die rechtliche Stellung der päpstlichen Legaten bis Bonifaz VIII.* (Görresgesellschaft zur Pflege der Wissenschaft im katholischen Deutschland: Veröffentlichungen der Sektion für Rechts- und Sozialwissenschaften 13; Paderborn 1912).

Russell, R. D. '*Vox Civitatis*': *Aspects of Thirteenth-Century Communal Architecture in Lombardy* (Ph.D. Princeton University, 1988).

Sacri canones servandi sunt: Ius canonicum et status ecclesiae saeculis XIII–XV, ed. Pavel Krafl (Opera Instituti historici Pragae C.19; Prague 2008).

Salonen, Kirsi . 'Marriage Disputes in the Consistorial Court of Freising in the late Middle Ages', *Regional Variations in Matrimonial Law and Custom in Europe, 1150–1600,* ed. Mia Korpiola (Leiden 2011) 189–209.

Santifaller, Leo. *Saggio di un elenco dei funzionari, impiegati e scrittori della cancellaria pontificia dall'inizio all'anno 1099* (2 vols. BISM 56–57; Rome 1940).

Saule, Kevin. 'L'officialité de Beauvais et l'enfermement des curés délinquants au xviie siècle: entre rigueur et indulgence', Beaulande /Charageat, *Les officialités* 205–224.

Sawicki, Jakub, *Concilia Poloniae: Źródła i studia krytyczne* (10 vols. Warsaw 1945–).

Sayers, Jane E. *Papal Judges Delegate in the Province of Canterbury, 1198–1254: A Study in Ecclesiastical Jurisdiction and Administration* (Oxford Historical Monographs; London 1971).

———. *Papal Government and England during the Pontificate of Honorius III (1216–1227)* (Cambridge Studies in Medieval Life and Thought, 3rd Series, 21; Cambridge 1984).

———. 'Proctors Representing British Interests at the Papal Court, 1198–1415', *Proceedings Strasbourg 1968* 143–163.

———. 'Canterbury Proctors at the Court of the "audiencia litterarum contradictarum",' *Traditio* 22 (1966) 311–345.

Schaller, Hans Martin. 'Der heilige Tag als Termin mittelalterlicher Staatsakte', DA 30 (1974) 1–24.

Schenk, Gerrit Jasper. *Zeremoniell und Politik: Herrschereinzüge im spätmittelalterlichen Reich* (Beihefte zu J.F. Böhmer Regesta Imperii Imperii 21; Köln-Weimar-Wien 2003).

Schieffer, Rudolf. *Die Entstehung von Domkapiteln in Deutschland* (Bonner Historische Forschungen 43; Bonn 1982).

———. '*Motu proprio*: Über die papstgeschichtliche Wende im 11. Jahrhundert', HJb 122 (2002) 27–41.

Schmale, F.-J. 'Synodus-synodale concilium-concilium', AHC 8 (1976) 80–102.

Schmidt, R. 'Zur Geschichte des fränkischen Königsthrons', *Frühmittelalterliche Studien* 2 (1968) 45–66.

Schmidt, Tilmann. 'Die älteste Überlieferung von Cencius' "Ordo Romanus",' QF 60 (1980) 513–522.

———. 'Liber censuum Ecclesiae Romanae', LMA 5 (1991) 1941.

———. 'Der ungetreue Notar', *Fälschungen im Mittelalter: Internationaler Kongress der Monumenta Germaniae Historica* (4 vols. MGH Schriften 33; Hannover 1988) 2.691–711.

Schimmelpfennig, Bernhard. *Die Zeremonienbücher der römischen Kurie im Mittelalter* (Bibliothek des Deutschen Historischen Instituts in Rom 40; Tübingen 1973).

———. *Das Papsttum: Von der Antike bis zur Renaissance* (6th ed. Darmstadt 2009, trans. into English New York 1992).

———. 'Die Bedeutung Roms im päpstlichen Zeremoniell', *Rom im hohen Mittelalter: Studien zu den Romvorstellungen und zur Rompolitik vom 10. zum 12. Jahrhundert: Reinhard Elze zur Vollendung seines siebzigsten Lebensjahres gewidmet*, ed. Bernhard Schimmelpfennig and Ludwig Schmugge (Sigmaringen 1992) 47–61.

———. 'Die Funktion des Papstpalastes und der kurialen Gesellschaft vor und während des Großen Schismas', *Génèse et débuts du Grand Schisme d'Occident (1362–1394)* (Paris 1980) 317–328.

———. 'Päpstliche Liturgie und päpstliches Zeremoniell im 12. Jahrhundert' *Das Papsttum in der Welt des 12. Jahrhunderts*, ed. E.-D. Hehl et al. (Mittelalter-Forschungen 6; Stuttgart 2002) 263–272.

———. 'Die Krönung des Papstes im Mittelalter, dargestellt am Beispiel der Krönung Pius' II. (3.IX.1458)', QF 54 (1974) 192–270.

Schimmelpfennig, Bernhard, and Ludwig Schmugge, ed. *Rom im hohen Mittelalter: Studien zu den Romvorstellungen und zur Rompolitik vom 10. zum 12. Jahrhundert: Reinhard Elze zur Vollendung seines siebzigsten Lebensjahres gewidmet* (Sigmaringen 1992).

Schmoeckel, Mathias. *Humanität und Staatsraison: Die Abschaffung der Folter in Europa und die Entwicklung des gemeinen Strafprozeß- und Beweisrechts seit dem hohn Mittelalter* (Norm und Struktur: Studien zum sozialen Wandel in Mittelalter und Früher Neuzeit, 14; Köln-Weimar-Wien 2000).

Schmutz, Richard A. 'Medieval Papal Representatives: Legates, Nuncios and Judges-Delegate', *Collectanea Stephan Kuttner* (SG 15; 1972) 441–463.

Schramm, Percy E. 'Die Imitatio Imperii in der Zeit des Reformpapsttums', *Kaiser, Könige und Päpste: Gesammelte Aufsätze zur Geschichte des Mittelalters* (4 vols. Stuttgart 1968–1971) 4.180–191.

———. 'Sacerdotium und Regnum im Austausch ihrer Vorrechte: "Imitatio imperii" und "imitatio sacerdotii",' *Kaiser, Könige und Päpste* 1.57–106.

Schulte, Johann Friedrich von. 'Der *Ordo judiciarius* des Codex Bambergensis P.I.11," *Sb. Akad. Vienna* 70 (1872) 285–326.

Schulz, Fritz. *History of Roman Legal Science* (Oxford 1953).

Schwab, Christian. *Das Augsburger Offizialatsregister (1348–1352): Ein Dokument geistlicher Diözesangerichtsbarkeit: Edition und Untersuchung* (Forschungen zur kirchlichen Rechtsgeschichte und zum Kirchenrecht 25; Köln 2001).

Schwarz, Brigide. 'Die römische Kurie, Teil Mittelalter', TRE 20 (1990) 343–347.

————. 'Die Erforschung der mittelalterlichen römischen Kurie von Ludwig Quidde bis heute', *Friedensnobelpreis und Grundlagenforschung: Ludwig Quidde und die Erschließung der kurialen Registerüberlieferung*, ed. M. Matheus (BDHI 124; Berlin-New York 2012) 415–439.

Seidel Menchi, Silvana and Diego Quaglioni, ed. *Coniugi nemici: La separazione in Italia dal XII al XVIII secolo* (I processi matrimoniali degli archivi ecclesiastici italiani, 1: Atti del Primo, Secondo e Quarto Seminario della Serie 'I Processi Matrimoniali degli Archivi Ecclesiastici Italiani', Annali dell'Istituto storico italo-germanico in Trento, Quaderni 53; Bologna 2000).

————. *Matrimoni in Dubbio: Unioni controverse e nozze clandestine in Italia dal XIV al XVIII* (I processi matrimoniali degli archivi ecclesiastici italiani 2; Annali dell'Istituto storico italo-germanico in Trento, Quaderni 57; Bologna 2001).

————. *Trasgressioni: seduzione, concubinato, adulterio, bigamia (XIV–XVIII secolo)* (I processi matrimoniali degli archivi ecclesiastici italiani 3; Annali dell'Istituto storico italo-germanico in Trento, Quaderni 64; Bologna 2004).

————. *I tribunali del matrimonio (secoli XV–XVIII)* (I processi matrimoniali degli archivi ecclesiastici italiani 4; Annali dell'Istituto storico italo-germanico in Trento, Quaderni 68; Bologna 2006).

Serrano Seoane, Yolanda. 'El sistema penal del tribunal eclesiástico de la diocesis de Barcelona en la Baja Edad Media', *Clio y Crimen*, 3 (2006) 334–428; 430–508.

Sheehan, Michael M. *The Will in Medieval England: From the Conversion of the Anglo-Saxons to the End of the Thirteenth Century* (Studies and Texts 6; Toronto 1963).

————. 'The Formation and Stability of Marriage in England in the Fourteenth Century: Evidence of an Ely Register', *Mediaeval Studies*, 53 (1971) 228–263.

————. *Marriage, Family, and Law in Medieval Europe: Collected Studies*, ed. James K. Farge (Toronto 1996).

————. 'Marriage and Family in English Conciliar and Synodal Legislation', *Essays in Honour of Anton Charles Pegis*, ed. J. Reginald O'Donnell (Toronto 1974) 205–214, reprinted *Marriage, Family, and Law*, 77–86.

————. 'The Influence of Canon Law on the Property Rights of Married Women in England', *Mediaeval Studies* 25 (1963) 109–224.

Shoemaker, Karl. *Sanctuary and Crime in the Middle Ages, 400–1500* (New York 2011).

Silverman, Lisa. *Tortured Subjects: Pain, Truth, and the Body in Early Modern France* (Chicago–London 2001).

Sinisi, Lorenzo. 'Mascardi, Giuseppe', DBI 71 (2008) 538–541.

Skierska, Izabela. 'Źródła do badania praktyk religijnych w średniowiecznej Polsce: Akta kapituł I sądów kościelnych', *Archiwa, Biblioteki i Muzea Kościelne* 87 (2007) 173–195.

Slatter, M. D. 'The Records of the Court of Arches', JEH 4 (1953) 139–153.

Smail, Daniel Lord. *The Consumption of Justice: Emotions, Publicity, and Legal Culture in Marseille 1264–1423* (Conjunctions of Religion and Power in the Medieval Past; Ithaca–London 2003).

Smith, David M. 'The "Officialis" of the Bishop in Twelfth and Thirteenth Century England: Problems of Terminology' *Medieval Ecclesiastical Studies in Honour of Dorothy M. Owen* ed. M. J. Franklin and C. Harper-Bill (Woodbridge 1995) 201–220.

Soetermeer, Frank P. W. 'Un professeur de l'Université de Salamanque au XIIIe siecle, Guillaume d'Accurse' *AHDE* 55 (1985) 753–765.

———. 'La "taxatio peciarum et quaternorum" de l'Université de Bologne', *Estudis de dret romà i d'historia del dret comparat en homenatge a Ramon d'Abadal i de Vinyals pel seu Centenari* ed. J. Sobrequés and M. J. Peláez (Barcelona 1989) 175–192.

Somerville, Robert ed. *Scotia pontificia: Papal Letters to Scotland before the Pontificate of Innocent III* (Oxford 1982).

Spiess, Pirmin. 'Ordo iudiciarius antequam', *Palatia Historica: Festschrift für Ludwig Anton Doll zum 75. Geburtstag,* ed. P. Spiess (Quellen und Abhandlungen zur mittelrheinischen Kirchengeschichte 75; Mainz 1994) 155–226.

Squibb, George D. *Doctors' Commons: A History of the College of Advocates and Doctors of Law* (Oxford 1977).

Stein, Peter. 'Vacarius and the Civil Law', *The Character and Influence of the Roman Civil Law: Historical Essays* (London 1988) 167–185.

Stelling-Michaud, Sven. 'Le transport international des manuscrits juridiques bolonais entre 1265 et 1320', *Mélanges d'histoire économique et sociale en hommage au professeur Antony Babel à l'occasion de son soixante–quinzième anniversaire* (2 vols. Geneva 1963) 1.95–127.

Stelzer, Winfried. 'Aus der päpstlichen Kanzlei des 13. Jahrhunderts: Magister Johannes de Sancto Germano, Kurienprokurator und päpstlicher Notar' RHM 11 (1969) 210–221

———. 'Beiträge zur Geschichte der Kurienprokuratoren im 13. Jahrhundert', AHP 8 (1970) 113–38.

Stern, Laura Ikins. *The Criminal Law System of Medieval and Renaissance Florence* (Johns Hopkins University Studies in Historical and Political Science, 112; Baltimore-London 1994).

Stickler, Alfons. 'Ordines judiciarii', DDC 6 (1957) 1132–1143.

Storey, R. L. *Diocesan Administration in Fifteenth-century England* (2nd ed. St. Anthony's Hall Publications 16; York 1972).

Straub, Heinrich. *Die geistliche Gerichtsbarkeit des Domdekans im alten Bistum Bamberg von den Anfängen bis zum Ende des 16. Jahrhunderts: Eine rechtsgeschichtliche Untersuchung* (Münchener Theologische Studien, Kanonistische Abteilung 9; München, 1957).

Sydow, Jürgen. 'Untersuchungen zur kurialen Verwaltungsgeschichte im Zeitalter des Reformpapsttums', DA 11 (1954) 18–73.

———. 'Il 'consistorium' dopo lo scisma del 1130', RSCI 9 (1955) 165–176 reprinted *Cum omni mensura et ratione: Ausgewählte Aufsätze: Festgabe zu seinem 70. Geburtstag,* ed. Helmut Maurer (Sigmaringen 1991) 53–64.

———. 'Cluny und die Anfänge der Apostolischen Kammer: Studie zur Geschichte der päpstlichen Finanzverwaltung im 11. und 12. Jahrhundert', *Studien und Mitteilungen des Benediktinerordens und seiner Zweige* 63 (1951) 45–66; reprinted *Cum omni mensura* 31–53.

Szentirmai, Alexander. 'Die ungarische Diözesankurie im Spätmittelalter', ZRG Kan. Abt. 48 (1962) 164–221.

Tabacchi, Stefano. 'Grassi, Achille', DBI 58 (2002) 591–595.

Tabbagh, Vincent. 'La pratique sacramentelle des fidèles d'après les documents épiscopaux de France du Nord (XIIIe–XVe siècle)', *Revue Mabillon* 12 (2001) 159–204.

———. 'Recherches sur l'adultère et sa répression par les officialités de France septentrionale a la fin du moyen âge', *La petite délinquance du Moyen Age à l'époque contemporaine,* ed. B. Garnot (Dijon 1998) 393–402.

———. 'Rouen 1438: de l'extension du champ de la répression judiciare en situation de crise', *De la déviance à la délinquance, XVe–XIXe siècle,* ed. Benoît Garnot (Dijon 1999).

————. 'Le prince face aux communautés ecclésiales: René, Charles, Louis, Philippe et les autres', *René d'Anjou (1409–1480): Pouvoirs et gouvernement,* ed. Jean-Michel Matz, Noël-Yves Tonnerre (Rennes 2011) 355–372.

Taliadoros, Jason. *Law and Theology in Twelfth-Century England: The Works of Master Vacarius: (1115/20–c.1200)* (Disputatio 10; Turnhout 2006).

Tamba, Giorgio. 'Giovanni d'Andrea' 55 DBI (2001) 667–672.

Tangl, Michael. *Die päpstlichen Kanzleiordnungen von 1200 bis 1500* (Innsbruck 1894, reprinted Aalen 1959).

Tate, Joshua C. 'The Origins of *Quare Impedit', Journal of Legal History* 25 (2004) 203–219.

————. 'The Third Lateran Council and the *Ius Patronatus* in England', *Proceedings Esztergom 2008* 589–600.

Taylor, Scott L. 'Survival of Customary Justice', *Crime and Punishment in the Middle Ages and the Early Modern Age,* ed. Albrecht Classen and Connie Scarborough (Fundamentals of Medieval and Early Modern Culture, 11; Berlin-New York 2012) 109–130.

Tellenbach, Gerd. *Die westliche Kirche vom 10. bis zum frühen 12. Jahrhundert* (Die Kirche in ihrer Geschichte: Ein Handbuch 2 F 1; Göttingen 1988), trans. Timothy Reuter *The Church in Western Europe from the Tenth to the Early Twelfth Century* (Cambridge Medieval Textbooks; Cambridge 1993).

Teske, Gunnar. 'Ein neuer Text des Bulgarus–Briefes an den römischen Kanzler Haimerich: Zugliech ein Beitrag zum Verhältnis von Saint-Victor in Paris zur Kurie', *Vinculum societatis: Joachim Wollasch zum 60. Geburtstag,* ed. Franz Neske et al. (Sigmaringendorf 1991) 302–313.

Thomas, Paul. *Droit de propriété des laïques sur les églises et le patronage laïque au moyen age* (Bibliothéque de l'École des Haute Études, Sciences Religieuses 19; Paris 1906).

Timbal, Pierre-Clément, and Bernadette Auzary. 'Visites décanales faites dans l'archidiaconé de Paris en 1468–1470', *Revue d'histoire de l'Église de France* 62 (1976) 349–360.

Timbal Duclaux de Martin, Pierre. *Le droit d'asile* (Paris 1939).

Toubert, Pierre. *Les structures du Latium médiéval: Le Latium méridional et la Sabine du IXe siècle à la fin du XIIe siècle* (2 vols. Bibliothèque des Écoles Françaises d'Athènes et de Rome 332; Rome 1973).

Trumbull, H. C. *The Threshold Covenant or the Beginning of Religious Rites* (New York 1896).

Trusen, Winfried. ed. 'Die gelehrte Gerichtsbarkeit der Kirche', Coing, *Handbuch* 467–504.

————. 'Forum internum und gelehrtes Recht im Spätmittelalter', ZRG Kan. Abt. 57 (1971) 131–157.

————. 'Advocatus – Zu den Anfängen der gelehrten Anwaltschaft in Deutschland und ihren rechtlichen Grundlagen', *Um Recht und Freiheit: Festschrift für Friedrich August Freiherr von der Heydte zur Vollendung des 70. Lebensjahres,* ed. H. Kipp, F. Mayer, and A. Steinkamm (Berlin 1977) 1235–1248.

Turner, George J., and Theodore F. T. Plucknett. *Brevia Placitata* (Selden Society 66; London 1947).

Turner, Ralph V. 'Clerical Judges in English Secular Courts: The Ideal versus the Reality', *Medievalia et humanistica* 3 (1972) 75–98.

Twyman, Susan. *Papal Ceremonial at Rome in the Twelfth Century* (Henry Bradshaw Society. Subsidia 4; London 2002).

Ulanowski, Bolesław. *Acta capitulorum nec non iudiciorum ecclesiasticorum selecta, 2: Acta iudiciorum ecclesiasticorum dioecesium Gnesnensis et Posnaniensis (1403–1530) 3.1: Acta iudiciorum ecclesiasticorum dioecesium Plocensis, Wladislaviensis et Gnesnensis (1422–1533)*

(Monumenta medii aevi historica res gestas Poloniae illustrantia 16, 18; Kraków 1902–1908).

Ullmann, Walter. *The Growth of Papal Government in the Middle Ages: A Study in the Ideological Relation of Clerical to Lay Power* (London 1955)

———. 'The Bible and Principles of Government in the Middle Ages', *La Bibbia nell'alto medioevo* (Settimane di studio del Centro Italiano di studi sull'alto medioevo 10; Spoleto 1963) 183–227.

———. 'A Decision of the Rota Romana on the Benefit of Clergy in England', *Collectanea Stephan Kuttner* (SG 13; Bologna 1967) 455–489.

Valazza Tricarico, Marie-Ange. 'L'officialité de Genève et quelques cas de bigamie à la fin du moyen âge: L'empêchement de lien', *Zeitschrift für schweizerische Kirchengeschichte*, 89 (1995) 99–118.

Vallerani, Massimo. *Medieval Public Justice,* augmented edition, trans. Sarah Rubin Blanshei (Studies in Medieval and Early Modern Canon Law, 9; Washington, D.C. 2012).

Valois, Nöel. *Histoire de la Pragmatique sanction de Bourges sous Charles VII* (Paris 1906).

Vann Sprecher, Tiffany D., and Ruth Mazo Karras. 'The Midwife and the Church: Ecclesiastical Regulation of Midwives in Brie, 1499–1504', *Bulletin of the History of Medicine* 85 (2011) 171–192.

Valsecchi, Chiara. 'Menochio, Giacomo (Jacopo)', DBI 73 (2009) 521–524.

———. 'Menochio, Jacopo', DGI (2013) 2.1328–1330.

Varin, Pierre. *Archives législatives de la ville de Reims* (Collection de documents inédits sur l'histoire de France; Paris 1840).

Vauchez, André. *Histoire du christianisme des origines à nos jours, 5: Apogée de la papauté et expansion de la chrétienté (1054–1274)* ed. André Vauchez et al. (Paris 1993).

Verger, Jacques.'Les étudiants slaves et hongrois dans les universités occidentales (XIIIe– XVe siècles)' *L'église et le peuple chrétien dans les pays de l'Europe du Centre-Est et du Nord (XIVe–XVe siècles)* (Roma 1990) 83–106.

Verzár Bornstein, Christine. *Portals and Politics in the Early Italian City State: The Sculpture of Nicholaus in Context* (Parma 1988).

Vetulani, Adam. 'Die Einführung der Offizialate in Polen: Ein Beitrag zur Verbreitungsgeschichte des bischöflichen Offizialats im Mittelalter', *Collectanea Theologica* 15 (1934) 277–322. Vilar, Hermínia Vasconcelos. 'In Defence of Episcopal Power: The Case of Bishop Egas of Viseu', *Carreiras eclesiásticas no Ocidente Cristão: Séc. XII–XIV* (Estudos de história religiosa 5; Lisbon 2007) 221–244.

Villari, Gianfilippo. *Il sarcofago dell'imperatore: Studi, ricerche e indagini sulla tomba di Federico II nella Cattedrale di Palermo* (2 vols. Palermo 2002).

Visky, Károly. 'Retribuzioni per il lavoro giuridico nelle fonti del diritto romano', *Iura* 15 (1964) 1–31.

Vleeschouwers, Cyriel, and Monique van Melkebeek. *Liber sentenciarum van de officialiteit van Brussel (1448–1459)* (2 vols. Verzameling van de Oude Rechtspraak in België 7; Brussel 1982–1983).

———. *Registres de Sentences de l'Officialité de Cambrai (1438–1453)* (2 vols. Recueil de l'ancienne jurisprudence de la Belgique; Bruxelles 1998).

Vleeschouwers van Melkebeek, Monique. 'Aspects du lien matrimonial dans le *Liber sentenciarum* de Bruxelles', TRG 53 (1985) 43–97.

———. 'Conflits de jurisdiction au niveau diocésain dans les Pays bourguignons de par deça', *Les juristes dans la ville: Urbanisme, société, économie, politique, mentalités,* ed. Jean-Marie Cauchies (Publication du Centre Européen d'Études Bourguignonnes 40; Neuchâtel 2000) 33–47.

———. *Documenten uit de praktijk van de gedingbeslissende rechtspraak van de Officialiteit van*

Doornik: Oorsprong en vroege ontwikkeling (1192–1300) (Iuris scripta historica, uitgeven door het Wetenschappelijk Comité voor Rechtsgeschiedenis van de Koninklijke Academie voor Wetenschappen, Letteren en Schone Kunsten van België 1; Brussel 1985).

———. 'Incestuous Marriages: Formal Rules and Social Practice in the Southern Burgundian Netherlands', *Love, Marriage, and Family Ties in the Later Middle Ages,* ed. Isabel David et al. (International Medieval Research 11; Turnhout 2003) 77–95.

———. 'Marital Breakdown Before the Consistory Courts of Brussels, Cambrai and Tournai: Judicial Separation *a mensa et thoro*', TRG 72 (2004) 81–89.

———. *De officialiteit van Doornik: Oorsprong en vroege ontwikkeling (1192–1300)* (Verhandelingen van de Koninklijke Academie voor Wetenschappen, Letteren en Schone Kunsten van België, Klasse der Letteren, 47.117; Brussel 1987).

———. 'Self-Divorce in Fifteenth-Century Flanders: The Consistory Court Accounts of the Diocese of Tournai', TRG 68 (2000) 83–98.

Vodola, Elisabeth. *Excommunication in the Middle Ages* (Berkeley 1986).

Wakefield, Walter L. *Heresy, Crusade and Inquisition in Southern France, 1100–1250* (London 1974).

Walravens, Christelle. 'Insultes, blasphèmes ou hérésie? Un procès à l'officialité épiscopale de Troyes en 1445', BEC 154 (1996) 485–507.

Wasner, Franz. 'Fifteenth Century Texts on the Ceremonial of the Papal "Legatus a latere",' *Traditio* 14 (1958) 295–358, and 16 (1960) 405–416.

Weber, Max. *Wirtschaft und Gesellschaft (5th ed. Tübingen 1976,* trans. Keith Tribe, *Economy and Society: The Final Version,* ed. Sam Whimster, London 2008).

Weigand, Rudolf. *Liebe und Ehe im Mittelalter* (Biblioteca eruditorum 7; Goldbach 1993).

———. 'Zur mittelalterlichen kirchlichen Ehegerichtsbarkeit: Rechtsvergleichende Untersuchung', ZRG (KA) 98 (67) (1981) 213–47, reprinted *Liebe und Ehe* 307–342.

———. 'Die Rechtsprechung des Regensburger Gerichts in Ehesachen unter besonderer Berücksichtigung der bedingten Eheschließung nach Gerichtsbüchern aus dem Ende des 15. Jahrhunderts', AKKR 137 (1968) 403–63, reprinted *Liebe und Ehe* 245–306.

Weiß, Stefan. *Die Versorgung des päpstlichen Hofes in Avignon mit Lebensmitteln (1316–1378): Studien zur Sozial- und Wirtschaftsgeschichte eines mittelalterlichen Hofes* (Berlin 2002).

Wetzstein, Thomas. *Heilige vor Gericht: Das Kanonisationverfahren im europäischen Spätmittelalter* (Forschungen zur Kirchlichen Rechtsgeschichte und zum Kirchenrecht, 28; Köln-Weimar-Wien 2004).

Whitman, James Q. *The Origins of Reasonable Doubt: Theological Roots of the Criminal Trial* (New Haven 2008).

Wickham, Chris. *Courts and Conflict in Twelfth-Century Tuscany* (Oxford 2003).

Wieben [Lampert], Corinne. *A Kind of Marriage: Marriage in Dispute in Medieval Lucca (1341–1361)* (Ph.D. dissertation, University of California at Santa Barbara, 2010).

Wilks, Michael. *The Problem of Sovereignty in the Later Middle Ages: The Papal Monarchy with Augustinus Triumphus and the Publicists* (Cambridge Studies in Medieval Life and Thought, 2nd series, 9; Cambridge 1964).

Winkelmann, Wilhelm. 'Die Königspfalz und die Bischofspfalz des 11. und 12. Jahrhunderts in Paderborn', *Frühmittelalterliche Studien* 4 (1970) 398–415.

———. 'Der Schauplatz', *Karolus Magnus et Leo Papa: Ein Paderborner Epos vom Jahre 799,* with contributions by H. Beumann, F. Bunhölzl and W. Winkelmann (Paderborn 1966) 99–107.

———. 'Est Locus Insignis, quo Patra et Lippa Fluentant: Über die Ausgrabungen in den karolingischen und ottonischen Königspfalzen in Paderborn', *Beiträge zur Frühgeschichte Westfalens: Gesammelte Aufsätze* (Veröffentlichungen der Altertumskommission im Provinzialinstitut für westfälische Landes- und Volksforschung 8; Münster 1984) 118–128.

Winroth, Anders. *The Making of Gratian's Decretum* (Cambridge Studies in Medieval Life and Thought, 4th Series, 49; Cambridge 2000).

Wolf, Armin. 'Das öffentliche Notariat', Coing, *Handbuch* 1.505–514.

Wood, Charles. *Joan of Arc and Richard III* (Oxford 1988).

Wood, Emily W. *The Execution of Papal Justice in Northern France, 1145–1198* (Ph.D. dissertation, Harvard University, 2009).

Woodcock, Brian L. *Medieval Ecclesiastical Courts in the Diocese of Canterbury* (London 1952).

Worby, Sam. *Law and Kinship in Thirteenth–Century England* (Royal Historical Society Studies in History, New series; Woodbridge–Rochester 2010).

Wormald, Patrick. 'A Handlist of Anglo-Saxon Lawsuits', *Anglo-Saxon England* 17 (1988) 247–281.

Wunderli, Richard M. *London Church Courts and Society on the Eve of the Reformation* (Speculum Anniversary Monographs 7; Cambridge, Mass. 1981).

Wunderlich, Agathon 'Beiträge zur Literärgeschichte des Prozesses im zwölften und dreizehnten Jahrhundert', *Zeitschrift für geschichtliche Rechtswissenschaft* 11 (1842) 84–89.

Zenker, Barbara. *Die Mitglieder des Kardinalskollegiums von 1130–1159* (Würzburg 1964).

Zey, Claudia. 'Entstehung und erste Konsolidierung: Das Kardinalskollegium zwischen 1049 und 1143', *Geschichte des Kardinalats im Mittelalter*, ed. J. Dendorfer and R. Lützelschwab (Päpste und Papsttum 39; Stuttgart 2011) 63–94.

———. 'Die Augen des Papstes: Zu Eigenschaften und Vollmachten päpstlicher Legaten', *Römisches Zentrum und kirchliche Peripherie: Das universale Papsttum als Bezugspunkt der Kirchen von den Reformpäpsten bis zu Innozenz III.* ed. Jochen Johrendt and H. Müller (Abh. Akad. Göttingen 2; Berlin 2008) 77–108.

———. 'Gleiches Recht für alle? Konfliktlösung und Rechtsprechung durch päpstliche Legaten im 11. und 12. Jahrhundert', *Rechtsverständnis und Konfliktbewältigung. Gerichtliche und außergerichtliche Strategien im Mittelalter*, ed. S. Esders (Cologne-Weimar-Vienna 2007) 93–119.

Zoepfl, F. 'Brauttüre', *Reallexikon zur deutschen Kunstgeschichte*, ed. Otto Schmitt (Stuttgart, 1948) 2.1134–1137.

Zutshi, Patrick N. R. 'Petitioners, Popes, Proctors: The Development of Curial Institutions, c. 1150–1250', ed. Giancarlo Andenna, *Pensiero e sperimentazioni istituzionali nella societas Christiana (1046–1250): Atti della sedicesima Settimana internazionale di studio, Mendola 26–31 agosto 2004* (Milan 2007) 265–293.

General Index

Note: Medieval and early modern (to 1600) persons are alphabetized by first name.

A. B. C. judices, 240
Aachen, 34
Abbots: and deposition, 412
Act of Union, 63
Actio: civil, 355–56; definition of, 139
Actorum synodalium, 410
Ad reprimendum, 25–29
Ad summariam notitam, 144, 420
Adam and Eve, 138–39, 142
Adelbertus of Constance, 132
Adrian V, pope, 152
Adultery, 332, 340, 409
Advocate, 59, 129, 265–66; cameral, 214; college of advocates, 63; consistorial, 217; in the Curia, 178, 219–220, 224–225; definition of, 55; duties, 70–72; fees, 68; *instigatores*, 439; king's 320
Advowson, 270, 359
Aethelbert, king of England, 80–81
Aiud, 454
Aix-en-Provence, 309; officiality records, 311
Alba Julia, 445–46
Albericus de Porta Ravennate, 87
Albertus de Morra, 195
Albertus Gandinus, 6–10, 15
Albi, 318
Alexander III, king of Scotland, 25
Alexander III, pope, 99, 135–36, 181, 190, 194, 233–35, 303, 418; and marriage, 293; papal chancellor, 195
Alon, bishop of Astorga, 412
Alfonso IV, 415
Alfonso X, king of Castile, 399, 409, 419, 421
Alfonso de Cusanca, 403
Alfonso Díaz de Montalvo, 419

Amiens, 303, 309
Andover, 101
Andrew I, king of Hungary, 431
Angelus de Ubaldis, 112
Angers, 303
Anglo-Saxon law, 81
Angoulême, 309
Antequam dicatur de processu iudicii, 144
Annulments, 366–68, 406
Apostoli, 231
Appeals, 230–34, 282–83; court of appeals, 218; tuitorial, 353
Apt, 309
Aragon, 392, 402
Arbitration, 128, 410
Arcadius Charisius, 89–90
Arcarius, 163–64
Archdeacon, 253, 267–268, 312, 349, 405
Arias de Balboa, 419–20
Arles, 309
Armand de Fayno, 327
Arms bearing, 408
Arnulfo de Paris, 420
Arras, 303, 318–19
Ars notaria, 455
Assessores, 192, 265–66
Assize *Utrum*, 270–71
Astorga, 406, 425
Asylum, right of, 40–41, 408
Aube, 312
Audentia litterarum contradictarum, 233–34, 209–13, 218–19, 224
Auditor, 57, 193, 199, 402; *litterarum contradictarum*, 210–12, 233
Augsburg, 339, 342